# CONSTRUCTION LAW AND MANAGEMENT

Related titles

*Delay and Disruption in Construction Contracts*
Third Edition
by Keith Pickavance
(2005)

*Partnering and Collaborative Working*
edited by David Jones, David Salvage and Rona Westgate
(2003)

*Construction Claims: Current Practice and Case Management*
by Jeremy Hackett
(2000)

*Professional Negligence in the Construction Industry*
by Jeffrey Brown, Ian Yule and Mark Arrand
(1998)

*What is Dispute Resolution?*
by Peter L d'Ambrumenil
(1998)

# CONSTRUCTION LAW AND MANAGEMENT

EDITED BY

KEITH PICKAVANCE

Routledge
Taylor & Francis Group
LONDON AND NEW YORK

First published 2007 by Informa Law

Published 2016 by Routledge
2 Park Square, Milton Park, Abingdon, Oxon OX14 4RN
711 Third Avenue, New York, NY 10017, USA

First issued in hardback 2015

*Routledge is an imprint of the Taylor & Francis Group, an informa business*



A catalogue record for this book is available from the British Library.

ISBN-13: 978-1-843-11671-4 (pbk)
ISBN-13: 978-1-1-381-3587-1 (hbk)

Typeset by
Interactive Sciences Ltd, Gloucester

# PREFACE

Construction law continues to develop and evolve at, at times, a demanding pace, and never ceases to be one of the most interesting areas of law in which to specialise.

Recent developments have taken place not just in the law itself but also in the methods by which disputes are resolved, both in the UK and overseas.

**In the UK**

In the last 18 months, there have been developments in the areas of adjudication, arbitration, construction management, health and safety, and costs.

In adjudication, it was decided in the case of *Connex South Eastern Ltd* v. *M J Building Services*[1] that, subject to circumstances where the right to refer a dispute to adjudication might have been waived, there is nothing to prevent a party from referring a dispute to adjudication at any time.

Very recently, in January 2007, H.H.J. Havery QC held in the cases of *Epping Electrical Company Ltd* v. *Briggs and Forrester (Plumbing Services) Ltd*[2] and *Aveat Heating Ltd* v. *Jerram Falkus Construction Ltd*[3] that, respectively, neither the CIC Model Adjudication Procedure nor the GC/Works/Sub-Contract complied with the requirements of Section 108 Housing Grants, Construction and Regeneration Act 1996 ("HGCRA"). The fallback provisions of the Scheme for Construction Contracts therefore applied instead.

In arbitration, the House of Lords held in *Lesotho Highland Development Authority* v. *Impregilo Spa and Others*[4] that a "mere error of law" did not amount to an excess of jurisdiction under the Arbitration Act 1996.

Technology and Construction Court ("TCC") judgments have been given in relation to construction management, in *Great Eastern Hotel Company Ltd* v. *John Laing Construction Ltd*[5] and project management in *Scheldebouw BV* v. *St James Homes (Grosvenor Dock) Ltd.*[6]

Reported decisions have been given in relation to costs incurred during adjudication,[7] costs arising from a claimant's refusal to mediate a claim,[8] and costs incurred by a defendant at the pre-action protocol stage of a case when

1. [2005] EWCA Civ 193.
2. [2007] EWHC 4 (TCC).
3. [2007] EWHC 131 (TCC).
4. [2005] UKHL 43.
5. [2005] EWHC 181 (TCC).
6. [2006] EWHC 89 (TCC).
7. *John Roberts Architects Ltd* v. *Parkcare Homes (No. 2) Ltd* [2006] EWHC Civ 64.
8. *The Wethered Estate Ltd* v. *Davis and Another.*

dealing with, and responding to, issues which were subsequently dropped when proceedings were instituted.[9]

Following a report by a working party set up by the TCC to consider whether any changes should be made to the Pre-Action Protocol for Construction and Engineering Disputes, a second edition of this Protocol has now been finalised, and will come into effect in April 2007.

Also in the TCC, research is currently being carried out, firstly by questionnaire survey, and then by follow up interviews, to investigate:—

1 In what circumstances is mediation an efficacious alternative to litigation;
2 Whether, and at what stage, the court should encourage mediation in future cases, and
3 Which mediation techniques are particularly successful.

The purpose of the research is to ascertain at what stage in the litigation cycle most parties settle by way of mediation, in order that the Judges may become better informed as to when they should encourage and/or direct parties to mediate.

In addition to this survey, the TCC has recently launched a new mediation service which is currently being piloted by the TCC Judges. Judges who have received appropriate training will offer to resolve disputes using conventional mediation techniques. If settlement is not achieved, and the case proceeds, the Judge who acted as mediator will have no further role in the proceedings. However, they will be able to set out their views on the dispute and their evaluation of the likely outcome of the case, if the parties request them to do so.

Another mediation alternative launched by CEDR and Fenwick Elliott is the Project Mediation Initiative. "Contracted mediation" or "project mediation" aims to fuse team building, dispute avoidance and dispute resolution in one procedure. Two mediators are appointed at the outset of a project or major business relationship, to act as the point of contact when problems are anticipated or arise. The panel, which will have a working knowledge of the project and the individuals working on it, can provide an immediate forum for the confidential discussion and potential mediation of all manner of differences or disputes.

The government is currently continuing its consultation process over its proposals to amend Part II of the HGCRA. The majority of the proposed changes relate to the payment provisions but there are also a number of proposals concerning adjudication. There are no current proposals to introduce a compulsory single standard adjudication procedure, although it may well be the case that the two recent decisions by H.H.J. Havery QC to which we refer above may make this proposal a late entry in the consultation process.

The JCT 2005 Suite of Contracts has gained more widespread use, and NEC/3 has been chosen as the preferred form of contract by the Olympic

9. *McGlinn* v. *Waltham McGlinn Contractors Ltd and Others* [2005] EWHC 1419.

Delivery Authority. The use and misuse of Letters of Intent continue to give opportunity for legal challenge.

Collateral warranties are still generally preferred for third party rights, particularly by funders.

There is no current proposal by the government to address the question of the status of PFI/PPP subcontracts following the judgment of Mr Justice Jackson in the case of *Midland Expressway* v. *Carillion Construction Limited.*[10] The Construction Committee of the City of London Law Society has published guidance for those engaged in advising on the first tier construction and facilities management subcontract of PFI projects in connection with their interaction with section 113(1) HGCRA, encompassing best practice recommendations for PFI subcontracts and alternative approaches to be considered.[11]

Other developments include the introduction of the Public Contract Regulations 2006 and the case law building up under the EU Public Procurement Directive, in relation to the procurement of both Part A and Part B services, including new regulations relating to framework agreements employed by contracting authorities.

## Overseas

Adjudication is developing apace throughout the world, most recently in the Far East. It is also increasingly provided for in contracts, such as FIDIC, through the use of Dispute Review Boards and Dispute Adjudication Boards. Each comprises three independent people, who evaluate disputes during the course of a project. A Dispute Review Board will make a settlement recommendation to the parties which, depending on the wording of the contract, may become binding; the Dispute Adjudication Board will issue a written binding decision, with which the parties will have to comply.

## Conclusion

Innovation in dispute resolution continues to challenge those involved in the field, but also provides myriad opportunities to resolve construction disputes throughout the world far more economically than has ever been the case. The increase in use of mediation, and project mediation, help to avoid an adversarial approach and assist in preserving working relationships for the future; evolving methods of procurement should help to ensure smoother delivery of construction projects, on time and to budget. The impact of the EU Public Procurement legislation should not be under estimated and it is likely that this is the area of law which will give rise to some of the largest disputes in the future.

10. [2005] EWHC 2963 (TCC).
11. www.citysolicitors.org.uk.

Continuing developments in all aspects of construction law mean that the construction practitioner can never stand still. We hope this book will assist in understanding the concepts involved.

Victoria Russell and Nicholas Gould
Fenwick Elliott LLP, London
February 2007

# AUTHORS' BIOGRAPHIES

**Dr Hamish Lal**
Hamish Lal B.Eng., B.A. (Oxon), Ph.D is a partner in the London Construction & Engineering Group of UK Law Firm Dundas & Wilson LLP. Hamish is a specialist in construction, engineering and project finance law. He has significant experience of and expertise in many forms of construction procurement (including PFI, project finance, construction management, partnering and target cost contracting) and has practised in the oil, nuclear, energy and PFI sectors. He has particular expertise in the legal analysis of delay and is the author of *Quantifying and Managing Disruption Claims* published by Thomas Telford Limited. In 2006 Hamish was awarded the inaugural Norman Royce Prize by The Society of Construction Arbitrators.

**Anders Axelson**
Anders is a senior consultant with the Asia-Pacific division of international consulting firm Nielsen-Wurster, and is based in Melbourne, Australia. He holds degrees in engineering and law, from the Universities of Melbourne and London respectively, and specialises in consulting work relating to dispute resolution and risk management.

**Mark Hackett**
Mark Hackett, M.A., M.Sc., FRICS, ACIArb has been a partner in Davis Langdon LLP since 1992 and he heads that practice's legal support group. The work of the legal support group is primarily aimed at assisting lawyers in the dispute resolution process arising out of which Mark has been involved in numerous high profile and large value disputes both at home and abroad. Together with Geoff Trickey, the former senior partner of Davis Langdon & Everest, Mark is the co-author of *The Presentation and Settlement of Contractors' Claims* (2nd edn), published by Spon Press in 2001. Mark is also the co-editor of the Aqua Group's *Procurement, Tendering and Contract Administration*, published by Blackwells in 2006.

**David Risbridger**
David Risbridger is a Partner at Denton Wilde Sapte and heads the Construction and PFI unit of the Milton Keynes office. David leads a team of 9 lawyers, involved in all aspects of non-contentious construction law. David trained as a quantity surveyor before joining the legal profession and has worked for a number of contractors on both building and civil engineering projects. Since qualifying as a solicitor he has specialised in non-contentious construction

work and PPP/PFI. David has a Masters degree in construction law and management from Kings College London, the leading academic institution in this area. David is a regular lecturer at the Construction Law Summer School and the Construction Law Master Class.

**Keith Pickavance**

Keith Pickavance, director of Pickavance Consulting and senior vice president of Hill International, is a chartered architect with a legal education. He specialises in overcoming delay and disruption-related issues through change management and critical path analysis. The first edition of his book *Delay and Disruption in Construction Contracts* (now in its third edition, Informa Professional 2005) attained the silver award at the CIOB Literary Awards. He is also the author of many articles on the subject. He is a Fellow of the Academy of Experts, FCIOB, member of the PMI, a founding member of the Expert Witness Institute, Associate of the American Bar Association, and member of the SCL Protocol drafting panel.

**Nick Carnell**

Nick Carnell is a partner at Kennedys Law. He is experienced in a wide range of contentious and non-contentious construction matters on behalf of employers, contractors, sub-contractors, members of the design team and their insurers; particularly in relation to disputes involving communication systems and infrastructure projects. He acted for the main contractor on the Central line recabling dispute and for the communications package sub-contractor in relation to the Jubilee line extension. He has wide experience of adjudication particularly relating to railway renewal works and acted in the reported case *Kitsons* v. *Matthew Hall* in relation to Heathrow Terminal 4. He is a regular contributor of articles to journals and has frequently lectured. He is the author of *Causation and Delay in Construction Disputes*. He is a Fellow of the CIArb, and an accredited mediator, as well as a member of SCL and TeCSA.

**Dr Julian Critchlow**

Dr Julian Critchlow has specialised in construction law for most of his career, joining Fenwick Elliott as a partner on 1 January 1999. He has acted in both contentious and non-contentious matters for a wide variety of construction clients including employers (both private and institutional), contractors, sub-contractors, consultants and PFI consortia. He has also sits as an arbitrator, an adjudicator (TeCSA registered) and a mediator (CEDR accredited). Dr Critchlow is also the author of numerous books and other publications including *Making Partnering Work in the Construction Industry.*

**Nicholas Gould**

Nicholas Gould is a partner in Fenwick Elliott LLP. Nicholas conducts a mix of dispute resolution and non-contentious work. He is a solicitor, chartered surveyor and CEDR Solve lead mediator, predominately advising institutions and companies who own, finance, invest, build and facilitate development opportunities and construction projects. He acts in a wide range of construction sectors including office, retail, leisure, residential, hotel, industrial, process plant and petrochemical. His dispute resolution experience spans litigation, arbitration (domestic and international), adjudication, mediation, early neutral evaluation and expert determination. He regularly acts as lead mediator in construction and property related disputes. He is the Senior Research Fellow at the Centre of Construction Law, King's College London, visiting lecturer at the National University of Singapore, an assessor for the commercial M.Sc. at UMIST, and external examiner for the construction law M.Sc. at Wolverhampton. Nicholas is the secretary of the Society of Construction Law and a committee member of the Adjudication Society. He has published widely in the area of construction law and won a Silver Award at the CIOB Literary Awards for his book *Dispute Resolution in the Construction Industry*. The Rt. Hon. Sir Philip Otton described the book as "the most fascinating publication to come across [his] desk for many a year".

**Victoria Russell**

Victoria read law at Exeter University. After qualifying as a solicitor in 1981, she joined the specialist construction law practice, Freedmans, becoming a partner in 1985. She joined Fenwick Elliott in 2000. Victoria's contentious work focuses on litigation, arbitration and adjudication claims for a wide range of clients. She also has extensive experience of all forms of ADR. She is a practising adjudicator, arbitrator and mediator and has for many years been identified as one of the country's leading construction lawyers by *Chambers Guide to the Legal Profession*. Victoria is a Fellow of the Chartered Institute of Arbitrators, the Chartered Institute of Building and the Faculty of Building. She is a past chairman of the Society of Construction Law and past president of the European Society for Construction Law.

# CONTENTS

CHAPTER 1

# INTRODUCTION TO THE ENGLISH AND EU LEGAL FRAMEWORKS

Hamish Lal

## AN OVERVIEW OF THE ENGLISH LEGAL SYSTEM

### *An overview*

English law is divided in a number of ways. It may be divided into substantive law and procedure:

- Substantive law refers to all the branches of law which define a person's rights and duties, such as contract, tort and crime.
- Procedure deals with the complex rules by which the process of law is set in motion to enforce some substantive right or remedy. In the context of construction disputes, procedure includes arbitration and other dispute resolution processes, particularly adjudication.

A further division of law is into common law and statute law; that is, into judge-made law and legislation. Then there is another type of division between common law and equity, which is a distinction based upon the two independent roots of English law.

Another division is between private law and public law, sometimes called administrative law:

- Private law relates to rights exercisable between individuals (including corporations and other legal entities).
- Public law, however, relates to the powers and duties exercisable by public bodies, which may affect the rights or expectations of individuals.

Another division exists between so-called domestic and international law. International law itself falls into two distinct categories: private international law, which applies to disputes having an international character but concerning individuals or other legal entities; and public international law, which applies primarily between states. Private international law comprises the rules applied in a particular country and of other countries whose laws may affect a dispute.

### The common law

English law is based upon the common law system. The common law means literally the law which was applied in common over all parts of the realm. It was created in the twelfth and thirteenth centuries by the King's judges and has been developed and handed down to the present time.

> The essential feature of the common law which distinguishes it from other systems is that it is based on evolving precedent, with no written principles from which the precedent stems.

The common law is not written down. It is stated each time a judgment is given at the end of a case, when the judge gives reasons for the legal principles embodied in his decision. In practice, the common law is found in the reports of judgments, and the law on any topic is to be discovered by reading those cases which turn on related facts.

To understand some of the complexities and apparent inconsistencies of English contract law it helps to have an understanding of how the law developed. In the Middle Ages, the courts of common law failed to give remedies in some cases. A Court of Chancery was set up to deal with such cases and the rules applied by the Court of Chancery also became law, known as "equity" (as opposed to the common law). The remedies available in equity (but not in common law) include specific performance of obligations (other than an obligation to pay money which was a remedy available at common law) and injunctions. Although all courts can now administer both common law and equity, the rules which apply to equity are still relevant. For example, a person seeking an equitable remedy is said to have to "come to equity with clean hands" (in other words they must not have done something which ought to deprive them of the remedy sought).

### Statute law

While the judges declare and apply the common law, Parliament in its legislative capacity passes enactments to change the law. Since the seventeenth century Parliament has had supreme authority and can in theory make or unmake any law. The passing of a Bill through Parliament and the debate at different stages in its passage can be followed in the media and in *Hansard.*

### EU law

In addition to Common Law and Statute Law, the European Economic Community has, since 1973, formed a third independent and increasingly major source of law applying throughout the United Kingdom. The foundation of the Community was and remains the Treaty of Rome, signed by the original six members in 1957. Membership of the Community has grown since then and continues to do so. Development in the 1980s was towards the Single European Market, for which 1992 was set as the target.

The European treaties form a "framework" of measures, expressed as broad aims to be achieved, which are intended to be filled in by detailed measures. Areas for detailed legislation include: competition law and public procurement, health and safety, environment and consumer protection, and the more general harmonisation of the laws of Member States to the extent required for the functioning of the common market.

The EEC is unique in having achieved more in terms of interstate integration than any comparable organisation in history. It operates in some ways as an international body and in other ways as a federal government. The principal institutions through which it operates are:

(i) The European Parliament, which is now a directly elected body which exercises defined powers, but falling far short of a full legislative assembly;
(ii) The Council of Ministers, which is a fluctuating body of Ministers from individual Member States who meet when required and generally represent the interests of their own governments. Presidency of the Council circulates among the Member States. When the Ministers are heads of state, the Council is referred to as the Council of Europe;
(iii) The European Commission, which is the equivalent of the European Civil Service, headed by permanent Commissioners who, although drawn from the Member States, should represent the interests of the Community, unlike the members of the Council. Every Member State contributes one Commissioner and the larger States, two;
(iv) The European Court of Justice, which comprises judges appointed by each Member State and has the function of interpreting and applying Community law.

European legislation emanates from the Council and the European Commission, principally in the form either of a Regulation or a Directive.

> Regulations have direct binding force on all Member States and comprise fully detailed measures.

> Conversely, Directives specify the result to be achieved and are intended to be acted upon through individual legislation enacted in each Member State.

### Procurement legislation

Since the 1970s, there has been much complicated Community legislation regulating the procurement procedures of public or government bodies. This has been replaced by recent directives which consolidate the existing legislation, extend it to cover utilities and add it to the remedies available for breach of procurement law as expressed either by the Treaty or the legislation. The principal Community legislation is as follows:

(i) Council Directive 93/37 concerning the coordination of procedures for the award of public works contracts ([1993] OJ L199/54) as amended by Directive 97/52 ([1997] OJ L328/1);
(ii) Council Directive 93/36 coordinating procedures for the award of public supply contracts ([1993] OJ L199/1) as amended by Directive 97/52 ([1997] OJ L328/1);
(iii) Council Directive 92/50 relating to the coordination of procedures for the award of public service contracts ([1992] OJ L209/1) as amended by 97/52 ([1997] OJ L328/1);
(iv) Council Directive 89/665 on the coordination of laws, regulations and administrative provisions relating to the application of review procedures to the award of public supply and public works contracts ([1989] OJ L395/33) as amended by Directive 92/50 above;
(v) Council Directive 93/38 coordinating the procurement procedures of entities operating in the water, energy, transport and telecommunications sectors ([1993] OJ L199/84) as amended by Directive 94/22 ([1994] OJ L164/3) and Directive 98/4 ([1998] OJ L101/1); and
(vi) Council Directive 92/13 coordinating the laws, regulations and administrative provisions relating to the application of Community rules on the procurement procedures of entities operating in the water, energy, transport and telecommunications sectors ([1992] OJ L76/4).

This EU legislation is implemented in the law of the United Kingdom by the following regulations:

(i) The Public Works Contracts Regulations 1991 ((SI 1991 No. 2680), as amended);
(ii) The Public Supply Contracts Regulations 1995 ((SI 1995 No. 201), as amended);
(iii) The Public Services Contracts Regulations 1993 ((SI 1993 No. 3228), as amended);
(iv) The Utilities Contracts Regulations 1996 (SI 1996 No. 2911).

## ENGLISH CONTRACT LAW

As discussed above, the English law of contract derives mainly from the common law (as opposed to statute)—there is no code or single source which sets out the various rules. There are also some statutory provisions which are relevant. This Module gives an overview of the main areas in English contract law but does not cover all the various (often complex) relevant areas.

## *Creating a contract*

### Agreement

There are three basic essentials to create a contract:

- agreement;
- contractual intention; and
- consideration.

Normally the question of whether the parties have agreed something is tested by asking whether one party has made an offer which the other has accepted. Agreements may not give rise to a binding contract if they are incomplete or not sufficiently certain. The courts apply an objective test in deciding if the parties have reached agreement.

### Offer

It is important to distinguish between offers, which can be accepted, and an "invitation to treat" which is an invitation to someone for them to make an offer, which the first party can then accept. An invitation to treat gives the party who issues the invitation control over when (and if) the contract is made. There is no requirement to have an invitation to treat: a valid contract can be formed when an offer is accepted. On auctions, it is the bid which is the offer.

### Acceptance

An acceptance is agreement to the terms of an offer. Offers can be accepted by conduct. If someone purports to accept an offer, but does so on different terms, that will be a counter-offer, rather than an acceptance.

The acceptance must normally be communicated to the offeror. There are special rules for when an offer is accepted by post (the general rule is that acceptance takes effect when the letter is posted) or some instantaneous mode of communication, e.g. telephone or telex (where the normal rule—that the acceptance must be communicated—applies).

Generally, silence cannot be treated as an acceptance. In exceptional circumstances (for example, where the offeree has invited the offeror to make an offer on the basis that silence will constitute acceptance or if there is a course of dealing between the parties that silence constitutes acceptance) silence may be treated as an acceptance.

An offer can be terminated in various ways: by withdrawing it before it is accepted, by lapse of time where it said it had to be accepted by a certain time, by a condition occurring if it said it was conditional (for example the employer providing possession of a site on or before a specified date), on something not happening or by being rejected.

An agreement may be incomplete, for example where the parties have agreed on essential matters of detail but have not agreed other important points, although an agreement may be complete even if it is not worked out in meticulous detail. There is nothing like "*essentialia negotii*" or "*accidentalia negotii*" to help determine which elements are essential and which are merely ancillary.

There will usually be no contract if the parties agree "subject to contract" but never agree on the terms of the contract. A provision that certain terms are to be agreed from time to time, with no fallback as to what is to happen if agreement is not reached, may make an agreement so uncertain as to be unenforceable.

> Although the courts will not enforce an agreement which is too vague or uncertain, they do not expect commercial documents to be drafted precisely. Custom and usage may help to resolve uncertainty.

## Intention

Some agreements are not enforceable contracts because there is no intention by one of the parties to create legal relations. Generally it is assumed that the parties do intend to create legal relations and there is a heavy burden to discharge if a party alleges it did not intend to do so. It is safer to make it clear if no enforceable contract is to be created, e.g. when heads of agreement are signed.

## Deeds

In general, a promise to do something must be either made in a deed or supported by "consideration".

> A deed is a document under seal which either (i) transfers an interest, right or property or (ii) creates an obligation which is binding on someone or some persons or (iii) confirms an act which transferred an interest, right or property.

Not all documents under seal are deeds. There are special requirements on execution and delivery of deeds. A contract under seal is an example of a deed. No consideration is required for a contract contained in a deed. A person identified in the deed as someone to benefit from a promise in the deed can enforce a promise to pay money or can seek damages if the promise is not performed. However, it should be noted that equitable remedies (for example, specific performance of obligations other than to pay money) are not available if there is no consideration.

## Consideration

This can be something of benefit to the person who has the obligation or who makes a promise to do something (called the promisor) or something which is a detriment to the promisee (the person who wants to enforce the obligation or who has the benefit of the promise).

As long as some value is given for the promise, the courts will not consider whether "adequate" value is given. Contracts to transfer something valuable for £1 are enforceable. However, if the promisee has already done the act that is said to be the consideration, that is usually "past consideration" and is not treated as being good consideration.

The consideration must be provided by the party who wants to enforce an obligation in the contract (or, possibly, by someone else as his agent) but need not be provided to, or benefit, the promisor. A promise not to sue on a valid claim can be good consideration.

### Capacity

Normally, the law presumes that a party to a contract has capacity to contract. Minors (children under 18) and mentally disordered people do not have full capacity to contract. It is for the person claiming the incapacity to prove it.

There are special rules which apply to corporations (including companies), unincorporated associations (including clubs and trade unions), the Crown (including any government department or officer of the Crown), public authorities (including local government bodies, bodies set up by Parliament to regulate privatised utilities, and bodies set up to provide social services or to implement the policy of a particular statute), the European Community, foreign states, sovereigns, international organisations and enemy aliens (anyone who voluntarily resides or carries on business in any enemy country or enemy-occupied country during a war in which the UK is engaged, regardless of their nationality).

## *Privity of contract*

### The general rule

> As a general rule, a contract cannot confer rights or impose obligations which arise under the contract on anyone other than one of the parties to the contract. So if A enters into a contract with B under which he agrees to pay money to C (who is not a party to the contract), B can enforce A's promise but C cannot.

### Contracts (Rights of Third Parties) Act 1999

Since the enactment of the Contracts (Rights of Third Parties) Act 1999, the parties to a contract can agree that someone who is not a party to the contract can enforce a term of the contract. In some cases the Act will apply to give a third party a statutory right to enforce a contract term where the term of the contract purports to confer a benefit on that third party. It is not possible to use a contract to impose an enforceable obligation on someone who is not a party to the contract. However, a similar effect may be achieved by conferring a benefit subject to the third party meeting a condition.

### *Mistake*

This is a complex area. There are rules which deal with what happens if the parties have agreed the terms of a contract on the basis of a shared (or mutual) and fundamental misapprehension as to the facts (e.g. where the goods to be sold have been destroyed). This is referred to as mistake.

Mistake can also occur where there is a misunderstanding in the communications between the parties (for example, the parties misunderstand each other or one party makes an offer on terms which the other party knows the first party did not intend) which prevents there being an effective agreement. The parties may misunderstand each other or one party may know that the other does not intend the terms he has offered (e.g. where he offers to sell goods at a price per tonne instead of per pallet) or there may be a mistake about the identity of the parties.

> Normally the effect is that the contract is void *ab initio* (i.e. there was never any contract between the parties).

However where, at common law, the court would decide that the mistake was not enough to make the contract void, it may then consider whether grounds exist for relief in equity. For example, it could refuse to grant specific performance or could grant rectification of a written agreement or agree to rescind the contract (i.e. bring the contract to an end).

### *Misrepresentation*

The law on misrepresentation is a complex mixture of the rules of common law, equity and statute law. It is also complicated by the fact that it may be possible to bring an action in tort (discussed below) for a misrepresentation, as well as in contract which can lead to the amount of damages awarded being different. There are three categories of misrepresentation:

- innocent misrepresentation,
- negligent misrepresentation, and
- fraudulent misrepresentation.

A person can always rescind for a fraudulent misrepresentation. If the misrepresentation is negligent or wholly innocent, the court has a discretion to refuse to allow the person to whom the misrepresentation was made to rescind the contract, but to award him damages instead.

## Misrepresentation Act 1967

It used to be the case that if someone was induced to enter a contract by a misrepresentation, he could rescind the contract subject to certain conditions but could only claim damages if the misrepresentation was fraudulent. However, since the Misrepresentation Act 1967, a person can claim damages for a negligent misrepresentation if he could have claimed damages if the misrepresentation had been fraudulent. The Misrepresentation Act applies whether or not the misrepresentation also becomes a term of the contract.

The misrepresentation can be a misstatement of a fact. In some cases, for example if a representation is made about an opinion or intention which is not honestly held, a statement of opinion or intention can also be actionable. Statements of law can also be a misrepresentation although this is a difficult area.

The general rule is that mere non-disclosure is not a misrepresentation as there is generally no duty on a party to a contract to disclose material facts to the other party. There are exceptions to this, for example, where there is a fiduciary relationship between the parties or where failure to disclose a fact distorts a positive representation. If a statement which is true when made subsequently becomes untrue, a failure to notify the change can itself be a misrepresentation in some cases.

To obtain relief, a person must be able to show that the misrepresentation was made to him or his agent, or that the person making it expected it to be passed on or made to the public at large. The person must also show that he relied on it or was affected by it.

## Main remedies for misrepresentation

The main remedies for misrepresentation are:

- damages or
- rescission.

The amount of damages for fraudulent misrepresentation differs from the normal damages for breach of contract.

> Damages for negligent misrepresentation can be reduced (under s. 1 of the Law Reform (Contributory Negligence) Act 1945) if the person claiming was contributorily negligent—i.e. the loss is partly his fault.

Rescission may not be awarded:

- if it is not possible to put the parties back to their original positions,
- if the party has affirmed the contract,
- because of lapse of time, or
- because a third party has acquired rights.

### *Duress and undue influence*

A contract which has been entered into as a result of duress can be avoided by the party subject to the duress (i.e. that party can choose not to be bound by the contract provided he has not affirmed or ratified the contract). In addition, a contract may be avoided if one party has abused his influence over the other or betrayed a position of confidence.

Equitable relief may also be granted for unconscionable bargains (where the "bargain" or transaction is so oppressive that it shakes the conscience of the court: for example where the complainant has got nothing out of a transaction or has sold property for much less than it was worth) or where there was in equality of bargaining power. This is not normally relevant to commercial contracts between businessmen.

### *Collateral contracts*

In some cases, the courts will be prepared to treat a statement intended to have contractual effect as a separate contract or warranty, collateral to another transaction.

> For example, A employed B to paint a pier and instructed B to buy paint from C, relying on a statement by C that the paint would last seven years. It lasted three months. The court held that there was a collateral contract between A and C that the paint would last seven years.

The courts usually find that there is a collateral contract if one party refuses to enter a contract unless the other party gives him an assurance on a particular point. Consideration for the collateral contract is normally provided by entering into the main contract but a collateral contract may be actionable even if the main contract is unenforceable. A collateral contract can also arise where the main contract is between A and B and the collateral contract is between either A or B and a third party.

### *Terms of a contract*

Normally a party signing a written contract is bound by its terms, whether or not he has read them. However, contracts can be oral, partly oral and partly written or written. There are special rules for standard form or term contracts, particularly if they contain exclusions or restrictions of liability.

#### **Conditions and warranties**

Traditionally, English contracts have differentiated between terms of a contract which the courts have described as "conditions" and those which the courts have described as "warranties". Note that "condition" in this sense is different from a condition which has to be satisfied before a contract exists or a particular obligation becomes enforceable. Warranty in this sense is also different from the way it is used to describe a representation in the contract, for example that the vendor is the legal and beneficial owner of the goods to be sold.

> If one party to a contract is in breach of a term which is a condition, this entitles the innocent party to choose not to perform his obligations under the contract and claim damages for loss as a result of the breach. Alternatively, the innocent party can decide to proceed with the contract.

> If a party to a contract is in breach of a term which is a warranty, the innocent party can only claim damages for breach of warranty, but cannot treat himself as discharged from the contract.

Terms are sometimes described as "intermediate terms" (breach of these may, depending on the nature and consequences of the breach, entitle the innocent party to treat himself as discharged from the contract) and "fundamental" terms (which go to the heart of the contract, where the substance of the agreement is destroyed if the term is not met). A representation (i.e. a statement made before the contract is entered into) can become a term of the contract and can then be a "condition", a "warranty" or an "intermediate term".

## Conditional agreements

An agreement is conditional if an obligation depends on an event which is not certain to happen (e.g. X agrees to award the contract to Y subject to obtaining planning approval). The law is generally unclear as to whether, before the condition is satisfied, there is any right to withdraw from the contract, a duty not to prevent the condition being satisfied or a duty to use reasonable diligence to bring about the event in question. Where the condition is for the benefit of one party, normally the party can waive it. It is also possible for parties to agree that there will be no binding contract between them unless a condition is satisfied.

### *Rules of contractual interpretation*

These are the rules a court applies to decide the meaning and legal effect of a contract. They apply to oral contracts as well as written ones. The object of the rules is to discover the parties' intention, as ascertained objectively.

The starting point is that words are to be given their ordinary and natural meaning, but technical words are usually given their technical meaning. Commercial contracts are construed in a business fashion. Certain words have a statutory meaning—month, person, the singular includes the plural and the masculine includes the feminine.

Evidence of prior negotiations is not usually admissible. Words usually prevail over numbers. If a deed or other instrument is ambiguous it is construed more strongly against the person who drafted the provision or for whose benefit the provision was drafted (*contra preferentem*). This is particularly relevant in guarantees, exclusion clauses and indemnities.

Where general wording is used after specific wording the "*ejusdem generis*" rule means the general words only guard against the accidental omission of a particular example from the list; it does not extend the list to something completely different. An express reference to something particular (e.g. a person) may show an intention to exclude everything else.

## Admission of extrinsic evidence

Generally, where a contract is in writing the parties cannot adduce extrinsic evidence (i.e. evidence of matters outside the document) to affect the document's content. However, this is subject to various exceptions, including to show the contract is not valid or binding. Entire agreement clauses are intended partly to prevent extrinsic evidence being used.

## Implied terms

The law will imply terms in a contract in some cases. Examples of this include, where it is necessary in the business sense, to give efficacy to the contract; and where it is obvious from the contract that the parties would, as reasonable men, have agreed it if it had been suggested when the contract was made.

Terms may also be implied by custom, usage or statute. For example, undertakings as to title, quality and fitness for purpose (amongst others) are implied into contracts of sale of goods by the Sale of Goods Act 1979, contracts of hire purchase by the Supply of Goods (Implied Terms) Act 1973 and contracts for the hire of goods by the Supply of Goods and Services Act 1982.

## Exemption clauses

Exemption clauses are clauses by which one party seeks to exclude or restrict liability under the contract or for a tort connected with the contract. Generally, they must be clearly expressed and unambiguous or they may be ineffective. Doubts and ambiguities will be resolved against the party seeking to rely on the clause. Whether an exclusion clause protects a party, even if there is a breach of a fundamental term, is a question of construction of the contract.

The extent to which one party can exclude or restrict liability is affected by the Unfair Contract Terms Act 1977 (UCTA) and various other statutory provisions.

UCTA controls contract terms which restrict or exclude liability for negligence, breach of certain terms implied by statute or common law in contracts of sale or goods, hire purchase, and other contracts for the supply of goods.

In some circumstances UCTA also controls other contract terms which restrict or exclude liability for breach of contract or purport to allow a party not to perform a contractual obligation or to do something substantially different from what was reasonably expected of him.

In some cases the exclusion clause is wholly ineffective and in other cases it is only effective if the term satisfies a reasonableness test. Some contracts are exempted from the Act's ambit, including:

- contracts of insurance;
- contracts relating to the creation or transfer of an interest in land;
- contracts relating to the creation or termination of a right or interest in intellectual property rights;
- contracts relating to the formation or dissolution of a company or its constitution; and
- contracts relating to the creation or transfer of any right or interest in securities.

### *Force majeure* clause

This is a provision which allows one or more parties not to perform the contract in whole or part or to delay or suspend performance if a specified event beyond his control occurs. *Force majeure* is not a term of art in English law and is wider than acts of God or *vis major*.

### Arbitration clauses

Parties to a contract can agree to refer disputes between them to a tribunal they have chosen, rather than to a court. There are special rules which apply to such agreements including whether the arbitration agreement is valid, its scope, how such agreements are enforced, appointment and removal of arbitrators, conduct of the arbitral proceedings and the court's ability to assist the process and enforce the award. The Arbitration Act 1996 governs much of this.

## *Illegality and public policy*

In some circumstances a contract will not be enforced because of public policy. One or more parties may not be able to enforce the contract or a particular undertaking in the contract. It is for the party alleging that the contract is illegal to prove this. Again this is a complex area.

The illegality can arise from statute or common law. It can affect both a party's ability to make a contract and performance of the contract. Examples include:

- a contract to do something which is a crime;
- to conceal a crime;
- to sell or transfer a public appointment;
- to do something which is illegal under the foreign law governing the contract; or
- to interfere with the course of justice.

It is also against public policy to support litigation in which a person has no legitimate concern without just cause or excuse (legally known as "maintenance"). More relevantly, contracts in restraint of trade are enforceable only if they are reasonable with reference to the interests of the parties concerned and the public. It is easier to enforce a restrictive covenant (e.g. not to carry on a business competing with the business sold for three years) between a vendor and purchaser of a business than between an employer and employee.

### *Joint and several liability*

> If two or more people (A and B) each agree with another (C) that they will each do something (e.g. pay £10), their promises are several, i.e. each of A and B is liable to pay C £10 and payment by A does not discharge B from his obligation to pay.

Joint liability arises where two or more people jointly agree to do the same thing. In this case there is only one obligation to C to do the same thing. If either (or any) of the joint obligors (i.e. the people who have the obligation) performs the obligation, the others are discharged from their obligations.

There are strict technical rules of law which apply to joint liability.

A liability can also be joint and several. Two or more people jointly promise to do the same thing and also severally agree to do the same thing. Performance by one will discharge the liability of all of them.

It is presumed that liability is joint where a promise is made by two or more people. If this is not the intention, express wording should be included to make the obligation several.

## Assignment

Rights under a contract are personal rights of property which can only be claimed or enforced by action (rather than by taking physical possession). These rights are known in legal terms as "choses in action". Rights under a contract can be assigned in accordance with s. 136 of the Law of Property Act 1925.

The main statutory requirements are

(i) that the assignment is absolute (and not just by way of charge);
(ii) it must be in writing under hand of the assignor and
(iii) express written notice of the assignment must be given to the debtor or person with the obligation.

An assignment which fails to meet the statutory requirements may still take effect as what is known as "an equitable assignment". The main difference is that if rights have been assigned in accordance with the above Act, the assignee can sue to enforce the debt or other obligation without joining the person who assigned the right (the assignor) as a party to the action. An assignee under an equitable assignment normally has to join the assignor in any proceedings.

If a contract states that rights under it cannot be assigned, a purported assignment is not valid. Some assignments are prohibited by statute or public policy. Some personal contracts (e.g. an author's right to have a book published by his publisher) cannot be assigned. Normally, commercial contracts can be assigned (unless there is a prohibition).

The burden of a contract cannot be transferred without the consent of the person subject to the obligation. However, a party to a contract can arrange for someone else to perform his obligations under the contract and the other party will have to accept that performance if it is in accordance with the contract (unless it is a personal contract). However, the contracting party remains liable for any breach by its sub-contractor (in the absence of specific provisions to the contrary).

## Novation

Whether both parties to a contract agree, one party can transfer all rights and obligations under the contract to a third party who agrees to take the place of the transferring party, who is then released from the contract. The original contract is brought to an end and replaced by a new contract. There must therefore be consideration (discussed above) for the new contract.

## Performance

There are various rules about how someone must perform an obligation under a contract. For example, where the contract is to be performed (if it does not say) and when.

A provision in a contract as to time (e.g. that the contract must be completed at a particular time) is not treated as being "of the essence" unless

(i) this is either expressly agreed in the contract or
(ii) by necessary implication this was intended by the parties or

(iii) where one party has not performed the obligation, the other gives notice that the contact must be performed within a reasonable period.

If time is originally agreed to be of the essence, failure by the relevant party to perform at the relevant time allows the other party to end the contract and claim damages (as though the obligation were a "condition"). This right to terminate may be lost if the innocent party affirms the contract or waives the right to terminate. If time is made of the essence by giving notice, the innocent party cannot turn the relevant obligation into a "condition". As a result, he can only terminate the contract if the failure to comply with the notice goes to the root of the contract.

## Discharge by agreement

A party can be released from his obligations under a contract by the other party. This can be done by deed or by "accord and satisfaction". Accord and satisfaction involves the party being released providing some new consideration in return for the release.

If neither party has yet performed all their obligations under a contract, they can agree, expressly or impliedly, to rescind the agreement.

The parties to a contract can agree to change its terms. This can be agreed orally or in writing, unless the original contract had to be in writing, in which case it can only be varied in writing. The agreement to vary must be supported by consideration, but this may be the parties agreeing to give up their rights under the existing contract or agreeing to confer any benefit under the new agreement.

Where a contract provides that one party can change an obligation in the contract unilaterally, this is enforceable (subject to any statutory restraints, e.g. on consumer contracts).

If one party voluntarily agrees to a request not to insist on the other party performing his obligations, the court may hold that he has waived his rights. Similarly, if a party tells the other party that he will not insist on an obligation being performed, and the other relies on this representation, the court may also hold that there is a waiver.

## Waivers

Waivers can be given orally or in writing and can be given for repudiatory breaches of contract. Where a party promises or represents to the other party that he will not enforce his rights under the contract and intends the other party to rely on this, which the other party does, the courts will stop the party from reasserting his rights unless this is inequitable. This is sometimes referred to as "promissory estoppel". The party to whom the promise or representation is made can rely on it even if he gave no consideration for it. Promissory estoppel is very similar (if not identical) to waiver.

A contract can itself provide that either party or one party can terminate the contract in any circumstances the parties agree (subject to any statutory restrictions, e.g. in UCTA).

### Frustration

If something happens after a contract is made which makes it physically or commercially impossible to fulfil the contract or changes the obligation under the contract into something radically different, the contract may be frustrated (i.e. the contract is discharged). So, if goods that are the subject of a contract are destroyed after the contract is made, the contract is frustrated. The doctrine of frustration operates within narrow limits and cannot easily be relied upon.

### Discharge by breach

A breach of contract may arise because a party fails to perform an obligation, by a party stating that he will not perform his obligation (known as repudiatory breach) or evincing an intention not to do so, or by a party making it impossible to perform his obligation by his own act or default. The other party to the contract may (depending on the facts) be entitled not to perform his obligations under a contract and to refuse the other party's performance of his obligations under the contract if the first party is in breach of the contract.

Not every breach of contract gives the innocent party this right. The innocent party can choose to claim damages and waive his right to treat the contract as discharged. If he chooses to treat the contract as continuing this is known as "affirming" the contract. This can be done expressly or impliedly (e.g. by some unequivocal act from which it can be inferred that he has elected to continue with the contract). Once a contract has been affirmed and this has been communicated to the other party, the innocent party cannot change his mind. The innocent party does not necessarily lose his right to claim damages for any loss suffered as a result of the breach just because he affirms the contract.

## *Remedies for breach of contract*

### Damages

Normally the parties to a contract can agree what remedy the innocent party can have if the other party breaches the contract. This can include an agreement to exclude a right to damages. What the parties can agree is, however, subject to the law on penalties' statutory restrictions, for example under the Unfair Contract Terms Act 1977, the Unfair Terms in Consumer Contracts Regulations 1994 and the Consumer Credit Act 1974 and general principles of law (e.g. illegality). If the parties do not agree, the general law applies to determine what compensation is payable for a breach.

The general rule is that the innocent party is to be put in the same position, as far as is possible by paying money, as if the contract had been performed. This means that if the innocent party is in a better position as a result of the breach, this must be taken into account when calculating the damages.

Damages can be awarded as well as, or instead of, an order for specific performance or an injunction (see below). The court will assess damages even if it is difficult to do so.

The parties can agree the amount of damages payable for a breach (known as liquidated damages). This arrangement is common in construction contracts. If the parties have not done this, the innocent party can seek unliquidated damages (in other words an amount which has not been agreed in advance and is instead determined by the court).

### Cause and effect

The innocent party must show that there is a causal connection between the defendant's breach of contract and the loss he has suffered. This is especially complex in the area of delay and disruption claims in the construction industry.

> The breach must be the "effective" or "dominant" cause of the loss.

Normally, if there is an intervening act by a third party between the breach of contract and the loss, this will break the chain of causation. The innocent party's own acts can also affect causation.

### Remoteness of damage

The law sets out the types of loss caused by breach of contract for which damages can be awarded. This is referred to as "remoteness of damage". The leading cases in this area are *Hadley* v. *Baxendale* (1854) 9 Exch. 341, *Victoria Laundry (Windsor) Ltd* v. *Newman Industries Ltd* (1949) 2 K.B. 528 and *Koufus* v. *C Czarnikow Ltd (the Heron II)* [1969] 1 A.C. 350.

> In *Hadley* v. *Baxendale* the court said the innocent party should be able to recover such damages as may fairly and reasonably be considered either as arising naturally, i.e. according to the usual course of things from the breach or such as may reasonably be supposed to have been in the contemplation of both parties, at the time they made the contract, as the probable result of the breach (known as the first limb of *Hadley* v. *Baxendale*). If the contract is made in special circumstances which are known to both parties the damages for breach would be the amount of injury which would ordinarily follow from a breach of contract under those special circumstances (known as the second limb of *Hadley* v. *Baxendale*).

Following further interpretations by the courts, the rule is now said to be that if a type or kind of loss was within the parties' reasonable contemplation as a not unlikely result of a breach (assuming that the parties foresaw the breach in question), then it is not too remote and the innocent party can recover damages for it. This means that a plaintiff can recover loss of profits where a reasonable man would have foreseen that this would be the result of the breach. He can also claim for wasted expenditure incurred in reliance on the contract or because of the breach.

## Duty to mitigate

The innocent party cannot recover damages for any loss he suffered if he could have avoided the loss by taking reasonable steps. If, in fact, the innocent party avoids the loss, he cannot recover damages for the loss avoided even if the steps he took went beyond what was reasonable. However, he can recover loss or expense incurred in the course of taking reasonable steps to mitigate the loss suffered. There is no duty to mitigate loss—but if the claimant does not do so he cannot recover damages to the extent he has failed to mitigate his loss.

## Penalties

When the parties agree that, if there is a breach of contract, the party in default has to pay a specified amount to the innocent party the courts will enforce such a provision (as liquidated damages) unless it is a penalty.

> If there has been a genuine attempt to estimate in advance the loss which the innocent party would suffer as a result of the breach, the amount will be enforceable (even if it is more than the loss actually suffered). If the amount is extravagant or unconscionable in amount in comparison with the greatest loss which could conceivably have been proved for, it is likely to be a penalty.

## Specific performance

The common law would only specifically enforce a contractual obligation to pay money. However, it was possible to get specific performance of other contractual obligations in equity. The result of this is that specific performance is subject to a number of limitations. The court will only award specific performance if it is satisfied that it is not just, in all the circumstances, for the innocent party to be confined to a remedy in damages. This test is sometimes stated to be that specific performance will not be granted if damages are an adequate remedy. Sometimes specific performance will be granted if damages would be only of a nominal amount or it would be difficult to quantify them.

Specific performance will not generally be ordered where

- the innocent party can easily get what he contracted for from another source;
- where a contract which involves personal service (e.g. a contract of employment);
- whether or not damages is an adequate remedy.

Specific performance is a discretionary remedy and so the court can refuse to grant it in various circumstances. These include:

- where the innocent party's conduct is reprehensible in some way—even if the conduct does not involve any breach of the contract;
- specific performance of a gratuitous promise (i.e. one for which consideration is not given) even if it is enforceable at law because it is made in a deed or supported by nominal consideration.

### Injunctions

An injunction is a court order to do something or not to do something. Like specific performance it is an equitable remedy and so is discretionary. If a contract contains an agreement not to do something an injunction may be granted to prevent a breach of that obligation. If a party has already breached an obligation in a contract a mandatory injunction may be granted to require him to put the breach right.

> The court will apply a "balance of convenience" test in deciding whether to grant a mandatory injunction. If the party in breach will suffer significantly more if he has to undo the breach than the benefit the innocent party will receive if the injunction is granted, the court may refuse to grant the injunction. Similarly, the court will use the balance of convenience test when deciding whether to grant a prohibitory injunction to stop the party in breach committing future breaches of the contract.

Injunctions will not usually be granted if:

- it would be oppressive to the party in breach;
- if the loss to the innocent party can easily be compensated by damages; or
- to prevent breaches of contracts of personal service.

### Restitution

In some situations, the law imposes a duty on a person to pay a sum of money or (exceptionally) to deliver specific property to another where there is a special relationship between the two persons. This is separate from contract law and is called quasi-contract or restitution.

Where restitution is granted, the defendant has to make restitution of a benefit which he ought not, in justice, to retain at the expense of the person making the claim. It is thought this action is based on a principle of preventing unjust enrichment.

It can be used, for example, to recover money paid under a mistake by the payer as to a material fact or to recover money paid by the payer where the consideration for the payment has totally failed (e.g. an employer can recover money paid for work but not completed or commenced).

*Quantum Meruit*: In some cases, the courts will make a person who has received a benefit pay for that benefit on a "*quantum meruit*" basis. For example, if a party to a contract refuses to perform his part of a contract, the other party who has performed his part of the contract can sue on a quantum merit for the work actually done. It may be possible to recover even if the contract is unenforceable.

## ENGLISH TORT LAW

### *An overview*

The English law of tort, like the English law of contract, imposes obligations on individuals or other legal entities (such as construction companies) towards other individuals or legal entities giving rights to the latter against the former. It is important to understand that the rights and obligations in tort arise independently of any contract. Instead they are derived in the main from the product of decisions by the court (discussed above as the common law) or alternatively from statute law enacted by Parliament.

The law of tort covers a wide spectrum of wrongs including:

- trespass;
- assault;
- libel; and
- statutory torts.

Some civil torts are also criminal offences. A criminal offence will arise from obligations that are owed to the state at large and proceedings are usually brought by the State.

The wronged individual/company is usually the person who raises legal proceedings against the wrongdoer or what is referred to in legal terms as a "tortfeasor" in respect of the "tortious" duty or obligation that is alleged to have been breached.

In the next sections we provide a general introduction of the key areas of tortious liability in so far as they are relevant and impact on the construction industry.

### *Negligence*

For a cause of action in negligence to arise:

(a) there must be a duty of care owed by the tortfeasor to the injured person;
(b) a breach of that duty of care must have taken place; and
(c) that breach must have caused the injured person to suffer loss.

The wronged individual/company should have suffered some form of loss or damage. It is important to understand that in the present context, the word "injured" is not intended to suggest that tortious duties are in any way limited to the realm of personal injury. Indeed, the range of duties in tort is vast.

In the early case law, liability for negligent conduct was recognised only in discrete categories where particular circumstances were said to give rise to a "duty of care". Often these situations were readily identified as being analogous to those where a contract would be said to arise. Today, identifying when a duty of care in tort law will arise is a difficult legal exercise.

### *Nuisance*

#### Introduction

Nuisance can be divided into two categories:

- private; and
- public.

The best description of nuisance is:

> "An act or omission which is an interference with, disturbance of or annoyance to, a person in the exercise or enjoyment of
>
> (a) a right belonging to him as a member of the public, when it is a public nuisance, or
> (b) his ownership or occupation of land or of some easement, profit, or other right used or enjoyed in connection with land, when it is a private nuisance."

Nuisance and negligence share some of the same qualities, but there is an important difference between the two. Negligence is concerned with the protection of personal rights and nuisance is concerned with the protection of proprietary rights; However, both:

- impose a similar standard of care on the potential tortfeasor; and
- are subject to similar rules of causation and remoteness of damage.

It should be noted that damages for nuisance differ slightly to those for negligence because injunctive relief rather than damages is more often the desired remedy.

### Public nuisance—who can sue?

Public nuisance is actionable in both criminal and civil law.

| |
|---|
| A person can sue for public nuisance without the requirement of an interest in land, unlike private nuisance. |

A person can sue for public nuisance in civil law if it can be shown that he or she suffers special damage beyond inconvenience suffered by others who have also been affected (for more details see *Harper* v. *Haden & Sons* [1933] Ch. 298 at p. 308).

In order for an action to exist, the claimant must also show that a "class" of people has been affected by the defendant's activities. The definition of a class has been held to be a matter of fact and degree.

### Private nuisance: who can sue?

The case of *Thompson-Schwab* v. *Costakis* [1956] 1 W.L.R. 335 at p. 338 stated that private nuisance can be divided into three categories:

(i) causing an encroachment on another's land;
(ii) causing physical damage to another's land or building works or vegetation upon it; and
(iii) unduly interfering with the comfort and convenient enjoyment of another's land.

In the case of *Hunter* v. *Canary Wharf* [1997] 2 W.L.R. 684, the House of Lords took the opportunity to reaffirm this area of law.

| |
|---|
| The House of Lords restated that the tort of nuisance is a tort directed against the plaintiff's enjoyment of rights over land and, accordingly, an action in private nuisance will only lie at the suit of a person who has a right in the land affected. |

## *Rylands v. Fletcher*

### Overview

The rule in *Rylands* v. *Fletcher* (1866) L.R. 1 Ex 265 at 276 is an offshoot of the law relating to nuisance. It encompasses "escaping liability". The main difference between private and public nuisance and *Rylands* v. *Fletcher* liability is that it was considered that the rule in *Rylands* imposed liability on defendants regardless of foreseeability of damage.

## The rule in *Rylands* v. *Fletcher*

In *Rylands* v. *Fletcher* the defendants built a reservoir on their land. Water collected and flowed into the plaintiffs' mine causing damage. The defendants were held liable on the ground that they kept the water on their land at their own peril. Blackburn J. said:

> ". . . the person who for his own purposes brings on his land and collects and keeps there anything likely to do mischief if it escapes must keep it in at his peril, and, if he does not do so, is *prima facie* answerable for all the damage which is the natural consequence of its escape."

In the House of Lords this was refined to bring in the concept of the "non-natural user". That is to say, that the defendant must be using his or her land for a non-natural use. The rule was interpreted to impose strict liability, and foreseeability of damage was not necessary to establish liability.

## The abolition of the rule

The abolition of this rule was considered by the House of Lords in a judgment delivered on 19 November 2003 in *Transco plc* v. *Stockport Metropolitan Borough Council* [2003] All E.R. (D) 255.

In *Transco*, Stockport supplied a multi-storey block of 66 flats with water for domestic use by the residents. The water was carried by a pipe made of asbestos cement and had an internal diameter of 3 inches (this gave the pipe a capacity 16 times that of a pipe in common domestic use). Without negligence on the part of Stockport the pipe failed and water escaped. The nature of the land in the area was such that water percolated into an embankment that supported Transco's gas main. Part of the embankment collapsed and left the gas main exposed and unsupported. Transco saw an immediate and serious risk that the gas main may also fail and took prompt remedial measures costing £93,681. Transco then sought this cost from Stockport claiming that the authority was liable without proof of negligence under the rule in *Rylands* as discussed above.

The House of Lords did not abolish the rule in *Rylands*. The issue in this appeal was whether:

(i) the authority had brought onto its land something likely to cause danger or mischief if it escaped; and
(ii) whether that was as an ordinary use of land.

The House of Lords decided that piping a water supply from the mains to storage tanks in the block of flats was a routine function carried out by Stockport and that this function did not raise any special hazard and did not constitute a non-natural use of land.

Of perhaps greater interest is that their Lordships held that the rule in *Rylands* did have a role even in today's society. In particular it was emphasised that the strict liability imposed under the rule concerned only damage to property and did not apply to claims for personal injury.

## THE CONSTRUCTION ACT

### *An overview*

The Housing Grants, Construction and Regeneration Act 1996 (referred to here as the Construction Act) received Royal Assent on 24 July 1996. Interestingly, only eight pages of the Act (which itself runs to some 103 pages), relate to construction. The Act and supporting Statutory Instruments provided a new legal frame work of rules within which the construction industry had to operate. The Act did not come into force until 1 May 1998.

The Scheme for Construction Contracts (England and Wales) Regulations 1998 and the Construction Contracts (England and Wales) Exclusion Order 1998 also came into force on 1 May 1998. The Scheme for Construction Contracts is in two parts; Part I deals with adjudication and Part II sets out rules relating to payment. The two Statutory Instruments will be referred to in this Module as the Scheme and the Exclusion Order respectively. In practice, the Construction Act the Scheme and the Exclusion Order should be read together to understand the extent to which agreements relating to construction are covered by the Construction Act and the terms implied into construction contracts that fall within the ambit of the Construction Act.

The key sections of the Construction Act are:

- ss. 104–107 deal with the identification of which construction contracts are covered by the Act;
- s. 108 sets out the requirements for Adjudication Rules;
- ss. 109–111 set out the new payment provisions and requirements for Payment Notices and Notices of Intention to Withhold Payment;
- s. 112 deals with the right to suspend performance for non-payment;
- s. 113 restricts pay when paid arrangements;
- s. 114 enables the Minister to make by order the Scheme for Construction Contracts;
- ss. 115 and 116 set out the rules for service of notices and reckoning periods of time.

The Construction Act does allow the Secretary of State to make a number of changes by order approved by a resolution of each House of Parliament, for example, in relation to the definition of construction operations or construction contracts which are excluded from the Act. However, the only power exercised by the Secretary of State thus far has been to issue the Exclusion

Order which excludes from the scope of the Act various types of construction contract, for example, PFI agreements.

In September 2004, Sir Michael Latham's review of the Construction Act was presented to construction minister Nigel Griffiths. The review announced in the 2004 Budget looked at both the payment and adjudication provisions of the Construction Act. It is intended that the review will form the basis of the consultation document to be issued by the Department of Trade and Industry (DTI). It is noteworthy that there was a strong degree of consensus within the group reviewing adjudication, but far less so in the group reviewing the payment provisions. The review identified the following issues to be addressed in any reform of the Construction Act:

*On adjudication:*

- preventing the practice of one party requiring that the referring party pay both parties legal costs irrespective of the outcome of the adjudication;
- a reinforcement of the requirement for impartiality;
- the prohibition of trustee stakeholder accounts; and
- clarification of the requirement for a contract to be "in writing".

*On payment:*

- improving the effectiveness of the right to suspend performance in cases of non-payment;
- providing a right for a third party to pay all (or some of) the unpaid funds to the payee where the original payer is insolvent;
- resolving the confusion over what entitlement to be paid arises at the "due date" for payment, possibly to include removing or replacing s. 110(2) of the Construction Act; and
- limiting the right of cross-contract set-off.

### General effect on construction contracts

Ordinarily under English Contract Law, parties negotiating a commercial agreement are free to agree whatever terms they like (no matter how unreasonable), provided they are not illegal or in breach of the principles of public policy. In construction, parties have traditionally had a very wide scope for agreeing terms no matter how unreasonable they might appear, for example, pay when paid provisions. The scope of interference by statute with such agreements was very limited and was largely confined to circumstances where one of the parties involved was a consumer or dealt on the other's standard terms of business, for example, the Unfair Contract Terms Act 1977. The Construction Act retains the parties' freedom to negotiate and agree a wide range of matters.

The details of how the Construction Act operates in relation to specific issues, such as failure to provide notice of intention to withhold payment, are outside the scope of this Module. However, whilst the overall operation of the Construction Act is to retain the parties' freedom to negotiate, there are a number of limitations. For example, the Construction Act entitles a party to a construction contract where the duration of work is 45 days or more to payment by instalments, stage payments or other periodic payments (see s. 109 of the Construction Act).

The Employer and Contractor are, however, free to agree the amounts of the payment and the intervals or circumstances in which they become due. It is only if the parties fail to agree any provisions for payment by instalment, stage payment or other periodic payment that the relevant provisions of the Scheme apply. The Scheme also provides similar terms in relation to the need for:

- an adequate mechanism to determine what payments become due;
- an adequate mechanism to determine when payments become due;
- identification of a final date for payment.

The Employer and Contractor are free to agree the above matters and it is only to the extent that the contract does not contain the necessary provisions that the terms of Scheme become applicable. In practice, it is perfectly possible, therefore, for the Employer and Contractor to agree all necessary matters and for the Scheme not to apply to the resultant Construction Contract at all. This means that the Scheme is a default provision which is only likely to have any impact if the parties fail to agree one or more of the issues required by the Construction Act.

If the provisions of the Scheme do apply then those provisions have effect as what we call implied terms of the agreement between the parties.

## What is a construction contract?

"Construction contract" is defined in ss. 104 and 105 of the Act as meaning an agreement for carrying out construction operations (as defined), including sub-contracted work and (importantly) architectural design or surveying work or advice on building, engineering, decoration or landscape.

The term "construction operations" is widely defined but (significantly) excludes a long list of construction operations such as extraction of oil, gas or minerals, installation of plant for nuclear processing, power generation or water or effluent treatment, bulk storage of chemicals, oil, gas, steel, or food or drink. Also excluded is the manufacture or delivery of components, materials, plant and machinery unless the contract also provides for installation.

> The Act applies only to construction operations in England and Wales (and Scotland), whatever the applicable law of the contract.

## How to apply the Construction Act

Where an agreement might be deemed a "construction contract", there is a two-stage process for identifying how the Construction Act might be applied:

- First, we need to identify whether the agreement is within the definition of the type of agreement that can be a construction contract and, importantly, whether it relates to an activity which is a construction operation for the purposes of the Act.
- Second, we need to consider the various exceptions in the Construction Act and the Exclusion Order, to see whether or not any of those exclude the construction contract from the operation of the Construction Act in circumstances where the Construction Act would otherwise apply.

### *Effect on payment provisions*

- Construction contracts of 45 days or more must include an entitlement to stage payments.
- All construction contracts covered by the Construction Act must include an adequate mechanism to ascertain how much is to be paid and when payments fall due. A final date for payment must also be agreed.
- Pay when paid clauses will be effective only in very limited circumstances (for example, insolvency of the Employer).
- If the parties have drafted an agreement which is not Construction Act compliant, then the Scheme will impose various terms into the agreement.
- If the Scheme is implied into the agreement then the timetable for interim payments will be:
  - a relevant period for valuations of 28 days;
  - payment falls due seven days after the end of the relevant period;
  - a payment notice must be served five days from the date payment falls due;
  - a notice of intention to withhold payment must be served not less than seven days before the final date for payment;
  - the final date for payment will be 17 days after the date the payment falls due.
- Payment notices must be served within strict time limits whenever a payment falls due (and in some cases when a payment does not fall due).
- If payment is to be withheld notice of intention to withhold payment must be served within strict time limits or payment will have to be made irrespective of how good the counter-claim of the paying party.

## *Adjudication under the Construction Act*

Adjudication is dealt with in s. 108 of the Construction Act which provides as follows:

"108—Right to refer disputes to adjudication,

(1) A party to a construction contract has the right to refer dispute arising under the contract for adjudication under procedure complying with this section.
(1) For this purpose dispute includes any difference.
(2) The contract shall—
    (a) enable a party to give notice at any time of his intention to refer a dispute to adjudication;
    (b) provide a timetable with the object of securing the appointment of the adjudicator and referral of the dispute to him within 7 days of such notice;
    (c) require the adjudicator to reach a decision within 28 days of referral or such longer period as is agreed by the parties after the dispute has been referred;
    (d) allow the adjudicator to extend the period of 28 days by up to 14 days, with the consent of the party by whom the dispute was referred;
    (e) allow the parties to agree to extend the time in which the adjudicator is required to reach a decision;
    (f) impose a duty on the adjudicator to act impartially; and
    (g) enable the adjudicator to take the initiative in ascertaining the facts and the law.
(3) The contract shall provide that the decision of the adjudicator is binding until the dispute is finally determined by legal proceedings, by arbitration (if the contract provides for arbitration or the parties otherwise agree to arbitration) or by agreement. The parties may agree to accept the decision of the adjudicator as finally determining the dispute.
(4) The contract shall also provide that the adjudicator is not liable for anything done or omitted in the discharge or purported discharge of his functions as adjudicator unless the act or omission is in bad faith, and that any employee or agent of the adjudicator is similarly protected from liability.
(5) If the contract does not comply with the requirements of subsections (1) to (4), the adjudication provisions of the Scheme for Construction Contracts apply."

| |
|---|
| Clause 108 is not restricted to payment disputes, but includes disputes relating to time, quality and any other matter capable of giving rise to a difference between the parties. |

### Enforcement of decisions

Section 108 of the Construction Act further provides that a party to a construction contract has the right to refer a dispute for adjudication, that the contract is to provide that the decision of the adjudicator is binding until finally determined by arbitration or other means, and that the contract provides for immunity of the adjudicator

The Construction Act does not make provision for the enforcement of an adjudicator's award. Accordingly, one of the early questions raised by the Construction Act was the attitude of the court to enforcement.

In *Macob Civil Engineering Ltd* v. *Morrison Construction Ltd* [1999] B.L.R. 95 93 Morrison, the unsuccessful party in the adjudication, argued that given that the adjudicator's determination was challenged, it was not a "decision" within paragraph 23 of the Scheme. The judge, Dyson J., rejected this argument pointing out that, if it were correct, it would substantially undermine the effectiveness of the Scheme, which was intended by Parliament " . . . to introduce a speedy mechanism for settling disputes in construction contracts on a provisional interim basis . . . ". Finally, the judge indicated that the usual remedy for failure to pay in accordance with an adjudicator's decisions will be for the successful party to issue proceedings claiming the sum due, followed by an application for summary judgment.

Following *Macob* the courts have taken a robust approach to the enforcement of adjudicator's awards.

## CDM REGULATIONS

The Construction (Design and Management) Regulations were introduced in 1994 (the "CDM regulations").

### *Objectives of the CDM Regulations*

The regulations are devised to ensure that there is proper coordination of health and safety matters throughout the design, construction, occupation and demolition processes.

The regulations seek to ensure that:

- All parties are competent to carry out their respective functions.
- They allocate adequate resources for health and safety.
- A health and safety file will be prepared for each structure in the project and will ultimately be made available to future owners/tenants.
- A health and safety plan will be prepared before any construction work begins on site.

These issues are dealt with in more detail below.

### Competence and resources of the parties

The regulations oblige certain people to satisfy themselves that those whom they appoint are competent to perform their duties under these regulations. This test of competence applies to the client's appointment of any agent, planning supervisor, designer, contractor or principal contractor. However, it only refers to competence in performing requirements arising from statutory provisions and in doing work without contravening prohibitions.

In deciding what steps should be taken to achieve reasonable satisfaction, the Approved Code of Practice (ACOP) issued by the Health and Safety Executive says that enquiries are to be guided by "common sense".

### Health and safety plan

A health and safety plan must be prepared before construction work commences, and should contain:

- a general description of the project work;
- the timing of the project and any intermediate stages;
- details of any reasonably foreseeable risks to any person involved;
- information enabling a contractor to demonstrate adequate competence;
- details the principal contractor might need for maintaining and developing the health and safety plan;
- details any contractor might need in order to understand how to comply with any requirements in respect of welfare or statutory provisions.

The principal contractor also has obligations to maintain the plan and to include into it any arrangements for ensuring the health and safety not only of all those involved in the construction process, but also of those who may be affected by it.

At all times, the health and safety plan must be available for inspection by the Health and Safety Executive (HSE) during routine inspections and accident investigations.

## *Application of the CDM Regulations*

### Types of work

The regulations apply to most types of construction work, with few exceptions. Construction is defined as the carrying out of any building, civil engineering or engineering work and includes construction, alteration, fitting out, commissioning, renovation, repair, upkeep, redecoration, maintenance (including certain types of cleaning), decommissioning, demolition or dismantling.

Also included is preparatory work such as site clearance, exploration, investigation, excavation and ground works, as well as the assembly or disassembly of prefabricated elements.

Site surveys are specifically excluded.

Exclusions are the exploration or extraction of mineral resources, but only on sites specifically established for that purpose.

### Size of project

| |
|---|
| Only those projects that are either longer than 30 days or will involve more than 500 person days of construction work are included. When a project involves less than five people in construction work, only the obligations on designers apply. However, if the work is the demolition or dismantling of a structure, all the regulations will apply, regardless of the size of the project. |

## *Obligations of the parties*

### Client

The regulations define the client as any person for whom a project is carried out, whether carried out by others or in-house. The client may appoint an agent to act as the only client for the project, i.e. fully delegating all matters relating to health and safety.

Such an agent, for the purposes of these regulations, shall make a declaration to that effect to the HSE. An agent who makes no declaration is entitled to act as agent of the client but does not stand in the client's shoes to the same extent.

If a domestic client, who would normally be exempt from these regulations, appoints a person to act as a developer of land, then the developer is the client for the purposes of most of the regulations.

The client must:

- appoint a planning supervisor and principal contractor who are competent and who have allocated adequate resources for health and safety;
- provide information to the Planning Supervisor;
- prohibit the start of construction work until the Health and Safety Plan is fully developed; and
- make the Health and Safety File available to any person who requires it or who acquires an interest in the site.

### Planning supervisor

There is no particular qualification for a planning supervisor. The Royal Institute of British Architects (RIBA) has indicated that it considers architects to be suitably trained to take on this role. Indeed, the RIBA publishes a Standard Form of Appointment as a planning supervisor, for use by architects acting in this capacity.

The planning supervisor must:

- on request, advise the client and others on appointments;

- send notice of the project to the HSE;
- prepare the pre-tender Health and Safety Plan;
- prepare the Health and Safety File;
- supervise designers to ensure that they are fulfilling their statutory duties; and
- cooperate with the principal contractor.

## Designer

Designers are defined as anyone who carries on business or trade in connection with the preparation of drawings, design details, specifications, bills of quantity, and the like.

Designers are obliged to ensure that no-one causes a design to be prepared unless the client for that project is aware of duties arising from these regulations and of advice issues from time to time by the Health and Safety Commission.

The designer must:

- ensure that the client is made aware of his duties under the Regulations;
- prepare a risk assessment of designs;
- reduce foreseeable risk to health and safety in his designs;
- provide information to other parties on risks remaining in his designs; and
- cooperate with other designers and the planning supervisor.

## Principal contractor

The principal contractor must be a contractor: in other words, someone whose usual business or trade is contracting. The principal contractor must ensure that there is cooperation between all of the contractors and that everyone on site complies with any rules in the Health and Safety Plan.

The principal contractor must:

- coordinate the safety activities of the contractors on site;
- restrict access to the site to authorised persons only;
- develop the Health and Safety Plan;
- reasonably direct the actions of contractors in respect of safety;
- ensure that safety information and training about the risks and conditions are provided to all operatives working on the site;
- obtain and consider the advice and opinions of persons on site;
- provide information for the Health and Safety File, as appropriate; and
- obtain the advice and views of persons at work in respect of safety.

### *Failure to follow CDM Regulations*

Failure to comply with these regulations carries penalties arising under the Health and Safety at Work Act 1974. These may be personal or corporate. The liability is almost exclusively criminal; civil liability only arises in two instances.

Those exceptions are:

- the client's failure to prevent construction work from beginning until a Health and Safety Plan has been prepared and developed; and
- a principal contractor's failure to take reasonable steps to ensure that only authorised persons are allowed on to the construction site.

## TEST YOUR UNDERSTANDING

**1. Which of the following is not needed to create a contract?**

(a) agreement between the parties;
(b) contractual intention;
(c) consideration;
(d) adjudication provisions.

**2. What legislation has direct binding force on all Member States without each Member State having to enact legislation?**

(a) a Directive;
(b) a Statutory Instrument;
(c) a Regulation;
(d) a CDM Regulation.

**3. The Unfair Contract Terms Act 1977 (UCTA) does not apply in which type of contract?**

(a) contract of sale of goods;
(b) contract for insurance;
(c) contract for the supply of goods;
(d) contract for hire purchase.

**4. Which of the following is not a requirement to assign a contract in accordance with section 136 Law of Property Act 1925?**

(a) that it must be in writing;
(b) express written notice of the assignment must be given to the debtor or person with the obligation;
(c) assignment must be absolute;
(d) must relate to a contract dealing with land.

5. **Liquidated damages are:**

   (a) a sum of money stated in the contract to be damages payable in the event of a specified breach of contract;
   (b) the actual damages suffered by the wronged party;
   (c) damages only payable for late completion;
   (d) damages only payable if the parties are unable to quantify the actual loss suffered.

6. **Under the Construction Act, if your construction contract is not in accordance with the Scheme, which of the following is true?**

   (a) the terms of your construction contract will prevail;
   (b) the terms of the Scheme will override the terms in your contract;
   (c) the Scheme will not apply because you have excluded it;
   (d) you will need to go to court to resolve the matter.

7. **Under the Scheme what is the maximum length of time in which the adjudicator should reach a decision under the Construction Act?**

   (a) 28 days of a referral;
   (b) 42 days of a referral;
   (c) 14 days of a referral;
   (d) any period greater than all of the above as agreed between the parties.

8. **Which of the following is false?**

   (a) the decision of the adjudicator is binding on the parties until the dispute is finally resolved in legal proceedings;
   (b) the decision of the adjudicator is binding on the parties until the dispute is finally resolved in arbitration;
   (c) the decision of the adjudicator is binding on the parties until the dispute is finally resolved by agreement of the parties;
   (d) the decision of the adjudicator is always binding.

9. **Who does not have an obligation under the CDM Regulations 1994?**

   (a) the client;
   (b) the builder or contractor;
   (c) the design architect;
   (d) the concrete supplier.

**10. The CDM Regulations 1994 do not apply to which activity?**

(a) demolition on a site involving 35 days of work;
(b) construction of a car park involving more than 600 person days;
(c) site survey work lasting 1000 person days;
(d) fixing of pre-fabricated elements over a 40-day duration.

CHAPTER 2

# MATERIALS AND COMMUNICATIONS

Anders Axelson

## INTRODUCTION

This Module considers the legal aspects of the "materials and communications" that are associated with administering a construction contract and resolving the claims and disputes that might arise therefrom. "Materials" in this sense stands for matter that is produced through the construction process but which does not form part of the physical built environment—most notably, paper and electronic documentation. "Communications" stands for how such materials are applied—particularly from the standpoint of establishing a contract, managing it, demonstrating entitlement to the contractual claims that arise from it, and resolving the resultant disputes.

The objectives of this Module are:

- To discuss the different kinds of document that are normally incorporated into construction contracts and how such documents influence the legal rights of the contracting parties.
- To highlight how a contractor's documents can best provide evidence to support its claims.
- To describe how the programme and bill of quantities influence parties' contractual rights.
- To examine the implications that new theoretical and technological developments may have on how construction contracts are administered in the future.

### *Documents in construction—a checklist*

For contracts where the obligations of the parties are as complex as those provided by construction contracts, a wide variety of documents, whether forming part of the contract or not, will be pivotal in determining the outcome of the project in general and the result of any dispute in particular. The following is a checklist of the types of documents that arise in the construction process and, in particular, can be used to support claims[1]:

1. Taken from Pickavance, Keith (2003) *Delay and Disruption in Construction Contracts* (2nd edn) (London, Informa Professional), p. 380.

*Pre-Contract*

- Pre-tender correspondence
- Pre-tender minutes of meetings
- Invitation to tender or provide a quotation
- Tender drawings, specifications, bills of quantities and schedules
- Nominated subcontractor details
- Site investigation report
- Programmes
- Tender estimate worksheets, calculations and quantity takeoffs
- Manpower resources analyses and levelling curves
- Cash flow forecast curves
- Subcontractor tenders and quotations
- Supplier quotations
- Site photographs
- Method statement
- Contractor's tender programme
- Submitted tender

*Contract*

- Contract agreement or conditions of contract
- Contract drawings
- Contract specifications and schedules
- Contract bills of quantities
- Bills of reduction
- Letters of intent
- Subcontract documents
- Pre-contract minutes of meetings
- Telephone attendance records
- Instructions to commence work
- Drawings and specifications issued for consideration

*Contemporaneous*

- Correspondence
- Minutes of meetings
- Conversation memoranda
- Telephone attendance records
- Internal office correspondence and email
- Inspection notices
- Drawing specifications revisions
- Submission and approval of the contractor's design
- Fabrication drawing submission and approval records
- Drawing submission log
- Defects and snagging lists
- Clerk of Works' daily reports
- Clerk of Works' diaries
- Site agent's and foreman's diaries
- Daily labour records
- Equipment use reports
- Weather data
- Safety reports
- The contract administrator's written instructions (EIs & AIs)
- Confirmation of verbal instructions (CVIs)
- Variation orders
- Variation proposals
- Requests for information (RFIs)
- Request for variation orders (RFVs)
- Variation logs
- Plant and tool programmes
- Labour and plant daily allocation sheets
- Progress photographs
- Schedules of defects and snagging lists
- Certificates of Partial Completion
- Certificates of Sectional Completion
- Certificates of Practical Completion
- Certificates of Final Completion
- Notices of delay
- Programme information
- Method statements
- Bar charts

- Planned and actual manpower histograms
- Planned and actual plant histograms
- Tender programme
- Original master programme
- As-planned short-term programmes
- Programme update reports and logs
- Programme update narratives from progress reports
- Short interval/look-ahead programmes
- Planned and actual resource loading
- Programming meeting minutes

*Cost data*
- Tender analysis
- Control budget
- Daywork sheets and supporting records
- Weekly labour distribution records
- Labour timesheets
- Labour overtime records
- Payroll records
- Daily equipment cost records
- Purchase orders
- Material delivery notes
- Cancelled accounts payable cheques
- Applications for payments
- QS's recommendations
- Progress payment reports
- Project cost reports
- Subcontractor cost reports
- Job cost reports
- Subcontractor cost reports
- Revenue records
- Bank loans

*Independent standards and authorities*
- Codes of practice
- National and international standards

### *The purposes of documentation*

To project management staff the primary purpose of most construction documents is obvious: to facilitate the efficient management and execution of the project by providing and communicating the information that the parties need to fulfil their respective contractual obligations. From a legal perspective, however, documentation is essential for two other important purposes—firstly, showing what was agreed under the contract; and secondly, demonstrating the facts as they occurred during construction. Naturally, these objectives should be borne in mind by the project management team.

#### (a) Showing what was agreed under the contract

This is what the "contract documents" do. Primary contract documents (such as what are commonly referred to as "standard conditions" or "general conditions" and "special conditions"—together "conditions of contract") set out directly the respective obligations of the parties. Construction contracts invariably also incorporate into the contract a wide range of other documents (see those listed under the heading "Contract" in the checklist above). For proper incorporation to be guaranteed so that the document becomes effective in setting out the contractual obligations of the parties, the relevant documents will need to be referred to expressly within the text of the conditions of contract (see Module 1).

Apart from the contract documents, the rights and obligations of the parties will also be influenced by the decisions of the courts on relevant issues, by Acts of Parliament and secondary legislation, and, to a lesser extent, by custom and trade usage.[2]

### (b) Proving facts

For a contractor to make credible claims under the contract (or otherwise) and thereby protect its legal rights, the claims will need to be supported by factual evidence. To succeed in this regard, the contractor, as the claimant, will need to discharge the burden of proof that the law places upon it—on "the balance of probabilities".[3] It has been widely recognised that many contractors fail to discharge this burden of proof on the basis of insufficient project documentation.[4] For a document to be used in legal proceedings, it will also need to be "admissible" into evidence. Traditionally, site documents that could not be shown to have been created "in the regular course of business" may have risked being rendered inadmissible by the rules of hearsay evidence. Nowadays, with the relaxation of such rules, this is unlikely to present any practical problem. Documents that have been created in the context of communicating with lawyers about legal proceedings will be inadmissible, however, on the grounds of "professional legal privilege" (see Module 10).

### *Interpretation of contractual obligations*

To establish a contract, there needs to be some sort of shared intention or "meeting of the minds" as to each party's contractual obligations (see Module 1). The following principles are among the main ways courts seek to deduce what those intentions were[5]:

- Courts will construe intention objectively, from the words of the agreement as would be understood by a third party. A party's "subjective intent" (that is, the exact thoughts that someone has at the time) will be irrelevant, unless manifested in the contract documents.[6]
- Courts will approach the task of interpretation from the standpoint of an "objective bystander", sometimes characterised as a "reasonable man".[7]

2. See, e.g., Trickey, Geoffrey, & Hackett, Mark (2001) *The Presentation and Settlement of Contractors' Claims* (2nd edn) (London, Spon Press), p. 5.
3. In some jurisdictions the burden of proof is the "preponderance of evidence".
4. See, e.g., Bingham, Tony, "Capital Punishment", *Building Magazine*, 6 March 1998.
5. See, e.g., Uff, John QC (2002), Construction Law (8th edn) (London, Sweet & Maxwell), pp. 219–221.
6. *Ibid.*
7. *Ibid.*

- Courts will ascribe to the third party interpreter the relevant factual knowledge that the parties had at the time. This set of facts against which a contract is interpreted is sometimes termed the "factual matrix".[8]

These principles are further discussed in Chapter 6.

## TENDER DOCUMENTS

### *The tender process*

The formation of a traditional, construct-only construction contract will normally commence with the employer, having had tender documents prepared and having selected and amended an appropriate form of contract, issuing all of these documents bundled together in the form of an "invitation to tender" to prospective contractors. Among the tender documents issued in relation to such contracts are typically the following:

- The form of contract, typically an industry standard form with appropriate amendments.
- Drawings in sufficient detail for pricing purposes.
- An unpriced bill of quantities (BOQ) and/or schedule of rates for pricing variations.
- A specification prescribing the scope of the works and technical requirements.

These documents will be discussed in later sections of this Module. In the case of private sector employers, invitations are normally issued to contractors of the employer's choosing. Public sector employers in the UK, however, are usually required by legislation to advertise for tenders publicly. An employer, typically, to retain the bargaining advantages that arise from dealing with a contractor under pressure of competition, will seek to provide the tender invitation and accompanying documents in a form capable of immediate binding acceptance upon receipt of the bid (that is, complete save for the information that is to be provided by the contractor). This will not be the case, however, if a tender is "qualified" by a bidder (that is, made subject to qualifications that need to be resolved before a binding contract can come into existence). For an unqualified tender, a contract will therefore be formed when its acceptance is communicated (see Module 1 for offer and acceptance). For qualified tenders to be accepted, however, further negotiation will be required until the parties reach a common intention. Which party is ultimately the offeror and which is the offeree will have no effect on the eventual contractual rights of the parties.

8. *Ibid.*

### Selection and acceptance of tenders

Once an employer has received tenders, an employer may, depending on the circumstances, be under a contractual obligation to consider all conforming bids. This principle was established in the 1990 case of *Blackpool & Fylde Aero Club* v. *Blackpool Borough Council.*[9] In that case, tenders were sought by a council from several companies for the operation of pleasure flights from an aerodrome. The organisation which had operated the flights during several prior contract periods submitted a bid before the relevant deadline but, due to an administrative mistake, the paperwork was not received by those responsible for deciding the successful bid. The court held that the council owed the organisation a contractual duty to consider its bid. This decision suggests the existence of an implied "collateral" contract between the employer and prospective contractors that comes into existence before the main contract is agreed whereby:

- the employer offers to consider each conforming bid in a stipulated way;
- tenderers accept this offer by submitting a conforming bid;
- the consideration is the opportunity of entering into a further contract with the employer.

The extent to which the decision in *Blackpool & Fylde Aero Club* turns on the regular course of dealings that there had been between the two parties beforehand, however, remains unclear.[10] Note also that unless it has undertaken to the contrary, an employer will not, however, be under any obligation to accept the lowest tender or any tender at all.[11] This is the case irrespective of whether or not the terms of tender submission express this (as is commonly the case).

### Later formal agreement

Although the terms of an unqualified tender submission will create a contract upon acceptance, such contracts normally also stipulate that the parties shall later execute their contractual agreement formally under seal (that is, so as to create a deed). This step has importance for the purposes of limitation of damages—the period of time before which a party is time-barred from suing under a contract (as per the Limitations Act). If formally executed in a deed, the limitation period will double from six to 12 years.

### D&C contracts

Under "design and construct" (D&C) or similar contracts where the contractor assumes responsibility for design, the drawings, bills and specifications

9. [1990] 1 W.L.R. 1195.

10. Duncan Wallace, Ian, QC (1995) *Hudson's Building and Engineering Contracts* (4th edn), Vol. 1, p. 344.

11. See *Pauling* v. *Pontifex* (1852) 2 Saund. & M.

annexed to the invitation to tender in construct-only contracts are replaced by a document known as "employer's requirements", outlining the parameters of the design. This frequently takes the form of a performance specification (see "Drawings, Specifications and Method Statements" below). The contractor provided information, conversely, takes the form of a "contractor's submission" or "contractor's proposal" which, if unqualified, will normally be capable of immediate binding acceptance in the same way as for construct-only contracts. Examples of D&C standard forms are the *ICE7 Design & Construct* form, the *JCT98 With Contractor's Design* form, and the *FIDIC Plant & Design/Build* form.

## BILLS OF QUANTITIES

### *What is a bill of quantities?*

The Bill of Quantities (BOQ) is a schedule which categorises, details and quantifies the materials and other cost items to be used in a construction project. It is usually in tabular form. In columns corresponding to each cost item is typically the following information:

- a description of the item;
- the unit by which the item is measured (for instance, $m^3$ for excavation, tonnes for reinforcement etc.);
- the numbers of units estimated for each item on the project;
- the unit rate (i.e. price per unit);
- the estimated total cost (i.e. the unit rate multiplied by the quantity).

Some items, such as site "preliminaries", will have lump sums rather than calculated quantities associated with them. Allowance is also made for provisional sums (items for which the exact quantities are not known at the time of tender) and prime cost items (amounts accounting for works not undertaken by the contractor). The ways in which the fields of information in a BOQ are used in construction contracts vary markedly among the standard forms. This will be discussed below.

### *How is the BOQ used?*

The BOQ has multiple applications throughout the construction process. How it is to be used depends on the contract. It can be used before, during, and after construction works are in progress. Among the uses that standard forms contemplate are:

- Providing information to prospective tenderers about the quantities of work in a project (so that they do not have to calculate or estimate it themselves).
- Defining the extent of the work for which a lump sum is payable (and, as a consequence, whether or not work is a variation).

- Indicating an estimated or approximate contract sum.
- Providing a means for valuing variations (from the rates).
- Providing a means of assessing the progress payments due to the contractor (from the rates).
- Providing a means of assessing the final payments due to the contractor (by facilitating re-measurement of the works).

The BOQ also has the potential to assist in various other project management tasks such as tender comparison, planning, cost control, and claim preparation.[12]

### Historical context

When it first became widespread in the early nineteenth century, a BOQ would be prepared by a tendering contractor "taking off" dimensions and quantities from drawings. By pricing each individual item, contractors could use the BOQ as a device for pricing the contract works. From around the 1850s, taking off would typically be done by the employer's quantity surveyor (QS)—rather than the contractors themselves—to avoid a costly duplication of effort. In the first half of the twentieth century, the emergence of standard methods of measurement (see below) meant that BOQs had come to be prepared with increasingly scientific precision. By this time, BOQs were commonly adopted as contractual documents, with references to the standards of measurement incorporated. Such standardisation enabled the utilisation of BOQs in a new way—as a basis for financial control of the project. This was manifested in different ways for building and civil engineering contracts. In the building standard forms (the pre-decessors to what is now the JCT suite), the BOQ was commonly used to quantify the amount of work for which the contract sum was payable. This resulted in the "lump sum of which quantities form part" type of contract (see below). In civil engineering works, however, the quantities of work ultimately required are far more susceptible to the uncertainties of unforeseen ground conditions than is the case with building works. In this regard, a type of contract where the consideration varied in proportion to the actual quantities of works that had to be undertaken was developed—the measure and value contract. In both types of contract, the BOQ played a pivotal role (see below).

## Types of contract

If conventional, construct-only (as distinct from "design and construct") standard form contracts are classified by the general way in which they determine consideration, four distinct categories emerge:

### 1. Lump sum (with quantities forming part)

For this type of contract a single fixed price (or "lump sum") is agreed in consideration of the contractor performing a defined amount of work. A BOQ

12. See Lal, Hamish (2002) *Quantifying and managing disruption claims* (London, Thomas Telford), p. 37.

forms part of the contract documents. The scope of work for which the lump sum is payable is defined through the quantities in the BOQ. Variations are (typically, where applicable) valued through the rates in the BOQ. Examples of this sort of contract are the *JCT98 Private With Quantities*, the *JCT98 Public Works With Quantities* and the *NEC ECC Option B (Priced contract with bill of quantities)* forms.

**2. Lump sum (without quantities forming part)**

As with Type 1 above, a lump sum is agreed in consideration of the contractor performing a defined amount of work. A BOQ is not used in this case, however, as a contract document. Instead of a BOQ, other contract documents (such as drawings and specifications) are used to define the scope of works for which the lump sum is payable. Variations are priced using other criteria (although a schedule of rates in a similar format to a BOQ is often used). Examples are the *JCT98 Private Without Quantities*, the *JCT98 Public Works Without Quantities* and the *NEC ECC Option A (Priced contract with activity schedule)* forms.

**3. Measure and value**

For this type of contract (also known as a "re-measurement" or "schedule of rates" contract), the quantities of each cost item are measured after the relevant work has been completed. The BOQ rates are then applied to these "re-measurement" quantities to determine a corresponding amount that is payable to the contractor. Examples of this type are *ICE 7th Edition, FIDIC Red Book* and the *JCT98 Bills of Approximate Quantities* forms.

**4. Cost plus**

The "cost plus" type of contract involves the contractor simply being recompensed by the employer for the costs it incurs in undertaking the works—plus a margin for the contractor's overheads and profit. In such circumstances, a BOQ has no special application as a contractual document. An example is the *NEC ECC Option E (cost reimbursable)* form.

Note that, for Type 1 above, the quantities in the BOQ are of great significance whereas the BOQ rates are significant only for the secondary purpose of valuing variations. For contracts of Type 3, however, this situation is reversed: the rates become of paramount importance whereas the BOQ quantities prior to re-measurement are relatively insignificant.

### *Standard methods of measurement*

In the early twentieth century, standardised methods of measurement began to emerge. Previously, different quantity surveyors might have applied varying methods of measurement and description to similar work. In the case of brickwork for instance, some QSs might have allowed for "rough cutting", for example, to differing degrees within the quantity of bricks; others still may have included it as a separate item elsewhere.[13] The necessity of providing, firstly, a level playing field for tenderers, and secondly, clarity of contractual entitlement, resulted in, from 1922, the publication of the first Standard Method of Measurement (SMM). It is now in its seventh (1988) edition. From 1976, the ICE also published a standard method of measurement for civil engineering works (CESMM). That document is now in its third (1991) edition. The SMM and CESMM are incorporated by reference into the JCT and ICE form contracts, respectively.

The two standard methods are generally highly detailed documents, which set out in tabular form:

- A hierarchical classification of each thing that is measured, with detailed description.
- The units of measurement.
- The rules about how the measurement of each item is to be taken.
- The rules about how the item is defined.
- The rules about what is included or excluded in the measurement.
- Relevant supplementary information.

Whilst they are similar in approach for the most part, the philosophies of the SMM and CESMM differ in two important respects:

- The classification system of the SMM is far more detailed. In the CESMM, conversely, many difficult and complex operations are often rolled up into one item. This means that civil engineering BOQs tend to be smaller than those for building.[14]
- The CESMM makes some allowance for "method-related charges". This is where the costs of an operation are calculated in proportion to time or set in accordance with a particular construction method —rather than being calculated as strictly in proportion to quantity.[15]

### *Provisions in standard forms*

The provisions relating to BOQs of the most commonly used BOQ-based forms for building and civil engineering works respectively in the UK are set out below. These are the *JCT98 "With Quantities"* forms[16] and the *ICE 7th Edition*. Note that, as mentioned above, the former is a lump sum and the latter is a measure and value form.

13. Example taken from Dent, Colin (1978) *Construction Measurement 1: Elementary Substructures and Superstructures* (London, Granada), p. 5.
14. Uff, John QC, *op. cit.*, pp. 245–246.
15. Lal, Hamish, *op. cit.*, p. 36.
16. Both the "Private" and "Public Works" forms are similar here in all material respects.

### (a) The JCT98 With Quantities forms:

**14.1**
The quality and the quantity of the work included in the Contract Sum shall be deemed to be that which is set out in the Contract Bills.
. . .

**2.2.1**
Nothing contained in the Contract Bills shall override or modify the application or interpretation of that which is contained in the Articles of Agreement, the Conditions or the Appendix.

**2.2.2**
Subject always to clause 2.2.1:

**.2.1**
the Contract Bills, unless otherwise specifically stated therein in respect of any specified item or items, are to have been prepared in accordance with the Standard Method of Measurement of Building Works, 7th Edition . . .

**.2.2**
if in the Contract Bills . . . there is any departure from the method of preparation referred to in clause 2.2.2.1 or any error in description or in quantity or omission of items (including any error in or omission of information in any item which is the subject of a provisional sum for defined work) then such departure or error or omission shall not vitiate this Contract but the departure or error or omission shall be corrected; where the description of a provisional sum for defined work does not provide the information required by General Rule 10.3 in the Standard Method of Measurement the correction shall be made by correcting the description so that it does provide such information; and such correction under this clause 2.2.2.2 shall be treated as if it were a Variation required by an instruction of the Architect under clause 13.2.

From this it is apparent that:

- The "Contract Bills" is the term the JCT forms give to the BOQ. This will often also include the technical specification.
- Clause 14.1 provides for the primacy of the BOQ over other contract documents (such as the drawings and specification) insofar as defining the "quality and quantity" of work is concerned. Clause 2.2.1, however, ensures that the BOQ does not override the conditions of contract in other respects.
- Departures from the BOQ quantities are treated as variations, which are calculated by adjusting the BOQ to correct it and bring it up to

date. This applies to both errors in the original BOQ, and to discrepancies between actual and billed quantities. The employer therefore bears the risk of inaccuracies in the BOQ: the contractor is entitled to assume that the BOQ is accurate and has been prepared in accordance with the SMM.

### (b) ICE 7th Edition:

[Clauses 52(1) & (2) provide for variation prices to be agreed or, failing that, assessed by the Engineer.]

> 52(3) Failing agreement between the Engineer and the Contractor under either Sub-Clause (1) or (2) the value of variations ordered by the Engineer in accordance with [the clause providing for variations to be instructed] shall be ascertained in accordance with the following principles and be notified to the Contractor.
> (a) Where work is of a similar character and carried out under similar conditions to work priced in the Bill of Quantities it shall be valued at such rates and prices contained therein as may be applicable.
> (b) Where work is not of a similar character or is not executed under similar conditions or is ordered during the Defects Correction Period the rates and prices in the Bill of Quantities shall be used as the basis for valuation so far as may be reasonable failing which a fair valuation shall be made.
>
> . . .
>
> 55(1) The quantities set out in the Bill of Quantities are the actual estimated quantities of the work but they are not to be taken as the actual and correct quantities of the Works to be executed by the Contractor in fulfilment of his obligations under the Contract.
>
> 55(2) No error in description in the Bill of Quantities or omission therefrom shall vitiate the Contract nor release the Contractor from carrying out the whole or any part of the Works according to the Drawings and Specification or from any of his obligations or liabilities under the Contract. Any such error or omission shall be corrected by the Engineer and the value of the work actually carried out shall be ascertained in accordance with [the clauses providing for Variations]. Provided that there shall be no rectification of any errors omissions or wrong estimates in the descriptions rates and prices inserted by the Contractor in the Bill of Quantities.
>
> 56(1) The Engineer shall except as otherwise stated ascertain and determine by admeasurement the value in accordance with the Contract of the work done in accordance with the Contract.
>
> 56(2) Should the actual quantities executed in respect of any item be greater or less than those stated in the Bills of Quantities and if in

the opinion of the Engineer such increase or decrease of itself shall so warrant the Engineer shall after consultation with the Contractor determine an appropriate increase or decrease of any rates or prices rendered unreasonable or inapplicable in consequence thereof and shall notify the Contractor accordingly.

56(3) The Engineer shall when he requires any part or parts of the work to be measured give reasonable notice to the Contractor who shall attend or send a qualified agent to assist the Engineer or the Engineer's Representative in making such measurement and shall furnish all particulars required by either of them. Should the Contractor not attend or neglect or omit to send such agent then the measurement made by the Engineer or approved by him shall be taken to be the correct measurement of the work.

57(1) Unless otherwise provided in the contract . . . the Bill of Quantities shall be deemed to have been prepared and the measurements shall be made according to the procedure set out in the "Civil Engineering Standard Method of Measurement" . . .

Things to note here are that:

- As with the JCT form, the BOQ is deemed to be correct; additional work arising from any discrepancies is to be treated as a variation.
- Unlike the JCT, however, the BOQ quantities are not deemed to be automatically corrected where discrepancies arise: this is unnecessary for this form as they will be overridden by the re-measured quantities in any case.
- Importantly, by clause 56(2), not only can the contract prices for a work item be adjusted (by application of the rates to re-measured or "admeasured" quantities), but the rates themselves can be changed, if this is warranted in the opinion of the Engineer. This mechanism provides some flexibility if the original rates prove to be "unreasonable" or "inapplicable" for application to the actual quantities. Quantity surveyors refer to such changed rates as "star rates".
- By clause 52, the price for variation work is to be determined from the BOQ rates "where work is of a similar character and carried out under similar conditions", and, in circumstances where this similarity is absent "so far as is reasonable". As to the interpretation of this clause see below.

### *The approaches of courts*

As the above clauses in the JCT and ICE contracts indicate, the BOQ has become firmly entrenched in many contract forms as a primary device for financial and scope control, to the exclusion of other forms of documentation which might alternatively be used for such purposes. The use of BOQs has not been without its difficulties, however, and problems have arisen that have required the court's intervention on several occasions. Two issues in particular stand out. Firstly, the multitude of uses to which a BOQ can be put has, in the absence of express contractual words, sometimes resulted in ambiguity as to what the parties can be said to have intended. Secondly, problems have arisen in relation to contracts (the ICE as quoted above, for instance) which on the one hand contemplate valuations on the basis of BOQ information, but on the other hand allow for the BOQ-based valuations to be replaced by a "fair value" or other assessment where it is considered appropriate or reasonable to do so. In such circumstances, where should the line be drawn between using the BOQ and overriding it? Generally speaking, these uncertainties have tended to be resolved by the courts in favour of utilising the BOQ, thereby upholding the status of a document that has been said to be "sacrosanct".[17]

### (a) Presumed intention to re-measure in measure and contracts

Where a bill of quantities is incorporated as a contract document, in the absence of indications to the contrary, there will be a presumed intention that re-measurement based on the bill of quantities is intended by the parties. This principle was established in the 1902 case of *Patnam and Fotheringham Ltd* v. *Pilditch*.[18] The presumption will apply even when the rate suggested by the contract documents is excessive, as was illustrated in the Court of Appeal decision in *Henry Boot Construction* v. *Alstom Combined Cycles*, part of a stream of seemingly never-ending litigation over an ICE form contract for civil engineering works at a power station in Wales.

In that case, immediately before the contract was to be signed, the design was revised to require sheet piling in two large areas of the site. In post-tender (but pre-contract) correspondence, the contractor faxed a price to the employer for that work. The price had been calculated for both areas. Despite that, however, the contractor stated in its correspondence that it was for one area only. The employer (misguidedly) accepted the price and it became incorporated into the contract. The contractor relied on the fact that as the contract was a re-measurement contract, and there had been no agreement to the contrary, so that price should be combined with the quantities associated with the one area to infer a unit rate for sheet piling, and that unit rate should then be applied to reach an adjusted contract price for any additional sheet piling works (in the same way that it would be if it were a separate item in the bill of quantities). This would give the contractor a "windfall gain", as it would be extrapolating a price it had calculated for two areas on the basis that it applied to only one area. The court confirmed that the contractor's approach was indeed correct, refusing to interfere with the rates that the parties had agreed, albeit by presumption rather than expressly.

17. See *Henry Boot* v. *Alstom* [2000] B.L.R. 247.
18. Duncan Wallace, Ian QC, *op. cit.*, Vol. 1, p. 368.

### (b) Bill rates or fair valuation?

The case in *Boot* v. *Alstom* ultimately boiled down to the court's interpretation of Clause 52(3) of the ICE Conditions (see above), where, in the absence of similarity of character and conditions, the BOQ rates are nevertheless to be applied "so far as is reasonable"—otherwise there will need to be a "fair valuation". Could the engineer have regard to the fact that the rate for sheet piling was excessive (and so not reasonable on a commercial basis) in deciding whether a fair valuation was to be undertaken? The arbitrator thought that he could, on the grounds that "it would not be reasonable to enlarge the ambit of the original mistake, and therefore compound the effect of the error".[19] In a much debated decision, however, a majority of the Court of Appeal disagreed, adopting the proposition that "what is reasonable is to be decided purely by reference to the nature of the original and varied work". So once again, the revered status of the BOQ remained intact.

## *Problems with the use of BOQs*

Many distinguished commentators have criticised the typically English practice of incorporating bills of quantities into construction contracts, particularly for building works. In the words of Professor Ian Duncan Wallace QC, who has been particularly vehement in this regard[20]:

> "There is no apparent reason why lump sum . . . documentation should not be used for properly pre-planned building work, as in the United States and many other countries, and the rapid adoption and spread during the last 50 years of . . . of building contracts requiring . . . use of bills of quantities . . . has been the principal outstanding feature which has distinguished the English construction industry from other countries, not excluding those of the Commonwealth."

Some other criticisms of the use of BOQs are set out below:

### (a) That it inaccurately models actual cost

It is important to recognise that using a BOQ as a basis for re-calculating the amount payable to a contractor provides an imperfect model for predicting cost. As the example in the chart below shows, as a cost model the BOQ approach is typically restricted by its assumption that costs incurred are entirely in proportion to quantity, in this case, the SMM-stipulated measurement of the length that a concrete pile is cut back. In reality, however, cost is often highly dependent on several other factors (such as time and method, for

19. *Ibid.*
20. Duncan Wallace, Ian QC, *op. cit.*, Vol. 1, p. 966.

instance) and in any case, the relationship between cost and quantity is not necessarily linear and not necessarily asymptotic to zero cost and quantity.

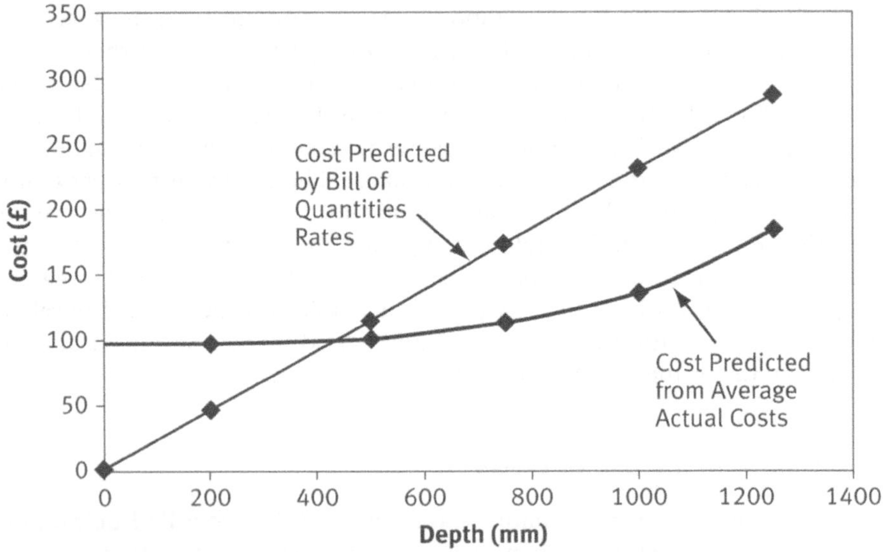


*Figure 1: Typical example of the relationship between quantity and cost based on (1) an averaged assessment of actual costs incurred and (2) as predicted by a corresponding BOQ. This example shows some of the limitations of the BOQ rate as a predictor of actual cost.*

The CESMM has alleviated this problem to a minor extent by the introduction of method-related charges; nevertheless, inaccuracies remain. This is one reason for the adoption by some contract forms of fallback provisions for "fair value" and "re-rating" assessments in circumstances where the failure of the BOQ model becomes too obvious (see, for instance, clauses 52(3) and 56(2) of the ICE form, as described above).

### (b) That the standard methods of measurement are too detailed and complex

Whilst the BOQ's mechanism of applying rates to quantities to derive costs is a simple one, the way in which BOQ items are broken down, as required by the standard methods (particularly the SMM), has been criticised for being excessively detailed and complex. Such detail and complexity has had adverse implications, it has been opined, not only on the time and cost of bill preparation, but also on accuracy. This has been supported by studies which have shown that around 90% of the bill preparation effort typically accounts for only around 10% of the priced total.[21] As one commentator has put it: "it is

21. Lal, Hamish, *op. cit.*, p. 40.

of major importance not to waste effort detailing to a greater degree than can be justified by the accuracy of the total."[22] Indeed, it has been claimed that the standard methods of measurement have "lost all touch with the far cruder realties of contractors' actual pricing methods."[23]

### (c) That it results in costly interim measurements and interim measurement disputes

The practice of basing a contractor's interim payment claims on a measured quantity survey assessed against a BOQ has also been criticised, again for the unnecessary cost and time that this incurs, as well as for the potential for disputes that this encourages. Fixed stage or milestone payments for the completion of pre-defined segments of the work have been cited as a preferable alternative. As Professor John Uff QC has put it[24]:

> "In the past few decades both natural evolution in forms of procurement and conscious policy have led to a move against bills of quantities, towards milestone interim payments and lump sum contracts of an increasingly turnkey nature. No one today wants to incur the cost of interim measurements, nor run the risk of interim payment disputes."

And, in the words of Professor Duncan Wallace QC[25]:

> "There are powerful commercial and administrative reasons why . . . interim payments should be based on fixed stage payments rather than periodical valuation."

### (d) That it encourages unbalanced bidding

One of the arguments in favour of using a BOQ in the tender process is that it supposedly provides a fair and even playing field for competing bidders to price the works. On the other hand, however, it also provides opportunities for contractors to engage in price manipulation—with a view to profiteering or "front-loading" their project cashflow. The former was alluded to in the case of *Sist Constructions* v. *State Electricity Commission of Victoria*[26]:

> "A tenderer may put down low rates for items he believes that the 'as-built' quantities are likely to be less than the billed quantities, and high rates for items where he believes that the 'as-built' quantities will exceed the quantities in the bill."

Employers who adopt a policy of selecting the lowest bid, irrespective of other factors, are particularly susceptible to such practices. In any case, according to Professor Duncan Wallace QC, such practices have, in the UK, reached a "high art" for contractors, and have been "the real driving force behind the

22. *Ibid.*, p. 35.
23. Duncan Wallace, Ian, QC, *op. cit.*, Vol. 1, p. 976.
24. Uff, Professor John, QC, *Are we all in the wrong job? Reflections on Construction Dispute Resolution*, Society of Construction Law, 3 July 2001, p. 3.
25. Duncan Wallace, Ian, QC, *op. cit.*, Vol. 1, p. 258.
26. [1982] V.R. 597, 606.

English industry's constant advocacy of contracts using bills of quantities".[27]

### (e) That it panders to the vested interests of quantity surveyors

Why has the contractual use of BOQs remained so prevalent in the face of all these difficulties and problems? Again, Professor Duncan Wallace QC provides an opinion[28]:

"[Quantity surveyors] represent in the UK, uniquely among Western common law countries, a powerful and successful vested interest operating effectively on both sides of the two industries and enthusiastically supported by contractor's organisations, favouring the universal use of measured contracts for work of any but the most modest size, and formal incorporation of the two industries' standard methods of measurement into the standard forms of contract in terms which not only represent serious financial risks to owners (by opening doors to a host of measurement claims of great ingenuity), but which lack obvious elementary safeguards to prevent abuse of the system."

## DRAWINGS, SPECIFICATIONS AND METHOD STATEMENTS

### *Drawings*

Drawings are incorporated into construction contracts to define the works that a contractor is to carry out. How the drawings interact with other contractual documents (such as the BOQ) in relation to that objective will be a matter for each individual contract: in the *JCT98 With Quantities* form, for instance, the bill of quantities overrides the drawings in respect of the contracted quantities of work (see "Bills of Quantities" above).

In all but the smallest and simplest of projects, once a contract incorporating drawings has been adopted, further drawings, or additional revisions to the existing drawings, will be required to revise or develop the design. In many cases this need arises in part because drawings will have been prepared only in sufficient detail to enable the contractor to price the work with a degree of reasonable certainty—not to specify definitively every aspect of the works. In reinforced concrete works, for example, bending schedules prescribing the layouts of the reinforcement bars within the concrete typically do not need to be issued until a relatively short time before the contractor is ready to commence placement. Design revisions creating additional work for the contractor ought to be distinguished from those that are merely detailing or developing the existing design—the former case will inevitably warrant a variation; the latter will not. In the words of *Hudson's Building and Engineering Contracts*, however[29]:

27. Duncan Wallace, Ian, QC, *loc. cit.*
28. *Ibid.*, p. 258.
29. *Ibid.*, pp. 420–421.

"Whether such everyday instructions involve an alteration of the original design and hence the contract price under a variation clause may be a difficult question of fact, but for some reason is only rarely the cause of a dispute. Whether they arrive in time to avoid delay and disturbance of the contractor's programme is, however, one of the commonest causes of building and engineering financial disputes."

To provide a degree of certainty in such instances contracts will typically seek to stipulate the due dates for the employer to provide the relevant drawings or other information via an "information release schedule".

## *Specifications*

Specifications set out the scope and technical requirements of the works, in varying amounts of detail, and generally tend to accompany the drawings as contractual documents.[30] As with drawings, the priority given to specifications *vis-à-vis* other contractual documents will be a matter of interpretation for each individual contract (although note that the *JCT98 With Quantities* form bundles specifications with the BOQs to form the "Contract Bills"). A specification will commonly cover some or all of the following:

- Construction details and standards of workmanship.
- Properties of materials (physical, chemical, acoustic, visual).
- How materials are to be procured or fabricated.
- Performance characteristics (such as equipment capability).
- Inspection, testing and certification requirements.
- External standards that are to be followed (commonly technical standards as well as those relating to quality, occupational health and safety, and environmental).

In general terms, the more detailed "physical" and less detailed "performance" specifications represent alternative philosophical approaches to specification drafting. Which is preferable will depend on the nature of the construction in question. In an office building refurbishment, for instance, the exact aesthetics and surface material properties are likely to be integral to an architect's design and so a precise physical specification is likely to be warranted. For a power station construction, conversely, it is the power output or wattage that is likely to be of prime importance—the precise physical characteristics can probably be left to the contractor. Hence in the latter case a performance specification would probably be the more appropriate alternative. In design and construct contracts, the "employer's requirements" will also typically be drafted in the form of a performance specification.

30. Note that whilst the term "specification" can connote an entire set of documents, it is in this instance used to refer to what might otherwise be known as a "technical specification" or "project scope and technical requirements".

### Method statements

In contracts that adopt them, method statements, setting out in detail the construction methods that a contractor intends to undertake for a part of the works, are in some instances included as a contractual document alongside the contract drawings and specification. Alternatively, the contract documents will merely stipulate in general terms what method the contractor is to use, subject to submission of a detailed method statement at a later date for the contract administrator's approval.

The established rule in relation to working methods is that, in the absence of contractual stipulation to the contrary, it is for the contractor to decide upon its method of construction. This was established in the case of *AMF International* v. *Magnet Bowling*, where it was held that[31]:

> "An architect has no right to instruct a builder how his work is to be done . . . It is the function and right of the builder to carry out his own building operations as he sees fit."

Where included as a contract document, a method statement, however, will override this general principle. Such a practice is not uncommon, particularly in relation to civil engineering contracts. Ostensibly, the purpose of specifying a particular construction method is to secure for the employer the quality that a given method will produce, and sometimes to control extraneous factors such as safety, noise and pollution. This has proved to be a double-edged sword for employers, however, as required changes to a method specified by the employer can sometimes give rise to variations.[32] In *Holland Dredging* v. *Dredging and Construction Co*, for instance, a contractor claimed a variation arising from a method statement for dredging that incorrectly presupposed a location from where backfill material would be available.[33] The Court of Appeal approved the claim, notwithstanding the principle of the *AMF International* case, on the grounds that the method statement had status as a full contractual document and specified a method that was impossible to achieve.

## PROGRESS RECORDS

### The purpose of progress records

Progress records are the documents in which a contractor records what it has done (or not done), and other associated information. They include both primary records, into which information is entered directly (for instance, site

31. [1968] 1 W.L.R. 1028.
32. Uff, John, QC (2002), *Construction Law* (8th edn) (London, Sweet & Maxwell), pp. 247–248.
33. (1987) 37 B.L.R. 1.

diaries) and secondary records that summarise the information in the primary sources (for instance, weekly, monthly and annual reports). Unlike drawings, specifications and BOQs, progress records are not normally contractual documents. This is because their purpose is to bear witness to the execution of contractual obligations—rather than define what those obligations are in the first place. The main purpose of progress records (in a legal context, at least) is therefore evidentiary—providing the necessary factual proof that a contractor's claims may require. The notion that the burden of proof lies on the claimant—as well as judicial resistance in the UK and most other jurisdictions to claims of a "global" nature—highlights the importance of good record-keeping.

### *What data should the primary records contain?*

The evidentiary importance of progress records is a compelling reason that provision for their form and style be made in a technical specification, notwithstanding the logic of the argument that good record-keeping is invariably in the contractor's best interests and so compulsion via a contractual document ought to be unnecessary. The SCL Protocol recognises this and provides a "Model Records Clause" (see "The SCL Protocol" below). Various other attempts have been made to codify best practice and stipulate the information that primary site records ought to contain.[34] In any case, such information might include the following:

- The date, the author of the records, the project.
- Weather conditions—temperature, precipitation, wind.
- The affect of the weather conditions on the work.
- The work that was started, completed and progressed (cross-referenced to programme activities), site location, drawing number, trade and subcontractor. How work undertaken is measured also needs to be considered.
- The time spent by each unit of plant, labour and equipment on each work item.
- Plant, labour and equipment downtime.
- The reasons for that downtime.
- Transfers of resources between work activities.
- Materials received on site.
- Whether each unit of work is programmed work, variation work or rework.

34. See, e.g., *The Daily Report*, Construction Claims Online, 29 December 2003 (*www.constructionclaims.com*); Hill, Peter A, and Morris, Richard (1995) *The Management of Project Information as an Aid to Effective Dispute Resolution* (*www.morris-associates.co.uk*); The Society of Construction Law Delay and Disruption Protocol (London, SCL), October 2002, p. 71.

- Any requests for information, variation orders, instructions etc., associated with that work.
- Non-negligible delays and disruptions, and the apparent reasons for them.
- The work and resources that those delays affected.
- Immediate requirements for upcoming work—and its impact on resources.
- Accidents.
- Visitors to the site and the purpose of their visit.
- Progress photographs.
- References to other documentation affecting the work (for instance site instructions, variation orders, health, safety, environmental, quality and testing documentation).

### *Evidentiary weight*

Since the removal of traditional restrictions on hearsay evidence in civil proceedings, all site records are generally likely to be admissible as evidence in legal proceedings, howsoever produced.[35] If the facts suggested by the records are in conflict with other evidence, a court or tribunal will need to decide how much weight to ascribe to the records. Among the factors which are likely to influence the perceived reliability and veracity of records are:

- *Contemporaneity*—records documenting events while they occur or shortly afterwards are more likely to be accurate than those recalling events some time in the past and relying on the memory of the recorder.
- *Neutrality*—records documenting events both adverse and favourable to the party recording them are more likely to be more factually reliable than those which only record facts favourable to the recorder.
- *Approval*—if a contractor can obtain signed approval or acceptance of its records by a putatively independent contract administrator, for example, they will be viewed as more reliable than otherwise might be the case.
- *Formal and consistent process*—a set of records produced as part of a formal and regular business process, by someone whose job it is to produce them, will appear more reliable than those produced on an ad hoc basis.
- *First-hand*—First-hand hearsay records are more likely to be treated favourably than multiple hearsay records. Records will be "first-hand hearsay" if the recorder creates them from what he or she sees or

35. See the Civil Evidence Act 1995.

perceives directly. Records will be "multiple hearsay" if the recorder relies on the assertions of others to produce them.

- *Security*—a recording process should minimise opportunities for subsequent fraud and manipulation. For instance, in the case of handwritten paper records, it may be prudent for the diarist to sign off at the end of each section of text so as to mimimise the ease with which underlying blank spaces can later be filled. Suspicions may also be aroused if the pen colour of paper diary entries changes frequently midstream.[36] It is also prudent to ensure security by maintaining multiple copies or backups of records, whether on paper or electronically stored.
- *Internal consistency*—the recording system should be set up so that facts are able to be confirmed in multiple ways. For instance, the activities that progress photographs suggest took place at a particular time should match what is suggested by resource allocation sheets and staff timesheets. Anomalies should be identified and either corrected or explained.

### *Use of technology*

Traditionally, record-keeping has been an onerous task for personnel whose primary focus has tended to be on the construction work itself—not on its manifestation through paperwork. Increasingly, however, contactors are turning to technological solutions that can revolutionise the speed, efficiency and reliability of record-keeping, as well as the potential for utilising the resultant information for other purposes. Initiatives such as the PIX Protocol (see "Project Data Exchange Systems" below) have the potential to assist in this respect. Among the practical ways in which a contractor can take advantage of today's technology are:

- Replacing paper records with electronic records. When entered electronically, the underlying formats of records can be streamlined, and consistency and completeness ensured. The entered data can then be used faster and more effectively for other purposes. The entry process can be made faster and more reliable with the use of dropdown lists. Background checking can also be established to prevent record errors such as duplicate entries and excess hours for labour and plant.
- Taking advantage of portable computing technology, including laptop or handheld computers, for convenient data entry. Electronic tablets and speech recognition software might also be used.
- Linking all site data into relational databases. This allows all relevant data to be analysed in a multitude of ways. Information need only ever

36. See, e.g., *Deangrove Pty Ltd* v. *Commonwealth Bank of Australia* [2001] F.C.A. 173.

be entered once. Ultimately, primary data can be integrated into company's secondary reporting systems, cost, payroll, invoicing, project management and programming software, in real time.[37]

- Using digital signature and security technology.
- Using digital camera and digital video technology to increase the frequency and ease with which progress photographs can be taken and used.

### Common deficiencies

Anecdotal evidence suggests that despite their evidentiary importance, deficiencies in progress records are not infrequent. Among the most common problems are[38]:

- Insufficient weather information.
- Missing reports.
- Not enough information.
- Not enough detail.
- Illegible handwriting.
- Inconsistency of format.
- Misleading information.
- Photographs not labelled and locations not identified.
- Records for subcontracted works not being produced to an adequate standard.

## PROGRAMMES

### Construction programmes—their purpose

The construction programme, most fundamentally, is a device that enables the contractor and employer to manage and monitor the progress of the works. It also, however, has vital importance in proving and supporting the contractor's claims for extensions of time (EOTs). That this is the case is evident from the following considerations:

- the burden of proof for demonstrating entitlement is on the contractor;
- to gain an EOT from a given event a contractor will need to show it resulted in a delay to completion[39];
- to prove a delay to completion, it needs to be shown that the delay in question was on the critical path(s) of the project when it occurred;

37. Bewsey, Geoff (2004) *Management, Analysis and Avoidance of Delay and Disruption in Construction Contracts: Record Keeping and Transmittal—Managing Records During Project Execution*, CIOB & Pickavance Consulting Masterclass, 18 November 2004, pp. 12–15.
38. *The Daily Report, loc. cit.*
39. Subject to the wording of the conditions of contract and notice requirements.

- and so: accurately showing the parts of the works that are critical will almost certainly require a construction programme in the form of a critical path network.

In other words, an accurate construction programme is essential for demonstrating entitlement to an extension of time.

### *Historical development of construction programmes*

The following are key stages in the historical evolution of the construction programme:

**(a) 1920s—Gantt/bar charts**

In the 1920s, the bar chart (as is described below) emerged. The Hoover Dam project in California was cited as the first recorded instance of its use. Credited with this innovation was the mechanical engineer and management consultant Henry Gantt. Hence bar charts are also known as "Gantt charts". Whilst it is not inconceivable that projects stretching back to medieval or even ancient times may have utilised some timeline or related graphical device to assist in organising construction work, this period nevertheless saw the first use of the bar chart as a formally recognised contractual document.

**(b) 1940s—Critical path method**

The critical path method (CPM—as is described below) then came into use after the Second World War. Cited as CPM pioneers were arms manufacturer DuPont-Remington and the US Department of Defense, in connection with the development of the Polaris missile from 1948. The CPM was first synonymous with manual calculations and hand-drawn arrow and box diagrams, and then with the use of computer software.

**(c) 1990s—Widespread use of computer software**

It was only in the early 1990s, in the UK construction industry, that software such as the Primavera products enabled activities to be displayed in the more user-friendly bar chart format, whilst still retaining CPM-associated logic. This meant that it was now practicable and cost effective for even the smallest projects to employ the critical path method for project planning.

### *What programmes show*

Nowadays, construction programmes are usually capable of showing the following:

- The work *activities* or tasks that make up the project scope of works. These are typically represented by bars or boxes.

- The timing of those activities.
- Individual completion dates and "milestones".
- *The logical relationships between the start and finish points of activities.* These are typically represented by arrows between the bars or boxes. Available link types include start-to-start, finish-to-start, finish-to-finish and, more rarely, start-to-finish links. Links can usually be "lagged", that is offset by a period of time, so that the logic generally takes the following form:

  > Activity X cannot [start/finish] until [+/–]Z days after Activity Y has [started/finished]

  Lags can be positive or negative. In the above example Z is the lag, Activity X is referred to as the *predecessor*, and Activity Y as the *successor.*
- *Critical path(s)*. When several activities are logically linked, they form "paths" between commencement and completion of differing lengths. One (or more) of those paths will be the longest, and thus determinative of overall project duration. This path is termed "critical" because any delays to it will delay the project as a whole.
- *Float.* Non-critical activities can be delayed by a certain amount of time before they become critical and therefore delay overall project duration. Such activities are referred to as being in "float". Most construction programming software calculates two types of float:

  > *Free float*—the amount of time that an activity can be delayed before one of its successors is delayed.
  > *Total float*—the amount of time an activity can be delayed before the completion of the project is delayed.

- *Coding* and a *work breakdown structure* assigned to each activity to enable the data to be organised.
- The proportion of each activity that has been completed, if at all, and the dates on which an activity started and finished, if at all, in relation to the programme date (or *data date*).
- *Resources* (plant, labour, equipment or materials) associated with each activity.
- *Costs* associated with each resource.
- *Constraints.* These are limitations on an activity's timing being determined by its logic. Such constraints might take the form of:

  > – activity X cannot start until date A;
  > – activity Y must finish on date B;
  > – activity Z cannot start until it is on the critical path.

- The days or hours that are set aside for working and non-working for a given activity, as shown in project *calendars*.

## *Construction planning software*

A construction programme is invariably prepared using an appropriate computer software package. A large number of packages are available. In the author's experience, the most popular are:

- Primavera Project Planner (P3)
- Primavera SureTrak
- Primavera Contractor
- Primavera Project Planner Enterprise Edition (P3E)
- Microsoft Project
- ASTA Powerproject
- ASTA Powerproject Teamplan

## *Issues in programme preparation*

### How much complexity?

"Complexity" in this context means the sophistication of the methods which the programme or software adopts in order to model the construction process.[40] It can be considered for most software packages there are around four levels of complexity, each of which represents an increased level of sophistication. These levels are, in order from least to most complex:

- the simple unlinked bar chart;
- the partially linked bar chart;
- the critical path method; and
- the resource levelled network.

Each of these levels incorporates the capabilities of the preceding level.

#### *(a) Level 1—The simple bar chart*

The longest established method of construction project planning is the simple (unlinked) bar or Gantt chart. It has the advantage of clarity, and the ease with which it can be understood. There is also a distinct lack of technological reliance; no computer is necessarily needed for its creation. Although there is no reason why new bars cannot be substituted for or superimposed upon the existing bars of the programme to reflect changes in the contractor's intentions as to timing or variations in work scopes, progress reporting and monitoring with unlinked bar charts is commonly undertaken by a visual comparison of

40. This is terminology used in Fenwick Elliott, Robert (2002) *Building Contract Disputes: Practice and Precedents*, para. 2–150.

a "zig-zag" progress line marking the current status of a each activity with a current date line.

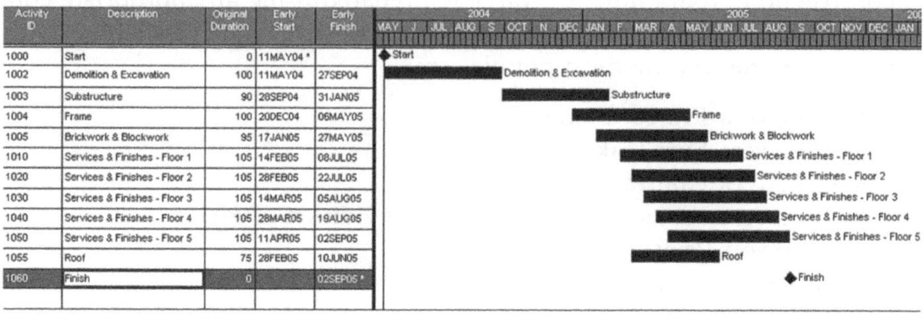


*Figure 2: An unlinked bar chart*

*(b) Level 2—The partially linked bar chart*

Most construction planning software has the potential to depict relationships between the activities that are represented in a bar chart by way of logic links. It is not uncommon for some relationships between some activities to be specified, but without going to the lengths of linking every activity to start and finish milestones. This practice is prevalent with users of some software products that allow activities with commencement dates in the future to remain in an updated or scheduled programme, notwithstanding that the reason for the future (rather than present) start has not been specified by way of either logic or constraint. The result here is what can be termed a "partially linked bar chart", a programme which, whilst showing some logical relationships between activities, does not do so to an extent sufficient to enable the critical path to be calculated from the programme. This is done presumably because of a desire to show only those logic links that are obvious and indisputable (see the links" described below), leaving out those links whose presence is less clear-cut.

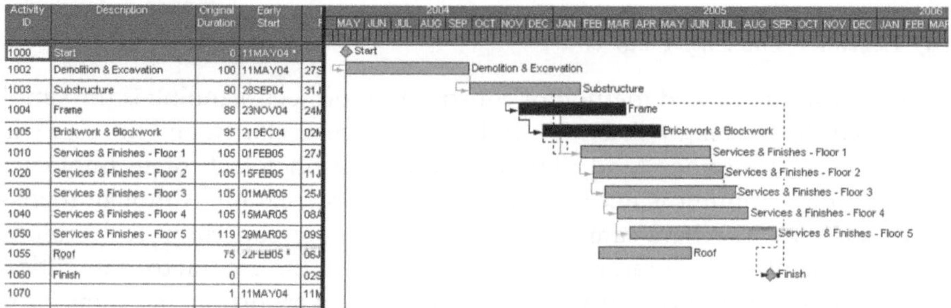


*Figure 3: A partially linked bar chart*

*(c) Level 3—The critical path method (CPM) network*

A construction project can be conceived as a means of getting from a start milestone to a finish milestone, where, directly or indirectly, every activity is a successor to the start and a predecessor to the finish. When all activities are fully (rather than partially) linked in a way that reflects this principle, a critical path network is formed. If properly prepared, the network enables the software to calculate arithmetically the longest path between commencement and completion: the path which is therefore determinative of the overall project duration whilst other paths are in float.

Whereas a partially linked bar chart may only contain one or two types of the above-mentioned classification of logic links, a critical path network, with its reliance on activities being strewn into competing paths, will most likely need to contain all four types of logic links (see below). This also means that, in the absence of updating and re-assessing the logic on a regular, periodic basis, the CPM network also has the potential to produce misleading results.[41] Thus, this method of planning is far more labour intensive than the previous two, if it is to be undertaken properly.

*(d) The resource levelled network*

Activities in a CPM programme which are in float may start later than the earliest possible date without causing a delay to completion. Where such activities have resources allocated to them, the latitude as to when activities can be commenced can be exploited so as to minimise the numbers of a given resource type that are required at any one time, using a "resource levelling" algorithm.

Whilst this is an option provided by most proprietary software packages today, anecdotal evidence suggests that, on building and civil engineering projects in the UK resource levelling is not often used unless there is a particular reason why the project is unusually resource-dependent.[42] There are various reasons which may explain this. One is that construction projects utilise a huge array of plant, labour and equipment. Keeping track of and entering all such details on a periodically updated programme is therefore likely to be at best time-consuming and at worst impractical. Secondly, there has been criticism about the appropriateness of the resource-levelling paradigm in a construction context, given that it takes no account of any arguments that there might be for retaining particular elements of float in order to protect the project against various unforeseen, or foreseen but unpredictable, events.

## How much detail?

A separate issue from methodological complexity is the level of detail that is adopted in the programme. Time is infinitely divisible. There is accordingly a

41. See Zack, James G. Jr., "Schedule 'Games' People Play, and Some Suggested 'Remedies'", *Journal of Management in Engineering*, Vol. 8, No. 2, April 1992.

42. For example, in the case of critical offshore oil platform work, where labour resources are constrained to the capacity of accommodation quarters.

huge spectrum of choices that can be made about how many activities a programme of work is to be broken into; on many projects this choice ranges between a few activities on the one hand and thousands on the other.

The greater the detail with which a CPM programme is created, the better the programme serves both as a record of how the contractor intends to perform the work and as a tool that can model and accurately predict the effects of changes to the work. The desirability of detail is, however, tempered by practicality—both in terms of the time and resources it takes to produce, review and update the programme, and in terms of how well a project team is able to estimate what it is likely to be happening at any given point in the future.

## *The importance of logic links*

A construction programme represents an attempt to derive a finite model from an often complex and chaotic process: the construction project. If a programme is to be used to determine extension of time (EOT) entitlement, the way in which logic links are inserted becomes of crucial importance. In general terms, a partially linked bar chart will be insufficient to determine with accuracy which activities are critical or in float, and so a fully linked CPM network will need to be created. If it is to reflect properly the reality of how the works will be progressed, an appreciation of the various reasons that exist for adding logic links to programmes is necessary.

Not all logic links are equal. Some can be regarded as fixed or "hard", and likely to remain unviolated throughout the project; others can be regarded as "softer" or "preferential", and are more likely to be violated when the programme is reconciled with reality. Various attempts that have been made to categorise these different types. One such classification scheme is as follows[43]:

### *(a) Physical links*

These are the strongest and most indisputable logic links. An example of a physical link might be the finish-start link between the fixing of reinforcement and the placing of concrete over that reinforcement—it would be impossible for this sequence to be reversed or for these activities to be undertaken in parallel.

### *(b) Resource links*

These are links determined by resource requirements. An (extremely simple) example is the finish-to-start link between the painting of Wall A and the

43. This classification scheme is suggested by McCaffrey, Gerry (1997) *LLM Construction Law Dissertation*, University of Strathclyde, pp. 21–25.

painting of adjacent Wall B, by a single painter. Such a link will need to be removed or altered either if the programme is re-sequenced (if, for example Wall A does not become available until after Wall B), or if there is a change in resourcing (such as the introduction of a second painter who can work in parallel with the first).

*(c) Contractual links*

These links reflect contractual requirements, which are not necessarily borne out of physical necessity. For example, a contract specifies that a piling contractor is not to commence work until after site welfare facilities and a canteen has been erected constitutes this type of link. If it is not also a physical link, this sort of link can be relaxed by entering into an overriding collateral agreement.

*(d) Strategic links*

These are relatively weak links which "seem like a good idea" but can probably be relaxed if necessary.[44] An example might be a decision to erect entirely a structural frame prior to commencing brickwork. This may be due to experience on previous projects where such concurrent working proved troublesome.

Clearly then, if a CPM network is to remain relevant throughout a project, not only will the activities need to be updated to reflect actual progress, but also the logic links, particularly the more "preferential" ones, will need to be reviewed, and revised if necessary.

## *Provisions in Standard Forms*

The following are extracts of the programme preparation provisions of the most widely used contract forms in the UK for building and civil engineering work respectively: the *JCT Standard Form of Contract 1998* and the *ICE Conditions of Contract (7th Edition) 1999*. These clauses can be considered typical of the approach adopted to programme provision by the JCT and ICE suites overall, and, more generally, the standard forms used in the construction industry as a whole.

### (a) In the JCT Standard Form of Contract 1998:

**5.3.1.2**

So soon as is possible after the execution of this Contract:

"The Contractor without charge to the Employer shall provide the Architect (unless he shall have previously been so provided) with 2 copies of his

44. *Ibid.*

master programme for the execution of the Works and within 14 days of any decision by the Architect [to extend the completion date or accept a variation quotation]."

**5.3.2**
"Nothing contained in . . . the master programme . . . shall impose any obligation beyond those imposed in the Contract Documents."

**(b) In the ICE Conditions of Contract 1999:**

14(1)

(a) Within 21 days after the award of the Contract the Contractor shall submit to the Engineer for his acceptance a programme showing the order in which he proposes to carry out the Works . . .

(c) Should the Engineer reject any programme [submitted in accordance with this contract] the Contractor shall within 21 days of such rejection submit a revised programme.

14(2) The Engineer shall within 21 days after receipt of the Contractor's programme:

(a) accept the programme in writing, or
(b) reject the programme in writing with reasons, or
(c) request the Contractor to supply further information to clarify or substantiate the programme or to satisfy the Engineer as to its reasonableness having regard to the Contractor's obligations under the Contract.

Provided that if none of the above action is taken within the said period of 21 days the Engineer shall be deemed to have accepted the programme as submitted.

14(3) The Contractor shall within 21 days after receiving from the Engineer any request under sub-clause (2)(c) of this Clause provide the further information requested failing which the relevant programme shall be deemed to be rejected. Upon receipt of such further information the Engineer shall within a further 21 days accept or reject the programme in accordance with sub-clauses (2)(a) or (2)(b) of this Clause.

14(4) Should it appear to the Engineer at any time that the actual progress of the work does not conform with the accepted programme referred in sub-clause (1) of this Clause the Engineer shall be entitled to require the Contractor to produce a revised programme showing such modifications to the original programme as may be necessary to ensure completion of the Works or any Section within the time for completion as defined in Clause 43 or extended time granted pursuant to Clause 44. In such event the Contractor shall submit his revised programme within 21 days or within such further period as the Engineer shall allow. Thereafter the provisions of sub-clauses (2) and (3) of this Clause shall apply. . . .

14(9) Acceptance by the Engineer of the Contractor's programme in accordance with sub-clauses (2), (3) or (4) of this Clause . . . shall not relieve the Contractor of any of his duties or responsibilities under the Contract.

When the importance of the construction programme in the context of proving EOT entitlement is considered, the brevity of treatment afforded by the JCT form seems surprising. Similarly, although the ICE form does provide for a more elaborate process of programme submission, acceptance and revision than the JCT form, it is still notably silent on other matters. So why this lack of provision? One reason may be that the contract drafting committees considered that further requirements for construction programming are best left to the drafters of the technical specification, as distinct from the main body of the contract itself. In any case, various attempts have been made to eradicate this shortfall, chiefly among them the SCL Protocol (see "The SCL Protocol" below) and what are known as the "PFE Change Management Supplements" (see Chapter 8).

### *The courts' approaches to programmes*

In the English and Commonwealth jurisdictions at least, there has been relatively little guidance from the courts as to how construction programmes affect legal entitlement. As has been noted[45]:

> "The use of critical path analysis in the proof of delay claims is a relatively recent innovation and the common law relating to the demonstration and proof of delay claims and the issues associated therewith is a developing area."

Although there have been relatively few UK cases that have dealt with these matters, with a few exceptions their outcomes have tended to be consistent, and, it can be argued, reflect a commonsense approach. Like many fields of contract law, it is difficult to generalise about the attitudes of judges in this area as any decision is likely to be highly dependent on the precise wording of the individual contract in question. Nevertheless, it might be concluded that the following questions have indeed been considered and answered[46]:

- **Is it appropriate to use critical path theory for programmes with a view to supporting or defending extension of time claims?**

45. See Burr, Andrew, *The Consideration of Critical Path Analysis in English Law*, Pickavance Consulting Masterclass in Delay and Disruption Management, November 2003.

46. Bearing in mind that these are undoubtedly somewhat contentious simplifications of highly complex factual and legal scenarios.

*Yes*. In the 1999 Technology and Construction Court (TCC) case of *Henry Boot (Construction) UK Limited* v. *Malmaison Hotel (Manchester) Limited*,[47] the court accepted the validity of a critical path analysis (in relation to a JCT form), holding that:

> "The respondent was entitled to respond to the claim both by arguing that variations, late information and so on relied on by the claimant did not cause any delay because they were not on the critical path . . . "[48]

These sentiments were lent further judicial support in 2002 by the Scottish case of *Motherwell Bridge* v. *Micafil*, among other cases.[49]

- **What does the programme need to show to support a contractor's EOT claim for a particular event?**

The extent to which the event in question impacted upon the contemporaneous critical path(s) and thereby caused, or was likely to cause, a delay to completion. Fundamentally, a successful EOT claim will need to show that the employer is liable to grant an EOT for the effects of the event in question. Then the claim will need to demonstrate what those effects were on the critical path and completion date. The programme assists in this second step. It is important to note the requirement of contemporaneity—the relevant critical path will be that as it exists at the time the event occurred—not at the start or finish of the project. These principles were first enunciated in several cases in the US Federal Courts, and have later been restated in the UK, Commonwealth, and other jurisdictions.[50]

- **Can inferences about EOT entitlement be drawn from logic and activities in the agreed contract programme—notwithstanding that there might be doubts about whether it is a proper representation of the contractor's true intention?**

*Yes* . . . In the 1999 TCC case of *Ascon Contracting Ltd* v. *Alfred McAlpine (Isle of Man) Ltd*,[51] a sub-contractor sought to base one element of its EOT entitlement on a series of two week start-to-start lags between a series of parallel overlapping activities, in a programme that had been created by a contractor. The contractor argued that it had inserted these links in an "arbitrary" fashion, and that the true logic was in fact only a one week lag. The court however, rejected this argument, stating:

> "I do not accept [the contractor's] attempts to disown the logic links in its own programme."

47. (1999) CILL 1527.

48. See also *John Barker Construction Ltd* v. *London Portman Hotel* (1996) 83 B.L.R. 31; *McAlpine Humberoak Ltd* v. *McDermott International Inc* (1992) 58 B.L.R. 1.

49. [2002] 81 Con. L.R. 44.

50. See for instance, *Brinderson Corp* v. *Hampton Roads Sanitation Dist*, 825 F.2d 41 (4th Cir. 1987), and the *Henry Boot* and *John Barker* cases (*loc. cit.*)

51. (1999) 66 Con. L.R. 119.

Thus there has been judicial support for a somewhat mechanistic or computational approach to EOT entitlement calculation.

*. . . But only up to a point.* In the 2004 judgment of *Skanska Construction Ltd* v. *Egger (Barony) Ltd*, the TCC criticised an employer's defence to an EOT claim that had relied on inferences drawn from programme logic, despite the fact that the programme in question had been updated (albeit by consultants, after the project had finished) to reflect each month's progress. The court suggested that such inferences could not be credibly drawn where "computer programme logic collided with demonstrable fact".[52]

## *Manipulation and abuse*

To maximise its commercial advantage, a contractor may try to manipulate its construction programmes so that when amended, it overstates the effects of any events for which it is entitled to an EOT or compensation, and understates the effects of contractor-caused delays. Whilst it is certainly not intended to imply that these tactics are necessarily widespread, it is nevertheless prudent for all contracting parties to become aware of the potential for such practices. Abuses to look out for include[53]:

### *Float eradication*

If two activities that are planned are to be undertaken in parallel (at the same time), for instance, are shown in a programme as taking place in series (one after the other), the period of time that the programme suggests is needed to complete both activities together increases. This technique, and other logic link manipulations, can be used to reduce or eradicate the float on a path in the programme, hence potentially changing criticality, which in turn will overstate the suggested EOT entitlement arising from an employer delay on that path. Increasing activity durations on the path will also have this effect.

### *Failing to provide a programme*

A contractor may deliberately omit to provide a contract administrator with a programme to review, irrespective of any contractual obligations to do so. This will mean not only that the employer and contract administrator will be left without a device to monitor the contractor's progress (including its failures), but also that the contractor will be left free to create whatever programme it needs to support its claims at the end of the project.

52. [2004] EWHC 248 (TCC). There is considerable argument, however, about whether the judge's interpretation of the facts in this case was correct.

53. See Zack, James G., *op. cit.*

*Failing to update the programme, or to submit it*

For similar reasons, a contractor may omit to update a construction programme, or otherwise fail to provide such an updated programme to the contract administrator. Again, this will allow the contractor more scope for later manipulation for the purposes of claims, and deprive the employer of information from which to judge the effects of its own actions.

*Misleading programme updates*

When a contractor does update a programme, it could do so in a way that reports activity actual start and actual finish dates, remaining durations or percentage progress inaccurately, and in essence change the project history. Some software programmes can allow this to happen inadvertently, with an "automatic update" function where the programme essentially guesses the progress during an update period. In any case, such manipulations can result in a false picture of float or criticality, invariably to the contractor's advantage if it is done deliberately.

*Exaggerated early completion*

A contractor may also, in the course of a project, produce a programme that shows an unrealistically early completion date. This will purportedly reduce the room for manoeuvre that the employer and contract administrator have for approvals and the provision of necessary materials and information. As a result, the programme will be more likely to invite inferences about employer-caused delays and disruptions (although the effectiveness of this tactic will depend on how questions of float ownership are resolved).

*Unrealistic or omitted delivery dates for free issue equipment or materials*

If a contract is silent about the particular dates that an employer is obliged to provide free-issue equipment or materials, the contractor may attempt to define these dates through the device of programme. It may further exploit this opportunity and specify unrealistically early dates, to maximise its chances of claiming EOTs for late delivery. Alternatively, a contractor might omit these dates from a programme altogether, for similar reasons. One commentator has termed this latter course of action "Star Trek scheduling", where the programme implies that equipment and materials are to be instantaneously beamed to the worksite, Star Trek-style![54]

*Unrealistic or omitted dates for information approval, review and release*

A similar ploy is to take advantage of imprecision in the contract about the dates by which a contract administrator is required to review and approve the

54. *Ibid.*

contractor's submissions, or release design information to maximise the contractor's chances of claiming associated EOTs. Again, the contractor could also, in the alternative, omit these dates from a programme altogether, with similar consequences.

*Failure to reflect variations*

Further scope for programme manipulation occurs when variations to project works are ordered. This provides an additional opportunity for contractors either to omit, to understate or to overstate the work that will be required, in order to change float and criticality to produce a result more favourable to itself.

*Legitimising a Manipulated Programme through Approval*

Once a programme has been manipulated in the contractor's favour in one of the aforementioned ways, the contractor might then attempt to buttress its legitimacy as a device for supporting its claims by disguising the changes and then seeking the contract administrator's approval or acceptance of the revised programme.

Note that such actions are not necessarily always deliberate, nor are they necessarily confined to contractors.[55]

### Technological and theoretical advances

It is unlikely that the evolution of the construction programme has come to an end. Although not widespread today, there are several theories and technological advances which may have the potential to gain acceptance and increase the technical sophistication of many construction programmes in the future. Three of these are:

- Taking into account the probabilistic element of activity durations and lags.
- Integration between construction programmes and three dimensional representations of the work (known as "four dimensional" or "4D" planning).
- Incorporation of Parkinson's Law in what is termed "critical chain" theory.

These methods may potentially invite different inferences about EOT entitlement to those suggested by a standard CPM network.

55. For instance, whereas a contractor may deliberately fail to submit programme's for the contract administrator's review, a contract administrator equally may deliberately fail to review or approve it.

### Probabilistic planning

Probabilistic project planning in theory overcomes one of the biggest weaknesses of CPM—the fact that, in the face of uncertainty about the future, it takes into account only one scenario (the most likely) at any one time. On any construction project, however, there are a range of random variables (the frequency with which weather events occur, the frequency of industrial action, variations in labour productivity, plant breakdown etc.) whose variation is predictable enough to be reliably modelled as a random process.

The Monte Carlo method can be used to model and simulate such variations in random events and in activity durations. When the resultant activities are logically combined, rather than deriving a single date for completion, a range of completion dates of different probability densities are computed.

> *Monte Carlo method*
>
> This is the term given to the method of obtaining information about the likely outcomes of fully or partially random processes by simulating them and comparing the frequency of each potential result. An example is flipping a coin 1000 times and comparing the relative frequency of heads and tails. The method was traditionally associated with checking the dice and roulette wheels for bias at the casino in Monte Carlo, Monaco.

This technique can also be used comparatively, to indicate how the impact of a relevant event affected the probability profile for practical completion, and assess the probability that a given delay impacted upon a project's critical path.

### Four dimensional planning

Software is available on the market which integrates the scheduling capabilities provided by Primavera P3 or similar with 3D design software such as AutoCAD or Microstation.[56] This has the potential to be more than simply a visual presentation device and allow the relationships between sections of work to be modelled in a more sophisticated way than the classical CPM can provide. For instance, whereas CPM requires work to be divided into discrete activities and the relationships defined entirely in terms of logic links, a 3D model potentially allows for a more realistic simulation that follows the way the work is actually constructed in three dimensional space, thereby enabling the different "types" of logic link (as described above) to be better differentiated.

### The 'Critical Chain' Method

Another development that has gained some popularity in the United States in recent years is the substitution of the CPM with the "critical chain method".[57]

56. See, e.g., *www.commonpointinc.com*
57. See, e.g,. *Critical Chain Concepts*, available at *www.scitor.com*

The key difference here is that the latter purports to take into account the effects of "Parkinson's law", the principle that work expands to fill the time available for its completion. A corollary of Parkinson's law is that critical or near-critical work is performed more efficiently than non-critical work.[58]

> *Parkinson's Law*
>
> This is the principle that work expands to fill the time available for its completion. This theory was proposed by management consultant C Northcote Parkinson in 1937, after undertaking time and motion studies of factory workers in the USA.

Whereas the CPM automatically assumes that activities are best performed as early as possible (so that they have the most float to absorb if anything goes wrong), the critical chain method suggests that there is actually an optimal point at which to start work that allows sufficient time for the activity to be completed but is nonetheless sufficiently close to criticality so as to harness Parkinson's law efficiencies. As programmes produced in accordance with the critical chain method suggest different answers to the CPM on questions of float ownership and what activity durations it is reasonable to allow for, they can also potentially produce different results if used to calculate EOT entitlement.

## THE SCL PROTOCOL

### *Purpose*

The *Society of Construction Law Delay and Disruption Protocol* (known as the "SCL Protocol") was introduced by the UK Society of Construction Law in 2002. It was produced by a drafting committee of members of the Society of Construction Law, and of the engineering, architecture, quantity surveying and legal professions.[59]

The Protocol was initiated to address certain perceived problems within the construction industry. These included:

- An industry tendency for excessive disputation in relation to delay and disruption claims.
- A perception that standard forms of contract do not make adequate provision for construction programmes.
- The lack of an industry consensus about the best method for contract administrators to deal with extensions of time for claims arising from delay and disruption.

58. *Ibid.*

59. *The Society of Construction Law Delay and Disruption Protocol*, SCL, October 2002, p. 3. Available at *www.eotprotocol.com*

- The lack of an industry consensus about the implications that float, concurrency, acceleration and mitigation have, or should be considered to have, on extension of time (EOT) entitlement.
- Uncertainty and ambiguities arising from the way that construction contracts typically address these issues.

The objectives and manner in which the Protocol was intended to be used were described in its introduction. As the Protocol puts it[60]:

"The object of the Protocol is to provide useful guidance on some of the common issues that arise on construction projects, where one party wishes to recover from the other an extension of time and/or compensation for additional time spent and the resources used to complete the project."

"It is not intended that the Protocol should be a contract document. Nor does it purport to take precedence over the express terms of a contract or be a statement of law. It represents a scheme for dealing with delay and disruption issues that is balanced and viable."

" . . . The Protocol contains guidance as to matters which should be addressed when the contract is being drafted and negotiated. The guidance is intended to be generally applicable to any contract that provides for the management of delay and disruption."

"Delay and disruption issues that ought to be managed within the contract all too often become disputes that have to be decided by third parties (adjudicators, dispute review boards, arbitrators, judges etc). The number of such cases could be substantially reduced by the introduction of a transparent and unified approach to the understanding of programmed works, their expression in records, and identifying the consequences of delay and disruption."

"The Protocol is not put forward as a benchmark of current (2002) good practice throughout the construction industry, though the aim is that the administration of contracts will in due course meet the standards of the Protocol. The cost of achieving this standard should be no more than is required for the best of current standard forms of contract."

In other words:

- It *is not* intended to be a separate contractual document.
- It *is*, however, intended to provide guidance on contentious issues for the drafters of contracts and specifications.
- It may assist contract administrators, adjudicators, and other tribunals of fact and law in providing guidelines for resolving these issues.
- It seeks to adopt a balanced view on the issues it addresses, having regard to the interests of each party to a construction contract.

### Structure

Aside from introductory and concluding remarks, the Protocol is divided into three parts[61]:

60. *Loc. cit.*
61. *Ibid.*, pp. 1–2.

1. Firstly, a statement of "Core Principles" relating to delay and compensation.
2. Secondly, "Guidance on the Core Principles". This guidance is delivered in three sections:
   (a) "Guidelines on the Protocol's position on Core Principles."
   (b) "Guidelines on preparing and maintaining programmes and records."
   (c) "Guidelines on dealing with extensions of time during the course of the project."
   (d) "Guidelines on dealing with extensions of time after completion of the project."
3. Thirdly, appendices. These consist of:
   (a) Definitions and glossary;
   (b) A model specifications clause;
   (c) A model records clause;
   (d) Graphics illustrating points in the Protocol.

## *Core Principles*

### What are the Principles?

Twenty-one "Core Principles" form the theoretical foundation upon which the other sections of the Protocol are based. To summarise the essence of each principle[62]:

1. That the programme should show the "manner and sequence" in which the contractor plans to undertake the works, and that there should be a process for its acceptance and for it to be updated.
2. That extensions of time (EOTs) under the contract are intended to relieve the contractor from damages for delay.
3. That EOT entitlement arises only from events for which the employer has assumed the contractual risk.
4. That EOT should be granted to reflect the extent that the event in question is "reasonably predicted" to prevent the works from being completed.
5. EOT can be granted before the event has begun to cause delay to the contractor.
6. After an initial award and where appropriate, the EOT granted for an event can later be increased as the effects of the event unfold.
7. EOTs should not be granted if the associated event only uses up float and so does not delay completion (unless there is contrary contractual provision).

62. *Ibid.*, pp. 5–9.

8. The contractor should be compensated for the direct costs it incurs as a result of an employer delay to its planned completion date (even if earlier than the contract completion date).
9. A contractor delay that is concurrent with an employer delay does not diminish the EOT entitlement arising from the latter.
10. An employer delay that is concurrent with a contractor delay only gives rise to an entitlement to compensation for prolongation costs for the contractor if such costs can be attributed solely to the employer delay.
11. A properly updated programme is needed for accurate identification of float and concurrency.
12. EOT entitlement should be determined from the standpoint of the contract administrator at the time the event in question occurred.
13. The contractor has a duty to mitigate the effect of employer events on its work (that is, take reasonable steps to minimise its loss and not take unreasonable steps to increase its loss) but need not normally add extra resources or work extra hours to fulfil this duty.
14. EOT entitlement does not lead automatically to compensation for the costs of the associated delay.
15. The compensation and EOT associated with variations should be pre-agreed, where practicable.
16. Compensation for prolongation should normally be based on the contractor's actual (rather than planned or projected) costs.
17. Because compensation for prolongation is based on actual costs, the allowances for site overheads planned for in the tender documentation are of limited relevance to its determination.
18. Compensation for prolongation should be calculated by reference to the period when the effects of the associated delaying event were felt—not to the extended period at the end of the contract.
19. "Global" claims, which do not substantiate the causes and effects of those claims, are discouraged.
20. If the contractor is to accelerate progress of the works and the contract does not explicitly provide for it, the associated compensation should be agreed in advance.
21. Disruption means a "disturbance, hindrance or interruption" to the works resulting in lower efficiency, and may give rise to a right to compensation based either under the contract or as a breach of contract.

These core principles are both descriptive and prescriptive. It might be considered that they fall into three somewhat overlapping categories:

- Those (principles 1, 2 and 3, for instance) that are in effect assertions as to how a typical construction contract does (or should) operate and how its provisions are (or should be) construed in law.

- Those that (11, 15, 17, 19 and 20) are more in the nature of practical guidelines to contracting parties.
- Those that are essentially restatements of or assumptions about how the law operates. These range from the relatively uncontroversial (2, 3, 13, 16, 18 and 21) to the controversial (7 and 9), or otherwise fall somewhere between these extremes (4, 5, 6, 8, 10, 12 and 14). Core Principles 7 and 9 are discussed further below.

## Float ownership (Core Principle 7)

Who owns float—the contractor or the project overall? If a contractor makes good progress so that it can expect to complete a project earlier than it needs to contractually, there will be a period of unallocated time ("terminal" float) between the expected and contractual completion dates. If an event for which the employer is liable then causes a delay to the early completion date, but which still falls before the existing contractual completion date, should the contractor be awarded an EOT and so preserve the end-of-project float period for its own use? Or should no EOT be awarded on the basis that the employer delay is simply absorbing float and not impacting the contractual completion date at all? These questions have proved highly contentious. Indeed there continues to be no consensus among judges, legal commentators or the drafters of contract forms about how these issues should be resolved.

To some extent, the SCL Protocol's Core Principle 7 (see above) avoids taking a firm position on this issue, advocating that parties address it themselves, one way or another, in their contracts. If that is not done, however, the Protocol provides a somewhat innovative compromise:

- Firstly, the contractor allocates or reserves float it is likely to need by creating contingency activities in the programme, the durations of which can be progressively depleted when the programme is updated and the float is used.
- Unallocated float, however, is available to the project—not exclusively to the contractor. In other words, it is available for whichever party uses it first. The Protocol recognises, however, that this stance can produce some unfairness or uncertainty (for the contractor in this instance, for the employer if the other approach is adopted)[63] but opines that this approach is the preference of "current judicial reasoning".[64]

This issue will be discussed further in Chapter 8 of this course. It is further complicated when different types of float are considered.

63. This is because, if an employer delay absorbs float which might otherwise be used in the future by the contractor and no adjustment to the contractual date for completion is made, the contractor has less margin of error for its own delays. Accordingly, the contractor placed in a worse position purely through the actions of the employer.

64. *Ibid.*, pp. 13–14.

## Concurrency (Core Principle 9)

Another problematic issue that arises in construction planning is how to deal with concurrent delay—that is, a contractor delay that occurs at the same time as an employer delay. Should the contractor be entitled to an extension of time in such circumstances, notwithstanding its own delay? Should the contractor be entitled to monetary compensation for the prolonged time it will have to be on site? The Protocol answers yes and no respectively to these two questions. In relation to the former, it essentially adopts this position based on the "prevention principle" of English law where an employer cannot take advantage (by imposing liquidated damages for late completion on the contractor) of its own breach of contract. On the other hand, the contractor considered not to be entitled to prolongation costs for an employer delay when, were it not for that employer delay, it would still incur those costs anyway.

These matters will also be further discussed in Chapter 8 of this course.

## *Guidelines on preparing and maintaining programmes and records*

This section in the Protocol is divided into two parts, dealing with programmes and records respectively. The policies outlined in the section are further codified by a "model [programme] specification clause" and a "model records clause", included in the Protocol as appendices.

### Content of programmes

As mentioned to in "Programmes" above, two variables that govern the content of a construction programme are: firstly, the level of methodological complexity, and secondly, the level of detail. The approach that the Protocol adopts in relation to each of these variables will be discussed in turn.

#### *(a) Complexity*

Insofar as methodological complexity is concerned, four possible alternatives can be identified: the unlinked bar chart, the partially linked bar chart, the CPM network and resource levelling (see "Programmes" above). Of these four, that which the Protocol promotes overwhelmingly "in all but the smallest of projects" is the third, the critical path method network.[65] This is unsurprising when the objective of the Protocol to facilitate "the analysis and management of change" such that "it can accurately predict the effects of change" is considered. For the purposes of calculating EOT entitlement, the "effects" of any change will be, firstly, whether the change causes any delay to progress, and secondly, whether such delay occurs on the critical path and thereby causes a delay to completion. Whilst tacitly conceding that a requirement for

65. "[I]t should be prepared as a critical path network using commercially available critical path method project planning software": see *SCL Protocol*, p. 35.

resources to be entered into the programme and continuously monitored may be asking too much, the Protocol recognises that having a means of assessing criticality is essential to achievement of this objective.[66] This therefore also rules out any support for the unlinked or partially linked bar charts, which, although potentially enabling a project's general status or progress to be reported satisfactorily, are incapable of providing anything but the most rudimentary picture of criticality.

*(b) Detail*

In relation to the level of programme detail, the Protocol stipulates:

- an activity should not encompass more than one trade or operation;
- no activity or lag should exceed 28 days duration;
- "excessive" leads and lags should be avoided.

This can be considered, at least for large projects, to represent a moderately high level of detail, but is excessively onerous by no means. It does, for instance, allow some leeway for programmes from project to project to be more or less detailed as may be considered appropriate. Nevertheless, the Protocol asserts that:

> "In principle, the procedure should be no different for small, medium or large projects (the smaller the project, the less this will involve). The Protocol does recognise that its recommendations may be thought to be onerous for smaller projects, but one of the Protocol's aims is to bring about a change in this attitude."[67]

*(c) Summary of the Protocol's approach to programme content*

In conclusion, in requiring a detailed breakdown of project works in a robust CPM network, the Protocol sets relatively high standards for both the complexity and detail of programmes, although this is tempered by some recognition of the practicalities of maintaining and updating such programmes. The following chart seeks to summarise this approach:

66. See, for example, clause 5A.3.6 of the *Pickavance Consulting and Fenwick Elliott Change Management Supplements*: "The Contractor and the Employer agree that the Master Programme shall be used for calculating the likely effect of any delay to progress on the Completion Date, if any, caused by an Employer's Time Risk Event."

67. See *SCL Protocol*, p. 35.

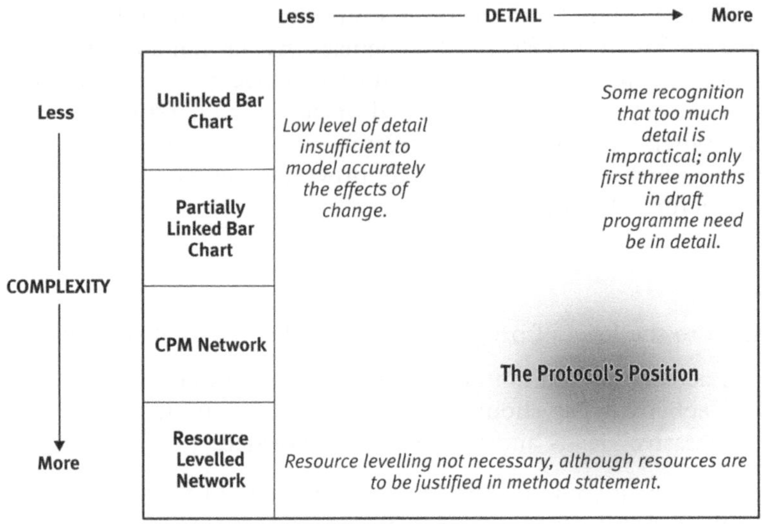


*Figure 4: Diagrammatical summary of the Protocol's approach to complexity and detail of programme preparation*

## Submission, approval and updating of programmes

The Protocol's approach to the submission and approval of programmes is summarised in the following extract[68]:

"As early as possible in the project, the Contractor should submit and the CA should accept a programme (using commercially available critical path method planning software) showing the manner and sequence in which the Contractor plans to carry out the works. In principle the procedure should be no different for small, medium or large projects (the smaller the project, the less this will involve). The Protocol does recognise that its recommendations may be thought to be onerous for smaller projects, but one of the Protocol's aims is to bring about a change in this attitude."

The Protocol goes on to emphasise the importance of parties reaching agreement about the programme is prepared and maintained, and stipulates that such agreement should cover:

- The form the programme should take.
- The interaction with method statement.
- The time within which the contractor should submit a draft for acceptance.
- A mechanism for obtaining the acceptance of the CA of the draft programme.
- Requirements for updating and saving the accepted programme.

Concession to the difficulties of specifying in detail an exact sequence of work before project commencement is made by allowing the possibility of

68. *Ibid.*, pp. 35–40.

separate draft and master programmes (or "initial" and "approved" programmes as the Protocol terms them). The Protocol requires that the initial programme need only show the requisite level of detail for the first three months of the project, before later adoption of the more detailed master programme when the project has commenced. Updates are also required at regular intervals. This procedure is codified in the Model Specification Clause at Appendix C. The *PFE Change Management Supplements*, which seek to adapt the principles of the SCL Protocol for specific standard forms, provide a useful flowchart for this procedure:

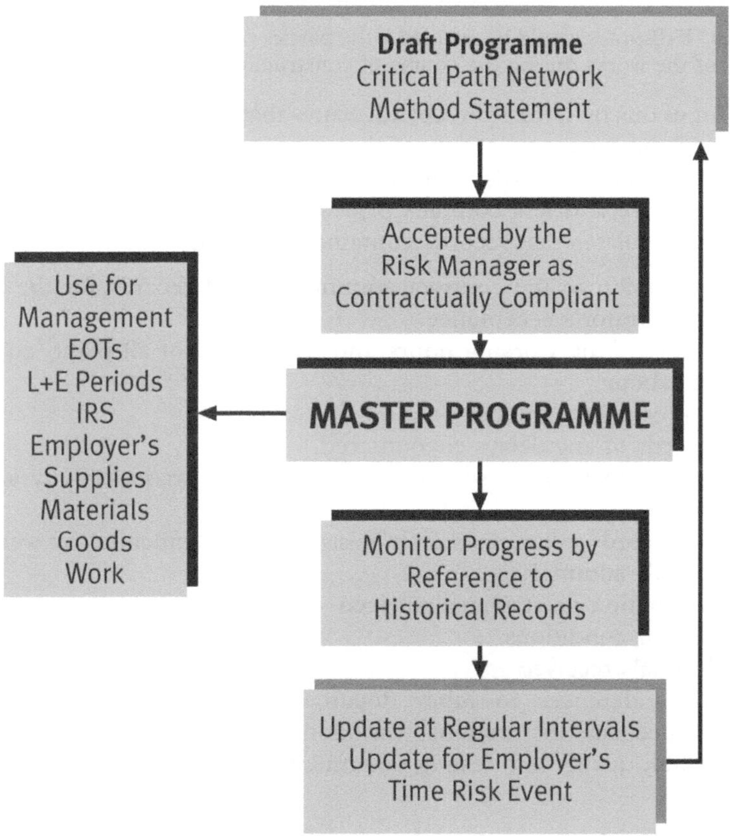


*Figure 5: The draft programme and updating process*[69]

## The programme method statement

A further feature of the SCL's approach to programme preparation is the stipulation that construction programmes be accompanied by a method statement detailing how the programme was prepared. This serves to buttress the

69. From *Practice Note for PFE Supplement*, p. 5.

legitimacy of programme as evidence and as a device for determining extensions of time. The method statement is intended to include:

- Substantiation of the durations of each activity. In most circumstances, this will require three things: the quantity of work, the number of resources dedicated to an activity, and the work productivity rates of those resources.
- The reasons of each logic link and any leads or lags.

## Guidelines on preparing and maintaining records

"Many EOT disputes would be avoided if the parties properly monitored and recorded progress of the works during the course of construction."

Cognisant of this fact, the Protocol advocates that agreement be reached in the contract on the form and nature of the contractor's progress records.[70] The appended "Model Records" clause suggests more and less detailed alternatives for more and less complex projects, respectively. The more detailed alternative stipulates that records contain, among other things[71]:

- Submission to the contract administrator of records for the contract adminstrator's acceptance.
- Details of the working hours and down-time of all plant, equipment and labour.
- Progress photographs.
- Records of any delays encountered.
- The numbers of persons working on site by trade, activity and location.
- Site records taken on a daily basis, but supplemented by weekly and monthly summaries.
- Information or drawings received.
- Weather conditions.
- Materials received.
- Cross-references to other documentation affecting the work (for instance site instructions, variation orders, health, safety, environmental, quality and testing documentation).

### *Guidelines for dealing with extensions time*

Important sections of the SCL Protocol are its guidelines for dealing with extensions of time, both during and at the conclusion of a project. These chapters will be addressed in Module 8 of this course, and so are not specifically discussed here.

70. *SCL Protocol*, p. 41.
71. *Ibid.*, p. 71.

## PROJECT DATA EXCHANGE SYSTEMS

### *What is project data exchange?*

"Project data exchange", is a relatively new concept for construction projects. It refers to the standardisation of the practices, policies and rules, across corporate and contractual boundaries, that parties have in relation to electronic data, software, and information technology generally. Central to a project data exchange system is a contractual document known as an "Electronic Data Interchange" (EDI) agreement. Although referred to as a separate agreement, in the context of a construction contract this document, it might be expected, would ideally be incorporated into the contractual documents between the respective contractors, subcontractors, suppliers and employers. In the UK, recognition of the benefits to the construction industry of efficient project data exchange systems has, with some government support, led to a movement for codifying and standardising procedures for their creation. Significant documents here include:

- *The PIX Protocol Guide and Toolkit.* This is intended to provide a practical template and guidance document for the creation of a data exchange system on construction projects. The resultant EDI agreement is termed a "PIX Protocol"; PIX here standing for "Project Information eXchange".[72]
- *EDI Association Standard EDI Agreement.* This document provides a standard form EDI Agreement. It is not specific to any industry, and is intended to be used either bilaterally or multilaterally (that is, among two or more parties).[73]
- *The European Model EDI Agreement.* As above but designed for use on Europe-wide basis.[74]
- *Uniform Rules of Conduct for Interchange of Trade Data by Transmission.* This set of rules were developed by the International Chamber of Commerce for the exchange of data in the context of international trade. The EDI Association Standard EDI Agreement and the European Model EDI Agreement incorporate these rules.[75]

Because of its practical orientation, its detail and because it is industry-specific, it is the PIX Protocol of these documents that is of most relevance in the context of construction projects.

72. Goodwin, Peter (2004) *The PIX Protocol Guide and Toolkit* (London, Building Centre Trust).
73. Thomas, Gillian, *IBC Construction Series: Dangers of Technology* (London, Lovells), 21 May 2002, p. 4.
74. *Ibid.*
75. *Ibid.*

### *The benefits of a project data exchange system*

If a project data exchange system can be implemented, it can, according to the promoters of the PIX Protocol, potentially save up to 10% of project cost.[76] Other benefits of such systems for construction projects include[77]:

- improvements in design efficiency;
- a reduction of errors on site;
- less time spent searching for and restructuring information;
- more interchangeability of successive revisions of drawings and CAD models;
- more reuse of project information; less redrawing, re-entry and re-keying;
- better communication of information; communications are not hindered by team members having sub-standard IT;
- facilitation of the transfer of information;
- the latest documents can be made available to everyone; team members need not work with old document revisions;
- as many persons can mark up or alter a document simultaneously as is necessary; systems for passwords and access privileges can ensure that this can be done without compromising security;
- provides a complete record of the project and so reduces the opportunity for mistakes or disputes;
- saves on copying and posting or couriering costs.

### *The wider industry context*

More generally, two key factors that also emerge in favour of the adoption of electronic data exchange systems in the construction industry are:

#### (a) Advances in technology

Firstly, IT and electronic communication capabilities have been notable for their exponential growth in recent years. This growth has occurred in relation to not only capacity but also the types of technologies that are available to businesses. Examples of the former are improvements in:

- the bandwith of internet connections;
- computer processing speeds;
- computer memory and data storage capacity;
- the capacity and bandwidth of mobile communications networks;

76. Goodwin, Peter (2004) *The PIX Protocol: A Risk Reduction Tool for Construction Projects* (London, SCL), p. 13.

77. Goodwin, Peter, *loc. cit.*; Thomas, Gillian, *op. cit.*, p. 2; Saddik, Farid W. (2004) *Outside the Box—Shared Project Control*, Construction Claims Online *www.constructionclaims.com*; 20 December 2004.

- the size and resolution of monitors.

Examples of the latter are:

- the emergence of the internet and worldwide web;
- the widespread use of email;
- improvements in mobile telephony;
- the emergence of wireless technologies such as Wi-Fi and Bluetooth;
- improvements in handheld and portable computing technology;
- digital camera technology;
- scanning and optical character recognition technology;
- voice recognition technology;
- improvements in data security such as firewalls and electronic signatures.

Such growth has been accompanied by a commensurate decay in the costs of such technologies. Despite the emergence of all of this technology, however, the construction industry, as many commentators have noted, has been slow to incorporate it into its usual practices. A 1999 survey commissioned by the UK Building Centre Trust, for instance, showed that at that time, some 80% of communications on construction projects were by paper.[78] Anecdotal evidence suggests that this percentage has not decreased dramatically since then. Thus, a key objective of the PIX Protocol and similar initiatives became, not only to facilitate better exchange of information among the parties to a construction project, but also to encourage it to improve its utilisation of these new technologies.

### (b) Trends towards greater collaboration between project parties

Secondly, project data exchange systems accord well with a tendency in the industry to promote more collaborative working arrangements. In the last decade or so, there has been, in the UK and elsewhere, a growing recognition of the long term advantages that can accrue when parties on a project join together in "a spirit of mutual trust and cooperation", as the NEC ECC contract form puts it.[79] This has manifested itself in new contract forms and in greater (although not universal) acceptance of the possibility of adopting "partnering" and "collaborative" project procurement arrangements. Such endeavours represent an attempted cultural shift away from what might be described as the traditional adversarial, contractarian and confrontational tendencies of parties to construction contracts. Project data exchange systems, therefore, it might be considered, represent some the technological aspects of that cultural shift.

78. Goodwin, Peter, *op. cit.*, p. 3.

79. *The Engineering and Construction Contract—Guidance Notes* (2nd edn, 1995) (London, Thomas Telford), p. 27.

## *What should a project data exchange agreement cover?*

### (a) Legal aspects

A project data exchange agreement such as the PIX Protocol (whether or not it is incorporated into a construction contract) will need to cover both legal and technical aspects of how the system is to work. Subject matter with legal implications that ought to be considered includes[80]:

- Security of data.
- Authenticity and integrity of messages.
- Confirmation of receipt of messages.
- Storage of data.
- Liabilities of the parties (including liability for use of third party intermediaries).
- Term and termination.
- Disputes and jurisdiction.

### (b) Technical aspects

Technical aspects for such an agreement to cover includes[81]:

- General Information and Company Policies on Information Exchange.
- Project Information Production and Distribution Policies.
- Drawing and CAD Management.
- Document Numbering Systems.
- Experience with Web-based Project Tools.
- Professional Indemnity Limitations.
- Email Distribution Policies.
- Policies on Internet Usage.
- IT Infrastructure.
- Operating Systems and Software Applications.
- Information Transport Capabilities.
- Disaster Recovery Systems and Procedures.
- Archiving Systems and Procedures.
- Security Systems.

## *What is the PIX Protocol?*

As far as the PIX Protocol system in particular is concerned, its key elements, according to its guidance document, are as follows[82]:

80. Thomas, Gillian, *op. cit.*, p. 4.
81. Goodwin, Peter (2004) *The PIX Protocol Guide and Toolkit* (London, Building Centre Trust), pp. 1–20.
82. *Ibid.*

- A definition of the client's information requirements, both during and at the end of the project
- Agreement within the team on which information is to be exchanged electronically; common formats for exchange and agreed rules for reuse of electronic information.
- Alignment of design management principles for the project. This means agreeing items such as drawing origins and grids and design coordination processes are followed.
- Alignment of document management principles such as file naming conventions and document numbering systems.
- Agreement on CAD standards to be used; this means agreeing alignment in areas such as common software platforms, CAD modelling approaches and layering conventions within CAD models.
- Agreement on standards for project communications, such as minimum speeds for internet communications, how electronic files are to be transported and agreement on maximum file sizes that can be produced for each communication channel.

Note the "team" in this context refers the collaborating entities on a project (the employer, its consultants, designers, suppliers, contractors and subcontractors etc.).

### *Agreeing a PIX Protocol*

In order for a PIX Protocol to operate, it needs to be agreed. The guidance document recommends that the Protocol form part of the contractual specification, to encourage higher levels of compliance and to avoid the prospect of "some team members only paying lip service to the concept".[83] To obtain the necessary information as to the capabilities of each party, standard questionnaires are issued by the employer for the other team members to complete. This process is termed the "team capabilities review". The review is intended to cover all relevant technical subject-matter of the data exchange agreement (see above).

Each questionnaire is designed to interrogate the minutiae of each team member's existing practices and capabilities the various subject areas listed above. For instance, the form on "Drawing and CAD Management" asks the following questions[84]:

- What are the drawing and CAD modelling approaches your organisation uses? What proportion of your output uses each method in a typical year?
- Are your CAD models drawn to scale with accurate dimensions or do you draw to approximate size and adjust dimensions to suit?

83. *Ibid.*
84. *Ibid.*

- Are standards used to produce your CAD models? If so what? Please attach.
- Would it be acceptable for your organisation to adopt project specific CAD standards that are different from your current standards?
- How do you resource the production of your CAD models?
- How are your CAD operator skills kept up to date?
- Do you use CAD for spatial and design co-ordination purposes?
- Describe your drawing issue process.
- Describe your file and document numbering systems for your drawings and CAD models.
- Is your organisation willing to use project standard title blocks which are different to your in-house standard?

The PIX Protocol can then be drafted and agreed taking this information into account. Typically, if it is not simply going be a case of all parties matching the lowest common denominator (which would in any case be inconsistent with the stated aim of achieving "best practice" across the project) for some team members conformance to the PIX Protocol will mean upgrading their existing capabilities. The guidance document recognises that such upgrades are likely to need to be negotiated on a commercial basis with the employer.

### *When should a PIX Protocol be implemented?*

The guidance document recommends that implementation should ideally commence in the feasibility stage of a project—before the team has been selected. That way, the team capability review can take place in conjunction with the tender selection process, and that the requirements for conformance with the Protocol be negotiated in the same way as any other part of the specifications.[85]

If this does not occur, and the team is already appointed the guidance document suggests that a "team leader" be appointed to conduct the team capabilities review, before publishing draft and final PIX Protocols in conjunction with the other team members. Alternatively, a meeting of all the team members can be held with the aim of agreeing a Protocol straight away.

## REFERENCES

Axelson, Anders (2004) *Preparing the Programme and Method Statement*, Pickavance Consulting Masterclass in Delay and Disruption Management, May 2004.

85. Goodwin, Peter (2004) *The PIX Protocol: A Risk Reduction Tool for Construction Projects* (London, SCL), p. 11.

Bewsey, Geoff (2004) *Management, Analysis and Avoidance of Delay and Disruption in Construction Contracts: Record Keeping and Transmittal—Managing Records During Project Execution*, CIOB & Pickavance Consulting Masterclass, 18 November 2004.

Bingham, Tony, "Capital Punishment", *Building Magazine*, 6 March 1998.

Burr, Andrew (2003) *The Consideration of Critical Path Analysis in English Law*, Pickavance Consulting Masterclass in Delay and Disruption Management, November 2003.

*Critical Chain Concepts*, *www.scitor.com*

*The Daily Report*, Construction Claims Online, 29 December 2003, *www.constructionclaims.com*

Dent, Colin (1978) *Construction Measurement 1: Elementary Substructures and Superstructures* (London, Granada).

Duncan Wallace, Ian, QC (1995) *Hudson's Building and Engineering Contracts* (4th edn).

Fenwick Elliott, Robert (2002) *Building Contract Disputes: Practice and Precedents* (London, Financial Times Publishing).

Furst, Stephen, QC & Ramsey, Vivian, QC (eds) (2001) *Keating on Building Contracts* (7th edn) (London, Sweet & Maxwell).

Goodwin, Peter (2004) *The PIX Protocol Guide and Toolkit* (London, Building Centre Trust).

Goodwin, Peter (2004) *The PIX Protocol: A Risk Reduction Tool for Construction Projects* (London, SCL).

Hill, Peter A., and Morris, Richard (1995) *The Management of Project Information as an Aid to Effective Dispute Resolution*, *www.morris-associates.co.uk*

*JCT Change Management Supplements* (2003) (London, Pickavance Consulting & Fenwick Elliott LLP).

Lal, Hamish (2002) *Quantifying and managing disruption claims* (London, Thomas Telford).

McCaffrey, Gerry (1997) *LLM Construction Law Dissertation*, University of Strathclyde.

Merritt, Frederick S., Loftin, M. Kent, and Ricketts, Jonathan T. (eds) (1995) *Standard Handbook for Civil Engineers* (4th edn) (New York, McGraw-Hill).

Pickavance, Keith (2000) *Delay and Disruption in Construction Contracts* (2nd edn) (London, LLP).

Pickavance, Keith (2004) *Putting the SCL Delay and Disruption Protocol Into Practice—Is It What the Industry Wants?* (London, SCL), September 2004.

Saddik, Farid W. (2004) *Outside the Box—Shared Project Control*, Construction Claims Online, *www.constructionclaims.com*

*The Society of Construction Law Delay and Disruption Protocol* (London, SCL), October 2002.

Thomas, Gillian, *IBC Construction Series: Dangers of Technology* (London, Lovells), 21 May 2002.

Trickey, Geoffrey, and Hackett, Mark (2001) The Presentation and Settlement of Contractors' Claims (2nd edn) (London, Spon Press).

Uff, Professor John QC (2002) *Construction Law* (8th edn) (London, Sweet & Maxwell).

Uff, Professor John QC, *Are we all in the wrong job? Reflections on Construction Dispute Resolution*, Society of Construction Law, 3 July 2001.

Zack, James G. Jr. (1992) "Schedule 'Games' People Play, and Some Suggested 'Remedies'", *Journal of Management in Engineering*, Vol. 8, No. 2, April 1992.

## SELF-TEST QUESTIONS

**1. Which of the following options best describes the purposes of documentation in the construction process?**

(a) setting out the legal rights and obligations of the parties;
(b) providing evidence for supporting later claims;
(c) providing the materials that project personnel need to manage the project;
(d) communicating information between project parties;
(e) all of the above.

**2. An employer and contractor agree on a contract based on the *JCT98 With Contractor's Design* form. Which of the following will normally be least likely to be included among the contract documents?**

(a) a performance specification;
(b) a statement of the employer's requirements;
(c) a bill of quantities;
(d) a statement of the contractor's proposals.

**3. A hastily assembled set of contract documents for a hotel project adopts the *JCT98 With Quantities* form. The contract bill of quantities specifies that 5000 m$^2$ of plasterboard is to be installed and remarks that it is to be painted with five coats of paint. The contract drawings indicate that 6000 m$^2$ of plasterboard will be needed and stipulates three coats of paint. In the absence of further contractual information, and with no additional instruction or variation, what has the contractor contracted to do?**

(a) install 5000 m$^2$ of plasterboard and paint five coats;
(b) install 5000 m$^2$ of plasterboard and paint three coats;

(c) install 6000 $m^2$ of plasterboard and paint five coats;
(d) install 6000 $m^2$ of plasterboard and paint three coats.

**4. A contractor argues that an engineer administering an *ICE7* contract form should dispense with BOQ rates and undertake a fair valuation to price some additional works. Which of these factors should the engineer give the least weight to in reaching his decision?**

(a) whether the BOQ rates are commercially reasonable;
(b) whether the work itself is of a similar type to that contemplated by the BOQ;
(c) whether the work is undertaken in a similar environment to that contemplated by the BOQ.

**5. An employer proposes to incorporate a contractor's method statement for some concrete piling works within a bundle of proposed contract documents. Which of these is least likely to be a good reason for doing so?**

(a) to ensure that the concrete is properly compacted;
(b) to minimise the risk of variation claims from the contractor;
(c) to provide a safeguard on the contractor's compliance with environmental standards;
(d) because the employer is concerned that the contractor will try and economise by using a cheaper method.

**6. Which of the following is not a form of progress record?**

(a) an annual report;
(b) photographs of the site;
(c) labour allocation sheets;
(d) a performance specification.

**7. How many days does the ICE Contract (7th Edition) allow the Engineer to reject a programme submitted by the contractor before it is deemed to be approved?**

(a) 14;
(b) 21;
(c) 28;
(d) 35.

**8. Which of the following changes to a contractor's programme will be least likely to increase the probability of the programme implying that an event for which the employer is responsible will delay the project completion date?**

(a) changing the programme logic so as to suggest that activities previously shown as taking place in parallel are now shown as taking place in series;
(b) inserting a new activity to reflect a variation;
(c) shifting the dates for the delivery of free-issue materials to later in the programme;
(d) increasing the durations of activities.

**9. A contractor is excavating a tunnel. The employer orders the contractor to stop all work on 1 July because it wants to reconsider the tunnel route. It orders the contractor to resume as before on 15 July. Immediately before the instruction to stop work was issued, the contractor's machinery breaks down due to the inexperience of its operators. No construction work could have taken place as a result, and the machinery was not fully repaired until 15 July. Which of the following best summarises the SCL Protocol's suggested solution to this problem?**

(a) the employer should grant the contractor a 14-day extension of time, but should not have to compensate the contractor for its site and head office overheads;
(b) the employer should have to pay the contractor's overheads, but should not have to grant the contractor any extension of time;
(c) the employer should grant a 7-day extension of time and the contractor should be compensated for half of its prolongation costs;
(d) the employer should not have to grant the contractor any extension of time, nor compensate it for any costs it has incurred.

**10. An employer's project manager is preparing invitations to tender and wishes to implement the PIX Protocol on the project. Which of these is least likely to be a good reason for such a choice?**

(a) he wishes to improve his organisation's it capabilities;
(b) he wishes to improve the it capabilities of the project's contractors and subcontractors;
(c) he wishes to encourage the lowest possible bids from tenderers;
(d) he wishes to improve the cost effectiveness of the project management process.

CHAPTER 3

# PROCUREMENT

Mark Hackett

## AN OVERVIEW OF PROCUREMENT

### *General introduction to procurement*

Procurement is the process of obtaining goods and services from one another. The vast majority of people in the developed world undertake the process of procurement without giving the process a second thought. The purchase of goods for a consumer is usually a simple transaction. One is usually able to view the goods in their finished state; purchase the goods instantly or in a short period; know the cost of the goods at the time of purchase; and if the goods were to prove faulty be able to return the goods and receive a full refund, exchange the faulty good for a new good in return or have the faulty good repaired.

The simplicity in procuring a good cannot be said to exist when procuring a construction project. The word construction might be said to have a number of different meanings:

- construction as a process—design and construction;
- construction as a category—building, civil engineering and process engineering;
- construction as a type—new build, refurbishment and maintenance; or
- construction as a project or range of projects.

Whatever context in which the word construction is used, each project will throw up its own challenges and each client will have his own view as to how those challenges should be managed; this will involve determining a procurement strategy which is matched both to the project's circumstances and to the client's requirements. Construction is a complex process in response to which numerous procurement strategies have evolved.

The complexity arising from projects is due to the prototypical nature of construction. With the exception of projects such as volume house building or supermarkets, each project is unique and is accompanied by varying degrees of risk. Consider here just how much the construction industry differs from the car manufacturing industry: with the latter, tens of millions of pounds are invested into research and development before a single car ever rolls off the production line, yet the cost to the consumer of the finished article is but a fraction of the cost of even the most modest of construction projects!

Clients who procure projects to fulfil their objectives will ordinarily expect the finished article to be:

- value for money;
- aesthetically pleasing;
- free from defects on completion;
- fit for the purpose;
- supported by worthwhile guarantees;
- reasonable as to running costs; and
- durable.

### *Selection of a procurement strategy*

The choice of procurement route is, in principle, driven by the client's business needs and objectives. In the majority of instances, construction is undertaken through physical necessity, commercial investment or to create a landmark building.

Hypothetically, all of the available procurement routes could achieve the same end result—namely a completed project. However, in practice, one route may be more appropriate than another in achieving clients' individual objectives.

Construction projects typically require that the client's project team should resolve three conflicting criteria (namely time, cost and quality) and do so in a manner which achieves the client's objective of value for money. These criteria, and any compromise, may be viewed as the eternal triangle. Successful balance and compromise should always be based on value for money over the life of the project and not merely on the capital spend alone. In assessing the procurement strategy, one must consider the best way forward to achieve the client's objectives for the project, whilst taking into account the risks and constraints. Such risks and constraints may include:

- client experience;
- attitude and ability to accept project risk;
- design responsibility and accountability;
- certainty of project outcome;
- ability to change the scope of the works; and
- public/private client.

### *Eternal triangle*

Time, cost and quality are the three ingredients which the client will have in mind when commissioning a project. Not surprisingly, the client will want his building constructed to the highest quality but in the shortest time and at the least cost. Such objectives are, perhaps, mutually incompatible but patient and thorough pre-planning coupled with a carefully considered procurement strategy can be used to obtain an optimum balance between these competing priorities.

In consultation with the client, it is essential to establish if the project is to be brief led or budget led. If the project is to be brief led, the primary focus will be on producing a design which meets the client's particular requirements and then seeking to obtain the best cost one can in relation to that. By way of illustration, a luxury hotel operator may need to achieve a certain standard of finish in his hotel to justify the forecast room rates and he will not be assisted by a design solution more associated with a youth hostel even if on the grounds that significant cost savings are thereby achieved. A budget led project, on the other hand, is one in which the client has a limit to his funds and requires a building which will be designed within his budget. By way of illustration, a manufacturing client operating from an industrial area is unlikely to require extravagant design solutions for his project no matter how aesthetically pleasing they may be. Of course, it is not unheard of that some clients may wish their project to be both brief led and budget led! One architect faced with this conundrum was once heard to respond: "Tell me what you want or tell me what you can afford but please don't tell me both."

*Figure 1: The eternal triangle*

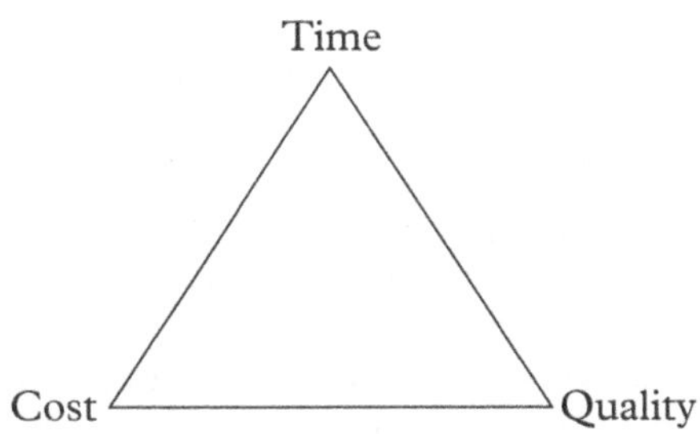


The ideal balance of criteria would be viewed in the shape of an equilateral triangle as the quality of the project would be appropriate to the cost of the project and completed in a reasonable timescale. Inevitably, the client will place the emphasis on one of the criteria in particular such that achieving that particular criterion may involve a compromise on another.

Should time be the priority, it might not be possible to tender the project competitively or to complete all of the design before the works start on site and this may lead to a premium in cost due to negotiating the contract price or due to rapid mobilisation of the workforce. By the same token, when time is the priority, quality may be compromised and this may have to be guarded against by implementing a strict quality control regime.

The importance and weight given to each criterion should be established in the briefing process and it is a fundamental prerequisite to deciding upon the procurement strategy.

Even the best planned of procurement strategies, once established having regard to the client's priorities, can be undermined by such things as:

- overly prescriptive briefs which give little flexibility to the design team;
- unnecessarily high standards;
- delays in decision making;
- use of one-off solutions rather than standardised products;
- scope changes somewhat beyond that considered at the time of selecting the initial procurement route;
- poor communication in the supply chain;
- conflicting agendas and objectives;
- doubling up of professional resources (as between the client and contractor teams);
- fixed mindsets and recycling of old solutions; and
- issue of design information which is late and/or inadequate and/or incomplete.

It is important to recognise the foregoing risks and to have, as part of the procurement strategy, management systems aimed at their eradication or, as a minimum, their control. Selection of a procurement strategy also influences the choice of which form of construction contract is used during the project. There are many standard forms available that complement the selection of a procurement route. However, it is worth noting that the selection of any particular form of contract is a secondary consideration to selecting a procurement route—the selected form of contract merely provides the administrative framework through which the procurement process can be achieved.

All procurement routes rely on the channelled communication of information. Traditional routes communicate clients' requirements through prescriptive specifications. Conversely, design and build utilises performance specifications. Each type of specification, together with the design drawings, varies in the length of time it takes to complete and this influences the selection of procurement route.

## DESIGN INFORMATION

### *Preface*

If the contractor is to quote a proper price for the project, and be kept to his contractual terms, he must always know his objectives. Initially, the basis for these will be set out in the contract documents. In terms of what is to be built and how it is to be priced, the contractor will look to such things as the drawings, specification and pricing schedule supplied by the design team—and the detail in which these documents are worked up will be governed by the selected procurement route. This latter consideration can be illustrated by reference to the detail in which a design should be worked up under a traditional contract when compared to that for a design and build contract.

In the case of a traditional contract (i.e. one in which all of the design details are provided to the contractor by the client), the handing over of a sparse design would be to invite problems since the contractor is entitled to a full design. On the other hand, providing the contractor with a full design under a design and build arrangement would defeat the object of giving the contractor the latitude to propose design solutions of his own which might be more economic.

It is important that the state of the design and the date by which it is released to the contractor are consistent with the chosen procurement route; any mismatches between these things will be a disservice to the client.

## *Drawings*

### Drawings generally

The traditional and most widespread method of conveying fundamental information regarding the project is by way of drawings. It is common for the architect to use drafting techniques and to detail plans and sections (general arrangements) on which can be superimposed:

- setting out dimensions;
- structural engineer's designs;
- services engineer's designs;
- specialist designs; and
- information for the development control submissions.

The clarity of drawings and other documents is fundamental to the smooth running of any project. Hence the goal of the design team must be to make the project information as simple and easy to understand as possible. It is suggested that one of the most effective ways of achieving this is to adopt the *Coordinated Project Information* (CPI) as set out in the guide first published by the coordinating committee for project information in 1987. Recommendations on the preparation of drawings, especially working drawings, are contained in BS 1192:1984. Also important are the principles defined in BS5750:1987 on quality assurance concerning the orderly preparation, dissemination and recording of design data and indeed all documentation relating to any form of manufacturing and production.

More recently, to accompany the high level increase in IT use by the construction industry and, specifically, the use of project extranets, the Building Centre Trust has developed a Project Information Exchange (PIX) Protocol Guide and Toolkit to help implement the protocol on all construction projects, if and when required. Key elements of the PIX Protocol are as follows:

- a definition of the client's information requirements, both during and at the end of the project;
- agreement within the team on which information is to be exchanged electronically, common formats for exchange and agreed rules for reuse of electronic information;
- alignment of design management principles for the project. This means agreeing items such as drawing origins and grids and design coordination processes to be followed;
- alignment of document management principles such as file naming conventions and document numbering systems;
- agreement on CAD standards to be used. This means agreeing alignment in areas such as common software platforms, CAD modelling approaches and layering conventions within CAD models; and
- agreement on standards for project communications, such as minimum speeds for internet communications, how electronic files are to be transferred and agreement on maximum file sizes that can be produced for each communication channel.

The PIX Protocol is further described in Chapter 2.

## Drawings for lump sum procurement

When tenders are to be obtained and a contract placed on the lump sum procurement route, with or without bills of quantities, it is necessary that all the drawings, schedules and specifications will be completed prior to obtaining tenders except when the contractor is provided with an information release schedule which states what information the architect will subsequently release and the time of its release. It should be borne in mind that where bills of quantities are used the SMM7R[1] general rules set out details of the drawings required for the purposes of tendering. The drawing production sequence is as follows:

- general arrangement drawings;
- services drawings by the architect (plumbing and drainage);
- construction details by the architect and specialist sub-contractors;
- assembly details;
- final coordination of drawings; and
- layout and site plans.

Many details and drawings will be changed during the course of the works and, in adjusting the contract sum in response to this, it will be necessary to

1. SMM7R is further described under the sub-heading Bills of Quantities which you will find set out below.

refer to the original information upon which the contract sum was based. It is therefore of the utmost importance to keep a record set of the drawings used in the agreement of what comprise the contract documents.

## Drawings for design and build procurement

Inasmuch as, under this arrangement, it is the contractor who is tasked with providing the detailed design, the drawings to be prepared by the client (and on which the contractor will base his tender) will be indicative or conceptual in nature and will provide the basic outline against which the contractor will work up the detail. Design and build procurement places a greater reliance on a performance/descriptive specification, usually by way of a set of employer's requirements, rather than fully detailed drawings.

## Drawings for management procurement

There are occasions when it is appropriate for the contractor to manage a contract in such a manner as will accelerate the rate of construction (even though it might increase the cost). In such circumstances, the preparation of the drawings will be geared not to the process of obtaining tenders for the whole of the works to be carried out by a single contractor but, rather, to obtaining a series of tenders for the various parts of the project, known as "packages".[2] The tenders for these packages will be obtained in a sequence related to the programme of the work to be carried out on-site, based on drawings and specifications and sometimes bills of quantities for each package. The order in which the drawings are produced will be related to the order of procurement and construction of each package.

Once the building is designed, the packages involved are also identified. The general arrangement drawings will have the same significance as the traditional procurement route but, once they are agreed, subsequent drawings will be of an elemental nature, i.e. concerned with the various and separate elements of the building. It is in the nature of management procurement that the works can commence on site before all elements of the design are complete. It is, however, essential to manage the completion of the remaining design if activities on site are not to grind to a halt. The management of the balance of the design must necessarily have regard to the time that it will take to (a) produce the design; (b) draw up the tender documents; (c) invite tenders; and (d) select the contractor to work on the package in question and allow him sufficient time to mobilise his workforce and procure the necessary plant and materials.

2. In a management contract arrangement, the party executing a parcel of the work is called a Works Contractor and is engaged by the Management Contractor. In a construction management arrangement, the party executing a parcel of the work is called a Trade Contractor and is engaged by the client but is controlled by the Construction Manager.

The following is an example of the order in which drawings, specifications and bills of quantities (when used) for packages might be required. Those items marked with an asterisk are likely to have a long lead-in period:

- general arrangement drawings;
- levelling and general site works;
- structural steel frame (steelwork)*;
- drainage;
- foundations (including piling);
- lifts (and escalators)*;
- proprietary walling*;
- roofing systems;
- windows and doors;
- brickwork details;
- mechanical and electrical engineering services*;
- plant and machinery details;
- partitions;
- staircases and other secondary elements;
- ceilings;
- fixtures and fittings; and
- external works.

The above list of packages is by no means exhaustive and, of those which are noted, it is often possible to combine them.

## *Specifications*

### Specifications generally

The types and uses of specification have changed dramatically in the past decade. They are no longer seen as documents that merely supplement drawings or bills of quantities but as key, stand-alone documents that define the scope and quality requirements of a construction contract.

In today's complex array of procurement, design and contractual methods, which seek to utilise the expertise of many contributors, the specification is the document that confirms precisely what one party agrees to provide to the other in respect of scope and quality. An inadequate clause or requirement that conflicts with other contractual statements will almost certainly lead to unwanted additional costs. Clients' demands for high quality, speed of construction and cost control increasingly lead to the need for off-site prefabrication where factory environments facilitate better quality control, economies of scale and less time on site. Traditional construction documentation is not always relevant to or understood by the manufacturing industry, and specifications therefore have to be adapted to suit.

Modern projects are very much a team effort, but legal responsibilities demand clear confirmation of who does what—the specification fulfils that requirement. There are three basic types of specification:

- Prescriptive.
- Performance.
- Descriptive.
- Output.

### Prescriptive specifications

Prescriptive specifications are more commonly known as a detailed materials and workmanship specification, this is a "do precisely as I say" specification. Such an approach pre-supposes that the design team know exactly what they want, have worked out exactly how it should be done, are allowed by European legislation to specify products, manufacturers, and are prepared to warrant the design, taking full responsibility for the end product being suitable for its intended use. Prescriptive specifications are most commonly written for smaller projects using well-tried and tested technology.

### Performance specifications

Performance specifications are used in circumstances where the design team have no particular visual requirements but wish the contractor to select suitable materials and install them to meet the stated criteria. A performance specification does not confirm what will be provided, only what has to be achieved and as such the employer does not necessarily know what he is getting when entering into the contract—the client's requirement is only that it performs and meets legislation and standard requirements. It is a "give me something that works" specification. Such performance specifications may be used to specify building services, lintols or other building elements which may not necessarily be seen and in respect of which meeting performance criteria is more important than the aesthetics.

### Descriptive specifications

A descriptive specification is a hybrid that has been developed to make best use of the skills of those involved in the process of delivering modern buildings. The main function of a descriptive specification is to define scope, design intent, procedures for completed detail design, quality control and to provide the contractor with a fair indication of the solutions that are acceptable. The contractor is required to use his specialist expertise to complete the detailed design (in consultation with the design team), manufacture and install the works and provide the necessary warranties and guarantees.

The need to prepare a contract specification which represents what the client is buying is fundamental to the successful use of descriptive specification if claims and variations are to be avoided at a later date. This requires a process of evaluating tenders in order to agree the key elements that reflect the scope of the works.

Descriptive specifications require that the design team and the contractor work in harmony and adopt a "help me to find the best solution" approach.

Large complex projects tend to require a descriptive approach whilst the more traditional design solutions lend themselves to the prescriptive approach.

### Output specifications

This type of specification is addressed in the "Procurement—The Options Evaluated" section of this chapter.

### *Bills of quantities*

The quality of the project sought is detailed in the drawings and the specification and is relayed to the contractor by the design team (acting on the client's behalf). The bills of quantities are documents that describe the quality and give the quantities of the constituent parts of the proposed construction works. They have two primary functions. Initially they are used as tender procurement documents to provide a uniform basis for competitive lump sum tenders. Subsequently they become the contract documents serving as the schedules of rates for the pricing of variations. It is therefore important that they contain at least the basic information required of them by the prevailing conditions of contract and that they are presented in a recognisable format that will facilitate their use.

Prior to the rising popularity of design and build, or projects being procured based on specification and drawings, the most popular standard form used in UK construction was the Joint Contract Tribunal Standard Form of Building Contract, With Quantities, 1998 Edition (JCT98 PWQ). This contract requires that bills of quantities be prepared in accordance with the current version of the Standard Method of Measurement of Building Works 7th edition, published by the Royal Institution of Chartered Surveyors and the Construction Confederation (SMM7R—at the time of publication).

The cost of producing bills of quantities is high and consequently their use as tender procurement and contract documents is often questioned and new techniques and procedures aimed at supplanting them are frequently tried. However, bills of quantities have survived thus far—no doubt because, in addition to their two primary functions, they contain vast amounts of information that can be of use in many ways. In preparing bills of quantities, the quantity surveyor sifts through and processes much detailed information that, although not required by SMM7R to be included in the bills of quantities, may be of use to tendering contractors and the building team in connection with project planning, administration and the compilation of historical cost data in the form of elemental cost analyses. It is therefore worthwhile, in the early stages, to plan the work and see what additional information can be readily gathered in the measurement process and/or presented in the bills of quantities to assist tenderers and the building team to operate more effectively and efficiently.

Bills of quantities are prepared by describing and quantifying, in accordance with the rules of SMM7R, the work shown on the drawings and given in the specification. Amongst other things SMM7R requires that "*Bills of Quantities shall fully describe and accurately represent the quantity and quality of the works to be carried out*".

## FACTORS INFLUENCING CHOICE OF PROCUREMENT

### *Preface*

The first section of this chapter addressed such influencing factors as the client's priorities as to time, cost and quality—priorities which will, in themselves, be influenced by whether the project is to be brief led or budget led. Numerous other factors combine to influence the client's choice of procurement.

### *Risk apportionment*

Any client's approach to the apportionment of risk will be coloured by wider business objectives than the project itself and might have regard to, for example, the number of projects with which he is involved and the state of his knowledge of the construction industry and how it operates.

A one off client involved in, say, a residential scheme for personal use may be particularly risk averse and may regard it as acceptable to pay a premium for a rigid contract which protects his interests and thereby spares him from financial disaster so he may "buy off" the risk with a rigid contract and will regard any premium paid as a worthwhile form of insurance. A "one off" client of the construction industry cannot rely on the promise of repeat business to influence the behaviour of the supply chain. In contrast, a regular, professional client (e.g. a major developer) might take the view that the cumulative effect of premiums on rigidly worded contracts might outweigh, on an actuarial basis, the risks which may eventuate in which case he might opt for a "softer" contract. Clearly, it is important to determine whether or not your client is risk averse (and, if so, to what extent) and then develop a procurement strategy which respects this.

In the event that things do go wrong, the client will want to know the nature of the remedies available to him. It could be that:

- the contractor is late in completing the works (and has no excuse for this) in which case the client may wish to recover the losses which he sustains as a result of the project overrun; or
- the contractor has produced sub-standard work in which case the client would want to have it condemned and put right; or

- delays and/or additional costs have been incurred due to the late issue of information in which case the client may look to recover his losses from the person whose fault it was that the information was late.

The client's attitude and ability to accept project risk should be reflected in which procurement route is chosen. "No construction project is risk free. However, risk can be managed, minimised, shared, transferred or accepted. It cannot be ignored."[3] Once the client's project objectives have been established, certainty of delivery is an important factor. Risks are events which may threaten the planned delivery of the project. They, therefore, need to be identified and managed. The basic principle of risk management is that risk should be allocated to the person most capable of controlling it. However, one must bear in mind that apportioning all risk, or as much risk as possible, on the contractor is likely to attract a premium in cost.

### *Risk management*

The focus of most risk management activity is on the project uncertainties (e.g. delays in planning consent or the effect of poor ground conditions). Early in the procurement process—and subsequently as part of an ongoing process—meetings should be held to address risk management issues as they will have a bearing on how the project will be procured and subsequently managed.

In mapping out a risk management strategy, the client and the project team should focus on identifying risks from the following sources:

- Quality and fit for purpose risks caused by failures to meet the specification, defects in construction, mismatches between client expectation and finished product.
- Cost risks caused by changes to the design, adverse market conditions or disruption to construction works resulting in claims for additional payment from contractors or sub-contractors.
- Time risks caused by delays to the planning process or production of design information, site conditions, the availability of labour, construction plant (machinery) and materials, or changes to client requirements.
- Health and safety risks, including accidents.

There are four principal strategies for dealing with specific risks:

(i) Eliminate—changing or cancelling the project.
(ii) Reduction—designing out risks or limiting the potential for risks.
(iii) Insure/transfer—reallocating risks to the design team, contractor or insurer through contracts and insurance policies.

3. Latham, Sir Michael (1994), *Constructing the Team, Final Report of the Government/Industry Review of Procurement and Contractual Arrangements in the UK Construction Industry*, HMSO.

(iv) Contain—either fully providing for or absorbing elements of risk or reacting only if risks become a reality.

In the elimination and reduction strategies, rational mitigation decisions can be made based on an assessment of the time, cost and quality implications of each risk. With transfer, the client will usually have to pay higher fees, costs and premiums whether the risks occur or not. With the contain and absorb strategies, the client should set aside a contingency fund, as part of the overall project budget, to cover the effect of risks should they eventuate.

All projects involve some form of passive risk management, usually associated with the expenditure of an unallocated contingency fund. As this fund is almost always expended, whether problems occur or not, the introduction of an active risk management strategy will result in improved financial management, as well as better planning and better responses to unexpected events. The principal benefits of active risk management are:

- Improved certainty—due to active risk mitigation and a greater understanding of project risk.
- Improved decision making—due to investment appraisals that incorporate an assessment of the project risk profile, or transfer to the party best placed to manage the risk.
- Improved management—through a focus on the issues that matter, a full record of the risks accounted for on the project, a focus on pre-planning and early risk mitigation, and effective control of budget allowances for risks.

### *Design responsibility*

A decision needs to be taken as to whether the client controls the design (as in the case of traditional procurement which envisages a fully worked up design accompanied by a prescriptive specification) or whether he devolves this responsibility to the contractor (as in the case of design and build procurement which envisages an indicative/conceptual design accompanied by a performance specification).

The timely production of design information is an essential ingredient to the works on site progressing satisfactorily. Where, in the case of traditional procurement, the flow of design information to the contractor is late and/or inadequate and/or incomplete, the contractor will be placed in a very strong position to obtain an extension of time (hence relief from liquidated and ascertained damages) and the reimbursement of any consequent loss and/or expense. It is because of this that some clients favour design and build procurement because all of the risks of producing the design information rest with the contractor.

A further attraction to clients of design and build procurement is what is referred to as "single point responsibility", so called because the responsibility for design, materials and workmanship rest with the contractor whereas the responsibility under traditional procurement becomes split between the design team (in respect of design matters) and the contractor (in respect of materials and workmanship matters) and this can cause difficulties in identifying who bears responsibility in the event of a building's failure.

Despite design and build procurement affording clients the opportunity to fix the contractor with single point responsibility, a grey area might still exist between those duties owed by the design team and those owed by the contractor. For instance, the design team may have a continuing responsibility for design carried out prior to the information being passed over to the contractor, such as drafting the Employer's Requirements. In terms of his dealings with the contractor, the client is contractually responsible for the performance of his design team and it may be that the client wishes to be absolved of any risk due to the performance of the design team. Where this is the case, the client may decide to novate his design team to the contractor.

Novation should allow for seamless responsibility for the design and construction of the project. However, each consultant's terms of appointment should be checked against the novation agreement to ensure that:

- The consultant's design responsibility matches the contractor's design responsibility under the construction contract.
- The consultants will be responsible to the contractor for design undertaken both pre-novation and post-novation.
- Adequate PI insurance is maintained.
- If liability is to be limited, it is not unreasonable.
- If consultants are to give warranties to the client, they do not prejudice the contractor's position by creating a conflict of interest.

For all of the benefits of placing the design responsibility with the contractor, the drawback to design and build procurement is that the client loses control over the project's aesthetics and the contractor is allowed to create a visual appearance of his choosing (subject, of course, to his meeting the performance standards set out in the contract).

The decision to place the design responsibility with the design team or the contractor is an important one. Sometimes, the design responsibility can be split as in the case where the Contractor's Designed Portion Supplement is used.[4]

## *The effect of legislation on procurement*

The extent to which legislation affects the procurement and tendering process largely depends upon whether the services, works, supplies or utilities are publicly or privately procured. There are few, if any, restrictions interfering

4. A document produced by the Joint Contracts Tribunal and which allows for the traditionally based Standard Form of Building Contract to be amended such that defined portions of the project will be designed by the contractor and will be subject to a contractual regime akin to that found with design and build procurement.

with the choice of procurement routes available to private clients. Conversely, all projects above EU procurement thresholds are subject to EU Procurement law.

The central objective of the European Commission has been to remove barriers of trade across the European Community. Four key principles have been addressed during the Commission's attempt to remove barriers to create a single market and thereby increase opportunities for competitive suppliers and contractors. The principles concern: (i) free movement of goods; (ii) free movement of services; (iii) free movement of labour; and (iv) free movement of capital.

The EU Directives affecting the public procurement of services and works were adopted between 1992 and 1993.[5] The Regulations implementing the Directives were enacted between 1991 and 1995[6] and were subsequently amended in 2000[7] and 2003.[8] Since these Directives were first adopted, the European Court of Justice has further developed the general principles of EC law and, in particular, the following areas:

- non-discrimination;
- proportionality; and
- transparency.

Where the EU Directives apply, no procurement route may be adopted which offends any of their principles—to take a simple example, it would be unlawful for a specification to require the preferential use of British products over other European products of equivalent standard. An example which is as simple as this but which is drawn from complex and evolving legislation hopefully demonstrates the impact which the EU Directives can have on determining one's procurement strategy.

## *UK public procurement*

### Preface

The Office of Government Commerce (OGC) has, since April 2000, issued government policy and advice for three recommended procurement routes for

5. Council Directive 93/37/EEC concerning the coordination of procedures for the award of public works contracts ("the Works Directive"), Council Directive 93/36/EEC 93 coordinating procedures for the award of public supply contracts ("the Supply Directive") and Council Directive 92/50/EEC concerning the coordination of procedures for the award of public service contracts ("the Services Directive").

6. Public Works Contract Regulations 1991 (SI 1991 No. 2680), Public Services Contracts Regulations 1993 (SI 1993 No. 3228) and Public Supply Contract Regulations 1995 (SI 1995 No. 201).

7. Public Contracts (Works, Services and Supply) (Amendment) Regulations 2000 (SI 2000 No. 2009).

8. Public Contracts (Works, Services and Supply) and Utilities Contracts (Amendment) Regulations 2003 (SI 2003 No. 46).

publicly procured projects. OGC guidance *Achieving Excellence in Construction*[9] defines and recommends instances when each of the three procurement routes should be used.

### Private finance initiative

This can be applied where the public sector contracts to purchase quality services (with defined outputs from the private sector) on a long-term basis, and including maintaining or constructing the necessary infrastructure so as to take advantage of private sector management skills incentivised by having private finance at risk. OGC states that PFI is only recommended for projects where the cost is likely to exceed £20m.

### Prime contracting

This involves the use of a single contractor to act as the sole point of responsibility to a public sector client for the management and delivery of a construction project on time, within budget (defined over the lifetime of the project) and fit for the purpose for which it was intended, including demonstrating during the initial period of operation that the operating cost and performance parameters are being met in accordance with a pre-agreed cost model.

### Design and build

This involves the use of a single contractor to act as the sole point of responsibility to a public sector client for the design, management and delivery of a construction project on time, within budget (taking account of whole-life costs) and in accordance with a predefined output specification.

Government policy permits the use of traditional procurement routes, i.e. where the design and construction are provided under separate agreements. However, OGC states that these routes should only be used where it can be clearly demonstrated that the traditional procurement route can provide better value for money than one of the three integrated procurement routes outlined above.

## PROCUREMENT—THE OPTIONS AVAILABLE

### *Selecting an appropriate standard form*

Recent developments in procurement routes have resulted in an increase in the number of standard forms available to cover such things as:

(i) traditional arrangements;

9. *Achieving Excellence in Construction Procurement Guide 06: Procurement and Contract Strategies*, (2003), Office of Government Commerce.

(ii) design & build arrangements;
(iii) management arrangements;
(iv) partnering arrangements; and
(v) prime contracting.

The Engineering and Construction Contract (aka NEC[10]) could be regarded as a contract which allows the selection of any of the above due to the numerous options which it provides. The flexible manner in which the NEC can cater for numerous procurement options is a subject in itself—and therefore beyond the scope of this chapter—but certain works are available which address this subject.[11]

## Traditional arrangements

The standard forms of contract presently available to cater for this procurement option are as follows:

- JCT Standard Form of Building Contract 1998 Edition.

| | | | | |
|---|---|---|---|---|
| • JCT98 | Private | With Quantities | CDPS[12] | SCS[13] |
| | | With Approx Quantities | | |
| | Local | Without Quantities | | |

- JCT Intermediate Form of Building Contract IFC98.
- JCT Agreement for Minor Building Works MW98.
- General Conditions of Contract for Building and Civil Engineering Works—GC/Works/1 With Quantities/Without Quantities 1998.
- General Conditions of Contract for Building and Civil Engineering Works—GC/Works/2 Minor Works 1998.
- Engineering and Construction Contract—NEC 2nd Edition.
- ICE Conditions of Contract—7th Edition (Measurement Version).
- ICE Conditions of Contract Minor Works—3rd Edition.
- FIDIC Conditions of Contract for Construction—1st Edition 1999.

## Design and build arrangements

The standard forms of contract presently available to cater for this procurement option are as follows:

10. This is the New Engineering Contract. It is almost universally referred to as NEC despite having been renamed as the Engineering and Construction Contract at the time of publication of the 2nd edition in 1995.
11. Trickey, Geoffrey and Hackett, Mark (2001), *The Presentation and Settlement of Contractors' Claims* (Chap. 12), Spon Press.
12. Contractor's Designed Portion Supplement as published by the JCT.
13. Sectional Completion Supplement as published by the JCT.

- Standard Form of Building Contract 1998 Edition With Contractor's Design (JCT98WCD).
- General Conditions of Contract for Building and Civil Engineering Works—GC/Works/1 Design and Build 1998.
- ICE Design and Construct Conditions of Contract—2nd Edition.
- Engineering and Construction Contract—NEC 2nd Edition.
- FIDIC Conditions of Contract for Plant & Design-Build—1st Edition 1999.
- FIDIC Conditions of Contract for EPC Turnkey Projects—1st Edition 1999.

### Management arrangements

The standard forms of contract presently available to cater for this procurement option are as follows:

- JCT Construction Management Contract plus Trade Contracts and CM Agreement.
- JCT Management Contract (JCT 98 MC) plus Works Contracts.
- Engineering and Construction Contract—NEC 2nd Edition.

### Partnering arrangements

The standard forms of contract presently available to cater for this procurement option are as follows:

- ACA Standard Form of Contract for Project Partnering PPC 2000.
- NEC Partnering Option X12, which can be used in all NEC contracts.[14]
- CIB Model Project Pact, which can be used with any contract.

### Selecting the right standard form

Whilst the selected contract must be appropriate to the procurement route, it is not an end in itself—it is often resorted to only when the parties seek remedies which are driven by disappointment or dissatisfaction. Accordingly, the emphasis in ensuring successful project outcomes should be on prevention rather than cure and this will largely be achieved by:

- involving the client during all stages of the evolving brief;
- selecting the right team to deliver the project;
- converting the brief into a detailed design which is sufficiently thought out (such that it will not have to be varied later on) and thorough in all respects (such that original concepts do not have to be amplified by way of subsequent drawing issues); and

14. Except the Adjudicator's Contract.

- placing risk with those best able to manage it.

No contract can make good the failure to observe these prerequisites—though it can go some way to mitigating the ensuing effects. If, despite the best laid of plans, problems are encountered then the contract should clearly set out the remedies available to the dissatisfied party in order that such remedies may be promptly implemented thus allowing attentions to be turned back to project delivery.

### Amendments to standard forms

Standard forms are generally forms of contract which have been drafted in one of two styles. They are either (i) drafted by a professional body with the sector in which that professional body operates in mind, e.g. Institution of Civil Engineers and the ICE Conditions of Contract[15] which focuses on the civil engineering sector or (ii) a representative panel of various professional bodies and clients with an element of negotiation to produce a standard form of contract, e.g. the JCT forms. Standard forms are exactly that—they are "standard". They do not and cannot cater for every project risk. Nor do they necessarily allocate risk to the party best placed to manage that risk. Consequently, it is the need to reallocate risk that leads to the amendment of standard forms.

### Other arrangements (non-standard forms)

There are also other procurement arrangements which are adopted by the industry but in respect of which there are not (presently at least) standard forms. These arrangements relate to such procurement routes as:

- Build Own Operate and Build Own Operate Transfer (more commonly referred to in the industry as BOO and BOOT).
- Private Finance Initiative and Public Private Partnership (more commonly referred to in the industry as PFI and PPP).

## *The emphasis created by the main options*

Whether one opts for the traditional, design and build or management options, each creates its own emphasis in terms of such things as:

- how best the time, cost and quality criteria are served;
- to whom design responsibility is devolved;
- the extent to which, if any, the design process can overlap with the construction process;
- whether the client enters into a single contract or multiple contracts; and

15. Now in its 7th edition, September 1999.

- the overall timescale from inception to completion.

A graphic representation of these issues is shown in the diagram below.

*Figure 2: Traditional, design and build, and management options*[16]

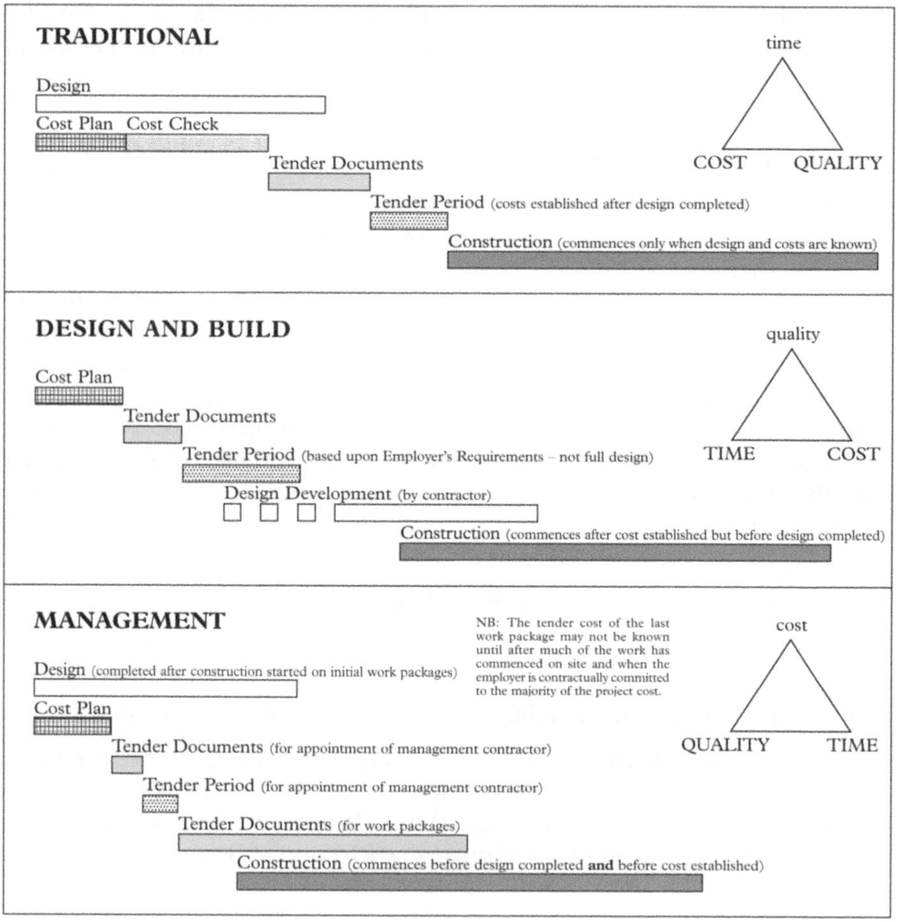


## PROCUREMENT—THE OPTIONS EVALUATED

The procurement options evaluated in this section represent those most commonly adopted by clients. Numerous other options are available to clients but it is beyond the scope of this chapter to address them here. Even with the options which are described, bespoke contracts (or amendments to standard

16. Hackett, Mark, and Robinson, Ian (2003), *Pre-Contract Practice and Contract Administration* (Blackwell Publishing).

forms) are frequently used to place a project-specific emphasis on the procurement option adopted by any client. Once the basic framework of the available procurement options is understood, one has as much flexibility to develop hybridised solutions as does an artist to mix different colours on his palette.

There is, however, a common strand to any procurement option. It is that there will always be someone to design what is to be built, someone to build it and someone to pay for it. What the different procurement routes do is to determine where any of the players sit in the contractual structure and to set out the timing and extent of the role that they are to perform.

## *Traditional procurement*

### Traditional lump sum (single stage)

A lump sum contract is one where the scope and quality of the work to be performed are determined from the outset such that the contractor can give a firm price in relation thereto and then be held to it. The lump sum approach is somewhat different from management arrangements (when the client's financial commitment can be no more than a forecast until such time as the final package is tendered) or remeasurement contracts (where the contractor will be paid on the basis of the quantity of work actually performed rather than the quantity of work forecast in the Bills of Quantities).

The above said, even under the traditional agreement, it is difficult to nail down every aspect of the design such that it is not uncommon to include provisional sums or approximate quantities in the contract sum[17] or to vary the works to respond to a change in the client's requirements.[18] This being so, many of those standard forms of contract which are intended to be lump sum in nature in fact contain numerous provisions dealing with how the contract sum will become subject to adjustment.

The traditional procurement route requires that a team of professional construction consultants be appointed by the client from the outset. This team is usually led by an architect or an engineer, depending upon which construction sector the project falls within. The traditional route requires that the design be completed in advance of inviting tenders.

The onus is on the client's design consultants to maintain the priorities established in the project brief and to extract and agree such further information as may be required from the client as the scheme progresses. All client and user decisions must therefore be made prior to the award of any contract, although provisional sums can be used where the design is incomplete.

17. Which sums and quantities become adjusted in the light of the precise requirements, once established, and which will correspondingly entail an adjustment to the contract sum that is commensurate with the way in which the budgetary provisions—which is what the sums and quantities amount to—compare with what was actually required.

18. Which will entail an adjustment to the contract sum that reflects the difference in value between what it was planned would be done with that which was in fact done.

Since it is a prerequisite to have the design very substantially—though ideally entirely—completed before tenders are invited, the procurement route is consequently one which involves the greatest period of time between inception and a physical start of the works on site. Whatever the complexity of the project, the detailed design will be undertaken by the design team rather than the contractor (and in respect of which the client is liable to the contractor for the design team's conduct) and the client's requirements will be particularised in such documents as detailed drawings, prescriptive specifications and bills of quantities.[19]

The traditional route has for a number of years been widely used in the building and civil engineering industries but its use in recent times has begun to decline at the expense of the design and build route. However, a large number of clients still use this route as the basis for guaranteeing quality due to the design definition being in great detail.

## Contractual structure under traditional procurement

The traditional procurement route and the use of standard forms paradoxically afford flexibility by virtue of the fact that the contractor may be required to undertake the design of certain elements. This, under the JCT 98 standard form, can be achieved by using the Contractor's Designed Portion Supplement (CDPS) or by having Performance Specified Work.

*Figure 3: Contractual structure under traditional procurement*

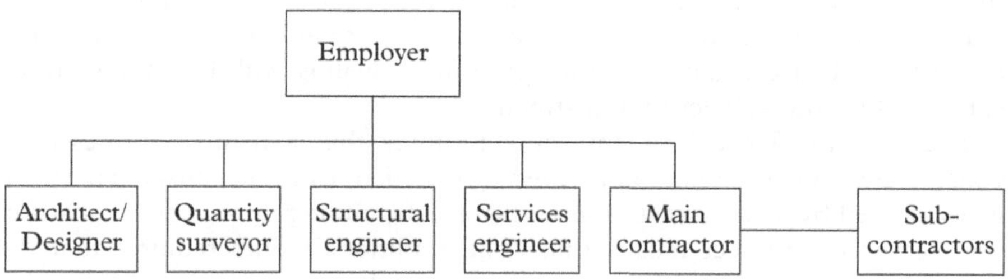


## Advantages and disadvantages of the lump sum procurement route

The advantages of lump sum contracting are:

- The ability to define quality requirements clearly at tender stage.
- The ability to make an appointment based on price competition.
- Early cost and time commitment.

19. These documents are described in "Design information" above.

- The ability to evaluate variations (changes to design or scope of works) based on known prices, without excessive cost and time penalties.
- Direct contractual remedy if consultants or contractor do not perform.
- The procedures, roles and responsibilities of the various players have become almost trade custom through usage.

The disadvantages of lump sum contracting are:

- The need to produce a fully detailed design before tender means that the sequential design/construct period is longer than with other procurement routes.
- Lack of continuity between design and construction unless a "two stage" approach is adopted.
- Uncertainty due to the sharing of cost and time risks between client and contractor.
- There is no "buildability" advice given by the contractor prior to the completion of the design.
- The adequacy and completeness of the design information is frequently a contentious issue, which increases the potential for claims.

In an effort to secure greater cost certainty, a number of major clients adopt both lump sum and two stage traditional routes by agreeing a fixed price. The fixed price is known as a guaranteed maximum price (GMP) contract. This is also an option when using other procurement routes and where responsibility for the design is transferred to the contractor. However, this is only feasible once, say, 70–80% of the work has been designed and tendered. It is only at this stage that a reasonable premium can be agreed with the contractor for those elements of work still to be designed.

### *Two stage traditional*

#### Preface

The two stage traditional process endeavours to maintain the benefits of single stage traditional (in terms of obtaining competitive prices in respect of a design which is in the client's control) but at the same time seeking to shorten the period of time between inception and the physical works starting on site.

The first stage of the process involves obtaining a fixed price tender based on having only the major elements of the project fully designed whilst the remainder of the design is still being completed by the client's design team. The pricing from the contractors at the first stage will necessarily focus upon key indicators such as the costs for management; plant and machinery; dayworks rates; overheads; and costings for such of the design as by then completed.

In order to minimise the cost of tendering in the first stage, the initial documentation should be kept to a minimum consistent with the need to[20]:

- provide a competitive basis for selection;
- establish the principles of layout design;
- provide unambiguous pricing documents, related to preliminary design and specification information, in a form sufficiently flexible for pricing the second stage tender (provision should be made for adjustment of price fluctuations during the first and second stage tenders);
- define the obligations and conditions of, and state the programme for, the second stage procedures; and
- establish the intended contract conditions.

The second stage of the process is undertaken following completion of the design by the client's design team, and possibly the contractor assisting on buildability issues. Only those contractors whose first stage tenders are commercially attractive would then be invited to participate in the second stage of the tendering process. Whilst it makes sense to narrow the field at this stage, the corollary is that the contractors who survive into the second stage of the tendering process no longer face the very competitive pressure which got them that far. Whilst the overlapping of design with the tendering process will save time there must also be the possibility that some of this is achieved at the expense of being able to maintain the competitive environment come the second stage which, in turn, may lead to premium costs being incurred.

## Advantages and disadvantages of two stage traditional

The advantages of two stage traditional are:

- The first stage tender price (not to be confused with the contract sum) is known before work commences.
- There can be a saving of time over single stage lump sum due to some element of overlapping the design production with the tendering process.
- Control of the design is retained by the client's design team.
- The procedure enables full tender competition of sub-contract works to be carried out as a parallel operation.
- The contractor's earlier involvement, perhaps in the design and document preparation, leads to a better understanding of the client's objectives and reduces the risk of disputes arising.
- Flexibility is possible for the latest procurement of finishes, in order to accommodate tenant requirements without penalty (because design can extend into the construction period).

20. The Aqua Group (1999), *Tenders and Contracts for Building* (London, Blackwell Science).

The disadvantages of two stage traditional are:

- Whereas certain costs may be determined competitively in the first stage, the reduced field of "competitors" in the second stage may lead to premium prices being paid such that the ultimately agreed price with the preferred contractor may be greater than would have pertained had the single stage approach instead been adopted.
- In the event of a breakdown of competition/negotiations in the second stage, the client may have to recommence the tendering process and this could substantially lengthen the time that it will take to reach a physical start of the works on site. In such a scenario, the time taken to get to an actual start on site could, far from being foreshortened, be extended.

### *Cost reimbursable*

A cost reimbursable contract is one where the client pays the contractor the actual cost of the work plus a management fee that includes the cost of overheads, supervision costs and profit. This type of contract permits the earliest start on site as there are very few items subject to a competitive tender and design work can continue whilst construction begins.

The client is exposed to a significant cost risk, as the cost of the works is no more than a forecast and the actual cost of the work will not be known until the final piece of the work has been finished. There is no incentive for the contractor to keep the costs down. However, if time permits, a degree of control over the cost might be exercised if one competitively tendered a schedule of rates and/or contractors' management fees.

If one were simply to tender competitively the management fee itself, there are three alternatives to determine that fee:

- Prime cost plus percentage management fee.
- Prime cost plus fixed management fee.
- Prime cost plus fluctuating management fee.

A stringent method of reviewing the prime cost put forward by the contractor should be employed. This will require the client to be involved in far more scrutiny of the contractor's applications for payment than compared with fixed price contracts. Such scrutiny will cover the following[21]:

- Supervision of the delivery of materials on to the site, their retention and use and checking of labour force and the activities performed.
- Checking of all records relating to the contractor's payments and transactions and certifying of amounts due to sub-contractors and suppliers.

21. Seeley, I. H. (1997), *Quantity Surveying Practice* (2nd edn) (Macmillan).

- Constant monitoring to ensure that no money is wasted by the use of unnecessary or unsuitable plant or the lack of coordination of services or discontinuity of work.

Whilst the contractor is not entitled to be paid for any defective work, there is a risk that this could happen under this type of arrangement unless there are strict quality control and checking procedures employed on site. This is because a sub-contractor being reimbursed on an hourly rates basis could submit a bill recording the total hours for executing defective work, dismantling it and then doing it again properly—the individual receiving the bill will see a request for payment and will also see works properly executed without necessarily appreciating the intervening events should a watchful eye not have been kept on the works as they were progressing.

## Prime cost plus percentage management fee

The prime cost plus percentage management fee is generally viewed as the highest risk to strategy for pro-curing a project. In this arrangement, the level of the contractor's fee will increase commensurately with increases in the cost of the works themselves. If, then, the contractor were to manage the works inefficiently then the prime cost of the works would increase as would his fee—such an arrangement could hardly be classed as one which rewards efficiency, on the contrary.

A further problem is that the contractor's fee could be disproportionate to the amount of work that he has to perform in order to earn it. For instance, if one were to supply and install a door costing £1000 instead of supplying and installing a door costing £200, the management fee for the door costing £1000 will be five times greater than the door costing £200, even though the management cost should be pretty much the same.

It is submitted that this procurement route should be reserved for situations of emergency.

## Prime cost plus fixed management fee

The prime cost plus fixed management fee is generally more acceptable than the percentage management fee due to the fact that the contractor is paid a fixed fee, which does not fluctuate in line with the prime cost of the works. The fixed fee provides the contractor with the incentive to finish the works as quickly as possible, thereby increasing the contractor's profitability on the project.

In order to avail of a fixed management fee, it would be necessary to provide a project plan to the contractor in sufficient detail to let him know the likely scope, complexity and duration of the work which lies ahead. Ironically, if a project plan could be provided in this sort of detail then those advising the client would be unlikely to suggest the prime cost approach in the first place.

### Prime cost plus fluctuating management fee

The prime cost plus fluctuating management fee is said to be the most appropriate of the three methods for reimbursing the contractor his fee. The fee paid to the contractor is determined using a sliding scale. The lower the final account for the project, the greater the management fee. This provides the contractor with the incentive to work efficiently and economically. However, for the fee scale to be set at an acceptable level, a reasonably detailed project plan is required.

### Advantages and disadvantages of cost plus

The advantages of cost plus are:

- The time taken for the preparation of tender documents and appointment of a contractor is minimised and therefore affords a quick start on-site.
- Work can start on site before the detailed design is complete.
- Good for carrying out investigative works.
- Flexible in coping with emergency repair type projects.
- The client does not pay a premium to cover any forecast of the contractor's risk and instead only pays actual cost if/when risks do materialise.

The disadvantages of cost plus are:

- Neither the client nor contractor can be sure of their respective commitments.
- The cost of construction to the client is typically greater than if other methods of procurement are used.
- Little incentive for the contractor to work efficiently and economically.
- The client carries the vast majority of the risk for the project.
- The requirement for supervision by the client of the contractor's activities is greater than with other methods of procurement and this can prove expensive.

## *Target cost*

Target cost contracts are similar to cost reimbursable contracts but they differ in that they are based on the "gain share/pain share" strategy. The money paid to the contractor is determined by the degree of the contractor's success in completing the works. If the contractor successfully completes the project below the target cost, the contractor will receive a percentage of the saving as a bonus. Conversely, if the contractor were to exceed the target cost, the contractor's payment would be reduced by a percentage of the cost overrun.

In essence, target cost contracts provide an incentive to the contractor to operate efficiently and economically and they transfer a proportion of the risk for doing so. If this type of arrangement were to be used, a realistic estimate would need to be agreed for the project to provide the target cost.

## *Design and build*

### Preface

Design and build as a procurement route has increased in use from 8% in 1985 to approximately 43% in 2001 for the combined value of all construction projects surveyed.[22]

The extent to which the design is entrusted to the contractor can involve either:

- the entirety of the design based upon a performance specification supplied by the client (referred to by some as "pure design and build" and something which is seldom encountered); or
- the development of the design advanced by the client's design team and which reflects the functional requirements, project objectives and planning constraints etc (this approach restricts the contractor's latitude to propose design solutions).

The latter of the above approaches is the one most frequently encountered and it has evolved in response to the criticism directed at design and build projects which is that design and build contractors are not capable of producing buildings of architectural flair and that the end product is generally of a lower quality than would be achieved using traditional procurement.

Design and build is viewed as being favourable in the following situations:

- Standard building types, especially for industrial warehousing where the early return on capital investment outweighs considerations of architectural flair.
- Buildings using proprietary systems.

22. RICS (2001), *Contracts in Use*, Davis Langdon & Everest and the Royal Institution of Chartered Surveyors.

- Building types in which contractors have become specialists such as highly serviced healthcare or laboratory buildings.

Where dealing with the "design development" approach to design and build, the design consultants initially develop an outline specification, a performance specification and/or drawings in varying degrees of detail which together are usually called the Employer's Requirements. From these requirements, the contractor is required to develop the Contractor's Proposals encompassing the Employer's Requirements. It is frequently the case that consultants appointed to develop the outline design and the Employer's Requirements are subsequently novated to the contractor and this is done to promote continuity of the design ethos.

The most commonly encountered standard form for design and build is the JCT's "With Contractor's Design" version. It is beyond the scope of this Module to address the features of this form but it is worth mentioning that there is no contractual obligation upon the contractor to obtain professional indemnity insurance in support of his design—this is in absolute contrast to the situation pertaining with design consultants whereby virtually all terms of engagement contain an express requirement to carry professional indemnity insurance in addition to which the maintaining of such insurance is a mandatory requirement of the various professional institutions.

For a diagram of the contractual structure under design and build, see Figure 4 on page 124.

### Advantages and disadvantages of design and build

The advantages of design and build are:

- Low cost of preparing the tender documents.
- Early cost and time commitments before commencing on site.
- Single point responsibility for design and cost risks.
- Economic construction due to early consideration of building methods (this may be at the expense of the client's aesthetic wishes).
- Shorter overall design and construction periods.

The disadvantages of design and build are:

- Lack of client control over design and quality standards.
- Variable design standards that may be further compromised if the design and build contractor incurs additional costs during construction.
- High cost and time penalties for changes to the scope of the works: design and build is unsuitable for complex, change-prone projects.
- Should the design team be novated to the contractor, conflicts of interest can arise.

- In the event that the design team are novated to the contractor, the employer has no direct means of checking or improving quality, unless he appoints other consultants at further cost.
- The costs of tendering are far greater for the contractor than with traditional procurement and this will be reflected in his price for the works.

*Figure 4: Contractual structure under design and build*

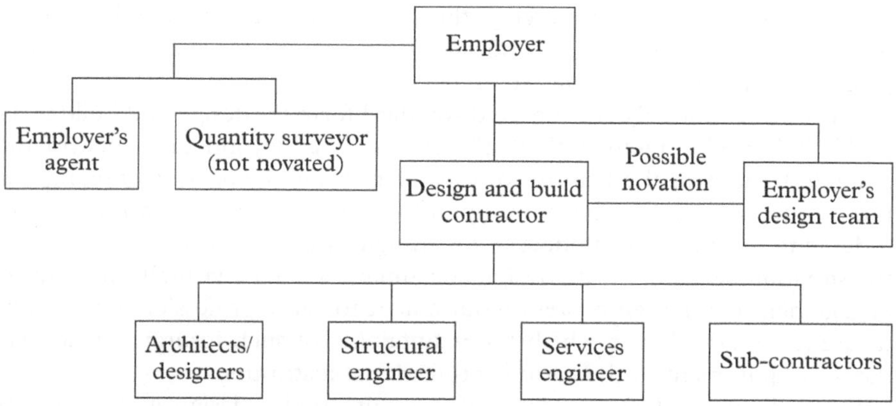


## *Construction management and management contracting*

### Preface

Construction management's approach to procurement is to place the client in a direct contract with each and every package contractor, which effectively means that the client assumes the role of the main contractor. As the vast majority of clients do not have sufficient construction management experience, the client usually employs consultants to carry out the role of construction manager. The sequential approach to designing the project on a package-by-package basis means that this form of procurement offers greater flexibility and greater operational speed.

The sequential approach to construction management can lead to clients acting as a conduit for claims for loss and/or expense. If one trade contractor were to cause delay by failing to complete a package on time, a client might receive a claim for loss and/or expense from a contractor whose work is reliant on the first contractor's completion. That client would then have to hope that he can recover such loss and/or expense from the delaying contractor if he is not to be left out of pocket.

Under the management contracting route, all of the works contractors have contractual links to the management contractor and it is the management contractor who is contracted to the client.

What both approaches have in common is that the cost of the works cannot be determined until the final package is let.

*Figure 5: Contractual structure under construction management*

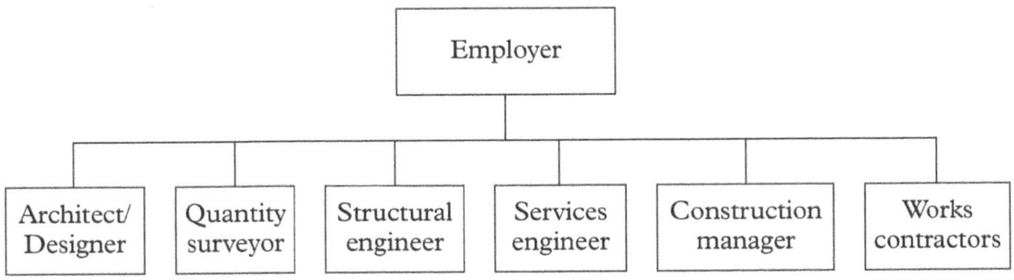


*Figure 6: Contractual structure under management contracting*

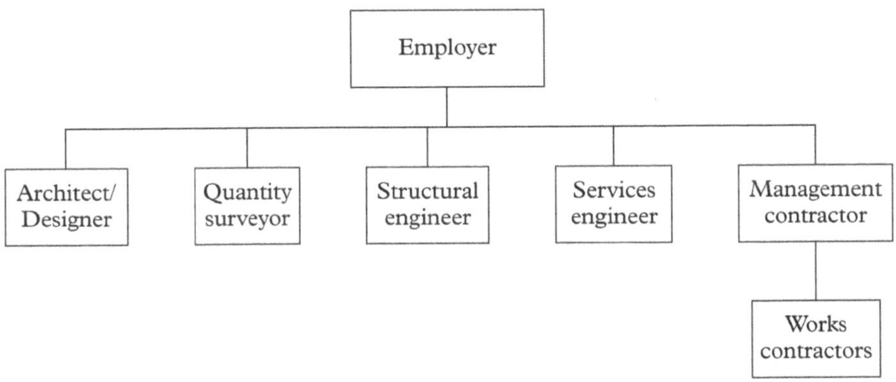


## Advantages and disadvantages of construction management and management contracting

The advantages of construction management and management contracting are:

- Overlapping of design and construction.
- Shorter overall design and construction period.
- Use of contractor's/construction manager's practical expertise and resources to improve the management of the construction process.
- Specialist design input from trade contractors.
- Suitability for complex, high quality projects.
- The administrative duties of the architect are lessened thus allowing him to place greater emphasis on design production and quality control.

The disadvantages of construction management and management contracting are:

- The cost of the works cannot be determined until the final package is let.
- Risk of any package contractor's lack of performance mainly with the client.
- Unsuitability for inexperienced, hands-off clients.

**Advantages of construction management over management contracting**

In construction management, there are direct contracts between trade contractors and the client which provides a smoother financial arrangement for the trade contractor (but which creates additional administration for the client). It is generally considered that for this reason there are tendering cost advantages in going down the construction management route rather than the management contracting route because the tenders will be keener.

The construction manager (who is usually the lead consultant) should be appointed early so that he is involved right at the start of the design path. A management contractor often comes onto the job last and, as such, is felt to be an outsider by the design team.

**Advantages of management contracting over construction management**

In construction management, the client has more hands on control of his project and must be prepared to exercise ultimate authority over the project. Management contracting is probably the better of the two routes for the less experienced client.

With management contracting, the client need only enter into one construction contract (because it is then the management contractor who engages all of the works contractors) whereas with construction management the client has myriad construction contracts to enter into which can create quite a burden in terms of making timely and periodic payments to all of the trade contractors.

***Table 1: Traditional, design and build and management compared***

| PROCUREMENT ROUTES | | | | | |
|---|---|---|---|---|---|
| **Selection Criteria** | **Traditional Lump Sum** | **Two-stage Traditional** | **Design and Build** | **Construction Management** | **Management Contracting** |
| Price certainty before commitment to build | 5 | 2 | 5 | 1 | 1 |
| Lowest construction cost | 4 | 3 | 5 | 2 | 2 |

| PROCUREMENT ROUTES | | | | | |
|---|---|---|---|---|---|
| **Selection Criteria** | **Traditional Lump Sum** | **Two-stage Traditional** | **Design and Build** | **Construction Management** | **Management Contracting** |
| Programme commitment from contractor before entering contract | 5 | 4 | 5 | 1 | 1 |
| Shortest overall programme (inception to completion) | 2 | 4 | 4 | 5 | 5 |
| Control over design and materials | 5 | 5 | 2 | 5 | 5 |
| Control over choice of trade contractors and sub-contractors | 3 | 4 | 1 | 5 | 5 |
| Input (during design) from contractor on programming and buildability | 2 | 4 | 3 | 5 | 5 |
| Control over programming/ planning on site | 2 | 2 | 1 | 5 | 5 |
| Single point of responsibility for design and construction | 1 | 1 | 5 | 1 | 1 |
| Direct contractual relationship between employer and designers | 5 | 5 | 1 | 5 | 5 |

| PROCUREMENT ROUTES | | | | | |
|---|---|---|---|---|---|
| **Selection Criteria** | **Traditional Lump Sum** | **Two-stage Traditional** | **Design and Build** | **Construction Management** | **Management Contracting** |
| Liquidated damages recoverable from contractor if he completes late | 5 | 5 | 5 | 1 | 1 |
| Ability to introduce and accommo-date changes | 4 | 4 | 2 | 5 | 5 |
| Suitability for complex design | 4 | 3 | 2 | 5 | 5 |

Source: British Council for Offices (2000), *BCO Guide 2000—Best Practice in the Specification for Offices.*

5 = Achieves criterion very well.
3 = Achieves criterion to an acceptable level.
1 = Does not achieve criterion.

### *Public Private Partnership/Private Finance Initiative*

Public Private Partnerships (PPP), of which Private Finance Initiative (PFI) is a constituent part, is a generic term describing the relationship of the public and private sector aimed at using private sector resources and/or expertise to deliver services which were traditionally provided by the public sector. Moreover, since PPP/PFI's inception, successive governments have proclaimed that private sector management expertise, competition and the transfer of risk from the public sector offer better value for money rather than the traditionally procured public sector infrastructure and services.

PPP/PFI is a method of conducting public procurement that serves to provide much more than a built asset. The main distinguishing feature of PPP/PFI is that it moves the emphasis away from the provision of a built asset to the provision of service in which construction of the asset is incidental to the provision of services. PPP/PFI projects are therefore primarily concerned with the purchase of services by the public sector. Thus, in the past where the public sector would have simply built a school building, the public sector is now procuring the service of educating people (together with hard and soft facilities management services) from the private sector. Typically, when construction of a facility is involved, the concession/project agreement may last between 25 and 30 years.

PFI was borne out of increased demand for investment in new and existing facilities at a time when public sector borrowing was restricted by EU criteria. The significance of using PFI is that the public sector does not own the new facilities and, as a consequence, these are not treated as a liability reported in the public sector accounts. This may be viewed both positively and negatively: positively, this may be viewed as freeing up resources for traditionally procured projects and, negatively, this may be viewed as understating the public sector's true liabilities.

PPP/PFI has developed similar principles to those established in private sector infrastructure projects, which are procured under the following provisions:

- Build Own Transfer (BOT).
- Build Own Operate Transfer (BOOT).
- Design Build Finance Operate (DBFO).

Practically, services provided under PFI amount to:

- providing finance and possibly land;
- design and construction of either new or upgraded assets, which are made available to the public sector;
- maintenance of these assets ("hard" facilities management services); and
- providing tertiary services such as cleaning and security personnel ("soft" facilities management services).

At the top of the PFI chain is a local authority that would usually, prior to the advent of PFI, provide a school building and be responsible for the day-to-day running and maintenance of the school. Under PFI, a local authority seeks to procure educational services from the private sector. Private sector services are traditionally supplied by a special purpose vehicle (SPV) which is a company set up specifically for a particular project and which may not trade for any other purpose. By analogy to the traditional procurement route, the awarding authority is the client and the SPV is the contractor. The SPV will, however, sub-contract the construction works to a contractor[23] using a contract which is back-to-back[24] with the project/concession agreement ensuring that the liability for construction is passed from the SPV to the construction contractor. Similarly, the SPV will also pass on the risk for providing the ongoing services to a facilities management contractor, which again uses a contract which is back-to-back with the project/concession agreement.

23. Using a procurement route which matches the SPV's requirements but which, very often, is a form of design and build.

24. Back-to-back is a term used to describe a sub-contract which requires the sub-contractor to perform his duties to the contractor such that the contractor can, in turn, perform his duties to the client without fear of the obligations across the range of contracts being inconsistent or missed out.

The key difference between PPP/PFI and the other procurement routes described in this chapter is that, under PFI/PPP, the ultimate client is procuring an operational facility and in respect of which construction is an incidental process.

*Figure 7: Contractual Structure Under PPP/PFI*

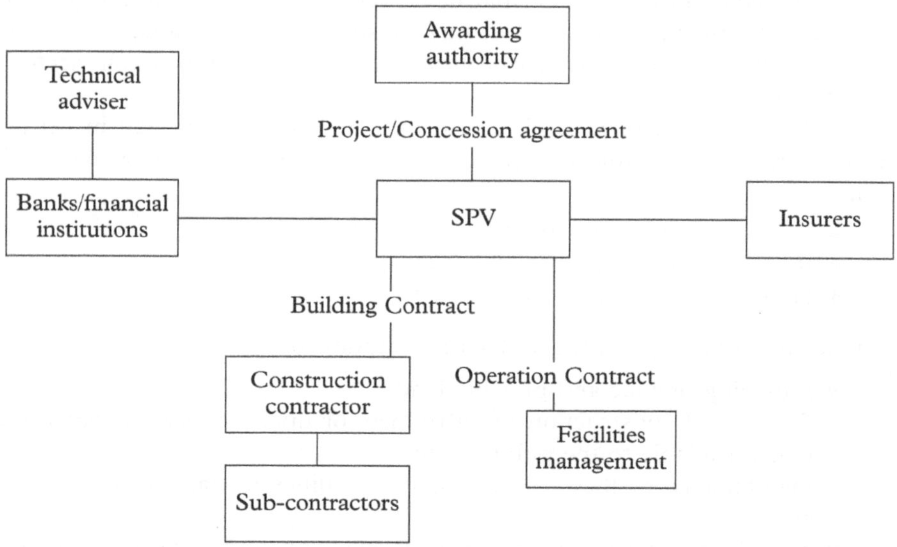


An essential component of PPP/PFI is the ability to competitively tender the initial bid for the project. However, in practice, this is not as simple as it first seems. Due to the fact that PPP/PFI is caught by the EC directives regarding procurement, all information must be communicated to tenderers in a transparent manner. This can cause some difficulties as the precise details of the project are something which are usually determined by negotiation after establishing the preferred bidder.

## Anatomy of a PFI agreement

Along with the service agreement, the output specification and the payment mechanism are essential elements of a PFI deal. The output specification describes the outcomes expected from a project, indicating the risk allocation between client and supplier, and explaining how the services provided will be integrated with public sector services.

## Output specifications

These present user requirements in a way that can free service providers to develop innovative proposals. This approach to stating purchaser requirements has been proved to work well in sectors such as transport, where needs can be converted into outputs such as a target road capacity.

In other sectors, such as health, where the design and process issues are more complex and where the service component includes only ancillary services, output specifications need to be prepared in greater detail.

As a result, the output specification tends to be more prescriptive, giving less scope for the PFI consortium to propose design or service innovations, which in turn can reduce the scope for PFI bidders to deliver value for money solutions. Irrespective of the level of detail in which the outputs are described, the output specification must be unambiguous, conveying sufficient information to enable the PFI service to be priced.

When developing an outline specification, essential issues that need to be addressed include:

- The objectives of the proposed facilities.
- The extent of, and performance requirements for, core facilities.
- The ranking of the importance of service provision, to both facility and function.
- The identification of areas of potential change.
- The identification of services not included in the PFI deal.

### Unitary payment

The unitary payment puts the agreed risk transfer into place. Accordingly its principal functions are:

- To pay the contractor and service providers.
- To provide an incentive for the provider to meet expected service standards.
- To ensure that services failures are remedied promptly.
- To encourage long-term efficiency gains.

Where unitary payment schemes are based on an established output specification model, monthly services payment levels will be related to the availability of facilities and the general quality of services provided. However, as broader social outcomes (such as targets to reduce hospital readmissions) start to be considered as an element of the output specification, further quality-led components of the unitary payment may be introduced.

Based on the established availability and service model, the main principles of the unitary payment are:

- No element of the monthly payment is guaranteed.
- All payments are related to the delivery of service.
- All payment follows the achievement of performance targets.

The main components of the conventional unitary payment model relate to the availability, performance and (to a lesser extent) the degree of usage of services.

### *Prime contracting*

The main objective of prime contracting is to achieve long-term value for money through active supply chain management incentivised by payment mechanisms, continuous improvement and economies of scale based on the ideology of partnering and collaborative working. Prime contracting requires a single point of responsibility between the client and the rest of the supply chain (designers, contractors and suppliers). The prime contractor has the responsibility for the management and delivery of the project or integrated service, which may include the provision of a new facility or the maintenance of existing infrastructure.

Key features of prime contracting include:

- Involvement of all parties in the prime contract on commencing the design process.
- A functional output-based specification rather than an input-based specification.
- Supply chain management and prompt payment of suppliers.
- Incentivised pricing arrangements.
- Open book accounting.
- Milestone payments based on achievable and measurable output.
- Clear allocation of risk.

Prime contracting relies on an output specification, similar to design and build (employer's requirements) and PFI, rather than a prescriptive specification which is relied upon under a traditional procurement route and which may be viewed as being suppressive of innovation. Conversely, the objective in using an output specification is to allow the prime contractor and supply chain to deliver innovative and more efficient services, which incorporate technological advances and operational experience.

*Figure 8: Contractual structure under prime contracting*

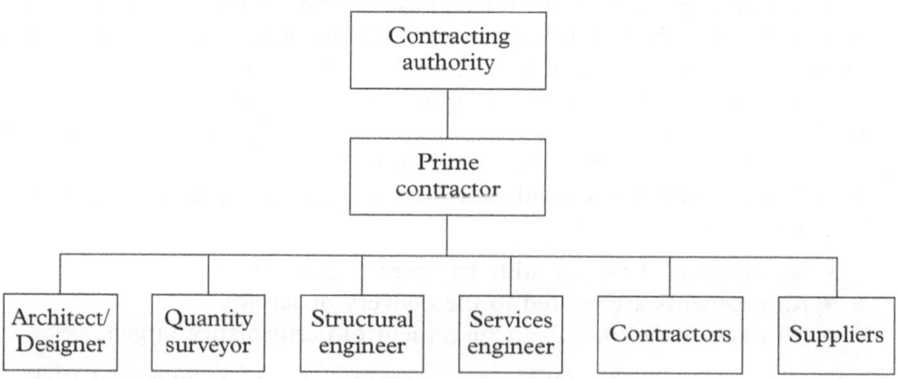

## SELF-TEST QUESTIONS

1. **Which of the following types of procurement requires a public sector client to make a case for its use?**

   (a) PFI;
   (b) traditional;
   (c) prime contracting;
   (d) design and build.

2. **Which procurement route would you recommend for a client who places more emphasis upon an early start on site than the cost of the project?**

   (a) prime cost plus management fee;
   (b) design and build;
   (c) construction management;
   (d) traditional.

3. **Which of these procurement routes does not fall under the PPP/ PFI banner?**

   (a) build own transfer;
   (b) traditional;
   (c) build own operate transfer;
   (d) design build finance operate.

4. **A prescriptive specification is particularly associated with which of the following procurement routes?**

   (a) build own transfer;
   (b) design and build;
   (c) traditional;
   (d) construction management.

5. **Which of the following is not an advantage to the use of prime cost procurement?**

   (a) work can start on site before the detailed design is complete;
   (b) flexible in copy with emergency repair type projects;
   (c) early commitment from the contractor as to project cost;
   (d) the client only pays for the risks that actually materialise hence no premium is paid for forecast events.

**6. Which type of specification is most associated the PFI projects?**

(a) prescriptive;
(b) performance;
(c) output;
(d) descriptive.

**7. Which factor represents the greater of the risks associated with construction management/management contracting?**

(a) the ability to introduce changes in the scope of the works;
(b) the client having a direct contractual link to the designers of the project;
(c) the certainty of project costs prior to commencing on-site;
(d) the ability to control the programme of works on-site.

**8. Which of the following is the most criticised aspect of the traditional procurement route?**

(a) clients' ability to have price certainty prior to commencing on site;
(b) the length of time taken to design the project before it can be put out to tender;
(c) the ability to control the quality of materials used in the project design;
(d) the ability of the client to recover liquidated damages if the contractor were to complete a project late.

**9. Which procurement route best serves a client if time and cost are a major influence in a client's decision?**

(a) traditional;
(b) construction management/management contracting;
(c) design and build;
(d) prime contracting.

**10. Design and build is not viewed as being favourable in which of the following situations?**

(a) designing and constructing standard building types;
(b) buildings using proprietary systems;
(c) building types such as healthcare or laboratory buildings where contractors have become specialists;
(d) buildings requiring a highly regarded aesthetic appearance.

CHAPTER 4

# STANDARD FORMS OF CONTRACT I

David Risbridger

## THE USE OF STANDARD FORMS

### *Standard form contracts—an overview*

Except for the bespoke construction contracts used in the field of Private Finance Initiative (PFI)/Public Private Partnerships (PPP) standard form contracts dominate the UK construction industry.

The dominance of standard forms is reflected in almost every other developed jurisdiction and is a common factor worldwide in the way the construction industry contracts. The exceptions to this generally relate to "one off" super projects such as Terminal 5 at Heathrow.

The reasons why standard forms dominate are easy to understand:

(1) huge economic advantage in not negotiating each individual contract;
(2) widespread knowledge amongst parties of the terms and conditions which have been agreed;
(3) standardisation of bargaining power and position.

The construction industry is not alone in its use of standard form contracts. Other industrial sectors including insurance, telecoms, banking and property use standard forms to a greater or lesser extent, usually with the same economic motive behind the adoption of such contracts.

The use of standard forms is not without its detractors and there are a number of issues surrounding standard form contracts which can and do create significant problems.

One of the criticisms which carries some weight is that use of standard forms produces a "one size fits all" mentality where a particular standard form is adopted simply because it was the form that was used previously. This then leads to insufficient thought being given as to how the terms and conditions set out in the standard form will operate for the particular project in question. This is not really a criticism of the standard form itself, or its use, but rather a criticism of the lack of intellectual rigour in the decision making process leading to the adoption of the particular standard form in question.

A useful indication of the trends in the use of standard forms can be obtained from the RICS Contracts in Use Survey,[1] the latest version of which was published in 2001.

That survey indicated that over 95% of the projects (by number) captured by the survey were carried out using standard forms, although this percentage dropped to just over 86% of the total value of the contracts examined. The survey concludes that the lower percentage by value is indicative of the use of procurement routes such as construction management for larger value schemes.

It is now proposed to look at, in turn, a number of the standard forms in common use today.

## JOINT CONTRACTS TRIBUNAL CONTRACTS

### *Overview*

By a large margin the majority of standard forms being used on projects in the UK are those produced by the Joint Contracts Tribunal commonly known at the JCT.

According to the latest RICS Contracts in Use Survey[2] 91% by number of the contracts covered by the survey employed one of the JCT Standard Forms. This was the same percentage as the survey found in 1998 which was itself the highest figure from all previous surveys. The RICS survey indicates that by value the proportion represents a figure of 79% only just below the highest percentage ever recorded. Again the RICS survey indicates that the likely reason for this variance is the predominance in higher value schemes of procurement routes such as construction management.

The influence of the JCT suite of contracts on the construction market's approach to standard form contracts cannot be overemphasised. Notwithstanding the many critics and the known faults, the JCT dominates the market.

The JCT is now, although it has not always been so, a company limited by guarantee. Prior to 1998 the JCT was an umbrella organisation for 11 industry bodies who operated by way of unanimity in their approach to drafting the suite of JCT contracts. The origin of the JCT contracts is hinted at by the name of its publisher, RIBA[3] Publications Limited. During the course of the nineteenth century the RIBA produced numerous standard form contracts culminating in the 1895 RIBA Conditions of Contract which were revised in 1902 to allow for with or without quantities options.

The JCT as an umbrella organisation was established in 1931 and has over the past 70 years produced standard forms of contracts, guidance notes and other standard documentation for use in the construction industry.

1. RICS Survey of Contracts in Use 2001.
2. RICS Survey of Contracts in Use 2001 Executive Summary Item 2.
3. Royal Institute of British Architects.

Modern day JCT contracts came into existence when the 1963 Standard Form of Building Contract was published. This was followed by the 1980 edition and then the consolidated current version contained in the 1998 edition.

As indicated above in 1998 the JCT incorporated itself as a company limited by guarantee (it is not a tribunal in any sense of the word) and its articles of association state that its main objective is:

"to procure the publication, revise and disseminate both in paper and electronic form suites and standard forms of contract, tender documentation and practice notes."

The current constituent bodies of the JCT are as follows:

- Association of Consulting Engineers
- British Property Federation
- Construction Confederation
- Local Government Association
- National Specialist Council
- Royal Institute of British Architects
- Royal Institute of Chartered Surveyors
- Scottish Building Contract Committee Limited

The JCT produce a variety of main contract and sub-contract documentation ranging from at one end of the spectrum the building contract for home owner/occupier (a contract designed to be used without professional assistance where the owner deals directly with the builder) right through to MC98, the standard form of management contract which provides a suite of contract documentation for use where the chosen procurement route is management contracting.

This section of the chapter will focus on six different JCT contracts.

### *JCT 98 Standard Form of Building Contract (JCT 98 SFBC)*

This is the core non-design and build contract produced by the JCT and is available in a number of forms including the Private Version (for use by the private sector) and Local Authorities Version. It is produced in a With Quantities option, a With Approximate Quantities option (a re-measurement contract) and a Without Quantities option (a specification and drawings contract).

The Private With Quantities version is the most common form from which all other JCT contracts largely derive. It is a lump sum traditional form procurement contract in which the design is carried out by designers employed by the project client who is referred to as the Employer in all JCT contracts. The contract requires that a full bill of quantities is prepared setting out a detailed breakdown of the various equipment, materials, plant and labour that is required and this is then priced by the Contractor so as to arrive at the lump sum which is inserted into the contract and defined as the Contract Sum.

The core provisions of the JCT 98 SFBC do not envisage the Contractor having design responsibility (this remains with the designers appointed by the project client) but the JCT does publish a supplemental option which allows for the introduction of contractor design by way of the Contractor's Design Portion Supplement (CDP) which provides for specific areas of design responsibility to be passed to the Contractor. Most commonly this operates where the Contractor is sub-contracting specific areas of design to its sub-contractors (very often in the mechanical and electrical engineering field).

The Contractor's Design Portion Supplement is published as a separate stand-alone supplement and it introduces a set of provisions which broadly match those contained within the JCT Standard Form of Building Contract With Contractor's Design (JCT 98 WCD). The design obligations only apply to the pre-specified portion of the design for which the Employer and the Contractor have agreed the Contractor will be responsible.

An alternative provision contained within the JCT 98 SFBC form allowing for partial design responsibility to be passed to a contractor by way of performance specified work. This is set out in Part 5 of the JCT 98 SFBC at Clause 42. This provision allows for work to be specified by way of a performance specification and for the Contractor to then produce a finished product which meets the performance specification.

The JCT 98 SFBC runs to over 110 pages and contains something in excess of 80,000 words. It is used on a wide range of projects and in many respects is considered to be the benchmark standard form. This has come about primarily because of the JCT's dominance of the standard form market for conventional building projects in the UK not because it is a good example of what contract drafting should look like.

## What the contract says about time

The primary obligation with regard to time in the JCT 98 SFBC is that the contractor must complete the works by the completion date. Should the Contractor fail to complete the works by the Completion date then the employer may levy liquidated and ascertained damages against the contractor at a rate specified in the contract appendix. It should be noted that Clause 24 of the contract contains a relatively cumbersome mechanism whereby prior to the deduction of liquidated and ascertained damages the certifying person under the contract (usually the Architect) must have issued a certificate of non-completion stating that the contractor has failed to complete the works by the completion date. This is a prerequisite to the deduction of Liquidated and Ascertained Damages.

Like all JCT contracts the completion date can be extended by any of a number of relevant events set out in Clause 25, the extension of time mechanism. The relevant events range from *force majeure* and exceptionally adverse weather conditions through civil commotion, to variations and lack of labour.

The list is relatively wide and it is common for employers to seek to reduce the scope of the relevant events by way of bespoke amendments to the contract.

Clause 25 also places on the contractor an obligation to use his best endeavours to prevent delay in the progress of the works (howsoever caused) and to prevent the completion of the works being delayed or further delayed beyond the completion date. Whilst on the face of it this provision might seem highly favourable to the employer the reality of its interpretation and use is such that it provides a relatively low level of protection against claims for extensions of time under Clause 25.

A sectional completion supplement is published along with the JCT 98 SFBC allowing for serial completion dates with liquidated damages applicable to each such date. The supplement is published in a composite supplement containing both the CDP and sectional completion wording.

The date that work is begun under the contract is defined as the date of possession (which is inserted in the appendix to the contract) and a mechanism exists in Clause 23 to enable that date to be put back by a maximum of six weeks albeit the contractor can claim additional costs as a consequence of such delay.

Certification of the achievement of practical completion is made by the architect or contract administrator. It should be noted that practical completion is not a defined term in JCT contracts, although it is relatively common to amend the contract so that a definition is included. There is nothing in the contract which prevents the contractor completing before the completion date and in such case practical completion will be certified on the earlier date. It should be noted, however, that the contract places no obligation on the employer to assist the contractor in achieving early completion. No bonus arrangement is included within the JCT 98 SFBC.

Provisions for use of an information release schedule are included at Clause 5.4.1. The contractor is obliged under Clause 5.3 to provide copies of his programme but the contractual programming provisions within the JCT 98 SFBC are not extensive.

## What the contract says about cost

The JCT 98 SFBC Private With Quantities version is a lump sum contract. The contractor's obligation is to carry out and complete the works described by the contract documents for the contract sum. This should be contrasted with the Approximate Quantities form of JCT 98 SFBC which is a remeasurement contract.

The JCT 98 SFBC Private With Quantities version relies on the production of a detailed bill of quantities which the contractor is then able to price. The approach of requiring a fully detailed bill of quantities, produced by the employer's quantity surveyor was common practice in much of the 20th century and was thought to provide comfort to the employer with regard to how the contractor had priced the Works and also to provide a mechanism for agreeing the valuation of variations. Bills of quantity are, however, less common now than they once were, partly because of a move away from traditional procurement towards design and build but also because of the view that they really added little to the Employer's ability to control costs, particularly where the form of contract made it clear that errors in the bills of quantities were always an employer's risk.

The payment provisions in the JCT 98 SFBC are set out in Clause 30. A detailed review of the payment provisions is beyond the scope of this chapter but the contract provides two alternative mechanisms for payment to the contractor, based either upon monthly valuations with payment being made monthly to the contractor or (if the appropriate appendix is completed) by way of stage payments at specified stages of the works as set out in the appendix.

In both payment arrangements payment is certified by the architect or contract administrator and the final date for payment is 14 days from the date of issue of each interim certificate.

Provisions are included within Clause 30 to deal with (i) advance payment for equipment that needs to be ordered early, (ii) retention (commonly at the rate of 5% until practical completion and thereafter 2.5%), and (iii) payment for off-site materials.

Detailed provisions with regard to the preparation of a final account are included within Clause 30.6; such account to be submitted by the contractor to the Architect no later than six months following practical completion. Clause 30.8 envisages the final task of the Architect under the contract to be the preparation and issue of the final certificate at the end of the defects liability period or the date of issue of the certificate of completion and making good defects, whichever is the later.

Although the JCT 98 SFBC Private with Quantities contract is a lump sum contract there are numerous contractual mechanisms by which the contract sum can be increased or decreased. Clause 13 contains extensive variation provisions which allow the Employer to alter or modify the design, the quality or the quantity of the work. Detailed mechanisms dealing with how such variations are priced are included within Clause 13 together with alternative arrangements for the pricing of variations (in advance of its carrying out) either by way of the contractor's price statement or assessment by the quantity surveyor (Alternative A/B) are set out in the Clause.

Under Clause 26 the contractor is entitled to claim loss and expense caused by matters materially affecting regular progress of the Works. The Clause 26 mechanism allows the contractor to claim such loss and expenses for a specified list of reasons including delay by the employer, variations and non-compliance by the employer with the CDM Regulations.

The loss and expense provisions are relatively widely drawn allowing substantial scope for the contractor to make claims. It is common for employers to seek to narrow the scope of the operation of Clause 26 by way of bespoke amendment.

In addition to variations and loss and expense claims optional fluctuation provisions are included in JCT 98 SFBC which allow for price inflation to certain items pursuant to a predetermined index increase. For many years these provisions were commonly excluded but recently, due to large increases in the cost of steel work primarily caused by demand in the developing world, particularly China, the reintroduction of the fluctuation mechanism for steel work costs has been seen.

### What the contract says about quality

The contractor, pursuant to Article 1, must carry out and complete the works shown upon, described by or referred to in the contract documents. That is the contractor's primary obligation under the JCT 98 SFBC.

Clause 2.1 requires the contractor to carry out and complete the works in compliance with the contract documents using materials and workmanship of the quality and standards therein specified.

Clause 2.3 sets out how divergence between or within the contract documents and/or the statutory requirements are to be resolved.

Clause 8 imposes an obligation on the contractor that all materials and goods shall, so far as procurable, be of the standards described in the bills of quantity and the contractor is expressly forbidden from substituting any materials or goods without the architect's written consent. An inspection mechanism and provisions for the opening up of work once completed is also included cross-referenced to the agreed code of practice dealing with opening up and inspection.

The contract sets out a defects liability period which commonly runs for 12 months from practical completion of the works. During this period the contractor is obliged to return to the site and correct defects which have arisen during the defects liability period.

## *JCT 98 Standard Form Building Contract with Contractor's Design (JCT 98 WCD)*

As indicated in the previous section the JCT 98 SFBC is not a design and build contract. The JCT cater for procurement via design and build by way of the JCT 98 Standard Form of Building Contract with contractor's Design Contract (JCT 98 WCD), the current version being the 1998 edition with the later amendments numbered 1–5.

The JCT 98 WCD was previously published and known as JCT 1981. The current JCT 98 WCD is the most widely used design and build contract in the UK.

The contracts runs to over 123 pages and has in excess of 80,000 words of detailed provisions, supplemental documents and appendices. In many of the detailed provisions the drafting is identical to that of the JCT 98 SFBC.

The JCT 98 WCD is a lump sum design and build contract. The primary obligation on the contractor is to complete the design for the Works and then to carry out and complete the construction of the Works. This is set out in Article 1. For the completion of the design and the carrying out and the completion of the Works the Employer pays the contractor the contract sum.

The JCT 98 WCD introduces the concept of the employer's agent. This is a person employed by the Employer to manage the project on the Employer's behalf. It should be noted that the employer's agent does not have a certification role in the same way that the architect has under the JCT 98 SFBC.

Contract documentation includes the employer's requirements (the document prepared by the employer setting out his needs and objectives) and the contractor's Proposals (setting out how the contractor proposes to meet the Employer's Requirements). The recitals to the Contract explicitly state that the Employer has examined the contractor's Proposals and is satisfied that they meet the employer's requirements.[4] It is a very common amendment to JCT 98 WCD to reverse the burden in this recital so that the contractor states that the contractor's Proposals meet the Employer's Requirements.

## What the contract says about design

The contractor's design warranty is set out in Clause 2.5 and is stated to be co-extensive to that of an architect or, as the case may be, other appropriate professional designer holding himself out as competent to take on work for such design. It can thus be seen that the level of design liability created by JCT 98 WCD and placed upon the contractor is that of reasonable skill and care (the same standard as applies to all professionals with regard to how they carry out their obligations) and not a fitness for purpose obligation which would otherwise be implied as a result of common law.

Negotiation of the imposition of a fitness for purpose standard for design liability upon contractors by way of bespoke amendment to JCT 98 WCD remains a contentious issue.

In addition to this level of design liability an express monetary cap on liability for breach of the design warranty is included within Clause 2.5.3. This operates as an overriding limit of liability for the contractor's liability for loss of use, loss of profit or other consequential loss arising in respect of a breach of the contractor's design liability. The amount of the limit agreed with the employer is inserted in Appendix 1.

4. Third Recital.

It is a relatively common, albeit not uncontentious amendment, to exclude Clause 2.5.3, thus altering the contractor's liability for defective design to an unlimited amount.

Perhaps surprisingly the JCT 98 WCD form makes no reference to professional indemnity insurance and it is an almost universal amendment to the contract to include a provision within it requiring the contractor to carry professional indemnity insurance to cover, *inter alia*, design liability.

### What the contract says about time

The broad position with regard to time is the same as JCT 98 SFBC albeit that some of the relevant events set out in Clause 25 are different. Given that the contractor is responsible for the production of the design the contractor is not entitled to an extension of time for delay in receipt of information in the same way that he is under JCT 98 SFBC.

No independent certification of practical completion occurs rather the contractor notifies the Employer when the contractor considers the works are complete. If the employer agrees he issues a written statement to that effect.

### What the contract says about cost

As indicated above, JCT 98 WCD is a lump sum contract under which the contractor contracts to complete the design and carry out and complete the construction of the works for the contract sum.

A detailed variation mechanism for changes to the employer's requirements is included within Clause 12 which mirrors that contained within JCT 98 SFBC. As no bill of quantity is prepared in connection with JCT 98 WCD the Employer is reliant upon the contractor's previously produced summary called the Contract Sum Analysis to price any such changes.

Clause 12 also includes detailed provisions dealing with provisional sums.

As with JCT 98 SFBC the payment provisions are set out in Clause 30. They envisage interim payments based either on monthly valuations or stage/milestone arrangements depending on whether Alternative A or Alternative B in Appendix 2 has been selected.

Unlike the JCT 98 SFBC there is no independent certification of amounts due by the architect, rather the contractor makes applications for interim payments which are assessed by the employer and either paid in full or in a reduced amount. Payments are made within 14 days from the date of receipt by the Employer of the contractor's application for interim payment.

As with the JCT 98 SFBC Clause 30 also contains provisions dealing with advance payment, retention and the Final Account.

Again, as with JCT 98 SFBC in the JCT 98 WCD contains various mechanisms to allow the contract sum to increase or decrease. These include a loss and expense mechanism in Clause 26 which follows the form of the loss and expense provision in Clause 26 of the JCT 98 SFBC and the JCT 98 WCD is similarly often reduced by employer amendment.

### What the contract says about quality

The primary obligation of the contractor is to complete the design for the works and carry out and complete the construction of the works. Clause 2.1 provides that the contractor is to carry out and complete the works referred to in the employer's requirements and must complete the design for the works including the selection of any specifications for any kinds and standards of materials and goods and workmanship as set out in the employer's requirements.

The nature of the contractor's design liability has already been discussed above.

Similar provisions with regard to work materials, goods, inspection and testing are included within Clause 8 of the JCT 98 WCD form as are found within Clause 8 of the JCT 98 SFBC.

The provisions governing a defects liability period are broadly the same as the JCT 98 SFBC.

## *JCT Intermediate Form (JCT 98 IFC)*

The JCT 98 IFC is aimed at works of simple content. The 1998 edition incorporating amendments 1 to 5 is the current version.

The JCT 98 IFC is issued for contracts in the range between those for which the JCT 98 SFBC and the JCT Agreement for Minor Building Works are issued. The form is broadly suitable where the proposed building works are:

(1) of simple content involving basic trades and skills; and
(2) without specialist or complex M&E work; and
(3) where the works are adequately specified and detailed in a bill of quantity prior to the invitation of tenders.

Guidance on the intended use of the form is set out in the JCT Practice Note 5 (Series 2) and this provides a helpful overview of the appropriate use of JCT 98 IFC.

The JCT 98 IFC is a lump sum contract based on a Price Specification/Schedule of Works/Bill of Quantity or if Option B is used a Contract Sum Analysis/Schedule of Rates.

It is a traditional procurement contract in that it does not envisage that the contractor will carry out any design whether by way of a full design and build obligation, a contractor's design portion supplement or performance specified work. It does not envisage that the contractor will have responsibility for any design carried out by any sub-contractor.

The contract comes in a single option form with no differentiation between private or local authority versions.

## What the contract says about time

Clause 2 of the JCT 98 IFC deals with possession and completion. The contractor is given possession of the site on the date stated in the Appendix and is thereafter obliged to begin and regularly and diligently proceed with the works and to complete the same on or before the date for completion which is again a date stated in the Appendix.

Should the contractor fail to complete by the completion date, Clause 2.7 provides for the levying of liquidated and ascertained damages for such non-completion but again it should be noted that prior to such levy the Architect or Contract Administrator must have issued a certificate of non-completion.

Clause 2.3 of the JCT 98 IFC allows for the granting of extensions of time and the relevant events listed are broadly the same as those under the JCT 98 SFBC except that there is no provision relating specifically to the exercise of statutory powers by the UK Government; the events relating to the non-availability of labour and materials are optional; and compliance with an instruction relating to a person named as a sub-contractor may be treated as a relevant event in an application for an extension of time.

As with the JCT 98 SFBC, practical completion is certified by the architect or contract administrator.

A Sectional Completion Supplement is published for use with the JCT 98 IFC and this is set out in a separate document entitled Sectional Completion Supplement and Guidance Notes. It operates in exactly the same way as the Sectional Completion Supplement for the JCT 98 SFBC (and the JCT 98 WCD form) in that each section has its own liquidated damages figure and the contract provisions which govern Practical Completion operate with regard to each sectional completion date.

The contract also usefully includes, at Clause 2.11, a partial possession provision.

## What the contract says about cost

The JCT 98 IFC has two mutually exclusive alternatives denoted A and B. Alternative A is used where a Specification or Schedule of Work, or Bill of Quantity which the contractor has priced in detail, is adopted which totals the Contract Sum under the contract.

Alternative B is a drawings and specification approach where no requirement exists for the contractor to price the Specification in detail but the contractor is obliged to provide either a contract sum analysis or schedule of rates setting out how the contract sum is calculated.

In either approach the contract is still a lump sum contract.

The payment provisions of the JCT 98 IFC are similar in principle to that of the JCT 98 SFBC. A retention provision is included which provides for 5% retention falling away to 2.5% during the Defects Liability Period. Whilst there is provision for an advance payment bond, and a bond in respect of payment for off-site goods, no mention is made of a retention bond.

Detailed Final Account mechanisms are included within the scope of the payment provisions.

### What the contract says about quality

The primary obligation of the contractor is to carry out and complete the works in accordance with the contract documents. The contract documents include the agreement, the conditions, the contract drawings and other documents describing the items of works.

Testing is covered by Clause 3.12 which contains provisions enabling the architect or contract administrator to issue instructions for inspection or tests of work or materials. Clause 3.13.1 provides detailed provisions dealing with opening up work for inspection.

The contractor carries full responsibility for all work that is sub-contracted including where sub-contracted to named sub-contractors.

Provisions for a defects liability period are included at Clause 2.10 with a period set by reference to the Appendix, usually 12 months.

## *JCT Minor Works Agreement 98 (JCT 98 MWA)*

The current version of the Agreement for Minor Building Works published by the JCT is the 1998 edition incorporating amendments 1–5.

This contract is available in one version only for use by both local authorities and private clients.

As the name suggests, this contract has been developed for works which are relatively straightforward for which it is felt the JCT 98 IFC is too elaborate. It is appropriate for use where the proposed works are to be carried out for an agreed lump sum and where an architect or contract administrator has been appointed. The JCT is at pains to stress that this agreement is only intended for use where the client has engaged a professional to advise on and to administer its terms. The JCT indicates that the form is suitable for contracts up to a value of £100,000 (2001 prices) but that it is not suitable for use where bills of quantity would be normally required. It should only be used where the work is simple in character.

The contract is based on drawings and/or specifications and/or schedules and the price is a lump sum with interim payments usually monthly.

There are no supplements available for use with the form which means there is no provision for sectional completion or design. It provides for limited fluctuations only.

## *JCT Major Projects Form (JCT MPF)*

The JCT MPF is the newest contract to be published by the JCT and was formally released in 2003. It represents a radical departure from previous JCT contracts and is the first to be drafted by an outsourced company, namely Brewer Consulting, and in particular Geoff Brewer.

The Guidance Notes indicate that the MPF is intended to respond to the specific needs of employers who have in-house contractual procedures and who regularly undertake major projects and the contractors with whom they work. As a consequence of such parties' familiarity with construction contracts it was possible to reduce the amount of detail in the MPF such that it is both shorter and simpler than the JCT 98 SFBC. This is amply demonstrated by the fact that the latter contains about 80,000 words whereas the MPF contains approximately 12,000 words.

The MPF is a contract which imposes greater risks and responsibilities on the contractor than under previously existing JCT contracts. Consequently the identification of risk at tender stage is critical. For the contract to work equitably the risk must be properly identified so that the contractor can price it. The contractor, at tender stage, must be able to understand the risk it is assuming.

It goes hand in hand with this approach to contractor risk that once the employer has defined its Requirements it should then allow the contractor to carry out the project without being reliant upon the Employer for anything more than access to the site, the review of design documents and payment. It is not anticipated that further information will be received by the contractor from the Employer as all design information beyond that contained in the Requirements will be the responsibility of the contractor.

In many respects the MPF represents the position that was often reached with either the JCT 98 SFBC or the JCT 98 WCD once it had been amended by the Employer's advisers. The drafters of the MPF identified the fact that both the JCT 98 SFBC and the JCT 98 WCD were not delivering what a particular type of employer wanted and as a consequence such employers were making substantial amendments to the published JCT forms.

The MPF comprises a number of sections and documents as follows:

1. The contract conditions.
2. The appendix (setting out all the project specific information relevant to the contract).
3. Third party rights schedule.
4. Pricing document.
5. The requirements.
6. The proposals.

## Design liability

The primary obligation on the contractor is to complete the works and the contractor is therefore responsible for any additional design work that is required beyond that contained in the requirements. As with the existing JCT

98 WCD form the contractor is not responsible for any designs within the requirements.

The level of design liability imposed on the contractor is that of reasonable skill and care. This is the same as the JCT 98 WCD. The Guidance Notes provide additional wording which can be added to Clause 5.3 if a fitness for purpose obligation is to be sought but the prevailing market opinion is that the norm for design liability under the MPF is reasonable skill and care.

The MPF includes a detailed design submission procedure that allows the employer to monitor the design documents being prepared by the contractor in order to satisfy itself that they are in accordance with the contract. This does not dilute in any way the design liability of the contractor.

A sensible addition to the design submission procedure is the referencing to a design programme which is rather like the information release schedule in other JCT contracts designed to encourage the orderly submission of design documents.

No limit of liability for breaches of the contractor's design liability obligations is included (a distinct change from the JCT 98 WCD).

No direct reference to professional indemnity insurance is made but the MPF deals with insurance in a very particular way; noting that in such projects insurance advisers are normally involved from an early stage and consequently all the contract proper needs to do with regard to insurance is provide a very broad framework. The Guidance Notes indicate that policy documents themselves or schedules setting out details of the policies may well be annexed to the contract, but that the contract itself does not attempt to define the scope or terms of the insurance that is to be provided. The Guidance Notes indicate that the role of the contract (insofar as insurance is concerned) is to sufficiently prompt the parties to make certain that the insurance remains in force for the benefit of the project to comply with the terms of the policy.

## What the contract says about time

Rather than being given possession of the site as is common in other JCT forms the MPF permits access to the site on a date stated in the appendix to the contract. This may well be sometime after the commencement of the project.

The contractor is required to use its reasonable endeavours to prevent or reduce delay to the progress and completion of the project and the contractor is required to complete the project by the completion date. Where the completion date has passed without practical completion being achieved the contractor will be liable to pay the employer liquidated damages at a rate stated in the Appendix. Usefully the preliminary notification of delay which is found in a number of other JCT forms is not present in the MPF.

Once the contractor believes it has achieved practical completion it notifies the employer and the employer then issues a statement recording the date of practical completion. No third-party certification is envisaged.

Partial possession terminology has been adapted to refer to the employer's right to "take over" parts of the project prior to Practical Completion of the whole. Taking over parts of the project is subject to contractor consent which is not to be unreasonably withheld or delayed. As with a partial possession the effect of a takeover is that practical completion occurs for that part of the Works which has been taken over.

Sectional completion requirements are dealt with in a much more straightforward way than other JCT Contracts. No separate supplement is published.

Under Clause 12 the contractor is entitled to an adjustment to the completion date to the extent that any of the delay events listed in Clause 12.1 have occurred. This list is narrower than under the JCT 98 WCD form; as for example, it excludes exceptionally adverse weather conditions, industrial disputes, the inability to obtain labour and/or materials and delays caused by statutory authorities. In this respect it represents the negotiated position that was often achieved by way of bespoke amendments to the JCT 98 WCD.

The grant of an extension of time is subject to the contractor complying with notification provisions and the supply of information. Any adjustment to the completion date may be subsequently revised in the light of either further documentation provided by the contractor or knowledge of the actual effects of an anticipated delay.

On the issue of concurrent culpable delay the contract provides for an adjustment to the completion date. Thus the MPF adopts the position set out in the Society of Construction Law Delay Protocol.

Alone amongst JCT contracts an acceleration provision is included which may be operated by agreement between the contractor and the Employer. It is important to note that notwithstanding lack of agreement it remains open to the employer to instruct specific additional measures to be taken with a view to achieving an earlier completion date. These measures would however be a change that the contractor is not obliged to achieve and the risk of whether the instructed measures actually work in fact rests with the Employer. Thus from a contractual perspective one can argue the acceleration provisions are of limited benefit.

As an option the MPF provides for the payment of a bonus if practical completion is achieved earlier than the anticipated completion date.

## What the contract says about cost

The MPF is a lump sum contract.

The contractor is required to make a detailed application for payment no later than seven days before the date the contractor considers that payment is due and a requirement is placed upon the Employer to issue a payment advice on a specified date each month that identifies a balance that is to be paid by one party to the other.

Uniquely amongst JCT contracts reference is made to a document called the pricing document which contains financial information concerning how the contract sum is calculated, how changes are to be valued and critically how payments of the contract sum are to be made to the contractor during the course of the works. The MPF makes it explicitly clear that costs such as loss and expense, liquidated damages, bonuses or costs incurred by the employer when the contractor has failed to comply with instructions are taken into account within the calculation of the amount due under the contract and not as a withholding from an amount due. Consequently a payment advice may require payments from either party to the other rather than simply from the employer to the contractor.

No provision for retention is made although the Guidance Notes refer to the possible need for additional security documents.

Replacing the Final Certificate seen in other JCT Contracts the MPF introduces the concept of the final payment advice issued either upon the completion of rectification of all defects or when the employer considers that a reasonable time has been allowed for such rectification and is not willing to delay issue of the final payment advice any further.

Clause 19 in the MPF sets out provisions dealing with costs savings and value improvement. These are novel approaches and very much welcomed. The provisions include allowing the employer to adopt contractor suggested changes with the instruction of such savings and/or improvement pursuant to the contractor's suggestion being made by way of a change.

The contract gives the contractor limited rights to be reimbursed loss and expense and the idea behind this is that the majority of such loss and expense is addressed as part of the valuation of changes.

Provisions for timely notification to the employer of such loss and expense issues are set out in Clause 21. The contractor must provide information that is reasonably necessary to allow the amount of the loss and expense to be ascertained.

## What the contract says about quality

The level of design liability imposed by the contract has been mentioned above.

The primary obligation on the contractor is that it shall execute the project in accordance with the contract.

Clause 5 sets out the standards of design materials and workmanship. In particular Clause 5.4 states that the contractor shall use in the execution of the project materials and goods of the kind and standards described in the contract. All materials and goods used on the project shall be of satisfactory quality.

Clause 5.5 states that all workmanship shall be of the standard described in the contract or if no such standard is described shall be executed in a good and workmanlike manner.

In keeping with the idea behind the contract that the contractor is responsible for everything other than the Requirements, Clause 4 provides detailed rules for dealing with conflict and discrepancy but it is made explicitly clear in the guidance notes that changes will be limited to those matters brought about by a genuine change of mind on the part of the employer rather than the correction of deficiencies or anomalies in the original information. This is crucial to understanding how the MPF works from the contractor's perspective as it represents a radical alteration from common industry practice and could have serious implications on contractors' approach to pricing MPF projects.

Mechanisms for pricing change and agreeing quotations in advance of change implementation are included within Clause 20.

### *JCT Management Contract 1998 Edition (JCT 98 MC)*

The 1998 edition is the current form of contract produced by the JCT for procurement via management contracting. It is the most complex of all the JCT contracts and an intricate network of contract documentation must be put in place to effectively operate the envisaged approach.

By the early 1980s, for large and complex contracts, the practice of engaging the contractor to be paid a fee to add to the management capacity for the construction of a building had become sufficiently widespread for it to be possible to standardise the procedures in a JCT form and consequently in 1987 the JCT published a standard form of management contract under which the contractor has a management function. The actual construction work is carried out by various other contractors (called Works contractors) using as a contract document the JCT Standard Form of Works Contract (now the JCT 98 WC), the use of which is an integral part of the management contract documentation. Since publication of the 1987 version and the subsequent 1998 version the use of management contracting in the UK has declined in popularity and in the latest RICS Contracts in Use Survey (2001) by number it accounted for 0.6% (by number) of projects surveyed and 2.3% (by value).

The JCT 98 MC is available in one version for local authorities and private clients.

The JCT 98 MC is appropriate for use of large scale projects where an early start and the earliest possible completion are required. One of the key advantages of management contracting is the ability to overlap the design and construction and thus shrink the overall timescale of the project. It must however be remembered that one of the implications of such shrinkage is that works may be procured when they are not fully designed and the cost implications of completing the design must be noted.

The core elements of the JCT 98 MC are the project drawings, the project specification and the contract cost plan. The services to be undertaken by the management contractor are set out in the third schedule.

It is critical that the management contract is used in association with the appropriate works contract. The works contract is based on drawings, specification and bills of quantities which are prepared by the employer's professional team.

Under the management contract price is based on the prime cost of the project plus a management fee. Consequently cost control is a critical issue for the use of the JCT 98 MC. Interim payments are monthly unless otherwise stated.

The employer is required to appoint the usual professional team and design liability usually remains with the employer's professional design team save for specified elements of work. The contract period is divided into two parts; the pre-construction period and the construction period. The rationale behind this differentiation is that the management contractor should be appointed as early as possible so that he becomes part of the professional team advising the client and thus benefits in terms of programming, formulating and agreeing construction methods and buildability flow to the employer. Critically the management contractor will have a vital role in agreeing the contract cost plan.

In the construction period the management contractor will manage, organise, supervise and secure the carrying out of the completion of the project through the works contractors which it directly employs. The works contractors remain sub-contractors of the management contractor, albeit the usual rule with regard to the contractor being responsible for its sub-contractors is subject to specific contractual exemption in the management contract.

## Design liability

As indicated above, the management contract does not envisage a design and build approach.

## What the contract says about time

Given the two specific contractual periods used in the JCT 98 MC (the pre-construction period and the construction period) the provisions governing time are more complicated than under traditional JCT forms.

Under Clause 2.1 of the management contract the management contractor only proceeds to construction of the project after written notice by the employer. At this point in time the provisions setting out possession and completion are confirmed by the employer.

Under Clause 2.3 of the management contract possession of the site is then given to the management contractor and the management contractor is under an obligation to secure the commencement of the project, the regular and diligent progress of the project and its completion on or before the completion date.

Completion of the project may be on or before the completion date. Should the management contractor fail to complete the project by the completion date the architect issues a certificate of non-compliance under Clause 2.9 and under Clause 2.10, following on from the certificate of non-compliance, the employer is entitled to deduct liquidated damages.

A relatively limited list of relevant events is included within Clause 2.13 and in Clause 2.12 there is an obligation similar to that found in many JCT contracts requiring the management contractor to use its best endeavours to prevent delay.

A sectional completion supplement (referred to as a phased completion supplement) is available for use with the contract.

## What the contract says about cost

Clauses 4.1–4.12 regulate payment with the primary obligation being set out in Clause 4.1, namely that the employer shall pay the management contractor the prime cost of the project (ascertained in accordance with the second schedule of the management contract) plus the management fee.

Payment is made by the employer to the management contractor at agreed and stated intervals on interim certificates issued by the architect. These certificates can be issued during both during the pre-construction period and during the construction period.

The prime cost is payable to the management contractor and the architect must direct the management contractor as to the amounts due with regard to works contractors. In addition the management contractor is paid the management fee. In addition the management contractor may be reimbursed for certain site staff and services depending on precisely what has been agreed.

The architect's payment certificates must set out the amount due to the management contractor and define how that amount has been calculated. The final date for payment by the Employer is 14 days from the date of issue of the certificate.

The final certificate provisions are included at Clause 4.12 with the architect issuing the final certificate not later than two months from occurrence of the latest of the events listed in Clause 4.12.

A loss and expense mechanism is included in JCT 98 MC under which the management contractor can pass up to the Employer those loss and expense claims made by its works contractors. If the architect is of the opinion that the application is valid and meets the conditions set out in the works contract then the quantity surveyor can be instructed to ascertain the amount of loss and expense (usually in collaboration with the management contractor).

As with any management contract it is critical to appreciate that no contract sum will exist at the start of the project and as such any employer adopting this procurement route must ensure adequate mechanisms exist elsewhere to control cost.

## What the contract says about quality

As indicated above, the management approach does not anticipate design liability lying with the Management contractor. Design liability in general remains with the professional team and is not passed to the management contractor under the management contract.

Clause 3.1 includes provisions with regard to the employment upon the project by the management contractor of named persons as set out in the second schedule to the contract consent from the architect is required to any changes to that schedule.

Detailed control mechanisms are included in Clauses 3.3, 3.4 and 3.5 dealing with instructions from the Architect so as to enable the management contractor to properly carry out the services that he has agreed to carry out as part of this management function.

Under Clause 3.7 the architect determines any levels which may be required but the management contractor is responsible for setting-out.

Under Clause 3.8 the obligation on the management contractor is that all goods and materials shall (so far as procurable) be of the respective kind and standards specified in the project specification, or as may be required in the specification or bill of quantities in any works contract. Workmanship should be of the standard described in the project specification.

Clause 3.11 provides detailed provision with regard to work or materials not in accordance with the contract and detailed provisions setting out the particular procedure to be adopted with reference to the Code of Practice (the same Code of Practice which is referred to in many JCT contracts) is set out.

For control of the works contractors the management contractor's obligations in respect of the employer (and the Employer's obligations in respect of the management contractor) are fully set out in Clause 3.21. Alleged breaches by the management contractor or by the works contractors are subject to explicit provisions in Clause 2.21. Ultimately, notwithstanding compliance by the management contractor with the works contract and the management contract, if the management contractor is not fully reimbursed by the works contractor then the employer shall pay to the management contractor the amount of any shortfall. Likewise with regard to claims against the management contractor by a works contractor the management contractor is entitled to complete reimbursement of the costs of settling or defending any such claim subject only to not being entitled to be reimbursed for costs directly arising out of the management contractor's breach.

The importance of understanding issues of liability between the management contractor and the works contractors cannot be overemphasised. Clause 1.7 of the management contract states that the liability of the management contractor for any breach of the management contract includes any breach occasioned by the breach of any works contractor is expressly subject to Clause 3.21. This is of critical importance in understanding the precise and limited nature of the management contractor's risks and liability.

Although there is no reference to performance specified work in the management contract, the works contract does refer to such elements of work.

## ICE CONDITIONS OF CONTRACT

### *Overview*

Some way behind the JCT in terms of volume of usage but equally well known in the UK domestic market and, because of certain similarities to FIDIC, in the international market as well, the Institute of Civil Engineers produces a family of standard conditions of contract for civil engineering work, the most well known of which is the Measurement Version 7th Edition (generally referred to as the ICE 7th Edition). This is a stand-alone contract for the carrying out of civil engineering works adopting re-measurement as the payment mechanism. It has been produced by the Institute of Civil Engineers (ICE) for over 50 years.

The Conditions of Contract themselves are jointly sponsored by the Institute of Civil Engineers, the Civil Engineering Contractors Association (CECA) and the Association of Consulting Engineers (ACE).

The ICE Conditions of Contract were designed to standardise the duties of contractors, employers and engineers and to allocate the risks inherent in civil engineering projects to those best able to manage them. Set up in 1975 the Conditions of Contract Standing Joint Committee (CCSJC) is an independent body that monitors the operation of the ICE Conditions of Contract. Its aim is to keep the use of the ICE Standard Forms of Contract under review and to consider any suggestions for amendment and also to undertake the drafting of new standard forms.

The suite of contracts produced by the ICE are as follows:

1. Measurement Version 7th Edition.
2. Design and Construct 2nd Edition.
3. Term Version 1st Edition.
4. Minor Works 3rd Edition.
5. Partnering Addendum.
6. Agreement for Consultancy Work in respect of Domestic or Small Works.
7. Archaeological Investigation.
8. Target Costs 1st Edition (due 2005).

In this chapter we are going to look specifically at three ICE contracts, namely the Measurement Version 7th Version, the ICE Design and Construct Contract and the ICE Minor Works.

The ICE also produce the ECC Form of Contract. This is covered in the next section.

### *Measurement Version 7th Edition*

The current version of this contract, the 7th Edition, was issued in September 1999. This updated the previous Sixth Edition (ICE 7th Edition) originally published in January 1991 and reprinted with amendments in November 1995 and November 1997.

As the name of the contract suggests, the ICE 7th is not a lump sum contract. Rather, like the JCT With Approximate Quantities Contract, it relies on re-measurement as the mechanism to calculate the final amount to be paid by the employer to the contractor for the carrying out of the works. In simple terms, the quantities which are included against any rates which the contractor has tendered are approximate only and are subject to re-calculation once the actual amount of work has been completed. It follows from this that any contract sum included in the contract may be a fairly accurate approximation of the final figure, but is not in any way contractually binding.

The contract does not place the main design liability on the contractor envisaging that the majority of design will have been carried out by the professional team employed by the Employer. As the standard form contract prepared by the Institute of Civil Engineers, its primary purpose is for large scale civil engineering projects and indeed the nature of the contract conditions would make its use unsuitable for building works.

The contract contains some 72 clauses spread over 53 pages. Usefully, like the GC/Works/1 Contract, a useful index is included setting out the location (by reference to clause number and page number) of various provisions.

The layout of the contract is totally different to JCT, although there are similarities between the ICE Conditions and FIDIC.

Of particular importance in the ICE Conditions is the engineer who is appointed by the employer and carries an important role in contract administration and dispute resolution.

### What the contract says about time

The core provisions with regard to commencement time and delays are found in Clauses 41 to 47 of the Conditions of Contract.

The contractor is obliged to start the works as soon as is reasonably practical after the works commencement date. The works commencement date is specified in the appendix to the form of tender.

Once started, the contractor is under an obligation to proceed with the works with expedition without delay in accordance with the contract.

Clause 42 allows the employer to prescribe that the contractor will only be given certain sections of the site from time to time and to restrict the availability and nature of access he needs to provide. In addition, the employer is able to prescribe the order in which the works will be constructed.

Under Clause 43, the whole of the works (including any section required to be completed within a particular time as stated in the appendix to the form of tender) shall be substantially completed within the time stated. The reference to any sections in Clause 43 allows for the concept of sectional completion to be introduced.

An extension of time mechanism is included at Clause 44 which provides that the contractor, within 28 days after the cause of any delay has arisen or as soon thereafter as reasonable, must notify the engineer and provide full and detailed particulars justifying the extension in order that it may be investigated contemporaneously with the actual delay. Clause 44 allows the engineer to assess the delay and to grant an interim extension of time which is subject to review once the works or relevant section of the works have been completed. Under Clause 44(5) the engineer is obliged within 28 days of the issue of the certificate of substantial completion for the works, or for any section thereof, to review all the extensions of time and to finally determine and certify the overall extension of time (if any) for which he considers the contractor entitled.

Clause 77 of the Contract Conditions makes the contractor liable for payment of liquidated damages for delay in substantial completion of either the whole or a specified section of the works and a capping mechanism is included at Clause 47(4) whereby a limit on the maximum amount of liquidated damages is inserted in the appendix to the form of tender. If no such limit is stated then there is no limit to the amount of liquidated damages.

Rather than referring to the concept of practical completion or completion, the contract refers to substantial completion and Clause 48 of the contract regulates how substantial completion is notified by the contractor to the engineer and then certified by the engineer.

Defects liability provisions are included within the contract as the defects correction period which runs from the date of substantial completion to the date stated in the appendix to the tender. The contractor is obliged to correct defects as soon as practicable. The defects correction certificate is issued by the engineer pursuant to Clause 61 of the contract when he is satisfied that the defects have been corrected.

## What the contract says about cost

As has already been mentioned, the ICE 7th is not a lump sum contract but a remeasurement contract where the approximate quantities included within the bill of quantities are subject to remeasurement and the tender total is consequently adjusted to reflect the actual amount of work involved in the project.

As a consequence of this, the contract does not refer to a contract sum but rather it refers to a tender total (which represents the approximate quantities multiplied by the agreed rates) and the contract price which is the final ascertained amount when the actual quantities have been multiplied by the rates. These are important concepts to understand when looking at the ICE

Conditions to differentiate a remeasurement contract from a lump sum contract.

Clause 60 of the Contract Conditions deals with certification and payments. The usual arrangement envisaged by Clause 60.1 is the submission of monthly statements by the contractor to the engineer showing, amongst other things, the estimated contract value of the permanent works carried out up to the end of the month.

Certification of payment is issued by the engineer and must occur within 25 days of the date of delivery of the contractor's monthly statement with payment by the employer following very quickly, only three days later giving a total of 28 days from the date of the submission for payment.

Provisions dealing with the rate and the limit of retention are included with 50% retention being released on the certificate of substantial completion and the remaining half at the end of the defects correction period.

Detailed final account provisions are included at Clause 60.4 with the receipt of the final account documentation and supporting evidence in the three-month period following the defects correction certificate with the engineer issuing the final certificate within a further three months.

The contract includes provisions at Clause 61 dealing with alterations, additions and omissions and the Engineer has a very wide scope to order variations.

Clause 55 of the contract makes it clear that the quantity set out in the bill of quantities are the estimated quantities of the work and Clause 56, by reference to the rather odd word "outer-measurement" introduces the concept of remeasurement for calculation of the actual quantities. The provision of Clause 56.2 is of note as this allows for some flexibility in the rate for a given item of work where the increase or decrease in the quantity is of such note that the engineer considers that it should warrant an appropriate increase or decrease in the rate.

Clause 58 deals with the use of provisional sums and prime cost items both of which may be utilised by the Engineer in his administration of the contract.

### What the contract says about quality

As indicated above, it is not generally anticipated that this form of contract places design liability on the contractor and express reference to this is made in Clause 8(2). It is important to note that the ICE Conditions differentiate between the permanent works and the temporary works but in neither case is the contractor liable for design.

The primary obligation of the contractor is, subject to express provisions of the contract, to construct and complete the works and provide the labour, materials, equipment, temporary work, transport and everything else necessary for completing the works. Thus the contractor is responsible for off-site operations and methods but not design.

Clause 13 provides that the contractor shall construct and complete the works in strict accordance with the contract to the satisfaction of the engineer and shall comply strictly with the engineer's instructions or those of anyone connected therewith. The mode, manner and speed of construction of the works are to be of a kind and conducted in a manner acceptable to the engineer. This is set out in Clause 13(2).

Under Clause 11(2) the contractor shall be deemed to have inspected and examined the site and under Clause 12, the contractor may claim additional time and/or money if during the carrying out of the works he encounters physical conditions (excluding weather) or artificial obstructions which could not in his opinion, reasonably have been foreseen by an experienced contractor. It can thus be seen that the risk of ground conditions is not totally allocated either to the employer or the contractor but is rather shared between them in a way which, during the existence of the ICE Contract, has created many disputes. It should be noted that this arrangement in respect of ground risk is broadly followed by the ECC Contract as well.

Clause 36 requires that all materials and workmanship shall be of the respective kinds as described in the contract and in accordance with the engineer's instructions. Clause 36 also deals with testing. Clause 38 covers examination of the works before covering up, uncovering and making openings and removal of unsatisfactory work.

### *ICE Design and Construct 2nd Edition*

The current version of the ICE Conditions of Contract Design and Construct is the 2nd edition published in September 2001. This updated the first edition published in 1992 which had been reprinted in 1997.

As the name suggests, this is a design and build contract based on the same rationale as the ICE Measurement Version 7th Edition for use on major civil engineering schemes.

Superficially the contract bears a great deal of resemblance to the ICE 7th but the similarity in terms of layout should not be misconstrued as the fundamental obligations under the contract are very different.

#### Design liability

Under Clause 8 the contractor's primary obligation to design, construct and complete the works.

Clause 8(2) sets out that the standard governing the contractor's design responsibility is the exercise of all reasonable, skill, care and diligence.

#### What the contract says about time

These are substantially the same as the ICE 7th although references to the engineer are replaced with references to the employer's representative.

### What the contract says about cost

The Design and Construct Contract is not necessarily a remeasurement contract. The form of tendering includes for a lump sum or such other sum as may be ascertained in accordance with the contract conditions. The contract price will include the design, construction and completion of the works. Otherwise the payment provisions broadly follow those of the ICE 7th.

### What the contract says about quality

Other provisions broadly follow the arrangement set out within the ICE 7th.

## *ICE Minor Works 3rd Edition*

The contract is aimed at engineering works and not building works. The Guidance Notes published along with the Minor Works edition indicate that the contract is for use on projects where the potential risks involved are small, where the works are simple and straightforward, where the design of the work is basically complete and where the contractor has no responsibility for the design of the permanent works other than possibly design of a specialised nature. It is also envisages that nominated sub-contractors are not employed, that the contract value does not exceed £500,000 and that the period for completion does not exceed six months.

### Design liabilities

As indicated above, it is not intended that the minor works contract covers a situation where the contractor carries full design liability but it is envisaged that it could cover a situation where the contractor carries some responsibility for design work of a specialist nature which would normally be undertaken by a specialist sub-contractor or supplier. If that is the case full details must be given in the specification, in the appendix to the contract, or in the drawings. The contractor's responsibility in respect of such works is limited to the exercise of reasonable skill and care and this is set out in Clause 7.3(c).

### What the contract says about time

Clause 4 of the Minor Works Conditions deals with commencement and completion.

The start date is either specified in the Appendix or notified by the engineer. The contractor begins as soon as reasonably possible after the start date. The period or periods for completion are as stated in the Appendix and commence on the start date.

Limited programme provisions are included in Clause 4.3.

An extension of time mechanism is included at Clause 4.4 with a fairly limited number of relevant events.

Practical Completion is defined to occur when the works reach a state when, notwithstanding any defects or outstanding items they are taken or are fit to be taken into use or possession by the Employer. Certification of Practical Completion is by the Engineer appointed by the Employer.

Liquidated damages are payable for a delay in completion pursuant to Clause 4.6.

Defect correction arrangements and the defects liability provisions are broadly as per the ICE 7th Edition.

### What the contract says about cost

The method of payment for the contract is stated in the Appendix to the Conditions of Contract but if a bill of quantities is used the method of measurement to be used must also be stated in the Appendix. No provision is made for fluctuations as it is not envisaged that the contract should be used for periods longer than six months.

The contract can be a lump sum contract or a measurement contract using a price bill of quantities. An appendix entry indicates which is applicable.

Monthly statements are provided from the contractor pursuant to Clause 7.2 and Clause 7.3 provides that the engineer shall certify claims within 25 days of receipt of the monthly payments, and such claims will be paid within 28 days. Again this is a relatively tight period.

Final account provisions are covered in Clauses 7.4 and 7.6.

Limited provision for the contractor to claim additional cost is included in the contract at Clause 3.8.

### What the contract says about quality

The employer is required to appoint an engineer to administer the terms of the contract.

The primary obligation of the contractor is to complete the works and this is set out in Clause 3.1.4.

## THE ENGINEERING AND CONSTRUCTION CONTRACT (ECC)

### *Overview*

Amongst standard forms in common use this is a relative newcomer, the first edition having been published in 1993 with the second edition published in 1995. It is anticipated that a further third edition will be published at some point during 2005. It is published by the ICE but has no relation to other contracts published by the ICE.

The ECC is a radical departure from existing standard form contracts both in terms of its underlying objectives and its drafting.

Both JCT and ICE standard forms owe their drafting style, to a large degree, to concepts and approaches that existed at the end of the 19th and for the majority of the 20th century. This goes some way to explaining the often lengthy and confused provisions contained within those contracts.

The ECC deliberately avoided the traditional style of drafting and terminology. The ECC introduces unique terminology such as Compensation Events (relevant events in JCT and ICE contracts), Works Information (drawings, specifications in JCT and ICE), contract data and site information. This reclassification is an attempt by the drafters of the ECC to move contract users away from the thought processes they have adopted on JCT and ICE contracts and to encourage more effective project management.

The ECC takes an entirely different and fresh approach when compared to the JCT and ICE contracts. The drafters of the ECC had three clear aims:

1. *flexibility*—the idea behind the ECC Contract is that it can be used for building and/or civil engineering works, and where the contractor has some, all or no design responsibility. It can also be used for a variety of pricing mechanisms ranging from target costs through lump sum procurement to management contracting and can be used both in the UK and abroad.
2. *clarity and simplicity*—the drafters of the ECC Contract wanted a distinct departure from the approach adopted, particularly in JCT and ICE forms and thus whilst the contract is a legal document and legally binding, it is written in ordinary language with words that are reasonably understood.
3. *a stimulus to good management.* The drafters of the ECC identified what they considered to be a weakness in many standard form contracts, namely that they did not encourage and promote effective project management and this was in part a reason why so many disputes and problems were encountered on major building and civil engineering contracts. In particular the cooperation of the key parties was an important and under-utilised technique for effective project delivery and the ECC Contract should, if used properly, encourage effective, cooperative project management so as to reduce the exposure to cost and time overruns and poor quality work.

The key to this approach and a central tenet to all the ECC contracts is how compensation events are dealt with and this will be looked at in more detail below.

### Structure of the ECC

To achieve the stated aim of flexibility the ECC Contract is published in six different payment options, lettered A to F. Each of these options will be looked at subsequently.

Following the six main payment options are a series of secondary options, lettered G to Z, covering such matters as performance bonds, advance payment, retentions, delay damages, changes in the law and trust funds. Some of these options will be looked at in more detail later.

## *Main options of the ECC*

### Option A—Priced contract with activity schedule

This is a lump sum contract which sets out a list of all the construction activities the contractor will be required to carry out (this is the activity schedule) and the contractor prices each of those activities. The total of the prices for each of the activities is the contractor's price for providing the whole of the works.

### Option B—Priced contract with bill of quantities

This, as the name suggests, is a lump sum contract but based on a bill of quantities rather than an activity schedule.

### Options C and D—Target contracts (with activity schedule or bill of quantities)

Again, as the name suggests, these are target cost contracts with pricing based either upon an activity schedule or a bill of quantities.

Target cost arrangements are of most use where it is not possible in advance of the contract to be completely certain about the extent of the work that is to be done. The primary purpose of such arrangements is to provide an economic incentive to the contractor to come in on target and also to provide an economic disincentive for the stated target to be exceeded. This is usually achieved by way of a pain/gain sharing arrangement with the contractor receiving a benefit if he comes in below the target cost or a penalty if he exceeds the target cost.

The terminology that the ECC Contract uses in this regard is relatively complex. The concepts of prices, the contractor's fee, actual cost and the price of work done to date need to be fully understood in order to understand the implications of the target cost arrangements. In particular actual cost is defined to mean a specific cost and is not the actual cost incurred by the contractor.

### Option E—Cost reimbursable contract

As the name suggests this is a contract where the contractor carries minimum risk in terms of cost and this option is commonly used in a situation where the nature of the works is so uncertain that even a target cost contract would not be appropriate.

### Option F—Management contract

This is a management contract where the contractor tenders his fee together with his estimate of the total of the prices of all the sub-contractors. Subcontract costs are paid as actual costs with the contractor providing management services.

The management contractor is paid a fee for the provision of those services which is subject to the compensation event mechanism.

### Design liability

As indicated above the ECC contract has been drafted to provide maximum flexibility. When it is applied to design liability, this has resulted in a contract which can be operated to make the contractor responsible for no part of the design, or the whole of the design or any intermediate stage in between those two extremes. The ECC contract itself is silent with regard to the level of design liability which results in the applicable standard being a fitness for purpose obligation, but Secondary Option M contains a mechanism to allow for the contractor's liability for his designs to be reduced to that of reasonable skill and care.

### Secondary options

As indicated earlier the secondary options are lettered G to Z, the secondary options are as follows:

| | |
|---|---|
| Option G | Performance bond |
| Option H | Parent company guarantee |
| Option J | Advanced payment to the contractor |
| Option K | Multiple currencies (not to be used with Options C, D, E and F) |
| Option L | Sectional completion |
| Option M | Limitation of the contractor's liability for his design to reasonable skill and care |
| Option N | Price adjustment for inflation (not to be used with Option E and F) |
| Option P | Retention |
| Option Q | Bonus for early completion |
| Option R | Delay damages |
| Option S | Low performance damages |

| | |
|---|---|
| Option T | Changes in the law |
| Option U | The Construction (Design and Management) Regulations 1994 (to be used in the UK) |
| Option V | Trust fund |
| Option Z | Additional conditions of contract |

Secondary Option Z refers to additional conditions of contract and these need to be drafted on an individual basis for each project taking into account the particular facts of the project.

## What the contract says about time

The clause numbering in all of the ECC main options is the same, and commencement and completion are dealt with in Clause 30. The contract sets out the start date and the completion date (both in the contract data). In the printed contract, words that are defined in the contract data appear in italics.

In addition the possession date is also inserted into the contract data. The possession date is the date the contractor commenced work on site.

The key representative for the employer is the project manager. The project manager is responsible for certifying completion within one week of completion occurring.

The ECC contains more extensive provisions concerning programmes than is common in many standard forms. Detailed information as to what is required to be included in the programme is set out in Clause 31.2 and the project manager has powers under Clause 31.3 to reject the programme for a list of defined reasons. Where the reason for rejection is one set out in the contract it is not a compensation event, otherwise it is. Clear time periods for responses are set out as is a provision for revising the programme.

Sectional completion or taking over are included within the contract and the contract data and works information will need to be included in order to operate those mechanisms properly.

An acceleration mechanism is included for Options C, D, E and F.

Compensation events as far as they relate to time are dealt with under a separate sub-heading in this chapter.

## What the contract says about cost

Payment is covered under Clause 50 and a detailed examination of the identified and defined terms and the payment arrangements for each of the ECC contracts is beyond the scope of this chapter.

Provisions with regard to assessing the amount that is due are common across the suite of contracts. Clause 50.1 defines the assessment date which is the date from which the dates of both certification and payment are calculated.

The first assessment date is fixed and thereafter assessment dates occur at the assessment interval.

The equivalent of the final account mechanism is set out in the final assessment and this date will be four weeks after the date when the supervisor issues the defects certificate or after a final decision of the adjudicator or tribunal.

The amount due to the contractor is the Price for Work Done to Date (PWDD). Sums are either added or deducted from this depending on which secondary options are used.

As indicated previously the latest dates for payment and/or certification by the project manager are tied back to the assessment date.

It should be noted, and this requires careful understanding when the contract is being used, that the definition of actual cost in Clause 11.2 varies depending on which main option is being used. It is absolutely critical to the successful use of the ECC Contract to fully understand the definition of Actual Cost in each of the options when the contract is being used. This is particularly the case with the target cost main option.

### What the contract says about quality

The specification documentation is contained within the works information. The contractor's primary obligation under the contract is set out in Clause 20.1, namely to provide the works in accordance with the works information.

Other information relevant to the contractor's quality obligations may be found in the site information and/or in the contract data Part 1 or Part 2. In using the ECC suite of contracts it is critical to understand what is contained within the works information and the contract data and not simply to assume that contract procedures or approaches that have previously been adopted in JCT and ICE contracts are automatically applicable to ECC contracts.

### Compensation events

Compensation events are, as the guidance notes indicate, events, which if they occur, and do not arise from the contractor's fault, entitle the contractor to be compensated for any effect the event has on the prices and the completion date.

As such these are analogous to the relevant events for extensions of time and grounds for loss and expense claims in JCT and ICE contracts.

The ECC Contract, by adopting an entirely new terminology has attempted to move thought processes away from the traditional approach towards a better understanding of what these mechanisms are trying to achieve. In essence the language adopted by the ECC Contract is designed to reinforce the fact that the compensation events set out risks that are with the employer and not the contractor. Consequently, should they occur, the contractor is entitled to be compensated for them. All of the compensation events may affect either the price or the completion date or both.

A detailed review of all of the compensation events is beyond the scope of this chapter, however, they include events such as delaying possession of the site, changes to the works information, delayed tests and inspections, unforeseen physical conditions and adverse weather.

Detailed mechanisms are included within the compensation event provisions dealing with notification of compensation events (Clause 61) quantities for compensation events (Clause 62) and assessment of the effect of compensation events. The assessment and the implementation of the assessment does vary between some of the main options.

## FIDIC

### *Overview*

FIDIC is the International Federation of Consulting Engineers (the acronym represents the French version of the name) which represents the international business of firms belonging to national member associations of engineering based consulting companies. FIDIC is based in Geneva, Switzerland and was founded in 1913. To date membership includes 64 member associations representing in excess of 500,000 professionals. FIDIC produces a number of contracts which are helpfully colour coded for ease of use. The FIDIC red book contains Conditions of Contract for Building and Civil Engineering Works which are designed by the Employer. The silver book is an Engineer Procurer Construct (EPC)/Turnkey Contract and the yellow book is for the procurement of plant and design build for electrical and mechanical plants and engineering works designed by the contractor.

FIDIC contracts are used predominately on international projects and are very much considered the standard form of contract for use on such projects, a fact that is recognised by international institutions such as the World Bank and the International Monetary Fund.

In addition to the above three forms, FIDIC also produces a short form contract known as the green book.

### *FIDIC (Red Book)*

Conditions of Contract for Construction (Red Book), which is recommended for building or engineering works designed by the employer or by his representative, the engineer. Under the usual arrangements for this type of contract, the contractor constructs the works in accordance with a design provided by the employer. However, the works may include some elements of contractor-designed civil, mechanical, electrical and/or construction works.

### *FIDIC (Silver Book)*

Conditions of Contract for EPC Turnkey Projects, which is recommended where one entity takes total responsibility for the design and execution of an engineering project. Under the usual arrangements for this type of contract, the entity carries out all the Engineering, Procurement and Construction: providing a fully-equipped facility, ready for operation (at the "turn of the key"). This type of contract is usually negotiated between the parties.

### *FIDIC (Yellow Book)*

Conditions of Contract for Plant and Design-Build, which is recommended for the provision of electrical and/or mechanical plant, and for the design and execution of building or engineering works. Under the usual arrangements for this type of contract, the contractor designs and provides, in accordance with the employer's requirements, plant and/or other works; which may include any combination of civil, mechanical, electrical and/or construction works.

### *FIDIC (Green Book)*

The FIDIC Short Form of Contract (Green Book) was first published in 1999 for engineering and building work of small financial value. There are circumstances, however, when the Green Book can be considered for works of a larger value; namely where the intended works are fairly simple or repetitive or of short duration and where they do not require the need for specialist subcontractors.

The Green Book aims to be as flexible as possible and essential commercial provisions are therefore included which can be adapted for use for all types of engineering and building work.

## What the contract says about time

The contractor is obliged to start the works on the commencement date (which the parties agree in advance and insert in the Contract Appendix) and complete the works within the time for completion (which is again agreed and inserted in the appendix). In the event the contractor is late in completing the works, he is obliged to pay to the employer liquidated and ascertained damages ("LADs") at the rate inserted in the appendix. The LADs are usually payable on a weekly basis although they can be pro-rated if the appendix makes this clear. The contractor will, however, avoid the obligation to pay LADs if the delay to the works has been caused by one or more of the employer's liabilities listed in Clause 6.1 of the contract. Employer's liabilities are events where the employer takes the risk of delay occurring to the works and includes events such as war, *force majeure* and any failure of the employer under the contract.

If the contractor believes an employer's liability has occurred which has caused delay to the works, he must apply to the employer for an extension to the Time for Completion. The employer is then obliged to consider all supporting details provided by the contractor and the employer must then extend the Time for Completion as appropriate in the circumstances.

Once the employer considers the contractor has completed the works in accordance with the contract, he is obliged to notify the contractor in writing stating the appropriate date when this has happened. This is known as the Taking Over Notice. The employer also has the option of taking over the works even though they are not fully complete. In such circumstances, the employer must notify the contractor of his intention to do so. The date on which this occurs constitutes the date of the Taking Over Notice. Notwithstanding the early issue of this notice, Clause 8.2 of the contract obliges the contractor to promptly complete any outstanding work and clear the site.

### What the contract says about cost

The contract is a lump sum contract. A variation mechanism is incorporated in Clause 10 which enables the employer to instruct changes to the original scope of works for an additional cost which is then added to the contract sum. The variations can be valued in a number of ways including as a lump sum price agreed between the parties or by comparison with rates set out in the contract.

Not only does the contractor get additional money for variations, he is also entitled to recover any costs he incurs as a result of any of the employer's liabilities. For both variations and claims for loss and expense arising out of employer's liabilities, the contractor must submit to the employer an itemised breakdown of the sums involved within 28 days of the costs being incurred or the instruction being given. The employer is under an obligation to check and agree the value of the variation or claim with the contractor but, in the absence of agreement, the value is determined solely by the employer.

The contract sum is paid to the contractor in monthly instalments with the final account being submitted by the contractor within 42 days of the expiry of the defects liability period or, if later, the date on which any defects notified to the contractor have been rectified. The employer is under an obligation to settle the final account within 28 days of its submission.

To encourage the contractor to both complete the works and rectify defects during the defects liability period, the Green Book provides for a retention of 5% of the contract sum (although the parties can, of course, agree a different percentage). One half of the retention is paid to the contractor within 14 days of the taking over notice being issued by the employer, with the remaining half of the retention being paid to the contractor within 14 days of the end of the defects liability period (or, if later, the date on which the contractor has rectified all defects notified to him during that time).

### What the contract says about quality

The contractor is under an obligation to construct the "works" in accordance with the terms of the contract. As the definition of "contract" includes reference to any specification, drawings, contractor's design or bill of quantities, there is obviously scope for the contract to be used in circumstances where the contractor will be expected to carry out some design work. Notwithstanding this, Clause 5.2 of the contract makes it clear that the contractor will only be responsible for his tendered design; the employer will maintain responsibility for any design set out in the specification (which details all of the employer's requirements for the project) and the drawings.

The employer certifies when the works are complete by issuing a taking over notice. The Green Book does not provide for an independent party to certify completion of the works although the employer may appoint an independent party to impartially certify should he wish to do so.

As is common with many construction contracts, the defects liability period is expressed to be 12 months from the date of taking over unless the parties state otherwise. During this 12-month period, the contractor must remedy at his own cost defects which are notified to him and due to the contractor's design, or materials, plant or workmanship not being in accordance with the contract. Defects arising from any other cause will be remedied by the contractor at the cost of the employer.

## ICHEME

### *Overview*

First published by the Institution of Chemical Engineers in 1968, the Red Book (so called because of its cover) is a lump-sum, turnkey contract for the procurement of process plant. It has a wide application across the chemical and materials industries. The 4th Edition embraces changes brought about by the Arbitration Act 1996, the Housing Grants, Construction & Regeneration Act 1996 and the Contracts (Rights of Third Parties) Act 1999.

The project manager performs most of the integral duties on behalf of the client (called the "purchaser") whilst the contractor's role goes beyond traditional expectations of design and build. Not only must it design and construct the plant but it must also carry out testing and commissioning to demonstrate that it is fit for its intended purpose. The technical information is contained in the specification and schedules to the contract and useful information is given in the Red Book's guidance notes to what the content of these schedules should be.

The IChemE also publishes a reimbursable form of the contract (the "Green Book") and the "Yellow Book" is a back-to-back sub-contract suitable for both the Red and Green Books.

## *How the Red Book deals with the key issues of time, cost and quality*

### What the contract says about time

There are two elements to completion before the plant is taken over by the purchaser—(i) completion of construction of the plant, and (ii) testing that the plant operates as required. The contractor is to complete the construction of the plant so that it is ready for the take-over procedures on or before the date specified as the time for completion (Clause 13.1). The contract allows for sectional completion if required.

Schedule 11 contains events related to liability for delay, and provides that the contractor is to submit to the project manager for approval a programme of work (once approved, the "approved programme"). The contractor uses reasonable endeavours to comply with the approved programme (Clause 13.3). However, if the time for completion is likely to be delayed as a result of the contractor's delay, the project manager may give notice and the contractor shall use best endeavours to remedy the potential delay at its own cost.

If the contractor is delayed by matters specified in Clause 14.1 or either party is delayed by *force majeure*, the party affected will give notice to the project manager. The contractor then notifies the project manager of any extension of time it believes is reasonable and the project manager within 14 days issues a Variation Order both to the purchaser and to the contractor stating the extension to the Approved Programme or, where appropriate, to the period in Schedule 16 (performance tests and procedures). Both parties are to use reasonable endeavours to minimise any delay in the performance of their obligations under the contract whatever the cause (Clause 14.3).

If the project manager wishes to issue a variation to the works or plant, its variation order will amend the approved programme and time for completion if appropriate (Clause 16.3). The approved programme and time for completion may also change as a result of any variation proposed by the contractor which is subsequently adopted by the project manager ("contractor's variation") (Clause 17.1). When the contractor is ready to conduct a pre-installation test, it notifies the project manager (Clause 22.3).

When the contractor believes the plant (or any part of it) is substantially complete and ready for inspection, it notifies the project manager. It then proposes a programme for inspection and testing commencing no sooner than seven days nor later than 14 days from the notice (Clause 32.2). Upon satisfactory completion of inspection and/or testing, the project manager issues the construction completion certificate. As soon as construction of the plant is demonstrated to be complete and is, in the contractor's opinion, ready for takeover procedures then upon notification by the contractor the project manager shall (within seven to 14 days of such notice) begin to conduct the procedures for take-over (Clause 33.2).

Should the plant then fail to pass a take-over test, the contractor makes adjustments and repeats the test. If the take-over certificate is endorsed with uncompleted items or omitted take-over procedures, the contractor shall complete these to the satisfaction of the project manager as soon as possible. Clause 33.9 also provides for partial completion where part(s) of the tested plant have not satisfied any take-over test.

The take-over certificate will be the acceptance certificate confirming that the plant or parts is/are satisfactory to the purchaser unless the contractor has made specific guarantees in respect of performance of the plant, in which case Clause 36 applies and the plant must then satisfy all performance tests before an acceptance certificate is issued. The acceptance certificate can be endorsed with any minor incomplete items or defects but is subject to revocation if these are not addressed within 28 days of the project manager giving notice. The defects liability period runs for one year from the take-over certificate. Following its expiry or where the contractor has made good all defects, the project manager issues the final certificate (Clause 38.1).

## What the contract says about cost

The purchaser pays the contract price and any sums specified in Schedule 19 (terms of payment) (Clause 39.1). Within 14 days of receipt of an interim statement (or, in the case of the final statement, within 56 days of receipt), the project manager shall issue a certificate in respect of that instalment. This shows the manner in which the sums specified had been calculated and lists all the sums which in its opinion are properly payable, separating any elements for nominated sub-contractors. Clause 39.5 specifies that the project manager may delete, correct or modify any sum previously certified as it considers proper.

Following receipt of the certificate, the contractor submits an invoice to the Purchaser for the sum certified as payable with a copy of the project manager's certificate. This is due on the date of receipt by the purchaser of such invoice and the purchaser pays the amount within 14 days of receipt (Clause 39.5) subject to any set-off.

If a variation is required (providing it is not a variation which is required to remove a defect or specific hazards to personal property, performance of the works or in the pre-operational use of the plant) then the contract price shall be adjusted (Clause 16.2). Clause 19 provides that the contractor should provide an estimate for each variation based on the rates charged in Schedule 18 (valuation of variations and claims) if applicable, or as may otherwise be reasonable, and the project manager and contractor shall agree the amount to be added or deducted in the contract price consequently. If the parties are unable to agree, the project manager decides the amount.

If the contractor fails to complete the plant or any specified section in accordance with Schedule 11 (time for completion), the contractor shall pay liquidated damages as described in Schedule 12 (Clause 15.1).

Clause 6.1 provides that, subject to the other provisions of the contract, the costs of executing the works are at the risk of the contractor and it is deemed to have obtained all information and taken account of all circumstances before agreeing to the contract price. The procedure for the contractor to seek any additional payment or adjustment to the contract price (which is not a contractor's variation under Clause 17) is set out in Clause 18. It must serve notice as a condition precedent to making a claim and the project manager will consider the claim in connection with the relevant circumstances and provisions of the contract. Should inaccurate information from the purchaser lead to increased cost to the contractor in performing its obligations, then the contractor is entitled to be paid its initial cost plus profit in addition to the contract price providing it submits a claim under Clauses 18 and 19.5. (Clause 6.2).

### What the contract says about quality

The contractor is required to carry out all work with sound workmanship and materials and in accordance with good engineering practice, applicable legislation and to the reasonable satisfaction of the project manager (Clause 15.2). The contractor is to set out the plant by references to points, lines and levels of reference provided by the project manager, and the contractor is responsible for the correctness of this information (Clause 3.3).

Clause 3.4 contains a fitness for purpose obligation in respect of the specification or any other provision of the contract. The contractor is under an obligation during the performance of the contract if it believes that a change to the works or design or method or operation of the plant is necessary to eliminate a potential defect or specific hazard as would otherwise be detrimental to the purchaser and to bring such matter to the attention of the project manager providing its reasons and to submit its proposals for a variation. The contractor shall itself maintain and require subcontractors to maintain a quality assurance system in accordance with any requirement under Schedule 6.

In the event of conflict between any of the contract documents, the order of precedence is set out in Clause 2.2.

The construction of process plant is likely to require specialist sub-contractors, and the Red Book provides that it is the contractor who is responsible for selecting sub-contractors and integrating their roles within the project. The contractor remains liable for any sub-contracted works (Clause 30.5). It is not permitted to sub-contract the whole of the works (Clause 9.2).

If the contract provides under Schedule 3 that the purchaser is to carry out any work or provide any materials, facilities or services necessary to permit the carrying out or the completion of the works by the contractor (unless otherwise provided in the contract), such work, facilities or services shall be carried out with sound workmanship and materials, safely and in accordance with good engineering practice, applicable legislation, in a manner compatible with the carrying out of the nature of works by the contractor and at a time specified in the contract or (if not specified) a reasonable time with regard to completion, the provisions of the approved programme of the actual progress of the works and all relevant circumstances (Clause 4.2). The purchaser provides personnel with adequate skills and experience to operate and maintain the plant from the date of the take-over certificate and makes them available for training in accordance with Schedule 9 (Clause 4.4).

The purchaser is responsible for the accuracy of the information provided by it or on its behalf (Clause 6.2). The purchaser takes the risk for all site conditions not reasonably foreseeable by the contractor or which could have obtained by visual inspection or by reasonable enquiry (Clause 6.3).

Should the contractor or sub-contractor supply any materials, the contractor should obtain in the names of both the purchaser and the contractor appropriate guarantees in respect of the materials for their construction, workmanship and fitness for purpose for either a year from the date of any take-over certificate or, if this is not possible and the project manager consents, for a period of not less than 540 days from the date on which title for such materials passes from the sub-contractor (Clause 9.4).

Upon issue of the final certificate, this will be taken as "conclusive evidence for all purposes and in any proceedings whatsoever" between the parties that the contractor has complied with the contract (subject to any fraud, misrepresentation or concealment) (Clause 38.4). The purchaser will thus be unlikely to succeed if it wishes to challenge the contractor for breach of the contract after the final certificate has been issued. There are mutual exclusions or limitations of liability set out, including for wastage, loss or contamination from use of the plant from any process consumable, and loss of profit, revenue, use or business interruptions (Clause 44).

In addition, the contractor's liability for loss or damage to the purchaser's (or its affiliates') property is limited to £5,000,000 in respect of any one incident or series of incidents arising out of any one event (unless another limit is agreed) (Clause 30.7). Above such limit, the purchaser is to indemnify the contractor and all sub-contractors. Clause 30.7 is subject to the contractor making good any loss or damage to the materials, plant or documentation prior to take-over or (after take-over but before final certificate) resulting from any cause, or from testing or other operations, carried out or supervised by the contractor or any subcontractor for the purpose of complying with the contractor's obligations. It is also subject to the purchaser's risks, which are outlined in Clause 30.4 and which include a number of neutral events.

## MF/1

### *Overview*

The current version of MF/1 is that published in 2000 and is generally referred to as MF/1 (MF/1(revision 4)/2000).

It is prepared by both the Institute of Mechanical Engineers and the Institute of Electrical Engineers.

The contract consists of a model form of General Conditions of Contract including forms of Tender, Agreement, Sub-Contract, Performance Bond and Defects Liability Demand Guarantee.

It is for use in connection with projects in the UK or overseas for the supply of electrical, electronic or mechanical plant including the erection of such plant.

It is specifically recommended by the Institution of Electrical Engineers, the Institution of Mechanical Engineers and the Association of Consulting Engineers.

The form of contract has a substantial history with the first edition being published by the Council of Institution of Electrical Engineers in 1903. During the course of the twentieth century it was substantially updated with the latest version, as indicated, being published in 2000.

The contract itself consists of 54 core clauses, additional Special Conditions covering supply of hardware and software, a Measurement Supplement, a Sectional Completion Supplement and a Supplement dealing with the Housing Grants Construction and Regeneration Act 1996.

MF/1 is a lump sum contract for the supply of electrical and mechanical plant. As indicated above a remeasurement option is available.

Under the MF/1 the contractor is responsible for the detailed design of the plant, based on the requirements of the specification. The contractor's overriding level of care is set out in Clause 13.1 namely that the contractor shall, subject to the provisions of the contract, with due care and diligence, design, manufacture, deliver to site, erect and test the plant and execute the works and carry out the completion tests within the time for completion.

Crucial to the understanding of this contract are the concepts of "tests on completion" and performance tests. The former is specified in the contract and must be taken and passed in order for the works to be taken over by the purchaser. The latter are optional; relevant only once the works have been taken over to demonstrate the performance of the works.

The inclusion of these tests are indicative of the type of work this contract is aimed at, namely process plant installations or other process driven or production driven plants where the output from the plant is the crucial requirement rather than the construction of the plant itself.

## What the contract says about time

Clause 32.1 deals with time. The contractor is required to execute the works so that they are complete and pass the tests on completion within the time for completion. Any performance tests are not required to be completed before completion.

Clause 33.1 provides for a relatively limited list of matters which, if they occur, can lead to an extension of time. Subject to the contractor providing a notice and full supporting information to the engineer as soon as reasonably practicable, the engineer will grant such extension of time for completion as may be reasonable.

Liquidated damages are dealt with in Clause 34.1 with the amount being set out in the Appendix. Rather unusually the liquidated damages are expressed as a percentage of the contract value. A capping mechanism is included so that the amounts so deductible or paid shall not exceed the maximum percentage stated in the appendix of the contract value.

Clause 34.2 deals with prolonged delay whereby once the maximum amount provided under Clause 34.1 has become payable, the purchaser may, by notice to the contractor require completion. A notice is served setting out a final time for completion and if the contractor fails to complete within such time the purchaser may by further notice to the contractor elect either to require the contractor to complete or to terminate the contract and in both situations recover from the contractor any loss set out by the failure up to an amount not exceeding the sum stated in the appendix.

This is a different approach to many standard forms and care must be taken in completing the appendix and understanding the implications of this layered approach to delay in completion and prolonged delay when using this contract.

Rather than adopting wording associated with completion or practical completion, Clause 29 refers to the concept of taking over. Subject to the works having passed the relevant Tests on Completion, the engineer issues a certificate to the contractor and to the purchaser (defined as a taking over certificate). This certifies that the works (or part of the works) have passed the tests on completion and are complete.

Specific provision is included in the contract for taking over by sections.

Clause 29.4 provides that the contractor shall rectify or complete to the reasonable satisfaction of the Engineer any outstanding or incomplete items of work. An interesting provision is included at Clause 30.1 which enables the purchaser to use any section or part of the works in respect of which a taking over certificate has not been issued because of default by the contractor.

Defects liability arrangements are included in the contract at Clause 36. The defects liability period is stated in the appendix from the date of taking over the works under Clause 29 (Taking Over) or if no date is set out in the appendix from the taking over date.

Clause 36 includes provisions dealing with notification of defects, delay in remedying defects and removal of defective works. Further testing provisions are also dealt with in Clause 36.7.

Clause 36.9 sets out an express limitation of liability for defects and states the contractor's liability under Clause 36 shall be in lieu of any other contract term implied by law as to the quality or fitness for any particular purpose of the workmanship of any part of the works once they have been taken over.

A further limitation is set out in Clause 36.10 which deals with latent defects which provides that within the period of three years after the date of taking over shall be made good by the contractor by repair or replacement provided that the defect was caused by the gross misconduct of the contractor. Gross misconduct is subject to a detailed definition.

Taken together Clauses 36.9 and 36.10 are clear restrictions on the purchaser which must be considered carefully when using this contract.

### What the contract says about cost

Payment is covered under Clause 39. The contractor makes application for payment in accordance with Clause 39.2 in the form of an invoice accompanied by supporting documentation. Under Clause 39.3, the Engineer issues an interim certificate within 14 days on receiving the relevant information from the contractor. Payment is to be made within 30 days after the date of the issue of the certificate of payment unless otherwise specified in the special conditions.

Clause 39.9 deals with the final certificate of payment and detailed provisions are set out with regard to the final account mechanism and the effect of the final certificate. It should be noted that the effect of the final certificate is that it is conclusive evidence that the works to which the certificate relates are in accordance with the contract and that payment of the amount certified in a final certificate of payment is conclusive evidence that the purchaser has performed all of his obligations under the contract. A saving provision is set out in Clause 39.12 indicating the final certificate is not conclusive where proceedings arising out of the contract are to commence within three months of the date of the certificate.

Clause 41 provides that the contractor may make claims for additional payment under a number of the provisions of the contract including sub-clause 5.7 (unexpected site conditions), sub-clause 11.8 (breach of purchaser's general obligations) and sub-clause 14.5 (revision of programme). The contractor has to provide appropriate back-up information and claims are assessed by the engineer.

The contract contains a number of important limitations on the contractor's liability in Clause 44 including at Clause 44.2 a limitation of liability with regard to indirect or consequential damage and at Clause 44.3 an overriding cap on liability on an amount stated in the Appendix or if no sum is so stated the Contract Price.

Unusually amongst construction contracts an exclusive remedy provision is included at Clause 44.4, limiting the remedies of the parties to those remedies stated in the contract unless specific exception allows for external remedies to be sought. This is an important restriction which users of the contract need to be fully aware of.

### What the contract says about quality

Clauses 30.1 and 30.2 deals with broad requirements to comply with the tests on completion and the obligation that the works shall be manufactured and executed in the manner set out in the specification or to the reasonable satisfaction of the engineer where work is not so specified.

The contractor's design liability has already been discussed.

Under MF/1 the engineer is given specific powers at reasonable times during manufacture, to inspect, examine and test (on the contractor's premises and elsewhere) the materials or workmanship and performance of all plant. This is again an unusual contractual provision compared with most construction contracts but does reflect the fact that MF/1 is designed for use where plant is the critical element being supplied and the building is secondary.

As discussed already, the contract sets out in Clause 28 detailed provisions with regard to tests which must be passed prior to taking over (tests on completion) and additional tests, referred to as performance tests, which are carried out post taking over by the purchaser.

Clause 35.8 sets out the consequences of a failure to pass such performance tests, namely either liquidated damages or in certain situations, determination based on contractor default.

The inclusion of liquidated damages for a failure to meet a given specification or pass a given test is not unique to MF/1. Similar provisions are included as an option within the ECC Contract.

Specific additional special conditions are provided within the MF/1 to deal with the incidental supply of hardware and software. In the process plant industry, computer operation is critical to success and thus provision dealing with installation of hardware, software and system acceptance, source codes, manuals and other documentation is included.

## PPC2000

### *Overview*

PPC2000 remains the only published standard form of team partnering contract. It was first published by the ACA in late 2000 and re-published with minor clarifications and adjustments in April 2003.

The contract draws from *A Guide to Project Team Partnering* published by the Construction Industry Council, itself is a response to *Rethinking Construction*, the report prepared by the Construction Task Force. It was also inspired by Sir Michael Latham's 1994 report *Constructing the Team*. In use, PPC2000 has found greater favour with the public sector than the private sector. A form of subcontract (SPC2000) has been published for use with PPC2000. Given its popularity with housing associations and councils with large property assets, it is rumoured that a term maintenance variant will be published later this year.

PPC2000 envisages that the main parties ("partnering team members") involved in a project (employer ("client"), contractor ("constructor"), employer's representative/project manager ("client representative"), professional team members ("consultants") and major design sub-contractors/sub-consultants ("specialists")) will enter into the contract together. The client should also appoint a partnering facilitator ("partnering adviser") to advise all the parties on relevant matters relating to the contract. Professional indemnity insurers should be aware that partnering team members owe each other mutual duties of care so there is the potential for greater exposure.

The terms and conditions are fairly short, anticipating that much of the detail on pricing and programme will be contained in the "Partnering Documents" (documents with contractual status). By adopting a partnered approach, PPC2000 aims to reduce disputes, reduce cost and time savings and achieve integrated design through the parties working together for the benefit of the project.

## What the contract says about time

PPC2000 is intended to be entered into from project inception. There is thus a timetable governing the activities of the parties prior to start on site (the partnering timetable) and a second timetable for dealing with subsequent activities (the project timetable). Both are partnering documents. Parties are required to carry out their agreed activities regularly and diligently in accordance with the partnering timetable (Clause 6.1). The project timetable sets out the date of possession, the date for completion and any sectional dates of possession/completion (Clauses 6.2, 6.3). It is prepared by the constructor and submitted to the client representative for approval by the core group (a group made up of representatives of all the partnering team members) and the client. Under Clause 6.3, the client representative may instruct acceleration, postponement or re-sequencing of any date or period stated in the project timetable, which will usually be a "change".

Clause 18.3 deals with extensions of time. The constructor is to use his best endeavours at all times to minimise any delay or increased cost in the project. However, the constructor should be granted an appropriate extension if, despite this, any one or more of the 16 events listed in Clause 18.3 has adversely affected the date for completion. The constructor must notify the client representative and submit appropriate evidence and detailed proposals for overcoming such an event and minimising their effect on cost, time for completion and quality of the project.

The constructor must give the client representative not less than five working days' notice when it considers that project completion will be achieved. Such notice will request the client's representative to attend, inspect and test as required under the project brief. Following such testing, the client representative will then issue a notice to the client and the constructor either confirming that the project has achieved project completion or stating what is necessary to do to reach project completion.

### What the contract says about cost

The client shall pay the agreed maximum price ("AMP") to the constructor. This is subject to change for agreed sharing of costs/savings and other increases or decreases set out in the contract. Although effectively lump sum, it is straightforward to redraft the price provisions so that the contract works as a reimbursable or cost plus contract. The build-up of the price is set out in the "price framework". There are no fluctuation provisions in the contract itself. If these are required, these should go into the price framework (in the case of the constructor) and in the "consultant payment terms" (for consultants). If it is intended that payment will be linked to achievement against key performance indicators, then the amount of adjustment is determined by the client representative (Clause 13.5).

Clause 18 deals with adjustments to the AMP in connection with extensions of time.

Time for payment is set out in the price framework (for the constructor), the consultant payment terms (for consultants) and any pre-possession agreement (a form of letter of intent) (Clause 20.2). However, if no intervals are stated payment will be at the end of each calendar month. Applications for payment must be accompanied by such details as are stated in the project brief with any further information as the client representative may reasonably require. Upon receipt of the constructor's application for payment, the client representative shall issue a valuation (Clause 20.3) specifying the amounts of the payment proposed to be made, to what that amount relates and the basis upon which that amount is calculated. The final date for payment of the amount stated is 15 working days from issue or 10 working days from date of receipt by the client of any required VAT invoice, whichever is later. Payment provisions are similar for consultants.

The client may give notice within two working days from the final date of payment of any amount due specifying any amount purposely withheld or deducted together with the ground(s) for such withholding or deduction and the amount attributable to each such ground (Clause 20.6).

The constructor shall pay all specialists unless they are appointed by the client under Clause 10.11. Specialists are paid in accordance with the "specialist payment terms". Full records of all amounts paid (and payable) to each specialist must be provided to the client representative upon request.

Within 20 working days following Project Completion (unless amended by the price framework), the client representative shall issue an account confirming the balance of the AMP due. Within 20 working days, the client representative shall then issue a valuation in the agreed amount or if there is no agreement then in such amount as is fair and reasonable (Clause 20.14). The final account follows defect rectification (Clause 20.15). The agreed final account is conclusive evidence of the balance of the AMP due between the client and the contractor. If the final account cannot be agreed, either the client or the contractor may invoke the dispute resolution procedure under Clause 27.

### What the contract says about quality

Under Clause 2.4, each partnering team member who prepares or contributes to any partnering document is responsible for any errors, omissions or discrepancy therein, except to the extent it has relied upon information from another Partnering Team member (provided this is stated in the partnering documents). Each Partnering Team member has a duty to warn others and the client representative of any error, omission or discrepancy it becomes aware of and to put forward proposals to resolve this without adversely affecting cost, time or quality (Clause 2.5). However, if no resolution can be reached in the event of a discrepancy, Clause 2.6 sets out the order of priority of the partnering documents.

Clause 8.1 requires the consultant chosen as lead designer and the other design team members to develop the design in the process of the project with the objectives of achieving the best value for the client. Clause 8.2 covers possible gaps in the design being prepared by partnering team members. It requires each design team member to contribute those aspects of design of the project that fall within its role, expertise and responsibilities as stated in the partnering documents. The design team is required to work together and individually under the coordination of the lead designer. Clause 8.8 provides that at each stage of design development the lead designer is to amend designs as necessary to adopt the results of any value engineering exercise providing the results are approved by the client after core group consultation.

Clause 22.1 requires all partnering team members to use the reasonable skill and care appropriate to its respective role, to achieve all responsibilities in all activities relating to the design, supply, construction and completion of the project. This is a mutual and co-extensive duty of care owed to all the other partnering team members. If agreed, the constructor's duty of care can be increased to single-point design liability and/or fitness for purpose.

## ACA BUILDING CONTRACT

### *Overview*

The Association of Consultant Architects Form of Building Agreement was originally issued in 1982, with a second edition in 1984 introducing significant improvements. The third edition was issued in 1998, which included amendments to take account of the payment and adjudication requirements of the Housing Grants Construction and Regeneration Act 1996.

It should be noted that in addition to this form the Association of Consultant Architects also publish PPC2000 but the two contracts are mutually exclusive and represent entirely different approaches to contracting between employers and their contractors. PPC2000 is covered in the previous section of this chapter.

It is difficult to gauge the number of projects on which this contract in the UK as it does not feature at all in the RICS Contracts in Use Survey. Anecdotal evidence would suggest that outside of a limited number of loyal users the ACA form is not widely used.

There is little or no guidance as to what type of project the contract can be used on. There is certainly no suggested contract sum limit beyond which the contract is inappropriate. It can be used with or without bills of quantity, and in situations where no quantity surveyor is appointed. No differentiation is made between private or local authority versions and the contract is capable of use by both public and private clients.

The format of the ACA Contract is notably for its relatively extensive use of options. Whilst this approach offers a high degree of flexibility (and in this regard it is not dissimilar to the ECC Contract) it leads to a contract which must be completed with a great deal of care. Not only must the correct options be chosen but compatibility between the selected options must be considered carefully.

### What the contract says about time

The primary obligation of the contractor is to carry out the works so that they are ready for taking over by the Employer by the agreed dates. Certification that the works have reached the appropriate stage is by the Architect. Liquidated damages may be payable depending upon which alternative contract option is used. Important dates are set out in the time schedule. Alternative 1 applies a single end date, alternative 2 for completion by sections.

The flexible nature of the options available under this form of contract are shown by the extension of time mechanisms where there are two alternatives, the first relating to delay caused solely by the employer or his consultants, and the second for neutral causes.

A provision not found in many standard forms is included enabling the contract administrator to accelerate and/or postpone the dates in the Time Schedule.

### What the contract says about cost

The contract is a lump sum contract but fluctuations can be used based on an ACA index. Again, the advantage of having a flexible contract with variable options on payment is to be welcomed but the care that needs to be taken upon completion of the contract to ensure the correct options are used in a harmonious manner cannot be over emphasised.

Interim payments are made by way of milestones or stage payments. The architect certifies by way of an interim certificate within 10 days of receipt of a contractor's application. The final account machinery is set out in Clause

19.1 where the contractor has 60 days to submit his final account following the end of the maintenance period. A 5% retention is held.

### What the contract says about quality

The primary obligation of the contractor with regard to quality is set out in Clause 1.1 under which the contractor is obliged to complete the works in strict accordance with the contract documents. Clause 1.2 indicates that the contractor is required to use the appropriate level of skill, care and diligence.

The Contract Documents are defined in Clause C.

The ACA Contract does envisage some contractor design responsibility, depending on whether Alternative 1 or 2 is used. Notably at Clause 3.1 the contractor is responsible for the accuracy of drawings and other information prepared by him and an absolute warranty is provided with regard to compliance with the performance specification and with regard to fitness for purpose. This is somewhat unusual in a standard form.

The contractor is primarily responsible for looking after the management of the construction process and the contract envisages appointment of a full time site manager by the contractor.

## PACE GC/WORKS/1

### *Overview*

The origin of the GC/Works suite of contracts goes back to centralised government property procurement via the Property Services Agency (the PSA). GC/Works/1 appeared originally in 1973 and was a form whose primary purpose was for use by government departments. The 1998 edition, known as GC/Works/1 (1998) follows on from the original form and is a contract for use in the procurement of construction projects and/or civil engineering projects adopting either a traditional procurement approach, a design and build approach or a management contracting approach.

Although primarily designed for use by Government, it has found favour with a number of private sector clients and non-central Government agencies, although its use in this regard is limited to a small number of loyal users.

### *Options*

It should be noted that whilst the Terms and Conditions in the 1998 edition look similar to those in the 1973 version (the Clause numbering is remarkably similar), there are crucial differences between the old and the new version. As indicated above, the early version was used almost entirely by Government departments.

The contract comes in six options:

- With Quantities.
- Without Quantities.
- Single Stage Design and Build.
- Two Stage Design and Build.
- With Quantities Construction Management Trade Contract.
- Without Quantities Construction Management Trade Contract.

### *Form of the contract*

The contract contains 66 core provisions along with a schedule of time limits annexed at the back. An extremely useful alphabetical index (something that is missing from a number of standard forms) is included.

The contract agreement is in two versions, one for Scottish law and the other where the appropriate governing jurisdiction is England & Wales.

The contract conditions are set out in a clear, concise and well-ordered manner and in terms of clarity it is a significant improvement on JCT drafting.

### What the contract says about time

The primary obligation placed upon the contractor with regard to time is that he is to proceed with diligence and in accordance with the programme so that the whole of the works (or any relevant section if sectional completion is utilised) is completed in accordance with the contract by the date for completion.

The date for completion is set out or ascertained from the abstract of particulars.

The programming requirements are more extensive than the JCT although not as extensive as those required under the ECC. Progress meetings are utilised as well as obligations to notify with regard to delay as soon as possible. Liquidated damages are payable at an amount specified in the abstract of particulars for late completion. There is no equivalent notification requirement for non-completion as is found in JCT contracts. A defects liability period in the form of a maintenance period is included with the period being set out in the abstract of particulars.

The contract includes provisions for completion of the works by sections and also provisions with regard to early possession.

### What the contract says about cost

The contract is a lump sum contract.

Relatively restrictive provisions are included with regard to delay and disruption costs with interest and finance charges specifically excluded.

Options for progress payments or milestone payments exist and the final account or final sum provisions require release of one half of the retention at completion with the balance being released at the point the final certificate is issued at the end of the maintenance period when the contractor has completed rectifying outstanding defects.

### What the contract says about quality

The primary requirement is for the contractor to execute the works with diligence, with all reasonable skill and care, and in a workmanlike manner. An additional requirement is that the works must be executed in accordance with the programme.

Quality is maintained by reference to the requirements of the specifications, bills and drawings. Satisfaction by the project manager with regard to the execution of the work, the appropriate level of skill and care and quality is a prerequisite.

Clause 31.6 makes it clear that if a part of the works does not comply with the contractor's obligations under the contract and is rejected by the project manager, then it must be replaced at the contractor's own expense.

Provisions for dealing with discrepancies between specifications and drawings are included at Clause 2.3.

A maintenance period is anticipated and will be described in the abstract of particulars. During the maintenance period the contractor is obliged to correct defects at his own cost to the satisfaction of the Employer. Interestingly a provision is included here with regard to disputes about liability and reimbursement during the maintenance period stating that such disputes must wait until after rectification of the defects.

## PRIVATE FINANCE INITIATIVE/PPP

The one area where standard forms have made very little progress is their use in connection with construction projects associated with either the Private Finance Initiative (PFI) or Public Private Partnerships (PPP).

It is common practice in PFI/PPP transactions for bespoke contracts to be drafted as between the project company and its construction sub-contractor. Usually these contracts reflect to a large degree the nature of the concession contract the project company has entered into with the central or local government agency requiring the facility (usually a hospital, a school or a prison) to be built.

The very high degree of risk transferred by such concession contracts and the specific nature of the obligations included within them would result in substantial amendments to standard forms being required before they were even suitable as a base document for the construction sub-contract. Moreover, the relatively complete nature of the transfer of risk from the project company to the construction sub-contractor would result in a level of amendment to the standard forms which would make their use impractical.

It has been suggested that the JCT Major Projects Form is a potential candidate for a contract which could form the basis of a standard construction sub-contract for use in connection with PFI/PPP transactions but to date the author is unaware of any actual project where the MPF is being used in such a way.

Both central and local government have sought to standardise the concession contracts and detailed guidance notes are published by the Office of Government Commerce in an attempt to improve the standardisation of concession agreements and consequently reduce costs in the billing process. Although reference has been made to standardisation of sub-contracts and in particular construction sub-contracts, no progress has been made in the production publication and issue of any standard form contracts to date.

## SELF-TEST QUESTIONS

1. **Explain the term "compensation event" in an ECC Contract.**
2. **Outline the key advantages and disadvantages of the adoption of standard form contracts in the construction industry.**
3. **How does the ICE 7th Edition measurement version deal with ground risk?**
4. **How is design liability dealt with in the JCT Management Contract suite of contracts?**
5. **What type of client/contractor is it envisaged that the JCT Major Projects form will be used by?**
6. **Where would you normally find the FIDIC set of standard forms being used?**
7. **Outline how PPC2000 attempts to encourage partnering and team work.**
8. **How do the extension of time events in the JCT Major Projects form differ from those found in the JCT 98 Private with Quantities form?**
9. **Explain the term "remeasurement" in context of a construction contract.**
10. **For projects below £100,000 in value with no design responsibility being placed on the contract or what contract form would you recommend?**

11. Provide an outline of the payment provisions within a JCT 98 Private with Quantities form.

12. JCT 98 Private with Quantities places no responsibility for design on the Contractor. Identify the two mechanisms which enable design responsibility to be placed on a contractor in the context of a Private with Quantities contract.

13. How does the ECC suite of contracts deal with the amount of design liability placed on the Contractor and the level or responsibility to be expected with regard to that design liability?

14. When would you use a target cost contract?

15. What were the main reasons behind the production of the ECC Form of Contract and what were the goals the drafters sought to achieve?

CHAPTER 5

# STANDARD FORMS OF CONTRACT II

Keith Pickavance

## CLASSIFICATION OF FORMS

In principle, the forms of contract discussed in this chapter can be separated into four main categories:

(1) build only forms for building and civil engineering work;
(2) forms for use with mechanical, electrical and process plant work;
(3) design and build forms for building and civil engineering work; and
(4) short forms.

However, this subdivision is rather simplistic and there are several subcategories into which it is often helpful to separate the forms. These are as follows:

### *Build-only forms*

The "build-only" forms of contract can be subdivided into three subcategories.

(1) Those said to be suitable for building work only. These include:

- the JCT Standard Building Contract;
- the JCT Intermediate Building Contract;
- the ACA Building Contract;
- PPC2000; and
- the JCT Management Contract.

(2) Those said to be suitable for civil engineering work only. This class includes:

- the ICE Form (7th edition).

(3) Those said to be suitable only for building or civil engineering work. These include:

- FIDIC Building and Engineering (red book);

- NEC3 Engineering and Construction Contract; and
- GC/Works/1 Building and Civil Engineering Form.

Whilst in all of these forms it is generally required that the works are to be designed by or on behalf of the employer and the contractor is only required to construct the employer's design, the forms envisage that either explicitly or by reference to a designated supplement, the works may also include some elements of contractor-designed work.

### *Mechanical electrical and process plant forms*

In regard to those suitable for mechanical, electrical and process plant work, it is generally required that the works are to be designed by or on behalf of the employer but the works may also include some elements of contractor-designed work. These forms include:

- IChemE Lump Sum (red book);
- MF/1; and
- FIDIC Plant Design and Build (yellow book).

Under the usual arrangements for this type of contract, the contractor designs and constructs plant or other works (which may include any combination of civil, mechanical, electrical or construction works). Whilst this class also includes FIDIC yellow book, this is discussed with the design and build categories below.

### *The short forms*

The short forms are generally suitable for building or engineering works of relatively small capital value. However, depending on the type of work and the circumstances, this form may also be suitable for contracts of greater value, particularly for relatively simple or repetitive work or work of short duration. In this type of contract, the contractor constructs the works in accordance with a design provided by the employer but can often also be used for contracts which include, or wholly comprise, contractor-designed works. As with the build-only forms these can be divided into three subcategories.

(1) Those said to be suitable for building work only:

- JCT Minor Works Building Contract.

(2) Those said to be suitable for civil engineering work only:

- ICE Short Form.

(3) Those said to be suitable only for building or civil engineering work:

- FIDIC Short Form (green book).

Whilst the remainder of the forms discussed are generally suitable for work carried out in the UK, FIDIC forms are recommended for general use where tenders are invited on an international basis and some of the conditions are not appropriate for use on domestic contracts without amendment.

### Design and build forms

In the design and build form of procurement the employer may provide a design brief describing basic requirements or it may provide a concept design for the contractor to develop into a detailed design. Generally, a single contractor (or in larger schemes a single contractor as a joint venture between contractors) assumes the risk and responsibility for designing and building the project, in return for a lump sum. The employer details its requirements to the contractor who then carries out the design and construction of the works.

| |
|---|
| There are two key concepts in design responsibility. They are reasonable skill and care, and fitness or purpose. |

Reasonable care and skill is usually imposed where the employer provides a design brief or a concept design for the contractor to complete. Fitness for purpose generally applies to those projects that are referred to as "turnkey" (all the employer has to do is turn the key) or "EPC" (engineer, procure and construct) in which the contractor, with little involvement of the employer, takes total responsibility for identifying what is necessary to achieve the project, designs the works and procures, installs and commissions the plant providing a fully-equipped facility, ready for operation.

In general terms reasonable skill and care is the duty imposed on a professional person. It is then a matter for the opinion of that professional's contemporaries as to whether the professional has exercised all the skill and care that can reasonably be expected. Only if "professional negligence" can be proven is the consultant liable for breach of duty. When fitness for purpose is the standard required there will only be liability for a failure if the product is proved unfit for the intended and mutually understood purpose for which it was supplied.

The design and build forms can thus be further subdivided according to the standard of care imposed:

(1) Fitness for purpose is imposed upon the contractor in

- FIDIC Plant Design and Build (yellow book); and
- FIDIC Turnkey (silver book).

(2) Reasonable skill and care is imposed upon the contractor in

- JCT Design and Build Contract;
- JCT Major Projects Form;
- ICE Design and Construct Form; and
- GC/Works/1 Design and Construct Form.

The word "design" is one which is not capable of precise definition in relation to a standard form of contract. Although there are obvious examples of conceptual work which it would be difficult to describe other than as design, design also encompasses selection and, to a degree, assembly of parts and products. *Walker-Smith* gives the example of the way joinery is fitted together, or the selection of a type of screw, which could be considered within the meaning of "design".

It was confirmed in the case of *Barker* v. *London Portland Hotel* that because forms such as the JCT Standard Building Contract and JCT Intermediate Building Contract and their kind rehearse in the recitals that the design drawings and specification are prepared by the CA, under the employer's direction, the contractor is not responsible for the design of the works and, except in regard to those matters of selection, where the materials selected must be fit for their purpose, the contractor is not required to build so as to be "fit for purpose". Under these forms the contractor is to build that which is described in the contract documents.

The distinction between the responsibilities of the contractor under a "build-only" form and those in a "design and build" form can be illustrated by the facts of *Rotheram* v. *Haslam* in which the contract administrator rejected an application for an EOT for the effect on time of an increase in fire stopping (measured as a series of provisional sums in a bill of quantities under JCT80 (a predecessor of JCT Standard Building Contract and a similar form of build-only contract) and measured in cost from a provisional sum of £6,000 to a final cost of £35,000) on the grounds that it was required by the Building Regulations, in conformity with which the contractor was contractually obliged to build. The court held that:

> "(the contract administrator's) rejection of (the fire stopping) as a relevant event on the ground that the contractor had full knowledge of the requirement for maintaining the one hour fire integrity of the shaft wall shows an error of law in relation to the respective responsibilities of the contractor and the employer (through the design team) . . . It was for the contract administrator (in conjunction with the mechanical and electrical consultants) to specify the necessary design".

Whether post-contract design required in relation to a design and construct contract amounts to design development that is at the risk of the contractor under the "design and build" type of form, or amounts to a variation of the employer's requirements, which is at the employer's risk was addressed to the Court of Appeal in *Skanska* v. *Egger*. In this, the second visit to the Court of Appeal the Court held that additional process plant steel work required as a result of a later drawing of the process plant provided by the employer was simply design development on which the employer was entitled to provide information. The court accepted that although it was poorly defined, there was an indication of a requirement for process steelwork on the tender drawings illustrating the employer's requirements and that it was part and parcel of the risk accepted by the contractor that the employer's requirements would be perfected at a later stage.

## STANDARD FORM PROVISIONS FOR EXTENSIONS OF TIME

Because of the differing nature of the forms, comparison is difficult; even the terminology in the forms is inconsistent. However, in an attempt to render it easier to interpret and compare the provisions of the forms the following terminology has been adopted.

- The employer and the contractor are the parties to the contract.
- The contract administrator is the employer's representative or other person charged with administering the contract.
- The risks as to time to be borne by the employer are called employer's time risk events.
- The risks as to loss and/or expense to be borne by the employer are called employer's cost risk events.

This chapter makes some comparisons between the forms under four headings:

- The risks imposed upon the employer in regard to extensions of time
- The requirements for a construction programme
- The requirements for acceptance or approval of the programme
- The requirements for updating the construction programme
- The scope for variations

> In all of the standard forms of contract considered here, the most important consideration in construing clauses that entitle the contractor to an extension of time (EOT) is that, no matter what the risk and no matter which form of contract, it is only a delay to a completion date, which will render the contractor liable in liquidated and ascertained damages (LADs), which ranks for an EOT.

### *Classification of forms by risk definition*

In the classification of types of employer's risk events, the standard forms of contract fall into three sub-groups. There are those which:

- provide no indication at all of the circumstances under which the contractor may be granted more time or be compensated for the effect of employer's risks;
- indicate a brief list of employer's risk events with reference to other clauses in the contract; or
- have a single clause which collects together either directly or by direct cross-reference all the circumstances which will give rise to a change in the rights of the parties.

In those forms such as the JCT Minor Works Building Contract which provide no indication at all as to the circumstances under which the contractor will be excused or compensated for change, the contractor is generally excused for any cause beyond its control. Whilst it would seem that on the face of it, by definition, that would exclude those matters which are within the employer's control (which it has generally been held must be clearly set out if they are to enable the employer to grant an EOT for its own acts). It would appear that there is room for a great deal of interpretative scope in determining what is and what is not within the contractor's control.

The second class of forms is that which, whilst having a brief list of employer's risk events, also includes a sweeping-up clause such as: " . . . and any other cause referred to in these conditions". This is the structure generally used for engineering contracts. So, for example, clause 44(1) of the ICE Form (7th edition) provides that the contractor is entitled to an EOT if completion is adversely affected by:

- any variation order;
- increased quantities;
- any cause of delay referred to in the conditions of contract;
- exceptional adverse weather conditions;
- any delay impediment prevention or default;

and then adds the same sweeping-up clause:

- other special circumstances of any kind whatsoever which may occur.

The FIDIC suite of contracts treats the excusable events in a similar, but not identical, way. Clause 8.4 of FIDIC Building and Engineering (red book), for example provides that the contractor is entitled to an EOT if completion is adversely affected by:

- a variation or other substantial change in quantity;
- a cause of delay referred to in the conditions;
- exceptional adverse climatic conditions;
- unforeseen shortages in personnel or goods caused by epidemic or government actions;

and then adds the sweeping-up clause:

- any delay, impediment or prevention caused by or attributable to the employer, the employer's personnel or the employer's other contractors on site.

The other "causes" under sub-clause (c) of the ICE Form (7th edition) and under the FIDIC suite of contracts are not easily located. Although there is a detailed index in both forms, nowhere is it possible to find a listing of the circumstances under which the contractor will be excused the consequences of delay, or which will provide for the contractor to receive compensation if, as a result of such events, it should suffer loss. The FIDIC and NEC3 Engineering and Construction Contracts are perhaps the most misleading in containing a clause entitled "employer's risks" which neither lists nor makes cross-reference to the employer's delay risk events set out in other parts of the contract but deal only with those catastrophes that are likely to cause physical damage to the works.

The difficulty of finding the risks, which are to be borne by the employer under this type of form, is caused by the drafting technique. The technique employed is that of specifying that a variation is at the employer's risk but then going on, in the body of the document, to specify that certain occurrences "shall be regarded as instructions", "shall be deemed to be a variation", "shall be treated as if it were a variation", "shall be treated as a change in the employer's requirements". Alternatively, whilst determining that the risk of delay caused by instruction shall be at the employer's risk, the draftsman specifies that for certain contingencies the contract administrator "shall issue instructions" or "the work and materials shall be treated as if they had been executed and supplied pursuant to an architect/contract administrator's instruction" which, in turn, will be deemed to be a variation. Without reading the document itself in its entirety and, in the case of JCT Management Building Contract, the documents together with the relevant Management Works Contract forms entirely, it is impossible to understand what those risks are.

The third category, where a single clause of the contract collects together either directly or by cross-reference all the circumstances which will give rise to a change in the entitlements of the parties, is made up principally of the JCT family of forms excluding JCT Minor Works Building Contract, but also includes NEC3 Engineering and Construction Contract, NEC3 Engineering and Construction Short Contract, FIDIC Short Form (green book) and the Change Management Supplements.

An attempt to achieve the clarity referred to above, has been made in the FIDIC Short Form (green book). Although in the guidance notes to the green book, FIDIC say that the employer's risks sub-clause gathers together in one place the grounds for EOTs and monetary claims, it is still necessary to read the document in full. For example clause 9.2 must be read in conjunction with clause 6.1(m) to understand that if work is opened up and found to be satisfactory, any delay to completion caused thereby will be an employer's time risk event. It is not possible to deduce that from reading clause 6.1. in isolation.

## CLASSIFICATION OF EMPLOYER'S TIME RISK EVENTS

There are four major classes of events in the practical standard forms which are sweeping-up clauses. There is then a number of detailed classifications. The four main classes of event causing changes for which the employer takes the risk are:

- voluntary and implied acts or omissions of the employer, or the contract administrator, or those employed by the employer, acting on the employer's behalf;

- acts and omissions of third parties;
- causes beyond the control of the contractor;
- *force majeure* and other special circumstances;

The phraseology used in regard to these clauses changes from form to form and must be looked at in some detail. Apart from the fact that all the foregoing may be deemed to be "causes beyond the control of the contractor" apart from the generic sweeping-up clauses, the clauses in general terms, deal with:

(1) Express, or implied instructions to:

- correct an ambiguity or discrepancy in the employer's requirements;
- correct an error in description (or quantity) in the bills, specifications or drawings;
- suspend the carrying out of the works;
- avoid a legal or physical impossibility;
- rectify any loss or damage arising from any of the insured risks;
- ensure conformity with any Act of Parliament, Regulation or Statute;
- investigate or dispose of archaeological findings; and
- uncover or make openings in work where the works are found to have been carried out in accordance with the contract.

(2) Other acts or omissions of the employer, the contract administrator or those employed by them, including:

- compliance with, or non-compliance with the CDM regulations;
- a failure to respond within due time to a contractor's submittal;
- a failure of the design team to issue in due time any information, drawings details or instructions (and under the JCT forms, that risk is not dependent upon whether such information is ever requested);
- a failure to give, or deferment of possession of, or access to, or egress from any part of the site;
- a failure to obtain any third party consents or licences necessary for the development;
- a failure to make prompt payment; and typically,
- any delay, impediment, or prevention caused by or attributable to the employer, the employer's personnel, or the employer's other contractors.

(3) Acts or omissions of third parties, including:

- civil commotion, strike or lock out;
- the default of a nominated sub-contractor or nominated supplier;
- the execution of work, or supply of materials, or goods by others;
- the contractor's unforeseen inability to obtain the labour or materials he needs;
- the execution of work under a statutory obligation.

Finally, there are those risks that are generally considered to be *force majeure* and similar risks, including:

- *force majeure*;
- exceptionally adverse weather;
- the discovery of unforeseeable ground conditions;
- the exercise of a statutory power that affects the supply or use of labour, plant, or materials;
- the use of, or threat of the use of terrorism; and
- insured risks such as fire, storm, tempest, flood etc.

### *Acts and/or omissions of the employer*

The employer's acts and/or omissions are generally specified as a generic excusable clause in many of the engineering forms and in some forms also used for building, for example, clause 32(6)(b) of GC/Works/1 and GC/Works/1 Design and Construct use the expression: any act, neglect or default of the employer, the contract administrator or any other person for whom the employer is responsible (not arising because of any default or neglect by the contrator or by any employee, agent or sub-contractor of his)".

Clause 44.1(d) of IChemE Lump Sum (red book) excuses "a breach of contract on the part of the employer", clause 33.1 of MF/1 excuses "any act or omission on the part of the employer or the contract administrator". Clause 4.24.5 of JCT Standard Building Contract excuses " . . . any impediment, prevention or default, whether by act or omission, by the employer, the architect/contract administrator, the quantity surveyor or any of the employer's persons [as defined] except to the extent that it was caused or contributed to by any default, whether by act or omission, of the contractor or any of the contractor's persons [as defined]." Clause 2.13.2 of the JCT Management Contract excuses "any default, whether by act or omission, of the employer or any persons for whom the employer is responsible in regard to the project". Under the ICE Form (7th edition), clause 44(1)(e) the employer is to take the risk of "any delay impediment prevention or default by the employer". Similarly, clauses 31(2) and 44(1)(b) of the ICE Design and Construct form excuse delay by the employer, by those employed by the employer or statutory bodies which could not be foreseen by an experienced contractor. Clause 11.5 alternative 1 of the ACA Building Contract excuses "any act, instruction, default or omission negligence of the employer or the contract administrator" which in the contract administrator's opinion has caused or is likely to cause delay to completion or, by clause 11.5(e), "any act, instruction, default or omission of the employer, or of the contract administrator" which the contractor proves has caused delay to completion.

Clauses 6.1(k) and 7.3 of FIDIC Short Form (green book) excuse "any failure of the employer". Clause 8.4(e) of FIDIC Building and Engineering (red book), FIDIC Turnkey (silver book) and FIDIC Plant Design and Build (yellow book) excuses "any delay, impediment or prevention caused by or attributable to the employer, the employer's personnel or the employer's other contractors on the site."

Clause 60.1(18) of NEC3 Engineering and Construction Contract excuses the contractor from any "breach of contract by the employer" other than compensation events referred to expressly within the contract. Earlier editions of the NEC3 Engineering and Construction Short Contract modified the scope of the generality of this to a compensation event comprising any "event" which:

- delays completion by more than two weeks,
- the contractor could not have reasonably prevented or controlled,
- an experienced contractor would have judged, at the date of the contractor's offer, to have such a small chance of occurring that it would have been unreasonable to have allowed for it and
- is not one of the other types of compensation event stated in this contract.

Rather confusingly, the clause added the rider: "In assessing this event the first two weeks are excluded." It was not at all clear whether the "two weeks" referred to in the rider is the same "two weeks" referred to in the first line and this provision has now been deleted from the current form.

"Negligence, breach of statutory duty or interference with any legal right by the employer" is also excused under NEC3 Engineering and Construction Contract by virtue of clause 80.1 and clause 60.1(14).

In common with other contracts of the 'partnering type, clause 18.3(xiv) of PPC2000 excuses a "breach of the Partnering contract by the employer or any consultant of which the contractor has given early warning".

## *Failure to pay*

By virtue of the provisions of the HGCRA there is now a statutory provision in the UK entitling anyone carrying out construction operations as defined by that Act to suspend the carrying out of the contract works if they are not paid promptly. The method by which the contractor is to be relieved of the effects of such a suspension differs between the contract forms. For example, under clause 4.24.3 of JCT Standard Building Contract the employer takes the risk of "suspension by the contractor [for failure to pay promptly a sum due] of the performance of his obligations under this contract, provided the suspension was not frivolous or vexations" and similar phraseology appears in the other JCT 2005 forms other than the Minor Building Works Contract:. GC/Works/1, PPC2000 provide for delay arising from a suspension by the contractor of the performance of his obligations under the contract.

Where other standard forms have not been reprinted, amendments have been made which, whilst not expressly providing for excusable delay as a result of "failure to pay", incorporate terms that will probably have the same effect.

For example, the FIDIC Building and Engineering (red book), FIDIC Turnkey (silver book) and FIDIC Plant Design and Build (yellow book) excuse "any delay, impediment or prevention caused by or attributable to the employer." MF/1 and IChemE Lump Sum (red book) on the other hand, probably because it is not envisaged by the draftsman that they are likely to be used for work falling within the definition of a "construction contract" within the Act, contain no provisions along these lines.

The NEC3 Engineering and Construction Short Contract appear to be alone amongst the new forms suitable for use for building works in making no provision for an employer's risk event to arise as a result of delay caused by suspension of work following the employer's failure to pay the contractor on time. Notwithstanding that the JCT Minor Works Building Contract acknowledges the contractor's right to suspend performance for the employer's failure to pay the contractor on time, in this form the only express redress for the employer's failure to pay promptly appears to be interest on late payment.

### *Circumstances beyond the contractor's control*

Both the engineering and building forms stipulate causes beyond the contractor's control as excusable events. So, for example, under clause 2.13.1 of the JCT Management Contract the contractor is excused for delay caused by "any cause which impedes the proper discharge by the management contractor of his obligations". In clause 2.7 of the JCT Minor Works Building Contract the contractor is excused for "any cause beyond the control of the contractor". Clause 36(2)(e) of GC/Works/l, dictates that the employer carries the risk of "any other circumstances (other than weather conditions) which are outside the control of the contractor or of any of his sub-contractors, and which could not have been reasonably contemplated". The expression used in clause 33.1 of MF/1 is simply "circumstances reasonably beyond the control of the contractor".

In the *Scott Lithgow* case, the Ministry of Defence had been unwise enough to agree to pay the contractor, the shipbuilder of a submarine, the cost of "exceptional dislocation and delay . . . due to alterations, suspensions of work or any other cause beyond the contractor's control". A sub-contractor installed a defective cable in a submarine which was discovered during construction and replaced with good cable. This caused delay and loss to the contractor and the contractor proceeded against the sub-contractor under the terms of the subcontract for the loss which it had suffered. However, the contractor compromised its claim for a sum less than its full loss and claimed the balance from the employer as being due to a "cause beyond the contractor's control".

Lord Keith of Kinkel upheld this contention briefly in one paragraph. He thought that *prima facie* it was not within the power of a contracting party to prevent breaches of contract as to quality on the part of a supplier or subcontractor such as might lead to delay. The contractor had no means in the ordinary case, or in this case on the facts, of supervising the manufacturing procedures of its supplier or detecting the defects in the cables prior to installation. It had correctly stipulated in the subcontract for delivery on time by the sub-contractor.

The obvious objection to this interpretation is that "contract" in this case has been interpreted in such a way that it effectively removes all risk from the contractor for the effects of the contracts the contractor enters into with its sub-contractors. Contrary to what was decided in this case, there appears to be good sense in saying that, in so far as the contractor is affected by the acts of its sub-contractors, its redress should be against its sub-contractors. In such a case the courts should not allow the contractor an action against the employer for a breach, the effects of which are entirely outside the employer's control. Lord Keith noted that Lord Jauncey, who, as a Judge of the Court of Session, had sat as arbitrator in the matter, made the point when he said:

> "Can it then be said that, in a situation where the contractor has responsibility for the supply of material, the failure by a Sub-contractor to perform his contractual obligations in relation to that material is a cause beyond the control of the contractor? I do not think it can. the contractor dictates his requirements to the Sub-contractor and can decide what contractual provisions he will or will not accept. He can proceed against the Sub-contractor in the event of the latter failing to perform his obligation. It would be curious if the Ministry had accepted the risk of a price variation caused by an event in respect of which, at the date of the contract, they would have had no recourse against a Sub-contractor, whereas the contractor would have had."

The Court of Appeal, in *John Mowlem* v. *Eagle Star*, considered, amongst other things, the meaning of the phrase "any cause beyond the control of the contractor, his sub-contractors or materials suppliers". In rejecting the rationale of the *Scott Lithgow* case, the Court of Appeal rejected Mowlem's claim for an EOT for delays caused by a sub-contractor.

### *Special circumstances*

The third class of sweeping-up provisions, that is, the "special circumstances" clause, is generally included in the engineering forms, but not in the building forms. So for example, clause 44(1)(f) of the ICE Form (7th edition) and clause 44(1)(e) of the ICE Design and Construct form excuse the contractor from "any special circumstances of any kind whatsoever". Clause 4.4(j) of the ICE Minor Works Form also excuses "other special circumstances of any kind whatsoever outside the control of the contractor".

### *Force majeure*

> *Force majeure* and the doctrine of frustration are inextricably linked so that in the absence of express terms to the contrary, force majeure frustrates the purpose of the contract and brings it to an end.

The expression *force majeure* is borrowed from continental usage and has been interpreted in the English courts by Bailhache J., in *Matsoukis* v. *Priestman & Co*, and by McCardie J., in *Lebeaupin* v. *Crispin*. It was formerly contended that *force majeure* was substantially the same as "Act of God" or "*vis major*". However, since *Matsoukis* v. *Priestman* it seems to be accepted that *force majeure* has a more extensive meaning than either *vis major* or Act of God. McCardie J., in *Lebeaupin* v. *Crispin*, quoted with approval Goirond's statement that war, inundations and epidemics are instances of *force majeure*. At common law, a strike of workmen is also a case of *force majeure*, but it is clear from the *Hackney Borough Council* v. *Doré* case that the reasonable apprehension of a strike is not. McCardie J., in considering the meaning of *force majeure*, said that: "any direct legislative or administrative interference would of course come within the term: for example, an embargo".

In the opinion of Bailhache J., such a thing as a breakdown of machinery through an accident would also be deemed to come within the meaning of *force majeure*. "Acts of God" or uncontrollable disasters including war, earthquakes, weather, strikes, lightning and the like would be obvious examples of *force majeure*.

However, most forms of contract deal with such specific risks as a category of employer's risk event and make more comprehensive provisions as to how the risk is to be borne. The purpose of this is, presumably, to expand the field of unforeseeable events that might otherwise be deemed to bring the contract to an end and to provide the contractor with relief as to time and/or cost in its place.

The building forms, for example, refer generally to "*force majeure*" as being an employer's time risk event, the effects of which entitle the contractor to more time, but do not bring the contract to an end, nor provide the contractor with compensation.

Neither PPC2000 nor the ICE forms nor contain any mention of *force majeure*, but the ICE forms do contain provisions entitling the contractor to an extension of time if the work is delayed by "any special circumstances of any kind whatsoever".

> Whereas under the JCT forms *force majeure* is generally undefined and a "neutral event", in that the employer takes the risk as to time and the contractor takes the risk as to costs caused thereby, under NEC3, the FIDIC Short Form (green book), FIDIC Building and Engineering (red book), FIDIC Turnkey (silver book), and FIDIC Plant Design and Build (yellow book) *force majeure* is defined as both a employer's time risk event and a employer's cost risk event.

Under clause 1.1.14 of the FIDIC Short Form (green book) *force majeure* is defined as:

"... an event or circumstance which makes performance of a party's obligations illegal or impracticable and which is beyond that party's reasonable control".

Clause 19 of FIDIC Building and Engineering (red book), FIDIC Turnkey (silver book), and FIDIC Plant design and Build (yellow book) define *force majeure* as including but not being limited to:

- (i) war, hostilities, (whether war be declared or not), invasion, act of foreign enemies,
- (ii) rebellion, terrorism, revolution, insurrection, military or usurped power, or civil war,
- (iii) riot, commotion, disorder, strike or lock out by persons other than the contractor's personnel and other employees of the contractor and sub-contractors,
- (iv) munitions of war, explosive materials, ionising radiation or contamination by radio-activity, except as may be attributable to the contractor's use of such munitions, explosives, radiation or radio-activity, and
- (v) natural catastrophes such as earthquake, hurricane, typhoon or volcanic activity.

It is clear from the phraseology employed that in these forms *force majeure* may in fact be anything that:

- is beyond the control of one of the parties to the contract;
- which such party could not reasonably have provided for before entering into the contract;
- which, having arisen, such party could not reasonably have avoided or overcome; and
- which is not substantially attributable to the other party

And that is the way the NEC3, rather tortuously goes about dealing with it so, without reference to *force majeure* at clause 60.1(19) NEC3 provides that it is a compensation event if the works are affected by:

"An event which

- stops the Contractor completing the Works or
- stops the Contractor completing the Works by the date shown on the accepted programme,

and which

- neither party could prevent,
- an experienced contractor would have judged at the contract date to have such a small chance of occurring that it would have been unreasonable for him to have allowed for it and
- is not one of the other compensation events stated in this contract."

Although the purpose of specifying *force majeure* as an excusable event is to avoid the contract being frustrated, many of the forms put a long-stop on this. So, for example, the FIDIC forms make provision for the contract to be terminated by either party if progress is suspended as a result of *force majeure* for a continuous period of 84 days or an aggregate period of 140 days as a result of the same *force majeure.*

Clause 46.1 of MF/1 defines *force majeure* as:

> "– war, hostilities (whether war be declared or not), invasion, act of foreign enemies;
> – ionising radiations, will contamination by radioactivity from any nuclear fuel, or from any nuclear waste from the combustion of nuclear fuel, radioactive toxic explosive, or other hazardous properties of any explosive nuclear assembly or nuclear component thereof;
> – pressure waves caused by aircraft or other aerial devices travelling at sonic or supersonic speeds;
> – rebellion, revolution, insurrection, military or usurped power or civil war;
> – riot, civil commotion or disorder;
> – any circumstances beyond the reasonable control either the parties."

However, this form, whilst making it clear that a *force majeure* event can be likely to cause delay to completion for which an extension of time has being granted, presumably along the lines of "circumstances beyond the reasonable control of the contractor", makes no provision for the allocation of costs, which presumably lie where they fall and if the circumstances last for more than 120 days, on the application of either party the contract can be terminated.

IChemE Lump Sum (red book) states that

"In the context of this clause, '*force majeure*' shall mean any circumstances beyond the reasonable control of either party would prevent or impede due performance of the contract my that party including, but not limited to, the following:

- government action or trade embargo
- war, hostilities or acts of terrorism;
- riot or civil commotion;
- epidemic;
- earthquake, flood, file or other natural physical disasters;
- exceptionally severe weather conditions or the consequences thereof;
- denial of the use of any railway, port, airport, shipping service or other means of public transport; or
- industrial dispute, other than any solely confined to the contractor and/or his sub-contractors or their employees including employees of any affiliate of the contractor or sub-contractor."

This form then goes on to say that 'the mere shortage of labour materials or utilities shall not constitute force majeure unless caused by circumstances which are themselves *force majeure.*

Clause 14.5 of IChemE Lump Sum (red book) expressly states that "in the event that either party is delayed by *force majeure* each party shall bear its own costs arising from such delay" but similarly to MF/1, it also provides at clause 14.6 for termination on the expiry of 120 days from notice of the occurrence of a force majeure event.

### *Errors and inconsistencies*

Irrespective of whether the form of contract has a general sweeping-up clause, contracts normally provide for excusable delay and compensation in the event that the contractor is adversely affected by errors or inconsistencies in the contract documents or instructions which are given during the course of the contract. There are exceptions, for example, in PPC2000 which states (at clause 2.4) that whoever created or participated in the creation of a document is responsible for its accuracy and the FIDIC forms (both of which get over the problem of inconsistencies between documents by a "priority of documents" clause) and the minor works forms (which generally make no express provision for delay arising out of correction of inconsistencies). Otherwise, generally, clause 2.13.2 of the JCT Management Contract and clauses 1.5 and 2.10.5.2 of the JCT Works Contract excuse the results of inconsistencies between contract documents and management contractor's instructions. Any discrepancy in or divergence between any two or more contract documents or between parts of any one of them is excused under clauses 5, 13(3) and 44(1)(c) of the ICE Form (7th edition), clauses 5(1)(c)(ii) and 44(1)(b) of the ICE Design and Construct form, clauses 2.15 and 2.29.1 of JCT Standard Building Contract, the JCT Management Contract and the Works Contract. Any departure from the standard method of measurement is excused under clauses 2.14.3 and 2.29.1 of the JCT Standard Building Contract, and clauses 2.13 and 2.20.1 of the JCT Intermediate Building Contract, the JCT Works Contract, and the JCT Management Contract. Under clauses 60.1(14) and 80.1 of NEC3 Engineering and Construction Contract, the contractor is excused delay caused by "a fault of the employer or a fault in his design". Any error in quantity or description or omission from the bills of quantities is excused under clauses 44(1)(b) and 51(4) of the ICE Form (7th edition), clauses 2.14.3 and 2.29.1 of JCT Standard Building Contract, and clauses 2.12.2, 2.13 and 2.20.1 of the JCT Intermediate Building Contract, clauses 1.10.2 and 2.10.5.1 of the JCT Management Contract and JCT Works Contract. Clause 3(3) of GC/Works/1makes provision for financial compensation for any error in quantity or description or omission from the bills of quantities but does not expressly make provision for relief from delay caused thereby.

Discrepancy in the employer's requirements is excused in Clauses 5(1)(c)(i) and 44(1)(a) of the ICE Design and Construct form, and any change in the employer's requirements is excused under clause 60.1(1) of NEC3 Engineering and Construction Contract and NEC3 Engineering and Construction Short Contract. Under clause 2.10.1 of the JCT Design and Build Contract any divergence between the employer's requirements and the definition of the site boundary is also excused.

Any discrepancy between what the employer requires and what the contractor offers is also excused under the JCT Design and Build Contract. Clause 2.13 provides that the contractor is to inform the employer as to how it proposes to overcome any discrepancy and that the employer may agree the contractor's proposals or decide itself how to overcome it. The clause goes on to say: "such agreement or decision shall be notified in writing to the contractor and such notification shall be treated as a change in the employer's Requirements". However, clause 2.26, which defines a "change in the employer's Requirements", provides, at clause 2.26.2.1, for instructions for such change which, if not objected to by the contractor, are excusable events under clause They are also reimbursable under clause 4.20.1. Thus, the failure of the contractor to get its design to conform to the employer's requirements is entirely at the employer's risk in regard to both time and cost. In view of the reputation of such forms for putting the risk of design with the contractor, it should not be necessary to trace these risks through four separate clauses in order to understand the true contractual position.

Illegal or impossible specification is excused under clauses 13(1), 13(3) and 44(1)(c) of the ICE Form (7th edition) and clauses 18.1 and 60.1(1) of NEC3 Engineering and Construction Contract. Unreasonably inaccurate approximate quantities are excused under clause 2.29.4 of JCT Standard Building Contract and clause 2.20.4 of the JCT Intermediate Building Contract, clauses 2.13.2 and Works Contract, clause 2.10.4 of the JCT Management Contract and clause 2.10.14 of the JCT Works Contract.

Clause 2.14.3 and 2.29.1 of the JCT Standard Building Contract, clauses 17(1) and 60.1(1) of NEC3 Engineering and Construction Contract, clause 2.13.2 of the JCT Management Contract and clauses 1.5A.1 and 2.10.5.1 of the JCT Works Contract excuse divergence between performance specified work and the contract administrator's instructions. Errors and inconsistencies in contract documents are excused under clauses 13(3), 5 and 44(1)(c) of the ICE Form (7th edition), clauses 1.5 and 11.5(e) of the ACA Building Contract, and clauses 2.4, 3.6 and 2.7 of the JCT Minor Works Building Contract, clause 2.13.2 of the JCT Management Contract, and clauses 1.5 and 2.10.2 of JCT Works Contract, clauses 2.29.2.1 of the JCT Standard Building Contract, and clause 2.20.2.1 of the JCT Intermediate Building Contract. Clause 17.1 and 60.1(1) of NEC3 Engineering and Construction Contract excuses "an ambiguity or inconsistency in or between the documents which form part of this contract". Discrepancy or divergence between the contract documents and any information provided under an IRS is added as an excusable event in clauses 2.11 and 2.29.6 of the JCT Standard Building Contract and clauses 2.10 and 2.20.6 of the JCT Intermediate Building Contract. Divergence between statutory requirements and the contract documents is excused under clauses 26(3)(b) and 44(1)(a) of the ICE Form (7th edition) and the ICE Design and Construct form, clauses 1.6 and 11.5(e) of the ACA Building Contract, clauses 2(3) and 36(2)(a) of GC/Works/1, clauses 2.17.2 and 2.29.1 of JCT Standard Building Contract, and 2.15.2 and 2.20.1 the JCT Intermediate Building Contract. Any divergence between the employer's requirements and the definition of the site boundary and any discrepancy in the employer's requirements is excused under JCT Design and Build Contract and similar provisions appear under clauses 4.7 and 8.4(b) of the FIDIC red book, where the employer is at risk as to "any error in the positions, levels, dimensions or alignment of the Works" in so far as those are specified or notified, but the contractor is under a duty to use its reasonable endeavours to verify their accuracy before use.

Clause 5.1 of the JCT Major Project Form states that the contractor shall not be responsible for the contents of the employer's requirements or the adequacy of the design contained in the employer's requirements and that "where a discrepancy is identified within the requirements, the contractor shall notify the employer which of the discrepant provisions it intends to adopt and proceed accordingly. If the employer wishes the contractor to proceed otherwise, it shall so instruct the contractor and that instruction shall be treated as giving rise to a change." By virtue of clause 12.1.5 such an instruction for change is an employer's time risk event but oddly, by reason of clause 21.1 is not an employer's cost risk event.

### *Instructed variations*

Most construction contracts include a clause permitting additions, deletions, and changes in obligations provided that the changes are within the scope of the contract. These are defined in IChemE Lump Sum (red book) as any change that in aggregate does not increase or decrease the contract price by more than 25 per cent or in the case of a variation order issued after the works have been taken over, does not increase the contract price by more than 5 per cent. In addition, such clauses usually provide a method of valuing changes and dealing with time for the execution of changes. In PPC2000 for example, clause 17 provides for the time and cost effect of changes to be pre-agreed between the employer and the contractor or pre-determined by the contract administrator according to the agreed price framework.

In most cases, the provisions permit written instructions for changes in detail to be given retrospectively (in emergency situations) in order to prevent personal injury or property damage. The adjustment in contract sum and/or contract time is usually either negotiated between the parties to the contract by acceptance of an agreed price or, by reference to the contractor's cost and a mutually acceptable fixed or percentage fee or by pro rata adjustment of the rates and charges set down in the contract bills or specification. Instructed variation and change are usually both an employers' time risk event and employer's cost risk event. In the event that they cause delay to completion they are also excusable causes of delay, provided that there is provision for the employer or the contract administrator to extend the contract period for that reason. Uniquely, in PPC2000, the provisions to extend time for performance are outside the extension of time clause and not cross related to it. In clause 17 it appears that the contractor is entitled to whatever additional time it can negotiate or to which the contract administrator says it is to be awarded, without any obvious structure for ascertainment. NEC3 Engineering and

Construction Contract, on the other hand, excuses any variation or change, contract administrator's change of instruction and the correction of an assumption about the nature of a compensation event but provides for the time effect to be ascertained by reference to its effect on an updated programme if one is provided and by reference to the contract programme in default.

Variation and change are expressly excusable under clause 12.1.5 of the JCT Major Project Construction Contract, clauses 51(1) and 44(1)(a) of the ICE Form (7th edition), and the ICE Design and Construct form, clause 11.5(e) of the ACA Building Contract, clause 36(2)(a) of GC/Works/1, clause 2.29.1 of JCT Standard Building Contract clause 2.20.1 of the JCT Intermediate Building Contract, clause 2.13.2 of the JCT Management Contract, and clauses 1.3.2.1 and 2.10.5.1 of the JCT Works Contract, clauses 6.1(m) and 7.3 of FIDIC Short Form (green book), clause 8.4a of FIDIC Building and Engineering (red book), FIDIC Turnkey (silver book), and FIDIC Plant design and Build (yellow book) and JCT Design and Build Contract refers to "any change in the employer requirements". In the JCT family of contracts variation and change are typically defined as a change involving:

- addition, omission or substitution of any work;
- alteration of the kind or standard of any materials or goods;
- removal of any work or goods which are not defective;
- imposition of obligation or restriction on access to any part of the site;
- limitation on working space or hours; and
- execution or completion of work in any specific order,

However, as is illustrated later in this book, this definition is expanded under the Change Management Supplements to include the alteration or modification of:

- the master programme so as to reduce, overcome, or avoid the likely effects of any delay to progress caused by one or a employer's time risk event;
- the duration, sequence or timing of any activity or activities;
- any period of time whether by reference to a lead, lag, or otherwise;
- the date of any milestone or key date;
- the resources to be used in connection with any activity or activities;
- the requirements of the schedules which specify how the networks and method statement are to be prepared, to whom they are to be distributed and how records are to be kept of the progress of the work on site.

A change in performance specified work caused by a change in the statutory requirements is excused under clauses 2.17.2.3 and 2.29.1 JCT Standard Building Contract, clause 2.13.2 of the JCT Management Contract and clause 2.10.16 of the JCT Works Contract.

Delay caused by the effect of expenditure of any provisional sums is excused under the JCT Design and Build Contract. Delay caused by the effect of expenditure of provisional sums only for undefined work is excused under clause 2.26.2.1. JCT Standard Building Contract, and clause 2.20.2.1 of the JCT Intermediate Building Contract. The significance of a defined provisional sum is set out in General Rules 10.1 to 10.6 of SMM7. This used to be reproduced as a footnote in earlier versions of the JCT Standard Building Contract but it has been omitted from the 2005 form. The note states:

"10.1 Where work can be described and given in items in accordance with these rules but the quantity of work required cannot be accurately determined, an estimate of the quantity shall be given and identified as an approximate quantity.

10.2 Where work cannot be described and given in items in accordance with these rules it shall be given as a Provisional Sum and identified as for either defined or undefined work as appropriate.

10.3 A Provisional Sum for defined work is a sum provided for work which is not completely designed but for which the following information shall be provided:

(a) The nature and construction of the work.
(b) A statement of how and where the work is fixed to the building and what other work is to be fixed thereto.
(c) A quantity or quantities which indicate the scope and extent of the work.

Any specific limitations and the like identified in Section A35.

10.4 Where Provisional Sums are given for defined work the contractor will be deemed to have made due allowance in programming, planning and pricing Preliminaries. Any such allowance will only be subject to adjustment in those circumstances where a variation in respect of other work measured in detail in accordance with the rules would give rise to adjustment.

10.5 A Provisional Sum for undefined work is a sum provided for work where the information required in accordance with rule 10.3 cannot be given.

10.6 Where Provisional Sums are given for undefined work the contractor will be deemed not to have made any allowance in programming, planning and pricing Preliminaries."

## *Weather*

The effects of weather on the progress of the work are excused under most of the forms in which there are not general sweeping-up clauses and also in some forms that have both *force majeure* and sweeping up clauses. However, the phraseology varies. The government contract forms GC/Works 1 and GC/works/1 Design and Construct expressly exclude bad weather as grounds for excusable delay and no provision is made for reimbursement of cost. Thus, so far as concerns this form and the UK government contracts, the risk of delay for bad weather rests entirely with the contractor.

Most of the standard forms excuse delay caused by the effects of "exceptionally adverse weather." This is broadly the phraseology used in clause 44(1)(d) of the ICE Form (7th edition), clause 44(1)(c) of the ICE Design and Construct form, clause 2.29.8 of the JCT Standard Building Contract, clause 2.20.8 of the JCT Intermediate Building Contract, the JCT Design and

Build Contract, clause 2.13.2 of the JCT Management Contract, and clause 2.10.2 of the JCT Works Contract.

Under these forms, a delay to completion caused by weather is only an employer's time risk event if the weather is "exceptionally adverse". It must, therefore, be out of the ordinary. The weather is often adverse during the winter but the weather must be worse than expected, e.g. in comparison to average previous years for the same location. The term "exceptionally adverse weather" covers any conditions in an exceptional different degree from those that could be expected and *prima facie* would thus also include extended periods of very hot weather. The problem however, remains that exceptional is a comparative term.

In practice, it is often difficult to establish at what point the adversity of the weather condition becomes exceptional because so many factors are involved. One source of information on which measurements may be based is Meteorological Office records. By comparing records over a period of time it may be demonstrated that the adverse weather conditions which have been experienced on the project under consideration have been above or below the average for the time of year in relation to the long-term average. However, these records do not normally take into account the time of day or night when the conditions occurred, nor do they take into account the nature of the site, which can lead to distortions of the picture.

> There is also a conceptual difficulty in determining that anything above or below the long term average automatically falls into the category of exceptional. It is doubtful whether exceptional in this sense can be construed to mean "above average" because, as "average" necessarily implies, it must be normal to experience levels of adverse weather both above and below the average in order to have an "average". Logically it seems then that 'exceptional' in this sense must thus be something in excess of the ultimate highs and lows used to calculate the average.

In some design calculations a 100-year period is the norm, however, it would seem that in relation to weather conditions, "exceptional" could reasonably be construed as, say, above the ten year high-point or, below the ten-year low point used to calculate the "average".

PPC2000 does not reduce the difficulty in using the expression in clause 18.3(v): "weather conditions which the Meteorological Office records for the area nearest the site indicate are exceptionally adverse for the time of year". This is because the Meteorological Office does not record "exceptionally adverse" weather it only records objective data of the actual weather conditions and calculates whether they are higher or lower than the long term average for the time of year.

Clause 60.1(13) of NEC3 Engineering and Construction Contract attempts more precision and refers to weather which "is shown to occur on average less frequently than once in 10 years" but the standard is measured by gauging whether the weather within a limited period of the date of tender is worse than normally occurs once in 10 years in relation to the place in which the weather is measured. Obviously, to be at all meaningful, the relevant weather conditions would have been measured, e.g. rainfall, frost, wind and temperature, and the place of measurement should be reasonably close to the site.

NEC3 Engineering and Construction Short Contract, on the other hand adopts the novel approach of focusing on the actual effect of weather conditions rather than its severity and providing a formula for balancing the risk between the parties. Clause 60.1(10) provides that the contractor is to be excused delay caused by weather conditions if:

> "the contractor is prevented by weather from carrying out all work on the site for periods of time, each at least one full working day, which are in total more than one seventh of the total number of days between the starting date and the completion date. In assessing this event, only the working days which exceed this limit and on which work is prevented by no other cause are taken into account."

However, causation in regard to exceptionally adverse weather is by no means straight forward. Take for example, the effect on tower cranes of exceptionally high winds. Bearing in mind that a tower crane might normally cease working if the wind speed exceeded 15–20mph (a speed which is not unusual and by no means exceptional), a wind speed of say 100mph, which might be exceptional, would have no effect on progress because the crane would have ceased working long before the wind reached that speed. On the other hand, if the wind maintained a speed in excess of 20mph for several days without dropping, it might be possible to show that to be exceptional. However, in England it is not unusual to have two or three windy days together or to have high wind at some time during every day for long periods.

Clauses 6.1(h) and 7.3 of FIDIC Short Form (green book) excuse delay, broadly caused by: "any operation of the forces of nature which is unforeseeable and against which an experienced contractor could not reasonably have been expected to take precautions". The notes to clause 6.1 of FIDIC Short Form (green book) say that there is no provision under this form of contract for an EOT for delayed completion as a result of adverse weather. Whilst it might reasonably be conceded that the "forces or nature" may extend to other things besides weather, it is difficult to understand how "weather" is not anything other than "the forces of nature" and thus, despite what is said in the guidance notes, by reason of clauses 6.1(h) and 7.3, is an excusable event. Clause 8.4 (c) of the FIDIC Building and Engineering (red book), and FIDIC Plant Design and Build (yellow book) provide for "exceptionally adverse climatic conditions" to be an employer's time risk event.

Whilst the JCT Major Construction Contract and FIDIC Turnkey (silver book) do not expressly refer to weather as being at the contractor's risk and make no express provision for it to be a employer's time risk event, the way the forms describe *force majeure* which, in FIDIC Turnkey is both a employer's cost risk event and a employer's time risk event, it would seem to be at the employer's risk. In this form clause 19.1, whilst setting out what *force majeure* can be deemed to include states that by definition, *force majeure* comprises an event

- which is beyond the control of one of the parties to the contract;
- which such party could not reasonably have provided for before entering into the contract;
- which, having arisen, such party could not reasonably have avoided or overcome; and
- which is not substantially attributable to the other party,
- which would seem to always include exceptional weather conditions.

### *Unforeseeable physical conditions*

Apart from the unforeseeability of weather conditions, in most of the engineering forms but not IChemE Lump Sum (red book), the contractor is also excused the effects on progress and cost of unforeseeable physical conditions. However, this provision does not extend to FIDIC Turnkey (silver book) which, at clause 4.12 states:

"(a) The contractor shall be deemed to have obtained all necessary information as to risks, contingencies and other circumstances which may influence or affect the Works;

(b) By signing the contract, the contractor accepts total responsibility of having seen all difficulties and cost of successfully completing the Works; and

(c) the contract price shall not be adjusted to take into account of any unforeseen difficulties or costs."

However, in other engineering forms this risk is variously circumscribed by such expressions as: "physical conditions . . . which an experienced the contractor would have judged at the contract Date to have such a small chance of occurring that it would have been unreasonable for him to have allowed for them" and "ground conditions which could not reasonably be foreseen by an experienced the contractor".

Clauses 7(3) and 36(2)(e). of GC/Works/1 define the risk adopted by the employer as:

" . . . ground conditions . . . which he did not know of, and which he could not reasonably have foreseen having regard to any information which he had or ought reasonably to have ascertained".

Clause 4.12 of FIDIC Building and Engineering (red book) and FIDIC Plant design and Build (yellow book) contain a slightly different definition, setting it down as meaning unforeseeable physical conditions which are:

" . . . natural physical conditions and man-made and other physical obstructions and pollutants, which the contractor encounters at the site when executing the works, including sub-surface and hydrological conditions but excluding climatic conditions."

Clauses 6.1(i) and 7.3 of the FIDIC Short Form (green book) excuses delays caused by:

"physical obstructions or physical conditions other than climatic conditions not reasonably foreseeable by an experienced the contractor and which the contractor immediately notified to the employer."

Finally, NEC3 Engineering and Construction Short Contract excuses delay caused thereby if

"the contractor encounters physical conditions which

- are within the site,
- are not weather conditions and
- which an experienced contractor would have judged, at the date of the contractor's offer, to have such a small chance of occurring that it would have been unreasonable to have allowed for them."

MF/1 is perhaps unique in attempting to specify what type of ground conditions are deemed to be unforeseeable. Clause 5.7 states:

"in the case of work underground or involving excavation where the actual conditions of the ground are not stated in the contract or if rock, rocky soil, solid chalk, water, running sound, slag, pipes, concrete or obstructions are found, and such conditions or obstructions could not reasonably be ascertained from an inspection of the site by the contractor before he prepared the tender or from information made available to the contractor for the purpose of the tender . . . .".

Clause 5.7 then makes express provision for any costs incurred to be an employer's cost risk event. However, for it to be an employer's time risk event it must be construed as "by reason of circumstances beyond the reasonable control of the contractor" under clause 33.1 which, of course, it obviously would be.

> On the whole, the "building forms" do not specify unforeseeable physical conditions as an excusable event, it being largely left to determination as whether what the contractor is ultimately required to do is something for which it has not been required to include in its price and which, thereby, becomes a variation.

Unusually amongst the "building forms" in clauses 2.6 and 11.5(e) of the ACA Building Contract, the contractor is excused delay caused by any "adverse ground conditions or artificial obstructions" whether or not they are foreseeable by the contractor or anyone else. JCT Major Project Construction Contract also makes provision for

"ground conditions or man-made obstructions in the ground that necessitate an amendment to the requirements and/or proposals"

of which the contractor is then bound to advise the employer and seek the employer's approval. However, by this form, depending upon which clause has been stated to apply, there is the possibility of such approval not constituting a change under clause 8.1 or constituting a change under clause 8.2 if the circumstances "could not reasonably have been foreseen by an experienced and competent contractor . . . having regard to any information concerning the site that the contractor had, or ought reasonably to have obtained."

> Generally, employers and contract administrators are under a duty to disclose to contractors all information in their possession regarding site conditions.

In the Canadian case of *Canadian Red Cross* v. *WN Developments* the contract administrator was contributorily negligent on a contract where, in the course of excavating for an extension to a building owned by the Canadian Red Cross Society, the contractor ruptured the water main, flooding part of the premises. It transpired that an as-built plan, in the employer's possession, showed the exact line and detail of the main. However, while the contract drawings indicated the position of the water main, they contained no information about it. Smith L.J. held that the reasonable degree of care and skill required of the contract administrator may not always include the duty to divulge all the information in its possession, but, in a general way: "if the contractor should have called for the as-built plans from the employer, *a fortiori*, the contract administrator should have done so".

It would also appear that, whereas general "soft-spots" may not be excusable under the engineering contracts (because the generality would be determinable by "information . . . which he ought reasonably to have ascertained"), an isolated or transitory soft-spot will provide the basis for excusable delay. In *Humber Oil* the Court of Appeal considered the meaning of clause 12 of the ICE 5th Edition in relation to the collapse of a lifting rig. The contractor was employed for the construction of mooring and berthing dolphins at Humberside. For the purpose of carrying out the work the contractor selected and used a jack-up barge equipped with a 300-tonne fixed crane. Whilst the crane was lifting a concrete soffit onto piles, the crane became unstable and collapsed, destroying the barge, causing extensive damage to plant and equipment and considerable delay and expense.

The contractor claimed that the collapse of the crane and the ensuing consequences were due to encountering physical conditions which could not reasonably have been foreseen by an experienced contractor. At paragraph 6.21 of his interim award on liability, the arbitrator answered the point as follows:

"6.21 Is the collapse properly to be regarded as merely an unforeseeable consequence of conditions which were in themselves foreseeable? In my opinion, the answer is No. Although the soil conditions at the base of the leg, taken in isolation, were foreseeable, and the geometry and the other details of the leg were well known, I do not consider that this requires me without more to reject the claim. It simply poses a different question: what was the condition that led to the failure of Stevin 73, and was that condition unforeseeable?

6.22 In my opinion taking into account particularly the unprecedented nature of this collapse, there must have been a very unusual combination of soil strength and applied stresses around the base of leg number 2 just before failure occurred. It is not possible to calculate or precisely to predict these strengths and stresses, but they must have existed for failure to have occurred, having regard to the findings that I have already made. Was this a physical condition? In my opinion it was. Clause 12 contains no limitation on the meaning of 'physical condition' and I can see no reason why a combination of strength and stress should not fall within the term. The 'condition' was thus a transient combination the elements of which existed at the time the contract was made but which came together only near the point of failure. I do not regard this as placing the condition outside the wording of Clause 12.

6.23 Was this condition such that it could not reasonably be foreseen by an experienced contractor? In my opinion, the answer must be yes. I do not believe that any amount of analysis, of the type put forward either by (the expert for the claimant) or (the expert for the respondent), would have led an experienced contractor to foresee this condition. Put more simply, I do not believe that the condition, which led to the collapse of Stevin 73, could have been foreseen. Of a certainty, it was not foreseen by anyone . . . "

In the Court of Appeal, Parker L.J., who referred to the arbitrator's award as "a model of clarity and lucidity", rejected the appeal shortly:

" . . . (Counsel) submits that the physical condition of the soil, which was found by the arbitrator to be foreseeable, really concludes the matter and that applied stress is not and cannot be any part of the physical condition.

Attractive as his argument appears to be at first sight, I cannot accept it. The arbitrator was in my view saying that the general soil conditions were foreseeable and well able to stand the applied loads and stresses. There was however here a peculiar characteristic, which could not have been reasonably foreseen, namely a liability to sheer at a much lower loading than had already been withstood.

The matter may perhaps be put in this way. General soil conditions were known and were foreseeable and foreseen. Such soil conditions would not have resulted in a sheer failure. There was thus an unforeseeable condition . . . "

> Where bills of quantity measure provide for costs to be inserted by the contractor at the time of tender for dealing with hidden obstructions or for working in different types of ground conditions then, apart from the adequacy or otherwise of the quantities the contractor is required to price, there can be no question of foreseeability in regard to those measured items. Certainly, the possibility of their existence is foreseen and priced for at the time of tender.

## *Access, ingress and egress*

Most of the building forms, for example clauses 42(3) and 44(1)(c) of the ICE Form (7th edition), clauses 42(3) and 44(1)(b) of the ICE Design and Construct form, clause 2.13.2 of the JCT Management Contract, and clause 2.10.12 of the JCT Works Contract, clause 18.3(i) and 18.3(xi) of PPC2000 expressly state that a failure by the employer to give access to the works is expressly described as a employer's time and cost risk event.

The failure to give or the prevention of the contractor from gaining access under the 2005 series of JCT forms falls under the "impediment, prevention or default" provision typically phrased in clause 2.29.6 of JCT Standard Building Contract

Clause 60.1(2) of NEC3 Engineering and Construction Contract and NEC3 Engineering and Construction Short Contract excuse delay resulting from a failure to give access to the site. Failure to give right of access to, and possession of, the site within the time stated in the Appendix to Tender is excused under clauses 2.1 and 8.4(b) of FIDIC Building and Engineering (red book), FIDIC Turnkey (silver book), and FIDIC Plant Design and Build (yellow book).

MF1/ provides that a breach by the employer of its general obligations to provide access to the site as specified is an employer's cost risk event. As to a time risk event, it falls to be construed under clause 33.1 as being "any act or omission on the part of the employer or (the contract administrator)," or "by reason of circumstances reasonably beyond the control of the contractor". Similarly, under IChemE Lump Sum (red book), a failure to give possession or access to the site as provided for in the contract would fall to be construed as a employer's risk event under clause 14.1(d) as a "breach of the contract by the employer". On the other hand, under JCT Major Projects Form, a failure to provide such access as is specified would rank as an employer's time risk event under clause 12.1.8 and an employer's cost risk event under clause 21.2.1 which provide for relief and compensation for "any other breach or act of prevention by the employer . . . "

Generally, relief is granted for the employer's failure to give, in due time, ingress to or egress from the site of the works, or any part thereof, through or over any land, buildings, way or passage adjoining or connected with the site and in the possession and control of the employer. This is not necessarily restricted to the whole of the works or only to the contractor. It could, for example, relate to a sub-contractor who might be denied access to a part of an existing building that was being renovated in stages, and to which it was essential that it had access in order to work.

### *Postponement*

Postponement of the works is the failure to release the site or parts of the site for commencement of the work or a part of the work. Postponement usually imposes a financial and time penalty on the employer and this is generally recognised in the forms analysed.

JCT Major Projects Form provides no power of postponement. Similarly, PPC2000 provides no express power of postponement, it being left to fall within the definition of change under Appendix 1, or to be construed as a breach under clause 18.3(xiv). Simple postponement or suspension is dealt with under clause 41 of IChemE Lump Sum (red book), clause 25 of MF/1, clauses 40(1) and 44(1)(c) of the ICE Form (7th edition), clauses 40(1) and 44(1)(b) of the ICE Design and Construct form, clauses 11.8 and 11.5(e) of the ACA Building Contract, clauses 3.15 and 2.29.2.1 of the JCT Standard Building Contract, clauses 3.12 and 2.20.2.1 of the JCT Intermediate Building Contract, clause 60.1(4) of NEC3 Engineering and Construction Contract and NEC3 Engineering and Construction Short Contract, clauses 6.1(j) and 7.3 of FIDIC Short Form (green book). Any instructions to postpone work due to safety conditions are also excused under the ICE Form (7th edition) and clauses 40(1)(c) and 44(1)(b) of the ICE Design and Construct form.

Deferment of possession of the site is excused under clauses 40(1)(c) and 44(1)(c) of the ICE Form (7th edition), clause 2.29.3 of JCT Standard Building Contract, clause 2.20.3 of the JCT Intermediate Building Contract, clause 2.26.3 of JCT Design and Build Contract, clause 2.13.2 of the JCT Management Contract, and clause 2.10.13 of the JCT Works Contract. In clauses 11.5(e) and 8.1(d) of the ACA Building Contract, the words used are: "the addition, alteration or omission of any obligation or restriction in regard to any limitations of working space or working hours, access to the Site or use of any parts of the Site." Whilst this goes a lot further than simple postponement, it would seem to probably include a postponement of the execution of part of the work.

### *Acts of third parties*

Delays caused by the acts or omissions of third parties include such things as works to be carried out at the employer's direct orders either by means of work, or supply of materials, or equipment, by other contractors, local authorities, statutory undertakings and government acts. They are variously described in the forms as "delay in . . . approval of any statutory body" or delay caused by a local authority or statutory undertaking "of work in pursuance of its statutory obligations . . . or the failure to carry out such work". JCT Major Project Form appears to provide no express relief for such a contingency. Clauses 18.3(iii) and 18.3(xv) of PPC2000 provide respectively for conditional relief in regard to:

"delay in the receipt of any of the third-party consents listed in the commencement agreement . . . " and

"damage or obstruction by any Specialist appointed by the employer"

"Delay in receipt of any necessary permission or approval of any statutory body which the contractor has taken all practicable steps to avoid or reduce" is also excused under clause 2.26.12 of the JCT Design and Build Contract.

In the UK, "statutory undertaker" is the expression used to describe the various "boards" that were formed to provide electricity, gas, water, etc. It also includes commercial enterprises doing works under statutory powers and transport providers acting under statutory powers. The cases of *Boskalis* v. *Liverpool* and *Henry* v. *CLNTDC* demonstrate that the contractor and subcontractors are entitled to an EOT only if the local authority or statutory undertaker causes the delay when executing the obligations imposed upon them by statute.

| |
|---|
| However, if they are acting in a contractual capacity, for example when carrying out electrical installation works under a contract with the contractor, the rules applicable to the sub-contractor will apply. |

Delay by local authorities and statutory undertakers is referred to in clause 18.3(vi) of PPC2000, clause 11.5(d) of the ACA Building Contract, clause 2.29.7 of the JCT Standard Building Contract, clause 2.20.7 of the JCT Intermediate Building Contract, clause 2.26.12 of the JCT Design and Build Contract, clause 2.13.2 of the JCT Management Contract and JCT Works Contract. Government acts are excused under clause 12.1.3 of the JCT Major Project Form, clause 18.3(x) of PPC2000, clause 2.29.12 of JCT Standard Building Contract, clause 2.20.12 of JCT Intermediate Building Contract, clause 2.26.11 of the JCT Design and Build Contract, clause 2.13.2 the JCT Management Contract and clause 2.10.9 of the JCT Works Contract. "Delay or disruption caused by a legally constituted public authority" is excused under clauses 8.5 and 8.4(b) of FIDIC Building and Engineering (red book). FIDIC Turnkey (silver book), and FIDIC Plant design and Build (yellow book) provide similar relief provided that the event

(a) is not caused by the contractor's failure to follow the appropriate procedures;
(b) delays or disrupts the contractor's work; and
(c) the delay or disruption to the contractor's work was unforeseeable.

Under clause 6.1 of MF/1, government acts are expressed to be employer's cost risk events the inference that they are also employer's time risk event can be drawn from the contractor being entitled to relief for any cause beyond its control. On the other hand, IChemE Lump Sum (red book), expressly defines government acts as *force majeure*, which is a employer's time risk event under this form but does not express it to be an employer's cost risk event.

Delay by other contractors and suppliers in the employer's direct employment is excused under Clause 31(2) the ICE Design and Construct form, JCT 2005 suite of contracts use the device of defining such parties as Employer's Persons' and then providing relief by way of impediment, prevention, default or breach as in, for example clause 2.29.6 of the JCT Standard Building Contract. Clause 60.1(5) of NEC3 Engineering and Construction Contract, provides that the contractor is to be excused delay caused by the failure by the employer or others to

- work within the times shown on the accepted programme
- within the conditions as stated in the Works Information, or
- if they carry out works not stated in the works information

In Clause 12.1.6 of the JCT Major Project Construction Contract the risk is expressed as "interference with the contractor's regular progress of the project by Others on the Site" where "Others" is defined as "persons whose presence on the site has been authorised by the employer other than the contractor its sub-contractors and suppliers and any other person under the control of the contractor".

Clauses 6.1(k) and 7.3 of the FIDIC Short Form (green book) uses the expression "any delay, impediment or prevention by the employer" and finally, clause 8.4(e) of FIDIC Building and Engineering (red book), clause 8.4(c) of FIDIC Turnkey (silver book), and clause 8.4(e) of FIDIC Plant design and Build (yellow book) provide for "any delay, impediment or prevention caused by or attributable to the employer, the employer's personnel, or the employer's other contractors on the site".

### *Nominated sub-contractors and suppliers*

FIDIC Turnkey (silver book), FIDIC Plant design and Build (yellow book), PPC2000, JCT Major Project Construction Contract, MF/1 and the JCT 2005 version of the Standard Building Contract make no provision for nominated sub-contractors. The effect of nomination or re-nomination of a sub-contractor or supplier is excused under clauses 35, 36 and 25.4.5 of the 1998 version of the Standard Form of Building Contract. The effects of the nomination or re-nomination of a supplier, but not of a sub-contractor are excused under clause 2.13.2 of the JCT Management Contract and clause 2.10.5 of the JCT Works Contract, and the renaming and replacing of a named sub-contractor are excused under clauses 3.7 and 2.20.2.2 of the JCT Intermediate Building Contract.

Clauses 14.1(e) and 10.7. of IChemE Lump Sum (red book) respectively provide for the appointment of nominated sub-contractors and conditionally for the failure of any nominated sub-contractor to perform its obligations to be an employer's cost risk event, and an employer's time risk event. Delay by a nominated supplier or sub-contractor is also excused under clause 25.4.7 of JCT 98 but no such provision appears in the 2005 Standard Building Contract. Delay by a nominated supplier is excused under clause 2.13.2 of the JCT Management Contract and clauses 8 and 2.10.7.2 of the JCT Works Contract. Delay caused by the default of a nominated sub-contractor but not a nominated supplier is excused under clause 59(4)(f) of the ICE Form (7th edition).

In regard to a delay to progress in the work of a nominated sub-contractor, clause 35.14.1 of the 1998 edition of the Standard form of Building Contract forbids the contractor from granting an EOT to any nominated sub-contractor without the written consent of the contract administrator who, in dealing with the notice, must apply the subcontract conditions. Clause 11.2.2.1 of NSC/4 requires that, with the consent of the contract administrator, the contractor should grant an EOT if the reason for delay is an employer's time risk event and:

"... any of the matters which are stated by the Sub-contractor to be the cause of the delay is an act, omission or default of the contractor, his servants or agents or his Sub-contractors, their servants or agents other than the Sub-contractor, his servants or agents or the occurrence of a relevant event."

NSC/4 and JCT Standard Building Contract create a three-sided arrangement where the contract administrator considers the nominated sub-contractor's notice, particulars and estimate which the contract administrator received via the contractor. If the contract administrator consents to the nominated sub-contractor's EOT then it does so via the contractor and the contractor then grants the EOT.

In *Jarvis* v. *Westminster* the House of Lords decided that "delay" on the part of a nominated sub-contractor should be considered in the light of the provisions relating to delay on the part of the employer under the main contract. Irrespective of whether the delay complained of results from dilatoriness or from bad workmanship, the provisions here only relate to the commencement of the nominated sub-contractor contract and hence cease on practical completion of the nominated sub-contractor work. Thus, in the event that a nominated sub-contractor has to return to the site to remedy defects in its work which has previously been taken over by the contractor, it cannot be said to be causing "delay" under these provisions.

The effects of the failure of the nominated sub-contractor to complete on time are the subject of NSC/4, clause 12, which reads:

"12.1 If the nominated sub-contractor fails to complete the sub-contract works (or any part thereof) within the period or periods for completion or any revised period or periods as provided in clause 1.1.2.2, the contractor shall so notify the contract administrator and give to the nominated sub-contractor a copy of such notification.

The nominated sub-contractor shall pay or allow to the contractor a sum equivalent to any loss or damage suffered or incurred by the contractor and caused by the failure of the nominated sub-contractor as aforesaid. Provided that the contractor shall not be entitled so to claim unless the contract administrator in accordance with clause 35.1.5 of the main contract conditions shall have issued to the contractor (with a copy to the nominated sub-contractor) a certificate in writing certifying any failure notified under clause 12.1."

The second paragraph, clause 12.2, leads to clause 35.13 in the 1998 version of the Standard Form of Building Contract which establishes that the contractor shall not grant to any nominated sub-contractor any extension of the period or periods within which the subcontract works are to be completed without the contract administrator's approval.

Clause 35.15 of that form is concerned with failure of the nominated sub-contractor to complete its works. It reads:

"If any nominated sub-contractor fails to complete the sub-contract works(or where the sub-contract works are to be completed in parts any part thereof) within the period specified in the sub-contract or within any extended time granted by the contractor with the written consent of the contract administrator and the contractor so notifies the contract administrator with a copy to the nominated sub-contractor, then, provided that the contract administrator is satisfied that clause 35.14 has been properly applied, the contract administrator shall so certify in writing to the contractor. Immediately upon the issue of such a certificate the contract administrator shall send a duplicate thereof to the nominated sub-contractor."

The certificate of the contract administrator under clause 35.15.1 is to be issued not later than two months from the date of notification to the contract administrator that the nominated sub-contractor has failed to complete the subcontract works or any part thereof. Its importance to both the contractor and nominated sub-contractor is that it enables the contractor to claim against the nominated sub-contractor for direct loss and/or expense which it may have suffered as a result of the nominated subcontractor's failure.

In the same way as sub-contracts are dealt with under the 1998 version of the Standard Building Contract, an EOT granted to a works contractor by a management contractor under the JCT Management Contract is granted not by the contract administrator but by the management contractor. The management contractor has a duty to advise the contract administrator in time for the latter to express dissent; if the contract administrator does express dissent it must be expressed before the time expires for the management contactor to decide the application by the works contractor. The JCT Works Contract is silent as to what happens if the contract administrator expresses dissent, but the management contractor goes ahead and grants on EOT to a works contractor, which thereby relieves it of its liability to pay LADs. The only safeguard appears to be the provision that: "no project extension item shall be considered to the extent that it was caused or contributed to by any default, whether by act or omission, of the management contractor". The employer's time risk events set out in clause 2.10 of the JCT Works Contract are virtually the same as those in clause 25 in JCT98 *mutatis mutandis.*

The FIDIC forms treat delay on the part of sub-contractors very much more simply. Clause 5 of the FIDIC Building and Engineering (red book) provides for the nomination of sub-contractors but does not provide for the contractor to obtain relief for any delay caused by them.

Delay caused by the employer or persons employed by the employer is excused under clause 2.29.6 of JCT Standard Building Contract, clause 2.20.6 of the JCT Intermediate Building Contract, clause 2.26.5 of JCT Design and Build Contract, clause 2.13.2 of the JCT Management Contract and clause 2.10.8.2 of the JCT Works Contract.

Delay caused by supply of materials by the employer or persons employed by the employer is excused under clause 2.29.6 of the JCT Standard Building Contract, clause 2.20.6 of the JCT Intermediate Building Contract, clause 2.26.5 of the JCT Design and Build Contract, clause 2.13.2 of the JCT Management Contract, clause 2.10.8.2 of the JCT Works Contract and Clause 60.1(16) of NEC3 Engineering and Construction Contract.

NEC3 Engineering and Construction Contract goes one stage further and ties in the employer's obligations to the programme itself, and excuses the employer's failure to carry out work "within the times shown on the accepted programme". Both NEC3 Engineering and Construction Contract and NEC3 Engineering and Construction Short Contract excuse delay caused by the employer's failure to "provide something which he is to provide by the date for providing it".

### *Delay in receiving information or instructions*

There are two aspects to the issue of whether and under what circumstances the contractor is entitled to relief from delay caused by it not receiving further information in good time.

> On the one hand there is the question of whether any further information, instructions, drawings, details or levels should be provided in relation to an agreed calendar date, or in relation to the date it is actually needed, or on a date it is expected to be needed. The second question is whether in order to render default an employer's risk, the contractor must make a specific request for such information and, if so, when such request must be made.

Throughout the pre-1998 versions of the JCT family of contracts it was provided that later information must be provided: "on a date which, having regard to the completion date, is neither unreasonably distant from nor unreasonably close to the date on which it was necessary for to receive it". In other words, on the date it is needed, in relation to an intent to complete by the completion date. The expression "having regard to the completion date" was considered in the *Glenlion* case. There, the contractor failed in its claim for disruption damages when the contract administrator did not provide the information when the contractor actually needed it in relation to a date for completion that was earlier than the completion date.

It was determined that the employer had no obligation to provide such information when it was *actually* needed if that need arose out of the contractor's acceleration of its programme. In that case the contractor's "*need*" arose at a time, which was not relative to the completion date, but in advance of the completion date because of the contractor's voluntary acceleration.

The other side of this coin is the question of what is the position if instead of being ahead of programme, the contractor is behind programme. If it has been agreed that information is to be provided on a date which had the programme been followed would have been timely but, because of a pre-existing contractor's delay to progress or an earlier employer's delay to progress is a date for provision of information that is well in advance of when it will then actually be needed, different questions are raised.

Whilst a delivery later than scheduled in relation to the schedule may or may not be an employer's risk event (depending upon the wording of the contract) in such circumstances, the late delivery in relation to the schedule cannot cause delay to progress (because at the time of delivery it is not yet needed) and if it does not cause delay to progress, logically, it cannot cause delay to completion.

The second point for consideration is whether any specific request must be made for such information. Generally, it is the contractor which has to carry out and complete the works and which is generally able to say when it will be necessary for it to place orders for goods or materials, or equipment or commence off-site manufacture of part of the work. For this reason, historically, the contractor's application has been required within a reasonable time of the information becoming necessary in order not to impede the progress of the works.

In *Merton* v. *Leach*, Vinelott J. considered that the purpose of the provision for an application from the contractor in writing at an appropriate date was:

- to spare the contract administrator from the requirement to furnish instructions too far in advance of the date when they were actually needed by the contractor as this would lead to unnecessary disruption of its work; and
- to ensure that the contract administrator would not be left with insufficient time to prepare them.

> It is an important consideration under many of the standard forms of contract considered, and one frequently overlooked by contractors and sub-contractors, is that they cannot just sit back and blame the contract administrator for delay in receiving information, expecting it to give them an EOT because they have not received necessary instructions in due time, unless (and it is an important "unless") they have specifically applied in writing for the instructions at an appropriate time.

The intention of restricting the timing of the applications for instructions is to assist the contract administrator and design team to plan their design work and order their priorities. There is in these forms a recognition that the contractor is in the best place to know when the information is likely to be needed and that the contract administrator is not expected to be able to provide "an instant drawing service".

The fact that some questions take time to research, time to price and to consider with the employer before instructions can be given is an important consideration. The fact that the contractor needs instructions by a particular date is itself not enough; the contractor needs to be able to ask for those instructions in time for the contract administrator to deal with its request.

On the other hand, since the 1998 versions of the JCT forms, JCT Standard Building Contract and the JCT Intermediate Building Contract (with the exception of the Minor Works Building Contract), the supply of further information has been dealt with quite differently from the way it was dealt with in the old editions and, in doing so, the JCT has adjusted, in the contractor's favour, the balance of risk of failure to produce further information at the appropriate time.

Under the 1998 and 2005 forms, there are two options for the provision of further information neither of which impose any obligation on the contractor to request it (at any time). The first possibility is that the contract administrator provides, as part of the contract documents, an Information Release Schedule (IRS) setting down exactly when every other piece of information, instructions, drawings, details or levels will be provided. Any failure to provide any of the information listed at the time set down in the IRS, irrespective of the contractor's need or actual progress on site, is deemed to be both an employer's time risk event and an employer's cost risk event. (See, for example, JCT98, clauses 25.4.6.1 and 26.2.1.1.)

If the contract administrator does not provide any of the information set down in the IRS (presumably in its entirety) or, in the event that there is a need for other information, instructions, drawings, details or levels, which are not referred to on the IRS (a contingency which, in practice, is probably inevitable) then the second limb of the new provisions cuts in. This second limb is perhaps the most pernicious change in the 1998 forms because no guidance notes have been provided to draw it to the attention of users and it effectively emasculates the force of Vinelott J.'s observations in Merton.

No longer does the obligation to provide such information arise conditional upon it being asked for in writing. In fact, the obligation to provide such information is no longer conditional upon the contractor asking for it at all, unless it is "reasonably practical to do so". Under the earlier forms, because of the requirement to request information in writing at a time "not to close to nor distant from" when it was needed, the risk of leaving it too late for the contract administrator to research, prepare and publish the further information requested was the contractor's. On the other hand, under the JCT Standard Building Contract and the JCT Intermediate Building Contract, the risk of delay caused because the contractor does not have information it has not asked for, or of delay caused by asking, at the last minute, for clarification or elaboration of information, instructions, drawings, details or levels or of any such information already given (as often happens in practice), now passes to the employer. The words "unless it is reasonably practical to do so" are weasel words. They have no effect in practice because the contractor, when in culpable delay, will never find it "reasonably practical" to give the contract administrator notice of its need so as to negate the possibility of extracting relief and compensation for its own default. If delay or disruption is caused by the contract administrator being unable to deduce the need or fulfil it instantaneously, the contractor is entitled to relief from damages for delay and compensation for loss and/or expense. (See, for example, JCT98, clauses 25.4.6.2 and 26.2.1.2.)

NEC3 Engineering and Construction Contract provides that it is both an employer's time and cost risk event if the employer:

- fails under clause 60.1(3) to provide something which he is to provide by the date for providing it; or
- under clause 60.1(6) the Project Manager or contract administrator does not reply to a communication from the contractor within the period required.

Clause 18.3(i) of PPC2000 refers to "a delay caused by a default or failure of the employer or any consultant . . . beyond any agreed time limit".

Clause 1.9 of FIDIC Building and Engineering (red book) contains express provisions to the effect that it is a employer's time and cost risk event if the contractor is delayed or disrupted as a result of "any necessary drawing or instruction is not issued to the contractor within a particular time, which shall be reasonable."

On the other hand, clause 35(3)(b) of the GC/Works/1 and GC/Works/1 Design and Construct forms specifically require the contractor, at monthly intervals, five days before each progress meeting, to set out in detail what further information, if any, it requires, and clause 35(4)(e) calls for the contract administrator to report, within seven days of the meeting, on how it intends to deal with the contractor's request.

### *Quality control*

Under this heading the effect of delay caused by the provision of samples is excused under clauses 3.5 and 11.5(e) of the ACA Building Contract and the delay in approving a contractor's quality system is excused under clauses 8(3) and 44(1)(b) of the ICE Design and Construct form. With the exception of GC/Works/1 and GC/works/1 Design and Construct, the standard forms generally identify as employer's time and cost risk events the effects of opening up or testing work which is not scheduled in the documents to be tested or opened up and which is later found to be satisfactory. This is phrased variously as: "additional testing of work found to be satisfactory" or "opening up of testing work found to be satisfactory" and "an ineffective search for defective work". In the latter case, clause 50 of the ICE Form (7th edition) does not expressly make provision for the time effects of an ineffective search for defective work. Clause 60.1(10) of the NEC3 Engineering and Construction Contract provides for an ineffective search for defective work to be both an employer's time and cost risk event. Clauses 36(4) and 50 of the ICE Form (7th edition) and clause 23(1) of the ICE Design and Construct form provide for compensation only for the additional testing of work found to be satisfactory. Clause 2.29.2.2 of JCT Standard Building Contract, clause 2.26.2.2 of the JCT Design and Build Contract, clause 2.13.2 of the JCT Management Contract, clause 2.10.5.3 of the JCT Works Contract and clause 60.1(11) of the NEC3 Engineering and Construction Contract and the NEC3 Short Contract and clauses 7.4 and 8.4(b) of the FIDIC Building and Engineering (red book), FIDIC Turnkey (silver book), FIDIC Plant Design and Build (yellow book) and clause 18.3(vii) of PPC2000 excuse delay caused by the opening up or testing of work found to be satisfactory. Clauses 9.2, 6.1(m) and 7.3 in the FIDIC Short Form (green book) also excuse delay caused where the contractor is prevented from carrying out tests and any additional tests on completion, boreholes or other exploratory and testing work.

There is also a strange provision in clause 3.13.2 of the 1998 version of the JCT Intermediate Building Contract (but not in any of the other JCT forms or the 2005 version of the same form) that purports to give to an adjudicator, arbitrator or the court (but not the contract administrator) power to extend the time for completion of the works, solely by reason of the contract administrator not withdrawing its instruction to open up and test work where a fault has been already found. The clause seems to bite if the contractor objects to compliance with the contract administrator's instruction to open up, stating its reasons in writing within 10 days of receipt of the instruction, and if, within seven days, the contract administrator does not in writing withdraw the instruction or modify the instruction to remove the contractor's objection. By way of contrast, clause 3.13.1 provides that if the contractor complies with the contract administrator's instruction and finds no defect then, by virtue of clause 2.4.6, if the instruction causes delay to completion the contractor is entitled to an EOT. However, under clause 13.3.2 not only is the question of delay to completion not a matter on which the contract administrator can decide but, irrespective of whether when carrying out the earlier investigation faults were found, or any further investigation is carried out, it seems that if the contractor objects, and in any subsequent adjudication, arbitration or court hearing the adjudicator, arbitrator or judge finds that the contract administrator behaved unreasonably in not withdrawing its instruction, then the adjudicator, arbitrator or judge may award the contractor more time to complete.

It seems odd that, if the work is found to be satisfactory, and the opening up caused delay to completion when opened up under clause 3.13.1, the contract administrator should be required to determine an appropriate EOT but not in the event that the contractor objects to the instruction. It appears that in the latter case, where the contractor objects to the instruction for further opening up, only the adjudicator, arbitrator or judge can determine an appropriate EOT and then the decision is based on whether the relevant tribunal finds the instruction to be fair and reasonable.

> Rationally, whether or not an EOT is granted should not depend upon whether an instruction was reasonable but, primarily, upon whether the opening up, the subject of the instruction, was actually carried out and, if so, whether it caused delay to completion. Entitlement to an EOT should then depend on whether the opening up showed the opening up to be unnecessary and, if so, caused delay to completion or, on the other hand, proved the work to be defective, or did not cause delay to completion.

### *Civil commotion*

Insofar as it is not expressly described as being included in the definition of *force majeure*, all forms except the ICE forms and NEC3 Engineering and Construction Short Contract expressly provide that the employer takes the risk of delay caused by riot, civil rebellion or insurrection. This matter is referred to in clauses 1(1)(d) and 36(2)(d) of GC/Works/1, clause 2.29.10 of JCT Standard Building Contract, clause 2.20.10 of the JCT Intermediate Building Contract, clause 2.26.9 of the JCT Design and Build Contract, clause 2.13.2 of the JCT Management Contract, clause 2.10.4 of the JCT Works Contract, clause 12.1.2 of the JCT Major Project Form, and Appendix 4, part 1, clause 19.1 and clause 18.3(viii) of PPC2000, clause 80.1 of NEC3 Engineering and Construction Contract, clauses 6.1(c) and 7.3 of the FIDIC Short Form (green book), clause 17.3(c) of the FIDIC Building and Engineering (red book), FIDIC Turnkey (silver book), FIDIC Plant design and Build (yellow book). In most forms, these are scheduled as insurable risks. In clause 20(2) of the ICE Form (7th edition) and the ICE Design and Construct form, there is provision only for financial compensation.

Similarly, insofar as it is not expressly described as being included in the definition of *force majeure*, the effect of strikes and lockouts is expressed as an employer's time risk event generally, but not under NEC3 Engineering and Construction Short Contract. Under clause 36(2)(c) of GC/Works/1 the employer only takes the risk of delay caused thereby provided the strike and/or lockout is outside the control of the contractor or its sub-contractors. Similar provisions are made in clause 18.3(ix) of PPC2000, clauses 80.1 and 60.1(14) of NEC3 Engineering and Construction Contract, clause 2.29.11 of JCT Standard Building Contract, clause 2.20.11 of the JCT Intermediate Building Contract, clause 2.26.13 of the JCT Design and Build Contract, clause 2.13.2 of the JCT Management Contract, clause 2.10.4 of the JCT Works Contract, and clauses 17.4 and 8.4(b) of the FIDIC forms which provide that the employer takes the risk of delay unless the riot or civil commotion is restricted to the contractor or its sub-contractors.

Again, insofar as it is not expressly described as being included in the definition of *force majeure*, the use or threat of terrorism is expressed as an employer's time risk event under clause 18.3(xiii) of PPC2000, clause 12.1.4 of the JCT Major Projects Form, clause 2.29.10 of the JCT Standard Building Contract, clause 2.20.10 of the JCT Intermediate Building Contract, clause 2.26.9 of the JCT Design and Build Contract, clause 2.13.2 of the JCT Management Contract, clause 2.10.15 of the JCT Works Contract, clauses 6.1(b) and 7.3 of the FIDIC Short Form (green book). Delay caused by the effects of war or hostilities are expressly excused in all the standard forms except the ICE forms, Government contracts, the Minor Works Forms and the JCT Intermediate Building Contract, and the JCT Management Contract and the Works Contract. Excusable delay for the effects of war is provided for in clause 11.5(c) of the ACA Building Contract, and clauses 6.1(b) and 7.3 of the FIDIC Short Form (green book).

Delay caused by "any unlawful, wanton or malicious act by a person or persons acting on behalf of or in connection with an unlawful association" is expressly at the employer's risk only under clause 22.2.3.5 of JCT98 although it is referred to in other forms in connection with work which is likely to be carried out in Northern Ireland, namely under clause 22.2.3.5 JCT With Contractor's Design Form, and clause 6.2 of the JCT Management Contract.

Clauses 1(1)(d) and 36(2)(d) of GC/Works/1 and clause 6.3.2 of the JCT Intermediate Form also provide that the employer takes the risk of delay caused by military and usurped power and an act of a foreign enemy, whether or not war has been declared.

### *Health and safety*

Safety provisions or the lack of them can give rise to excusable delay and this is expressly referred to in relation to the CDM regulations under clauses 71(3)(a), 13(3) and 44(1)(c) of the ICE Form (7th edition), clause 2.13.2 the JCT Management Contract and clause 2.10.17 of the JCT Works Contract. In clauses 40(1)(c) and 44(1)(c) of the ICE Form (7th edition) and the ICE Design and Construct form delay caused by instructions to postpone work due to safety conditions is also an excusable event.

The JCT 2005 forms do not treat this as a separate excusable event but identify that a breach of the CDM regulations by the employer is an employer's time risk event by the "impediment, prevention or default" clause, typically set out in the Standard Building Contract at clause 2.29.6.

### *Damage caused by carrying out the works*

Not unreasonably, the JCT forms generally provide that the contractor is responsible for financial loss arising out of damage caused by the carrying out of the works where it is due to its own negligence or breach of statutory duty. It may be required to insure against any such loss arising there from but there is no provision for relief from the effects of any delay caused thereby. However, delay caused by the "use or occupation of the site by the works" is an employer's time risk event under clauses 80.1 and 60.1(14) of NEC3 Engineering and Construction Contract. Delay resulting from "damage necessarily caused by the carrying out of the works" is excused under clauses 80.1 and 60.1(14) of NEC3 Engineering and Construction Contract. Finally, delay caused by a fault in the design of the works is expressly excused under clauses 80.1 and 60.1(14) NEC3 Engineering and Construction Contract, clauses 6.1(g) and 7.3 of the FIDIC Short Form (green book), and clauses 17.3(g), 17.4 and

8.4(b) of the FIDIC Building and Engineering (red book) and FIDIC Plant Design and Build (yellow book).

### *Catastrophes*

Essentially a catastrophe of any variety is a *force majeure*, and in some of the contracts the usual catastrophes are listed as being comprised in the definition *force majeure*. Catastrophes are generally those circumstances which are required to be insured either by the contractor, by the employer or by the parties jointly. Some of these risks, of course, are uninsurable. Intrinsically, so far as the contractor is concerned, the employer takes the risk of their occurrence, although for those uninsurable risks, should they occur, it is likely that the risk will be reimbursable under statutory provisions granting the licence to operate. Such risks generally include the likes of nuclear radiation or explosive nuclear assemblies and sonic or supersonic pressure waves. For extended discussion on the law relating to nuclear installations and damage caused thereby, see the judgment in the *Blue Circle* v. *MOD* case in which it was accepted that the reduction in value of property due to plutonium contamination of a nearby marsh was "damage to property" for the purposes of liability under the Nuclear Installations Act 1965.

> Catastrophes causing damage to the works, which are normally insurable, are such things as fire or explosion, storm, lightning, tempest, flood or earthquake, aircraft or other aerial devices or objects dropped therefrom, and bursting or overflowing of water tanks or pipes. They may also include such things as civil commotion, strike or lockout, acts of terrorism and so on.

In some contracts they will be referred to as the "specified perils", in others as "insured risks" and in others as "accepted risks" or "excepted risks" and in the new FIDIC forms and NEC3 Engineering and Construction Contract as "employer's risks". This can create a little confusion and it is prudent to read the relevant clause carefully. Generally, delay caused by these risks are at the contractor's risk under the government contracts, under the ICE forms they are not expressly referred to, but they are expressed to be at the employer's risk under the FIDIC, ACA, JCT and NEC forms. Unusually, NEC3 Engineering and Construction Short Contract provides that the contractor is to be excused delay caused by

"A loss of Plant and Materials or damage to the works, Plant and Materials which

- is not the fault or responsibility of the contractor or
- could not have been prevented by any reasonable action of the contractor"

but which are insured risks in the joint names of the contractor and the employer under clause 82.1, irrespective of whether the loss or damage is not the fault or responsibility of the contractor or could not have been prevented by any reasonable action of the contractor.

Uniquely, the effect of nationalisation or requisition or loss or destruction of or damage to any property by or under the order of any government is excused under clause 6.3.2 of the JCT Intermediate Form.

### *Fossils and antiquities*

There is one other discrete category of relief, the finding of antiquities or fossils. The effect of such finds is generally to suspend the carrying out of the works whilst the contract administrator gives instructions as to what should be done in regard to the exposure, restoration, or preservation of such antiquities or fossils. Whilst it can reasonably be construed that the discovery of unknown fossils or antiquities may well fall under the "unforeseeable physical conditions" clause there is separate express provision for financial compensation under the ICE and government contracts, relief for delay caused thereby is only provided for expressly in clause 18.3(ii) of PPC2000, clauses 2.13.2 and 3.27 of the JCT Management Contract coupled with clause 2.10.5.1 of the JCT Works Contract.

Rather confusingly, the 2005 series of JCT contracts deal with this matter in two completely different ways. Typically, clause 3.24 expressly provides that this is an employer's cost risk event but nothing is mentioned about time. To identify that it is also an employer's time risk event, reference first has to be made to clause 1.1 to identify that the "third party" referred to in the last sentence of clause 3.23 is defined as one of the "Employer's Persons", an "impediment, prevention, or default, whether by act or omission" by whom is an employer's time risk event under clause 2.29.6.

Clause 60.1(7) of the NEC3 Engineering and Construction Contract and clauses 4.24 and 8.4(b) of the FIDIC Building and Engineering (red book), FIDIC Turnkey (silver book) and FIDIC Plant Design and Build (yellow book) provide that such occurrences are both employer's time and cost risk events.

## STANDARD FORM PROVISIONS FOR PROGRAMMING

> Because it is only a delay to a completion date, which, if it is not met will render the contractor liable in liquidated and ascertained damages, that ranks for an EOT, it is of paramount importance to be able to distinguish between critical activities and those with float. Activities the timing of which is not planned to be critical to completion can shift in time without causing delay to completion and are thus unlikely to qualify for an EOT when delayed by an employer's time risk event.

However, as may be expected, there is no consistency of approach to the requirements for programming in the standard forms of building and civil engineering contracts. Some forms, such as the JCT Minor Works Building Contract do not require any programme from the contractor at all. Others, such as the JCT Standard Building Contract whilst requiring a programme, give no definition of its content or how it is to be prepared and monitored.

### *Programme required*

Clause 3.2 of the ACA Building Contract, whilst not referring to a contractor's programme, provides for a time schedule as a programme for the receipt by the contractor of the contract administrator's drawings and further information.

Clause 31.1 of the ICE Short Form and ECC Short Form whilst not requiring a programme under the contract conditions, makes provision for the specification for the way the programme is to be dealt with to be a contract condition if one is required in the works information. By virtue of clause 50.3 of NEC3 Engineering and Construction Contract and clause 50.7 of the ECC Short Form, in the event that the contractor does not comply with the contract requirements for the submission of the first programme, the employer may deduct 25 per cent retention of all valuations until it is submitted as specified.

It is significant that of all the standard forms considered, only 50 per cent refer to a programme at all and less than 30 per cent of those forms actually require the contractor to produce a construction programme for the works. GC/Works/1 Building and Civil Engineering Form, GC/Works/1 Design and Construct, FIDIC Short Form (green book), and ICE Short Form fudge the issue, and, whilst not actually requiring a programme to be prepared during the course of the works, give a specification of what the contract programme should include if, by the terms of the contract preliminaries, the contractor is required to prepare one.

None of the contract forms discussed here actually require the contractor to indicate the critical path, although clause 33(1) of GC/Works/1 Building and Civil Engineering Form and GC/Works/1 Design and Construct Form require the programme to indicate critical events and Clause 31.2 of the NEC3 Engineering and Construction Contract requires the programme to indicate float. Failure to require the programme to show the critical path to commence with and to state whether and when it changed seems a strange omission as it is principally by reference to the critical path, and changes in it, that the likely effect of delay to progress on the completion date can be identified.

The wording of these contract conditions does not prevent the contract administrator including specific requirements in the preambles or specification to the contract however as chapter 8 illustrates, this may not always be the most appropriate place to define the level of detail and type of programme required. Certainly, the planning, monitoring and record retrieval requirements should be reflective of the specific requirements for the project being undertaken but care is necessary when expanding upon provisions written into the contract conditions that in the process, conflicts and inconsistencies are avoided. Notwithstanding that there is the opportunity to do so, the sad fact is that in the majority of projects the contract administrator rarely particularises the requirements for the construction programme in sufficient detail or, with sufficient control to make sure that the specification is performed.

Bearing in mind that these are often used for major works and the JCT Major Project Construction Contract is said to be designed for that purpose alone, it is surprising that neither that nor the JCT Design and Build Contract require the contractor to prepare any programme at all. The only contract forms amongst those discussed that actually require a programme to be prepared are PPC2000, MF/1, IChemE Lump Sum (red book), JCT Standard Building Contract (although this is noted for optional deletion), the ICE Form (7th edition), ICE6DB, NEC3 Engineering and Construction Contract, FIDIC Building and Engineering (red book), and, unusually amongst the design and build forms, FIDIC Turnkey (silver book) and FIDIC Plant Design and Build (Yellow Book). In contrast, the PFE Change Management Supplements are far more prescriptive in the nature and detail of the construction programme required and the way it is to be used and, to that extent are similar to the approach taken by the U.S. government forms of contract.

### *Programme content*

GC/Works/1 Building and Civil Engineering Form deals with the requirements of programming at clause 33 and provides that the contractor should demonstrate on the programme:

"the sequence in which the contractor proposes to execute the works, details of any temporary work, method of work, labour and plant proposed to be employed, and events, which, in his opinion, are critical to satisfactory completion of the works; that the programme is achievable, conforms with the requirements of the contract, permits effective monitoring of progress and allows reasonable periods of time for the provision of information required from the employer; and that the programme is based on a period for the execution of the works to the date or dates for completion."

FIDIC Building and Engineering (red book) requires that the contractor should submit a detailed programme to the contract administrator including:

"(a) the order in which the contractor intends to carry out the works, including the anticipated timing of each stage of design (if any), contractor's documents, procurement, manufacture of plant, delivery to site, construction, erection and testing,

(b) each of these stages of work for each nominated sub-contractor . . .

(c) the sequence and timing of inspections and tests specified in the contract, and

(d) a supporting report which includes:

  (i) a general description of the methods which the contractor intends to adopt, and of the major stages, in the execution of the works, and

  (ii) details of the contractor's reasonable estimate of the number of each class of the contractor's personnel and of each type of the contractor's equipment, required on the site for each major stage."

Clause 8.3 of the FIDIC Turnkey (silver book) and FIDIC Plant Design and Build (yellow book) is similar and unusual amongst the design and build forms in requiring that the contractor should submit a detailed programme to the contract administrator including:

"(a) the order in which the contractor intends to carry out the works, including the anticipated timing of each stage of design, the contractor's documents, procurement, manufacture of plant, delivery to site, construction, erection and testing,

(b) the periods for reviews under clause 5.2 and for any other submissions, approvals and consents specified in the employer's Requirements,

(c) the sequence and timing of inspections and tests specified in the contract, and

(d) a supporting report which includes:

(i) a general description of the methods which the contractor intends to adopt, and of the major stages, in the execution of the works, and

(ii) details of the contractor's reasonable estimate of the number of each class of the contractor's personnel and of each type of the contractor's equipment, required on the site for each major stage."

FIDIC Building and Engineering (red book), FIDIC Turnkey (silver book) and FIDIC Plant Design and Build (yellow book) all require this programme to be submitted to the contract administrator within 28 days of receipt of the notice to proceed. Unless the contract administrator notifies the contractor within a further 21 days of its receipt that, in the contract administrator's opinion, the programme fails to conform to the contract requirements, the contractor is required to proceed in accordance with the submitted programme but "subject to his other obligations under the contract".

The provision that whatever is indicated in the contractor's programme is subservient to the contractor's other obligations under the contract is a normal provision in the standard forms whether or not the programme is subject to the agreement of, or acceptance by the contractor or the employer.

By way of contrast, NEC3 Engineering and Construction Contract gives an even fuller listing of what is required in the content of a construction programme. Clause 31 states:

"If a programme is not identified in the contract data, the contractor submits a first programme to the contract administrator for acceptance within the period stated in the contract data.

The contractor shows on each programme which he submits for acceptance:

- the starting date, access dates, key dates and completion date,
- for each operation, a method statement which identifies the equipment and other resources which the contractor plans to use,
- planned completion,
- the order and timing of:
  - the operations which the contractor plans to do to provide the works and
  - the work of the employer and others either as stated in the works information or as later agreed with them by the contractor
- the dates when the contractor plans to meet each condition stated for the key

dates and to complete work needed to allow the employer and others to do their work,

- provisions for:
  - float,
  - time risk allowances,
  - health and safety requirements, and
  - the procedures set out in this contract
- the dates when, in order to provide the works in accordance with his programme, the contractor will need:
  - access of a part of the Site if later than its access date
  - acceptances and
  - plant and materials and other things to be provided by the employer and
  - information from others
- for each operation, a statement of how the contractor plans to do the work identifying the principal equipment and other resources which he plans to use, and
- other information which the works information requires the contractor to show on a programme submitted for acceptance."

Because it comprises a list of activities priced by lump sum dividing the price for the totality of the work, the programme under NEC3 Engineering and Construction Contract is sometimes thought of as a replacement for the bill of quantities. It is, however, much more than that. In this form, the programme of activities should not only be the pricing document, but also a model of the intended sequence of works. It should obviously be based on all the activities required within easily identifiable works programmes.

If the contractor is to receive payment for off-site activities under NEC3 Engineering and Construction Contract, then activities that comprise off-site fabrication or those where the site work itself is only one of the cost/time components should be listed in the programme together with the constituent off-site parts. The NEC3 Engineering and Construction Contract Guide quotes, by way of example, structural steel, which may have a contractor design element, fabrication and site assembly.

Other than defined activities, which the contract may stipulate are to be included, the format and detail of the programme remain at the contractor's discretion. This offers the contractor an opportunity under NEC3 Engineering and Construction Contract to model cost in a way that ensures payment reflects actual expenditure, provided the work is executed as planned and to programme. Whilst this may reduce the risk associated with traditional valuation procedures, it certainly puts added pressure on the contractor to get its model activity durations right at the outset.

Although it does not dictate what is to be allowed for in the programme, by exclusion JCT Standard Building Contract does indicate what is not to be allowed for by the introduction of SMM7.

> In principle, unless SMM7 or similar provisions are incorporated by reference, it would appear that the contractor may be bound to include a time allowance in its programme for expenditure on contingencies and other provisional sums, no matter how badly they may be described.

On the other hand, the essence of rule 10 of SMM7 is that it specifically negates the obligation to include in the contract programme the time to execute work for which an element of cost is included in the contract sum, but for which the work is not described in detail. Under SMM7, the contractor is assumed to have made due allowance in its programme for the work involved in "defined provisional sums" so that the execution of work under this kind of provisional sum does not provide grounds for an EOT. On the other hand, if any of the information for such sums required by SMM7 rule 10.3 is not given in the contract bills then, irrespective of what it is called, the provisional sum amounts to an "undefined provisional sum". An instruction amounting to a variation must be given to expend an undefined provisional sum. Compliance with that instruction would then rank as a developer's time and cost risk event for which the contractor may be entitled to an EOT and the reimbursement of any loss and expense suffered as a result.

The developer's risk event regarding approximate quantities relates entirely to the effect of SMM7 rule 10.1. It is limited in effect to those items where the approximate quantities are not a reasonable forecast of the actual quantity of work required. If it is a reasonable forecast, no EOT can be required for the execution of the work covered by the approximate quantity.

These provisions are important because, in effect, they are the contractual provisions which dictate the content of the programme in terms of durations to be planned for activities comprised in approximate quantities and defined provisional sums. The execution of work comprised in an undefined provisional sum (even if described in the bills under the heading of "defined provisional sums") will entitle the contractor to relief from damages and to compensation for what may be the effect of change.

### *The programme as a contract document*

The contract programme is not a contract document under most of the standard forms including MF/1, IChemE Lump Sum (red book), the JCT, ICE, FIDIC and ACA conditions. On the other hand, incorporation of the programme within the contract is an express option in GC/Works/1 Building and Civil Engineering Form, GC/Works/1 Design and Construct Form and NEC3 Engineering and Construction Contract.

The programme under clause 38 of GC/Works/1 and GC/Works/1 Building and Civil Engineering Form must model sequence, timing, resources and critical events. It forms an integral part of the reporting process and the contractor must proceed with the works in accordance with the programme. These forms define the programme which the contractor is bound to follow as that which was "submitted prior to the acceptance of tender and agreed by the employer at that time" and thus imply that the programme is one of the contract documents with which the contractor and the employer are bound to conform.

In so far as the programme can be construed as a contract document, it appears that:

- the contractor is bound to start and finish every activity on the dates indicated on the programme. If it were not to do so it would be in breach of contract; and
- the employer (or the contract administrator as its agent) is bound to facilitate the contractor in carrying out the work in accordance with the programme. In particular, it must provide every piece of information in good time in order that the contractor is not prevented from carrying out its programmed obligations. Similarly, a failure to do so would be a breach of contract.

The effect of a breach of these obligations, which are distinct from the obligation to complete by the completion date leaves it open to the innocent party to terminate the contract. Whilst it will seldom be in the employer's interest to do so, simply because in most cases the employer is more interested in having the project finished if it is at all possible, where for commercial reasons the liquidated damages for non-completion have been set at a level below that which fairly represents the employer's likely losses, proceeding for actual damages for the breach of duty in failing to comply with the programme or, as in *Masons* v. *King* a failure to comply with instructions to accelerate may represent a better prospect of recovery than a late completion with recovery of depleted LADs but to obtain such relief, particular care must be taken in the drafting of the contract clauses.

### *Submission and acceptance*

Apart from the requirement to indicate critical activities and float, there is no indication in any of the standard forms as to how the programme is to be produced or in what form. Clause 2.9.1.2 of the JCT Standard Building Contract requires the contractor to submit its master programme "so soon as is possible after the execution of this contract". FIDIC Building and Engineering (red book), and FIDIC Plant Design and Build (yellow book) require the programme to be submitted to the contract administrator within 28 days of receipt of the notice to proceed and FIDIC Turnkey (silver book) provide that the programme be submitted within 28 days of the commencement date. The ICE Form (7th edition) requires the programme to be submitted within 21 days of the award of the contract. NEC3 Engineering and Construction Contract, on the other hand, more sensibly provides for a period within which the programme is to be submitted to be inserted in the contract data. In contrast, GC/Works/1 Building and Civil Engineering Form and GC/Works/1

Design and Construct provide no period for submission but define the programme which the contractor is bound to follow as that which was "submitted prior to the acceptance of tender and agreed by the employer at that time".

Apart from the fact that a detailed programme to be submitted with a tender tends to be based on nothing better than assumptions in regard to the contractor's performance on partially specified work, it is often of little value and can be unnecessarily expensive. The contractor should not be required to have a full working master programme available on the first day of the contract. A more pragmatic approach and one that can be both useful and informative is described in Chapter 8 as to require the contractor to complete its programming on different levels: tender programme, master programme and short-term-look-ahead, programme etc. This is the formula adopted by the Change Management Supplements.

Normally the contractor should be expected to submit, within a short period after appointment, an as-planned programme that covers in detail the first two to three months of a project and include a master programme of the remaining work. Within the first few months, the contractor can discuss the requirements of the plan with its sub-contractors and suppliers and develop its as-planed programme for the remainder for submission.

### *Monitoring updating and revision*

The standard forms of contract are diverse in their requirements for programme monitoring and revision. Under JCT Standard Building Contract, the contractor is required to reissue the programme with any amendments or revisions which the contractor decides to make only if an EOT is awarded. Whilst the contractor is required to notify the contract administrator of any cause of delay to the progress of the works, it appears that the contractor is not required to update its programme to demonstrate those changes of timing; the contractor is only required to amend or revise its master programme to meet the grant of an EOT. The editors of *Walker-Smith* say in reference to the 1998 form that whilst it may seem restrictive the intention is that the master programme is related to the contract period and only if that period is extended, by the fixing of a later completion date is an amendment or revision of the master programme required. However, that ignores its importance in regard to effective management of the works and the calculation of an appropriate extension of time.

> If there is not an as-planned updated programme that demonstrates the current state of the work and the contractor's current intentions, how, when a developer's time risk event has occurred, is the contract administrator supposed to ascertain that it has impacted the critical path the contractor is following and hence is likely to cause delay to completion? Delays to progress can shift activities, which were previously in float, to the critical path and *vice versa*.

## Provision of information

Consider also delays caused by the contract administrator's failure to provide drawings, instructions and details. In some forms of contract, if these delays are to constitute a developer's time risk event and thus to be excusable, by definition, the information must be requested at a time not too distant from, nor too close to the time at which the contractor actually needs it, not to the time the contractor might reasonably be expected to need it if everything went to plan. Of course, the contractor's actual need in this must usually be considered in light of the actual progress, not the theoretical progress the contractor might have made if it had been proceeding efficiently. Under the JCT forms published since 1998 the contractor's obligation has been to give due warning of its need for further information or instructions has been modified to an obligation to request the necessary information only if the contractor can reasonably anticipate that it will need it and it is reasonably practical to do so. However, the effect, if any, of the lateness (or otherwise) of delivery to the contractor of further information, drawings and details can only be calculated by reference to the state of the work at the time the information drawings or details are issued. Thus, the absence of an obligation to incorporate the effects of the substance of notices of delay to progress in an updated master programme seems to be a serious omission from JCT forms, an omission which is probably at the root of the difficulties some commentators appear to find with the status of the contractor's programme in this form of contract.

In order to resolve this inconsistency, some editing of the master programme requirements in JCT forms should be made. The programme requirements should specify not only the reflection of the effect of EOTs but also the effects of every prediction of, and the occurrence of, every occasion of interruption to or variation of the planned progress of the work. The Change Management Supplements should provide some useful guidance as to what might reasonably be required in this regard.

## Culpable delay

The contractor is also required to update its programme when it is inconsistent with its programme or when instructed to do so under clause 6.7 of PPC2000, and in clause 8.3 of each of FIDIC Building and Engineering (red book), FIDIC Turnkey (silver book), FIDIC Plant Design and Build (yellow book). More proactively, clause 14(4) of the ICE Form (7th edition) provides for the contractor to be required to update the programme at any time the actual progress does not conform with the accepted programme.

Under clause 32 of the NEC3 Engineering and Construction Contract, the contractor can revise its programme at any time but it must do so in accordance with the periods set down in the contract data and whenever instructed to do so and, if instructed to do so, it must submit its revised programme within the period for reply. This form calls on the contractor to revise and reissue its as-planned programme to show:

- the actual progress achieved on each operation;
- the effect of progress upon the timing of the remaining work;
- the effect of implemented compensation events;
- the effect of notified early-warning matters;
- the contractor's proposals for dealing with any delays;
- the contractor's proposals for correcting notified defects; and
- any other changes the contractor proposes to make to the accepted programme.

NEC3 Engineering and Construction Contract also requires the contractor to show on each revised programme:

- the actual progress achieved on each operation and its effect upon the timing of the remaining work;
- the effect of implemented compensation events and of notified early-warning matters; and
- how the contractor plans to deal with any delays and to correct notified defects and any other changes which it proposes to make to the programme.

Clause 4.3 of the ICE Short Form, also provides that the contractor should update the programme if, when behind programme, it is instructed by the contract administrator to do so. Clause 35 of the UK government contracts GC/Works/1 Building and Civil Engineering Form, and GC/Works/1 Design and Construct make specific reference to programme meetings at which the contractor is required to report on progress in relation to the project and to formulate proposals for accommodating any change in the programme. Under clause 35, the contractor is required to submit to the employer, five days before each progress meeting, a written report which, amongst other things, is required to:

- describe the progress of the works by reference to the programme and relevant instructions;
- explain any new circumstances arising since any previous progress meeting which in his opinion have delayed or may delay completion of the works or a section; and
- set out any reprogramming proposals to ensure the completion of the works or any section will be achieved by the relevant date for completion.

These forms however, do not require the contractor to report on or revise its programme for delays to progress which are not likely to affect completion. This seems to be a serious omission. Apart from problems of float and criticality, it is difficult, if not impossible, to calculate with any precision the damage which flows from disruption to progress if it cannot be demonstrated when it occurred and the effect it had on other activities.

| |
|---|
| Whether or not the contractor is obliged to update its programme, it will be in its interests to do so and to record all changes in the update, whether or not they are compensable and/or excusable. |

Finally, and perhaps rather unhelpfully, clause 14.4 of MF/1 states that "the contractor shall not without the (contract administrator's) consent make any material alteration to the approved programme".

## Redress in default

Whilst it is unusual to find detailed procedures for the monitoring and updating of programme information set down in a building contract, it is common for the methodology of any monitoring and updating to be set down in a specification. However, the degree to which attention is paid to monitoring and updating will depend, to a great extent, on what sanctions are available to the employer or the contract administrator in the event that the contract requirements for performance monitoring and updating are not followed.

## Early warning

In some contract forms, there are provisions for the contractor to identify in advance the prospective effect on time and money of proposed change and to enter into a collateral contract to accommodate the effects of the change. In such circumstances the ability to monitor and update the as-planned programme at regular intervals for the purposes of estimating the effects of a variation in progress is vital. Without such monitoring and updating the degree of accuracy with which the effects of such proposed change can be gauged for the purpose of collateral agreements will be minimal. Similarly, it is only by keeping the programme up to date that it is possible to record the effect of the collateral agreement on the programme.

Under clause 61.1 of NEC3 Engineering and Construction Contract and clause 61.2 of the ECC Short Form, for example, the contractor is required to provide an estimate of both the cost and time effect of each compensation event. The contract administrator may accept or negotiate on the estimate. Failure by the contractor to submit the estimate entitles the contract administrator to assess the compensation event. It is thus in the contractor's interest to provide "early warning" of the event as failure to do so permits the contract administrator to make due allowance in its assessment for the saving that could have been achieved had the contractor complied with the early warning requirement. Upon agreement or assessment of the event, the programme is then updated to take account of the likely effect of the change.

## THE POWER TO VARY THE WORKS

> The starting point in consideration of whether there is a change or variation the consequences of which are the responsibility of the employer is the necessary and implicit work which the contractor is required to do under the contract and the basis upon which that work be varied.

The standard forms deal with the contractor's obligations in different ways. Clause 20.1 of NEC3 Engineering and Construction Contract and ECC Short Form, for example, state rather enigmatically, that: "the contractor provides the works in accordance with the works information" and in so far as design responsibility goes, Clause 21.1 of NEC3 Engineering and Construction Contract states "the contractor designs the parts of the works which the works information states he is to design". Although there are various references in the form as to whether certain acts or omissions are implied changes in the works information, there appears to be no express limitation upon what changes to the works information can be imposed on the contractor.

### *Definition of variation*

Clause 15.2 of PPC2000, which requires only that the contractor should carry out and complete the works in accordance with the partnering documents within the contract period defines "change" rather circulatory as "a change in all or any part of the project by way of addition, omission or variation of any kind or by way of expenditure of a provisional sum identified in the price Framework". Clause 27.1 of MF/1 states simply that a variation is "any alteration of the works whether by way of addition, modification or omission".

Under clause 16.1 of IChemE Lump Sum (red book), a variation is defined as "any alteration to the plant, method of working, programme of work or to the type or extent of the works, which is an amendment, omission or addition thereto (other than an amendment, omission or addition which is necessary for the plant to comply with the specification)".

Clause 16 provides for the contract administrator to issue instructions for variations which, subject to conditions, the contractor is bound to follow but then goes on in clause 16.7 to provide that the contractor may object to any variation ordered or proposed upon the ground that compliance therewith would:

- when combined with all variations previously ordered, increase or decrease the contract price by more than 25 per cent;
- in the case of a variation order issued after the date of (practical completion) for all or part of the works, increase the contract price by more than 5 per cent;

- require the contractor to act in breach of any enforceable undertaking or agreement with a third party;
- cause the contractor to infringe any legal obligation, patent, registered design, design right, copyright or other protected right of any third party; or
- require the contractor to do work or to exercise skills which are not of the kind the contractor undertakes in the ordinary course of his business, unless the variation order specifies that the work shall be performed or those skills exercised by a (nominated) sub-contractor.

Similarly, clause 4.1 of FIDIC Building and Engineering (red book) require that the contractor should be responsible for

"... the adequacy, stability and safety of all Site operations and of all methods of construction. Except to the extent specified in the contract the contractor shall be responsible for all contractor's documents, temporary works, and such design of each item of plant and materials as is required for the item to be in accordance with the contract ..."

but then goes on to expressly exclude design of the works, stating that the contractor

"... shall not otherwise be responsible for the design or specification of the permanent works".

In these forms a variation is defined as "any change to the works, which is instructed or approved as a variation under clause 13". Amongst other things, clause 13 states:

"Each variation may include:

- changes to the quantities of any item of work included in the contract (however, such changes do not necessarily constitute a variation),
- changes to the quality and other characteristics of any item of work,
- changes to the levels, positions and/or dimensions of any part of the Works,
- omission of any work unless it is to be carried out by others,
- any additional work, plant, materials or services necessary for the permanent works, including any associated tests on completion, boreholes and other testing and exploratory work, or
- changes to the sequence or timing of the execution of the works."

As this is expressed permissively rather than exclusory, it is unclear whether the contractor is bound to execute a variation that does not include one of the above.

The ICE Form (7th edition), at clause 8.1, simply states that subject to the provisions of the contract the contractor shall:

"(a) construct and complete the works and

(b) provide all labour materials contractor's equipment temporary works transport to and from and in or about the site and everything whether of a temporary or permanent nature required in and for such construction and completion so far as the necessity for providing the same is specified in or reasonably to be inferred from the contract."

But then, as with the FIDIC forms, they go on to clarify what the contractor is not required to do and specifically, exclude design responsibility for anything other than its own design of temporary works stating:

"the contractor shall not be responsible for the design or specification of the permanent works or any part thereof (except as may be expressly provided in the contract) or of any temporary works designed by the contract administrator. The contractor shall exercise all reasonable skill care and diligence in designing any part of the permanent works for which he is responsible.

The contractor shall take full responsibility for the adequacy stability and safety of all site operations and methods of construction."

The ICE Form (7th edition) also deals with the issuance of instructions for change in a form which does not appear on its face to restrict the contract administrator's powers. Clause 51 states that the contract administrator must order a variation to any part of the works that is in his opinion necessary for the completion of the works and "may order any variation that for any other reason shall in his opinion be desirable for the completion and/or improved functioning of the works".

Without limitation, clause 51(1) of the ICE Form (7th edition) say that no variation shall vitiate the contract and that variations may include:

"additions, omissions, substitutions, alterations, changes in quality, form, character, kind, position, dimension, level, or line and changes in any specified sequence, method, or timing of construction required by the contract and may be ordered during the defects corrections period."

Clause 5.1 of the JCT Standard Building Contract defines a variation as:

".1 the alteration or modification of the design or quality or quantity of the works including

- The addition, omission or substitution of any work,
- the alteration of the kind or standard of any materials or goods to be used in the works,
- the removal from the site of any work executed or materials or goods brought thereon by the contractor for the purposes of the works other than work materials or goods which are not in accordance with this contract;

.2 the imposition by the employer of any obligations or restrictions in regard to the matters set out in this clause 5.1.2 or the addition to or alteration or omission of any such obligations or restrictions so imposed or imposed by the employer in the contract bills or in the employer's requirements in regard to:

- access to the site or use of any specific parts of the site;
- limitations of working space;
- limitations of working hours;
- the execution or completion of the work in any specific order."

Clause 1 of the ACA Building Contract, with slightly more detail, specify the contractor's obligations in relation not only to "contract documents", but also to bills of quantity.

"In consideration of the payments to be made by the employer to the contractor under this agreement, the contractor shall execute and complete the works in strict accordance with the contract documents and shall comply with and adhere strictly to the (contract administrator's) instructions issued under this agreement.

Without prejudice to any express or implied warranties or conditions, the contractor shall exercise in the performance of his obligations under this agreement all the skill, care and diligence to be expected of a properly qualified and competent contractor experienced in carrying out work of a similar scope, nature and size to the works . . ."

The ACA forms do not use the words "change" or "variation" and in the ACA Building Contract the requirement at clause 8(1)(e) is expressed slightly differently as:

"(e) the alteration or modification of design, quality or quantity of the works, including the addition, substitution, omission of any work, alteration of kinds and standards, or the removal of any materials or goods from site;"

Clause 18 of GC/Works/1 Building and Civil Engineering Form also makes provision for compliance with contract bills which are subject to re-measurement. The obligation in the 1998 version is not identical but substantially the same as that in the previous edition which, at clause 31, provides that the contractor shall execute the Works:

"(a) with diligence,
(b) in accordance with the programme,
(c) with all proper skill and care, and
(d) in a workmanlike manner.
(2) the contractor shall use the skill and care of an experienced and competent contractor to ensure that:
(a) the Works,
(b) any things for incorporation, whether or not the contractor is required to choose or select any of them, are of good quality for their intended purpose, and conform to the requirements of the specification, the bills of quantities and the drawings."

A Variation instruction under GC/works1/98 is defined under clause 40(2) as "any instruction which makes any alteration or addition to, or omission from, the works or any change in the design, quality or quantity of the works" where the works is rather circulatory defined as including "all modified or additional works to be executed under the contract." However, the contract administrator's power to issue instructions is very wide stating that instructions may be given in relation to all or any of the following matters:

- variation or modification of all or any of the specification, drawings or BOQ, or the design, quality or quantity of the works;
- any discrepancy in or between the specification, drawings and BOQ;
- removal from the site of any things for incorporation and their substitution with any other things;
- removal and/or re-execution of any work executed by C;
- order of execution of the works or any part of them;
- hours of working and the extent of overtime or night work to be adopted;

- suspension of the execution of the works or any part of them;
- replacement of any person employed in connection with the contract;
- opening up for inspection of any work covered up;
- amending and making good of any defects;
- cost savings in relation to acceleration;
- execution of any emergency work;
- use or disposal of material obtained from excavations, demolition or dismantling on the site;
- actions to be taken following discovery of fossils, antiquities or objects of interest or value;
- measures to avoid nuisance or pollution;
- quality control and the contractor's accreditation in regard to quality; and
- any other matter which the contract administrator considers necessary or expedient.

Under clause 5.1 of the JCT Design and Build Contract, change is defined as:

".1 A change in the employer's requirements which makes necessary the alteration or modification of the design, quality or quantity of the works, otherwise than such as may be reasonably necessary for the purposes of rectification (of defects) including

.1 the addition, omission or substitution of any work;

.2 the alteration of the kind or standard of any of the materials or goods to be used in the Works;

.3 the removal from the site of any work executed or materials or goods brought thereon by the contractor for the purposes of the works other than work materials or goods which are not in accordance with this contract;

.2 the imposition by the employer of any obligations or restrictions in regard to the matters set out in this clause 5.1.2 or the addition to or alteration or omission of any such obligations or restrictions so imposed or imposed by the employer in the employer's requirements in regard to:

.1 access to the site or use of any specific parts of the site,

.2 limitations of working space,

.3 limitations of working hours, or

.4 the execution or completion of the work in any specific order."

FIDIC Turnkey (silver book), makes reference to fitness for purpose and the developer's requirements stating:

"the contractor shall design, execute and complete the works in accordance with the contract, and shall remedy any defects in the works. When completed, the works shall be fit for the purposes for which the works are intended as defined in the contract.

The contractor shall provide the plant and the contractor's documents specified in the contract, and all the contractor's personnel, goods, consumables and other things and services, whether of a temporary or permanent nature, required in and for this design, execution, completion and remedying of defects.

The works shall include any work which is necessary to satisfy the employer's requirements, or is implied by the contract, and all works which (although not mentioned in the contract) are necessary for stability or for the completion, or safe and proper operation, of the works."

Clause 4.1 of FIDIC Plant Design and Build (yellow book) contains similar obligations but in the third paragraph brings in the contractor's proposals and schedules, stating that:

"The works shall include any work which is necessary to satisfy the employer's requirements, the contractor's Proposals and Schedules or is implied by the contract, and all works which (although not mentioned in the contract) are necessary for stability or for the completion, or safe and proper operation, of the Works."

In these two forms, variation is expressed as "any change to the employer's requirements or the works, which is instructed or approved as a variation under clause 13". Clause 13 of the forms contains no other restriction on scope of variation. It would thus appear that in these forms a variation is anything the employer wants it to be, without any contractual limitation.

Under clause 39.2 of the JCT Major Projects Form, "change" is defined as

"1. any alteration in the requirements and/or proposals that gives rise to an alteration in the design, quality or quantity of anything that is required to be executed in accordance with the contract; or
2. any alteration by the employer of any restriction or obligation set out in the requirements and/or proposals as to the manner in which the contractor is to execute the project, or the imposition of additional restrictions or obligations; or
3. any matter that the contract requires to be treated as giving rise to a change. Provided always that the alteration or matter referred to above is not required as a result of any negligence or default on the part of the contractor"

and the contractor's obligations are stated simply to be to "execute and complete the project in accordance with the contract, including the completion of the design, the specification or selection of materials and the execution of the construction works".

## BIBLIOGRAPHY

ACA Building Contract
NEC3 Engineering and Construction Contract 2005
FIDIC Building and Engineering (red book);
FIDIC Plant Design and Build (yellow book)
FIDIC Short Form (green book).
FIDIC Turnkey (silver book).
GC/Works/1 Building and Civil Engineering Form.
GC/Works/1 Design and Construct Form.
ICE Design and Construct Form
ICE Form (7th edition).
ICE Short Form.
IChemE Lump Sum (red book)
JCT Intermediate Building Contract (2005).
JCT Intermediate Form (1998)
JCT Major Projects Form (2003)

JCT Management Contract (1998)
JCT Works Contract (1998)
JCT Minor Works Building Contract (2005).
JCT Design and Build Contract (2005)
JCT Standard Building Contract (2005).
JCT Standard Form of Building Contract (1998)
JCT NSC/4 contract for nominated sub-contractors
MF/1
PPC2000
*Walker-Smith and Close on the Standard Forms of Building* contract (updated 1979, Charles Knight).
McGowan, Paul H., R. Malcolm, W. Horner, Denise Jones, and Peter A. Thompson, *Allocation and Evaluation of Risk in Construction contracts* (1992, Chartered Institute of Building). Occasional Paper No. 52 of The Chartered Institute of Building.
U.S. Army Corps of Engineers, "Section 01320A—Project Schedule", *Unified Facilities Guide Specifications*, (May 2002).
Housing Grants, Construction and Regeneration Act 1996 (HGCRA)

## Cases

*Blue Circle Industries* v. *Ministry of Defence* [1998] 3 All E.R. 385 (C.A.)
*Boskalis Westminster Construction Ltd* v. *Liverpool City Council* (1983) 24 B.L.R. 83
*Glenlion Construction Ltd* v. *The Guinness Trust* (1988) 39 B.L.R. 89
*Hackney Borough Council* v. *Doré* [1922] 1 K.B. 431
*Henry Boot Construction Ltd* v. *Central Lancashire New Town Development Corporation* (1980) 15 B.L.R. 1.
*Humber Oil Terminals Trustee Ltd* v. *Harbour and General works (Stevin) Ltd* (1991) 7 Const. L.J. 333.
*J. Jarvis & Sons Ltd* v. *Westminster Corporation* [1970] 1 W.L.R. 637.
*John Barker Construction Ltd* v. *London Portman Hotel Ltd* (1996) 83 B.L.R. 31
*John Mowlem & Company plc* v. *Eagle Star Insurance Co. Ltd* (1992) 62 B.L.R. 126
*Lebeaupin* v. *Crispin* [1920] 2 K.B. 714
*London Borough of Merton* v. *Stanley Hugh Leach Ltd* (1985) 32 B.L.R. 68
*Masons* v. *W.D. King and Ano.* [2003] EWHC 3124 TCC
*Matsoukis* v. *Priestman & Co*, [1915] 1 K.B. 681
*Peak Construction (Liverpool) Ltd* v. *McKinney Foundations Ltd* (1970) 1 B.L.R. 114 (C.A.)
*Perini Pacific Ltd* v. *Great Vancouver Sewerage and Drainage District* (1966) 57 the D.L.R. (2d) 307
*Rotherham Metropolitan Borough Council* v. *Frank Haslam and Co.* (1996) 12 Const. L.J. 333

*Scott Lithgow Ltd* v. *Secretary of State for Defence* (1989) 45 B.L.R. 6
*Skanska Construction UK Ltd* v. *Egger (Barony) Ltd.* [2002] EWCA Civ 1914
*The Canadian Red Cross Society* v. *WN Developments (Ottawa) Ltd and McLean & McPhadyen Ontario Supreme Court* (1983) 1–CLD–02–09
*Wells* v. *Army and Navy Co-operative Society* (1903) Construction Law Year Book Vol. 4 65

### Further Reading

Capper, Philip, "Overview of Risk in Construction" in *Risk Management and Procurement in Construction*, edited by John Uff Q.C and Martin Odams (1995, Centre of Construction Law and Management, King's College, London).

Abrahamson, M. W., *Engineering Law and the ICE Contracts* (4th edn, 1985).

Uff, John, Q.C. "*Standard Contract Terms and the Common Law*" (1993) 9 Const. L.J. 108.

## SELF-TEST QUESTIONS

1. **What forms require the contractor to design the works?**
2. **What is the standard of care in a design and build contract?**
3. **Which Forms of contract impose the standard of fitness for purpose?**
4. **Which forms of contract gather together, in a single clause, the employer's time risk events?**
5. **In which form of contract is the contractor entitled to an EOT only if either the contract administrator thinks that an employers act omission is likely to cause delay to completion or the contractor proves that it actually has caused delay to completion?**
6. **Which forms of contract do not expressly provide for an EOT for delay caused by suspension of the works when the contractor has suspended progress as a result of the employer failing to pay promptly?**
7. **Which forms make express provision for nominated sub-contractors?**

8. **What is the effect of the contractor accepting a nomination of a subcontractor under a form which has no provision for nomination?**
9. **In which forms of contract is a delay by a nominated subcontractor at the contractor's risk?**
10. **What is the effect of an Information Request Schedule issued by the contractor under JCT Standard Building Contract?**
11. **Which form of contract provides for an adjudicator, arbitrator or the court to grant an EOT but not the contract administrator?**
12. **In which forms of contract is the contractor to be compensated for loss and expense arising out of the discovery of historical artefacts?**
13. **In which forms of contract is the employer provided with sanctions for the contractor's failure to provide a programme?**
14. **Under what forms of contract is the programme a contract document?**
15. **Under which form of contract can the contract administrator not instruct variations that cause the contract value to increase by more than 25%?**
16. **In which forms is there no express contractual limit on the scope of a variation?**

CHAPTER 6

# POWERS AND DUTIES OF THE EMPLOYER AND CONTRACTOR—PART I

Nick Carnell

## INTRODUCTION

This chapter and the next chapter are intended to look at how some of the most commonly encountered features of any project are dealt with under Standard Form Building Contracts. It will be apparent after reading this book that different standard forms deal with these concepts in different ways. In part this is a matter of drafting. However, and more importantly, it is a question of allocation of risk. A contract, after all, is no more than a mechanism for allocating the risks which will be encountered by the parties during the course of the project. Thus it will become apparent that there is no right way of dealing with any particular issue and it is up to the parties to determine a means of dealing with matters which best suits the requirements of the particular project.

A side effect of this is that while considerable criticism has been levelled at the drafting of Standard Forms of Building Contract (see, for example, *Deck Construction (Liverpool) Limited* v. *McKinney Foundations Limited* (1970) All E.R. 114), the reality is that in many instances the problems which parties seek to blame on the way in which matters are dealt with under a particular form of contract are actually attributable to their own failure to properly understand how particular risks are allocated between those contracts.

## COMMENCEMENT, TRANSFER OF POSSESSION AND SITE ACCESS

The concepts of commencement, possession and site access are interlinked. Clause 23.1.1 of JCT 98 illustrates this:

"On the date for Possession, possession of the site shall be given to the Contractor who shall thereupon begin the Works and regularly and diligently proceed with the same and shall complete the same on or before the Completion Date."

The Date for Possession is inserted in Appendix 1.

It will be noted from this that if the Standard Form has not been amended to incorporate the requirements of the PFE Change Management Supplement or an equivalent provision regulating the sequencing of the works, and the management of change, the contractor is entitled to carry out the works in any order he chooses, provided completion is achieved by the completion date.[1] The contractor is entitled to complete the works prior to the completion date if he chooses, but cannot be required by the employer to complete prior to the completion date, nor can the contractor require the employer to permit him to complete prior to the completion date—see *Glenlion Construction* v. *The Guinness Trust* (1987) 39 B.L.R. 89.

This is to be contrasted with clause 33.1 of the NEC, which provides that possession will be given by the later of the possession dates or the date for possession shown in the *accepted programme*.

None of the standard forms define what is meant legally by possession. The expression "possession" was considered in *Whittal Builders* v. *Chester le Street DC* (1987) 40 B.L.R. 82, where it was held that under the 1963 form the expression meant possession of the whole site and that in giving piecemeal possession, the employer was in breach of contract. The proper view, therefore, is that possession means that the contractor has an exclusive licence to occupy the site for the duration of the works.

This view is supported by the provisions of clauses 20 to 22 and 23.3.1 of JCT 98 (and the equivalent provisions in other standard forms) which impose on the contractor the obligation to insure the works against the risk of, respectively, injury to persons or property on or adjacent to the works and damage to the property comprising the works and to maintain that insurance up to and including the date of practical completion. This is consistent with the notion that the contractor is responsible for the works and for mishaps which occur while he exercises that control. The last part of clause 23.3.1 provides that the subject to the provisions of clause 18 (partial possession) the employer shall not be entitled to take possession of any part of the site until practical completion.

By clause 23.1.2 of JCT 98, where this clause is stated in the Appendix as applying, the employer is permitted to postpone the date for possession by a period of up to six weeks. Where this clause applies, its effect will be that the contractor is entitled to an extension of time under clauses 25.3 and 25.4.13 and to loss and expense under clause 26.1. It does not disentitle the employer from recovering liquidated and ascertained damages. Where it does not apply the employer will not be entitled to recover liquidated and ascertained damages, and the contractor will of course be entitled to an extension of time under clause 25.4.5.1 and loss and expense under clause 26.2.5. These provisions, which are concerned with granting possession of the site for the purpose of commencing and carrying out the works, should not be confused with the

1. It is also the case—and this will be considered elsewhere—that the unamended standard form does not give rise to an entitlement to carry out the works in particular order, and that hence while an act by the employer may prevent the contractor from carrying out the works in a particular order, unless it gives rise to disruption or causes the works to be delayed beyond the contractual completion date, it does not—of itself—give rise to any entitlement on the part of the contractor.

provisions in clauses 25.4.12 and 26.2.6 which provide extensions of time and loss and expense where the employer fails to grant access to the site.

Clause 23.3.2 allows the employer with consent of the contractor to use or occupy the site either for the storage of materials "or otherwise" provided that the consent of insurers has been obtained for such use or occupation. This is a surprisingly little used provision, and indeed, the Appendix provides an option to delete this clause, which on its face might be used to overcome the problems which can occur where prior to practical completion, the employer wishes to make use of the works.[2]

Clause 28.1 of NEC provides that the contractor shall grant access to the project manager, the supervisor and others notified to him by the project manager. The equivalent provision in JCT 98 is found in clause 11 which provides that the architect

> " . . . shall at all reasonable times have access to the works and to the workshops where work is being prepared for this contract . . . "

By clause 12 the employer is permitted to appoint a clerk of works whose duty is to inspect the works on behalf of the employer.

Failure by the employer to grant possession on the date for possession is a relevant event for the purposes of clauses 25.4.12 and 25.4.13 of JCT 98, and is a compensation event for the purpose of clause 60.1.(2) of NEC. Under clauses 26.2.5 and 26.2.6 of JCT 98, failure to give access or possession, or to postpone possession or commencement will also give rise to an entitlement to direct loss and/or expense. An interesting contrast is provided by clause 34(1) of GC/Works/1. This simply provides that within the period specified in the abstract of particulars the employer shall notify the contractor when he may take possession of the site, which shall be not more than 14 days after the date specified. The contractor is then required to proceed with the works in accordance with the programme so that the whole of the works or any relevant section shall be completed in accordance with the contract. Under clause 36(2) failure to grant access on the date calculated under clause 34(1) is not specifically identified as a matter giving rise to an extension of time, but is likely to give rise to an extension by virtue of the saving provision on clause 36(2)(b), which provides for extensions of time to be granted in the event of any other circumstance any act, neglect or default of the employer.

A further interesting contrast is provided by clause 33 and 35 of GC/Works/1. The former provides that the contractor shall submit a programme in which he warrants that this shows the sequence in which he proposes to carry out the works, that this is achievable and that this permits effective monitoring of progress. This can be changed only with the consent of the project manager,

2. A commonly encountered problem occurs where the employer wishes to take over the works or part of them, prior to practical completion, where the provisions of clause 18 might not be appropriate. Examples occur where, in the case of a residential property, the employer wishes to use the property over a holiday period, or in the case of commercial premises, where he wishes to use part of the premises for the storage of equipment. Clause 23.1.2 provides a useful mechanism for this.

and such consent does not relieve the contractor of responsibilities. Clause 35 provides for progress meetings at which progress is monitored against the programme, and provides that within seven days of each progress meeting the project manager shall issue a statement identifying progress by reference to progress meetings and the programme; delays are to be identified and steps taken to reduce the affects of delays.

The contrast with JCT 98 is acute. This provision fills what has long been regarded as the single biggest hole in JCT 98, a hole which the SCA Delay Protocol and PFE Change Management Supplement attempt with mixed success to fill. The wider point is that whereas JCT 98 gives the contractor discretion to determine the sequence in which the works are to be carried out; under GC/Works/1, the ordering of the works is more closely originated.

## INFORMATION

### *Introduction*

Building contracts deal with the provision of information concerning the works in a variety of different ways. At its simplest, the information provided to the contractor dictates the nature of the works which the contractor is to carry out, and the end result which he is to achieve. The following approaches are among the most commonly used:

- Performance specification or turn key contracts—the employer describes the end result he wishes to achieve, frequently by reference to the performance which that end result is intended to produce. The contractor has absolute discretion as to how he achieves that end result.
- Design and build—similar to the above. The employer produces "employer's requirements" which describes what is to be built, generally by reference to certain design information. The contractor is responsible for producing the detailed design in order to fulfill the employer's requirements by means of "contractors proposals".
- Traditional construction—the employer remains responsible for the design of the works. The contractor is responsible for constructing the works in accordance with that design. This in turn is subject to two subdivisions: contracts "with quantities", where the works are described with precision by reference to bills of quantities, and contracts "without quantities", where they are not.

The particular choice of contracting regime will dictate the information which the contractor can require from the employer.

In JCT 98 (with quantities) the starting point is the articles of agreement. The first recital provides that "the employer is desirous of . . . " and space is left for the description of the project and its address, and goes on to say that the employer has caused drawings and, where appropriate, bills of quantities which "show and describe the work to be done".

The second and third recitals provide respectively that the contractor shall have provided a fully priced bill of quantities, and that particular identified drawings will be referred to as the contract drawings. These are referred to as "the contract bills" and "the contract drawings". Collectively these are "the contract documents".

Articles 1 and 2 provide that in consideration of payment of the contract sum, the contractor will carry out the work shown in the contract documents.

These definitions are important in understanding the nature of the parties' obligations, particularly with regard to information requirements. Two important points need to be taken on board:

- firstly by contrast with JCT 98 (WCD) the contractor's obligation is to carry out the works on the basis of the information provided to him by the architect. He has no design obligation;
- secondly that he is carrying out a precisely described amount of work in return for a finite payment. To the extent that what is eventually built differs from that description it will affect the sum to be paid.

Both of these principles are significant in terms of the information to be provided. Slightly different considerations apply where the contract does not incorporate bills of quantities. There are of course numerous ways in which the works can be described, but for present purposes the important consideration is that of identifying the works as described in the contract documents.

An important provision which should be noted here is clause 2.2.2.2 which provides that where any error or inconsistency is found it shall be corrected and the correction shall be treated as a variation and valued in accordance with clause 13.2. In other words, the employer bears responsibility for the correction of errors. It is common to see attempts made by employers to reverse the risk contained in this clause and equally common to see this proposed amendment being strenuously resisted.

### *Further information*

The contract envisages—sensibly—that as the works progress, the contractor will require information in order to carry out the works described in the contract drawings. The unamended form refers in clause 5.4.1 to the provision of an information release schedule. The precise form which this is to take is not defined (although it is very common indeed to find that the contract is amended to set out in some detail what it is to comprise). It should also be noted that this is an optional provision where the sixth recital to the contract has not been deleted.

Clause 5.4.1 provides that the architect shall release the information identified in the information release schedule on the dates provided in it, and clause 5.4.2 provides that the architect shall "as and when from time to time may be necessary" provide to the contractor such information as shall be necessary to "explain and amplify" the contract drawings. This shall be done at such time as is necessary to enable the contractor to carry out the works by the completion date, and if the contractor believes that the architect may not be aware of the need for such further information he shall notify the architect of the need for it.

In relation to an earlier version of this contract, the question of supply of further information was considered by Vinelott J. in *London Borough of Merton* v. *Leach* (1985) 32 B.L.R. 51. It was held that it must have been in the contemplation of the parties that the architect would exercise reasonable skill and care in supplying information to the contractor and that there was scope to imply a term to the effect that the information to be supplied by the architect would be correct.

### *Failure to provide information*

Failure to provide information in accordance with clause 5.4.2 will give rise to an entitlement to an extension of time under clause 25.4.6.2 and to loss and expense under clause 26.2.1.2.

It is worth remembering that the comments made above have focused on the provision of information by the architect. These comments will apply equally to information to be provided by other members of the design team. There is, however, a distinction to be drawn between drawings and information to be provided by the employer's design team, and drawings and information to be provided by nominated sub-contractors. In *H Fairweather* v. *LB Wandsworth* (1987) 39 B.L.R. 106, H.H.J. Fox-Andrews QC concluded in relation to the 1980 form that delay on the part of nominated sub-contractors in providing drawings could not constitute a breach by the employer of clause 5.4.2.

A further consideration, which is frequently encountered in practice, concerns the nature of the information actually provided. It is common in main contracts, and even more common in subcontracts where there is a design responsibility, to encounter the suggestion that the drawings provided do no more than provide "design development", and thus delay in providing them cannot be said to cause delay. Whether this is actually the case will be a matter of fact to be determined in each case.

Unsurprisingly, the NEC puts forward a rather simpler regime, albeit one which contains a number of gaps in the drafting.

Clause 11.2(5) defines "works information" as being that which either specifies or describes the works or specifies any constraints on how the contractor provides the works and which is either in the contract documents, or is in an instruction given in accordance with the contract. Clause 11.2(6) defines "site information" as information which describes the site and its surroundings and is in the documents which the contract says it is in.

Clause 20.1 provides that the contractor provides the works in accordance with the works information, and is responsible for the design of those parts of the works which the works information says he is to design.

It appears to be assumed that the works information is provided by the employer and that it is complete and accurate, and to date this has not been tested by the courts.

Clause 31.2 provides, amongst other things, that the contractor's programme shall show "other information which the works information requires the contractor to show . . . ".

Implicit in this approach is the assumption that the works information provides, in the case of those parts of the works which the employer is to design, all the information which is necessary to enable the contractor to deliver the works, and in the case of contractor-designed work, sufficient information to allow him to carry out that design. Unlike JCT 98 there is no provision for the works information to be augmented as the works progress, and this may be seen as a drafting oversight which ideally should be remedied.

This is reflected in the compensation events which provide at clause 60.1(1) that instructions changing the works information will be a compensation event except where the change is made to rectify a defect, or (significantly) the change is made to the information provided by the contractor and which is made at his request in order to comply with other works information provided by the employer. The effect of this is broadly to mirror that of clause 2.2.2.2 in JCT 98, considered above.

Other compensation events of note are clause 60.1(5) which covers where the employer or others do not work in accordance with the programme or the works information and clause 60.1(16) where the employer does not provide materials facilities or samples as provided by the works information. Again, the assumption is that the works information is complete at commencement.

It is also important to consider clause 60.1(12)—it is a compensation event where the contractor encounters physical conditions within the site, which an experienced contractor would at the contract date have judged to have had such a small chance of occurring that it would have been unreasonable to have allowed for them.

This must be read with clause 60.2 which provides that in judging physical conditions the contractor is assumed to have taken account of the site information, publicly available information referred to in the site information, obtainable from visual inspection of the site, and information which an experienced contractor could reasonably be expected to have or to obtain. It must also be read with clause 60.3, which states that where there is an inconsistency within the site information the contractor is assumed to have taken account of the physical conditions most favourable to doing the work.

This is unsatisfactory in several respects. Firstly, the definition of site information includes the surroundings to the site which are not referred to in clause 60.1(12). Secondly, no provision is made as to the source of the site information—is it to be provided by the employer? Thirdly and most importantly, it seems to be assumed that the risk of inaccuracy in the site information rests with the employer, but introduces the requirement that the contractor should satisfy himself as to the accuracy of that information, while introducing a vague notion of reasonableness to cover circumstances where the physical conditions are not as anticipated.

The approach adopted in NEC can be contrasted with that taken in the ICE 7th Edition. It is not difficult to see that the draftsman of the NEC clearly had the ICE 7th edition and its predecessors in mind and clearly attempted to recast the ICE form using "NEC-type" language. As indicated in the previous paragraph, the misfortune is that this has been done in a way which leaves a number of unanswered questions. The following therefore provides a relatively brief overview of the treatment of the supply of information under the ICE 7th edition.

Under clause 6(1) of the NEC 7th edition, upon the award of the contract the contractor is supplied with four copies of the contract conditions together with copies of all of the drawings referred to in the specification.

Under clause 7(1) the engineer is to provide the contractor with such further information or drawings as shall in his opinion be necessary for the proper construction of the works. If this involves a variation to the works it shall be deemed to have been issued pursuant to clause 51 of the conditions and valued accordingly.

Clause 7(2) provides that in the case of those parts of the works designed by the contractor, the engineer may require the contractor to provide such further documents as may be necessary for the proper construction of the works.

Clause 7(3) provides that the contractor shall give adequate notice to the engineer of any further drawing or specification which he may require and clause 7(4) provides that if the works are delayed by virtue of the late supply of information, this shall be taken into account by the engineer in assessing any extension of time to be awarded under clause 44 and any cost to be assessed under clause 60.

As with the equivalent provisions under JCT 98 (but unlike NEC) the ICE form recognises that the contract drawings and specification are unlikely to contain all the information necessary to enable construction of the works and that further information is likely to be required. In *Neodox* v. *Swinton* [1958] 5 B.L.R. 34 it was suggested that such information shall be supplied so as to enable the contractor to carry out his works within the timescale envisaged by the contract. It is important to note, however, that the contractor's entitlement to any form of relief, i.e. extensions of time or costs, is dependent upon an "adequate" notice being submitted under clause 7(3). The adequacy of the notice will be a question of fact.

The most important provision in the ICE 7th edition relating to information is clause 11, which is concerned with ground conditions. In essence this provides as follows:

- information in respect of ground conditions or pipes and cables in or over the ground, which has been obtained by the employer shall only be taken into account to the extent that it was made available to the contractor before the submission of his tender and it shall be the responsibility of the contractor to interpret that information;
- the contractor is deemed to have inspected the site and all information available in connection with it and to have satisfied himself as to both the ground conditions and the work necessary to carry out the works; and
- to have based his tender on his own inspection and to have satisfied himself as to its adequacy.

In relation to the first limb of this clause *Keating on Building Contracts* observes that the use of the word "only" is curious and fails to address the situation where information came into the possession of the employer but was not made available to the contractor.

What is clear, however, is that the risk remains substantially with the contractor who is responsible for satisfying himself as to the ground conditions. Subject to questions as to whether the employer knew of the conditions and could be said to have concealed them (which of course is the issue highlighted in the previous paragraph), the employer cannot be held liable in cases where the information he has supplied in good faith, while not inaccurate is nonetheless misleading and there is no scope to imply a term to the effect that the information supplied is complete or exhaustive (see, for example, *Thorn* v. *LCC* (1876) 1 App. Cas. 120).

Clause 12, of course, then goes on to provide relief in the event that the contractor encounters ground conditions which are not reasonably foreseeable. The question of what was reasonably foreseeable will be a question of fact.

A similar approach is adopted in clause 7 of GC/Works/1. Clause 7(1) places the onus firmly on the contractor to satisfy himself as to the "conditions affecting the works" which includes not only the ground conditions, but also existing roads, railways and other means of communication with access to the works, the site contours and boundaries; the risk of damage by reason of any work to any property adjacent to the works; the conditions under which the works will have to be carried out; the supply of and conditions affecting labour and (importantly) any other matters or information affecting or likely to affect the execution of or price tendered for the works. In the event that unforeseen matters are encountered, the contractor is required to give notice of these matters, and only if the project manager agrees that such matters are unforeseen is any redress available.

What is significant is that risk rests with the contractor not only in relation to the physical conditions under which the works are to be executed, but also in relation to constraints on the manner in which the works are to be executed.

Disputes over the provision of information are one of the most commonly encountered areas of contention. A typical example of this occurs where a contractor maintains that particular information is required in order to explain or amplify the contract drawings and this contention is disputed by the design team. It is unrealistic to believe that the precise scope of the information which is likely to be necessary will be capable of being exactly determined at the time of the contract. Accordingly, this area provides a good example of a principle contained in the introductory section of this chapter, namely that a contract is simply machinery for allocating risk. One may contrast the approach adopted in JCT 98 where the parties attempt to legislate the further information by way of the Information Release Schedule with that adopted in the ICE 7th edition where a reasonably comprehensive code is provided for the requesting and supplying of further information with that found in GC/Works/1, where the onus is placed firmly on the contractor to satisfy himself as to the further information to be required. It is suggested that each of these approaches, while different, has the benefit of clarity and each is to be preferred to the unsatisfactory vague approach adopted within the NEC 2nd edition.

## STANDARDS OF WORKMANSHIP/FITNESS FOR PURPOSE OBLIGATIONS AND DUTY OF CARE WARRANTIES

### *General*

The standard of care is a frequently misunderstood issue. In the context of building contracts, the question "to what standard is the contractor required to perform" will differ depending on whether the contractor is carrying out any works of design, whether the contractor is familiar with the purpose for which the works are being carried out, and whether the contractor is supplying materials.

In general terms English law recognises two distinct standards of care. Those are "reasonable skill and care" and "fitness for purpose". Reasonable skill and care was defined in *Bolam* v. *Friern Hospital Management Committee* [1957] 2 All E.R. 118 by McNair J. as follows: "A man need not possess the highest expert skill at the risk of being found negligent. It is well established law that it is sufficient if he exercised the ordinary skill of an ordinary competent man exercising that particular art." In the context of design professionals the matter was considered in *Eckersley & Others* v. *Binnie & Partners* (1988) 18 Con. L.R. 1. Lord Justice Bingham said "a professional man is to bring to any professional task he undertakes no less expertise skill and care than other ordinarily competent members would bring but need bring no more. The law does not require of a professional man that he be a paragon combining the qualities of polymath and prophet."

This has been taken to mean that the actions of a professional should be judged against a group of his peers acting reasonably. Undoubtedly, in most situations, there will be a range of possible ways of dealing with a particular task. If the professional's conduct falls within that range, then he has acted reasonably. It is, however, worth noting that the test is an objective one. The level of skill required is that of the typically competent member of that profession with experience of carrying out that particular type of work. It is no defence for the person accused of negligence to say that in fact he did not possess the skills to carry out that particular task, or that he lacked relevant specialist skills.

So what does this mean in practice? The point was considered by His Honour Judge Stabb QC in *Sutcliffe* v. *Chippendale & Edmondson* [1971] 18 B.L.R. 149 in relation to the duties of architects where it was said that the person who employs an architect is entitled to expect:

> "That the architect will perform his duties in such a manner as to safeguard his interests and that he will do what is reasonably within his power to ensure that the work is properly and expeditiously carried out so as to achieve the end result as contemplated by the contract."

The critical words are "reasonably within his power". If it is the case that the body of reasonably competent people would have acted in the same way, and the same result would have occurred, this would provide a defence to a claim that the conduct was negligent. Without exception, the effect of the Standard Forms of Building Contract is to require the contractor to exercise reasonable skill and care in the exercise of his duties under the building contract. This is to be contrasted with the position where works are carried out other than under Standard Form, where there is a term to be implied by law to the effect that the works will be reasonably fit for their intended purpose (see *Viking Grain Storage Limited* v. *TH White Installations Limited*). The difference between the two standards of care is illustrated in *George Hawkins* v. *Chrysler (UK) Limited & Burne Associates* (1986), a personal injury claim resulting from an accident where Chrysler's employee slipped on water in a shower room. It was alleged by the employer that the designer of the shower room would use reasonable skill and care in selecting the material to be used for the floor and that he impliedly warranted that the material used would be fit for its intended purpose. The difference between the two positions is therefore clear; an obligation to use reasonable skill and care requires only that the same level of competence should be displayed as the ordinarily competent practitioner in that field, whereas fitness for purpose equates with a warranty that the works will achieve their intended objective.

The issue is of particular importance where the contractor (or his subcontractors) is being required to provide collateral warranties to other persons involved in a building process.

### *Standards of care and fitness for purpose*

Under JCT 98, clause 2.1 provides that the contractor shall carry out and complete the works in compliance with the contract documents, using the materials and workmanship of the quality and standards specified therein provided that where and to the extent that approval of the quality of the materials or of the standards of workmanship is a matter for the opinion of the architect, such quality and standards shall be to the reasonable satisfaction of the architect.

In relation to the matters which are said to be to the reasonable satisfaction of the architect, it is not settled that the satisfaction of the architect applies only to that class of materials where the architects decision is expressed in his final certificate as being conclusive.

Otherwise, if the contractor is to supply materials, he warrants that the materials are (1) reasonably fit for the purpose for which they will be used, and (2) of good quality, unless the terms of the contract specifically provide otherwise. (See, for example, *Young & Marten* v. *McManus Childs* [1969] 1 A.C. 454.) Where the contractor knows the employer's intended end result, and represents that he is familiar with what the employer is seeking to achieve, and is capable of achieving it, it is likely if it can be shown that the employer relied on the contractor's skill and judgement that the contractor will be taken to have warranted the fitness for purpose of what he has offered to provide.

That will not be the case where someone other than the contractor has carried out the design, and the contractor has provided no specific promises that the works will achieve any particular purpose; in those circumstances, the contractor's obligation is simply to exercise reasonable skill and care in the performance of his works.[3]

### *Collateral warranties*

A collateral warranty is an ancillary agreement to a primary contract and it runs "side by side" with that contract. It is intended to provide contractual remedies to those who are not parties to the primary contract but who have an interest in the subject matter of the primary contract, e.g. parties with an interest in the land and/or the building to which the warranty relates. Typically the beneficiaries are funders, purchasers and tenants.

A warranty is necessary because, in English law, it is generally not permissible for someone to enforce rights arising out of a contract to which it is not a party.[4] The need for collateral warranties came about following the various decisions in the late 1980s and early 1990s which served radically to restrict

3. This should be contrasted with the position under clause 2.5.1 of JCT 98 (WCD). This provides that to the extent that the contractor carries out design works, he owes the same duty to the employer as he would if he was an architect engaged under a separate appointment. In other words, he owes a duty of reasonable skill and care.

4. Though recent legislation in the form of the Contracts (Rights of Third Parties) Act 1999 permits this in very specific circumstances.

the parties' rights to make claims in tort, in the absence of contractual relationships (see, in particular, *D & F Estates* v. *Church Commissioners for England* [1989] A.C. 177). In modern development projects, it is not uncommon to find parties reliant upon members of the construction and design term with whom they have no direct contractual relationship. It is now the rule rather than the exception for funders to insist on having a comprehensive suite of warranties before advancing funds for a project and for purchasers or tenants to require warranties as a precondition to acquiring interests in the property.

In construction, members of the design team, contractors and subcontractors will normally provide collateral warranties. Warranties are typically provided to the employers, funders and purchasers or tenants. The parties providing warranties and the number of warranties to be provided will vary from project to project.

Sub-contractors, for example, may be expected to provide warranties to the employer (i.e. the party who is in contract with the main contractor) and the intended owners/tenants of the building. The beneficiary will have a contractual right to recover damages directly from the sub-contactor.

A beneficiary may rely on a warranty if, for whatever reason, it cannot pursue the party with whom the primary contract was made or if for any reason it does not wish to. For example, an employer may rely on a warranty from a sub-contractor if the main contractor with whom it had entered into the primary contract has become insolvent. The beneficiary may, however, choose to rely on the warranty in any event.

## Collateral warranty provisions

Although there are standard forms of collateral warranty available the tendency is to use "bespoke" forms. In particular the British Property Federation has produced the BPF CoWaF Form for use by funders and the CoWa P&T Forms which have gained widespread usage. They have not, however, replaced the bespoke forms. Most of the major developers have over the past decade developed their own forms of warranty, the terms of which have become widely known. It is, however, not uncommon to encounter project specific forms. Consequently, the length and complexity of collateral warranties can vary greatly.

The purpose of a warranty is to provide contractual remedies to parties who would not otherwise possess them. The main objective is to make such contractual remedies available in respect of any failure by the warrantor to properly carry out its principal obligations under the primary contract, and to provide the beneficiary with a direct contractual right of action.

In the case of a sub-contractor, for example, the warranty will be seeking to provide contractual remedies to the beneficiary in respect of any failure on the part of the subcontractor to properly carry out the subcontracted works under the relevant subcontract. This will normally be achieved by inclusion of a provision that equates to a promise made to the beneficiary on the part of the sub-contractor to carry out the subcontracted works in accordance with the subcontract. The particular benefit of this arrangement can be seen in two distinct ways. Firstly it enables the beneficiary of the warranty to claim against the party who is actually responsible for the problem, thus avoiding the situation where, for example, the employer is obliged to bring proceedings against a contractor who in turn is required to join in the sub-contractor. Secondly, it avoids the situation where, if the contractor has become insolvent, the employer is deprived of a remedy.

The warranty may also contain a number of additional provisions that relate to issues other than the performance of works or services under the primary contract, such as insurance, prohibited materials, assignment, copyright, step-in rights, restriction on liability and the provision of further warranties. Again, this will afford the beneficiary contractual remedies if such provisions are breached. These are worth looking at in turn:

- *Insurance*—it is common to encounter provisions which require the warrantor to maintain insurance for a term equal to the limitation period. Such provisions usually limit the obligation to obtain insurance to circumstances where that insurance is reasonably available at commercial rates within the market place. The warrantor can be required to produce evidence of insurance at reasonable notice.
- *Prohibited materials*—it is not uncommon to encounter provisions prohibiting the use of a lengthy list of particular materials. While popular, such provisions can be regarded as misconceived. The place for such provisions is within the building contract.
- *Assignment*—particularly in warranties given in favour of tenants, it is common to provide that the warranty will be capable of a specific number of assignments. This is to ensure that the warranty is not capable of unlimited numbers and assignments, thus producing a situation where the warrantor finds himself owing obligations to parties whom he knows nothing about. A restriction on the number of possible assignments is commonly insisted upon by professional indemnity insurers.
- *Copyright*—warranties frequently contain a statement that the beneficiary shall not be entitled to use any design materials produced by the warrantor other than in connection with this particular project. Again this is a restriction commonly imposed by professional indemnity insurers and its merits are self evident.
- *Step-in rights*—particularly in warranties in favour of funders, it is common to find provisions which enable the funder to "step in" to the primary contract in the event of insolvency of, for example, the employer. This mirrors provisions within funding agreements whereby

if the employer becomes insolvent, the bank retains the right to step in and complete the works.

- *Provision of further warranties*—in the event that it is contemplated that the works may be let to an as yet unidentified third party, it is not uncommon to find a requirement that further warranties will be provided in due course in favour of that third party.
- *Restrictions on liability*—warranties frequently provided (sensibly) that the warrantor shall owe no greater duty under the warranty than he owes under the primary contract.

A further issue, which has been a source of great contention, is the use of so-called "net contribution clauses". Typically these take the form of providing that where a number of members of the construction team are each required to provide warranties the liability of any one of them will be limited to the sum for which they would have been liable had all of those required to provide warranties actually provided them and in the event that judgment was obtained against more than one, had each discharged the sum for which they had been held liable.

Put slightly differently, this is a requirement that the party providing the warranty shall be protected from the risk that other members of the team might become insolvent and thus be unable to contribute towards a claim made against several members of the professional team. At first sight this type of provision has certain attractions and it is popular with certain providers of professional indemnity insurance, some of whom insist upon the provision of such clauses. However, further consideration of this type of clause throws up certain difficulties. First, it is necessary to consider the concept of joint and several liability. This provides that where a claim is made against two or more defendants, and each is found liable, each of them is responsible for the full sum for which judgment is given. It is up to the defendants to bring contribution proceedings pursuant to s. 1 of the Civil Liability (Contribution) Act 1978 to ask the court to apportion liability between them. The important point to remember is that this covers situations where two defendants are responsible for causing the same damage. It does not cover a situation where different defendants have caused different damage. Accordingly, a typical example where joint and several liability would be relevant is where defects have occurred in construction, and liability is established against the contractor for poor workmanship and the supervising officer for failure to instruct the remedying defects. It does not cover the sort of situation which would arise where claims are made arising out of defects, some of which arise as a consequence of poor workmanship, but others are a consequence of negligent design for which the contractor bore no responsibility. Thus it can be seen that the argument that, but for a net contribution clause, the party providing the warranty risks being held liable for matters for which he had no responsibility is misconceived.

## Providing collateral warranties

It is first necessary to establish the nature of the warranty, i.e. the work that the warranty is to cover. A subcontractor, for example, will normally be required to warrant that it will comply with its obligations under the subcontract in respect of carrying out the subcontract works.

A warranty that requires the warrantor to commit to obligations beyond those included under the primary contract should be resisted. For example, the warranty may include provisions that are not included under the primary contract, such as consequential loss, indemnities, transfer of intellectual property rights and inappropriate lists of deleterious materials. The scope of the duty owed under the warranty should never be greater than that owed under the primary contract. That is to say, in a warranty provided by a contractor to a funder ordinarily the duty owed under the contract will be to use reasonable skill and care. It would be inappropriate to seek to require a contractor to warrant to the funder that he will achieve fitness for purpose.

It may be the case that providing a warranty will prejudice insurance policy cover carried by the warrantor. It is essential that proposed warranties be crosschecked with insurance policies and with insurers in this respect. Proposed warranty forms should be forwarded to insurers for approval if this is a requirement of the policy or if there is any doubt regarding the extent of policy cover.

Collateral warranties are normally executed as a deed and as such are subject to a 12-year limitation period. The same will normally apply in respect of the primary contract. However, it is possible for the limitation periods under the two agreements not to correspond, such as in the case where warranties are provided subsequently and the limitation period begins to run from the date of the warranty. In this situation the limitation period under the warranty may extend beyond the expiry of the limitation period under the primary contract.

As previously noted, it is now possible for parties outside a contract to enforce the terms of that contract under the specific circumstances set out in the Contracts (Rights of Third Parties) Act 1999. The Act does, however, include provisions allowing parties to exclude the Act from their contract. Such exclusion should be expressly included in both the primary contract and the warranty.

At the time this Act was introduced, it was suggested in some quarters that this would do away with the necessity for warranties. This has not proved to be the case. Although the Act restricts the persons who may benefit under the Act, it is common to find a "belt and braces" provision in warranties restricting any possibility that any right under the Act might be required.

APPENDIX

| | Time for possession | Information | Standards of workmanship | Quality of work |
|---|---|---|---|---|
| JCT 98 | Cl 23.1.1—On date for possession, possession given to contractor who shall complete works by date for completion. [Dates for possession and completion provided by Appendix.] | Cl 5.4—Information release schedule [form not specified]. Information to be provided on dates provided in Schedule. | | |
| ICE 7th Ed | | Cl 6(1)—On award of contract, copies of all drawings. Cl 7(1)—Engineer may issue any further information necessary for carrying out of works. | | |
| NEC 2nd Ed | Cl 33.1—Possession to be granted on date for possession shown in accepted programme. | Cl 11.2(5) —Works information: that which defines the works. Cl 11.2(6)—Site information: information which defines conditions under which works to be executed. | | |
| GC/Works/1 | Within the period identified in Abstract of Particulars, PM notifies contractor of date when may take possession. Contractor then carries out work as required by programme to completion by date shown on programme. | Cl 7—Contractor obliged to satisfy self as to all relevant site conditions. No separate provision for what information is to be provided. | | |

| | Variations | Certification and payment | Notice provisions |
|---|---|---|---|
| JCT 98 | Cl 13—additions, omissions or substitutions; alteration of kind or standards of work; in position of restriction by Employer variations to be valued under cls 13.4 and 13.8. | | Cl 25.2.3—Stage test<br>• Progress of work being delayed<br>• By relevant event<br>• Leading to delay to completion date<br>Notice shall be given for the works: providing all necessary parties. |
| ICE 7th Ed | Cl 51(1)—Alterations by way of additions, omissions, changes in form or quality character kind or position dimension line or level or change in sequence or timing. | | Cl 44.1—If matters in paragraphs (a)–(f) have occurred, contractor shall give notice within 28 days providing all necessary particulars. |
| NEC 2nd Ed | Cl 14.3—PM has discretion to order variations.<br>Cl 60.1—Variation instructions in compensation event. | | Cl 61.3—Contractor shall notify PM of event which he believes to be compensation event. |
| GC/Works/1 | Cl 40.1—PM discretion to order variations: addition, alteration or omission. | | Cl 36(1)—Where PM receives notice requesting EOT shall form decision within 42 days. |

| | Notice provisions—contd<br>1. Condition precedent | 2. Particulars | Completion |
|---|---|---|---|
| JCT 98 | Pre-practical completion—<br>Yes | Yes | Cl 71.1—"Practical completion" |
| ICE 7th Ed | No | Yes | Cl 48—"Substantial completion" |
| NEC 2nd Ed | Unclear | No | Cl 30.2—"Completion" |
| GC/Works/1 | No | No | Cl 34/(1)—"Completion" |

| | Defects and defect correction |
|---|---|
| JCT 98 | Cl 17.2—Architect shall be entitled to instruct correction of defect. |
| ICE 7th Ed | Cl 49—Upon substantial completion contractor shall provide undertaking to carry out works outstanding at no cost to employer. |
| NEC 2nd Ed | |
| GC/Works/1 | Cls 21 and 34—PM has wide discretion to order correction of defects. |

## TEST YOUR UNDERSTANDING

**1. Possession of the site means:**

(a) the contractor has the keys to the site;
(b) the contractor has sufficient access to the site to enable him to proceed with his works;
(c) the contractor is the only person permitted to have access to the site;
(d) the contractor and those persons authorised by him to come onto the site are the only persons permitted onto the site.

**2. Works information (an expression occurring within the NEC) means:**

(a) information concerning local sources of manufactured goods;
(b) information which describes the works and the way in which they are to be carried out;
(c) information concerning the site and its surroundings;
(d) information concerning the contract documents.

**3. When works have been said to be fit for their purpose it means that:**

(a) the materials used to construct them are appropriate;
(b) the builder has exercised reasonable professional skill in carrying out his works;
(c) the works will achieve the purpose for which they are said to be constructed;
(d) the works will be long lasting.

**4. Which of the following statements about collateral warranties is not true?**

(a) collateral warranties provide funders and employers with direct contractual relationships with designers and subcontractors;
(b) in the absence of a collateral warranty, purchasers and tenants are often unable to sue subcontractors in respect of defective work;
(c) collateral warranties simply confirm the obligations which the parties already owe;
(d) collateral warranties should always be checked with professional indemnity insurers to ensure that no higher duties are assumed.

CHAPTER 7

# POWERS AND DUTIES OF THE EMPLOYER AND CONTRACTOR—PART II

Nick Carnell

The purpose of this chapter is to build on the information introduced in the previous chapter. It considers the relationship between the contractor and the employer under the principle standard forms, together—as appropriate—with the role of the contract administrator/certifier.

In this chapter the student will learn more about how the most commonly encountered concepts within the construction process are dealt with in the various standard forms. The issues encountered include:

- variations;
- certification and payment;
- notice provisions;
- time for completion;
- partial possession and section completion;
- completion;
- defects, defects correction and latent defects.

## VARIATIONS

### *What do we mean by "variation"?*

Before looking at the provisions of the various standard forms it is worth considering what we mean by "varied work". One of the most frequently encountered areas of dispute is over whether particular activities give rise to an entitlement to additional payment or extensions of time. In part this is because there is no universally applicable definition of what constitutes a variation. This is exacerbated by the fact that different considerations apply depending upon the precise nature of the contract. Different considerations will apply where the works are precisely defined from those where the contractor's obligation is to achieve a specific end result and he is given latitude as to how to achieve that result.

The latter—contracts where the contractor's works are widely defined—are perhaps more difficult. *Keating* suggests at para 4-29, that where, for example, the contractor has agreed to provide a particular product, such as a house, answering a particular description, his obligation is to do all things "indisputably necessary to complete the whole work", that is to say, a house answering the description in the specification. (See, for example, *Williams* v. *Fitzmaurice* (1858) 3 H&N 844.)

An interesting parallel is provided by contacts for professional services. It is not uncommon to encounter circumstances in which designers inadvertently commit themselves to the design and contract administration of a project in consideration of a fixed fee without consideration of the precise scope of the work required to achieve the end result.

Accordingly, in these circumstances, unless the contractor indicated that his bid was based upon specific assumptions as to how the works were to be carried out or he can show that the employer expressly warranted that the works could be carried out in a particular manner; the fact that the works proved more arduous than he had assumed will not assist the contractor. There are a large number of Victorian authorities identified by *Keating* where unexpected difficulties in executing the works were held to be at the risk of the contractor. See, for example, *Bottoms* v. *York Corporation* (1892) HBC (4th edn) Vol. 2, 208—unexpectedly encountering running sand; and *Sharpe* v. *San Paolo Railway* (1873) L.R. 8 Ch. App. 597—inadequacies in the Engineer's drawings leading to additional excavation.

Particular care is needed in determining whether information provided in the employer's invitation to tender can be taken as to a warranty as to the accuracy of that information. In *Bacal* v. *Northampton Development Corporation* (1975) 8 B.L.R. 88, the Court of Appeal found that the employer had intended to warrant the accuracy of the information provided and as a consequence it has become commonplace for tender invitations to provide that the tenderer should satisfy himself as to the accuracy of any statement in the tender invitation documents. It should, however be noted that such a disclaimer needs to be worded with care since any ambiguity will be construed against the employer.

### *Defining the works*

This should be contrasted with the situation where the works are precisely defined by way of bills of quantities or the equivalent. In this situation, if the quantities of work to be executed differ from that stated in the bills, on the face of it, this will give rise to an entitlement to additional payment. The issues which will face a court or arbitrator in this situation are firstly whether it can be said that the bills actually form part of the contract; and secondly whether it really can be said that the bills are intended to be an exact quantification of the work which needs to be done. In each instance this will be a question of fact to be judged on the circumstances of each individual case.

Different considerations again will apply where the works are carried out on a "measurement and value" basis. Since the basis of payment will generally be by reference to what the contractor actually does, the issue of what is stated in the contract will usually be of little consequence.

A further point of interest arises in relation to contracts for professional services. Where the services to be provided are defined by reference to particular work stages, it may be difficult for the consultant to argue that actual amount of effort put in exceeds that for which he had contracted. At the most extreme end of the scale, if, for example, an architect has agreed to a lump sum for providing design and supervision services to a project, he may find himself in difficulties if he finds that the level of effort required exceeded that which he had anticipated. The lesson is clearly to define with as much precision as possible what is included within a fee or a particular work stage, such that if something additional becomes necessary, this does not fall within the "all-in" fee.

A final consideration is that of the authority to order additional or varied work. While the standard forms expressly empower the employer or his agents —usually the architect or engineer to order varied work, without express authority this will not be implied. However, in the context of what *Keating* refers to as a contract for "whole work" that authority will not usually extend beyond the "whole work". In other words, the power to order variations does not extend to ordering something which goes wholly beyond the scope of the original project.

Thus far we have been concerned with the question "additional to what?" However, even if it can be shown that the works are different to that provided by the contract, that does not of itself give rise to an entitlement to additional payment. Two considerations arise. The first is that the works must have been required by the employer, or where this is not the case, the contract must provide for "variations by reason of necessity". The second is that the work must be of a type identified in the contract as giving rise to a right to additional payment. Both are easier to identify in practice than they are to describe.

The first arises when works have been carried out which differ from that specified without a specific instruction. Of course, the starting point is that the contractor is vulnerable to the claim that the works do not comply with the contract and hence the employer may have the right to order their removal. It is also the case that the mere fact that the altered works may be better than that contracted for does not give rise to any entitlement to additional payment. However, it may be that the contractor will argue that since the employer has received a benefit of the "improvement" it would be unjust to deny him payment. The issue is addressed (not entirely clearly) in a number of Victorian cases (e.g. *Bottoms* v. *York Corporation*) and the moral seems to be that the contractor departs from the agreed works at his peril. An exception may arise where the varied works were required as a result of an emergency, and in these circumstances, it seems likely that the contractor will be entitled to payment for the additional work. Again there is an absence of clear modern authority on the point.

The second arises where the contract specifically provides that the term "variation" shall have a particular meaning. In these circumstances, it will be difficult for the contractor to argue that works which although different to that specified in the contract do not fall within the definition of variations can be valued as varied work—see *Kitsons Sheet Metal Ltd* v. *Matthew Hall Mechanical & Electrical Engineers* (1989) 47 B.L.R. 90.

A further interesting consideration arises in relation to provisional sums. These arise where a particular aspect of the works has not been fully designed or is for some other reason incapable of being designed, and accordingly priced with precision. A sum is inserted with the contract sum, and is substituted by the actual price when this is capable of being ascertained.

Slightly different considerations apply in respect of the with and without quantities versions of JCT 98. In particular, the former introduces the concept of the "defined provisional sum". This is defined by Rule 10 of the 7th edition of the Standard Method of Measure. In essence this defines a defined provisional sum as one where the quantities can be ascertained, but the works have not been fully designed. Importantly, it also provides that in pricing the provisional sum, due allowance shall have been made for preliminaries and programming of the works.

Subject to this important distinction, instructions to expend provisional sums are to be valued as variations under clause 13.5.3 of JCT 98, and will be a relevant event under clause 25.4.11 giving rise to an extension of time and will be a relevant matter under clause 26.2.7 giving rise to an entitlement to loss and expense.

## *JCT 98—Variations and instructions*

All of these points are, to an extent, dealt with in clause 13 of JCT 98. Clause 13.1 defines the term "variation" as

> "1. the alteration or modification of the design quality or quantity of the works including
>
> 1.1. the addition, omission or substitution of any work
> 1.2. the alteration of the kind or standard of any of the materials or goods to be used in the works the removal from site of any work executed . . . other than works not in accordance with the contract
>
> "2. the imposition by the employer of any restrictions in regard to the matters set out in clauses 13.1.2.1 to .4 or the addition to or alteration or omission of any such restriction . . . in regard to
>
> 2.1 access to the site or use of any specific part of the site
> 2.2 limitation on working space
> 2.3 limitation on working hours
> 2.4 the execution or completion of work in a specific order."

Clause 13.1.3 excludes any instruction for the nomination of any subcontractor where the measured quantities of work are set out in the contract bills.

It will be noted that clause 13.1.1 deals with what might be termed "physical variations," while clause 13.1.2 deals with variations in the way in which the works are carried out or the conditions under which they are carried out.

Clause 13.2 provides that the architect/contract administrator shall be entitled to issue instructions requiring a variation. This is stated to be subject to the contractor's right of reasonable objection which is provided in clause 4.1.1. In the event that such objection is made in writing clause 4.1.2 provides that where the architect/contract administrator issues an instruction requiring compliance with the instruction, and the contractor does not comply within seven days, the architect/contract administrator may employ others to carry out the work so specified and the cost of so doing may be deducted from the contract sum or recovered from the contractor as a debt. A question arises here—where an instruction requiring a variation comprising additional work is issued and not complied with—a strict application of this provision means that the contractor runs the risk that the additional work thereby required will be executed at his cost, thus producing a windfall for the employer.

Clause 13.2.3 provides that variations shall be valued in accordance with the provisions of clause 13.4 or 13.8 as the case may be—see below.

Clause 13.2.4 provides that the architect/contract administrator may sanction in writing any variation made other than by way of an instruction given under this clause. Clause 13.2.5 provides that no variation required by the architect/contract administrator and subsequently sanctioned by him shall vitiate the contract. These are significant provisions.

The first gives the architect the right retrospectively to approve a variation even though the contractual procedure has not been followed. This is important where the works have been varied by *ad hoc* actions taken as the works progress.

The second prevents the contractor from arguing that such was the scope of the changes that the original contract can be taken as having been rescinded. The point was considered in *McAlpine Humberoak* v. *MacDermott International* (1992) 58 B.L.R. 1 where the Court of Appeal overturned an earlier finding that the volume of variations had the effect of discharging the contract and entitling the contractor to be paid on a *quantum meruit* basis.

### *ICE 7th edition—Procedure for ordering variations.*

The scheme for ordering variations under ICE 7th edition is essentially similar to that encountered in JCT 98. Under clause 51(1) the engineer has power to order any variation which in his view is necessary for the completion of the work or which for any other reason shall in his view be desirable for the completion or improved functioning of the works. Such variations may include alterations by way of additions, omissions changes in the form, quality character kind position dimension level or line and changes in any specified sequence method or timing of the works. Clause 51(2) provides that any variation shall be ordered in writing. Clause 2(6) however provides that if it is considered necessary for instructions to be given orally they shall be complied with and where such instructions are given orally they shall be confirmed in writing and if confirmed in writing by the contractor and not contradicted by the engineer or his representative shall be deemed to be instructions in writing. Clause 51(3) provides that no instruction ordering a variation shall invalidate the contract.

### *NEC—Variations—procedure and payment*

The procedure under the NEC form is commendably uncomplicated. By clause 14.3 it is provided that the project manager may give instructions which changes the works information—and thereby changes the works. Clause 29.1 provides that the contractor shall obey an instruction given in accordance with the contract. What is left unclear is whether there shall be such a thing as an instruction not in accordance with the contract. Under clause 60.1 an instruction changing the works information is a compensation event and therefore gives rise to an entitlement to payment.

### *GC/Works/1*

A slightly different approach is taken in GC/Works/1. Clause 40(1) gives the project manager complete discretion to issue further instructions and information. These may take effect as a variation instruction. This is defined narrowly as an alteration or addition to or omission or any change in the design quality or quantity. This does not, accordingly, include alterations in the sequence in which the works are to be carried out (which is dealt with in clause 33 of this contract) or the conditions under which the works are to be carried out, which under clause 7 is a risk which rests with the contractor.

### *Payment for varied work*

Payment for varied work is dealt with in the next section.

## CERTIFICATION AND PAYMENTS

### *Payment certificates*

"... I accept the importance of 'cash flow' in the building industry. In the vivid phrase of Lord Denning MR: 'It is the very lifeblood of the enterprise ...' "

### Introduction to payment

It was once a basic principle of English law that when a contractor undertook to do work for a fixed sum, he was not due any payment until the whole of the work had been completed, but once the work was complete he was due full payment of the fixed sum. Whilst this arrangement may have been appropriate for small projects, construction work can involve large sums of money being expended over a number of months—or even years. Thus, in order to provide cash flow to the contractor, this basic principle was usually varied by specific agreement between the parties to allow interim payments to be made as the work proceeded.

The Housing Grants, Construction and Regeneration Act 1996 (hereinafter the "Construction Act") came into effect on 1 May 1998 and requires that all construction contracts, defined within the Construction Act, contain payment provisions which are consistent with the Construction Act.

When considering the subject of interim payments, it is worth bearing in mind that the contractor has similar obligations to his suppliers and sub-contractors as does the client to the contractor. Timely payment to the contractor means that he may, in turn, fund his payment obligations to his suppliers and sub-contractors.

Provided that the minimum requirements of the Construction Act are met, interim payments can take one of the following forms:

- payments of pre-determined amounts at regular intervals;
- payments of amounts at regular intervals calculated by a detailed valuation process as the work proceeds (a periodic payment); or
- payments of pre-determined amounts when the work reaches pre-determined stages of completion (a stage payment).

### Payments of pre-determined amounts at regular intervals

This is a method where, for example, a construction project of £120,000 is contracted to take 12 months and it is determined that the contractor will be paid £10,000 per month, adjusted to account for authorised variations, fluctuations, loss and/or expense and retention. This method has the advantage, to both parties, of minimal administration and cash flow certainty. However, it can lead to problems if the contractor falls behind programme or executes defective work, whereupon overpayment to the contractor for the work done is a probability, which would certainly lead to problems in the event of the contractor going into liquidation before completing the project.

### Payments of amounts at regular intervals calculated by a detailed valuation process as the work proceeds

This method of determining the amounts of interim payments is the fairest and most commonly adopted in construction contracts. The implications of defective work, delays, authorised variations, materials on and off site, fluctuations, loss and/or expense and retention can all be readily taken into account in each payment. This procedure does, however, require a regular and substantial input from most members of the building team.

## Stage payments

This is a method whereby pre-determined amounts, adjusted to account for authorised variations, fluctuations, loss and/or expense and retention, become due for payment upon the proper completion of a pre-determined stage of work. For example, the pre-determined amount of (say) £100,000 becomes payable upon the proper completion of all work up to damp-proof course level.

Determining the amount of interim payments in this way keeps down the parties' administration costs and (unlike the method of paying pre-determined amounts) does not lead to overpayment to the contractor if he falls behind programme or if he executes defective work. It can, however, be disadvantageous to the contractor as it does not take into account the value of unfixed materials and goods either on or off site.

It is worthy of note that JCT 98 With Contractor's Design provides for the optional use of this method of payment under clause 30.2A, Alternative A—Stage Payments.

## Which payment mechanism is more beneficial?

Periodic payments can be more beneficial because they operate to a given cycle and can produce for the contractor a better liquidity than stage payments. In simplistic terms, the gross valuation due to the contractor will bear the same relationship to the contract sum as the amount of work then executed bears to the overall work to be done for the project to be completed.

The drawback with periodic payments is that so valuing the work can be a time consuming task (if it is to be carried out accurately) whose use is short lived indeed (because no sooner is the valuation determined then it is time to start the exercise again).

Stage payments, as the name suggests, have the advantage that payments are tied to particular stages of work completed. Once the stage of work in question has been completed, the pre-agreed payment in respect thereof can be made without time consuming debate as to what exactly should be paid.

The drawback with stage payments is that if the contractor falls behind programme, he will not receive any payment until the particular stage of work has been completed even though a high value of work may have been executed. The corollary of this drawback, though, is that contractors may be particularly careful to stay on programme and this will operate to the mutual benefit of both the contractor and the client.

## Items to be included in payment

Clause 30.2 of JCT 98 PWQ provides a "checklist" of those items which may be included in an architect's interim certificate and distinguishes between those items which either are or are not subject to retention.

Implicit in this is the fact that the inclusion of any items in a contractor's application for payment which are not also to be found in clause 30.2 must fall outside the scope of the application which is to be considered by the architect (or the quantity surveyor on his behalf).

Each type of contract (i.e. JCT, ICE, GC/Works, NEC/2 and FIDIC) contains its own detailed rules as to what items are eligible for payment. The rules for each type of contract are not overly different though you are, of course, referred to each of the contracts for their precise terms and effect.

Items eligible for payment *and subject to retention* are generally as follows:

- the total value of work properly executed by the contractor, including variations and, where applicable, any adjustment for fluctuations by use of the price adjustment formulae;
- the total value of materials and goods delivered to or adjacent to the works and for incorporation therein by the contractor;
- the total value of materials and goods or items prefabricated, which have been listed by the client, before their delivery to site;
- the total amount of the above three points but in respect of each nominated subcontractor;
- the profit of the contractor upon the total amount included for each nominated sub-contractor, including their fluctuations and any other monies due to them under the terms of the subcontract; and
- advance payments (where applicable).

Items eligible for payment but not subject to retention are generally as follows:

- any amount which becomes due to the contractor under the terms of the contract in respect of statutory charges priced in the contract bills, opening up work for inspection and testing or the like;
- any amount due to the contractor by way of reimbursement of loss and/or expense arising from matters materially affecting the regular progress of the works or from the discovery of antiquities;
- any amount due to the contractor for the replacement or repair of loss or damage and removal and disposal of debris which is treated as a variation;
- the amount of any final payment to a nominated sub-contractor;
- any amount due to the contractor for fluctuations calculated other than by use of the price adjustment formulae; and
- any amount properly payable to a nominated sub-contractor for the replacement or repair of loss or damage and removal and disposal of debris which is treated as a variation and for fluctuations calculated other than by use of the price adjustment formulae.

## Items to be excluded from payment

Put simply, items to be *excluded* from payment are those whose characteristics do *not* conform with the items to be *included*.

Items to be excluded from payment are generally as follows:

- work not yet executed;
- work not executed in accordance with the contract;
- the value of variations for which no proper authorisation has been given; and
- loss and/or expense which has not been ascertained.

With specific regard to JCT 98 PWQ, the contractor's entitlement to payment for a variation whose value was agreed in accordance with clause 13A is capped at the pre-agreed amount. Clause 12A of JCT 98 WCD contains a similar provision.

The above exclusions might all make perfectly proper sense but the design and build version of the JCT contract (i.e. JCT 98 WCD) provides that the contractor will be paid all that he asks for (even if this includes several inadmissible items) in the event that the client (or the employer's agent) does not issue a withholding notice in due time. If, therefore, a contractor engaged on a JCT 98 WCD submits an application for payment which is inflated and/or contains inadmissible items, it must be met promptly with a withholding notice in the proper form.

NEC/2 proposes a novel exclusion. Clause 50.3 of NEC/2 provides that if the contractor does not produce a programme for the works then 25% of the monies due to him will be withheld until such time as he does.

## *JCT, ICE, GC/WORKS, NEC and FIDIC—compared and contrasted*

### General

As already observed, when looking at items to be included in or to be excluded from payment, the standard forms of contract take a broadly similar approach.

The real difference between the standard forms does not so much lie in the subject matter of the payment but, rather, the manner in which the payment is calculated. This is best demonstrated when looking at how variations are to be paid for.

JCT 98 PWQ makes a clear distinction between the valuation of the variation (clause 13) and the ascertainment of any loss and/or expense (clause 26). Clause 13.5 of JCT 98 PWQ states that " . . . no allowance shall be made under clause 13.5 for any effect upon the regular progress of the Works or for any other direct loss and/or expense . . . " such matters being dealt with according to the somewhat different set of rules contained in clause 26. For a consideration of the difference between "valuation" and "ascertainment", see Chapter 8 "Changes and its Effects" below.

Condition 41(2) of GC/Works 98 is in striking contrast with the position under JCT 98 PWQ. Under condition 41(2), the *value* to be ascribed to any instruction for a variation " . . . shall include any disruption to or prolongation of both varied and unvaried work . . . ".

For the purposes of this overview, ICE and FIDIC are sufficiently close to the scheme of things under GC/Works 98 for no further mention of them to be made here.

NEC/2 provides at clause 60.1(1) that where the " . . . project manager gives an instruction changing Works Information . . . " (which is NEC/2 speak for a variation), this shall be treated as a compensation event. NEC/2's approach to working out the payment due to a contractor in the event of a variation is materially different to both JCT 98 PWQ and GC/Works 98—this is a subject worth expanding upon.

### Assessing a compensation event under NEC/2

Clause 63.1 of NEC/2 provides that the changes to the contractor's price are assessed as the effect of the compensation event on the actual cost of the work already done, the forecast actual cost of the work not yet done and the resulting fee.

Clause 63.1 of NEC/2 stipulates that the prices are changed to reflect the effect which a compensation event has on actual cost. In simple terms, this is done by calculating the difference between the actual cost both with, and without, the effect of the compensation event. The contractor's tendered rates and prices are not relevant to the exercise. Unlike JCT 98 PWQ, therefore, the contractor will not be tied to his tender rates (or even the familiar concept of "fair rates and prices") in the event of varied work.

The guidance notes to NEC/2 explain that " . . . the reason for this policy is that no compensation event for which a quotation is required is due to the fault of the contractor or relates to a matter which is at his risk under the contract. It is therefore appropriate to reimburse the contractor his forecast additional costs or actual additional costs if work has already been done arising from the compensation event. Disputes arising from the applicability of contract rates are avoided . . . ".

## NOTICE PROVISIONS

### *Introduction*

All of the major standard form of contracts contained provisions requiring the contractor to give notice to the employer in the event that certain events occur. The most important of these provisions concern the obligation to give notice in the event that delays occur or loss and expense or its equivalent has been incurred. The rational behind this requirement is an obvious one; if delays have occurred, or are likely to occur, it is desirable that the employer should know about them at the earliest opportunity, first so that these matters do not take him by surprise at a later date; second so that he can if he wishes attempt to take measures to lessen their impact. Put slightly differently, they should not simply be seen as a hurdle placed in the path of the contractor seeking extensions of time or direct loss and expense. This section is therefore concerned to examine exactly what the notice requirements comprise, and what happens in the event that notices are not given.

### Machinery

Clause 25.2 of JCT 98 sets three hurdles for obtaining an entitlement to an extension of time:

- progress of works is being delayed;
- by a relevant event (as defined by clause 25.4);
- effect must be to delay *completion of works* beyond presently fixed completion date.

[NB: Obvious inference to be drawn is that if the delay event will not cause delay to completion of works, i.e. is not a critical delay, no extension of time will be granted.]

Clause 44.1 of ICE 7th edition is similar in effect:

- if contractor considers that matters listed at (a) to (f);
- entitle him to an extension of time for substantial completion of the works.

[That is, the event listed in the contract leads to delay to completion.]

### Notice requirements

Essentially similar under both forms:

- where circumstances identified in clause 25.2 of JCT 98 or clause 44.1 of ICE 7th edition become apparent;
- contractor shall (under JCT 98 forthwith) (under ICE 7th edition within 28 days of it becoming apparent) give notice of the effect;
- providing all necessary particulars to enable architect/contract administrator or engineer to make a decision.

[Comment—intention here is plainly to enable extensions of time to be dealt with as the works progress.]

### Procedure

At this point the onus switches:

- JCT 98 clause 25.3: if on receipt architect/contract administrator considers any of matters contained in notice 2 constitute relevant events and those relevant events will delay completion date;

- then he shall (note mandatory wording) fix new completion date identifying the relevant events he has taken into account.

In fixing a new completion date the architect/contract administrator must "if reasonably practicable" and "having regard to the sufficiency" of the particulars provided

" . . . fix a new completion date with 12 weeks, or if the completion date is less than 12 weeks away, not later than the completion date."

[NB: Wherever notice seeking the extension of time is delivered on the day before completion date, the architect/CA is probably saved by the words "if reasonably practicable".]

Under clause 25.3.3 within 12 weeks of Practical Completion ("PC") the architect/contract administrator is obliged to fix a new completion date by reference to all of the relevant events, whether or not specifically notified by the contractor.

The position is broadly similar under ICE 7th edition.

Under clause 44.2 (a) upon receipt of particulars the engineer shall make an assessment of the delay caused and fix a new date for substantial completion and (b) in the absence of any claim he may make an assessment of the delay.

Under clause 44.4 he has a duty to review previously granted extensions of time.

### *Practical differences*

At first sight these are limited.

- Under JCT 98 the power to review after practical completion is mandatory, notwithstanding the absence of a notice.
- Under JCT 98 the duty to review in the absence of a notice only arises after PC.

### *Failure to give notice*

#### Condition precedent?

Is the giving of notice a condition precedent to entitlement to an extension of time ("EOT") or does the failure to give notice disentitle a contractor from obtaining an EOT? The answer will depend on the precise words used. See, for example, *City Inns* v. *Shepherd Construction* (Court of Session). In *City Inns* an equivalent provision to clause 25.2 was amended to make plain that giving of notice was a pre-condition to entitlement to extension (Lord MacFadyen—failure to give notice will disentitle contractor from entitlement to EOT).

Extremely common in amendments drafted on behalf of major developers to find amendments to clause 25.2, the clear purpose of which is to make giving of notice a condition precedent—vigilance is obviously called for.

### In unamended JCT 98

*Keating* suggests that prior to PC notice may be a condition precedent—clauses drafted in mandatory form.

After PC plainly it is not—the architect has duty to review whether or not notice is served.

*However*, the fact that after PC the architect has a mandatory duty to review whether or not the notice is served means that the mandatory notice prior to PC is unlikely to be of much consequence.

Under ICE 7th edition engineer's discretion under clause 44.2 suggests that notice is not a condition precedent.

### *London Borough of Merton* v. *Stanley Hugh Leach Limited*

This case still offers a definitive discussion of the issue—despite being concerned with the 1963 JCT form which contains slightly different (and simpler) wording.

The judgment of Vinelott J. has the merit of considerable practical common sense.

As is well known on the 1963 wording, Vinelott J. held that notice is not a condition precedent to entitlement to EOT.

Just as importantly, it was held that requirement to give notice only applied when the delaying event had happened. No requirement to give notice applied when there was a perception that the delaying event was going to happen. This is probably still the case.

### Effect of failure to give notice is treated as follows

- Post PC architect is under a duty to assess EOT whether or not a notice is given. This duty was owed to the employer and contractor; but
- failure to give notice is constituted a breach by contractor.

Hence:

(a) the contractor cannot benefit from the consequences of own breach so if the effect of failure to give notice has prejudiced employer, that may be taken into account in assessment of EOT awarded, and

(b) the contractor cannot obtain greater EOT than would have been obtained had notice been given.

[Comment—if as a consequence of failure to give notice the contractor feels he has received less than his due, he will face an uphill struggle if the court or arbitrator concludes he could and should have given notice.]

## Contents of notice

So what should the notice provide? Vinelott J. in *Leach* was at pains to say that notice had no particular formal requirements.

Practical issue—notice should provide whatever information contractor feels necessary in order to persuade the architect of entitlement.

Where works are planned using project network techniques, it would seem an excellent idea to produce an updated programme to show the effect of delaying events.

## Considerations

The next question is what the architect can/should take into account in considering his award.

Is he constrained by relevant events, or can he take account of other matters which may have led to the delay—whether or not they are relevant events?

Taking the exact wording of both clause 25.2 of JCT 98 and clause 44.2 of ICE 7th edition, this is plainly a measure of ambiguity.

A practical approach suggests that the architect or engineer should look at the big picture—he should determine what has actually caused the delay and proceed accordingly.

This was the approach taken by Dyson J. in *Henry Boot Construction (UK) Ltd* v. *Malmaison Hotels (Manchester) Limited* (1999) 70 Con. L.R. 32: a question of whether account could be taken of relevant events alone (the claimant's view) or relevant events and other matters which caused delays which were not relevant events (the defendant's approach).

Dyson J., adopting in large part the views expressed by Malmaison's counsel, Finola O'Farrell QC, approached the latter on the basis of what he termed the negative and the positive basis.

- Negative—relevant events did not cause a critical delay.
- Positive—the real cause of delay was not a relevant event but another matter which was not a relevant event.

## How should he do it?

In *John Barker Construction Ltd* v. *London Portman Hotel Ltd* (1996) 83 B.L.R. 35, the architect had taken an impressionistic approach. This was clearly sincere but there was no sense of having made a logical analysis of what had actually caused delay.

This is in contrast to the approach taken by the claimant's delay analyst.

An interesting sidenote is provided by *Ascon Contracting Ltd* v. *Alfred McAlpine Construction Isle of Man Ltd* (1999) 66 Con. L.R. 119—a dewatering contract. No doubt that both parties' experts adopted a systematic analysis as what they saw as being the causes of delay. Unfortunately, both delay claims were seriously flawed. So much so that in assessing the extensions of time due, H.H.J. Hicks QC described himself as "left to his own devices".

[Comment—the decision in *John Barker* has potentially serious ramifications wherever the architect/contract administrator has approached the questions of extensions of time on the basis of "a finger in the air". More often than not, however, his defence will be that put forward by Hicks J. in *Ascon*, namely that the quality of the information provided to him was such that he did all he could and made the best of a bad job.]

### A conundrum

Where the architect is satisfied that the delay has been caused by two matters, where

- one is a relevant event and the other is not; or
- both are relevant events but only one gives rise to an entitlement to loss and expense, how should he proceed?

There are two possible approaches that he can take:

- dominant cause approach: if can be shown that one cause is the effective cause of delay that will be sufficient to entitle him to an extension of time for the whole of the period of the delay;
- burden of proof approach: the claimant is entitled to an extension of time for as much of the delay as he can show was caused by the delay (in practice this generally leads to the Court or Arbitrator required to undertake an apportionment).

The SCL Protocol favours the dominant cause approach.

However, authority on the point is minimal and such as there is offers some support for the burden of proof method.

In *H. Fairweather & Co.* v. *London Borough of Wandsworth* (1987) 39 B.L.R. 106, the arbitrator had adopted the dominant cause approach. H.H.J. Fox Andrews QC offered observations which seemed to support the burden of proof approach (although these must be regarded as *obiter*).

This is an issue on which clear guidance is needed.

Under the NEC Form, by clause 61.3 a contractor is obliged to notify the project manager of an event which has happened or which he expects to happen as being a compensation event if he believes the event to be a compensation event, if less than two weeks have passed since he became aware of the event and the project manager has not notified him. It will be noted that there is no requirement that the notice should take any particular form or should indicate any particular consequences which flow from the compensation event. The flaw in this wording is that in the event that more than two weeks have passed, it cannot be said that the contractor owes any obligation to notify.

It will also be noted that the project manager does not have power to request the contractor to explain or amplify any notification given.

The treatment of this issue under GC/Works/1 is worth considering. Under clause 36 it is provided that where the project manager receives notice requesting an extension of time from the contractor (which shall include the grant for the request) or where the project manager considers that there has been or is likely to be a delay, he shall as soon as possible and in any event within 42 days notify the contractor of his claims regarding the extension of time.

It is clear from this wording that notice is not a condition precedent; the onus is on the project manager to take the initiative. Unlike clause 25.2 of JCT 98 there is no requirement that any particulars can be required, and it is also worth noting the provisions of clause 36(3) which provides for an interim or final decision to be made depending on the information available. It is also worth noting in clause 36(4) which provides that no extension of time may be requested after completion of the works and the project manager shall make a final decision on all outstanding and interim decisions within 42 days of completion. This may not go quite as far as it first appears since power is given within the arbitration clause to review any decision made. What is clear is that it is incumbent on the contractor to get notices in promptly. Those familiar with this contract will also be aware that clause 35 provides a regime for progress meetings to be conducted at which detailed provision is made for assessing progress by reference to the contract programme. On the basis that this approach is followed, there is little excuse for the contractor not to give notice of delays as they occur.

## TIME FOR COMPLETION

As we have seen, clause 23.1 of JCT 98 provides that following the giving of possession the contractor shall proceed regularly and diligently with the works and shall complete the works on or before the completion date, which includes the impact of extensions of time.

It is of course the case that the contractor is entitled, should he so wish, to complete the works prior to the completion date, but he cannot contend that the Employer is under any duty to perform in such a way as to permit him to do this. See *Glenlion Construction* v. *Guinness Trust* (1987) 39 B.L.R. 89.

Clause 8(1)(a) of the ICE 7th edition is in simple terms—the contractor is obliged, subject to the provisions of the contract, to construct and complete the works. Clause 43 provides—equally simply—that the works shall be substantially completed by the date dated in the Appendix, subject to any extensions granted under clause 44.

Under the NEC 2nd edition, Clause 11.2(13) simply provides that the works will be provided by the date for completion.

GC/Works/1 provides that the works will be completed by the date set out in the abstract of the particulars.

An issue of some importance here is that the contractor is entitled as well as obliged to carry out his works by the date for completion. In *Wells* v. *Army & Navy Stores* [1902] 2 H.L. 346 Vaughn Williams L.J. held, in effect, that not only was the contractor obliged to carry out his works by the date for completion, he also had that time in which to complete the works. This has two significant practical consequences. First, in the event that the employer commits some act of prevention or obstruction, under each of the Standard Forms, that is likely to give rise to an extension of time. Secondly, except where specifically provided, there is no entitlement on the part of the employer to accelerate the works.

What it does not do, as we have seen in Chapter 5, is to provide the contractor with the right to carry out the works in any particular order, unless, as is the case under clause 33 of GC/Works/1, the contract makes specific provision for this.

A further consideration is that of time become "at large". This can be defined as the situation where circumstances have arisen such that the contractor cannot be held to the original completion date. There are a number of Victorian authorities where the courts held that the circumstances of the contract had so altered that the completion date could be regarded as being of no effect. Those, however, are cases where the contract contained either no or no effective mechanism for extending time and it is likely to be the case that those cases would not be followed today. An exception to this might arise if a contract contained no provision for an extension of time and an act of prevention or delay was committed by the employer. In those circumstances, time might be said to become at large. An example is provided by the decision in *McDermott International* v. *McAlpine Humberoak* [1990] 24 Con. L.R. 68. Although at first instance H.H.J. John Davies QC held that the contract had been so varied that time could be said to be at large, in the Court of Appeal Lloyd L.J. concluded that, although extensive variations had occurred, they could not be said to have made the extension of time provision inoperable.

## PARTIAL POSSESSION AND SECTIONAL COMPLETION

The concepts of partial possession and sectional completion can sometimes be confused. In the context of JCT 98, the former refers to the situation where prior to practical completion the employer takes possession of some part of the works less than the whole of the works. The latter occurs in JCT 98 where the parties have agreed that the works will be sub-divided into sections; separate completion dates are agreed for those sections and a sectional completion supplement is completed to give effect to this sub-dividing of the works.

Clause 18.1 of JCT 98 provides that:

"If at any time or times before the date of issue by the Architect/the Contract Administrator of the Certificate of Practical Completion the Employer wishes to take possession of any part or parts of the Works and the consent of the Contractor (which consent shall not be unreasonably withheld) has been obtained then ... the Employer may take possession thereof. The Architect/Contract Administrator shall thereupon issue to the Contractor on behalf of the Employer a written statement identifying the part or parts of the Works taken in possession ... ".

Clause 18.1.1 provides that for the purposes of clauses 17.2, 17.3 and 17.5 (practical completion) and 30.4.1.2 (defects liability); practical completion shall be deemed to have occurred and the defects liability period shall be deemed to commence for the part of the works taken into possession by the employer when that part of the works is taken into possession.

Clause 18.1.3 makes similar consequential amendments to the requirement to insure the works and clause 18.4 provides that liquidated and ascertained damages shall be abated *pro rata* as between the parts of the works taken into possession and the parts which remain in the custody of the Employer.

It is clear that this does not amount to sectional completion. *Keating* makes it clear that in order for the contract to provide for sectional completion the contract (as opposed merely to the Bills) must be amended to provide for sectional completion. (See also *Gleeson Ltd* v. *London Borough of Hillingdon* (1979) 215 E.G. 165.) Similarly, to avoid confusion, if the parties wish to allow the employer use of some part of the site, falling short of partial possession it is essential that the contract should be amended to reflect precisely what the parties intend. (See *English Industrial Estates* v. *Wimpey* [1973] 1 Lloyd's Rep. 118.) It is also clear from the decision in *Bramall & Ogden* v. *Sheffield City Council* (1973) 29 B.L.R. 73, that the provision of clause 18.1.4 need to be operated with caution. That case was concerned with construction of housing and the contract provided for liquidated damages at the rate of "£20 for each uncompleted dwelling". The court held that this was unworkable since the appendix to the contract did not provide for the calculation which would be required—namely the ascertainment of the amount of work remaining to be completed after deducting the houses taken into possession. This apparently harsh decision shows the care which needs to be taken.

The position is simpler under the ICE 7th edition sub-paragraph (u) of clause 1—the definitions section defines Sectional Completion as any part of the works separately identified in the Appendix. The completion obligation in clause 43 defines the "whole of the works and any section required to be completed within a particular time" and clause 47 provides that where sections are defined the Appendix shall be completed to provide for liquidated damages to be divided among the sections. Clause 48(3) deals with partial possession in similarly brief terms providing that if any substantial part of the works shall have been taken into possession by the employer the engineer shall issue a certificate to that effect. It is suggested that this is permissive in effect, i.e. the employer may take over parts of the works. In that event it probably follows that liquidated damages should be abated to reflect the proportion which has been taken over, but in order to avoid *Bramall & Ogden*-type difficulties it makes sense for the contract to be amended to make clear what effect this will have. Further, it would seem prudent to amend this clause to make clear that the effect of taking over part of the works will be that the part taken over is deemed (substantially) completed unless specifically stated otherwise.

Under the NEC form, clause L1.1 of the secondary options simply provides that references to the works, completion and the completion date shall apply either to the whole of the works or as the case may be to any section, and it is therefore left to the parties to determine whether a particular reference is to the whole or to a section. In the case of delay damages which are dealt with at Secondary Option R, it is therefore up to the parties to ensure that sections are appropriately dealt with.

Clause 35.1 largely mirrors clause 48 in the ICE 7th edition, by providing that possession of the site returns to the employer when he takes over the part of the works which occupies it. It goes on to say that the employer does not have to take over the works prior to completion if the contract data indicates that he is unwilling to do so. Clause 35.3 indicates that he may use any part of the works prior to completion, and clause 35.4 provides that the project manager shall issue a certificate certifying the date upon which the works have been taken over.

As indicated above, clause 35(1) of GC/Works/1 deals simply with time for completion. The drafting of the contract is designed to enable the works to be divided into sections. A minor shortcoming of the drafting is that whilst the time for completion of sections and indeed liquidated damages applicable to sections is provided for, the contract form itself does not contain any designated place to define what the sections actually comprise.

## COMPLETION

The JCT family of contracts all make reference to "Practical Completion". In JCT 98 this is found in clause 17.1 which provides that:

> "When in the opinion of the Architect Practical Completion of the Works is achieved . . . he shall forthwith issue a certificate to that effect and Practical Completion of the Works shall be deemed for all purposes of this contract to have taken place on the day named in such certificate."

By contract clause 30.2 of NEC 2nd edition provides that:

> "The Project Manager decides the date of completion. The Project Manager certifies completion within one week of completion."

The expressions "Practical Completion" and "Completion" are not defined in either form. The term "practical completion" gives rise to conceptual difficulties. Does it mean "nearly complete" or "complete for all practical purposes"? As *Keating* puts it: "Practical completion is perhaps easier to recognise than to define."

The authorities are limited to observations of the House of Lords in *Jarvis & Sons* v. *Westminster Corporation* [1970] 1 W.L.R. 637 and *PM Kaye* v. *Hosier*

*& Dickinson* [1972] 1 W.L.R. 146; and two decisions of H.H.J. Newey QC; *HW Nevill (Sunblest) Ltd* v. *William Press* (1981) 20 B.L.R. 78 and *Emson Eastern* v. *EME Developments* (1991) 55 B.L.R. 114.

Newey J.'s comments in the latter two cases suggest that the best view is that "practical completion" should be defined as meaning "complete but for minor of *de minimis* items". This will be a question of fact in the circumstances of each case. It will be noted, however, that the term "snagging" does not appear and is not used in the contract. *Keating* makes the sensible point that while the works can be practically complete notwithstanding the presence of latent defects, they should not be certified as practically complete if there are patent defects.

To avoid uncertainty it is increasingly common for the standard form to be amended to set out a series of minimum standards to be achieved in order for practical completion to have occurred. This will commonly include:

- delivery of operation and maintenance manuals;
- testing and commissioning to have been successfully completed;
- finishings to have reached an agreed standard (usually to enable a tenant to carry out his fit-out works);
- health and safety documentation to have been delivered.

Does the expression "completion" as used in NEC mean something different? At present there is no authority on this point, but it is suggested that it does not. The fact that (like JCT) NEC includes provision for a defects liability period and the rectification of defects, that it is envisaged that completion can occur, notwithstanding the presence of minor items of defective or incomplete work.

In addition to marking the point at which the works are physically complete (but for minor defects or items of incomplete work) practical completion (under (JCT) and Completion (under NEC) also mark the point at which the Employer's right to liquidated damages for delay ceases. Liquidated damages for delay cannot be deducted for periods after practical completion. This is a point which needs to be carefully considered by an architect in deciding whether the works should be certified as being practically complete.

In clause 48 of the ICE 7th edition, the term used is "substantial completion". This expression has been used in previous editions of the form. *Keating* indicates that the reference in this clause to "outstanding works" to be carried out during the defects correction period suggests something short of literal completion, although it is difficult to see any logical reason why this should be differentiated from the position under JCT 98 which provides the same contractual "scheme" for the correction of defects and completion of outstanding works after practical completion.

GC/Works/1 deals with the matter simply. Clause 34(1) refers to "completion" without otherwise defining the expression. Clause 21, however, provides for the rectification of defects appearing during the maintenance period. It is suggested (albeit that there is no decided authority on the point) that completion under this form probably means the same as practical completion under JCT98, substantial completion under ICE 7th edition or completion under NEC.

It is clear that these provisions set the bar at a high level. While it is no doubt often tempting for a contract administrator to certify that the works are complete, subject to an often extensive list of matters to be completed or remedied, and this will often be done as a result of pressure from both the employer and the contractor, this should be approached with caution. The reason for this is very simple. Once practical completion has been granted, the right to deduct liquidated damages disappears. The employer's principle sanction to pressure the contractor into completing the works accordingly vanishes.

## DEFECTS, DEFECTS CORRECTION AND LATENT DEFECTS

Under JCT 98 the position is stated clearly in clause 2.1 as follows:

"The contractor shall upon and subject to the conditions carry out and complete the Works in compliance with the Contract Documents using materials and workmanship of the quality and standards therein specified provided that where and to the extent that approval of the quality of materials is a matter for the opinion of the Architect/the Contract Administrator such quality and standards shall be the reasonable satisfaction of the Architect/the Contract Administrator."

A useful starting point is the proviso which takes up the last part of the clause. This is now understood to apply only to those matters specifically reserved to the architect, and not generally (thereby reversing the effect of the decision in *Crown Estates Commissioners* v. *John Mowlem & Co. Ltd* (1994) 70 B.L.R. 1).

In summary then, the contractor's obligation is to carry out the works strictly in accordance with the contract documents and where the works do not comply with the contract documents, on the face of it they are defective.

As we have seen above, clause 8 deals with the quality of workmanship and the contractor's obligation to carry out the works in accordance with the contract as well as the architect/contract administrator's entitlement to order the opening up of works which he believes do not comply with the contract, and the removal of works found not to comply, and/or the adjustment of the contract sum.

We have also seen above that clause 30.2.1.1 provides that the value to be included in any interim certificate shall be that of work properly carried out.

It is suggested that the word "properly" can be used interchangeably with "in accordance with the contract".

The question of how defective or non-compliant work is to be valued is the subject of Chapter 9. However, at this point it is relevant to consider a number of issues facing the parties.

- First, the provisions of clause 8.1 provide the architect with limited discretion—as we have seen in relation to clause 2.1 the "reasonable satisfaction" of the architect is confined to matters stipulated as being subject to his approval.
- Where works are found to be non-compliant the architect has an absolute right to order their removal, subject to the discretion to allow them to remain and make an appropriate adjustment to the contract sum. It follows that the contractor is not entitled to argue that the Architect must allow the non-compliant work to remain, or even that a reasonable Architect would allow these works to remain (see *William Cory & Son* v. *Wingate Investments* (1980) 17 B.L.R. 104). At best this may go to arguments concerning mitigation of loss in subsequent proceedings.
- The right to call for opening up under clauses 8.3 and/or 8.4.4 provided it is properly exercised does not carry with it any entitlement to remuneration if the works are found to be compliant. It does convey a right to an extension of time.

It is also the case that practical completion of the works should not be certified in the event that there are patent defects in the works (see above). Put slightly differently, unless and until the works have been carried out in accordance with the contract, the architect is under no duty to certify practical completion. The common practice of certifying practical completion, subject to a (sometimes lengthy) list of outstanding "snagging" items, while understandable is not to be encouraged.

This leads to consideration of the defects liability period. The duration will be specified in the Appendix. Most commonly this will be 12 months from practical completion. Clause 17.2 provides that:

"Any defects shrinkages or other faults which shall appear within the Defects Liability and which are due to materials or workmanship not in accordance with this contract . . . shall be specified by the Architect/the Contract Administrator in a schedule of defects which he shall deliver to the Contractor as an instruction of the Architect/the Contract Administrator not later than 14 days after the expiration of the said Defects Liability period and within a reasonable time after receipt of such schedule, the effects shrinkages and other faults shall be made good by the Contractor at no cost to the Employer. . . . "

The clause also provides that the architect/contract administrator has a discretion to instruct that such defects shall not be made good, in which case an appropriate deduction can be made from the contract sum. This is an option which is seldom used.

Clause 17.3 provides that notwithstanding the provisions of clause 17.2 at any time (within the defects liability period) the architect/contract administrator may issue instructions for the putting right of any defect, shrinkage or other fault appearing within the defects liability period. Clause 17.4 provides that when in the opinion of the architect/contract administrator have been put right, he shall issue a certificate to that effect "the certificate of making good defects". Upon issue of this certificate, the second half of the retention is released (as provided by clause 30.4.1.3).

An important consideration here is that the architect's power to issue instructions for the putting right of defects will only extend to defects appearing within the defects liability period. If a defect was not apparent during the defects liability period, the architect cannot be expected to issue instructions for its remediation. The reverse side of this is that if a defect is apparent, but no instruction is issued with regard to it prior to the issue of the certificate of making good defects, the likelihood is that that the employer will face arguments that he has waived any subsequent right to require the contractor to put it right, although he may well have a right of action against the architect. Obviously this will not apply where the instruction has been given and the contractor has either concealed the fact that he has not addressed the problem or has not addressed it properly. Where the defect is not one which could have been identified within the defects liability period, the employer's rights will, subject to limitation, be unaffected.

Under the ICE 7th edition a slightly different regime applies. Clause 48(1) provides that where the contractor considers that the works are substantially complete he shall give notice to that effect and shall accompany that notice with an undertaking to put right any outstanding work. Upon the issue of a certificate of substantial completion, the defects correction period, the duration of which is specified in the Appendix, shall commence. Clause 49(1) provides that by agreement this undertaking shall provide a period for the execution of outstanding work, and clause 49(2) indicates that as soon as practicable, the contractor shall carry out this work at no cost to the employer.

Clause 50 requires that if the employer so directs in writing, the contractor shall carry out searches or tests at his own cost to determine the cause of any defect. This is a sensible provision given the concealed nature of many civil engineering works. Clause 61(1) provides that where all works required to be carried out under clause 48 and any defects appearing and covered by clauses 49 and 50 have been carried out, the Engineer shall issue a Defects Correction Certificate.

As indicated above, under GC/Works/1 a simple regime is provided by clauses 21 and 34.

## SELF-TEST QUESTIONS

**1. True or false?**

In the event that a contractor finds that his works are much harder than he had originally anticipated, he is entitled to argue for the incorporation of an implied term entitling him to additional payment.

**2. Retention monies are released:**

(a) whenever the element of work to which the retention money relates has been completed;
(b) when the architect issues a certificate saying it is fair and reasonable to do so;
(c) half on practical completion, half on making good of defects;
(d) at the end of the limitation period.

**3. Which of the following statements is true?**

(a) notices specifying that delays have been suffered are available from HM Stationery Office;
(b) under JCT 98, notice of delay is a condition precedent;
(c) the requirements for a notice are strict and failure to comply with the correct form of notice will be penalised;
(d) serving notice can be dispensed with where the contractor considers this would be excessively "contractual".

**4. Practical completion means that:**

(a) the works are completed but for minor items;
(b) the works are very nearly complete;
(c) the works are complete, but for snagging items, which can number into hundreds;
(d) the works are complete in every respect.

**5. Latent defects are:**

(a) defects which are underground;
(b) defects which are not considered serious;
(c) defects which were not known about at the time of practical completion;
(d) defects which nobody ever knew about.

CHAPTER 8

# CHANGE AND ITS EFFECTS

Mark Hackett

## AN OVERVIEW OF CHANGE AND ITS EFFECTS

It is unrealistic to attempt to ban variations or design changes. A building project is usually a complicated, unique venture erected largely in the open, on ground the condition of which is never fully predictable, and in weather conditions which are even less so. There is a considerable time span between making the initial decision to build and the completion of works on site. During this period technology, fashion and the client's requirements inevitably change. The standard forms of contract recognise these possibilities and attempt to ensure that variations are valued fairly in accordance with rules which are known at tender stage, rather than leaving the establishment of those rules until the problems occur at which time one party would most probably be in a more advantageous position than the other.

On a contract that is beset with delays and disruption, much of the blame for this will be put on the implementation of variations or design changes. On a contract so affected, and where the targets of time and monetary entitlement are temporarily undermined, it is understandable, if not contractually supportable, for the contractor to turn his back on his obligations and divert his energies to building a claim rather than building the project.

This is not to say that variations or design changes should not be implemented, but where they are necessary the effect both on time and monetary entitlement should be quickly evaluated so that the project objectives are repaired. This is where many building projects fail. Albeit that many of the standard forms of contract have had features introduced into them aimed at agreeing the valuation of variations prior to their implementation, all too often contracts do not provide the necessary procedure for speedy resolution of these matters; and where they do the parties or their representatives do not implement them properly.

There is, however, an intrinsic difficulty in framing the provisions for valuing variations on the principle adopted by, for example, the JCT Standard Form of Building Contract. This principle is that variations introduced by the client shall be paid for at rates analogous to those in the tender; that is to say at the rates that the contractor might reasonably be expected to have used had those works been incorporated or described in the tender documents. Such a provision is an invaluable asset to the client; without it he may find himself paying penal amounts for variations, the value of which would be set by a contractor well established on site and with all the advantages. However, for such a provision to operate effectively it must operate fairly. Thus the JCT Standard Form of Building Contract provides for changed conditions or changed character to be taken into account when valuing the variation; in just the same way that one might presume that the contractor's estimator would take such conditions and character into account at tender stage had that work been included. Such a proviso is reasonable as is the other proviso to be found in the JCT Standard Form of Building Contract which is that "fair valuation" may be undertaken where the tendered rates would not do justice to the variation or design change. However equitable and necessary such provisos are, they can also be used by the unscrupulous to avoid the detailed rules of valuation to be found elsewhere in the contract.

The lesson to be learned here is that the time and monetary effects of variations should, where at all possible, be agreed in advance of their implementation. If this is not done, the matter might not be addressed until months after the event and this may be at the very point when the contemporary evidence necessary to make a proper valuation is no longer to hand. It is the absence of contemporary evidence which is one of the single most important reasons for the valuation of variations and/or the settlement of claims degenerating into an expensive game of poker.

## VALUATION v. ASCERTAINMENT

### *Preface*

Viewed from the perspective of JCT Standard Form of Building Contract Private with Quantities 1998 Edition—and, indeed, the whole family of JCT Contracts—establishing the appropriate level of payment due to the contractor can involve assessment techniques such as valuation and ascertainment. Valuation and ascertainment are two very different things and care must be taken not to mix them up!

### *Clause 13—valuation of variations*

It is a common feature of construction contracts that the originally intended scope and/or quality of the project will be varied from time to time—it is with this in mind that any of the standard construction contracts contain detailed clauses governing what is to be done when variations arise. On its simplest analysis, the valuation of variations at contract rates (or at rates analogous thereto having made adjustments to suit the particular circumstances under review) allows for a replication of the contractor's pricing assumptions at tender stage thus holding the contractor within the confines of the very pricing structure which led to his being awarded the contract in the first place.

As any project progresses, a contractor may find that certain of the rates are insufficient to cover his costs. Whilst contractually bound by these rates, commercial pressures dictate that the contractor may then try to recover the shortfall by maximising the return on all variations which he is asked to carry out. Contractors often put the thesis this way: "I don't mind sticking by my pricing errors for the work covered by the contract sum but it is unreasonable to expect them to be used if the client changes his mind about the scope and/or quality of the work to be executed." On the face of it, this is not an unreasonable point of view. However, it indicates a fundamental misunderstanding of both the intent and the wording of the standard construction contracts. Taking JCT in particular, the rates in the contract form part of that contract exclusively for the purposes of valuing variations and remeasured work; that these rates were also used in the compilation of the contract sum is not contractually relevant. The contractor offers to complete the whole of the work called for under the contract in exchange for the contract sum; in addition, he offers to undertake variations at the rates entered into the contract. Plainly, it is not the intention of JCT that the rates be overturned and set aside on the very occasion for which they were designed.

Authority on this point was provided by H.H.J. Humphrey Lloyd QC in the case of *Henry Boot Construction Ltd* v. *Alstom Combined Cycles Ltd.*[1] In that case, the plaintiff sought to benefit from an exceptionally high rate on the occasion of a variation being ordered in respect of a category of work which was the subject of that rate; the defendant, faced with the prospect of paying somewhat over the odds for the varied work, sought to avoid that exceptionally high rate by arguing that the varied work should instead be valued by reference to a fair and reasonable level of pricing—it was also apparent that the rate was high by reason of an error in the compilation of the plaintiff's tender and the defendant saw the valuation of the variation as presenting an opportunity to correct this error. The plaintiff, a contractor, was in the relatively unusual position of seeking to be held by the pricing in the contract bills and received support for this stance from H.H.J. Humphrey Lloyd QC whose judgment was that a variation could not be used as a pretext to unravel and correct mistakes made by a contractor in his pricing since this would "be completely inconsistent with the wording of such a contract and the philosophy to be derived from it". As noted from the 11 April 2000 edition of *The Times*, H.H.J. Humphrey Lloyd QC's judgment has since been confirmed by the Court of Appeal. Once the contract is entered into there can, by definition, be no such thing as "errors" in the contract bill rates or prices.

In effect, when valuing a variation, the quantity surveyor is trying to arrive at the answer which the contractor would have given at tender stage had he been aware of the variation. At tender stage, the contractor's estimator will have been operating in the climate of wanting to win the work which is the subject of the tender and this will lead to competitive pricing which is reflected in the rates. The inherently competitive aspect of the rates should not then be abandoned if there are variations.

1. (1999) 64 Con. L.R. 32.

### *Clause 26—Ascertainment of loss and/or expense*

Just in the same way that any of the standard construction contracts will provide a regime for maintaining the integrity of the contractor's original undertakings as to price, those contracts also recognise that there will be occasions where rate adjustments alone will not provide appropriate recompense to the contractor in respect of those risks which eventuate and for which the client is responsible. Accordingly, in addition to the recovery by the contractor through his rates (and derivatives therefrom) in the circumstances described above, JCT provides that the contractor is entitled to recover any loss and/or expense he suffers for acts of hindrance or prevention on the part of the client (or those for whom he is responsible).

In this situation, and to use the usual parlance in the construction industry, the contractor will make a "claim" which, if validly made, will entitle him to recover his actual, as distinct from tendered, costs and arriving at the computation of same will involve a process analogous to that of establishing general damages at common law. Consequently, the individual charged with establishing the contractor's entitlement will need to satisfy himself that the following conditions precedent have been satisfied:

- the matter complained of is something for which the client is responsible;
- the contractor has actually, as distinct from theoretically, suffered loss and can provide an audit trail in support of this;
- there is a causative link between the last two items;
- the contractor has mitigated the effects of the matter complained of; and
- there is no duplication in respect of monies which may already have been received under any other clause of the contract between the parties.

The right to make a claim sometimes gives rise to the argument from contractors that the claim itself can be used to "top up" any shortfall on the valuation process; this argument is flawed since if any shortfall on a valuation could be resurrected elsewhere under the contract then the comprehensive and widely drafted variation clauses to be found in JCT would be rendered meaningless.

### *Ascertaining loss and/or expense*

Too often, claims for reimbursement of direct loss and/or expense are initiated by the contractor who submits a seemingly detailed build up of his alleged entitlement at or towards the end of a project. Although clause 26.1 now recognises that " . . . the contractor may give his quantification . . . " it does not require that he shall do so. It is for the architect (or quantity surveyor if so instructed by the architect) to ascertain the amount due and to request from the contractor such details as he believes are necessary to fulfil this obligation. In the case of *London Borough of Merton* v. *Stanley Hugh Leach*,[2] it was stated that "The Contractor must clearly cooperate with the architect or the quantity surveyor in giving such particulars . . . to enable him to ascertain the extent of that loss and/or expense". Moreover, the fact that it may be difficult to arrive at an accurate ascertainment cannot be a barrier to making as proper an assessment as the available data permit. Indeed, from the case of *Wood* v. *Grand Valley Railway Co.*,[3] it is clear that even when it is " . . . impossible . . . to estimate with anything approaching mathematical accuracy the damages . . . (this) . . . cannot relieve the wrongdoer of the necessity of paying damages . . . and its (the judge or jury) conclusion will not be set aside even if the amount of the verdict is a matter of guess work".

In the case of *F G Minter* v. *Welsh Health Technical Services Organisation*,[4] it was emphasised that it was cost, as distinct from the rates and prices given in the contract bills, that should be the basis of any ascertainment. However, the damages payable by a party committing a breach should be no more than he anticipated would be the consequence of such a breach at the time he made the contract. Thus, where a contractor's costs are materially different from the rates quoted in the contract bills, there must be a good reason for that difference otherwise any significant unjustifiable increase in costs might have to be disallowed from a claim for reimbursement of direct loss and/or expense on the grounds that to include them would result in the client paying more than he anticipated at the time he signed the contract.

Where, however, the contractor does submit a monied out claim, the architect's or quantity surveyor's task is not to challenge or reduce that submission but, rather, his role is to build up an entitlement quite independently under the terms of the contract by ascertaining the amounts due, given the contract conditions and the established facts. In building up the contractor's entitlement, the architect or quantity surveyor should start with a comprehensive list of possible headings under which such an entitlement might arise. This list is as follows:

(a) materials;
(b) labour disruption;
(c) attraction money and bonus payment (in certain circumstances);
(d) preliminaries and supervision;
(e) inflation;
(f) head office overheads and profit; and
(g) interest charges.

2. (1985) 32 B.L.R. 51.
3. (1913) 30 O.L.R. 44.
4. (1980) 13 B.L.R. 1.

Other items often appearing in a contractor's submission which generally would not be admissible are:

(h) cost of accelerating the works;
(i) cost of overtime; and
(j) cost of preparing a claim.

In ascertaining the amounts properly payable as direct loss and/or expense, it is advisable to ask the following questions, the answers to which will provide useful background against which to make an evaluation:

(a) did the event occur and was it the direct result of the cause claimed?;
(b) is the cause one which is recognised by the contract, i.e. is it either one of the matters listed in clause 26.2 or deferment of possession of the site under clause 23.1.2?;
(c) have the conditions laid down by the contract been complied with, e.g. was the contractor's application in writing and was it made as soon as it became, or should reasonably have become, apparent to him that the regular progress of the works had been materially affected?;
(d) what are the costs directly attributable to the cause?; and
(e) is any part of the cost reimbursed elsewhere under the contract?

Application of some of the above questions may lead one to conclude that the problem is not covered by the contract terms, in which case neither the architect nor quantity surveyor is empowered to deal with it even if the contractor has a general right to sue the client for breach of contract. The application of some of the other questions may demonstrate that only part of the costs alleged are reimbursable.

In any event, the contractor's entitlement is that amount which is ascertained as the difference between the costs properly and directly incurred in carrying out the work (albeit disrupted by the event) and what those costs would have been had the event not occurred. In practice, this may be very difficult to establish and will always involve an element of judgment rather than established fact: "what the costs would have been" will always be a matter for conjecture—a fact not always recognised by those who have to accept the consequences of the ascertainment.

Any such ascertainment will havc to ignore:

(a) any errors in the level of pricing in the tender; or
(b) any extra costs in executing the work not directly associated with the claim, i.e. mismanagement.

This part of the chapter has followed upon the JCT form. To compare the manner in which payment is calculated across the standard forms, readers might like to turn back to Chapter 7 to the section entitled "JCT, ICE GC/Works, NEC and FIDIC—compared and contrasted".

# DISRUPTION

## A definition

The term "disruption" is used in both the Association of Consultant Architects Form of Building Agreement 1998 and the GC/Works/1 (1998) standard form contracts at clauses 7.1 and 46 respectively to describe an effect on the "regular progress of works".

More recently, the Society of Construction Law's Delay and Disruption Protocol defined disruption as:

"(as distinct from delay) disturbance, hindrance or interruption to a contractor's normal working methods, resulting in lower efficiency. If caused by the employer, it may give rise to a right to compensation either under the contract or as a breach of contract."

From the above, two key points emerge:

- disruption can (but not necessarily) result in lower efficiency for the contractor; and
- disruption is distinct from the allied concept of "delay".

In reality, claims involving disruption are the more difficult to quantify.

## Disruption in practice

Disruption during a working day is often of small duration, involving slowly working down or stopping work for periods ranging from 10 minutes to several hours, and can lead to an overall productivity loss.

The productivity loss can, in turn, lead to time (and cost) overruns. Contractors of all tiers concerned that they have lost money, troubled by the threat of liquidated damages or simply because the conditions of contract allow, are tempted to submit claims for extensions of time and loss and/or expense. The temptation for contractors to submit a claim for an extension of time (instead of loss and/or expense) is heightened when they cannot readily demonstrate cause and effect to progress associated with the alleged disruption. In such cases, contractors, probably because they do not possess tangible records, are simply unable to prove or quantify the loss and/or expense incurred as a direct result of the disruption. Nevertheless, keen to recover some costs (or time), they are "forced" (or resigned) to submit an extension of time delay claim, whereas they should have submitted a loss and/or expense disruption claim.

## Loss and/or expense or extension of time?

Generally speaking, contractors do in fact know that disruption should only lead to claims for loss and/or expense and that delays should lead to claims for an extension of time. They also fully understand that delay and disruption require different tests and that a successful claim in one is not a condition precedent for a successful claim in the other.

It is vital to appreciate that it is disruption occurring during the working day that is the most contentious and difficult to quantify. Longer, more tangible delays involving stoppages of work for days and weeks, usually at the start of the project, are more straightforward in terms of duration and lend themselves to the various delay analysis techniques described later in this chapter.

Of course, this is not to say that issues such as ownership of float, concurrency and the actual method of delay analysis are settled in practice or within the construction industry or in English Law. The quantification of such delay claims has one distinct advantage over the quantification of disruption claims, namely that quantification of disruption claims requires the measurement of site labour/resources productivity. In contract, although not a major advantage, it is nevertheless generally accepted that in the quantification of delay claims, there is usually some level of factual agreement about the length of the actual stoppage. In disruption claims, the parties usually cannot agree on even the crude level of disruption, or indeed on the actual time lost due to the various small interruptions/stoppages.

## *The treatment of disruption in case law*

Following *Ascon Contracting Ltd* v. *Alfred McAlpine Construction Isle of Man Ltd*,[5] the *Construction Law Reports* (February 2000) commented, " . . . the failure of both parties to demonstrate to any real extent their contentions in respect of delay again reinforces the importance when pursuing claims for delay of some form of technical delay analysis demonstrating cause and effect".

A series of relevant cases in this area from *Wharf Properties Ltd* v. *Eric Cumine Associates*[6] to *Ascon Contracting* v. *Alfred McAlpine Construction Isle of Man Ltd* has increased the construction industry's attention to linking cause and effect. In practice, it is highly unlikely that the courts will consider disruption claims based simply upon the global overspend on plant/labour for the whole of the contract. There is a need to isolate (to some degree) the cause and effect of disruption.

The most convincing method of quantifying the effect of disruption is a comparison of actual hours and output, during a period known to be unaffected, with those in the affected period. An almost identical approach is advocated by the Society of Construction Law's Delay and Disruption Protocol which states " . . . the starting point for any disruption analysis is to understand what work was carried out, when it was carried out and what resources were used".

The Protocol also states:

> "The most appropriate way to establish disruption is to apply a technique known as the 'Measured Mile'. This compares the productivity on an un-impacted part of the contract with that achieved on the impacted part. Such a comparison factors out issues

5. (1999) 66 Con. L.R. 119.
6. [1991] 52 B.L.R. 1.

concerning unrealistic programmes and inefficient working. The comparison can be made on the man hours expended or the units of work performed."

### *Quantifying disruption*

The key point of both methods discussed above is that, as recognised in the Protocol, care must be exercised to compare like with like. In the absence of actual measured productivity records, the courts have used other (crude) methods and data to obtain an indication of actual site productivity loss.

For example, in *Whittal Builder Company Ltd* v. *Chester-le-Street DC*,[7] the contractor was disrupted by the client with the result that " . . . ordinary and economic planning and arrangement of work was rendered impossible". However, a stage was reached in November 1974 when no further disruption occurred. The court had to decide, in the absence of site resource/labour productivity records, upon the appropriate method of quantifying the effect of the disruption. In this case, the contractor was able to illustrate that the value of work done was £108 per man-week during the period of disruption and that the value of work done rose to £162 per man-week during the period after November 1974. The court held that the loss in productivity caused by the disruption was therefore one-third.

Mr Recorder Percival QC accepted this method of comparing the value of the work done per man in the whole period during disruption with the value of the work done under non-delayed conditions as the " . . . best approach open to me". There should be little difficulty in calculating such man-hours using the contractor's accounts and interim certificates.

However, it should be noted that this manipulation of costs could be at variance with reality, since it does not allow for the contractor's own defaults and it fails to take account of the natural variability in site resource/labour productivity.

The courts prefer an accurate method of assessment but case law indicates that the difficulties of accurate assessment cannot relieve the wrongdoer of the duty to pay damages. The problem is that an assessment on that basis is not objective and may not be accurate.

Although programmes have been used, the courts have shown a dislike for their use in the evaluation process. In *Glenlion Construction Ltd* v. *The Guinness Trust*,[8] Judge Fox-Andrews QC said:

"In regard to claims based on delay, litigious contractors frequently supplied to architects or engineers at an early stage in the work highly optimistic programmes showing completion a considerable time ahead of the contract date. These documents are then used (a) to justify allegations that the information or possession has been supplied late and (b) to increase the alleged period of delay, or to make a claim possible where the contract completion date has not in the event been extended."

7. [1988] 40 B.L.R. 82.
8. [1987] 39 B.L.R. 89.

It may be concluded that the courts would welcome a system of using the actual site resource/labour productivity measurements to quantify the effects of disruption in terms of loss and/or expense. The measurement and comparison of actual site productivity is the key to quantifying the effect of disruption.

Thomas[9] states:

"Comparison between actual productivity and the allowance in the tender may not be appropriate as a basis of calculation. This method does not take into account errors in the tender. Further, the project team may have changed the method of construction assumed by the estimator. What needs to be considered is the actual productivity with that which ought to have been achieved using the proposed method and sequence that the contractor would have used if there had been no disruption."

What Thomas does not say, but presumably intends, is that the actual productivity is itself reasonable and not influenced by inefficient working methods.

### *Use of productivity measurements*

The need to use actual site productivity records was also highlighted in *Foundation Co. of Canada* v. *United Grain Growers Ltd.*[10] In this case, the claimant's sub-contractor employed an "expert" to calculate retrospectively the site production levels before, during and after the alleged disruption. The judge dismissed these calculations, saying that they were inconsistent and did not reflect the sensitivity to delay in the different methods of construction and in the various activities. The judge suggested that actual site productivity was vital in the accurate and realistic assessment of damages. He said:

"In my view a productivity loss claim should be supported to the fullest extent possible by evidence as to what was occurring as the job progressed. If the employees sit idle because material did not arrive, or on arrival did not fit, the loss of time can be documented. If employees are forced to move to another area, the time lost in that exercise can also be recorded. If the pace at which employees complete their tasks is reduced because of extended overtime hours, that as well can be noted by the supervisors at the time."

### *The role of productivity measurements*

The present position in construction disruption-based claims and disputes is that settlement is often reached after extensive, and sometimes highly subjective, negotiations. The parties' positions are usually severely weakened by a

9. Thomas R., *Construction Contract Claims* (The MacMillan Press Limited).
10. (1996) Foundation Co. of Canada 62 All Canada Weekly Summary (3d) 29.

lack of records that may actually demonstrate the effect of a "disruptive" event on the contractor's work operations. If the contractor's productivity could be recorded sufficiently accurately and simply, it could be used as objective evidence accurately to demonstrate the effect the disruption has actually had on the site productivity. The equating of productivity loss to disruption may represent a realistic and objective measure of the effect of disruption on the contractor's progress of work.

It is not only the courts who have recognised the vital importance of productivity measurements. Pickavance[11] has concluded that delay and disruption claims of necessity require productivity analysis:

"Labour and equipment are the two major performance variables by which a party can manage to achieve timely performance. Much of the impact of such timely and efficient performance (or lack thereof) is manifested in labour and equipment performance, of which productivity is the management measure."

But:

- How do we measure productivity?
- Do we monitor all site activities?
- Or do we monitor only a few?
- If so, which ones do we actually monitor?
- And how do we then translate or relate the productivity measurements to loss and/or expense and, in particular, the time-related charges?

### *Developing a disruption measurement scheme*

Most practitioners will readily appreciate that, in reality, there are numerous factors that can influence site labour productivity on the construction site. A precise or detailed definition of productivity would need almost one observer to every site operative. However, because the cost of providing an observer for every worker would clearly be prohibitive, the search for precision must be tempered with economic and practical reality. The construction site is not a science laboratory. It is not possible to change one variable at a time and study its effect on site labour productivity. Even academic researchers who have tried have found it almost impossible to reach conclusions of practical merit.

The way in which site labour productivity should be measured is influenced by the purpose for which the results will be used. In this part of the Module, we are concerned with the effects of disruption in order to facilitate agreement between, typically, the client and main contractor involved in a claim for loss and/or expense. It follows, therefore, that in order to determine the incidence,

11. Pickavance K., (1997) *Delay and Disruption in Construction Contracts*, 1st edn, Construction Practice Series, LLP Reference Publishing.

cause and effect of disruption, the proposed site labour productivity measurement scheme must collect site information on the nature, duration and possible cause(s) of disruption.

### *Labour productivity measures*

The area of site labour productivity appears to have consumed a significant amount of academic's time. This appears to suggest that labour productivity could be measured using the following three types of time input:

**1. Total time**
Output where total time is total paid time.

**2. Available time**
Output where available time is total time minus unavoidable delays (i.e. meal breaks and weather).

**3. Productive time**
Output where productive time is available time minus avoidable delays.

- Total time/output defines the total labour cost of the job. It does not differentiate between time spent working or idle time. It is the global figure often required by the estimator for tendering purposes and the measure used to assess whether or not the contractor has made a profit.
- Productivity measured using available time is influenced by the quality of site management, through its ability to minimise the frequency and duration of disruption. This measure is also affected by the effect of design on the potential for continuity of work and by changes in the scope of the works that cause delays and disruption. It is naturally the measure around which all claims for delay and disruption are based.
- Productivity measured using the productive time/output represents the actual time input and provides a measure of the intrinsic factors relating to a particular job. Such factors include the quality of the labour (e.g. skill, attitude), the design (e.g. buildability) and the site environment (e.g. scale of project). In theory and in practice, it is the most detailed level at which site labour productivity can be economically and practically measured without the continuous presence of an (expensive and often intrusive) observer.

Another method of representing a productivity measure is earned value. Earned value relies on the establishment of a set of standard outputs or "norms" for each unit operation. A number of "earned hours" is associated with each unit of work completed. Productivity can then be defined as the ratio of earned hours to actual hours, i.e.:

$$\frac{\text{Earned hours}}{\text{Actual man-hours}}$$

### *Some practical considerations*

In any event, the contractor's entitlement is that amount which is ascertained as the difference between the costs properly and directly incurred in carrying out the work (albeit disrupted by the event) and what those costs would have been had the event not occurred. In practice, this may be very difficult to establish and will always involve an element of judgment rather than established fact: "what the costs would have been" will always be a matter for conjecture (see Example 1)—a fact not always recognised by those who have to accept the consequences of the ascertainment.

Any such ascertainment will have to ignore:

(a) any errors in the level of pricing in the tender; or
(b) any extra costs in executing the work not directly associated with the claim, i.e. mismanagement.

An example of such a calculation, of the need for conjecture and of the element of inadmissible costs, is given at Example 1.

The provision of these data by the contractor as required by clause 26.1.2 is dependent upon the architect or quantity surveyor requesting them. Therefore where disruption to progress is likely to occur, or where direct loss and/or expense due to a variation is likely, the architect would be well advised to inform the contractor immediately what data he expects to be recorded. It would be sensible to ensure that such records were agreed between the contractor and the clerk of works.

If such proper records are kept they will be the best evidence for calculation of loss of output and must be preferable to any subsequent assumptions.

However, there are dangers. First, the request to keep such records must not be mistaken for an acceptance that the client will pay all or any of the costs involved whatever they may be; the contractor may generally be inefficient or part of his labour might be expended on carrying out the work incorrectly or in remedying defective work; to that extent such costs will not be reimbursable and, therefore, they should be isolated. Secondly, steps must be taken to ensure that the records extend only to the work which is or may properly be the subject of a claim. Thus the architect should agree with the contractor precisely what is to be recorded and how, and then alert the clerk of works to monitor the manner in which this work is carried out and the efficacy of the cost records. Once these safeguards have been properly implemented, the records should be compared with an assessment of what costs would have been incurred had the delay or disruption not taken place; the difference being reimbursable to the contractor as the following Examples 1 and 2 show.

***Example 1: Ascertaining the loss of output from records***

A variation to part of a foundation to a building delays the erection of one bay of the pre-cast concrete frame. This prospect is predicted well before it takes place and the clerk of works and the contractor, at the request of the architect, agree records of output both before and after the period of disruption. These are as follows:

| | |
|---|---|
| (a) Recorded cost of an erection gang per week | £3,500 |
| (b) Recorded output of the gang prior to the disruption | 1.50 bays per week |
| (c) Recorded output of the gang during disruption | 1.15 bays per week |
| (d) Output of the gang assumed at tender stage deducted from the contract bill prices | 1.30 bays per week |
| (e) After discussion with the clerk of works it is decided that the contractor did not manage the disrupted work as well as he should have done. Had he done so the output at (c) above would have been | 1.25 bays per week |

Thus the reasonable cost per bay during disruption is (a) ÷ (e)

$$\frac{£3,500}{1.25} = £2,800$$

Whereas the cost per bay before disruption (i.e. that which should have prevailed had disruption not taken place) is (a) ÷ (b)

$$\frac{£3,500}{1.5} = £2,333$$

Therefore the direct loss and/or expense is £467 per bay (£2,800–£2,333) and this is the contractor's entitlement.

The following points should be noted:

(a) the level of pricing deduced from the contract bills is not relevant—at an actual output of 1.50 bays per week the contractor was beating his tender assumption of 1.3 bays per week and thus reaping an additional profit which should not be eroded; and

(b) the contractor can only recover the direct loss; that is to say to the extent that mismanagement added to the contractor's costs (i.e. the reduction in output from 1.25 to 1.15 bays per week) those costs are not reimbursable as they are not the direct result of the variation.

In practice, rarely is one in such a privileged position of having accurate records of the costs before disruption in the form envisaged above; and in any event an element of conjecture is always inevitable as to what the costs would have been had the variation not disrupted the progress of the works, i.e. the costs at (e) must almost inevitably be the subject of conjecture—and contention! Moreover, it will be noted that neither of the two figures that are actually available—the contract bill prices at (d) and the recorded prime costs at (c)—are directly relevant to the ascertainment. On the other hand, the contractor might have priced the contract bills on the assumption that the gang would erect only 1.25 bays a week. In the event, the 1.50 bays they achieved bettered this; the disruption did no more than restrict him to his original target of 1.25 bays a week. He is nevertheless entitled to the same reimbursement of his loss of output as calculated above for he should not be denied the potential for profit implicit in the rate.

It is the disruption to the regular progress of the frame that is dealt with here in accordance with clause 26 (i.e. by reference to the contractor's costs). It is assumed that the variation to the foundations would have been dealt with separately under clause 13.5, which sets out the valuation rules.

***Example 2: The cost of out of sequence working from records***

A contractor undertakes work which includes erecting blockwork to form ducts for mechanical services described as isolated casings in the contract bills. He programmes his work so that this element can be carried out at the same time as his general blockwork. In the event, instructions related to the mechanical services are delayed and, as a result, the enclosing blockwork has also to be delayed and thus executed out of sequence and in a piecemeal fashion. The quantity surveyor requests under clause 26.1.3 that the contractor keeps records at the time of executing the duct enclosures and agrees them with the clerk of the works. The records show that 40m$^2$ of blockwork in ducts are erected by a gang comprising two bricklayers and one labourer in two days whereas 60m$^2$ of general blockwork is erected by a similar gang in a similar period. It is judged that this work was as well managed as the circumstances permitted, i.e. that no element of these costs was attributable to poor management. The price in the contract bills for blockwork in walls and partitions is £10.50/m$^2$ and isolated casings is £11.50/m$^2$ of which the labour element is estimated to represent £6.50/m$^2$ and £7.50/m$^2$, respectively. An evaluation of the loss of output might take the following form:

(a) Assessment of labour costs actually incurred on 40m$^2$ of isolated casings:

| | £ |
|---|---|
| Bricklayers, 2 for 2 days at £75 per man per day | 300 |
| Labourer, 1 for 2 days at £65 per man per day | 130 |
| | 430 |

Therefore labour cost per m$^2$ = £10.75

(b) Assessment of labour costs actually incurred on 60m$^2$ of general blockwork:

Total cost as before, namely: £430

Therefore labour cost per m$^2$ = £7.17

(c) Estimated labour element of the contract bill price for general blockwork = £6.50/m$^2$

(d) Summary:

| | | |
|---|---|---|
| (i) | Labour rate/m² of general blockwork in Contract Bills prices | £6.50 |
| (ii) | Ditto but as achieved | £7.17 |
| (iii) | Shortfall in achievement by comparing (i) and (ii) above | 10.3% |
| (iv) | Labour rate/m² of blockwork in ducts in Contract Bills prices | £7.50 |
| (v) | Labour rate/m² of blockwork in isolated casing as achieved | £10.75 |
| (vi) | Assessed labour rate/m² of blockwork in isolated casing as might have been achieved had it not been varied £7.50m² at (iv) + 10.3% at (iii) | £8.27 |
| (vii) | Direct loss/m²: (v)–(vi) | £2.48 |

(Inflation is dealt with separately.)

Note again that the comparison is between what the proper costs were and what they would have been had the disruption not taken place; not a comparison between the costs incurred and the price in the contract bills. Thus an assessment of likely performance on undisrupted work has to be made. In this example, this is achieved by reviewing progress on the general blockwork, i.e. it is assumed that the general shortfall in productivity at (iii) would have applied to the isolated casings in any event. Moreover, it is assumed that the particular delay referred to did not materially affect the regular progress on other work. The contractor may have sub-let this work at prices dissimilar to those in the contract bills with either a greater or lesser profit. This, as has been suggested above, is not relevant because an ascertainment of loss and/or expense should not be used to upset the profit that the contractor would have earned nor to remedy the loss that he would have incurred.

### *Conclusions*

- Quantifying disruption purely in terms of lost time or man-hours is not an accurate reflection of loss in efficiency.
- Measurement of site productivity does, however, provide a more realistic picture of the effect of disruption.
- Site productivity does not always reduce during the incidence of disruption.
- Comparison of productivity measurements on "disrupted days" with "standard" (undisrupted) days can provide sufficient data to establish the effects of disruption and quantify loss in efficiency.
- The "measured mile" approach is not always possible and may involve too many subjective factors.
- The contractor's entitlement is that amount which is ascertained as the difference between the costs properly and directly incurred in carrying out the work (albeit disrupted by the event) and what these costs would have been had the event not occurred.

# EXTENSIONS OF TIME

## *The purpose of extension of time clauses in standard contracts*

For those who are familiar with construction contracts, the extension of time provisions contained therein are often taken for granted and it is therefore worth considering the position were they not included.

All the standard forms of construction contract contain a provision for the insertion of a date for completion which, if not achieved, renders the contractor liable to the client for damages which almost invariably are in the form of liquidated and ascertained damages. The client must not do anything lawfully or unlawfully to prevent the contractor from completing the works by the due date or he will forfeit his right to liquidated and ascertained damages unless time can be, and is, properly extended under express contractual provisions. This follows the "prevention principle"—followed in a trio of cases, namely *Holme* v. *Guppy*,[12] *Wells* v. *Army & Navy Cooperative Society*[13] and *Dodd* v. *Churton*[14]—that a party loses his right to insist on the performance of an obligation where it is through that party's own fault that the obligation cannot be performed, e.g. the late issue of instructions. In the case of the JCT Standard Form of Building Contract, Amendment 4 (January 2002) now incorporates this common law position, stating that " . . . any impediment, prevention or default, whether by act or omission, by the client or any person for whom the client is responsible except to the extent that it was caused or contributed to by any default, whether by act or omission, of the contractor or his servants, agents or sub-contractors" is a "Relevant Event"[15] qualifying for an extension of time, and, quite separately, a "Matter"[16] relating to loss and/or expense.

In the absence of express contractual provisions enabling the client to allow additional time to the contractor in recognition of default, the completion date and the right to levy liquidated and ascertained damages are displaced and time is "at large" as soon as the client, through his default, prevents the contractor achieving that completion date.

In his work *Liquidated Damages and Extension of Time*,[17] Brian Eggleston excellently summarises the meaning of "time at large" in the following way:

"The phrase time at large is much loved by Contractors. It has about it the ring of plenty; the suggestion that the Contractor has as much time as he wants to finish the Works. This is not what it means. Time becomes at large when the obligation to complete within the specified time for completion of a contract is lost. The definition

12. (1838) 3 M. & W. 387.
13. (1902) 86 L.T. 764.
14. [1897] 1 Q.B. 562.
15. This is JCT terminology referring to a circumstance which may allow the contractor to be granted an extension of time.
16. This is JCT terminology referring to a circumstance which may allow the contractor to recover loss and/or expense which he incurs.
17. Eggleston, B. (1997), *Liquidated Damages and Extension of Time* (Blackwell Science).

then becomes to complete within a reasonable time. The question of what is a reasonable time . . . is most certainly not as and when the Contractor sees fit."

From the above, it may be seen that the extension of time provisions within the standard forms of construction contract override the position which would otherwise pertain at Common Law and provide the client with a means of extending the date for completion in a measure commensurate with his own default, thus setting a new date from which liquidated and ascertained damages may run.

### *Clause 25 of the JCT Standard Form of Building Contract*

Clause 25 is a widely encountered and legally tested mechanism and which also illustrates well how the granting of extensions of time should be approached.

As previously observed, at common law if a client or his agent prevents a contractor from completing his work by the contracted completion date then the contractor's obligation is transformed from one of having to complete by that date to one of completing within a reasonable time, unless there is an express power in the contract for the client to set a new date for completion in the new circumstances and that this power is properly implemented: clause 25 contains that express power.

It will be seen, therefore, that the existence and proper operation of the clause is, insofar as a breach by the client or his agent has caused the delay, for the benefit of the client in order to preserve his rights. Thus the client who seeks to hide behind a technical failure of the contractor fully to comply with the provisions of clause 25 as a means of denying an extension of time might find his euphoria short-lived; he may well lose all entitlement to liquidated and ascertained damages for delay. Architects also should be aware that failure to properly implement the provisions of clause 25 may, rather than set the scene for Adjudication, Arbitration or Legal Proceedings on the amount of an extension of time, set the seal on the client's prospect of claiming any liquidated and ascertained damages at all. It is for this reason that architects, when operating under the JCT Standard Form of Building Contract, must remember that when giving their final decision on extensions of time they are required to take into account all Relevant Events whether they have been previously notified or not.

Clause 25 is best seen as comprising six parts:

(a) the requirement for the contractor to give timeous notice of delay, and to give further details to assist the architect in establishing any extension of time (clause 25.2 refers);

(b) the requirement for the architect in certain circumstances to grant extensions of time during the construction period or to notify the contractor that an extension of time is, in his view, not justified (clause 25.3.1 refers);

(c) the requirement or permission for the architect to review the completion date after completion (clause 25.3.3 refers);
(d) the effect of omissions upon extensions of time (clauses 25.3.2 and 25.3.3.2 refer);
(e) the list of events which entitle the architect to consider granting an extension of time—these are termed Relevant Events (clause 25.4 refers); and
(f) the general obligations imposed upon the architect and contractor in relation to their conduct (clauses 25.3.4, 25.3.5 and 25.3.6 refer).

### *Relevant events: client default v. neutral events*

In determining the extent to which delays and claims should be allowed within the terms of a contract (as opposed to being left to be resolved in the courts), the draughtsmen of the JCT Standard Forms clearly had in mind two criteria, namely:

(a) events which are in the control of, or are caused by, the act or default of the client or his agents are to give the contractor an entitlement to an extension of time for completion and also an entitlement to be reimbursed the loss and/or expense arising; or
(b) events which are outside the control of either party, often termed "neutral events", to give the contractor an entitlement to an extension of time for completion but not to recover any loss and/or expense.

Broadly speaking, the first criterion is in line with the provisions that apply in Common Law; any default by the client or his agents will be legitimate grounds for a claim by the contractor. But the second criterion goes much further. In general, unless the terms of the Contract provide otherwise, a Completion Date would only be set aside or subject to review where an act or default of the client or his agents prevented its achievement. But the JCT Standard Form of Building Contract, and many other standard forms of building contract, extend this facility to causes of delay outside the control of either party, e.g. exceptionally adverse weather conditions. Clearly, the second criterion benefits the contractor since it provides him with grounds for an extension of time (and thereby relief from liquidated and ascertained damages) which would not exist at Common Law. Another view of the second criterion is that it is a fair apportionment of risk in that the client is denied the right to levy liquidated and ascertained damages during the period of delay caused by a "neutral event" whilst the contractor bears the costs of prolongation without the right to recover these costs from the client.

It is important to point out that the contractor receiving an extension of time does not automatically carry with it an entitlement to be reimbursed his loss and/or expense—for that he must show that he has actually suffered loss and that it owes its cause to the circumstance giving rise to the extension of time. The corollary of this is that the contractor receiving loss and/or expense consequent upon disruption (as distinct from delay) will not necessarily be entitled to an extension of time.

The table below illustrates the comparison in the JCT Standard Form of Building Contract between clause 25 (which deals with the contractor's entitlement to extension of time for completion) and clause 26 (which deals with the grounds for which he is able to claim reimbursement of his loss and/or expense).

***Table 1: Comparison of the JCT Standard Form of Building Contract circumstances listed in clause 25 with those in clause 26***

| **Extracts from clause 25.4—grounds for extension of time for completion (termed Relevant Events)** | **Clause** | **Comparable extracts from clause 26.2—grounds for reimbursement for loss and/or expense (termed List of Matters)** | **Clause** |
|---|---|---|---|
| Force majeure | 25.4.1 | None | |
| Exceptionally adverse weather conditions | 25.4.2 | None | |
| Specified perils | 25.4.3 | None | |
| Civil commotion and strikes | 25.4.4 | None | |
| Architect's instructions under clauses: | 25.4.5.1 | | |
| 2.3 and 2.4.1 Discrepancies | | Discrepancies (see note 1) | 26.2.3 |
| 13.2 Variations (including variations instructed under clause 13A.4.1) | | Variations (including variations instructed under clause 13A.4.1) (see note 2) | 26.2.7 |
| 13.3 Provisional sums | | Provisional sums (see note 3) | 26.2.7 |
| 23.2 Postponement | | Postponement | 26.2.5 |
| 34 Discovery of antiquities | | Discovery of antiquities | 34.3.1 |
| 35 Nominated sub-contractors | | None | |
| 36 Nominated suppliers | | None | |
| Architect's instructions requiring opening up for inspection | 25.4.5.2 | Architect's instructions requiring opening up for inspection (see note 4) | 26.2.2 |
| Where an information release schedule has been provided failure of the architect to comply with clause 5.4.1 | 25.4.5.2 | Where an information release schedule has been provided failure of the architect to comply with clause 5.4.1 | 26.2.1.1 |
| Failure of the architect to comply with clause 5.4.2 | 25.4.6.2 | Failure of the architect to comply with clause 5.4.2 | 26.2.1.2 |
| Nominated sub-contractors or nominated suppliers | 25.4.7 | None | |
| Work by the employer or those for whom he is responsible | 25.4.8.2 | Work by the employer or those for whom he is responsible | 26.2.4.1 |
| Supply of materials by the employer | 25.4.8.2 | Supply of materials by employer | 26.2.4.2 |
| Restriction in the availability of men, materials, fuel or energy due to government exercising its statutory powers | 25.4.9 | None | |

| Extracts from clause 25.4—grounds for extension of time for completion (termed Relevant Events) | Clause | Comparable extracts from clause 26.2—grounds for reimbursement for loss and/or expense (termed List of Matters) | Clause |
|---|---|---|---|
| Contractor's inability to secure: | | | |
| Such labour as is essential for the works | 25.4.10.1 | None | |
| Such materials as are essential for the works | 25.4.10.2 | None | |
| Work by statutory authorities | 25.4.11 | None | |
| Failure to give ingress to or egress from the site | 25.4.12 | Failure to give ingress to or egress from the site | 26.2.6 |
| Deferment of giving possession of the site (where this option has been selected) | 25.4.13 | Deferment of giving possession of the site (where this option has been selected (see note 5)) | 26.1 |
| Approximate quantities proving not to be an accurate forecast of the work actually required | 25.4.14 | Approximate quantities proving not to be an accurate forecast of the work actually required | 26.2.8 |
| Change in statutory requirements requiring changes to performance specified work | 25.4.15 | None | |
| Terrorism or threat of same and/or activity of authorities in dealing with this | 25.4.16 | None | |
| Compliance or non-compliance by employer with his obligations arising out of the Construction (Design and Management) Regulations 1994 | 25.4.17 | Compliance or non-compliance by employer with his obligations arising out of the Construction (Design and Management) Regulations 1994 | 26.2.9 |
| Suspension by the contractor of the performance of his obligations under the contract to the employer | 25.4.18 | Suspension by the contractor of the performance of his obligations under the contract to the employer (see note 6) | 26.2.10 |
| Any impediment, prevention or default, whether by act or omission, by the employer or agents, except to the extent that it was caused or contributed to by any default, whether by act or omission, of the contractor or his servants, agents or sub-contractors | 26.4.19 | Any impediment, prevention or default, whether by act or omission, by the employer or agents, except to the extent that it was caused or contributed to by any default, whether by act or omission, of the contractor or his servants, agents or sub-contractors | 26.2.11 |

Notes to the foregoing table:

1. The documents, in or between which discrepancies or divergences might give rise to an extension of time under clause 25.4.5.1, are those listed in clause 2.3 namely:

   (a) the contract drawings;
   (b) the contract bills;

(c) architect's instructions (except those requiring a variation);
(d) architect's drawings or documents issued under clauses 5.3.1.1 (descriptive schedules and the like), 5.4 (information referred to in the information release schedule and further drawings or details) or 7 (setting out drawings);
(e) the numbered documents (documents annexed to the articles of nominated sub-contract agreement). (The documents, in or between which discrepancies or divergences might give rise to an extension of time under clause 25.4.5.1, are also referred to in clause 2.4 namely the contractor's statement in respect of performance specified work and any instruction of the architect issued by him after receipt by him of the contractor's statement).

Only discrepancies in or between (a), (b) and (e) above (the contract drawings, the contract bills and the numbered documents) give rise to an entitlement to claim reimbursement of loss and/or expense under clause 26.2.3.

2. Excluding a variation to work for which there has been a confirmed acceptance of a quotation given under clause 13A.
3. Excluding the expenditure of provisional sums through the contractor as a result of a tender by him under clause 35.2.1.
4. There is some restriction on the contractor's entitlement to claim reimbursement of any direct loss and/or expense *vis-à-vis* the "opening up" provisions in clause 8.4.
5. This is not one of the Matters listed in clause 26.2 but is included in the introductory clause 26.1 as a ground for claiming reimbursement of direct loss and/or expense.
6. The suspension must not be frivolous or vexatious.

In the table above, all items which appear under the first column but not in the second column represent causes beyond the control of either party (i.e. they are "neutral events"); whereas items which appear under both (with the exception of the discovery of antiquities) represent causes due to the act or default of the client.

It is this apparent leaning towards the contractor by way of introducing "neutral events" as grounds for granting an extension of time that has resulted in certain criticism, particularly from the private sector, of the JCT Forms of Contract. It can, of course, be argued that to make "neutral events" a contractor's risk (e.g. *exceptionally adverse weather conditions*) would result in a disproportionate increase in the contractor's tender to cover those damages for the delay that might ensue. On the other hand, the pressures of competition will control the tenderer's temptation to overload this and the party in control of the works on site (the contractor) is the better placed to mitigate the effects on progress of any event particularly if he has the incentive to do so. Contractors will point out that they already have such an incentive, in that they get no recompense for the extra costs to them, such as the extended use of their site establishment due to any such delay, only relief from damages for delay which they will say is the much lesser amount.

Whatever the merits or otherwise of the present strategy relating to clause 25, it has currently been drawn so widely as to persuade some contractors and their advisers that the onus is now on the client to prove that any delay is due to the contractors' default before the client can levy liquidated and ascertained damages—or at least to claim that any cause of delay outside the contractor's control is a proper ground for extension of time. This is not so. The contractor undertakes to complete the works by the completion date which will only be extended for the reasons given in the contract and then only to the extent that such recognised events cause an inevitable delay to the completion date. As long as clauses 24 and 25 have been properly implemented, then if the date of practical completion occurs after the completion date the client will be entitled to liquidated and ascertained damages for that period of delay.

### *Extension of time provisions compared*

On receipt of a proper and valid notice of a client's time risk event that causes or, at its lowest, is likely to cause delay to completion, the contract administrator must grant the contractor an appropriate extension of time for completion of the works. Under the standard forms, it is generally not the contractor's duty to ascertain the reason for an extension of time. On the contrary, the standard forms tend to provide that the question of whether, and if so, on what ground an extension of time should be granted is a matter for the opinion of the contract administrator, based upon his own knowledge and upon any additional information given to him by the contractor. Many of the standard forms contain no express provisions and give no guidance at all upon what basis the contract administrator should award the extension of time. For example MF/1 refers to such extension of time " . . . as may be reasonable".[18] The ICE engineering forms provide that the contract administrator is to grant an extension of time provided he is satisfied that " . . . the delay suffered fairly entitles the contractor to an extension of time".[19] IChemE simply says that the contract administrator should grant " . . . the appropriate extension of time".[20]

Similarly, the ICE Short Form[21] requires that the contract administrator shall " . . . upon a written request by the contractor promptly by notice in writing grant an extension of time for the period of completion of the whole or part of the works that may in its opinion be reasonable".

FIDIC Building and Engineering (red book), FIDIC Plant Design and Build (yellow book), and FIDIC Turnkey (silver book) approach the point by dealing with the contractor's subjective entitlement as opposed to the contract administrator's duty measured by an objective standard. They all contain the same provision, stating that " . . . the contractor shall be entitled to . . . an extension of time if and to the extent that the completion date is or will be delayed . . . ". Virtually identical phraseology is also used in the JCT Major Project Form.[22]

18. Clause 33.1.
19. Clause 44(3).
20. Clause 14.1.
21. Clause 4.4.
22. Clause 12.1.

ECC is much more prescriptive and states that a delay to completion for which the contractor is entitled to relief from liquidated and ascertained damages and reimbursement of its costs " . . . is assessed as the length of time that, due to the compensation event, planned completion is later than planned completion as shown on the accepted programme".[23] By reference to clause 32.1 an "accepted programme" is defined as one which includes updates and reviews incorporating progress actually achieved, the effects of any preceding events and any re-sequencing.

Under the JCT forms of contract, the contract administrator is to determine "a fair and reasonable" extension of time. During the course of the works, the JCT forms generally provide that:

"if the completion of the works is likely to be delayed (as a result of a client's risk event) beyond the completion date the (contract administrator) . . . shall in writing to the contractor give an extension of time . . . as he then estimates to be fair and reasonable."[24]

After the completion date has passed, the contract administrator may also grant an extension of time " . . . if in his opinion the fixing of such later completion date is fair and reasonable . . . ".[25]

Contrary to what is thought by some commentators, the clause does not require that the contract administrator should be fair and reasonable in forming his opinion but that the extension of time awarded should be fair and reasonable.

Before the contract administrator may grant an extension of time under ACA Building Contract,[26] the contract requires that the contractor shall " . . . prove to the satisfaction of the contract administrator that the taking over of the works or any section . . . is prevented . . . " by any of the scheduled events. ICE Form (7th Ed) and ICE Design and Construct[27] provide that the contract administrator shall " . . . consider all the circumstances known to it at that time and make an assessment of the delay (if any) that has been suffered by the contractor as a result of the alleged cause . . . ".

GC/Works/1 Building and Engineering[28] provides that the contractor should be granted "an extension of time . . . if the (contract administrator) is satisfied that the delay or likely delay to completion is, or will be due to . . . a specified event". JCT Standard Form of Building Contract With Contractor's Design[29] states that " . . . if the works are delayed beyond the completion date by (a client's time risk event) the client shall make an extension of time for completion of the works as is then fair and reasonable . . . ". The JCT Intermediate Form,[30] as with JCT Standard Form of Building

23. Clause 63.3.
24. Clause 25.3.1.2.
25. Clause 25.3.3.2.
26. Clause 11.5, alternative 2.
27. Clause 44(2)(a).
28. Clause 36(2).
29. Clause 25.3.1.
30. Clause 2.3.

Contract, requires the contract administrator to " . . . make in writing a fair and reasonable extension of time for completion of the work".

In the FIDIC Short Form (green book),[31] the basis upon which the contractor should be entitled to an extension of time is not set out. However, in the guidance notes FIDIC say, rather unhelpfully, that the test of whether the contractor is entitled to an extension of time " . . . is whether it is appropriate . . . " and they go on to say: " . . . this means that if an event under sub-clause 6.1 causes critical delay to the work and it is fair and reasonable to grant an extension of time, the client should do so . . . " "Critical delay to the work" is not defined nor is there any guidance of when it would be "fair and reasonable". The use of such vague expressions in preference to the otherwise almost universal expression "delay to completion" and a "fair and reasonable extension of time" is almost certain to cause dispute. Bearing in mind that it is intended that this form should be used without the benefit of a professional third party to decide claims, such loose phraseology might be regarded as unhelpful.

### *Likely or actual delay to completion*

So far as concerns relief for the effect of delay by the grant of an extension of time, there is generally a three-part chain of causation to be proved:

- a client's time risk event must occur;
- the event must cause a delay to progress; and
- the delay to progress must have a knock-on effect on the completion date.

In the absence of express terms to the contrary, the occurrence of the client's time risk event alone is insufficient to provide an entitlement to an extension of time—the event must also have an effect. The second part of the causation equation is that the event must have an adverse effect on progress. If it does not in fact cause a delay to progress then the occurrence of the event alone is generally of no consequence because it logically must follow that, if it does not delay the progress of the works in any way, it cannot delay the completion of the works in any way. The third part of the causation equation for entitlement to an extension of time is thus that the delay to progress must cause, or at it lowest, be likely to cause a delay to completion of the works or a defined section of the works.

The reason why the delay to progress must cause a delay to completion is that, generally, under the standard forms of contract, the contractor is not obliged to maintain any particular planned duration, start or finish dates for discrete activities—and liquidated and ascertained damages are not deductible for a simple departure from the programmed sequence of individual activities. Liquidated and ascertained damages are generally only deductible if a delay to

31. Clause 7.3.

progress caused by the contractor also has a knock-on effect and causes a delay to completion of a defined part of the work by a contractually binding date in respect of which the failure to perform will render the contractor liable to pay liquidated and ascertained damages. It is thus only a delay to progress caused by an event at the client's risk as to time that causes, or at its lowest is likely to cause, a delay to completion for which the contractor may be awarded an extension of time.

Some forms of contract do not make it at all clear as to from where entitlement springs. Others are overly prescriptive in addressing time-related relief. The standard forms of contract tend to fall into three categories. These are those providing relief in the event that completion of the works:

- is likely to be delayed;
- is likely to, or has been delayed; or
- has been delayed.

For example, the JCT Standard Form of Building Contract uniquely expressly states that an extension of time may be awarded only if completion of the works " . . . is likely to be delayed . . . ".[32] Common amongst the prescriptive forms, including the remainder of the JCT forms, the GC/Works/1 forms, IChemE and the FIDIC forms is the possibility, in the alternative, of likely or actual delay to completion determining the right to an extension of time. So, for example, the FIDIC forms use the expression " . . . is or will be delayed . . . ".

There is a third category that restricts analysis for the purposes of entitlement to a calculation based upon actual delay to completion alone. This class includes MF/1, which requires that the contractor " . . . shall have been delayed in the completion of the works".[33]

Where the standard forms provide for analysis based on the likely effect on the completion date, the forms generally also provide for a retrospective assessment on the basis of a "fair and reasonable" extension of time and, where one is restricted to relief for an actual delay to completion, the forms also usually provide for an interim assessment on a similar basis (although this does not appear to be the case with MF/1, which makes no reference to interim assessments prior to the completion date).

With regard to most of the forms which provide only for relief on the basis of what actually delayed completion, the idea is presumably that during the course of the works the contract administrator may make a fair and reasonable assessment on the basis of the best information available to him at that time and, after completion, entitlement can then be calculated on the basis of what actually happened. If entitlement was previously underestimated, the contract administrator can add something on and, if he had overestimated entitlement

32. Clause 25.3.1.2.
33. Clause 33.1.

during the interim period, that is just hard luck on the client! It is submitted that this is not a satisfactory way to go about determining entitlement.

The SCL Protocol recommends that assessment of entitlement to an extension of time should always be upon the basis of the likely effect upon the completion date at the time the client's time risk event occurred.

## *The timing of an award*

In the absence of express conditions to the contrary, the contract administrator cannot merely take a passive role in the extension of time process. Even if he has not received notice, he must consider whether a client's time risk event has occurred. In *Holland Hannen and Cubitts (Northern) Ltd* v. *Welsh Health Technical Services Organisation*,[34] design defects in windows supplied by a nominated subcontractor under a JCT form of contract led to delays, but the contract administrator, in the mistaken belief that the problem lay between the contractor and the nominated sub-contractor, declined to issue a variation order or an extension of time. In the action which followed, Judge John Newey QC, sitting as an Official Referee, said[35]:

> " . . . I find it impossible to believe that (the contract administrator) in charge of a great building project, which has been brought to a stop by an unexpected difficulty, [is] entitled to adopt a passive attitude . . . (the contract administrator's) failures were ones of omission rather than of commission, but I think that they nonetheless amounted to a breach of contract. The same conclusion as I have reached in regard to the issue of a Variation Instruction applies, I think, to the grant to the contractor of an extension of time . . . "

The contract administrator should act as soon as he practicably can in dealing with the award of an extension of time: he must give the contractor an adequate opportunity to plan his resources for completion in the light of the events that have occurred. Unreasonable delay in dealing with the extension of time could result not only in the contractor incurring acceleration costs which, as a result of the later grant of an extension of time might prove to have been either unnecessary or unwanted, but it may also affect the client's entitlement to liquidated and ascertained damages for a client's delay to completion. In *Peak Construction (Liverpool) Ltd* v. *McKinney Foundations Ltd*[36] Salmon L.J. said:

> "The liquidated damages clause contemplates a failure to complete on time due to the fault of the contractor. It is inserted by the employer for his own protection; for it enables him to recover a fixed sum as compensation for delay instead of facing the difficulty and expense of proving the actual damage which the delay may have caused him. If the failure to complete on time is due to the fault of both the employer and the contractor, in my view, the clause does not bite. I cannot see how, in the ordinary course, the employer can insist on compliance with a condition if it is partly its own fault that it cannot be fulfilled."

34. (1982) 18 B.L.R. 80.
35. (1982) 18 B.L.R. 80 at pp. 127–128.
36. (1970) 1 B.L.R. 114 at p. 121.

However, it is entirely foreseeable that the effects of a client's time risk event may not be finite in time until completion. In such circumstances, the actual extension of time cannot be gauged until the contract has been completed, hence the contract administrator is in some difficulty in regard to quantification of the extension of time before completion. On the other hand, it is equally entirely possible that if the contract administrator acts too quickly, he might award an extension of time based on assumptions which later prove to be unfounded and which result in the contractor getting an irrevocable extension of time for delay to completion which plainly did not occur.

The JCT Standard Form of Building Contract requires that a decision should be conveyed to the contractor, in writing, within a time-limit of 12 weeks from the date of notification of the delay or by the original completion date, whichever is the sooner.[37] The GC/Works/1 forms[38] require the contract administrator to deal with the notice . . . as soon as possible and in any event within 42 days from the date any such notice is received. The FIDIC Short Form[39] (green book) makes no mention at all of any limitation on the time allowed for reaching a decision. However, the other FIDIC contracts contain a new provision in clause 20.1 stating:

"Within 42 days after receiving a claim or any further particulars supporting a previous claim, or within such other period as may be proposed by the (contract administrator) and approved by the contractor, the (contract administrator) shall respond with approval, or with disapproval and detailed comments. He may also request any necessary further particulars, but shall nevertheless give his response on the principles of the claim within such time."

The JCT Standard Form of Building Contract clearly contemplates that the contract administrator can only deal with delays that occur before the completion date in an interim decision and that he will also make his decision as to whether such delays entitle the contractor to an extension of time before that completion date.[40] Thus, if the contract administrator has less than 12 weeks between receipt of sufficient particulars from the contractor and the completion date, the contract administrator will still have to make his interim decision by that completion date. This seems a pretty unreasonable position for the contract administrator to find himself in but some element of respite comes in the form of the requirement that he need only act where it is " . . . reasonably practicable having regard to the sufficiency of the . . . (contractor's) notice . . . ".

As to the effect of continuing causes, the ultimate quantification of which cannot be dealt with until after completion, it seems that the contract administrator might contemplate three possibilities:

(1) the grant of an unquantified extension of time for the cause, on the basis that it will be quantified after completion;

37. Clause 25.3.1.
38. Clause 36.
39. Clause 20.1.
40. Clause 25.3.1.

(2) the grant of a quantified extension of time for the likely effects up to the date of the extension of time followed by updates of that assessment at regular intervals throughout the remainder of the contract and up to completion; or
(3) the grant of an estimated extension of time on the basis of the best information available at the time of the assessment but with the facility to reduce awards at a later date in the light of further and better information.

The first, it seems, is highly unsatisfactory from everybody's point of view and should be avoided: an extension of time which does not tell the contractor the date by which he must complete is useless and in any event would not comply with any of the standard form provisions.

### *The effect of omissions*

On completion of the contract, most of the forms require the contract administrator not only to review the progress of the works generally, whether or not any notice of delay has been given, but also require that the contract administrator should review any awards for extension of time that may have been made. In relation to this, the ICE forms[41] state " . . . no such final review of the circumstances shall result in a decrease in an extension of time already granted by the contract administrator". GC/Works/1 forms[42] state that the contract administrator " . . . shall not in any final decision withdraw or reduce any interim extension of time already awarded, except to take account of any authorised omission . . . that he has not already allowed for in an interim decision". The JCT Intermediate Form[43] provides that in regard to any later review " . . . such an extension of time shall not reduce any previously made". The JCT Standard Form of Building Contract With Contractor's Design Form[44] provides that the client may " . . . fix a completion date earlier than that previously fixed . . . if the fixing of such earlier completion date is fair and reasonable having regard to the omission of any work or obligation instructed by the (client) after the last occasion on which the (client) made an extension of time". FIDIC/Build 99, FIDIC Turnkey (silver book) and FIDIC Plant Design and Build (yellow book) all contain the same provision at the same clause 8.4, which states that the determining party " . . . shall review previous determinations and may increase but shall not decrease, the total extension of time".

From the contractor's point of view, there is thus good sense in giving prompt notice of delay and making sure that the contract administrator has all the information available to him to deal competently with it. On the other

41. ICE Short Form, clause 4.4 and ICE Form (7th edn), clause 44(5).
42. Clause 36(4).
43. Clause 2.3.
44. Clause 25.3.

hand, from the client's point of view, the problem of dealing with the effects of delay too quickly is that (save for omissions made from the works in particular circumstances) in most standard forms of contract the contract administrator is forbidden from reducing the extension of time in any subsequent review of an award.

All of this begs the question, can any extension of time be curtailed in the event that certain of the works or obligations are omitted? Under the JCT Standard Form of Building Contract, the contract administrator can only take account of instructions omitting work where those instructions were issued since the contract administrator's last decision on an extension of time. In other words, the contract administrator cannot use this provision to "second guess" his previous awards; he can only take into account the effect on time of the later instructions to omit work or obligations.

The JCT Standard Form of Building Contract provides that the contract administrator may fix a date earlier than that previously fixed in these circumstances:

(1) by acceptance of a quotation under clause 13A including a reduction of time; or
(2) having regard to the omission of any work after the last occasion when the contract administrator fixed a completion date, but in any event, the contract administrator may not fix a time for completion earlier than that stated in an accepted quotation under clause 13A.

Whilst the intention of clause 25.3.1 of the JCT Standard Form of Building Contract is that the contract administrator shall make a decision on all the contractor's applications for an extension of time not later than the completion date, clause 25.3.3 allows the contract administrator a further opportunity, in the 12 weeks immediately following practical completion, to review (or confirm, as the case may be) his previous decisions on the extension of time, but not to reduce them.

### *Client's delay in period of culpable delay to completion*

Culpable delay is a term used to describe the state in which the contractor's lateness is not caused by an event for which the client is responsible—and in consequence of which the contractor will be answerable to the client for liquidated and ascertained damages. Culpable delay is the period between the passing of the completion date by the contractor and his achieving practical completion.

Where the contractor is in culpable delay, the contract administrator must still grant an extension of time if a client's time risk event occurs in that period. Generally, under most standard forms of contract, there is no restriction on the type of client's time risk events which entitle the contractor to an extension of time in a period of culpable delay. They may therefore include those client's time risk events which are deemed to be at the client's risk plus the "neutral" client's time risk events, such as exceptionally adverse weather conditions.

There appears to be nothing in the standard forms of contract that would indicate on what basis it would be possible to calculate the likely effect of a client's time risk event occurring during a period of culpable delay, after the completion date has passed. If the approach taken were dependent upon the primacy of the critical path (as it is submitted it should be before the completion date) then the contractor would not be entitled to an extension of time for such an event occurring that did not impact upon the critical path to the ultimate date for completion.

The SCL Protocol considers this to be unfair and recommends that after the completion date has passed, the contractor's entitlement to more time should not be calculated by reference to its effect upon the critical path to the then date for completion but by reference to the period of time taken up on site by the work or suspension caused by the client's risk event.

## LIQUIDATED AND ASCERTAINED DAMAGES

In a contract where completion to a declared time is a requirement, the entitlement to damages in the event of delay can take one of two forms. Either it can be left to be determined, if necessary by the courts, if and when the delay occurs; this is referred to as general damages. Alternatively, the rate of damages can be resolved in advance by estimating the damage the client would suffer due to delay; these are known as liquidated (i.e. calculated, agreed) damages; or in the language of the JCT Standard Form of Building Contract "liquidated and ascertained damages".

Once the parties have decided on the use of liquidated and ascertained damages and the amount has been determined, the Courts will generally not set these aside. For them to be set aside they must be shown to have been pitched at such a level as to be a penalty on the contractor rather than being a reasonable attempt at a pre-estimate of the damage that will be suffered by the client if there is delayed completion. The fact that it might be difficult to determine such loss in advance is no ground for avoiding this facility of liquidated damages. On the contrary, this is one good reason for introducing it; namely that both parties agree at the outset of the contract that element which it might be difficult to calculate at a later date so as to reduce an area of uncertainty. Consequently, the fact that the damages actually suffered by the delay differs from the amount of liquidated and ascertained damages is no ground for setting them aside.

The view is often expressed that if a building is destined never to create a tangible profit for its owner then no liquidated damages can be claimed in the event of delayed completion.

However, this is to take a very narrow view of the benefits of a building. Consider the building of a church for example, the benefits of which may be difficult to evaluate, at least in this world. Nevertheless, those who commission such a project have taken the view that investing money in this way is more worthwhile than any alternative, e.g. a commercial building which would give a more tangible return. Delay in completion in any event will increase the cost of financing the work. Moreover, on those buildings which require a subsidy to operate, one cannot argue that the cost of the subsidy is saved by any delay: the life of the building (and therefore the total burden of the subsidy) is not reduced by late completion; it is only postponed. Thus there are good reasons for calculating liquidated and ascertained damages on an apparently loss-making project based on the average commercial venture.

### *Distinguishing liquidated damages from penalty clauses*

As to distinguishing between liquidated damages (which are enforceable) and a penalty (which is not enforceable), the principles relating to each were summarised by Lord Dunedin in *Dunlop Ltd* v. *New Garage Co. Ltd*[45] in the following way:

> "(1) Though the parties to a contract who use the words 'penalty' or 'liquidated damages' may *prima facie* be supposed to mean what they say, yet the expression used is not conclusive. The court must find out whether the payment stipulated is in truth a penalty or liquidated damages . . .
>
> (2) The essence of a penalty is a payment of money stipulated as in terrorem of the offending party; the essence of liquidated damages is a genuine covenanted pre-estimate of damage.
>
> (3) The question whether a sum stipulated is a penalty or liquidated damages is a question of construction to be decided upon the terms and inherent circumstances of each particular contract, judged as at the time of the making of the contract, not as at the time of the breach.
>
> (4) To assist this task of construction various tests have been suggested, which if applicable to the case under consideration may prove helpful, or even conclusive. Such are:
>
> (a) It will be held to be a penalty if the sum stipulated for is extravagant and unconscionable in amount in comparison with the greatest loss that could conceivably be proved to have followed from the breach.
>
> (b) It will be held to be a penalty if the breach consists only in not paying a sum of money, and the sum stipulated is a greater sum than the sum which ought to have been paid . . .
>
> (c) There is presumption (but no more) that it is a penalty when 'a single lump sum is payable by way of compensation, on the occurrence of one or more or all of several events, some of which may occasion serious and others but trifling damage'.[46]
>
> (d) It is no obstacle to the sum stipulated being a genuine pre-estimate of damage that the consequences of the breach are such as to make precise pre-estimation almost an impossibility. On the contrary, that is just the situation when it is probable that pre-estimated damage was the true bargain between the parties."

45. [1915] A.C. 79 (H.L.).
46. Referring to *Lord Elphinstone* v. *Monkland Iron and Coal Co.* (1886) 11 App. Cas. 332 (H.L.).

### *Issues to consider when calculating liquidated and ascertained damages*

Against the backdrop of the principles advocated by Lord Dunedin, it is not practicable to give examples which wholly exhaust the range of calculations for liquidated and ascertained damages but the following check list of items to be considered may be helpful:

(1) It should be a genuine pre-estimate of damage (it does not matter that a precise pre-estimate is not possible as the Court will not take an overly technical and/or pedantic approach in the construction of a liquidated and ascertained damages charge).[47]
(2) It should be the damage naturally arising from the delay and what the parties might reasonably have supposed, at the time the contract was signed, was likely to be the outcome of the delay.
(3) It must not be a penalty.
(4) It should comprise the loss that the client may suffer in the event of delay and therefore the following should be considered in the calculation:

    (a) interest payable during the period of delay on cash paid out, i.e. on land costs (including purchase of old properties on the site), on interim payments on the building contract, professional fees and direct contracts carried out by the client (e.g. demolition, diversions, soil investigation);
    (b) loss of profit or return on the new building;
    (c) loss of rent;
    (d) rent of alternative premises and the cost of decanting;
    (e) extra payments under the fluctuations clauses (the amount is dependent upon which clauses of the contract are used);
    (f) inflation or postponement costs of later direct contracts, e.g. installation of machinery, fitting out contracts, removal; and
    (g) alternative costs incurred in failing to take possession on the agreed date, e.g. staff costs.

It is sometimes argued that to put anything approaching a realistic rate in for liquidated and ascertained damages will encourage the contractor to turn his energies to undermining the client's right to claim damages by pressing heavily for extensions of time, rather than trying to meet his obligations to complete on time. The fallacy of this argument is that it implies that extensions of time are there for the asking; they are not. There has to be delay, the delay has to be such as to be likely to affect the completion date and has to have been caused by one or more of the permitted circumstances envisaged by the contract. These will be matters of fact. Although constant demands for extensions of time from a contractor can be time consuming for the design team to

47. See *Philips Hong Kong Ltd* v. *AG of Hong Kong* (1993) 61 B.L.R. 41.

deal with, as long as their house is in order and most demands are responded to resolutely but reasonably, the contractor will almost certainly return his attention to meeting his contractual obligations rather than trying to obscure them.

All too often the client's needs in this matter of timely completion are overlooked or at least undervalued in either the formulation of the contract documents or in the management of the contract and the contractor's difficulties are given pride of place. This is a short sighted view; the decision to build, upon which the building industry depends, must be largely influenced by the confidence that a prospective client may feel for the venture. Part of this confidence will come from a realisation that the industry will take seriously its obligation to complete on time or, failing this, be prepared to make adequate amends.

There may, however, be circumstances in which the real damage to the client due to delay will be out of proportion to the value of the building, e.g. when it is planned to install expensive machinery after completion of the building contract to a complex programme and the cost of that machinery can dwarf the cost of the building. The cost of such a delay can be real and very extensive and, moreover, the contractor could be aware or made aware of this possibility before entering into the contract and thus in theory be made liable for swingeing liquidated and ascertained damages. The cost of meeting this obligation, or of covering the risk of failing to do so, may itself result in a disproportionate amount being added to the contract sum; the contractor is, after all, in the building business not the insurance business. If it is felt that this overpricing is a real prospect on any project, a satisfactory compromise may well be to reduce the liquidated and ascertained damages to a figure generally commensurate with the losses due to delay on an average building of comparable value and introduce a commitment on the contractor regularly to monitor and report upon the progress of his work and to insist that he notify, in a structured way, all potential delays of which he ought to be aware. In this way the client will be forewarned of any delay and can take steps to mitigate his resultant losses.

## DEMONSTRATING CAUSE AND EFFECT

### *Preface*

There are a number of project management techniques used in the construction industry to demonstrate the cause and effect of events in the project programme. These techniques demonstrate the effect of an event occurring by applying logic to contemporaneous project records and recollections of project staff. Non-programme-based techniques rely on written descriptions and only produce logical explanations of the data. Non-programme based techniques do not provide a calculation of the causative effect, nor do they provide the visual benefits (picture); both of which a programme based analysis provides.

### *The nature of proof required*

In order to identify to what extent an activity affects the date for completion, it is necessary to separate those events which have to be carried out sequentially on the critical path and those events which are capable of completion without interference with the critical path. Whilst a delay to progress of the works may be self evident, in many cases it is not, and the effect of a client's time and/or cost risk event should be calculated or deduced, in isolation from any other cause. When calculating the time related loss it is of paramount importance to establish:

- the period of delay actually suffered;
- the activities affected; and
- the calendar period in which the delay to progress was suffered.

These are always material considerations in relation to the calculation of the knock-on effect on a key date.

Occasionally, restricted working calendars or restricted resource calendars have greater causative effect on the progress or sequence of another activity. For example, during the wet season when the ability to progress groundworks may be limited, say, from the end of October to the end of March the following year, a delay to completing an activity to which the groundworks are dependent will prevent the groundworks from being completed as planned during dry season.

None of the standard forms of contract expressly states how entitlement to an extension of time or to time-related compensation is to be proved. In principle, however, whether the proof is offered contemporaneously, or retrospectively, in order to demonstrate a causal relationship between a client's time and/or cost risk event, a structured process is recommended:

(1) If the programme is based on the as-planned programme, check and verify the base line programme as being a reasonable method of construction, and that it was updated from time to time to conform to the progress actually achieved.
(2) Identify whether at any time the programme has been amended or revised to accommodate changed methods of working, changed resources or to achieve accelerated progress.
(3) If the programme is based on the as-built programme, check and verify the as-built programme.
(4) Develop a comprehensive listing of all changes or unanticipated events that occurred during the project and relate those impacts to specific points in time.
(5) Review the contract documents to confirm that the change or unanticipated event is a client's time and/or cost risk event.

(6) Identify the date of initiation of the causal event.
(7) Calculate the effects on progress of the variances in work sequences, activities and durations, manpower and resources.
(8) Calculate the effects of identified delays to progress on key dates.
(9) Prepare a complete written description of each major change or event.
(10) Write up the narrative explaining the process and results.

### *Critical path methods of analysis*

Critical path method techniques are used for calculating the effect of a causal event rather than merely perceiving the causal effect. In principle, there are three static methods of analysis which rely on a single fixed base line and, in addition, a dynamic method which is dependent on a shifting baseline. The static methods of analysis comprise:

(1) As-planned v. as-built.
(2) As-planned impacted.
(3) As-built but-for.

The dynamic method is known as time-impact.

Andrew Burr, in an article in the *Construction Law Journal*,[48] made the following observation regarding critical path methods of analysis:

> "Critical path analysis can only ever be regarded as a model that approximates the sequence and duration of the operations and activities on site. The perfect model would follow each resource around the site and show what it was doing and in what location and the sequence in which it carried out its work. Records are invariably not available at this level of detail, and further a programme at this level may involve tens of thousands of operations, any meaningful analysis of which would be impossible. Critical path analysis therefore has, at each level, to be a summation of groups of like operations. The higher the level of the analysis and the smaller the number of activities shown on the analysis, the easier it is to follow and understand but the higher the level of summation and therefore probably the higher the level approximation. There is always therefore likely to be some level of impressionistic assessment applied to decisions about the extent of extensions of time, even where critical path delay analyses form the basis of such decisions."

### *As-planned v. as-built*

The essence of an as-planned v. as-built methodology is that two programmes are compared and inferences drawn from differences. This methodology differs from an impact method which depends upon an addition or subtraction of a factual matrix from a base line and does not rely on the calculation of impacts.

48. Burr, Andrew (2004) "Critical Path Analysis in English Law: the Present State of Play", 20 Const. L.J. 222.

### *As-planned impacted*

As-planned impacted methodology exploits the critical path method based planned programme and reacts dynamically to changes on the baseline. Calculations are made by adding causal events, which are represented by a fragnet or sub-network to the base line. The effect of the causal event on the key date is calculated as to the difference between the key date before the event and that following the addition of the fragnet or sub-network.

The methodology for an as-planned impacted analysis is as follows:

(1) establish that the as-planned programme is reasonable and fit for use as a base-line;
(2) take activities or durations comprised in the causal event;
(3) estimate the reasonable resources necessary to complete the task on the same basis as the calculation for those resources that were calculated at the time of tender;
(4) identify the period of time which it would normally take to carry out those activities or durations comprised in the event during the ordinary working period and in those circumstances anticipated at the time of tender;
(5) add the causal event to the base line programme; and
(6) recalculate the completion date.

The essence of an as-planned impacted analysis is that it is referable only to the objectively assessed impact of change to the contractor's planned programme. Its use is very limited because:

(1) the base-line must be a programme which is relevant to the contractor's intentions at the time the event occurs; and
(2) the effects of the events calculated are not related to the time they actually occurred.

The second of the two issues causes a serious problem with the as-planned method of analysis. This is due to the fact that the impact on the as-planned programme is an objective assessment as to the likely effect of the event on the contractor's programme, rather than the actual effect. In contrast, the critical path method based on the as-built but-for analysis generally requires relevant current material to be taken into account in the as-built programme. Accordingly, the as-planned impacted method usually takes no account of the contractor's acceleration or culpable delay during the progress of the works when calculating the completion date. Instead, it merely looks objectively at the assumed effect of change on the contractor's intended method of working. This method simply determines the period for an extension of time which should be granted to the contractor or the date from which the client may deduct any liquidated and ascertained damages, once the contractor has failed to complete his work.

The result of an as-planned impacted analysis cannot reasonably be used for demonstrating a period of time for which loss and/or expense will have arisen because the assessment of a period in which disruption occurred cannot be properly identified without good contemporaneous records.

### *As-built but-for*

The as-built but-for method, sometimes referred to as the "collapsed as-built" method, is another impact technique which, when properly used, produces acceptable proof of the effect of a causal event. It is a static method of analysis which utilises the base line on a final as-built programme to calculate the causal effect by subtracting the factual matrices of events.

The as-built but-for analysis is typically more difficult to perform than the as-planned impacted analysis because project planning software regards as-built dates as historical events fixed in time. As a result, this type of analysis cannot be executed on programmes containing actual dates. To create a programme using "but for" simulations, fixed dates must be removed from the computerised as-built programme and substituted by planned dates and a logic network created that calculates the start and finish dates actually achieved and which replicates the historical start and finish dates. When completed, the simulated as-built programme will allow activities to move and interact within the bounds of their logical predecessors and successors and will reflect the effects of the causes identified.

### *Time-impact*

As its name suggests, time-impact methodology, sometimes referred to as the "snapshot" method, is another impact technique that calculates the effect of a causal event rather than relying on the perceived effect of an event. When properly used, this method produces the most thorough and reliable technical proof of the effect of a causal event. The method of analysis is stipulated in US Government contracts and is acknowledged by the SCL Protocol as being the most appropriate method of contemporaneous analysis and, also, the most comprehensive method for retrospective analysis.

It is a dynamic method of calculation which utilises the base line on the contractor's programme compiled contemporaneously during the course of the works. The factual matrices of events which occur during construction are added to the programme to calculate their effect on the programme and, in doing so, the programme makes reference to the changing pattern of float and shift in the critical path.

The essential characteristics of time-impacted methodology are that:

(1) There is a critical path method based as-planned programme that will react dynamically to change.
(2) That programme is updated to a date shortly before a client's time or cost risk event was initiated to identify the effects of any delay or

acceleration by the contractor not related to the event and to establish the contractor's implied intent for the future conduct of the works.

(3) The factual matrix of the event is then added to the updated programme, linked logically with the programme and its effect calculated on progress and on a key date in the same way as in an as-planned impacted analysis. This identifies the putative effect of the event as the difference between the key date calculated before the event was subtracted, and that calculated after the event is subtracted.
(4) The impacted programme is then updated again with as-built records to determine whether the dates on which activities were started, completed or key dates were achieved is actually greater than or less than the delay to progress or completion that was likely to occur as a result of the event. From this it can be deduced whether the contractor was in concurrent delay to progress or completion or achieved acceleration.
(5) Whenever the contractor changes his planned sequence, the new planned sequence is impacted by substituting the new for the old and recalculating the completion date as a new base line. In the event that this indicates an earlier planned completion date it illustrates the contractor's intent to accelerate progress. In the event that it illustrates a later completion date, it illustrates the contractor's intent to delay completion.

This simple contemporaneous approach to cause and effect analysis allows assessment to be made of three important aspects, which tend to be unavailable with other methods:

(1) the actual state of progress at the time the event was initiated;
(2) the changing nature of the critical path as a result of delays to progress and acceleration; and
(3) the concurrency of delays to progress and to completion.

The methodology for a time-impact analysis is as follows:

(1) Identify the as-planned network and gather together the relevant records and documents.
(2) Make a chronological list of those events, along with supporting documentation, which are to be considered.
(3) Identify the first event that is:

    (a) a client's time and cost risk event;
    (b) a client's time risk event;
    (c) a contractor's risk event; and
    (d) identify the dates on which the events were initiated.

(4) Identify the progress-records for the date or just prior to the date on which the causal event occurred.
(5) Using the progress data, update and re-analyse the network and recalculate the critical path.
(6) Using the updated network add the causal event and connect its logical predecessors (if any) and successors.
(7) When the causal event has been added, the network is re-analysed and the critical path recalculated. If the causal event was on or near the critical path, the forecast end date (calculated by the progress update) will be extended. The difference between the forecast end date and the finish date now calculated is the delay to progress or to completion likely to be caused by the event.
(8) Once all activity delays have been quantified, the origins and causes can then be researched and responsibility for the consequences of each event can be allocated to either the contractor or the client.

When executed retrospectively, this technique works well on projects in which the programme has been affected by a small number of events. It can lead to a vast amount of data if the project experienced high number of project delays, and is recognised as a practical problem when executed other than in time "windows".

### *Windows and watersheds*

Each method of analysis can make use of the whole construction period from start to finish, or a discrete period of construction, for its base-line. The analysis can be performed on each identified period in succession and the effect on the earlier period being carried forward to the next. This is called the "windows" method of conducting an analysis and is an approach to conducting an analysis rather than a method of analysis itself.

### *Selecting a method of proof*

What constitutes acceptable proof of causation in each particular case will generally depend upon a number of factors. These may comprise:

(1) The terms of the contract.
(2) The subject matter of the proof.
(3) The factual materials available.
(4) Proportionality.

#### Terms of the contract

In principle, whenever the contract requires entitlement to be gauged in relation to what is likely adversely to affect the completion date, the proof will be based upon the contractor's planned programme of the works. That is because it indicates the likely sequence of activities up to the point of completion.

The actual date for completion is unlikely to be the planned date for completion. Reasons for any such divergence may comprise:

- the effects of latent errors in the contractor's planned programme;
- the effects of the absorption of float;
- unnecessary fixed lags or express or implied contingency activities;
- the effect of subsequent re-sequencing or changes in resources; and
- the effects of subsequent contractor's or client's time risk events.

Thus, in order to identify the actual effect on completion, as opposed to the likely effect of a delay to progress caused by a client's time risk event, the base-line must be an as-built programme.

With regard to likely delay to completion, the base-line of the planned programme of work is usually updated to a point before the event occurs, taking into consideration what has gone before and predicting, in the light of that, what is likely to happen in the future. In these circumstances, the effect of the event is calculated in relation to its likely impact on the planned programme for the future conduct of the work. Conversely, an event causing delay to completion cannot be calculated by reference to a planned programme that predicts no more than what is likely to happen. Delay to completion cannot occur until after the completion date has passed and an effect upon it can only be calculated in relation to what actually happened as opposed to what was planned to happen.

## The subject matter of the proof

The actual effect of an event can only be proved by reference to the sequence in which the works were actually built, not by reference to the way the works were planned. Thus, the as-built programme is usually the base-line from which the causal effect of an event is measured, either by reference to a planned completion date (an as-planned v. as-built analysis) or by reference to an as-built programme but for the effect of the client's cost risk events (an as-built but for analysis).

A time-impact analysis can demonstrate the likely impact of events through subsequent impacts, updates and rescheduled programmes to identify the residual effect of those events that continue to affect the sequence of events from initiation through to the impacted key date.

## The factual materials available

The first consideration that should be borne in mind when considering adopting a method of delay analysis is the quality of the as-built programme or the records from which such a programme could be retrospectively built. If there are no satisfactory as-built records then an analysis on the basis of as-planned

v. as-built, as-built but-for or time-impact will be impossible to perform and the analyst must then consider the availability and reliability of the planned material available. If a planned critical path method network is available then an as-planned impacted analysis might be performed. If all the evidence that exists is represented by a simple bar chart, it might be possible, with additional reasonable logic, to convert the bar chart to a critical path method network.

In the event that as-built records or planned programmes are non-existent, the analyst must revert to whatever contract documentation exists in a bid to produce a reasonable critical path method network for the works that might reasonably have been envisaged at the time of entering into the contract.

A time-impact analysis should be considered whenever a contractor's programme (based on a critical path method network) has been updated during the course of the works. This method is more appropriate when the contractor has suffered concurrent delays, which are of the contractor's and the client's making, or where the contractor has re-sequenced his planned programme and has attempted acceleration to overcome delays. In these circumstances, a time-impact analysis is more likely to produce a meaningful calculation for each party's respective entitlements than any other method available.

## Proportionality

It is a general principle to be observed in all formal dispute procedures (in which the losing party can be ordered to pay the winning party's costs) that the parties should act reasonably to keep costs proportionate to the nature and gravity of the case and the stage the claim has reached. In practice this generally means that complicated and expensive methods of analysis should not be applied to matters that have little in dispute or at a time when it is unnecessary for the purpose to be achieved.

The obligations of the contract administrator, when considering the contractor's entitlement for an award of an extension of time, are usually defined in subjective terms. The contract administrator is usually required to award an extension of time that is fair and reasonable. In *John Barker Construction* v. *London Portman Hotel Ltd*[49] Mr Recorder Toulmin QC said that the application of an impressionistic (rather than a calculated and rational) assessment is not sufficient to discharge the contract administrator's duty to make a fair and reasonable award. Those observations have been interpreted by some to imply that all extension of time assessments must be arrived at by carrying out some form of critical path method network analysis. One might contend that this is incorrect. Apart from anything else, there are many small building contracts performed in which there is either no workable programme or one that is not fully networked. In Barker, however, there was a fully networked critical path method programme which formed the basis of the acceleration agreement on

49. (1997) 83 B.L.R. 31.

which the dispute ensued. It was thus in that case entirely appropriate to assess the contractor's entitlement by reference to that programme.

## GLOBAL CLAIMS

There have been a number of cases in recent years centring around whether claims must be calculated by dealing with each item—each instruction even—or whether a claim can be presented by lumping together all the problems and making a global claim. It seems clear that rarely, if ever, are the several causes of a claim or their effects indistinguishable one from the other albeit that there will be circumstances where the cost effects of those causes are impossible to isolate item by item. This being the case the response to this question of the ability of the contractor to make and sustain a global claim may be summarised as follows:

(a) a contractor must give the proper notice on each occasion that an entitlement to make a claim arises;
(b) each of these notices must conform fully with the rules written into the contract about them (e.g. the timing, the need for them to be in writing and to be sent to the architect);
(c) there must be a clear demonstration of the relationship between cause and effect in each case;
(d) the contractor must keep such records as are required of him in relation to every such event;
(e) he must make available all the relevant cost data to enable the architect or quantity surveyor to carry out a proper ascertainment; and
(f) only where the effect of a series of claims events (e.g. the late issue of instructions or the instructing of variations) is such as to create extra costs which by their nature are indistinguishable one from the other, can an ascertainment on a global basis be entertained. Simply because there is, say, a series of variation instructions which create overlapping or contiguous disruption it does not follow that all other claims on that project can be lumped into a global claim. The facility to present a claim should be restricted solely to the events which inevitably create indistinguishable costs.

Thus no contractor should be penalised by being denied reimbursement simply because he was caused to incur extra costs which could not by their nature be particularised. On the other hand, no contractor should be allowed to abuse that facility—to make a global claim—by using it to mask facts and figures that could and should properly have been particularised and presented. The notion that a contractor should be put to quite a burden of proof to particularise his claim was seen in *Crosby & Sons* v. *Portland UDC*[50]; in that

50. (1967) 5 B.L.R. 121.

case, Donaldson J. was considering the award made by an arbitrator and accepted that, in principle, the loss attributable to each cause should be separately identified and particularised but in those circumstances where such separate identification was difficult, or even impossible, then (and only then) a lump sum award may be made in relation to those circumstances. Whilst the *Crosby* case has mistakenly been taken as authority for launching so called "global claims" (i.e. claims which do not attempt to establish the nexus between the matters complained of and a line by line explanation of the damages flowing therefrom), another more recent case (*Wharf Properties* v. *Eric Cumine Associates*[51]) was to breathe life back into the proposition that every effort must be made separately to identify those damages flowing from each of the matters complained of.

### Events for which the client is not responsible

The decision of *Crosby and Sons Ltd* v. *Portland Urban District Council*[52] and the decision in the notable case of *London Borough of Merton* v. *Stanley Hugh Leach Ltd*[53] were both based on the premise that the client was responsible for all of the events for which loss and/or expense was claimed by the contractor. The basis for succeeding in a global claim was recently restated in the case of *John Doyle Construction Ltd* v. *Laing Management (Scotland) Ltd*[54] by the Inner House of the Court of Session in Scotland. The court said:

> "If . . . the contractor is able to demonstrate that all of the events on which he relies are in law the responsibility of the employer, it is not necessary for him to demonstrate causal links between the individual events and particular heads of loss. In such a case, because all of the causative events are matters for which the employer is responsible, any loss and expense that is caused by those events and no others must necessarily be the responsibility of the employer that is in essence the nature of a global claim. A common example occurs when a contractor contends that delay and disruption have resulted from a combination of the late provision of drawings and information and design changes instructed on the employer's behalf; in such a case all of the matters relied on are the legal responsibility of the employer. Where, however, it appears that a significant cause of the delay and disruption has been a matter for which the employer is not responsible, a claim in this manner must necessarily fail. If, for example, the loss and expense has been caused in part by bad weather, for which neither party is responsible, or by inefficient working on the part of the contractor, which is his responsibility, such a claim must fail. In each case, of course, if the claim is to fail, the matter for which the employer is not responsible in law must play a significant part in the causation of the loss and expense."

It is, therefore, clear that if a contractor is to succeed with a global claim, the contractor must eliminate causes of claims for loss and expense for which the contractor is not responsible. The court in *John Doyle* did, however, make three qualifications (*obiter*) to the global claim doctrine:

51. (1991) 7 Const. L.J. 251.
52. (1967) 5 B.L.R. 121.
53. (1985) 32 B.L.R. 51.
54. [2004] 1 B.L.R. 295; (2004) CILL 2135.

> "(1) . . . it may be possible to identify a causal link between particular events for which the employer is responsible and individual items of loss."

One might argue that if causal links between items of loss caused by the client can be established, why would a contractor prejudice his chances of recovery of his loss by obscuring such an event, causal link and loss within a global claim.

> "(2) The question of causation should be treated by the application of common sense to the logical principles of causation.[55] In this connection, it is frequently possible to say that an item of loss has been caused by a particular event notwithstanding that the order of events played a part in its occurrence. In such cases, if an event or events can be described as the dominant cause of an item of loss, that will be sufficient to establish liability, notwithstanding the existence of other causes that are to some degree at least concurrent."

Presently, there is no English case law covering the second qualification in the context of a global claim, although *John Doyle* v. *Laing Management* might be persuasive to an English court.[56] There is also a practical issue as to how a court would recognise a dominant cause in the context of a global claim. By its very nature, it would not be possible to identify a dominant cause. If it were, the claim would seem to fall within the first qualification above.

> "(3) Even if it cannot be said that the events for which the employer is responsible are the dominant cause of the loss, it may be possible to apportion the loss between the causes for which the employer is responsible and other causes."

There is no English or Scottish authority to support the apportionment of loss in the context of a global claim. The court did, however, recognise that "this procedure [apportionment] does not, however, seem to be fundamentally different in nature from that used in relation to contributory negligence or contribution among joint wrong doers." The Court cited two decisions from the United States that it considered might be persuasive authority, *Lichter* v. *Mellon-Stuart Company*[57] and *Phillips Construction Co. Inc* v. *United States*.[58] The court's view on apportionment was, however, very much *obiter*, as was the view of Lord MacFadyen at first instance, whose view was disparate to that of the Inner House. Lord MacFadyen considered that the two US cases were simply instances of the first qualification identified above, where evidence was sufficient to find a causal connection between individual losses and individual events. The opinion of Lord MacFadyen in the Outer House and the opinion given by Lord Drummond-Young in the Inner House identify that

55. *John Holland Construction & Engineering Pty Ltd* v. *Kvaerner RJ Brown* (1997) 82 B.L.R. 81; *Leyland Shipping Company Ltd* v. *Norwich Union Fire Insurance Society* [1918] A.C. 350.

56. Decisions from the Scottish courts, where the law is similar but not identical, are not binding as precedent on the English courts though English judges have careful regard to what Scottish judges have to say (and vice versa).

57. 305 F 2d 216 (1962).

58. 394 F 2d 834 (1968).

it would take a brave and wealthy contractor, unperturbed by risk, to pursue a global claim based on apportionment.

### *The risk of pursuing a global claim*

Whereas the Inner House[59] differed in certain respects to what Lord MacFayden had to say in the Outer House, it nevertheless considered that Lord MacFayden's legal analysis of the nature of a global claim was very much correct in recognising the risk of pursuing such a claim:

"The logic of a global claim demands . . . that all the events which contribute to causing the global loss be events for which the defender[60] is liable. If the causal events include events for which the defender bears no liability, the effect of upholding the global claim is to impose on the defender a liability which, in part, is not legally his. That is unjustified. A global claim, as such, must therefore fail if any material contribution to the causation of the global loss is made by the factor or factors for which the defender bears no legal liability . . . The point has on occasion been expressed in terms of requirement that the pursuer[61] should not himself have been responsible for any factor contributing materially to the global loss, but it is in my view clearly more accurate to say that there must be no material causative factor for which the defender is not liable.

Advancing a claim for loss and expense in global form is therefore a risky enterprise. Failure to prove that a particular event for which the defender was liable played a part in the global loss will not have any adverse effect on the claim, provided the remaining events for which the defender was liable are proved to have caused the global loss. On the other hand, proof that an event played a material part in causing the global loss, combined with failure to prove that the event was one for which the defender was responsible, will undermine the logic of the global claim. Moreover, the defender may set out to prove that, in addition to the factors for which he is liable founded on the pursuer, a material contribution to the causation of the global loss has been made by another factor or other factors for which he has no liability. If he succeeds in proving that, again the global claim will be undermined."

Much has been said and written on the subject of global claims. Generally, they are frowned upon by the courts—albeit that the courts have recognised the exceptional and carefully qualified instances in which they might succeed. The exceptional circumstances in which global claims might be admitted have, unfortunately, been seized upon by certain claims consultants as amounting to far reaching authority for the proposition that a contractor can claim anything that he likes against the client and then place the onus upon the client (or his advisers) to wade through it all and identify those areas which are not the client's responsibility. Were such an analysis correct, and it certainly is not, it would amount to saying that the burden of proof is removed from the claimant and is instead placed on the defendant.

59. Scotland's equivalent of the Court of Appeal and hence superior to the Outer House (which is equivalent of the High Court).

60. The Scottish term for defendant.

61. The Scottish term for claimant.

## CLAIM TACTICS

No compilation of notes touching upon the subject of loss and/or expense would be complete without some reference to the tactics sometimes resorted to by one or both parties in either the presentation, response or negotiation of a claim.

Not all the following devices are employed all of the time; nor does everyone resort to them some of the time. In the same way as a medical text book, crammed with the real or potential physical maladies of the body, is not typical of the majority of the human race, the following examples are not included because they are typical of the building industry!

There follows a short selection of claim tactics which might be encountered:

- *The Solomon Syndrome*—At the root of too many negotiations is the bland acceptance that, if two contrary views are expressed on a claim, there must be some merit in both and the real truth lies somewhere in between; moreover, the nearer the middle that the answer is judged to be, the more sensitive and sophisticated has been the adjudicator. This, of course, is nonsense. But the more widely it is practised the more it is exploited, with each side stretching ever wider the boundaries of their imagination in order to establish a base in as extreme a position as can be tolerated without totally losing credibility. Before concluding that "there is no smoke without fire" one must be able to differentiate between smoke and hot air, and in any event to recognise that the amount of smoke is no measure of the real intensity of the fire. The amount of the entitlement is by no means pro rata to the amount of paper generated; often the converse is the case.

  This predisposition to split the difference can be particularly distressing when attempting to reconcile the contractor's with the architect's or quantity surveyor's view on entitlement to reimbursement of loss and/or expense. Their respective roles in the run up to any such confrontation are quite different and this difference is often not recognised by the client nor, regrettably, by his legal advisers. In arriving at his figure, the architect or quantity surveyor will have been under a duty to operate the terms of the contract as best he can as between client and contractor. The contractor, on the other hand, has no such constraint and is perfectly entitled to express every item in dispute in a way which is to his advantage. Given such a situation it is quite clearly wrong to assume that the view of each side has equal merit, because the architect or quantity surveyor has been representing the contract, whereas the contractor has been representing himself. Any temptation to split the difference should be resisted. The contractor and the architect or quantity surveyor are not at opposite ends of a tug-of-war rope; the latter are standing where they judge the centre marker to be.

- *The Clandestine Cost Plus*—In this type of claim, the text will present undeniable facts relating to the running of the Contract, trace the remedy to the correct clause in the Contract, and then finish with a calculation of loss and/or expense which turns out to be no more than a comparison between what the contractor alleges his costs to be and what he claims to have recovered through the Contract to date; he is in effect seeking reimbursement of all his costs under this heading which is not the test to be applied however just his cause or claim. Indeed, this approach is often camouflaged by a distracting detour through fascinating formulae. Converting the alleged labour content of the final account into a percentage of the total value and describing this as the "tender output", relating the alleged labour costs incurred to the same value and describing this as the "achieved output", comparing the two and describing the difference as the "disruptive loss" is a typical route as illustrated in the following tables.

***Table 2: Claims based upon the labour cost incurred***

| | | | £ |
|---|---|---|---|
| 1. | Value of final account | | |
| 2. | Less preliminaries | | 4,586,327 |
| | | | (432,313) |
| 3. | Subtotal | | 4,154,014 |
| 4. | Tender labour content | 38.43% | |
| 5. | Actual labour cost incurred | | 2,103,296 |
| 6. | Therefore achieved labour output (Item 5/Item 3) | 50.63% | |
| 7. | Therefore loss of output (Item 6 Item 4) | 12.20% | |
| 8. | Resultant disruption of labour 12.20% × £4,154,014 | | 506,790 |

This approach is quite unacceptable because:

(a) it makes no attempt to relate cause to effect;
(b) it does not seek to ascertain the direct loss and/or expense attributable to each matter listed in clause 26.2 of the JCT Standard Form of Building Contract;
(c) it applies a global formula to total labour costs; and
(d) the global formula is deduced entirely from the total costs said to have been incurred on the scheme and is not an ascertainment of the effect upon specific labour elements of the individual items of disruption.

A nice touch is often added by making a modest deduction for fluctuations charged elsewhere by the introduction of sophisticated but irrefutable calculations. But at the end of the day it is no more nor less than a claim for reimbursement of all labour costs, however they were caused, and this is irrelevant in the ascertainment of direct loss and/or expense.

- *The Veneer of Precision*—No-one is impressed by a claim of such generality as £25,000; one's suspicions are aroused as to its authenticity. On the other hand, a total of £24,787.32 does concentrate the mind wonderfully. Peeling back the veneer, however, the following details may be revealed:

***Table 3: The veneer of precision***

| | |
|---|---|
| Claims by domestic sub-contractors | £ |
| (a) A Smith & Co's claim | 4,787.32 |
| (b) Provisional allowance for claims likely to be forthcoming from other sub-contractors, say | 20,000.00 |
| To Summary | 24,787.32 |

- *"Double Bubble" on variations*—Where variations are ordered, the valuation of some may involve the recovery of a contribution to profit and overheads. If and insofar as this is the case, and if the contractor is also delayed and/or disrupted by these variations, care must be taken to ensure that the ascertainment of loss and/or expense does not include monies already recovered by virtue of the valuation process.
- *Build up the claim*—Contractors have a fondness for presenting their claims in a light that best suits their position and those who accept such submissions find themselves in the situation of knocking out those parts which they find unacceptable—and who is to say that they will even find all the bits which duplicate other items and/or which are not contractually recoverable?

What ought in fact to happen is that the architect (or the quantity surveyor when, as is so often the case, the architect delegates this responsibility to him) builds up the claim from first principles and by reference to the contractor's contemporaneous records of actual costs.

CHAPTER 9

# PROVISIONS FOR MANAGING CHANGE

Keith Pickavance

## INTRODUCTION

The time and cost risks of the effects of voluntary change cannot be transferred to the contractor. So long as the employer relies on the right to vary the works it must necessarily carry the liability for the effects of any change so ordered; that applies irrespective of whether the contract is "build only" such as JCT 98 SFBC, "turnkey" or "EPC" such as FIDIC silver book, "design and build" such as JCT 98 WCD or JCT MPF, "the one stop shop" as design and build is sometimes called, "management contracting" as with JCT 98 MC, "partnering" as with PPC2000, or even if the contract is a bespoke concoction with the wonderfully reassuring (but deceptively misleading) title of "guaranteed maximum price". The contract in *Skanska Construction Ltd* v. *Egger (Barony) Ltd* [2002] EWHC 773, for example, was a "Guaranteed Maximum Price Contract" for a £11.5 million factory finished six months late and resulted in a claim for an additional £12 million over and above the £13.5 million actually paid.

It is a generally accepted principle of risk management that those who are most able to manage a particular risk should bear that risk. Clause 6 of the introductory notes to the 1998 version of GC/Works/1 Design and Build Contract puts it simply:

> "Different contract strategies allocate risk differently between the parties. Generally, responsibility and risk should go together so that the party responsible for performing a task is accountable for the outcome. Ideally each risk should be allocated to the party with the greatest ability to manage and minimise its effects."

However, under the standard forms of contract this principle that risk should be allocated to the party most able to manage it is in conflict with the informational strategy that leaves the programme and records in the hands of the contractor and the obligation of the employer to give the contractor more time and more money if it is affected by one of the employer's risks.

| |
|---|
| Time and change are inseparable. It is unrealistic to think that change over time can be avoided, or that it is unnecessary, or uneconomical, or unwieldy to facilitate the management of the risk of it within the contractual framework. |

Clearly if the effects of the risks giving rise to delay to progress and disruption are not competently managed, increased costs and delay to completion inevitably follow. We now live in a different society than that envisaged by the administrative structure of the majority of the standard forms of contract currently available and improvements in technology have made it now both possible and eminently sensible for employers to take a structured and disciplined approach to the management of the effects of their own risks of change and for contractors to manage the construction process more professionally than they have ever been possible before.

## *The employer's risks*

When considering risk under a construction contract, and particularly the risk of change, it is common to think of that as encapsulated in the employer's power to vary the works voluntarily. However, in connection with the prospect of managing the risk of change it is perhaps more prudent to consider "change" in its broadest sense as being anything that involves a departure from the quantity, quality, timing or sequence of work for which the contractor tendered and upon which the contract is based.

In principle, there are four major classes of change in the principal standard forms:

(1) voluntary and implied acts or omissions of the employer, or thecontract administrator, or those employed by the employer, acting on the employer's behalf;
(2) acts and omissions of third parties;
(3) causes beyond the control of the contractor; and
(4) *force majeure* and other special circumstances.

In ECC all these are referred to as "compensation events" conditionally entitling the contractor to both compensation (by way of loss and expense) and also relief for the time effects (by way of an extension of time). However, under most standard forms it is only those risks that are actually or ostensibly in the employer's control at items 1 and 2 that carry with them the risk of having to pay compensation and under those conditions, the risks at items 3 and 4 above are employer's time risks only with the contractor carrying the risk of any financial loss incurred in connection therewith.

### Voluntary acts or omissions

These are what are generally referred to as variations and their scope and the consequences in terms of time and cost are usually expressly referred to in the contract. Effective pre-planning will obviously minimise the risk of the need to give instructions for voluntary variations. However, it is impractical to think that any construction project can be so well thought out in advance that it can be built without any voluntary change at all.

### Implied variations

Implied instructions are often referred to in connection with other clauses that stipulate that instructions must either be given, or are deemed to have been given, which constitute a variation in the works. Typically, these will cover such things as express or implied instructions to:

(1) correct an ambiguity or discrepancy in his requirements;
(2) correct an error in description (or quantity) in the bills, specifications or drawings;
(3) suspend the carrying out of the works;
(4) avoid a legal or physical impossibility;
(5) rectify any loss or damage arising from any of the insured risks;
(6) ensure conformity with any Act of Parliament, Regulation or Statute;
(7) investigate or dispose of archaeological findings;
(8) uncover or make openings in work where the works are found to have been carried out in accordance with the contract.

### Employer's other acts or omissions

The contract forms generally provide that acts or omissions of the employer, the contract administrator or those employed by them, which otherwise would be an act of prevention or breach of contract, are grounds for extending the time for performance and compensating the contractor for losses flowing therefrom. Depending upon the form of contract in use, these risks generally cover such events as:

(1) compliance with, or non-compliance with the CDM regulations;
(2) a failure to respond within due time to the contractor's submittal;
(3) a failure of the design team to issue in due time any information, drawings details or instructions (and under some forms, that risk is not dependent upon whether such information is ever requested);
(4) a failure to give, or deferment of possession of, or access to, or egress from any part of the site;
(5) a failure to obtain any third party consents necessary for the development;
(6) a failure to make prompt payment;
(7) any delay, impediment, or prevention caused by or attributable to the employer, the employer's personnel, or the employer's other contractors.

### Acts or omissions of third parties

Apart from responsibility for the acts of those employed by the employer, the employer is usually required to take the risk of default by others involved in the works not employed by the employer. They may be but are not necessarily employed by the contractor. These are referred to as "third parties" and depending upon the form of contract, the risks may include:

(1) civil commotion, strike or lock out;
(2) the default of a nominated sub-contractor or nominated supplier;
(3) the execution of work, or supply of materials, or goods by others not employed by the employer;
(4) the contractor's unforeseen inability to obtain the labour or materials he needs;
(5) the execution of work under a statutory obligation.

### *Force majeure* and associated risks

Then, finally, there are those other risks, generally considered to be not in the control of either the employer or the contractor, which are generally left at the risk of the employer under the standard forms. These include:

(1) *force majeure*;
(2) exceptionally adverse weather;
(3) the discovery of unforeseeable ground conditions;
(4) the occurrence of insured risks such as fire, storm, tempest, flood, etc;
(5) a change in the law;
(6) the exercise of a statutory power that affects the supply or use of labour, plant, or materials;
(7) the use of, or threat of the use of terrorism.

In JCT 98 the obligation to give notice of the need for further information has been modified from the absolute obligation in JCT 80, to one of practicality in the contractors' favour. Under clause 5.4.2 of JCT 98, the contractor is only obliged to give notice of its need for further information if it is reasonably practical for it to do so.

Where there is no express requirement in the contract that a sub-contractor must ask for any further information it needs, then it would appear from *J & J Fee Ltd* v. *The Express Lift Company Ltd* (1993) 34 Con. L.R. 147 that the court will readily imply a term to the effect that the contractor would:

"provide [the sub-contractor] with correct information concerning the works in such a manner and at such times as was reasonably necessary for the [sub-contractor] to have in order for him to fulfil his obligations under the contract."

## PROGRAMMES, METHOD STATEMENTS AND RECORDS

Programmes, method statements and records are the three tools which are essential to the employer and its consultants if the employer is to be able to manage its risks during the currency of a construction contract.[1]

1. For further guidance, see Chapter 2, Materials and Communications.

> The value of a complete and well thought-out master programme of the way the work is planned to be carried out in principle cannot be over-emphasised.

At any one time, the master programme is the base-line from which is established:

(1) the intended periods of activity and sequence of the works;
(2) the dates and logic by which the flow of design information will be planned;
(3) the dates and logic by which the procurement of major items of plant or goods or equipment on long delivery will be planned;
(4) the dates and logic by which the arrival on site of materials goods or contractors employed by the employer will be planned;
(5) any time contingency required by the contractor and it sub-contractors;
(6) the free float and total float available (if any) which may be used by the contractor and/or the employer for managing the expenditure of their respective time contingencies.

> Programming is really no more than putting the decisions made at the planning stage into a database that will enable the planner to allocate calendar periods to the various sections of the work.

It follows that from a well thought out programme, the contractor can make decisions as to preferred sequences, logical precedents and successors, the calculation of float in relation to resources available and to present the plan in a form acceptable to the design team as a process management tool. In the process of converting the plan into a programme, the planner should determine:

(1) the duration of the activities;
(2) the party who will perform the activities;
(3) the resources to be applied to the activities;
(4) how any one or more activities are to be sequenced in relation to other activities.

> For the purposes of change management, the programme should not be thought of as the product of a single finalised intent embodied in one product for all purposes.

In principle, there are at least three basic programmes, the tender programme, the master programme for the works and the updated master programme incorporating amongst other things, the short term look-ahead programmes, referred to as the as-planned programme. Only one of these is frozen in time—the tender programme. The others can and should change significantly as the works proceed and more information becomes available.

Finalisation of the design of the works actually required to be carried out and selection of the resources available to construct it will inevitably change the contractor's intent as to how the works should proceed and hence: how it is programmed to proceed.

> Without a competent, current master programme to act as a baseline, proper management of a project is difficult, if not impossible.

Apart from a programme, method statements and records are also vital equipment in the change manager's toolbox.

Method statements put flesh on the bones of the programme. They set out what work is to be carried out under the activity descriptions on the programme, the resources necessary to achieve the productivity required and the interface between the different activities.

Construction records are needed to record the progress actually achieved in relation to the programme and to update the programme for the purposes of identifying the effect of change in its broadest sense. Without progress records, little can be done to update the programme accurately and without accurate updates the programme will not indicate the true pattern of work and will rapidly fall into disuse.

## NOTICES AND EARLY WARNINGS

The purpose of notices and early warnings is to give the contract administrator an opportunity to deal with the possible consequences of the delays to progress, in so far as that is possible under the standard forms of contract.

> It is one of the potential benefits of the conventional contracting system that the contract administrator is often in a position to mitigate the effects of delay.

For example, the contract administrator may be able to give instructions for the omission of work; or, by redistributing or increasing its own resources the contract administrator may be able to speed up the supply of drawings; or, in order to provide an alternative source of work for the contractor, the contract administrator may be able to persuade the employer to release possession of other parts of the site earlier than was intended; and, in the event of anticipated delay due to protracted delivery of materials, he may be able to give instructions for the substitution of materials on shorter deliveries.

### *What the contracts say about notices*

Most forms of contract require the contractor to give notice of delay to progress that it considers is likely to cause delay to completion and which have been caused by an event at the employer's risk. Sometimes this is phrased as a claim for an extension of time. Other forms require the contractor to give considerably more information about delays to progress and do not distinguish between those at the employer's risk and contractor's risk, or those that are likely to affect the completion date and those which are not so likely to affect it.

## JCT forms

The JCT family of contracts for example requires the contractor to advise the contract administrator of all delays and likely delays to the contract irrespective of their causes. In particular, clause 25.2.1.1 of JCT 98 SFBC states:

> "If and whenever it becomes reasonably apparent that the progress of the works is being, or is likely to be delayed, the contractor shall forthwith give written notice to the architect of the material or circumstances including the cause or causes of the delay and identify and give such notice of any event which in his opinion is a [employer's time risk event] . . . "

## ICE 7th edition

Some contracts contain provisions which require not only that the contractor is to advise the employer of delay to progress that has occurred or is likely to occur but also that the employer or the contract administrator on its behalf should advise the contractor of any circumstances that it becomes aware of, or should reasonably be aware of that might adversely affect the cost or timing of the project. The guidance notes to ICE 7th edition for example, advise that "the contract is drafted bearing in mind the benefits of team working and current procurement initiatives. If its procedures are followed the parties to the contract will be provided with an "early warning" of circumstances that may give rise to additional costs or delay in a stage or completion of the contract" but it is not apparent how within the terms of that contract that is supposed to operate other than by the contractor advising the contract administrator of delay to progress within 28 days of its occurrence under clause 44(1).

## FIDIC

Although it comes under the heading of "early warning" and is more in the nature of a notice of delay, the FIDIC short form of contract contains the requirement that:

> "the contractor shall notify the employer in writing as soon as he is aware of any circumstance which may delay or disrupt the works, or which may give rise to a claim for additional payment. To the extent that the contractor's failure to notify results in the employer not being unable to keep all relevant records or not taking steps to minimise any delay, disruption, or cost, or the value of any variation, the contractor's entitlement to extension to the time for completion or additional payment shall be reduced."

## ECC

More extensive provisions appear in ECC, which states that:

"the contractor and the [contract administrator] give an early warning by notifying the other as soon as either becomes aware of any matter which could:

- increase the total of the Prices,
- delay Completion or
- impair the performance of the works in use.

Either the [contract administrator] or the contractor may instruct the other to attend an early warning meeting. Each may instruct other people to attend if the other agrees.
At an early warning meeting those who attend cooperate in:

- making and considering proposals for how the effect of each matter which has been notified as an early warning can be avoided or reduced,
- seeking solutions that will bring advantage to all those who will be affected and
- deciding upon actions which they will take and who, in accordance with this contract, will take them.

The [contract administrator] records the proposals considered and the decisions taken at an early warning meeting and gives a copy of his record to the contractor."

Whilst there is no penalty in default of an early warning imposed upon the employer if it fails to warn the contractor other than it will have to face the time and cost consequences of whatever follows, clause 63.4 of ECC provides that:

"If the [contract administrator] has notified the contractor of his decision that the contractor did not give an early warning of a compensation event which an experienced contractor could have given, the event is assessed as if the contractor had given an early warning."

## PPC2000

Similar but not identical provisions appear in PPC2000. There it states at clause 3.1 that:

"The partnering team members shall work together and individually, in accordance with the partnering documents, to achieve transparent and cooperative exchange of information in all matters relating to the project and to organise and integrate their activities as a collaborative team."

PPC2000 then goes on, in clause 3.7, to require that:

"The partnering team members shall operate an early warning system, whereby each partnering team member shall notify the others as soon as it is aware of any matter adversely affecting or threatening the project or that partnering team member's performance under the partnering contract, and shall include in such notification proposals for avoiding or remedying such matter. The [contract administrator] shall convene a meeting of the core group within five working days from the date of any such notification unless all core group members agree an alternative course of action."

### GC/Works/1

Clause 35 of GC/Works/1 requires progress meetings to be held. Five days before each progress meeting the contractor must submit a detailed report describing the progress of the execution of the design and works by reference to the programme. The report should explain any new circumstances arising since the previous meeting which, in the contractor's opinion, have delayed or may delay completion of the works or a section thereof and setting out any re-programming of proposals to ensure that completion of the works or any section thereof will be achieved by the relevant completion date.

> Giving adequate notice to the contract administrator of the likelihood of occurrence of delay is obviously one of the reasonable steps that the contractor can take to prevent or reduce delay.

*Hudson's Building Contracts*[2] takes a slightly more robust view, however, and suggests that whilst not ranking as a condition precedent to the grant of an extension of time the absence of notice might be actionable in damages, saying:

> "So far as failure by the contractor to give a required notice of a claim for an extension is concerned, it has been held that such a contractual requirement will not usually be interpreted as a condition precedent, although lateness or failure to give the notice in time may entitle the employer, on appropriate facts, to damages."

## THE SCL PROTOCOL AND CHANGE MANAGEMENT SUPPLEMENTS

### *The SCL Protocol*

The Protocol[3] came into being because there was widespread dissatisfaction from all interest groups within the Society of Construction Law as to how delay and disruption was being treated both during the course of the works and in disputes after the contract was completed.

> The idea of the Protocol is to provide a scheme for the management of change which was fair and balanced as between the differing interests of the parties to the contract and which is clear and comprehensive.

### Structure of the Protocol

It is not always appreciated that conceptually there are four aspects to the Protocol:

2. Edited by Ian Duncan Wallace QC (11th edn, 1995, Sweet & Maxwell).
3. For further guidance on the Protocol, see Chapter 2, Materials and Communications.

(1) definitions of terms in use;
(2) contemporaneous calculation of entitlement to extensions of time and compensation;
(3) retrospective calculations of entitlement to extensions of time and compensation;
(4) contemporaneous management of the effects of change.

The Protocol's recommendations for the contemporaneous management of the risk of change is not on all fours with the provisions of any of the standard forms of contract currently available, and it cannot be put into practice without substantial amendments being made to standard forms.

### *The Change Management Supplements*

In the absence of any significant movement on the part of any of the drafting bodies of the standard forms of contract, in 2004 the PFE Change Management Supplements were published privately, by Pickavance Consulting Ltd and Fenwick Elliott LLP.

#### Availability

The PFE Change Management Supplements are currently available for use with JCT 98 SFBC, JCT 98 WCD, JCT 98 IFC and JCT 98 MWA. Those for use with ICE 7th Edition and GC/Works/1 are to be published shortly.[4]

#### Application

In the same way that other supplements to the standard forms such as "sectional completion" and "contractor's design" are not suitable for all projects, the PFE Change Management Supplements will not always be appropriate conditions of contract for all projects. On the other hand, it seems that for those departments of the state and local government who spend public money, those responsible for the use of trust funds, and those private employers such as the defendant in *Masons* v. *WD King* [2003] EWHC 3124 (TCC) where completion on time is far more important than the choice between a "horse-deal" and retrospective litigation, the Supplements may produce a more acceptable way of managing the employer's risks under a construction contract.

The standard forms of contract contain a liquidated damages clause which provides that in the absence of an employer's time risk event having an adverse effect on completion, if the contractor fails to complete by the contract completion date, it will pay liquidated and ascertained damages at a fixed rate, usually per week, that the works remain incomplete. Liquidated damages, if

4. All published editions are available from the RIBA Bookshop and by electronic order from *www.pickavance.net*

they are to be enforceable must be no more than the loss that can reasonably be estimated at the time of contract to be likely to flow from a failure to complete by the completion date although they may be less than the loss foreseeable.

Provided that the estimate does not exceed the foreseeable loss, then in common law jurisdictions liquidated damages will be payable whether or not the estimated loss is actually suffered. However, it is sometimes the case that a reasonable estimate of the losses that are likely to flow from delayed completion is simply not commercially viable. In areas of high land value, for instance, the interest running on the purchase price of the land alone may be hundreds of thousands of pounds per week.

In such circumstances, the commercial risk of quantifying the losses likely to occur at a sum that properly represents the employer's likely losses carries with it the attendant risk of adversely affecting the contract price. It is understandable that the employer may not then seek to recover by way of liquidated and ascertained damages its likely losses but a sum considerably less than what is reasonably foreseeable.

> Notwithstanding the possibility of recovering liquidated damages, there are some circumstances in which it is far more important to achieve completion on time rather than to receive compensation for the failure.

Take for example, the opening night of a new theatre, university halls of residence that must be completed before the beginning of an academic year, hotels in which reservations are often taken for function rooms and bedrooms on the basis of a planned completion date and those projects planned to be opened to celebrate a particular date. A similar recurring deadline which has often caused problems is in relation to completion of the stadia, accommodation and transport facilities for the Olympic Games, every four years.

## Content

Each Change Management Supplement contains different conditions according to the contract it is intended to amend, but there are some common themes:

(1) the management information structure;
(2) changed definitions;
(3) new definitions;
(4) the role for the risk manager;
(5) change management;
(6) programme preparation;
(7) programme update;
(8) additions to the appendix to the contract; and
(9) schedules of project specific requirements.

## Changed definitions

The standard forms are inconsistent in the way they define the date by which the contractor is to complete the works and the do not recognise that the contractor could plan to complete by any other date. For example, JCT 98 defines the "completion date" as:

> "the date for completion as stated in the appendix or any date fixed (under the provisions for an extension of time) or in a confirmed acceptance of a (collateral agreement)."

The definition of "date for completion" does not provide for a planned completion date independently of a contractual obligation. In contrast, the PFE Change Management Supplements define the "completion date" as the date set down in the appendix as that by which the works are to be completed, or a variation of that date fixed by means of an extension of time, or by collateral agreement. On the other hand, the "date for completion" is identified as that indicated on any programme by which the contractor plans the work to be finished. In other words, the "date for completion" is what the contractor's programme indicates will be the date on which the works are likely to be finished, irrespective of the date by which the contractor is contractually obliged to complete the works.

## The management information structure

For the Supplements to give effect to the recommendations of the SCL Protocol, it is generally the case that some significantly different arrangements from those contemplated by the standard forms must be made for construction programming, record keeping, provisions for extension of time and compensation. The Supplements also introduce some new concepts relating to information gathering and electronic exchange and acceleration. The provisions will replace, augment or amend some obligations or impose new obligations in addition to those in the standard form.

## Contract requirements for a programme

It was observed by the plaintiff in *Masons* v. *W. D. King* [2003] EWHC 3124 (TCC) that:

> "as a matter of general practice within the industry it is quite common for contractors not to produce satisfactory programmes as a matter of course throughout the job but rather to produce them retrospectively at the end of the job when they actually begin to litigate or arbitrate extension of time claims."

> The PFE Change Management Supplements recognise that producing a programme retrospectively at the end of the job when the contractor actually begins to litigate or arbitrate extension of time claims is of little use at all to the employer who wants to be able to manage its exposure to the risk of delay.

The PFE Change Management Supplements define the "Programme" as a critical path network, together with a method statement, the two of which are to be read together. The requirements for the critical path network and the method statement are set down in appended schedules. Initially, the network and method statement are together referred to as the "draft programme". Once accepted they together become the "master programme".

The Supplements recognise that the programme is to be prepared in stages and regularly reviewed and updated, and because it is impossible, at the outset, to get all the information necessary to plan the whole of the works to an adequate level, the programme is to be prepared in differing levels of density and regularly reviewed and revised as a rolling programme.

The activities on the critical path network must be identified as precisely as possible in the light of the information available at the time it is prepared. Each activity and its relationship with each other activity is to be set out in a method statement that explains the sequence of activities on the critical path network.

## Monitoring the progress of the work

None of the standard forms makes provision for the employer to be able to monitor or control the progress of the work in any way. Whilst they do make provision occasionally for the contractor to manage and to monitor its progress, how that is generally to be accomplished is left for the contractor to determine.

Whilst it is common to think of monitoring the effect of change by reference to the completion date or one or more sectional completion dates, the Supplements recognise that it is also often desirable to monitor, independently of sectional or overall completion, the start or completion of individual activities or chains of activities. A "key date" that is not necessarily a sectional or overall completion date against which liquidated damages and extensions of time apply, may be monitored in such a manner.

Apart from final completion dates, it is not unusual in building and civil engineering projects to have multiple sectional completion dates. Sometimes these are based upon completion of defined zones of operation such as "Zone A ready for plant installation" but can equally be defined in relation to a state of completion required for a follow-on contractor to be able to commence. In major projects it is not unknown for there to be 20 or more sectional completion periods specified, each with a separately calculated liquidated damages provision for failure to complete on time.

The sort of activities typically chosen as milestones would be physical operations on the site such as the completion of a particular floor slab, the commencement of the installation of plant, "power-on" or "weather-tightness". Non-physical stages may also be selected like the approval of design drawings.

Unless performance under the programme to which it is working is contractually enforceable, control of the method and speed of working in the interim stages of the project is entirely in the hands of the contractor. It is up to the contractor, for example, to marshal its resources in whatever way it sees fit and, if that means some parts, phases or other sections of the work go faster or slower than the employer would like, in the absence of express terms giving the employer some power over progress there appears little that the employer can do about it save terminate the contractor's employment for breach of the obligation to proceed regularly and diligently. It will readily be appreciated that such draconian measures are unlikely to achieve completion any faster, indeed in most cases such a procedure is likely to delay completion by more than it would otherwise have been delayed.

Recognising this, the PFE Change Management Supplements introduce the power to control the progress of the works not only by reference to completion or sections carrying liquidated damages but by reference to key dates that can be referable to virtually anything that is project specific and identifiable.

> Whilst it is common to think of monitoring the effect of change upon the completion date or one or more sectional completion dates, it is often desirable to monitor independently of the completion of the works or a defined section of the works, the start or completion of other activities or chains of activities.

Under these recommended amendments to the UK standard forms, a key date is the date by which the start or finish of any defined process, delivery, activity, work package, section, or part of the works defined in a schedule to the amendment is to be monitored. A key date, for example, could be represented by a milestone called "power-on" or "watertight" or describing the start or finish or a point in the duration of the work of one or more particular specialist contractors or direct works contractors.

In this regard, the Supplements require that the key dates are identified on the master programme by milestones logically linked to the activity or activities, preceding and/or succeeding them.

Those key dates which the employer requires to be monitored are to be specified in a schedule to the supplement, however, if the contractor wishes others, there is no reason why it should not introduce them into his master programme; in theory, there is no limit to what can be monitored.

The provisions for monitoring a key date do not translate it into a sectional completion date or the completion date for which liquidated damages may be deducted and for which extensions of time may be awarded. Whereas both a sectional completion date and the completion date are key dates, a key date is not necessarily a completion date; it is simply a date of something that the employer or the contractor particularly wishes to monitor.

## Provisional sum

Traditionally, contractors have been required to include in their tender their anticipated costs of complying with the requirements set down in the tender documents for the preparation of programmes, historical records and other managerial information. In many construction contracts this has proved to be an unsatisfactory arrangement. It is a fact that the less work a contractor plans to do, the less will be his costs and the lower the costs, the more attractive the tender. The result is that contracts have tended to be awarded to those contractors who do not plan to spend much time or money managing the works. The result has generally been manifest in confusion, delay and claims. The purpose of the provisional sum is to take out of the tendering equation the costs of planning and recording the construction process and to make the cost of those elements a common factor amongst all tendering contractors.

The Supplements require the contract administrator to include a provisional sum in the tender documents for the provision of the management information to the employer. The provisional sum must provide for the costs of the preparation of:

(1) the first critical path network for the construction of the works;
(2) the first method statement describing the network;
(3) the number of reviews of the programme necessary to provide a number of updates required by the Supplements within the contract period; and
(4) the number of progress records required by the schedule necessary to fulfil the requirements of the Supplements within the contract period.

The provisional sum is not required to include the costs of:

(1) the correction of any part of any submittal that fails to comply with the schedules to the Supplements; and
(2) the resequencing or replanning, or the taking of any other steps to manage the delay to progress or the predicted effects thereof, whether such delay is caused by the contractor or by the employer.

## Liquidated damages for failure to produce management information

The failure to provide management information is dealt with by new powers to recover any losses as liquidated damages if, as a result of the contractor failing to supply the employer with the information he needs, he is inhibited from managing his risks. The principle for the deduction of liquidated damages is broadly similar to that for the deduction of liquidated damages for delay.

The losses that can be expected to flow from a failure to provide the management information necessary to enable the employer to follow the progress of the work and to manage his risks are those costs that will be expended in the event of a dispute about a claim for reimbursement of loss and/or expense or for an extension of time which, because of the absence of contemporaneous information, then has to be calculated retrospectively. The Supplements provide for a graded liquidated damages provision over six periods but there is no intrinsic reasoning why there should not be more or less periods, or for that matter, why the liquidated damages could not be formulated according to a "bell curve" graph demonstrating little foreseeable loss at the beginning and end of a contract but maximum in the middle.

## Roles and relationships

The management of the construction process so as to deal with the risks of change, consequent disruption and delay to progress and to manage them so as to minimise or avoid entirely their effects on the completion date requires the ability to use techniques that may not always be found among staff normally employed. That is not to say that the architect, contract administrator, project manager, quantity surveyor, engineer or clerk of works in any particular case will not have the skills to conduct the tasks anticipated by the Supplements. Much will depend upon each individual case.

> The PFE Change Management Supplements specify that, by default, the role is played by a separate individual who is referred to as the risk manager.

The role of the risk manager is to look after the employer's interests as to extensions of time, time related compensation periods and recovery from the effects of delay to progress.

By analogy, the role of the risk manager is as to time what the role of the employer's quantity surveyor is to construction economics, interim valuation and final account.

In relation to recovery measures, the risk manager's task is to provide a structure and discipline to the performance of the contractor's overriding obligation to complete the works by the completion date.

## The process of change management

The PFE Change Management Supplements recommend that the strategic management of time should commence during the latter part of the design stage in identifying, in conjunction with the employer and its advisers, those significant features of the project design in relation to the intended method of procurement which are likely to be important in the management of time during the course of the construction process.

The risk manager will advise the employer and its design team on the techniques to be used to prepare the programme, the software to be used and the general shape and feel of the management information that will be required from the contractor.

Once the contractor has been appointed and the programme has been prepared and is submitted for acceptance, it is the risk manager's task to examine the contractor's submittal and to advise the contract administrator whether the updates and amendments prepared during the course of the works comply with the contract.

Once the works have commenced on site, the contractor is required to produce progress information in conformity with the schedule to the Supplement. It is then the risk manager's task to examine the progress information submitted and to advise on whether it complies with the contract requirements for the proper monitoring of the progress of the works by means of updating the master programme.

With the provisions of the Supplements in place, the employer is also able to control the risk, not only of a delay to completion or sectional completion, but also of delay to a key date. Simply put, the project does not have to run late simply because the contractor has been awarded an extension of time. The provisions for delay management in the Supplements require the risk manager and the contractor to work together to investigate whether, and if so, how, the future programme of work can be re-sequenced or reprogrammed or the resources modified or the works be otherwise re-organised so as in whole or in part to overcome or avoid the delay that was likely to occur as a result of the change. In effect, the task of the risk manager under these circumstances is to provide the employer and his advisers with the information they need in order for the contract administrator to be able to give appropriate instructions to the contractor in order to overcome or reduce the effects of those employer's time risk events for which the employer takes the risk of time and/or cost.

Once the works have been completed, then it is the risk manager's task to check the contractor's final calculations of delay to progress, disruption, prolongation and concurrency and to advise the contract administrator and/or the quantity surveyor of those time periods for which the contractor may properly be reimbursed loss or expense, if applicable.

## MONITORING, UPDATING AND REVISING THE PROGRAMME

Monitoring progress is really no more than keeping score and identifying whether activities have started and/or finished as they were planned to start and/or finish as a matter of fact. Updating a programme requires the conversion from planned data to as-built data and the correction of logic that has not been followed. It is only by updating a programme that the effect of progress actually achieved in relation to the future plan can be gauged. Amending a programme involves the reassessment of the data upon which the programme was prepared and the reconsideration of method, sequence and resources so as to arrive at a more satisfactory intent than was previously planned.

## Monitoring progress

Whichever method of monitoring is selected it will involve an attempt to compare some planned progress of activity with actual progress as it occurs. This inevitably requires specific knowledge and judgement and whether a programme is produced as a simple bar chart or a cascade diagram or other method of network analysis will dictate, to a large extent, the method or methods of monitoring available.

## Updating the programme

During the course of the works, actual progress will have departed from planned progress for many reasons and it would be wrong to see such a departure as "fault". At its most serious it can be no more than a symptom of absence of reasonable foresight, but it is simply because it is so rare to have accurate foresight of what our needs will be in the future and how others are likely to conduct themselves that some differences between planned and actual progress will always occur.

Programmes have often fallen into disuse during construction projects not necessarily because of inaccuracy in programming logic, but because of a failure to update the programme regularly to reflect actual progress and changed intent. But if the programme is to be of any further use, it must be updated regularly.

Notwithstanding the contract requirements, there appears to be a widespread tendency amongst contractors to be reluctant to alter their first master programme to account for changing circumstances. Indeed, it seems that some contractors sublet the production of their construction programmes to companies or individuals that offer a "project planning" service, which are simply not commissioned to update the programme.

> Frequently, site management will adopt a method considered more "cost-effective" but without reference to the programme and without considering a revision of the issued programme.

Thus, often, programmes become so far divorced from the way the project is actually being built as to be useless for control of the project, let alone as a basis for the management of change.

Apart from problems of float and criticality, it is difficult, if not impossible, to calculate with any precision the damage which flows from disruption to progress if it cannot be demonstrated when it occurred and the effect it had on other activities.

Whether or not the contractor is obliged to update its programme, it will be in its interests to do so and to record all changes in the update, whether or not they are compensable and/or excusable.

### Revising the programme

The recommendation of the SCL Protocol is that the accepted master programme is not "cast in stone"; it is a dynamic management tool that will model the timescale of the contract scope of work and produce a prediction of the sequence of activities to completion based upon the best information then available. Information will improve as the project goes forward, and as better information becomes available, so the programme is to be revisited and revised.

### The as-built programme

A complete and regularly updated CPM programme provides the contractor, the employer and the contract administrator with a management tool to monitor the time and cost of contract performance which can be a vital element in the proof of delay or entitlement to damages. It is not always appreciated that a construction programme updated on a periodic basis creates an as-built record of the project that will be invaluable in demonstrating the relationships between root causes and ultimate effects if the occurrence of an event results in a claim.

## *What the contracts say about monitoring and updating*

The standard forms of contract are diverse in their requirements for programme monitoring, updating and revision. Notwithstanding that a programme that is not updated is of little use in ascertaining the contractor's intent or predicting the completion date, none of the standard forms contain any description of what an "update" should entail and some do not require the programme to be updated at all.

### JCT forms

Under JCT 98 SFBC, the contractor is required to reissue the programme with any amendments or revisions which the contractor decides to make only if an extension of time is awarded. Whilst the contractor is required to notify the contract administrator of any cause of delay to the progress of the works, it appears that the contractor is not required to update its programme to demonstrate those changes of timing. The contractor is only required to amend or revise its master programme to meet the grant of an extension of time. The editors of Walker-Smith justify this by saying that whilst it may seem restrictive the intention is that the master programme is bound only to the contract period and only if that period is extended, by the fixing of a later completion date is an amendment or revision of the master programme required. However, this fails to recognise the importance of shifts in timing changing the critical path and failing to properly predict the sequence and timing of the works.

> The absence of an obligation to incorporate the effects of the substance of notices of delay to progress in an updated master programme seems to be a serious omission from JCT 98 SFBC, an omission which is probably at the root of the difficulties some commentators appear to find with the status of the contractor's programme in this form of contract.

## FIDIC

FIDIC is unusual in stating, as a condition of contract, what is required by way of progress monitoring. In this form, the contractor is required to produce a monthly report accompanied by:

"(a) charts and detailed descriptions of progress, including each stage of design (if any), the contractor's documents, procurement, manufacture, delivery to site, construction, erection and testing; and including these stages of work for each nominated sub-contractor . . .
(b) photographs showing the status of manufacture and of progress on site;
(c) for the manufacture of each item of plant and materials, the name of the manufacturer, manufacture location, percentage progress, and the actual or expected dates of:

(i) commencement of manufacture;
(ii) the contractor's inspections;
(iii) tests; and
(iv) shipment and arrival at the site;

(d) the details described in Sub-Clause 6.10[5];
(e) copies of quality assurance documents, test results and certificates of materials;
(f) safety statistics, including details of any hazardous incidents and activities relating to environmental aspects and public relations; and
(g) comparisons of actual and planned progress, with details of any aspects which may jeopardise the completion in accordance with the contract, and the measures being (or to be) adopted to overcome delays."

5. Clause 6.10 requires the contractor to provide to the contract administrator at monthly intervals, a report of the number of each class of the contractor's personnel and of each type of the contractor's equipment on the site.

## PPC2000/FIDIC

Under PPC2000 and in clause 8.3 of each of FIDIC, the contractor is also required to update its programme when it is inconsistent with its programme or when instructed to do so.

## ICE forms

The ICE minor works form and ICE design and construct also provide that the contractor should update the programme if, when behind programme, it is instructed by the contract administrator to do so.

More proactively, clause 14(4) of ICE 7th edition provides for the contractor to be required to update the programme at any time the actual progress does not conform with the accepted programme.

## ECC

Under ECC, the contractor can revise its programme at any time but it must do so in accordance with the periods set down in the contract data and whenever instructed to do so. If instructed to do so, it must submit its revised programme within the period for reply. Furthermore, this form calls on the contractor to update and revise and reissue its as-planned programme to show:

(1) the actual progress achieved on each operation;
(2) the effect of progress upon the timing of the remaining work;
(3) the effect of implemented compensation events;
(4) the effect of notified early-warning matters;
(5) the contractor's proposals for dealing with any delays;
(6) the contractor's proposals for correcting notified defects; and
(7) any other changes the contractor proposes to make to the accepted programme.

ECC also requires the contractor to show on each updated and revised programme:

(1) the actual progress achieved on each operation and its effect upon the timing of the remaining work;
(2) the effect of implemented compensation events and of notified early-warning matters; and
(3) how the contractor plans to deal with any delays and to correct notified defects and any other changes which it proposes to make to the programme.

## GC/Works/1

GC/Works/1 makes specific reference to programme meetings at which the contractor is required to report on progress in relation to the project and to formulate proposals for accommodating any change in the programme. Under clause 35, the contractor is required to submit to the employer, five days before each progress meeting, a written report which, amongst other things, is required to:

> "(a) describe the progress of the works by reference to the programme and relevant instructions;
>
> . . .
>
> (c) explain any new circumstances arising since any previous progress meeting which in his opinion have delayed or may delay completion of the works or a section;
>
> . . .
>
> (e) set out any reprogramming proposals to ensure the completion of the works or any section will be achieved by the relevant date for completion."

### MF/1

Finally, and perhaps rather unhelpfully, MF/1 states that "the contractor shall not without the [CA's] consent make any material alteration to the approved Programme".

## COMPUTERISED PROJECT PLANNING PROGRAMMES

Ultimately, the use of project planning computer software enables more effective management of projects than was the case before the prevalence of such technology. Network analysis can be used to control the work as it proceeds by using it rapidly to update and amend the planned programme at intervals, throughout the project to take account of changes in work content and timing. With all the data available on databases, it is possible to know, virtually instantaneously, what stage a project is at, who is involved, how progress is proceeding and what resources are available or being used or proving inefficient.

| |
|---|
| It is not at the planning stage, but in project monitoring, updating and predicting delay that the use of project planning computer software becomes invaluable. |

To prepare a revised plan it is necessary to ascertain which activities have been completed, the time required for completion of activities currently in progress and the revised times of future activities if these have changed. The revised earliest and latest times can then be calculated for each activity, a revised critical path traced by analysis, and the process of resource allocation repeated to produce the revised programme.

Modelling "what if?" scenarios, tracking costs, reprogramming projects suffering from delay to progress and reallocating people and resources can help to analyse defaults and to work towards putting things right. However, very detailed consideration of resources takes time; judgement is therefore required in deciding the degree of detail to be employed that will retain the value of rapid revision without introducing unacceptable errors into the updated as-planned programme.

## Difficulties with project planning software

Before modern Windows-based project planning software became available, the programme logic of a network normally would be corrected in the next update to reflect the actual sequence of activities on site. The reason for this was that if the logic was not corrected, the update would report incorrect results. In some cases, an out-of-sequence report would prevent further processing of the programme. However, many of the modern computerised project planning software products permit the user to by-pass inconsistencies in the progress data and programme. For example, PowerProject project management software permits the user to maintain the programmed start and finish dates for activities independent of their actual status at the data date by manipulating the date line around the planned dates. This is sometimes put forward by contractors as an "updated" programme. However, whilst it may identify which activities have started, finished or are in progress, it does not do so in relation to a data date that enables the contractor, the employer and the contract administrator to identify the effect of progress actually achieved on the contractor's programmed intent.

Most project planning software products have the facility for "automatic updates" the theory of which is that once the data date is entered on the computer, an update executed "automatically" will then simply convert any as-planned data that is chronologically earlier than the data date to as-built data. Thus, if an activity was planned to be started and finished between 1 February and 15 March, an "automatic update" carried out at the end of March will show that the activity actually started on 1 February and actually finished on 15 March. This is so irrespective of what the progress records indicate simply because the update has not been carried out by reference to progress records but as a product of a computerised process independent of the facts.

## Relationship between records and updates

The PFE Change Management Supplements require that progress records to be kept electronically in a way that will enable them to be used efficiently and be handed over contemporaneously to the employer, the contract administrator and other parties involved to enable them to check that programme updates at regular intervals. It is readily apparent that without such contemporaneous data as to progress actually achieved, the employer is in some difficulty if the contractor misreports progress as it did in *Sauer* and *Great Eastern Hotel.*

## PROGRAMME MONITORING AND UPDATING

The following sequence of diagrams illustrate the danger of relying on programme "monitoring" passed off as a programme "update".

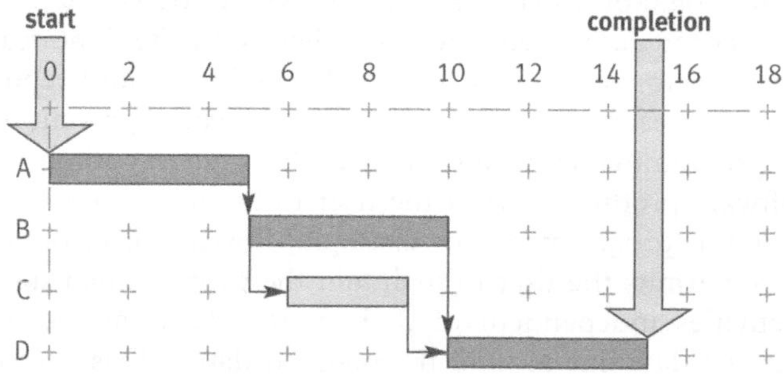


*Figure 1: The planned programme*

Figure 1 illustrates a programme of four activities. Activity "A" is to start on the commencement date and continue for five weeks. When that is completed activity "B" is planned to start and one week after activity "A" has finished and one week after activity "B" has started, activity "C" can start. Activities "B" and "C" must both be finished before activity "D" can start, although, as planned, activity "C" has 1 week of free float and the completion of activities "A", "B" and "D" on time is critical to completion on time, the critical path running through those three activities.

For the purposes of this example, at the end of week 7, a review of progress indicates that activity "B" is still in progress and still has two weeks' work left to complete. On the other hand, it was found in practice that activity "B" did not have to wait until all of activity "A" had finished before it could be started and was in fact started one week early, at the beginning of week 5 and only had two weeks left to complete. However, because activity "C" could not commence until one week had elapsed after the completion of activity "A"had been achieved, activity "C" had not started.

At the end of week 7 on the basis of this progress report, a "jagged line" progress report would look like that illustrated in Figure 2. This demonstrates that in relation to the date line at week 7, activity "A" which still has two weeks' work to complete is still scheduled to be completed in week 5 (*sic*!) and activity "C", which should have started, but has not, is still planned to be completed by week 9, and activity "D" is still planned to be completed on time at the end of week 15.

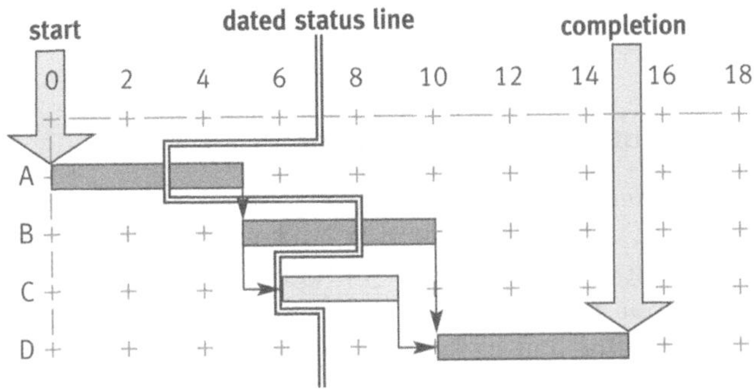


*Figure 2: "Jagged line" progress monitoring*

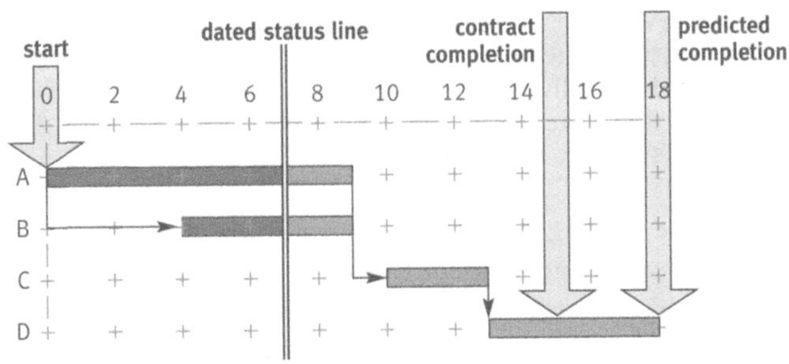


*Figure 3: Programme updated*

A competent update at the end of week 7, based upon the same review of progress as that for Figure 2, is illustrated at Figure 3 above. This indicates that activity "A" is still in progress and still has two weeks' work left to complete. On the other hand, activity "B" did not have to wait until activity "A" had finished before it could be started and was in fact started one week early, at the beginning of week 5 and, at the end of week 7, has only two weeks' work left to complete. However, because activity "C" cannot commence until one week has elapsed after the completion of activity "A", activity "C" cannot in fact start until week 11 (at the earliest). Because activity "D" cannot start until activity "C" is finished and, taking into account the absorption of the planned float at the end of week 7, activity "D" could not be expected to start until week 14. This update then predicts that completion is not likely to be achieved on time as shown on the jagged line progress monitoring report but in fact, in the absence of recovery measures, is likely to be three weeks late.

As can be observed from the illustrations above, the jagged line progress monitoring report fails to illustrate the effect on completion of the contractor's progress and, whilst it may seem incredible some contract administrators accept such progress monitoring reports as contractually compliant updates.

## *The courts' view of programme updates*

In *Great Eastern Hotel Company Ltd* v. *John Laing Construction Ltd* [2005] EWHC 181 (TCC) the court came to the conclusion that not only was competent updating of the contractor's programme relevant to the cause and effect of events, but that in failing to properly update its programme the management contractor had in fact caused all the losses which were claimed against it. In this case the employer claimed £17m in losses against the management contractor for delayed completion of the refurbishment of a large hotel in London.

H.H.J. Wilcox observed that a competent management contractor requires knowledge of the exact status of the project on a regular basis in order that he can ensure that the employer is kept fully appraised, and that the management contractor can deal with problems that have arisen, anticipate potential problems that may arise and make provisions for the proper carrying out of the work.

In finding that the management contractor's failure to competently update its programme and report accurately the state of the works from time to time had caused all the employer's losses, H.H.J. Wilcox said:

"From November of 1997 [the management contractor] seriously unreported [*sic*] the delays on a monthly basis occurring to the project, against the master programme. The most flagrant example according to [the employer] occurred in December of 1998 when the recovery programme . . . was presented. [The management contractor] reported a 20 weeks delay as against 34 weeks assessed by the experts. During October of 1997 to February of 1998 inclusively a five-month period, [the management contractor] reported monthly delays to the project of eight weeks only. Alterations were made to the updated copies of the master programme, which had the effect of showing that no further critical delays were occurring during that reporting period, when in fact because of [the works contractor's] performance the delay to the temporary roof and the consequential effects were much greater."

H.H.J. Wilcox then addressed how the management contractor had sought to interpret the information arising from its reporting systems:

"No satisfactory explanation has been given on behalf of [the management contractor] as to why this institutionalised misreporting occurred. [The management contractor was] served by a professional planning team . . . The intended use made of the construction planning system as it evolved throughout the project seemingly to provide a transparent tool to accomplice [*sic*] a timely completion of the project, contrasted with its use by [the management contractor] as a source of selective data to mask delay and management incompetence. The [management contractor's] project managers and their team were clearly privy to the use made of the data extracted from the programmes, and presented to [the employer] as construction bench marks accomplished, or as the basis for forecasting the path and timing of the construction yet to be achieved to complete the project. Where the electronic programme is shown to have had its logic changed to the end of producing data capable of masking incompetence, the likelihood is that such sophisticated technical manipulation was unlikely to have been part of the detailed knowledge of those other than the dedicated professional planners . . .

I accept that from time to time that (*sic*) professionals including the architects and the engineers voiced concerns about delay, and were aware that some delay was occurring, but I am satisfied that the [the management contractor] failed to comply with their contractual obligation to report candidly and objectively as to the extent of the delay which was known to them, and to seek to assuage those concerns."

His Honour then added the following criticism:

"Furthermore on the evidence before me I am driven to the conclusion that [the management contractor's planners] knew full well what they were doing when they permitted misleading delay information to be furnished to [the employer] and their advisors. They were all of them intelligent and experienced personnel who were well able to perceive the advantage to [the management contractor] of suppressing the true extent of the delay for as long as that remained possible, and giving themselves the opportunity to 'manage the way out of the difficulty' or to safeguard the financial interests of [the management contractor]."

Finally, His Honour concluded as follows:

" . . . in my judgement there is no doubt that [the management contractor] did deliberately submit incorrect information on the delays and causes of delays. It translates into causal effect . . . I accept that had [the management contractor] accurately reported delays and faced up to them there would have been little difficulty reorganising the contract before trade contracts commenced, so that they were properly coordinated in accordance with the actual progress of the project . . . I accept that is one of the key skills which a [management contractor] is supposed to bring to a project, and that their failure to properly report progress meant that they were unable to do this, and [the employer] and the professional team were not in a position to push [the management contractor] to do so. In consequence [the employer] was exposed to the inevitable claims for prolongation, delay and disruption as a direct consequence of [the management contractor's] breaches."

In the earlier case of *Royal Brompton Hospital NHS Trust* v. *Frederick A Hammond* [2001] 76 Con. L.R. 148, it was expressly recognised that because planned activities rarely start and finish on the dates they were planned to start and finish, the critical path (and hence the activities critical to completion) will change. That is why the programme must be updated as a result of progress actually achieved. If the master programme is to identify the contractor's intent for the future conduct of the works, it must also be reappraised, where necessary, in the light of later information becoming available and the occurrence of other changes. In this case the court held that:

"In order to make an assessment of whether a particular occurrence has affected the ultimate completion of the work, rather than just a particular operation it is desirable to consider what operations, at the time the event with which one is concerned happens, are critical to the forward progress of the work as a whole. On the evidence of [the experts] the establishment of the critical path of a particular construction project can itself be a difficult task if one does not know how the contractor planned the job. Not only that, but the critical path may well change during the course of the works, and almost certainly will do if the progress of the works is affected by some unforeseen event."

On the same point, in relation to JCT 98 SFBC, in *Balfour Beatty Construction Limited* v. *The Mayor And Burgesses of The London Borough of Lambeth* [2002] 1 B.L.R. 288, H.H.J. LLoyd QC observed:

"By now one would have thought that it was well understood that, on a contract of this kind, in order to attack, on the facts, a clause 24 certificate for non-completion (or an extension of time determined under clause 25), the foundation must be the original programme (if capable of justification and substantiation to show its validity and reliability as a contractual starting point) and *its success will similarly depend on the soundness of its revisions on the occurrence of every event*, so as to be able to provide a satisfactory and convincing demonstration of cause and effect. *A valid critical path (or paths) has to be established both initially and at every later material point since it (or they) will almost certainly change.*" (Emphasis added.)

Similarly, in *Henry Boot Construction (UK) Ltd* v. *Malmaison Hotel (Manchester) Ltd* (1999) 70 Con. L.R. 32, in which the contractor had claimed that its entitlement to an extension of time was to be calculated by reference to the putative effect of the employer's risk events on its earlier planned programme regardless of the evidence of the effect that its own culpable delays were alleged to have had on the programme. The court rehearsed the issues thus:

"[the employer] denies that the Works were delayed by the matters alleged by [the contractor], and asserts that [the contractor's] analysis of delay is 'misconceived and flawed' . . . In short, [the employer] says that the events relied on by [the contractor] did not in fact delay progress of the Works for various reasons. These include the fact that [the contractor's] assessment of delay was based on a revised programme which ignored the true state of the works at the date of issue, the part of the work affected by the [employer's time risk events] was not on the critical path, and the fact that '[the contractor's] delay analysis does not take into account any culpable delay on its part or actual progress at the time of the events relied upon' . . . "

Dyson J. accepted the employer's point saying:

"I accept the submissions of [counsel for D]. It seems to me that it is a question of fact in any given case whether a [employer's time risk event] has caused or is likely to cause delay to the works beyond the completion date in the sense described by Colman J. in the Balfour Beatty[6] case."

6. This is a reference to *Balfour Beatty Building Ltd* v. *Chestermount Properties Ltd* (1993) 62 B.L.R. 1 in which Colman J. said that the purpose of the power to grant an extension of time was to fix the period of time by which the period of time available for completion ought to be extended having regard to the incidence of the employer's time risk events, measured by the standard of what is fair and reasonable. The completion date as adjusted was not the date by which the contractor ought to have achieved practical completion, but the end of the total number of working days starting from the date of possession within which the contractor ought fairly and reasonably to have completed the works.

## The American approach

> The Boards of Contract Appeals in the US have consistently taken the view that unless the contractor's programme is properly updated, it cannot safely be used as a baseline from which to measure delay to progress.

For example, in *Kemron Environmental Services Corp.* (1999) ASBCA 51536, in which the contractor attempted to recover liquidated damages on the basis that it had not been responsible for the subsequent delay to completion, the Board found that:

"[the contractor] could not begin work until its . . . design was approved and it submitted its second design within a reasonable period of time after [the employer] improperly disapproved its first design. The only evidence which suggests that [the contractor] might not have been delayed is found in its revised project schedule. However, inasmuch as it is apparent that the schedules were not updated to reflect contemporaneous events and the record contains no relevant explanations, we find them to be inherently unreliable for purposes of determining the number of days [the contractor] was delayed."

Similarly, in *W. G. Yates & Sons Construction Company*, ASBCA Nos 49398 and 49399 (2001), where the contractor had failed properly to update its programme, it was held not to have any intent by which delay could be measured and not entitled to adduce evidence as to what was really its intent so as to demonstrate delay to progress caused by government changes. The Board said:

"Based on [the contractor's] failure to segregate the steel work performed after 26 March 1993 into structural steel and miscellaneous steel work, [the contractor's] failure to provide an updated work schedule for the period after 3 October 1992, and [the contractor's] own (site diary) entries characterizing much of the work performed after 26 March as 'misc[ellaneous] steel work' and structural steel for shops B and the contractor, pumphouse, and administrative offices we conclude that the erection of the structural steel, i.e. the truss erection and fill-in steel, was substantially completed on 26 March 1993 when [the contractor's supervisor] left the site; and that the work after 26 March did not follow a single critical path but ran through a number of different activities including masonry, carpentry, skin, metal decking and roofing.

. . . [the contractor's] contention that a study was performed from which it was determined it took 4 men 10–11 hours to change one splice plate segment is at best questionable . . . We conclude the alleged study is nothing more then generalized unsupported self-serving opinion testimony which we have held does not reach the level of credible proof."

Furthermore, in *The Gassman Corporation*, ASBCA Nos 44975 and 44976 (1999), where the contractor attempted to demonstrate its entitlement to more time in relation to its original planned programme without regard to sequence actually followed, the court observed:

" . . . neither [the contractor] nor its expert ever modified the CPM schedule to reflect [the contractor's] change in logic regarding erection of steel. The schedule's usefulness in evaluating the alleged slab 'delay', therefore, is limited . . . [The] CPM schedule must be current to evaluate project . . . whether a 'change' affects the critical path must be determined on basis of conditions existing immediately prior to its occurrence . . . [The] CPM schedule must reflect actual performance to be reliable basis for evaluating delay."

In the case *L & C Europa Contracting*, ASBCA No. 52848 (2004), the Board went further still and declined to accept oral testimony that was not supported by an updated impacted programme saying:

"In no instance, has [the contractor] attempted to identify and track the allegedly delayed work in the daily reports and account for the delay period. Only the (pre-construction planned programme) is in evidence. There are no updated (programmes) in the record that might demonstrate the relationship of the alleged delays to other work at the site, or the timing and impact of alleged delays on overall completion of the contract. The record does not permit segregation of any delays attributable to [the employer's] fault from other non-compensable delays including delays caused by [the contractor] and/or delays extending over unexplained gaps in [the contractor's] on-site performance.

With respect to the nature of the proof offered by [the contractor] generally, [the contractor] for the most part relies on general, unspecific and conclusory testimony that was not credible."

Generally, the courts in England and the US have acknowledged the dynamic nature of the project programming process.

> In the US, courts and tribunals have often placed great reliance on an analysis of delays affecting the critical path being assessed contemporaneously as the project unfolds by using the programme updating process as the reference point. This is also the recommendation of the SCL Protocol.

The approach taken in the English cases in *Chestermount*, *Malmaison*, *Balfour Beatty* v. *Lambeth*, *Brompton Hospital* and *Great Eastern Hotel* and that of the US Courts of Claims and Boards of Contract Appeals is correct in holding that in the face of persuasive evidence that it has not been followed, any programme (whether a tender programme, "contract" programme or otherwise) cannot safely be used as a baseline from which to measure the effect of an employer's time risk event on progress, or on completion.

## THE CHANGE MANAGEMENT PROCESS

It is readily apparent that the most effective method of monitoring a network programme and measuring the effects of change is to ensure that the programme is continuously updated after each progress review by indicating by reference to the date of review, the data date, which activities have started, finished or are in an estimable state of progress. In order to make sure that the results are reliable, the contractor should check the progress records against the as-built data on the programme and should not rely on any computerised "jagged line" progress monitoring, "progress override" or "retained logic" update to by-pass inconsistencies.

> The contractor should reassess de novo the logic of any shift in timing of planned activities as well as any changed work so as to render progress and logic consistent and make the appropriate corrections before running any recalculation of the planned completion date.

If a recalculation of the critical path demonstrates a projected overrun and the contractor is not entitled to an extension of time to that extent then, before completing the update, the contractor must reassess its resources and planned sequences to see if some improvement can be made by additional resources and re-programming to maintain the existing completion date.

The PFE Change Management Supplements envisage that the programme update and review process will always have three steps to it and may have four, or five, depending on the circumstances prevalent at the time.

### First step

The first step in the updating process is to identify what has actually happened since the programme was last compiled. Those activities that have started must be changed from planned activities to activities with actual start dates. Where activities that had been overlooked have started, they must be incorporated into the programme with appropriate logic. Where planned activities have started in an order or sequence different from that planned, they must be corrected to illustrate the sequence actually followed. Those activities in progress must have their degree of completion estimated. Those activities that have finished must have their planned finish date changed to an actual finish date. Where contingency periods have not been absorbed entirely, they must be reallocated in whole or in part, or discarded.

### Second step

The second step in the updating process is a review of the information upon which the planned programme was produced. The purpose of this is to see if there was any error in the master programme or whether, because of information now available that was not available earlier, there should be additions or changes to the planned sequence. For example, amongst other things, the master programme should be reviewed to see whether there is now any better information than before about how sub-contractors, statutory undertakings or utilities are likely to perform. When that review has been completed, the critical path (and hence the likely date for completion in the light of that update) must be recalculated. At that point, the risk manager, the contractor, the employer and any other persons identified in Schedule 1 will know where the contractor is in relation to where he planned to be.

## Third step

The third step in the updating process is that in which the first phase of the change management can be applied (at this point there has not yet been any consideration of the occurrence of an employer's time risk event). This is where the contractor must consider what to do concerning the progress actually achieved in regard to the master programme. If the master programme illustrates that the works are ahead of schedule the contractor should ask himself whether all successive activities have been allotted sufficient time. If so, will the design team have to produce information more quickly to keep up? And can they do that? If so, at what cost? Alternatively, should additional time be allowed for the provision of information? If the recalculated date for completion illustrates that progress is behind schedule, have any activities and their sequences been overestimated? Can they be executed any quicker with the same resources? Can the resources sensibly be increased to achieve faster progress than was planned? Can areas of work be taken off the critical path by resequencing? Or, can the contingency periods allotted safely be used to absorb the lost time? And so on.

The object of this reassessment must be to reorganise the programme where it can be changed, to identify what needs to be done to achieve completion on time and to set the train in motion by re-programming the work. This is a step that is called for by most standard forms of contract. Sometimes it is called mitigation. Sometimes it is referred to as "the contractor's overriding duty to overcome or avoid delay". Nowhere, in any standard form of contract, is there any guidance or structure for doing it. However, the Supplements call for this to be done regularly during the update process and requires that whatever decisions are taken, they must be recorded in an updated critical path network and method statement and be accepted by the risk manager. In other words, the Supplements require structure and discipline to be given to the mitigation process.

## Potential fourth step

The fourth step in the updating process only arises in connection with the occurrence of an employer's time risk event. In the fourth step, the contractor must identify what has happened to change the works in a way that is at the employer's risk as to time or cost. The contractor must identify in a sub-network the new activities and/or durations comprised in the employer's time risk event, what sequence they must follow, and the interface between that sub-network and the updated programme. Having done that, the contractor must again recalculate the date for completion. It is the recalculation that determines what is the effect (if any) of the employer's time risk event on progress, what is likely to be the effect on future progress and what is likely to be the effect on the date for completion and/or the completion date. If the calculated impact of the employer's time risk event demonstrates a likely adverse effect on the date for completion after the completion date, the contractor will be entitled to an extension of time.

### Potential fifth step

The employer or the risk manager will generally instigate the fifth and final step in the updating process but this really cannot be achieved without the contractor's cooperation because, if this step is to be achieved at all, its success will depend upon the contractor's active involvement. This step is the management of the effect of an employer's time risk event. It is the review of the contractor's master programme and consideration of what must be done to overcome the likely effect of change. This step is closely allied in its process to the third step, although the consequences are radically different.

In the third step, the programme was to be reviewed to overcome the contractor's likely culpable delay to completion, and hence, any changes made to the master programme were made at the contractor's expense. However, this cannot be so for the fifth step. In the fifth step of the update, the review of the contractor's activities, durations, sequence and resources is made to overcome the effect of a change that is at the employer's risk. Obviously, the contractor cannot be expected to carry the cost of this, and it should not do so. That does not mean that there will necessarily be a significant cost attached to it but, whatever it is, the employer should bear it, as it will arise out of the employer's liability for change in the master programme.

The sort of change that may be instructed could be re-sequencing activities that were sequential to be carried out in parallel, increasing resources where practicable, or the omission of time allowed for work associated with provisional or prime cost sums, or the omission of parts of the measured works.

The fifth stage of the update process is a collaborative process to manage change. It requires active participation of the risk manager, the design team and the employer and the contractor, working together to manage change in the construction process. It is truly partnering.

## MITIGATION

Mitigation is the process of making less severe. In construction and civil engineering contracts it is a term usually used to describe the process of avoiding circumstances that are likely to cause delay to progress or of minimising the likely knock on effect of delay to progress upon completion dates.

## The position at common law

Whilst there is no general common law duty upon a claimant to mitigate its loss, the contractor cannot recover from the employer losses that it could reasonably have avoided, nor will it be entitled to additional time which with reasonable diligence would not have been necessary. This position was enunciated most authoritatively by Viscount Haldane L.C. in *British Westinghouse* v. *Underground Electric Railways* [1912] A.C. 673 and his comments form the basis for the modern law relating to loss mitigation. In that case His Lordship stated that:

"I think that there are certain broad principles which are quite well settled. The first is that as far as possible, he who has proved a breach of a bargain to supply what he contracted to get is to be placed, as far as money can do it, in as good a situation as if the contract had been performed. The fundamental basis is thus compensation for pecuniary loss naturally flowing from the breach; but this first principle is qualified by a second, which imposes on a plaintiff the duty of taking all reasonable steps to mitigate the loss consequent on the breach, and debars him from claiming any part of the damage which is due to his neglect to take such steps."

But it is axiomatic that a claimant cannot owe a duty to himself. This was made quite clear by Donaldson M.R. in *The Solholt* [1983] 1 Lloyd's Rep. 605 when he stated that:

"A plaintiff is under no duty to mitigate his loss, despite the habitual use by lawyers of the phrase 'duty to mitigate'. He is completely free to act as he judges to be in his best interests. On the other hand, a defendant is not liable for all loss suffered by the plaintiff in consequence of his so acting. A defendant is only liable for such part of the plaintiff's loss as is properly caused by the defendant's breach of duty."

## The American approach

In the US case *R. P. Wallace Inc.* v. *The United States*, COFC No 96–222 the contractor (2004), for example, the US Federal Court of Claims identified that where delay is caused by something it deemed the contractor could have avoided, the delay is not caused by an event at the the employer's risk at all. In this case it was the contractor's evidence that once it had taken the first submittal from the supplier of windows and found the specification defective, it was out of his hands and whatever time the supplier subsequently took was not the contractor's problem. Having found that apart from anything else, the contractor had caused a concurrent delay to progress in wasting a month in approval of one of its own supplier's samples, the court observed:

"The factual flaw of this argument, however, is that [the contractor] produced no evidence, beyond the self-serving statements of its officers, that, once the defective specifications were corrected, it had no reasonable choice but to subcontract with [the supplier]. The lack of proof on this point is all the more startling as trial revealed that [the contractor] apparently knew, at or around the time it initially authorized [the supplier] to proceed, that the latter would need 22 weeks to complete a job that [the contractor] had originally estimated and represented would take, at most, eight. Yet, there is no indication that [the contractor] even considered going elsewhere . . .

As such, for the fabrication period, [the contractor] plainly has neither shown that the delay in completing the work was 'beyond [its] control,' nor that the 'delays' experienced by [its supplier] in delivering the windows were 'from unforeseeable causes beyond the control and without the fault or negligence of both [the contractor] and the subcontractors or suppliers . . . Rather, donning rose-colored glasses, [the contractor] seems to operate now, as it did then, on the assumption that once the original design of the windows was found to be defective, both it and the [the employer] were 'stuck' with whatever schedule [the supplier] could provide. That sticky assumption is counterfactual, particularly given the apportionment rule, discussed above, under which the [the employer's] initial delay did not absolve [the contractor] from having to obtain the windows in a timely manner, so as to minimise further delay in the completion of the contract."

## *What the contracts say about mitigation*

Some forms of contract require the contractor to prevent or avoid delay to the progress of the works as well as delay to completion. Most forms also contain some provision requiring the contractor to proceed diligently and to inform the contract administrator of any likelihood of delay.

### JCT forms

JCT 98 SFBC, JCT 98 IFC, JCT 98 WCD, and the works contract for use with JCT 98 MC require the contractor not only to "prevent delay" but also to "prevent the completion of the works being delayed". These forms impose two obligations whilst using the word "delay" to describe both. On the one hand the contractor is required to prevent delay in the course of the works, i.e. to prevent a delay to progress caused by the work falling behind programme and, on the other, to prevent delay to completion caused by the period of work continuing beyond the contractual completion date. However, JCT 98 MC requires the management contractor, not to "prevent", but to "avoid or reduce" delay without being specific as to which type of delay. Here it is not merely an obligation to avoid delay occurring, but also to moderate the effects of delay (presumably to progress) that has already occurred.

### GC/Works/1 and ICE forms

A further variation on this theme appears in GC/Works/1 and ICE minor works form, which require that the contractor should "prevent delays" and "minimise unavoidable delays", again without being specific as to whether either refers to delay to progress only or also delay to completion.

## PPC2000

PPC2000 requires that the contractor "shall use its best endeavours at all times to minimise any delay or increased cost in the project".

## Demonstrating mitigation

When the contractor is in culpable delay, clause 8.6 of the FIDIC red book goes much further and requires the contractor actually to demonstrate what recovery steps are to be taken and how they are to be implemented, requiring the contractor to present:

"a revised programme and supporting report describing the revised methods which the contractor proposes to adopt in order to expedite progress and comply with the contract."

ICE 7th edition and the FIDIC forms make it clear that the contract administrator is to consider the rate of progress in relation to any section of the works as well as the works as a whole, and, in forming the opinion that the rate of progress is too slow to ensure "substantial completion" by the contract completion date, it may issue a notice to the contractor to that effect who, " . . . shall thereupon take such steps as are necessary and to which the [CA] may consent to expedite the progress so as substantially to complete the works or such section by that prescribed time or extended time . . . ".

IChemE provides that the contractor is to revise its programme and use its "best endeavours to remedy the potential delay". At clause 13.5 it states:

"If at any time the performance of the contract falls behind the approved programme, or it becomes clear that it will so fall behind, then the [contract administrator] may require the contractor either to take such steps as may be practicable in order to achieve the approved programme or to revise the approved programme in the light of the circumstances and to re-submit it to him for his approval. If the [CA] approves the revised programme it shall thereafter be the approved programme.

Without prejudice to Sub-clause 13.5, if the [*contract administrator*] decides that the rate of progress by the contractor in carrying out the Works is likely to prejudice [the contractor's] ability to complete the construction of the plant, or any specified section thereof, in accordance with the provisions of Sub-clause 13.1, and that this is due to a cause for which the contractor is responsible, the [*contract administrator*] may give notice to that effect to the contractor. Following such notice the contractor shall use his best endeavours to remedy the potential delay at his own cost. If when the [*contract administrator*] requires the contractor to revise the approved programme, the contractor fails to submit such revised programme within a reasonable time, or if the contractor submits a revised programme which the [*contract administrator*] is unable to approve for good reason, the [*contract administrator*] may instruct the contractor in writing to make reasonable revisions to the programme, and the contractor shall forthwith make such revisions and the revised programme shall thereafter be the approved programme."

By way of contrast, the obligations generally imposed by the standard forms are not absolute. So the ICE Minor Works form, for example, requires the contractor to "take all reasonable steps".

JCT 98 SFBC and its fellows, referred to above, require the contractor to work out for itself whether it is suffering or likely to suffer delay and the contractor's obligation is then qualified in that it is not required to do more than "use constantly his best endeavours" to achieve the objective.

## Definition of best endeavours

> It is generally the case that conformance with such express obligations to use best endeavours to overcome or avoid delay is made a condition precedent to entitlement to an extension of time.

The expression "best endeavours" was interpreted in the case of *IBM* v. *International Business Machines (UK) Ltd* v. *Rockware Glass Ltd* (1980) F.S.R. 335 in regard to an agreement to sell some land by a contract that included a condition that IBM would use its best endeavours to obtain planning permission. Permission was initially refused and IBM did not appeal to the Secretary of State. It was held that even though making an appeal would cost a significant amount, the parties would have considered that an initial refusal at local level would not be the end of the matter. The test of "best endeavours" in that case was that purchasers of land:

> " . . . are bound to take all those steps in their power which are capable of producing the desired results, namely the obtaining of planning permission, being steps which a prudent, determined and reasonable [employer], acting in his own interests and desiring to achieve that result, would take."

It was further stated that the criterion was not that of someone under a contractual obligation, but someone who was considering his own interests. In *Sheffield District Railway Company* v. *Great Central Railway Company* (1911) 27 T.L.R. 451 the court said the words did not mean second-best endeavours nor did they require that the limits of what is reasonable must be overstepped with regard to the cost of the service, but that the defendant must, broadly speaking, "leave no stone unturned".

## Examples of mitigatory action

Typically an example of reasonable mitigation of delay might be that if the contractor has to construct 10 pad foundations and it intends to proceed from 1 to 10 in that order but finds a soft spot on pad 1, providing it is practical to do so it must move to construct the other pads while clearing the soft spot and cannot hold everything up for no better reason than the eclectic order in which it was first planned that the pads should be constructed.

In terms of its costs the contractor should also consider whether economies of plant can be effected by taking off hire, or removing from site, those items of plant which, with reason, would be stood idle. Items such as dumpers, forklift trucks, small mixers, etc., may easily be released. However, it might be unreasonable to expect the contractor to release a tower-crane or some complicated scaffolding, on the basis that it may be standing idle for a few days or so when the costs involved in removing such items would outweigh the hire charges if they were allowed to remain on site. Thus for the avoidance of doubt, it is advisable for the contractor to discuss these matters with the contract administrator and agree, if possible, which items of plant may be removed in the furtherance of mitigation of loss and/or expense.

## ACCELERATION

Acceleration is the obverse of delay; that is to say that for a given work content, acceleration is really no more than the difference between an intention and reality as to the timing of the work where the reality is an improvement upon the intent. Dictionaries will indicate that to accelerate means "to cause to move more quickly" or, "to increase in rate, amount, or extent", "to move faster" or "to happen faster".

> As with "delay", acceleration has no intrinsic quality; it is a comparative term and cannot have an existence independently of an objective standard by which it can be measured.

There are two common applications of the term acceleration. On the one hand, it tends to be used to describe the act of completing the works in a shorter time than that anticipated by the contractor at the time of tender in light of the resources planned, in the degree, disposition and under the circumstances anticipated by the contract documents. On the other hand, the term acceleration is also used to describe the act of recovery where the date for completion is likely to be delayed but the contractor applies more resources than planned to overcome or reduce the likely delay to the date for completion.

### The common law position

Over 100 years ago it was expressly stated by the Court of Appeal in *Wells* v. *Army and Navy Co-operative Society* (1903) 86 L.T. 764, C.A. that the imposition of a contract date for completion means that the contractor has a positive right to have the stipulated period in which to complete. Thus where there is no provision in any of the standard forms for the contract administrator to have the power to instruct acceleration, no such term can ever be implied out of some generalised provision for work to be done under the contract administrator's directions or to the contract administrator's satisfaction, or giving the contract administrator power to order or control the methods of working. It follows from this that in these circumstances any instruction for acceleration must expressly or impliedly emanate from the employer and any agreement for acceleration must be concluded between the contractor and the employer if the employer is to be liable for the ensuing costs.

### *What the contracts say about acceleration*

The standard form provisions for the power to instruct acceleration must be considered according to whether the acceleration is intended to:

(1) achieve a completion date earlier than that which the contractor is obliged to complete under the contract;
(2) maintain a completion date that the contractor is obliged to achieve under the contract;
(3) achieve a completion date earlier than that by which the contractor is entitled to complete as a result of any extension of time to which it is entitled.

### *Acceleration to overcome culpable delay*

The standard forms rarely use the word acceleration in connection with recovery of lost time that is at the contractor's risk. The structure of the forms varies, some requiring that the contractor puts into operation recovery measures in respect of culpable delay as a condition precedent to its entitlement to an extension of time; others requiring the contract administrator to issue instructions for such recovery. On the other hand, many of the standard form of engineering contracts and some of the standard forms of building contracts contain provision for the contract administrator to instruct the contractor to accelerate when it is in culpable delay.

Typically, however, the clauses which provide for recovery of lost time under these circumstances are not called "culpable delay", "power to accelerate" or anything equally explicit, they are usually entitled something reasonably innocuous such as "rate of progress".

### FIDIC

For example, under the heading of "rate of progress", the FIDIC forms contain the following:

> "If at any time actual progress is too slow to complete within the time for completion and/or progress has fallen (or will fall) behind the current programme . . . other than as a result of a (employer's time risk event), then the [contract administrator] may instruct the contractor to submit . . . a revised programme and supporting report describing the revised methods which the contractor proposes to adopt in order to expedite progress and complete within the time for completion."

### ICE forms

Some forms do not specifically require that the contractor should re-programme the work or revise its method statement, requiring simply that the contractor should take whatever steps are necessary to get back on programme. For example, under the heading of "rate of progress", ICE 7th edition, clause 46 provides that:

"If for any reason which does not entitle the contractor to an extension of time the rate of progress of the works or any section is at any time in the opinion of the [contract administrator] too slow to ensure substantial completion by the time or extended time for completion prescribed by Clauses 43 and 44 as appropriate or the revised time for completion (as a result of an interim award of an extension of time) the [contract administrator] shall notify the contractor in writing and the contractor shall thereupon take such steps as are necessary and to which the [contract administrator] may consent to expedite the progress so as substantially to complete the works or such section by that prescribed time or extended time. The contractor shall not be entitled to any additional payment for taking such steps."

Additionally, under the heading of "revision of programme", ICE 7th edition, clause 14(4) also requires specifically that the programme should be revised for the contract administrator's approval:

"Should it appear to the engineer at any time that the actual progress of the work does not conform with the accepted programme referred to in sub-clause (1) of this clause the engineer shall be entitled to require the contractor to produce a revised programme showing such modifications to the original programme as may be necessary to ensure completion of the works or any section within the time for completion as defined in clause 43 or extended time granted pursuant to clause 44. In such event the contractor shall submit his revised programme within 21 days or within such further period as the engineer may allow . . . "

## IChemE

IChemE requires, at clause 13.5, that the contractor is to revise its programme and use its "best endeavours to remedy the potential delay". At clause 13.5 it states:

"If at any time the performance of the contract falls behind the approved programme, or it becomes clear that it will so fall behind, then the [contract administrator] may require the contractor either to take such steps as may be practicable in order to achieve the approved programme or to revise the approved programme in the light of the circumstances and to re-submit it to him for his approval. If the [contract administrator] approves the revised programme it shall thereafter be the approved programme.

Without prejudice to Sub-clause 13.5, if the [contract administrator] decides that the rate of progress by the contractor in carrying out the Works is likely to prejudice [the contractor's] ability to complete the construction of the plant, or any specified section thereof, in accordance with the provisions of Sub-clause 13.1, and that this is due to a cause for which the contractor is responsible, the [contractor] may give notice to that effect to the [contract administrator]. Following such notice the contractor shall use his best endeavours to remedy the potential delay at his own cost. If when the [contract administrator] requires the contractor to revise the approved programme, the contractor fails to submit such revised programme within a reasonable time, or if the contractor submits a revised programme which the [contract administrator] is unable to approve for good reason, the [contract administrator] may instruct the contractor in writing to make reasonable revisions to the programme, and the contractor shall forthwith make such revisions and the revised programme shall thereafter be the approved programme."

Generally, the standard forms require the contractor to carry the costs of devising a programme and/or method statement and of putting it into practice to recover the contractor's lost time. The FIDIC forms also require the contractor to pay the employer's costs in regard to any losses it may suffer as a result of putting into effect the recovery methodology. For example, at clause 8.6, the FIDIC forms provide that:

"If these revised methods cause the employer to incur additional costs, the contractor shall . . . pay these costs to the employer, in addition to liquidated and ascertained damages for delay, if any."

### *Bespoke acceleration clauses*

It is not unusual to find bespoke clauses added to the standard forms to provide for acceleration to achieve recovery of culpable delay in more forceful terms. Typically, such bespoke clauses may be along the lines of that used in *Masons* v. *W. D. King* [2003] EWHC 3124 (TCC):

"In the event that the project manager is of the opinion that the contractor's rate of progress in carrying out the works is likely to prejudice completion of the works or any section by its completion date, and to the extent that in the opinion of the project manager this is due to a cause which is not a [employer's time risk event] the project manager, acting reasonably, and taking account of the contractor's representations, may instruct [the contractor] as to the measures he requires the contractor to take to retrieve the position and the contractor shall comply with the same at no cost to the employer. Without prejudice to the foregoing, such instructions may include the requirement to resequence work, to accelerate completion of a part of the works and/or require the contractor to increase its on and off site resources.

The project manager shall give the contractor notice in writing of an intention to issue an acceleration instruction no later than 5 working days before such instruction is intended to be issued, and the contractor may submit to the project manager representations in relation to the proposed instruction no later than 4 working days thereafter. In taking account of the contractor's representations, and making a decision to issue an acceleration instruction the project manager shall have regard to the progress of the works against the completion date for the works and each section thereof current at the relevant time."

In some contracts bespoke clauses will be inserted that provide for the contract administrator to instruct acceleration to overcome both contractor's culpable delay to progress and delay to progress arising as a result of an employer's time risk event. Typically, such clauses differentiate only in regard to liability for costs of the acceleration. For example:

"the contractor shall upon the written instruction of the [contract administrator] accelerate the progress of the works or any part thereof in such a manner as the [contract administrator] may consider necessary. The contractor shall be entitled to be paid the net extra cost (if any) incurred in giving effect to the [CA's] instruction hereunder, provided always that, should, in the opinion of the [contract administrator], the acceleration be necessary as the result of the contractor's failure to meet any of its obligations under the contract, all additional costs of the required action, including, but not limited to, the working of overtime, employment of additional labour and/or the use of additional construction equipment or other resources, shall be borne by the the contractor."

In so far as such a clause does not require the contract administrator expressly to differentiate between its power of instruction when the contractor is entitled to an extension of time from that when the contractor is not so entitled, the result is often that liability for the delay to progress and the consequential costs of recovery are left to be disputed after the contract has been completed.

### *Acceleration to achieve early completion*

This aspect of acceleration is probably the easiest to get to grips with as the date which it is intended to be improved upon is that which is encapsulated in the contract documents. It is an identifiable date, it is certain and fixed and, if it is improved upon, the acceleration is self-evident.

### *What the contracts say about early completion*

#### ACA form

Clause 11.8 of the ACA form is unusual in providing that the contract administrator can instruct that any of the dates in the schedule for taking over the works may be "brought forward" and that the contractor "shall immediately take such measures as are necessary to comply with such instruction"; it also makes provision for a payment of any damage or direct loss or expense arising out of that acceleration.

#### JCT 98 SFBC

If the employer wishes to achieve an earlier completion date than that to which the contractor is entitled to complete then it may also do so under JCT 98 by reference to a collateral agreement under clause 13A.2.2, which states that a quotation provided under that clause shall include:

"Any adjustment to the time required for completion of the works (including where relevant stating an earlier completion date than the date for completion given in the appendix) . . . "

#### GC/Works/1

Clause 38 of GC/Works/1 also provides for the contractor to offer to bring forward the completion date and for the right to require the contractor to provide its proposals to do so. It does not however require the employer to adopt any such proposals whether instructed or voluntarily provided, it does not require the contractor to comply with any such direction to provide such proposals, nor does it provide for any specific redress in the event that whilst it may have been entirely practicable to achieve an early completion, the contractor fails to comply with the contract administrator's direction to plan to bring forward the completion date. Under the heading of "acceleration and cost savings", so far as concerns directed acceleration, this form provides that:

> "1. If the employer wishes to achieve completion of the works or any relevant section before the (completion date), he shall direct the contractor to submit to him within the period specified in the direction—
>
> (a) the contractor's priced proposals for achieving the accelerated completion date, together with any consequential amendments to the programme, or
>
> (b) the contractor's explanation why he is unable to achieve the accelerated completion date."

## ECC

Other forms require the contractor, on invitation, to provide an estimate of costs of acceleration, which upon acceptance will become a term of a collateral contract. Typically, for example, ECC states:

> "The [contract administrator] may instruct the contractor to submit a quotation for acceleration to achieve completion before the completion date. A quotation for acceleration comprises changes to the prices and the completion date and a revised programme."

## *Acceleration to overcome an employer's delay*

### The common law position

In the absence of express words to that effect, there is generally no obligation upon the contractor to overcome the effects of a delay caused by an excusable event. That is, an event which entitles the contractor to an extension of time and relieves the contractor of the obligation to pay liquidated damages. This was brought out in the case of *Ascon Contracting Ltd* v. *Alfred McAlpine Construction Isle of Man Ltd* (1999) 66 Con. L.R. 119 in which Ascon was the concreting sub-contractor to the contractor for the redevelopment of the Villiers Building on the shorefront at Douglas in the Isle of Man. The sub-contractor alleged that seawater ingress below ground (for which it was agreed that the contractor was liable) had caused the sub-contractor the delay it had suffered in constructing the concrete substructure. In attempting to demonstrate, by way of counterclaim that culpable delay by the sub-contractor had caused the contractor to delay completion, the contractor had argued that whatever was the initial delay caused by the ingress of seawater, the sub-contractor nevertheless had had plenty of time to overcome it. In rejecting this argument, H.H.J. Hicks QC said:

> "It is difficult to see how there can be any room for the doctrine of mitigation in relation to damage suffered by reason of the employer's culpable delay in the face of express

contractual machinery for dealing with the situation by extension of time and reimbursement of loss and expense."

> In effect this meant that the contractor was not entitled to rely on the sub-contractor to overcome the knock-on effect of delay to progress caused by events for which the sub-contractor was entitled to an extension of time and to recover compensation for loss or expense suffered.

## Overview of the potential problems

Thus, unless the employer gives enforceable instructions requiring the contractor to re-sequence the work or to take other accelerative action in those circumstances, the delay to progress or disruption will inevitably mature into a delay to completion and a claim for reimbursement of prolongation costs.

This is potentially the most difficult area of acceleration to deal with and this is particularly so when the contractor has not updated its programme competently so as to identify what it has actually achieved in relation to what was planned and what its intentions are for the future of the project at the time any employer's time risk event occurred. Bearing in mind that the first thing to establish in regard to acceleration is the date that the contractor would be likely to finish in the absence of such acceleration, the absence of a programme by which that can be established prior to the nature of the acceleration required being considered and instructed, can render the employer's position extremely precarious.

### *What the contracts say about overcoming employer's delay*

It is rare to find in any standard form of contract for use with building, express provisions entitling the employer to manage the consequences of delay to progress caused by an employer's time risk event.

#### PPC2000

In PPC2000, for example, whilst clause 5.3 permits the contract administrator to issue any instruction that is not contrary to any partnering document and providing for the risks as to time to be the employer's liability, states at clause 18.2 that the contractor is to manage all risks associated with the project and the site. It provides nothing by way of information or power of instruction that would enable the employer to manage its own risks and for the contractor to receive more time and more money through the extension of time and compensation provisions if it fails to manage the employer's risks.

#### JCT forms

JCT 98 SFBC, JCT 98 WCD, JCT 98 IFC and JCT 98 MC do not contain any power of instruction in regards to the revision of the sequence of activities, resources to be applied, or methodology. The only provision available to the employer under JCT 98 SFBC, if it wishes to achieve an earlier completion date than that to which the contractor is entitled to complete is a collateral agreement under clause 13A.2.2, which states that a quotation provided under that clause shall include any adjustment to the time required for completion of the works. How such acceleration (if any) is to be achieved under those provisions and at what cost is then entirely for the contractor to decide. Again, there is nothing in the contract which provides for the employer to have access to the information it would need, or the powers of instruction necessary to manage the effect of its own risks.

### MF/1

Some of the UK engineering forms also have provisions that will, if implemented, enable the employer to manage its risks. For example, MF/1 provides that:

> "In all cases where the contractor has given notice [of an employer's time risk event that is likely to cause delay to completion, the contractor shall consult with the [contract administrator] in order to determine the steps (if any) which can be taken to overcome or minimise the actual or anticipated delay. The [contract administrator] shall thereafter comply with all reasonable instructions which the [contract administrator] shall give in order to overcome or minimise such delay. If compliance with any such instruction shall cause the contractor to incur additional cost and the contractor is entitled to an extension of time, the amount thereof shall be added to the contract price."

## PUTTING RECOVERY MEASURES INTO EFFECT

Although the power to instruct acceleration may be provided, it cannot reasonably be exercised without the contract administrator and the employer having access to the contractor's programme, method statement and progress records in order to ascertain what might reasonably be achievable and hence what might reasonably be instructed. It must also be borne in mind that it is the contractor who is in control of the site and its resources and, irrespective of the contract conditions and the information available, acceleration cannot reasonably be achieved in fact without the active cooperation of the contractor and his sub-contractors.

This problem is recognised by the PFE Change Management Supplements, which take account of these issues and provide the risk manager with the information it needs and with the powers necessary to give effect to the third and fifth stages of the programme update process[7] which are to give both the contractor and the employer the power and machinery to control their risks. The provisions deal separately with:

7. See above at page 374.

(1) the power to instruct acceleration when in culpable delay;
(2) the power to instruct acceleration when in excusable delay.

| |
|---|
| Where acceleration is required to overcome the effects of delay to progress not caused by an employer's time risk event the contractor bears the costs, but where it is required to overcome the effects of an employer's time risk event, the instruction is a variation for which the employer is to bear the costs of preparing any proposals and of putting them into effect. |

Wherever the power to instruct acceleration is contemplated, the PFE Change Management Supplements provide for a consultative process requiring the contractor's cooperation.

## PFE Change Management Supplements

The standard forms of contract are generally inadequate for the purposes of risk management. For this reason, the PFE Change Management Supplements incorporate amendments setting out the employer's powers and liabilities in regard to instructed acceleration as follows:

"*Acceleration when in culpable delay*

If in accordance with [the clause requiring the programme to be updated], as a result of delay to progress caused by events other than . . . [employer's time risk events], the contractor publishes a programme indicating that any part or parts of the works are likely to be completed later than a key date or dates or the completion date, the risk manager shall consult with the contractor as to possible means to overcome or avoid the envisaged delay to the key date or dates or the completion date. The risk manager shall [using his discretion but having regard to the consultation] deliver to the [contract administrator] written proposals and state whether in his opinion the contractor may reasonably be instructed to:

(1) reschedule one or more specific activities or sequence of activities or parts of the programme;
(2) change the resources to be applied to one or more specific activities; or
(3) take any other action necessary properly to re-sequence the programme so as to illustrate [the contractor's] revised intentions.

Provided always that the risk manager is reasonably of the opinion that it is practicable for the contractor to comply therewith (though, for the avoidance of doubt, compliance shall not be regarded as impracticable solely by reason of the cost likely to be incurred by compliance) and the [contract administrator] is of the opinion that it is reasonable to do so, within 7 days of receipt of the risk manager's proposals he shall instruct the contractor to publish the proposals in a revised master programme and the the contractor shall comply therewith at no cost to the employer.

*Acceleration when entitled to an extension of time*

If, as a result of any delay to progress caused by [an employer's] time risk event, the contractor publishes a programme indicating that any part of the works is likely to be completed later than a key date or dates or the completion date then, at any time thereafter, the [contract administrator] may instruct the contractor to consult with the risk manager to assist the risk manager in drafting proposals to overcome or avoid the likely delay, in whole or in part, to the key date or dates or the completion date. The risk manager shall (using his discretion but having regard to the consultation) deliver to the contract administrator written proposals to overcome or avoid the envisaged delay and state whether in his opinion the contractor may reasonably be instructed to:

(1) reschedule one or more specific activities or sequence of activities or parts of the programme;
(2) change the resources to be applied to one or more specific activities; or
(3) take any other action necessary properly to resequence the programme so as to illustrate [the contractor's] revised intentions.

provided always that the risk manager is reasonably of the opinion that it is practicable for the contractor to comply therewith and [the contract administrator] is of the opinion that it is reasonable to do so, within 7 days of receipt of the risk manager's proposals the [contract administrator] shall instruct the contractor to publish the proposals in a revised master programme . . .

Any instruction given under [this clause] is a variation instruction. the contractor shall keep such records as are reasonably necessary to substantiate the costs of preparing any proposals required by the [contract administrator] under [this clause] and of complying with any instruction issued by the [contract administrator] to implement such proposals . . . "

## *Compensation for failure to recover from delay*

Whilst it is unusual to find detailed procedures for the monitoring and updating of programme information set down in a building contract, it is common for the methodology of any monitoring and updating to be set down in a specification. However, the degree to which attention is paid to monitoring and updating will often depend, to a great extent, on what sanctions are available to the employer or the contract administrator in the event that the contract requirements for performance monitoring and updating are not followed. As is apparent from the case of *Masons* v. *W. D. King* [2003] EWHC 3124 (TCC), it is one thing to have the power of instruction and another thing entirely to have some meaningful redress if the instructions are not obeyed.

In the circumstances envisaged by clauses giving the employer the power to require the contractor to accelerate to overcome the likely effects of its own culpable delay to progress, the contemplated acceleration, if effective, will achieve no more than the contractor's primary underlying obligation under the contract, which is to complete the works on time.

> A failure on the part of the contractor either to plan such acceleration or to perform it in accordance with the instruction properly given would clearly be a breach of contract, but the redress that flows from that breach other than a right to terminate the contractor's employment under the contract is unspecified under most standard forms of contract.

It can readily be appreciated that the ultimate result of a failure to accelerate in accordance with such instructions may well be a delay to completion but, in regard to recovery for the breach, three difficulties flow from that:

(1) appreciation of the likelihood of a delay to completion is often a condition precedent to the right to instruct such acceleration;
(2) if the acceleration is not carried out, the delay to completion that was likely to result from the pre-existent delay to progress will occur; and
(3) the redress for delay to completion is the liquidated and ascertained damages identified in the contract.

It is trite law that a party that fails to perform its obligations under a contract must compensate the wronged party for the loss it suffers as a result of the breach. The difficulty in this case is to identify the loss that flows from the breach.

At the point in time at which the instruction to accelerate is given, although delay to progress has occurred, the likely effect of that delay on the completion date has not materialised. A party that is properly instructed to take action to avoid the likely effect on the completion date of a delay to progress that has already occurred where such action in compliance with the instruction, had it been taken, would have avoided the delay to completion, does not, simply by failing to take such action, cause the delay to completion. The object of compliance with the acceleration instruction is that, if put into effect, the acceleration achieved will break the chain of causation so as to prevent the delay to progress from having its likely effect on the completion date.

> As it happened, the contractor fell into culpable delay, and so the contract administrator exercised its contractual power to instruct acceleration. The contractor, however, failed to comply with that instruction and the project was ultimately finished late. This caused the employer to suffer hundreds of thousands of pounds in losses in excess of that which was recoverable via liquidated damages.

In *Masons* v. *W. D. King* [2003] EWHC 3124 (TCC) the claimants were lawyers claiming recovery of unpaid fees for the drafting of specific clauses to a contract for the development of halls of residence for Bath University. At contract, relevantly, it had been decided that for commercial reasons the employer's likely losses in the event of non-completion would be only partially recovered through liquidated damages provisions, and so a lesser rate than what the true loss might have been estimated to be had been set down. The contract also contained provisions for the contract administrator to instruct acceleration to overcome culpable delay to progress but no specific redress for failure to comply with such an instruction.

The defence to the claim was put on the basis that the lawyers had been negligent in not having provided for specific damages in the contract for a failure to comply with the instruction to accelerate. Having found that, amongst other things, the lawyers had not been negligent, H.H.J. LLoyd QC opined that:

"In my judgment failure to meet the obligation to comply with an instruction [to accelerate to overcome culpable delay] does not of itself give rise to any claim for damages. The primary obligation to complete on time remains. The additional obligation created by the instruction does not supersede that primary obligation. It is created to secure its due performance. If it is not observed the consequence may (or may not) be a failure to complete on time. The obligation is therefore preliminary, ancillary or subservient to that primary obligation. It overlaps that obligation. Failure to comply with it means only that the contractor has not remedied non-compliance with its general obligation to execute the works with diligence or with the programme . . .

The result may not be that the works are finished late. If they are, the true cause (if one need be found) lies in [the contractor's] failure to proceed with diligence or to comply with the programme, or some other failing or mishap for the consequences of the risk of which the contractor is contractually responsible but which the contractor did not correct or surmount and not the failure to comply with the instruction [to accelerate to overcome culpable delay]."

At paragraph 83, the point was summarised by H.H.J. LLoyd QC thus:

"Failure to comply with the instruction given when it is probable or likely that delay in progress will result in delay in completion merely means that the chain of causation that started with the event which has caused the delay in progress is not broken by lack of the compliance that is expected from the instruction, although it would be broken had there been compliance which averted the delay to completion."

Even if it were to be possible to rationalise circumstances in which a failure to accelerate did cause the delay to completion the anticipation of which the acceleration was instructed to overcome, the position then would be that the employer required compensation for the delay to completion. The remedy for culpable delay to completion is liquidated damages. Those liquidated damages are the very same liquidated damages as would have been suffered in any event, as a result of the contractor's culpable delay to completion, which were likely to follow from the delay to progress, that raised the spectre of instructed acceleration in the first place. In other words, the failure to accelerate does not interrupt the pre-existent chain of causation, and causes no identifiable and separable loss.

The question then arises as to whether in such circumstances it is possible to claim that the contractor is liable for the losses that actually flow from delayed completion instead of or as well as the agreed liquidated and ascertained damages.

## The effect of liquidated damages provisions

At common law, the affect of an agreement for liquidated damages is to place an agreed limitation on the contractor's liability for damages for delay to completion no matter how that should arise. In *Pigott Foundations* v. *Shepherd Construction* (1993) 67 B.L.R. 48 H.H.J. Gilliland QC said:

"The effect of a provision for the payment of liquidated damages for delay in a building contract has been considered in a number of recent authorities from which it is clear that not only does such a clause have the effect of imposing a liability upon the party who is responsible for the delay to pay damages at the stated rate but also it has the effect of precluding the other party to the contract from seeking to avoid the limitation on any amount of damages contained in a liquidated damages clause by claiming damages for delay or disruption arising from delay in completing the works as damages for the breach of some other provision of the contract."[8]

Thus, unless it is expressly provided for in the contract in unambiguous terms, the employer cannot recover time-related damages in excess of the liquidated and ascertained damages for delay to completion.

## Liquidated damages or compensation for actual loss

Generally, it should not be open to the contractor to choose between, on one hand, complying with an instruction to accelerate that has been validly given or, on the other, paying liquidated and ascertained damages. Provided the losses flowing from the failure to accelerate can be identified as other than delay-related losses it seems that they should be recoverable.

In *Aktieselskabet Reidar* v. *Arcos Ltd* [1927] 1 K.B. 352, where a charterer was obliged to pay demurrage at an agreed rate for the detention of a vessel for longer than a stipulated period, the issue was whether the charterer was also required to pay compensation for a breach of contract arising out of a defective load. In this case the Court of Appeal decided that the provisions for demurrage provided the remedy not for all breaches of contract but only for the loss which would normally arise from longer detention of the vessel, and not for the dead freight caused by the separate breach of loading less than full cargo. The Court of Appeal essentially thought that the demurrage only applied to one form of loss, but that there were two forms of loss involved, one compensated by demurrage, the other not. Accordingly, they allowed the charterers to recover general damages for the breach of contract in failing to load the appropriate cargo quantity in addition to demurrage for the additional lay days in port.

## Termination for breach

It would thus appear that in the absence of express provisions identifying the damages that will flow from a failure to accelerate following instructions validly given under the contract the employer's only redress would be to proceed to terminate the contractor's employment for the breach. In the *Masons* case, H.H.J. LLoyd declined to accept that in the absence of specific damages for the failure to comply with an instruction to accelerate, such a contractual obligation to comply therewith was "mere verbiage" as had been

8. See also *Cellulose Acetate* v. *Widnes Foundry* [1933] A.C. 20, H.L.; *Temloc* v. *Errill Properties* (1988) 39 B.L.R. 30, C.A. at 38–39; and *Surrey Heath BC* v. *Lovell Construction* (1988) 42 B.L.R. 25 at p. 37.

thought by at least one learned author,[9] and felt that the possibility of termination was a significant sanction saying:

> "Both the ICE Conditions and GC/Works/1 (in common with many other standard forms) contain provisions for the determination of the contract or the employment of the contractor under it for non-compliance with instructions. As is apparent from an examination of such clauses (and the references in them such as to time or progressing with diligence) the instructions include those to make up lost time (or to accelerate) . . .
>
> Although determination is not achieved swiftly (since it is necessary to give the contractor a last clear opportunity to comply before such the drastic sanction can be effectively and lawfully be applied), nevertheless the threat of such a sanction is conducive to realism. The cynical, such as those who have only a jaundiced view of the performance of contractors, tend to dismiss the commercial utility of determination provisions. In my view, they do not recognise that contractors, certainly those of some standing, will do everything possible to avoid a determination. Expulsion from a site is not just bad for [the contractor's] finances but affects [the contractor's] reputation and it can have significant consequences in terms of relationships with bankers and insurers. It will lead to a bond being called with immediately detrimental effect."

However, H.H.J. LLoyd QC also recognised that termination was unlikely to be of any assistance to the employer in achieving the purpose of the acceleration order, which is to reduce or avoid entirely the likely delay to completion by the key date. Clearly, before terminating the contractor's employment for failure to comply with an instruction to accelerate, the employer would have to be certain that the works would not be finished on time which, depending upon the information available, might not be capable of being established until close to the completion date. The notice of termination itself would be in breach if given unreasonably, or vexatiously, a point that might also be difficult to establish where the termination would not only not satisfy the object of the instruction given but also where the termination would in fact exacerbate the difficulty that was intended to be ameliorated by the instruction.

In the light of the reasoning given in *Masons* v. *W D King* there can be no doubt that in those circumstances where it is more important to the employer to have the project completed on time rather to recover liquidated damages for non-completion, the structure of the standard forms of contract is inadequate to protect the employer's interests.

On the other hand, the PFE Change Management Supplements take account of the effects of this case in making specific provisions for delay management and for the recovery of the employer's actual losses in the event of a failure to obey an instruction to accelerate that is reasonably given. By the terms of this amendment to the standard forms, the contractor will be liable in damages to the employer for the losses that are actually suffered as a result of failure to conform to an instruction to accelerate, over and above the liquidated damages specified in the contract for a failure to complete on time.

9. This was a reference to Duncan Wallace, Ian, QC (ed), *Hudson's Building and Engineering Contracts* (11th edn, 1995, Sweet & Maxwell) p. 127.

For example, clause 25C of the PFE Change Management Supplement for JCT 98, states:

"Notwithstanding the provisions for default in compliance with an instruction under clause 4.1.2, if the contractor fails to comply with an instruction (for acceleration), the contractor shall reimburse [the employer] for all the loss and expense, costs and damages that [the employer] thereby incurs. [The employer] shall be entitled to deduct such sums from any monies due or to become due to the contractor or may recover them as a debt. For the avoidance of doubt, [the employer's] entitlement hereunder is distinct from and not included within any entitlement to liquidated damages recoverable or deductible . . . However, in computing its losses, [the employer] shall give credit for any liquidated damages that have been deducted or paid . . . "

## VALUE OF RECOVERY MEASURES

Essentially, the purpose of acceleration must be to save time and money. There are a number of such measures, all of which may be described as acceleration, in which the contractor can reduce the effects of potentially delaying events. Of these, some may, however, increase the contractor's costs, some will certainly increase the contractor's costs and some, whilst taking some administrative time to implement, may not directly affect the contractor's costs at all.

Generally, in descending order of the usual ratio of cost to benefit, the following are potential methods of accelerating progress:

(1) changing the sequencing of the activities or increasing the overlap between activities;
(2) other logic changes to the method of working: using a different process to carry out the activity to that originally envisaged;
(3) increasing the motivation of the workforce to achieve higher production levels;
(4) increasing the resources allocated to an activity or group of activities on or near the critical path; and
(5) increasing the hours worked above the level originally assigned to the activity.

### Changing the sequence of activities

Changing the sequencing of the activities or the method of working may include reassessing the principles underlying the way that the work is to be carried out.

However, a change in construction logic, whilst it may increase costs, may also prove more efficient and actually save costs.

In the American case of *Canon Construction Corporation*, 72.1 B.C.A. (CCH) para. 9404, ASBCA No. 16142 (1972), for example, the layout of roads was to precede the construction of buildings but the design of the roads was changed delaying the works by over three months, the contractor claimed compensation for accelerating the work to avoid an anticipated rainy season. The claim for extended overheads and costs was measured according to the difference between the actual date of completion and the date the contract would have been completed but for delays which might have been due either to government fault or the performance of changed work. The contractor was held to be entitled to the compensation claimed which arose out of increased sub-contract prices and overtime costs incurred in an effort to avoid the rainy season.

## Other logic changes

Other logic changes such as increasing the overlap between activities will result in more work being carried out within the available time. Suppose, for example, in a hospital building it had been intended to complete all cabling, throughout, before commencing plastering. Instructions were then given to install a special set of services that could not be fitted until after those services originally included in the contract were completed. On the face of it, the time to install the special services will take a period between completion of cabling and commencement of plaster, thereby inevitably delaying the contract. However, if the contractor re-sequenced its work pattern so that, instead of the cabling being carried out on all floors simultaneously, it was done floor-by-floor, the following work by the plasterers could be brought forward on a floor-by-floor basis, reducing, or even eliminating, the effect on time of the additional special services.

Building works are particularly susceptible to acceleration by operating in parallel zones of operation that were planned to be sequential. This is in fact what was done in the acceleration programme in the case of *John Barker Construction Ltd* v. *London Portman Hotel Ltd* (1996) 83 B.L.R. 31. The contractor had 11 storeys of hotel bedrooms to complete and in order to accelerate to overcome delays to progress it had experienced, it decided to split the tower into two separate parts: eleventh storey down to sixth under one supervisor with one set of sub-contractors, and fifth floor down to the ground under another supervisor and with another set of sub-contractors.

The cost benefit of acceleration in relation to the time saving achieved depends to a large extent upon how the acceleration is planned to be put into effect. In most projects that have multi zones of operation and multiple trades in progress, there can be no doubt that acceleration achieved by re-sequencing (sometimes referred to as "crashing the programme") is by far the most easily achieved and cost effective method of saving time on a project.

However, not all projects are multi-zonal with multiple zones in progress. For example, a pipe-line through a forest may have only two points of access, one at each end and the process of pipe-laying is linear. That is to say, it must follow a regular cyclical path of clearance, pipe-stringing, welding, excavation, laying, backfill, testing, replanting. The works cannot be carried out in any other order. In projects such as this the only way that sequential accelerative measures can be put in place is to increase the number of work fronts. For example, an additional access at, say, the midpoint between the two ends, will double the number of work fronts and reduce the non-productive travelling time to each work front.

Some cyclical trades are particularly easy to accelerate by an increase in work fronts for example piling, which is dependent for its progress upon the number of piling rigs in operation may be accelerated if the site is big enough to accommodate it simply by increasing the number of piling rigs and zones of operation.

## Using a different method of working

Using a different process to carry out the activity from that originally envisaged could, for example, include using a pump to place concrete instead of a tower-crane and skip, or the use of dehumidifiers to dry out the works more quickly than could be achieved with natural ventilation. It may well transpire, for example, that where a twin-cage passenger goods hoist has been installed primarily for economic transportation of personnel at peak times, the spare hoisting capacity at off-peak times may be utilised for work previously envisaged for a crane, and result in increased service capacity.

## Increasing motivation

The motivation of the workforce to achieve higher production may be achieved, as an obvious example, by offering a bonus. The existence of bonus provisions can put pressure on the developer and the designers to avoid change and provide details early, and on supervisors to provide prompt approval or rejection.

If the nature of the project lends itself to incentives, they should not be overlooked. There are potentially significant benefits to be achieved from bonuses. For example, bonuses can be attached to intermediate stages of completion or milestones. Generally, it can be perceived that attitudes fostered by the prospect of a bonus are much more positive than those induced by the threat of damages or removal. However, incentive schemes fall to the ground where supervisors make adjustment to standards to make sure that bonuses are paid in any event, perhaps out of fear that the labour force will walk off unless they receive them! In such circumstances bonuses become just another way of calculating wages, irrespective of performance.

## Increasing resources

Increasing the resources allocated to an activity or group of activities on or near the critical path may be achieved by increasing the number of operatives and/or the amount of plant above that originally allotted to the activity.

If the sequence of operations is to be changed, this requires reprogramming in advance and closer management control. In the *Barker* case, the contractor had to condense three months' work in finishing the refurbishment of a tower block of hotel bedrooms into six weeks. The decorators could not work in the corridors and bedrooms if other trades were involved, so the contractor arranged for the decoration to be done at night whilst other work went on during the day.

Generally, it can be assumed that an activity duration is inversely proportional to the level of resource attributed to it in general, and the level of labour resources in particular. So, for instance, the amount of work constituted in an activity will commonly be estimated as a number of man-hours, and the duration will be accordingly determined by dividing that figure by the number of dedicated labour.

In other words, the more resources are applied, the shorter the activity duration. Such a simplistic view, however, is unrealistic. For all trades, there is a level at which an increase in resources ceases to be reflected in a reduction in the activity duration. The point at which that is reached will depend not only on the type of work, but also the working area, the proximity of other trades and the degree of coordination required from others. If the resources exceed the optimum level, the reduction in activity duration will begin to decrease proportionately until the activity duration begins to increase again in relation to the number of parties allocated to the task. In summary:

(1) after a certain point has been reached, any further increase in resources will become an decreasingly effective because of the various inefficiencies that result;
(2) after a certain point, the time the activity takes will stop decreasing and may actually start to increase.

## Increasing the working time

Although this method of acceleration is potentially the most expensive and wasteful of all methods of acceleration it is also usually the method first offered by contractors to overcome delay when progress is adversely affected as a result of a developer's time risk event.

Increasing the working hours in a given period may reasonably be expected to produce a loss of efficiency so that the costs incurred do not bear the same relationship to the benefit achieved as was anticipated at the time of tender. The law of diminishing returns tends to apply to increasing the hours worked above the level originally assigned to the activity. When working hours are increased for long periods, productivity is likely to reduce significantly. Changing working patterns may or may not be more effective than increasing the resources or working hours, depending on the circumstances. For instance instead of one shift working 80 hours per week, the contractor may use two separate teams each working 40 hours per week or, by a triple-day shift of three separate teams, reduce the activity duration even further. However, there always remain the inherent problems of continuity, quality control and management of resources in all but the simplest of cases.

In compiling estimates of acceleration costs it is often forgotten that the loss of productivity is relative to an increase in activity duration and is not accounted for simply by increasing the cost by the productivity loss coefficient. In *Skanska Construction Ltd* v. *Egger (Barony) Ltd* [2002] EWHC 773 for example, in considering a claim in which the subcontractor had said:

> "Any instruction to [the sub-contractor] to accelerate their works will have to incorporate agreement of their substantiated NPO[10] costs and an agreement to reimburse their reduction in productivity based upon 25% of the outstanding working hours."

It was held by the court to be interpreted as a mark up of 25% on their working rates on top of the non-productive overtime, His Honour Judge Wilcox observing:

> "In my judgement [the defendant's expert] is in error, the uplift to reimburse their 'reduction in productivity' was to be 'based upon 25% of the outstanding working hours'. This does not mean additional overtime hours or additional overtime plus normal hours worked on the same day, it relates to all of the working hours outstanding. The uplift must be applied to all hours worked."

It is suggested that a more logical interpretation is that the parties agreed that the overtime would cause a 25% loss of productivity during the period and in connection with the activities in which the overtime was actually worked. The effect of this would be to fix an agreed factor for lost productivity caused by acceleration at 25% and not to uplift the chargeable labour rates by 25% for whatever hours were worked which, in effect gives the contractor double recovery.

## BIBLIOGRAPHY

Povey, Philip J. (ed.), *Walker-Smith on the Standard Forms of Building Contract* (2001 update, Charles Knight).

Duncan Wallace, Ian, QC (ed.), *Hudson's Building and Engineering Contracts* (11th edn, 1995, Sweet & Maxwell).

Scott, K. L., "The management of contractual claims" (1992) in *Studies in contractual claims 14* (The Chartered Institute of Building).

British Standard BS 6079–2:2000 Part 2.

Society of Construction Law, *Delay and Disruption Protocol* (October 2002) *www.eotprotocol.com*

*PFE Change Management Supplement for use with JCT98 SFBC* (2003) Pickavance Consulting Ltd and Fenwick Elliott LLP, *www.pickavance.net*

10. Non-productive overtime, i.e. the enhanced rate of 1.5 or 2 times the normal labour rate for overtime worked is stipulated in the UK in the building and engineering industries by the various sets of National Working Rules legislation.

Lehmann, Mike, P. E. "CPM Schedule development, review and analysis guidelines" Accelerated Construction Strategies Guideline, Texas Department of Transportation (2003) *www.dot.state.tx.us/cst/construction_strategies.htm*

Wickwire, Jon M. and Ockman, Stuart, "Use of Critical Path Method on Contract Claims—2000", in *The Construction Lawyer*, Vol. 19, No. 4.

## TEST YOUR UNDERSTANDING

**1. Under which type of contract does the contractor usually take the risk of variations required by the employer?**

(a) all the standard forms;
(b) guaranteed maximum price contract;
(c) design and build;
(d) JCT98 SFBC;
(e) none.

**2. In connection with change management, the word "change" means:**

(a) variations instructed by the employer;
(b) contractor's errors;
(c) changes in the law;
(d) any departure from the contract documents;
(e) anything different from what the parties intended.

**3. A CPM programme is important to change management because:**

(a) it is the baseline from which to measure the effect of change;
(b) its difficult to get right;
(c) it always needs updating;
(d) nobody can understand it;
(e) the contract administrator always asks for one.

**4. The activities on a CPM programme should always be logically linked so that they are:**

(a) critical;
(b) no more than a week in duration;
(c) fixed so that they cannot move;
(d) of different maximum duration;

(e) able to react dynamically to change.

5. **The Change Management Supplements are:**

(a) conditions of contract;
(b) a guide to good practice;
(c) an appendix to the SCL Protocol;
(d) vitamin pills for elderly ladies;
(e) none of the above.

6. **The failure to produce a programme can be compensated by means of:**

(a) nothing;
(b) key dates;
(c) sectional completion dates;
(d) liquidated damages;
(e) bonus provisions.

7. **The role of the risk manager during construction is to:**

(a) transfer the risks under the contract;
(b) manage the employer's risks for him;
(c) advise on the time effects of change;
(d) replace the project manager;
(e) assist the contract administrator.

8. **The contractor should amend the programme from time to time because:**

(a) it will conceal contractor's delays;
(b) it will keep everyone on their toes;
(c) it is impossible to get it right first time;
(d) it is not a contract document;
(e) the employer has varied the works.

9. **The employer can always mitigate the effects of employer-caused delays by:**

(a) not granting an extension of time;
(b) agreeing with the contractor appropriate measures;
(c) instructing the contractor to accelerate;
(d) insisting they did not happen;
(e) paying the contractor compensation.

**10. Acceleration is usually most cost effectively achieved by:**

(a) working extended hours in critical path activities;
(b) working extended hours on all activities;
(c) resequencing the work to change the critical path;
(d) improving morale on site;
(e) bringing onto site additional resources.

CHAPTER 10

# REMEDIES FOR BREACH

Julian Critchlow

## INTRODUCTION

Where one party breaches his legal obligations to another, the injured party may be entitled to any of a number of forms of relief. Often, the parties will agree their own remedies. As to the common law position, the entitlement to damages is prominent. Where the parties are in contract, termination, repudiation, or rescission may also be options. Sometimes, an injunction will be available. The obligation breached may have its foundation in contract, tort, or statutory duty. Even where no obligation has been breached, if one party performs services for another at his request, an entitlement to be paid a reasonable sum is likely to arise. This chapter considers each of the above while concentrating on damages for breach of contract.

## FINANCIAL REMEDIES AGREED BY THE PARTIES

As a general rule, the parties to a contract may themselves determine the remedies applicable in case of breach. In construction contracts, the standard forms make express provision. Such remedies may include termination, which is discussed later. They may also include financial entitlements, such as the grant of an express right to the employer to obtain liquidated damages for late performance by the contractor, or a contractor's right to recover loss and expense for employer default.

### *Liquidated damages*

The overwhelming majority of standard form contracts and, indeed, bespoke contracts, entitle the employer to liquidated damages where the contractor fails to complete the contract works by the time stipulated. The contractor's delays must be culpable, i.e. delays that are his responsibility and for which he is not entitled to an extension of time. Typically, damages will be expressed as an amount per day, although sometimes an amount per week is stated.

The advantage of providing for liquidated damages is that they obviate the employer's necessity to prove the actual losses he has suffered in the event of delay. Thus, the damages that will typically be incurred by a developer will include the costs associated with being unable to sell the development so that he is kept out of his money, and the additional cost of financing the works. Establishing quantum of such costs can be an uncertain process. A pre-agreed figure for liquidated damages can greatly reduce that uncertainty.

From the contractor's point of view, the advantage of liquidated damages is that they provide greater certainty as to what his losses will be for any period of culpable delay, thereby enabling him to price his tenders with greater confidence.

There are a number of traps for the unwary with regard to liquidated damages.

### Genuine pre-estimate of loss

If the sum stipulated for liquidated damages exceeds the amount that the employer might reasonably expect to suffer for the delay, the liquidated damages clause will be struck down as constituting a penalty. The rationale for that principle is to prevent employers from taking advantage of contractor default so as to obtain a premium. The seminal case respecting penalties is *Dunlop Limited* v. *New Garage Company Limited* [1915] A.C. 79 H.L. That case made it clear that the courts will look to the true nature of the clause and not to what the parties have called it (e.g. "liquidated damages clause" or "penalty clause"). Thus, they will investigate whether the designated sum exceeds a reasonable pre-estimate of damages. There is no objection to agreeing a sum for liquidated damages that is less than a reasonable pre-estimate: where a contractor's exposure to unliquidated damages is so extensive that he is not prepared to assume all of the risk consequent upon delay, a lower liquidated damages figure may be agreed to limit his liability.

### Unintended limits

It is open to the parties to a construction contract to agree that liquidated damages are not to be an exhaustive remedy for delay. Whether or not they are depends upon the construction of each clause. However, where the clause represents the entire entitlement to damages, the employer will experience difficulties where damages are set unintentionally low. An extreme example appears in *Temloc* v. *Errill Properties* (1988) 39 B.L.R. 30. In that case, liquidated damages were expressed to be "£ nil". It was held that this did not mean that there was, in effect, no liquidated damages clause at all so that damages became "at large" (i.e. were available to the extent that they could actually be demonstrated); instead, it meant that the employer lost all rights to damages for delay.

Careless drafting can also unintentionally restrict recoverable damages where the period for recovery of damages is stipulated with insufficient precision. Thus, where liquidated damages are expressed to be, say, £10,000 per week, damages will only be recoverable for each full week of delay: there is no automatic apportionment for part weeks. To avoid this situation liquidated damages clauses are often stated to require payment "per week or part thereof" or provide for a daily rate.

Where a liquidated damages clause is agreed, should it cease to be operable, e.g. because time becomes at large (see below) so that the employer seeks to recover the actual damages that he can prove, the liquidated damages figure will nevertheless act as a cap on the amount of damages he can recover—*Rapid Building Group* v. *Ealing Family Housing Association* (1984) 24 B.L.R. 5.

### Time at large

The right to liquidated damages may be lost where time becomes "at large". Thus, the underlying principle is that if the employer himself delays completion, e.g. by ordering additional or different work, or by failing to give necessary instructions within the time required, he loses the right to insist on completion by the agreed date. The rationale is that he should not be able to insist on timely performance where he himself is responsible for the default.

However, well-drawn contracts invariably make provision for time for completion to be extended where delays are not the fault of the contractor. By way of example, the JCT family of standard forms lists certain "relevant events" that entitle the contractor to extensions of time when they occur. Some of those relevant events arise by way of default by the employer or his agents, e.g. failure to give instructions timeously; most arise from neutral events such as "exceptionally adverse weather conditions". Other standard forms go further and allow the contractor an extension of time for any circumstances beyond the contractor's control (e.g. the GC Works forms). Some of the events contained in the standard forms, e.g. the contractor's inability for reasons beyond his control to secure labour or materials, as provided for in the JCT family, are almost invariably struck out in practice as placing too much risk on the employer.

Certain delaying events also entitle the contractor to time as well as money. The list is generally more restrictive than the JCT Relevant Events and is largely limited to matters of specific employer default such as failure to give possession of the site. It is important to recognise that where any incidence of employer default does not give rise to an extension of time, time may well become at large and the employer will lose his right to liquidated damages. Thus, the extension of time mechanism is at least as much of the benefit of the employer as for the contractor. Further details appear in Chapter 7.

### Damages at large

Where, for whatever reason, damages have become at large, the employer's entitlement to recover them will depend upon his ability to establish when the contractor should have completed, and that the failure to complete on time was a consequence of the contractor's culpable delay. These matters are also dealt with in Chapter 7.

### *Contractor's entitlement to monies as provided for in the contract terms*

As observed above, it is open to the parties to a contract to decide their own remedies for breach (subject to certain exceptions such as the "penalty clause" referred to above). So far as the contractor is concerned, recovery of losses attendant upon employer default is frequently provided for expressly. In the JCT Forms, the entitlement is referred to as loss and expense, the ICE forms refer to cost, and the NEC provides for adjustment to the prices as a result of the effect on actual cost and the resulting fee arising from so-called compensation events. The advantage of making such express provision for breach is, again, increased certainty. Thus, it may be easier for the contractor to establish a money claim under a contractual mechanism where, for example, the employer has hindered or prevented his carrying out of the works, than to demonstrate breach by the employer of an implied term to the same effect. Such greater certainty may also be a benefit to the employer.

In practice, there is usually little distinction to be drawn between loss and expense available under the contract on the one hand, and common law damages for breach of contract arising out of the same event on the other. By way of example, if the contractor suffers disruption as a result of work being carried out on site by a third party, the "expense" that he stands to recover pursuant to clause 46(1) of the GC Works Single Stage Design and Build Contract, or direct loss and/or expense pursuant to clause 26.1 of the JCT Standard Form, is likely to be much the same as the damages that he might recover for breach of the term commonly implied into construction contracts that the employer will not hinder or prevent the contractor's completion (*London Borough of Merton* v. *Leach* (1985) 32 B.L.R. 51).

However, there are certain distinctions to be drawn between the entitlement provided by the contract and common law damages. Thus, the existence of the entitlement to recover financing charges (i.e. the contractor's cost of being kept out of his money, such as bank overdraft interest incurred or loss of investment opportunity) may be clearer under the contract terms than for breach of contract. The position is, however, blurred since the decision in *Wadsworth* v. *Lydall* [1981] 1 W.L.R. 598, C.A. That case decided that financing charges may be recovered as common law damages for breach of contract where they are reasonably within the contemplation of the parties at the time the contract was made as being the probable result of breach—i.e. they arc recoverable pursuant to the second limb of *Hadley* v. *Baxendale* (1854) 9 Ex. 341 (see below). In the absence of an available claim for special damages, the contractor's entitlement at common law will be limited to interest.

It is also the case that common law damages may need to be proved with a greater degree of precision than claims pursuant to the contract terms. For example, where the claim is for loss and/or expense, formulaic methods of calculation such as Emden's or Hudson's formulae may be permissible to establish claims for overheads and profit in the event of delay (see Chapter 7), but are likely to have to be proved strictly in an equivalent claim for common law damages.

Interest will, however, generally be available. The contract itself may make express provision for it (e.g. clause 30.1.1.1 of the JCT standard form), or the entitlement may arise pursuant to Statute such as the Late Payment of Commercial Debts (Interest) Act 1998, or section 49 of the Arbitration Act 1996. It has also been decided recently that an adjudicator has an inherent entitlement to award interest—*Carillion Construction Limited* v. *Devonport Royal Dockyard* (2005) L.T. 13.6.05.

Finally, under this head, it should be noted that it is open to the parties to agree that their rights should be restricted to those expressly stipulated by the contract itself and to exclude any equivalent common law right to damages. There are limits on the right to exclude remedies (see below) but, in the more usual types of construction contract between commercial parties, such a limitation is likely to be effective.

## COMMON LAW DAMAGES FOR BREACH OF CONTRACT

English law proceeds on the fundamental principle that "the governing purpose of damages is to put the party whose rights have been violated in the same position, so far as money can do, as if his rights were observed"—*Victoria Laundry Limited* v. *Newman Limited* [1949] 2 K.B. 528. However, not all losses sustained as a consequence of breach are recoverable. If no limit were placed on the right to recover damages, their extent would become unworkably open-ended and include losses far beyond those that could normally be expected to arise as a result of default. Therefore, the courts have developed restrictions on recoverability. The principle stems from *Hadley* v. *Baxendale* (1854) 9 Ex. 341 which stipulates two limbs for recoverability. Damages must fall within the ambit of one limb or the other; otherwise they will be disallowed on the grounds of being too "remote".

In that case it was stated that:

> "Where two parties have made a contract which one of them has broken, the damages which the other party ought to receive in respect of such breach of contract should be such as may fairly and reasonably be considered either (1) arising naturally, i.e. according to the usual course of things from such breach of contract itself or (2) such as may reasonably be supposed to have been in contemplation of the parties at the time they made the contract, as the probable result of breach of it."

Thus, the first limb requires the damages to be of the sort that would generally be expected to arise as a result of a breach. For example, if a contractor, in breach of contract, fails to complete a building, the additional costs of having the work carried out by others and of the employer's being kept out of the use of the building will "arise naturally" and be recoverable.

The second limb requires knowledge of what losses the parties themselves might expect to be incurred as a consequence of breach having regard to their knowledge at the time of contract. For example, if a contractor were to fail to construct on time accommodation that he knew was intended for the 2012 Olympics, the losses arising from that failure would be recoverable even to the extent that they did not arise "naturally" from the breach.

If, however, a contractor's late completion lost the employer the opportunity to participate in, and profit from, a further project of which the contractor was unaware at the time of contract, that loss of profit would probably be too remote to be claimable: it would neither arise naturally from the breach nor have been reasonably supposed to be in the contemplation of the parties at the time of contract.

### *Mitigation*

The innocent party to a breach of contract is obliged to take reasonable steps to mitigate the losses he has suffered. For example, if a contractor's workmanship proves after completion to be subject to latent defects of a progressively worsening nature, the employer can be expected to deal with those defects promptly rather than allowing them to deteriorate: the employer's recoverable losses will be restricted to those he would have incurred if he had acted with the speed that prudence requires. The obligation does not, however, extend to taking unreasonable or uncommercial steps; and the costs of reasonable mitigation are themselves recoverable.

### *Reasonability*

It was noted above that the general principle of damages for breach of contract is to put the injured party into the same position as he would have been in if the breach had not occurred. However, recent case law indicates an exception to that principle, namely that the injured party cannot insist upon being placed in precisely the same position that he would have been in but for the breach if the cost of doing so would, in all the circumstances, be disproportionate. Thus, in *Ruxley Electronics* v. *Forsyth* [1996] A.C. 344, H.L. it was held that where a swimming pool was built with a deep end of 6ft instead of 7$\frac{1}{2}$ft, and the cost of rebuilding it would have been £21,560, the owner was not entitled to have the pool rebuilt precisely to specification because it was suitable for its intended purpose and there was, therefore, no diminution in its value.

### *Betterment*

The level of recoverable damages is also restricted in that the entitlement will only extend to the actual loss. Thus, if an employer rebuilds or reinstates a defective structure to a better standard than was contracted for, he will not be able successfully to claim the cost of the betterment. However, that principle will not apply where the injured party had no choice: if new build to replace old is an unavoidable consequence of the breach of contract in question, the injured party will not have to give credit for obtaining a better product.

### *Exemption clauses*

It was seen earlier that the parties to a contract can pre-determine the extent of damages payable for delay by agreeing liquidated damages and that a liquidated damages figure will normally act as a cap on recovery even where damages become at large. Beyond that, the parties may agree specific limits on liability known as exemption or exclusion clauses. Such clauses may place restrictions as to what behaviour is to be regarded as a breach of contract, e.g. by requiring one party or the other to disregard certain faults in performance such as errors in description of goods; or they may restrict the entitlement of a party to recover damages where a breach has occurred. A fairly common example is limitation by a consultant, such as an architect, on the amount of damages that may be recovered by his client should he breach the consultancy. Often, a limit so stipulated will be coextensive with the consultant's insurance cover.

Another common restriction on claims relates to the obligation of the design and build contractor. The general rule is that a contractor who agrees to be responsible for both design and build of a structure assumes a duty to ensure that it is fit for its intended purpose as communicated to the contractor —*Greaves* v. *Baynham Meikle* [1975] 1 W.L.R. 1095. Accordingly, the contractor's responsibility is stricter than that of a consultant carrying out design, where the implied design obligation is usually only one of reasonable competence. Since it is difficult for contractors to obtain insurance for a fitness for purpose obligation, both standard forms and bespoke contracts often limit the contractor's design responsibilities to those of the consultant's standard of reasonable competence, or similar. That is the case in the JCT Design and Build version, although the Design and Build version of the GC Works form gives the parties an option to select either fitness for purpose or the lesser, competent designer, standard.

Where an exemption clause is extremely onerous, the courts will scrutinise it carefully to ensure that its wording is adequate to effect the exclusion in question and, in this respect, they will apply the *contra proferentem* rule. That rule provides that where a clause in a contract is ambiguous, it will be construed against the interests of the party that drafted or tendered it.

Further, there are certain statutory limits on the effectiveness of exemption clauses the most important of which being contained in the Unfair Contract Terms Act 1977 (see Appendix 1). Of particular significance for construction is s. 3 which provides that where one party to a contract deals:

(a) as a consumer; or
(b) on the other's written standard terms of business,

the other party cannot exclude or restrict liability for his breach of contract, render substantially different performance from that reasonably expected, or render no performance at all, except so far as the exclusion is "reasonable".

Occasionally, the parties to a contract will seek to exclude "consequential losses". Such exclusions may be intended to extinguish the entitlement to recover losses that are not direct. Thus, where a building fails, the cost of rebuilding might, in ordinary terminology, be regarded as "direct", and loss of profits from expected rental "consequential". However, the courts have not construed the term in that way. Instead, they have held that it covers damages falling within the second limb of *Hadley* v. *Baxendale* (see above), i.e. damages reasonably supposed to be in the contemplation of the parties at the time of contract as likely to arise from breach, and does not exclude damages arising naturally from the breach.

## DAMAGES IN TORT

Chapter 1 outlines the distinctions to be drawn between contract and tort. For a period in English law it appeared to be the case that where damages were available for breach of contract, the party in breach would have no concurrent liability to the injured party in tort. It now seems clear that, in principle, such concurrent liability can arise i.e. so the injured party can elect to proceed pursuant to either basis, or both. This can be significant as the rules for demonstrating breach of an obligation, of deciding the extent of damages, and the applicable limitation periods, can all differ for each. There are a number of different torts. That most commonly (though by no means uniquely) met in construction is the tort of negligence. A particularly important distinction between recovery of damages in contract and in negligence lies in their respective tests for remoteness. The contractual test was outlined above and encapsulated in the two limbs of *Hadley* v. *Baxendale*. In negligence, available damages are those that constitute a reasonably foreseeable consequence of breach—*The Wagon Mound No. 1* [1961] A.C. 388. Thus, the test for remoteness in tort, in practice, can sometimes be more restrictive than in contract because losses that are a direct consequence of the breach will not necessarily be foreseeable. In *The Wagon Mound No. 1* itself, oil was negligently allowed to spill into the sea and then set alight by welding operations, damaging the plaintiff's wharf. It was held that the damage was irrecoverable because, although it arose naturally from the negligence, on the scientific evidence then available, the fire was unforeseeable.

However, a major advantage of proceeding in tort is that the time limit for commencing proceedings may sometimes be longer than in contract. That is because the right of action arises at the date the damage was suffered as opposed to the position in contract where time runs from the date of the breach; and that period in tort may be lengthened still further where the negligence in question concerns latent defects (see below).

A major restriction on the ability to claim in tort that is of particular relevance to the construction industry concerns the recovery of pure economic loss, i.e. loss that is not a result of physical damage. Where pure economic loss is consequent upon the giving of negligent advice, e.g. as given by an architect or other consultant, there is no inhibition on its recovery provided that the other requirements for recovery are present including, in particular, the existence of a "special relationship" between the negligent party and the claimant. The position is different where the negligence arises out of a contract that includes physical construction. Thus, where a claim is made against a contractor or sub-contractor by a person who was not in contract with them, and the damage that that person suffers is "to the thing itself", the loss will be characterised as purely economic and irrecoverable. For example, if a purchaser of a dwelling discovers defective plaster and commences proceedings in negligence against the plastering sub-contractor (who was employed by the developer from whom the purchaser purchased) the purchaser's proceedings against that sub-contractor will fail—*D&F Estates* v. *Church Commissioners* [1989] A.C. 177, H.L. That is because the cost of repairing or replacing the plaster is purely economic—the damage claimed for is to the "thing itself", i.e. the plaster.

However, proceedings will be successful against a contractor or sub-contractor with whom a party does not have a contract where the damage is to "other property". Thus, if the cladding to a dwelling is defective and a piece falls from the building thereby damaging the car of the purchaser of the dwelling, the damage to the car will be recoverable from the contractor or sub-contractor responsible for the cladding failure. That is because the car is "other property" and not "the thing itself".

A question that remains to be resolved by the courts arises where the "thing itself" is a "complex structure" such as a building. It is arguable that one part of the building, say the foundations, is distinct from the other parts, such as the superstructure, so that if the foundations of a structure fail owing to negligence, a purchaser not in contract with the contractor may be able to sue the contractor responsible for the foundations in respect of the damage that has been caused to the superstructure—see *Murphy* v. *Brentwood City Council* [1991] 1 A.C. 398.

## RECOVERY IN THE ABSENCE OF A CONTRACT

It was seen in Chapter 1 that, sometimes, a contractor will carry out valuable work for an employer without a contract being in place between them. In such circumstances the contractor will generally be entitled to be paid a reasonable commercial sum—see, e.g. *Laserbore Limited* v. *Morrison Briggs Wall Limited* [1993] CILL 896. Sometimes, this entitlement is said to be pursuant to a quantum meruit ("the amount he deserves"), and sometimes the entitlement is seen as a function of the legal principles of restitution or unjust enrichment.

Calculation of a reasonable commercial sum will depend upon the facts of the individual case. Relevant factors may include any prices referred to in negotiations, or valuation by experts.

This head of recovery is to be distinguished from the situation where the parties have entered into a binding contract but have not agreed a price. Again, the contractor's entitlement will be to recover a reasonable sum. However, that reasonable sum will be assessed against the background of the contract as a whole.

## BREACH OF STATUTORY DUTY

Much English legislation affects construction, whether directly or indirectly. Some statutory provisions are intended merely to give rise to liability, where they are impinged, to the state, but others give rights to third parties. The Construction (Design and Management) Regulations 1994 appear to fall within the former category. The Defective Premises Act 1972 falls into the latter category and fixes contractors and developers with liability to any person who acquires an interest in a dwelling where the construction work is not done in a workmanlike or professional manner, or carried out with proper materials, as a consequence of which the dwelling is unfit for habitation. The Act is silent as to how damages are to be calculated but have been held to comprise losses arising from loss of use of the dwelling. *Keating on Building Contracts* (7th edition) suggests that all reasonably foreseeable losses that are a natural consequence of breach are recoverable.

The Housing Grants Construction and Regeneration Act 1996 contains a number of important rights with attendant consequences of breach. They include a contractor's entitlement to periodic payments and to certain contractual notices respecting payment, as well as the right to suspend work for non-payment. It also gives each party the right to adjudicate disputes. (See Appendix 2.)

The Building Act 1984 includes a right to compensation (by s. 38) for a contractor's breach of the building regulations.

## OTHER REMEDIES

### *Termination/repudiation*

Where one party defaults on his contractual obligations several possible consequences arise:

(i) the injured party obtains a right to damages or other relief pursuant to the contract's terms, but the contractor's obligation to proceed with the works continues;

(ii) the injured party obtains a right to damages or other relief at common law (or pursuant to statute) but the contractor's obligation to continue with the works subsists;
(iii) the injured party acquires the entitlement to treat the contractor's employment under the contract as at an end; or
(iv) the injured party acquires the entitlement to treat the contract as being repudiated so that both parties are discharged from further performance of it.

This section deals with the latter two categories.

## Termination of the contractor's employment under the contract

Apart from restrictions imposed by certain public policy considerations, the parties can designate any matter a reason for automatically terminating the contractor's employment under the contract or, alternatively, giving one party the discretion to terminate. Most of the standard forms, and many bespoke forms, provide that if a party commits any of a list of specified defaults, the other party can give notice requiring the default to be remedied within a certain period and, in the absence of remedy, the injured party may terminate. The list of specified defaults may differ according to the party—the employer's primary default will be failure to pay monies due under the contract; the contractor's will be failure to proceed diligently with the works or to remedy defective work. Insolvency of one or other party is also often designated a terminating or terminable event.

The remedies available on a termination will vary according to the parties' agreement and as to which party is in default, but may well include such matters as vacation of the site by the contractor, use of the contractor's plant and equipment by the employer, and the taking of an account as to monies due from each party to the other after the works are complete.

It should be noted that where the termination occurs as a result of a party's insolvency, the parties' agreement cannot supersede the provisions of the insolvency legislation, which is non-excludable.

Termination of the contractor's employment under the contract is distinguishable from repudiation (see below) in that the parties may well agree that certain contractual rights and obligations will survive that termination, e.g. an employer's right to use the contractor's plant and equipment in the completion of the works.

## Repudiation

Repudiation may occur where a party has breached a condition of the contract or, in certain circumstances, an "intermediate" term. "Condition" is used in a special sense in this context. It is a term of the contract that, if breached, allows the other party to treat the contract as repudiated because (a) statute so provides, (b) the parties have agreed that the breach should have that effect, or (c) the courts regard the term as being of the quality to have such an effect because it goes "so directly to the substance of the contract". Breach of condition is to be juxtaposed with breach of warranty, the latter being a term of the contract that may give the injured party certain rights, but not the right to treat the contract as repudiated. In between breach of condition and breach of warranty lies the intermediate term. That is a term breach of which may or may not be capable of operating as a condition that entitles the injured party to terminate depending upon whether the breach is sufficiently serious.

Thus, in the broadest terms, breaches of contract not expressly stipulated to be breaches of condition are likely to give rise to an entitlement to treat the contract as repudiated where their effect on performance is extremely serious. Such a breach may be of the sort whereby one party acts in such a manner as to evince an intention no longer to be bound by the contract. In the case of the employer, this could encompass evicting the contractor from site; for a contactor, it could encompass abandoning the site.

### Consequences of repudiation

The injured party is not bound to accept that a repudiatory breach terminates the parties' respective further obligations: he may instead affirm the contract, in which case, whilst he will still have the right to recover damages resulting from the breach, the parties' obligations for future performance will continue. However, the right to affirm will, in reality, be illusory where, for example, an employer has dismissed a contractor from the site, or a contractor has deserted the site. In this regard it should be noted that, usually, a contactor cannot compel an employer to continue to allow him access to the site even where the employer is in repudiatory breach—*Bath and North East Somerset District Council* v. *Mowlem Plc* [2004] EWCA Civ 115.

In the case of repudiation by the contractor, the employer will generally have an entitlement to recover all his losses resulting from the contractor's leaving site such as any additional cost of having the works completed (beyond what it would have cost to complete in any event) and losses resulting from any delay to completion.

In the case of repudiation by the employer, the contractor will generally be entitled to his loss of profit on the works that remain incomplete. Both parties will retain all the rights they had accrued up to the date of repudiation. Whilst both parties will be discharged from further performance, any arbitration clause or right to adjudicate will survive in most cases.

## *Rescission*

Repudiation must be distinguished from rescission. Rescission is an entitlement to treat a contact not merely as terminated, but extinguished as if it had never been entered into in the first place. It arises where a party has been induced to enter into a contract on a representation that is untrue. The law in this area is regulated by the Misrepresentation Act 1967. The right to rescind is subject to certain restrictions. In particular, the court has the discretion to grant damages instead of rescission, and rescission will not generally be available where it is no longer possible to put the parties back in their original pre-contract positions.

### *Injunctions*

Rather than seek damages, the injured party to a contract that has been breached may wish to compel performance. However, there is usually little scope for doing so in construction contracts. That is because, except in respect of a very limited category of contracts, such as those involving the transfer of land, the courts will not order specific performance of contractual obligations where damages are adequate compensation. For this reason, as noted above, a contractor will not normally succeed in obtaining an injunction restraining his wrongful eviction from site.

However, injunctions undoubtedly do have a role in relation to construction contracts. They may be used, for example, to evict a contractor from site, or by an owner to recover goods wrongfully retained by a third party. Injunctions may be either interim, i.e. granted to hold the position between the parties pending a full investigation by the court, or final, i.e. granted once that full investigation has taken place. Whether or not an interim injunction will be granted will frequently depend upon the "balance of convenience" test which involves determining which party would be most prejudiced by an interim injunction being granted or withheld—*American Cyanamid Co.* v. *Ethicon* [1975] A.C. 396.

## TIME LIMITS

The entitlement to relief for beach is subject to the defence of limitation. In contract, the time limit for commencing proceedings is six years from the time the breach of contract occurred, or 12 years if the contract was made by deed. In construction contracts, claims for defective work will often, in practice, run from the time of practical, or substantial, completion.

In tort, the period is usually six years form the time the damage was suffered (unless the claim is for personal injury where the period is three years). However, of particular importance to construction contracts is the Latent Damage Act 1986. In broad terms, the Act extends the limitation period in tort beyond the initial six years to a further three years after any latent damage is discovered or could have been discovered using reasonable diligence, subsequent to a long stop of 15 years from the date of the act of negligence in question.

In construction, establishing precisely when damage has been suffered can sometimes be a highly difficult question of fact—see *Pirelli* v. *Oscar Faber and Partners* [1983] 2 A.C. 1 H.L. and more recently in *Abbott and another* v. *Will Gannon & Smith Limited* (1995) CILL 2226.

Time is also prevented from running for limitation purposes in cases of fraud, concealment, or mistake by the Limitation Act 1980.

Where proceedings are brought beyond the relevant limitation period, limitation will generally operate as a complete defence. However, where the claim is for a debt and, subsequent to the debt's arising, liability is acknowledged by the debtor or he makes a part payment in respect of the same, time runs from that later point.

# APPENDIX 1

## Unfair Contract Terms Act 1977*

*1977 Chapter 50*

An Act to impose further limits on the extent to which under the law of England and Wales and Northern Ireland civil liability for breach of contract, or for negligence or other breach of duty, can be avoided by means of contract terms and otherwise, and under the law of Scotland civil liability can be avoided by means of contract terms.

*[26th October 1977]*

BE IT ENACTED by the Queen's most Excellent Majesty, by and with the advice and consent of the Lords Spiritual and Temporal, and Commons, in this present Parliament assembled, and by the authority of the same, as follows:

*Scope of Part I*

**1.**(1) For the purposes of this Part of this Act, "negligence" means the breach—

(a) of any obligation, arising from the express or implied terms of a contract, to take reasonable care to exercise reasonable skill in the performance of the contract;
(b) of any common law duty to take reasonable care or exercise reasonable skill (but not any stricter duty);
(c) of the common duty of care imposed by the Occupiers' Liability Act 1957 or the Occupiers' Liability Act (Northern Ireland) 1957.

(2) This Part of this Act is subject to Part III; and in relation to contracts, the operation of sections 2 to 4 and 7 is subject to the exceptions made by Schedule 1.

(3) In the case of both contract and tort, sections 2 to 7 apply (except where the contrary is stated in section 6(4)) only to business liability, that is liability for breach of obligations or duties arising—

(a) from things done or to be done by a person in the course of a business (whether his own business or another's); or

* Reproduced with the kind permission of the Department of Trade and Industry.

(b) from the occupation of premises used for business purposes of the occupier; and references to liability are to be read accordingly [but liability of an occupier of premises for breach of an obligation or duty towards a person obtaining access to the premises for ecreational or educational purposes, being liability for loss or damage suffered by reason of the dangerous state of the premises, is not a business liability of the occupier unless granting that person such access for the purposes concerned falls within the business purposes of the occupier.

(4) In relation to any breach of duty or obligation, it is immaterial for any purpose of this Part of this Act whether the breach was inadvertent or intentional, or whether liability for it arises directly or vicariously.

*Negligence liability*

**2.**(1) A person cannot by reference to any contract term or to a notice given to persons generally or to particular persons exclude or restrict his liability for death or personal injury resulting from negligence.

(2) In the case of other loss or damage, a person cannot so exclude or restrict his liability for negligence except in so far as the term or notice satisfies the requirement of reasonableness.

(3) Where a contract term or notice purports to exclude or restrict liability for negligence a person's agreement to or awareness of it is not of itself to be taken as indicating his voluntary acceptance of any risk.

*Liability arising in contract*

**3.**(1) This section applies as between contracting parties where one of them deals as consumer or on the other's written standard terms of business.

(2) As against that party, the other cannot by reference to any contract term—

(a) when himself in breach of contract, exclude or restrict any liability of his in respect of the breach; or
(b) claim to be entitled—

(i) to render a contractual performance substantially different from that which was reasonably expected of him, or
(ii) in respect of the whole or any part of his contractual obligation, to render no performance at all,

expect in so far as (in any of the cases mentioned above in this subsection) the contract term satisfies the requirement of reasonableness.

*Unreasonable indemnity clauses*

**4.**(1) A person dealing as consumer cannot by reference to any contract term be made to indemnify another person (whether a party to the contract or not) in respect of liability that may be incurred by the other for negligence or breach of contract, except in so far as the contract term satisfies the requirement of reasonableness.

(2) This section applies whether the liability in question—

(a) is directly that of the person to be indemnified or is incurred by him vicariously;
(b) is to the person dealing as consumer or to someone else.

*"Guarantee" of consumer goods*

**5.**(1) In the case of goods of a type ordinarily supplied for private use or consumption, where loss or damage—

(a) arises from the goods proving defective while in consumer use; and
(b) results from the negligence of a person concerned in the manufacture or distribution of the goods,

liability for the loss or damage cannot be excluded or restricted by reference to any contract term or notice contained in or operating by reference to a guarantee of the goods.

(2) For these purposes—

(a) goods are to be regarded as "in consumer use" when a person is using them, or has them in his possession for use, otherwise than exclusively for the purposes of a business; and
(b) anything in writing is a guarantee if it contains or purports to contain some promise or assurance (however worded or presented) that defects will be made good by complete or partial replacement, or by repair, monetary compensation or otherwise.

(3) This section does not apply as between the parties to a contract under or in pursuance of which possession or ownership of the goods passed.

*Sale and hire-purchase*

**6.**(1) Liability for breach of the obligations arising from—

(a) section 12 of the Sale of Goods Act 1979](seller's implied undertakings as to title, etc);
(b) section 8 of the Supply of Goods (Implied Terms) Act 1973 (the corresponding thing in relation to hire-purchase),

cannot be excluded or restricted by reference to any contract term.

(2) As against a person dealing as consumer, liability for breach of the obligations arising from—

(a) section 13, 14 or 15 of the 1979 Act (seller's implied undertakings as to conformity of goods with description or sample, or as to their quality or fitness for a particular purpose);
(b) section 9, 10 or 11 of the 1973 Act (the corresponding things in relation to hire-purchase),

cannot be excluded or restricted by reference to any contract term.

(3) As against a person dealing otherwise than as consumer, the liability specified in subsection (2) above can be excluded or restricted by reference to a contract term, but only in so far as the term satisfies the requirement of reasonableness.

(4) The liabilities referred to in this section are not only the business liabilities defined by section 1(3), but include those arising under any contract of sale of goods or hire-purchase agreement.

*Miscellaneous contracts under which goods pass*

**7.**(1) Where the possession or ownership of goods passes under or in pursuance of a contract not governed by the law of sale of goods or hire-purchase, subsections (2) to (4) below apply as regards the effect (if any) to be given to contract terms excluding or restricting liability for breach of obligation arising by implication of law from the nature of the contract.

(2) As against a person dealing as consumer, liability in respect of the goods' correspondence with description or sample, or their quality or fitness for any particular purpose, cannot be excluded or restricted by reference to any such term.

(3) As against a person dealing otherwise than as consumer, that liability can be excluded or restricted by reference to such a term, but only in so far as the term satisfies the requirement of reasonableness.

(3A) Liability for breach of the obligations arising under section 2 of the Supply of Goods and Services Act 1982 (implied terms about title etc in certain contracts for the transfer of the property in goods) cannot be excluded or restricted by references to any such term.

(4) Liability in respect of—

(a) the right to transfer ownership of the goods, or give possession; or
(b) the assurance of quiet possession to a person taking goods in pursuance of the contract,

cannot [(in a case to which subsection (3A) above does not apply)] be excluded or restricted by reference to any such term except in so far as the term satisfies the requirement of reasonableness.

(5) This section does not apply in the case of goods passing on a redemption of trading stamps within the Trading Stamps Act 1964 or the Trading Stamps Act (Northern Ireland) 1965.

*Effect of breach*

**9.**(1) Where for reliance upon it a contract term has to satisfy the requirement of reasonableness, it may be found to do so and be given effect accordingly notwithstanding that the contract has been terminated either by breach or by a party electing to treat it as repudiated.

(2) Where on a breach the contract is nevertheless affirmed by a party entitled to treat it as repudiated, this does not of itself exclude the requirement of reasonableness in relation to any contract term.

*Evasion by means of secondary contract*

**10.** A person is not bound by any contract term prejudicing or taking away rights of his which arise under, or in connection with the performance of, another contract, so far as those rights extend to the enforcement of another's liability which this Part of this Act prevents that other from excluding or restricting.

*The "reasonableness" test*

**11.**(1) In relation to a contract term, the requirement of reasonableness for the purposes of this Part of this Act, section 3 of the Misrepresentation Act 1967 and section 3 of the Misrepresentation Act (Northern Ireland) 1967 is that the term shall have been a fair and reasonable one to be included having regard to the circumstances which were, or ought reasonably to have been, known to or in the contemplation of the parties when the contract was made.

(2) In determining for the purposes of section 6 or 7 above whether a contract term satisfies the requirement of reasonableness, regard shall be had in particular to the matters specified in Schedule 2 to this Act; but this subsection does not prevent the court or arbitrator from holding, in accordance with any rule of law, that a term which purports to exclude or restrict any relevant liability is not a term of the contract.

(3) In relation to a notice (not being a notice having contractual effect), the requirement of reasonableness under this Act is that it should be fair and reasonable to allow reliance on it, having regard to all the circumstances obtaining when the liability arose or (but for the notice) would have arisen.

(4) Where by reference to a contract term or notice a person seeks to restrict liability to a specified sum of money, and the question arises (under this or any other Act) whether the term or notice satisfies the requirement of reasonableness, regard shall be had in particular (but without prejudice to subsection (2) above in the case of contract terms) to—

(a) the resources which he could expect to be available to him for the purpose of meeting the liability should it arise; and
(b) how far it was open to him to cover himself by insurance.

(5) It is for those claiming that a contract term or notice satisfies the requirement of reasonableness to show that it does.

*"Dealing as consumer"*

**12.**(1) A party to a contract "deals as consumer" in relation to another party if—

(a) he neither makes the contract in the course of a business nor holds himself out as doing so; and
(b) the other party does make the contract in the course of a business; and
(c) in the case of a contract governed by the law of sale of goods or hire-purchase, or by section 7 of this Act, the goods passing under or in pursuance of the contract are of a type ordinarily supplied for private use or consumption.

(2) But on a sale by auction or by competitive tender the buyer is not in any circumstances to be regarded as dealing as consumer.

(3) Subject to this, it is for those claiming that a party does not deal as consumer to show that he does not.

*Varieties of exemption clause*

**13.**(1) To the extent that this Part of this Act prevents the exclusion or restriction of any liability it also prevents—

(a) making the liability or its enforcement subject to restrictive or onerous conditions;
(b) excluding or restricting any right or remedy in respect of the liability, or subjecting a person to any prejudice in consequence of his pursuing any such right or remedy;
(c) excluding or restricting rules of evidence or procedure;

and (to that extent) sections 2 and 5 to 7 also prevent excluding or restricting liability by reference to terms and notices which exclude or restrict the relevant obligation or duty.

(2) But an agreement in writing to submit present or future differences to arbitration is not to be treated under this Part of this Act as excluding or restricting any liability.

*Interpretation of Part I*

**14.** In this Part of this Act—

"business" includes a profession and the activities of any government department or local or public authority;

"goods" has the same meaning as in [the Sale of Goods Act 1979]:
"hire-purchase agreement" has the same meaning as in the Consumer Credit Act 1974;
"negligence" has the meaning given by section 1(1);
"notice" includes an announcement, whether or not in writing, and any other communication or pretended communication; and
"personal injury" includes any disease and any impairment of physical or mental condition.

*International supply contracts*

**26.**(1) The limits imposed by this Act on the extent to which a person may exclude or restrict liability by reference to a contract term do not apply to liability arising under such a contract as is described in subsection (3) below.

(2) The terms of such a contract are not subject to any requirement of reasonableness under section 3 or 4 . . .

(3) Subject to subsection (4), that description of contract is one whose characteristics are the following—

(a) either it is a contract of sale of goods or it is one under or in pursuance of which the possession or ownership of goods passes; and
(b) it is made by parties whose places of business (or, if they have none, habitual residences) are in the territories of different States (the Channel Islands and the Isle of Man being treated for this purpose as different States from the United Kingdom).

(4) A contract falls within subsection (3) above only if either—

(a) the goods in question are, at the time of the conclusion of the contract, in the course of carriage, or will be carried, from the territory of one State to the territory of another; or
(b) the acts constituting the offer and acceptance have been done in the territories of different States; or
(c) the contract provides for the goods to be delivered to the territory of a State other than that within whose territory those acts were done.

## *SCHEDULE 1*
## *SCOPE OF SECTIONS 2 TO 4 AND 7*

*Section 1(2)*

**1.** Sections 2 to 4 of this Act do not extend to—

(a) any contract of insurance (including a contract to pay an annuity on human life);
(b) any contract so far as it relates to the creation or transfer of an interest in land, or to the termination of such an interest, whether by extinction, merger, surrender, forfeiture or otherwise;
(c) any contract so far as it relates to the creation or transfer of a right or interest in any patent, trade mark, copyright [or design right], registered design, technical or commercial information or other intellectual property, or relates to the termination of any such right or interest;
(d) any contract so far as it relates—

(i) to the formation or dissolution of a company (which means any body corporate or unincorporated association and includes a partnership), or

(ii) to its constitution or the rights or obligations of its corporators or members;

(e) any contract so far as it relates to the creation or transfer of securities or of any right or interest in securities.

**2.** Section 2(1) extends to—

(a) any contract of marine salvage or towage;
(b) any charterparty of a ship or hovercraft; and
(c) any contract for the carriage of goods by ship or hovercraft;

but subject to this sections 2 to 4 and 7 do not extend to any such contract except in favour of a person dealing as consumer.

**3.** Where goods are carried by ship or hovercraft in pursuance of a contract which either—

(a) specifies that as the means of carriage over part of the journey to be covered, or
(b) makes no provision as to the means of carriage and does not exclude that means, then sections 2(2), 3 and 4 do not, except in favour of a person dealing as consumer, extend to the contract as it operates for and in relation to the carriage of the goods by that means.

**4.** Section 2(1) and (2) do not extend to a contract of employment, except in favour of the employee.

**5.** Section 2(1) does not affect the validity of any discharge and indemnity given by a person, on or in connection with an award to him of compensation for pneumoconiosis attributable to employment in the coal industry, in respect of any further claim arising from his contracting that disease.

## *SCHEDULE 2*
## *"GUIDELINES" FOR APPLICATION OF REASONABLENESS TEST*

*Sections 11(2), 24(2)*

The matters to which regard is to be had in particular for the purposes of sections 6(3), 7(3) and (4), 20 and 21 are any of the following which appear to be relevant—

(a) the strength of the bargaining positions of the parties relative to each other, taking into account (among other things) alternative means by which the customer's requirements could have been met;
(b) whether the customer received an inducement to agree to the term, or in accepting it had an opportunity of entering into a similar contract with other persons, but without having to accept a similar term;
(c) whether the customer knew or ought reasonably to have known of the existence and extent of the term (having regard, among other things, to any custom of the trade and any previous course of dealing between the parties);
(d) where the term excludes or restricts any relevant liability if some condition is not complied with, whether it was reasonable at the time of the contract to expect that compliance with that condition would be practicable;
(e) whether the goods were manufactured, processed or adapted to the special order of the customer.

# APPENDIX 2

Housing Grants, Construction and Regeneration Act 1996*

*1996 Chapter 53*

Arrangement of sections

## Part I
## Grants, &c. For Renewal of Private Sector Housing

### Chapter I
### The Main Grants

*Introductory*

**Section**

1. Grants for improvements and repairs, &c.
2. Applications for grants.

*Preliminary conditions*

3. Ineligible applicants.
4. The age of the property.
5. Excluded descriptions of works.
6. Defective dwellings.

*Renovation grants*

7. Renovation grants: owner's applications and tenant's applications.
8. Renovation grants: certificates required in case of owner's application.
9. Renovation grants: certificates required in case of tenant's application.
10. Renovation grants: prior qualifying period.
11. Prior qualifying period: the ownership or tenancy condition.
12. Renovation grants: purposes for which grant may be given.
13. Renovation grants: approval of application.

*Common parts grants*

14. Common parts grants: occupation of flats by occupying tenants.
15. Common parts grants: landlord's and tenants' applications.
16. Common parts grants: certificate required to accompany application.
17. Common parts grants: purposes for which grant may be given.
18. Common parts grants: approval of application.

*Disabled facilities grants*

19. Disabled facilities grants: owner's and tenant's applications.
20. Disabled facilities grants: the disabled occupant.
21. Disabled facilities grants: certificate required in case of owner's application.
22. Disabled facilities grants: certificates required in case of tenant's application.

23. Disabled facilities grants: purposes for which grant must or may be given.
24. Disabled facilities grants: approval of application.

*HMO grants*

25. HMO grants: the interest of the applicant in the property.
26. HMO grants: certificate required to accompany application.
27. HMO grants: purposes for which grant may be given.
28. HMO grants: approval of application.

*Restrictions on grant aid*

29. Restriction on grants for works already begun.
30. Means testing in case of application by owner-occupier or tenant.
31. Determination of amount of grant in case of landlord's application.
32. Apportionment in case of tenants' application for common parts grant.
33. Power to specify maximum amount of grant.

*Decision and notification*

34. Decision and notification.

*Payment of grants*

35. Payment of grants: general.
36. Delayed payment of mandatory grant.
37. Payment of grants: conditions as to carrying out of the works.
38. Payment of grants: conditions as to contractors employed.
39. Payment of grant to contractor.
40. Applicant ceasing to be entitled before payment of grant.
41. Change of circumstances affecting disabled occupant.
42. Cases in which grants may be re-calculated, withheld or repaid.
43. Repayment where applicant not entitled to grant.

*Grant conditions and repayment*

44. Grant conditions: introductory.
45. Condition for repayment on disposal: renovation grants.
46. Condition for repayment on disposal: common parts grants.
47. Condition for repayment on disposal: HMO grants.
48. Condition as to owner-occupation: renovation grants.
49. Condition as to availability for letting: renovation grants.
50. Conditions as to occupation: HMO grants.
51. Conditions as to repayment in case of other compensation, &c.
52. Power to impose other conditions with consent of Secretary of State.
53. Meaning of relevant disposal.
54. Meaning of exempt disposal.
55. Cessation of conditions on repayment of grant, &c.

*Supplementary provisions*

56. Provisions relating to death of applicant.
57. Power of local housing authority to carry out works which would attract grant.
58. Minor definitions: Chapter I.

59. Index of defined expressions: Chapter I.

## Chapter II
## Group Repair Schemes

*Introductory*

60. Group repair schemes.
61. Qualifying buildings.
62. Scheme works.
63. Approval of scheme by Secretary of State.

*Participation in group repair scheme*

64. Persons eligible to participate in group repair scheme.
65. Scheme consent and restriction on works.
66. Certificate of completion date.
67. Contributions by participants.

*Variation of group repair scheme*

68. Variation of group repair scheme.

*Conditions of participation*

69. Conditions of participation: general.
70. Condition as to payment of balance of cost on disposal.
71. Conditions as to occupation.
72. Meaning of relevant disposal and exempt disposal.
73. Payment of balance of cost, &c: cessation of conditions.

*Supplementary provisions*

74. Power of Secretary of State to modify operation of Chapter.
75. Index of defined expressions: Chapter II.

## Chapter III
## Home Repair Assistance

76. Home repair assistance.
77. Entitlement to home repair assistance.
78. Assistance in respect of house-boats and mobile homes.
79. Power to make further provision by regulations.
80. Index of defined expressions: Chapter III.

## Chapter IV
## Deferred Action Notices, &c.

*Deferred action notices*

81. Deferred action notices.
82. Service of deferred action notices.

83. Appeals against deferred action notices.
84. Review of deferred action notices.
85. Guidance by Secretary of State.

*Power to improve enforcement procedures*

86. Unfitness for human habitation &c.: power to improve enforcement procedures.

*Power to charge for enforcement action*

87. Unfitness for human habitation, &c.: power to charge for enforcement action.
88. Recovery of charge for enforcement action.

*Supplementary provisions*

89. Power to prescribe forms.
90. Minor definitions: Chapter IV.
91. Index of defined expressions: Chapter IV.

Chapter V
Supplementary Provisions

*Contributions by Secretary of State*

92. Contributions by the Secretary of State.
93. Recovery of contributions.

*Consent of the Secretary of State*

94. Consent of the Secretary of State.

*Parsonages, charities, &c.*

95. Parsonages, charities, &c.

*Interpretation*

96. Meaning of "reasonable repair".
97. Fitness for human habitation.
98. Members of a person's family and connected persons.
99. Meaning of "owner" of dwelling.
100. Disabled persons.
101. Minor definitions: Part I.

*Transitional and consequential provisions*

102. Transitional provisions.
103. Consequential amendments: Part I.

Part II
Construction Contracts

*Introductory provisions*

104. Construction contracts.
105. Meaning of "construction operations".

130. Regeneration and development: Welsh Development Agency.

*Relocation grants in clearance areas*

131. Resolution by local housing authority to pay relocation grants.
132. Relocation grants: applications and payments.
133. Relocation grants: qualifying persons and qualifying dwellings.
134. Relocation grants: amount.
135. Relocation grants: condition for repayment on disposal.
136. Relocation grants: conditions as to owner-occupation.
137. Relocation grants: cessation of conditions on repayment of grant, &c.
138. Relocation grants: liability to repay is a charge on dwelling.
139. Relocation grants: contributions by the Secretary of State.
140. Minor definitions relating to relocation grants.

Part V
Miscellaneous and General Provisions

*Miscellaneous provisions*

141. Existing housing grants: meaning of exempt disposal
142. Home energy efficiency schemes.
143. Urban development corporations: pre-dissolution transfers.
144. Housing action trusts: orders for dissolution.
145. The Commission for the New Towns: orders for dissolution.

*General provisions*

146. Orders, regulations and directions.
147. Repeals and revocations.
148. Extent.
149. Corresponding provision for Northern Ireland.
150. Commencement.
151. Short title.

*Schedules:*

Schedule 1—Private sector renewal: consequential amendments.
Schedule 2—Architects.
Part I—New First Schedule to the 19311931 Act.
Part II—Other amendments.
Part III—Transitional provisions and savings.
Schedule 3—Repeals and Revocations.
Part I—Grants, &c for renewal of private sector housing.
Part II—Architects.
Part III—Financial assistance for regeneration and development.

## TEST YOUR UNDERSTANDING

1. (a) What are the advantages of a liquidated damages clause?
   (b) On what basis can a liquidated damages clause be held to be invalid?

(c) How can the right to liquidated damages be lost?

2. (a) What is the fundamental basis upon which the common law right to damages for breach of contract is founded?
   (b) Explain the concept of remoteness in the context of recovery of contractual damages.
   (c) Give two instances when the full extent of losses otherwise legally recoverable as damages for breach of contract may be disallowed.
   (d) To what extent can liability for breach of contract be restricted by the contract terms?

3. (a) With regard to time bars for claims, what is the distinction between contract and tort?
   (b) What kind of damage recoverable in contract cannot be readily recovered in tort?

4. (a) Name two important statutes having an important impact on construction and set out their principal features.

5. (a) When may a contract be lawfully terminated?
   (b) What are the main differences between termination, repudiation, and rescission?

CHAPTER 11

# CLAIMS AND DISPUTE RESOLUTION

Nicholas Gould and Victoria Russell

## DISPUTE RESOLUTION

### *Introduction*

As you will have read in the previous chapters, disputes can arise for many different reasons at any point in a project. Thus it is important to understand how to resolve such problems. This final chapter deals with the range of dispute resolution techniques that are available in the construction industry. This is considered in three main parts. First a general overview of the spectrum of dispute resolution techniques and consideration of the ADR movement. Second, an examination of the individual techniques, including:

- negotiation;
- mediation and conciliation;
- adjudication;
- arbitration;
- litigation.

Finally, a consideration of the hybrid processes, such as MedArb and other contractual dispute escalation approaches, and project based dispute resolution such as dispute review boards.

This chapter explains the three core processes of dispute resolution before introducing the range of frequently encountered techniques. Each of the main dispute resolution techniques are then considered in turn. The purpose is not to delve into the detail of each technique, but to provide an overview and draw out the main distinctions between the processes, whilst setting out the key characteristics of the techniques.

### *Spectrum of dispute resolution techniques*

The "conventional" model of dispute resolution is one of an adjudicative process, most frequently fulfilled by the courts. According to Schapiro (1981) the ideal court, or more properly the prototype of the court, involves:

"(1) an independent judge applying (2) pre-existing legal norms after (3) adversarial proceedings in order to achieve (4) a dichotomous decision in which one of the parties was assigned the legal right and the other found wrong."

He goes on to say that an examination of the courts across a range of societies reveals that the prototype "fits almost none of them". Nonetheless, this does provide a suitable starting point for what one might call the conventional model of dispute resolution. This is clearly at the formal binding end of the spectrum. At the other end of the scale, two-way problem solving between the parties represents the informal, non-binding, approach, the successful outcome of which is an agreement to "settle".

In its most basic form direct negotiation provides a simple party based problem solving technique. A further dimension is added when either party introduces advisers. Nonetheless, the essential feature of this process is that control of the outcome remains with the parties. Litigation and arbitration require the parties to submit their dispute to another who will impose a legally binding decision. Negotiation is a "process of working out an agreement by direct communication. It is voluntary and non-binding". The process may be bilateral (between two parties) or it could be multi-lateral (many parties). Each party may utilise any form of external expertise it considers necessary, and this is often described as "supported negotiating".

Mediation is a "private, informal process in which parties are assisted by one or more neutral third parties in their efforts towards settlement". The new and distinguishing feature here is the addition of a neutral third party who aids the disputants towards settlement. A further important factor is that the mediator does not decide the outcome; settlement lies ultimately with the parties. A distinction is often made between styles of mediation which are "facilitative" and those that are "evaluative". During a facilitative mediation, the mediator is trying to re-open communication between the parties and explore the options for settlement. The mediator does not openly express his or her opinions on the issues. If, on the other hand, the mediator is called upon to state his opinion on any particular issue then he/she is clearly making an evaluation of that issue.

Mediation or conciliation refers to a process in which an independent third party re-opens or facilitates communications between the parties and so aids the settlement process. The process can be facilitative in that the third party merely tries to aid the settlement process, or evaluative in that the third party comments on the subject matter or makes recommendations as to the outcome. In the UK, the facilitative style of third party intervention is most frequently referred to as mediation, and conciliation is reserved for the evaluative process.

ACAS is most widely associated with this evaluative style of conciliation in labour disputes, and more recently the ICE in connection with conciliation in civil engineering disputes. On the other hand, CEDR promotes a style that is more focused towards the facilitative end of the spectrum and refers to this as mediation. The position is not necessarily the same internationally. Mediation refers to a more interventionist evaluative approach in some parts of the world.

*Table 1: Facilitative and evaluative processes*

| Mediation or conciliation | |
|---|---|
| **Facilitative** | **Evaluative** |
| The mediator/conciliator aids the negotiation process, but does not make recommendations. | The mediator/conciliator makes a recommendation as to the outcome. |

In practice a mediation that starts off in a purely facilitative way may become evaluative in order to try and reach a settlement. This may occur intentionally, at the request of the parties or with forethought on the part of the mediator, or unintentionally by the words or actions of the mediator. The boundary is clear in theory, but not necessarily in practice. Nonetheless, at a basic level a distinction can be made between "settlement" processes and "decision" imposing processes. Control of the outcome, or the power to settle, rests with the parties during negotiation, mediation and conciliation. By contrast, "adjudicative" or "umpiring" processes, such as litigation, arbitration and adjudication, rely on the judge, arbitrator or adjudicator having the power to impose a decision.

*Table 2: Settlements and decisions*

| Control of the outcome rests with the parties | Decisions are imposed |
|---|---|
| Negotiation<br>Mediation<br>Conciliation | Litigation<br>Arbitration<br>Adjudication<br>Expert determination |

What we have then, are three core techniques, which may be employed in the resolution of disputes. First, negotiation, which refers to the problem solving efforts of the parties. Second, third party intervention, which does not lead to a binding decision being imposed on the parties, and finally the adjudicative process, the ultimate outcome of which is an imposed binding decision. Such an approach has been adopted by Green and Mackie (1995), who refer to the "three pillars" of dispute resolution. The discrete techniques may be introduced under one of the three pillars, depending upon the main characteristics of the particular technique; see Figure 1, following.

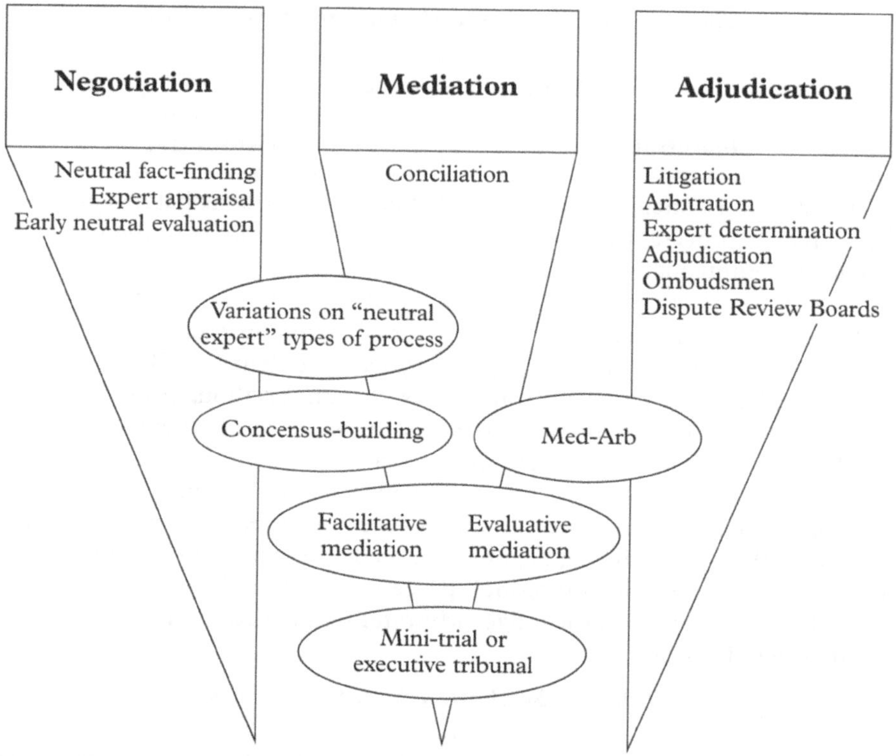


Source: Mackie, K., Miles, D., and Marsh, W. (1995) *Commercial Dispute Resolution: An ADR Practice Guide* (London, Butterworths), p. 50. The chart was derived from a chart by Professor Green of Boston University (1993).

*Figure 1: "The Dispute Resolution Landscape"*

Arguably, all dispute resolution techniques are built upon three basic principal methods: negotiation, mediation/conciliation, and some form of adjudicative umpiring process.

Essentially, categorisation can be by way of any number of core characteristics. An alternative approach to the one considered above could quite simply involve listing those techniques that lead to a binding outcome, and those which are non-binding. Further categorisation could be by way of those techniques which relate to dispute avoidance or the management of conflict, and those which relate to the resolution of disputes. Such an approach expands the range of techniques that need to be considered to include the broader view of "dispute response" (see Chapters 3 and 4).

The rest of this chapter considers each of the core and most frequently encountered techniques in turn.

## *Alternative Dispute Resolution—the subjective debate*

The term ADR has attracted a great deal of attention in legal and quasi-legal fields since the mid 1980s. However, the 1990s appear to have witnessed an enormous growth in the "ADR debate" with an ever increasing sphere of academics, lawyers and consultants entering the arena. Although the concept of dispute resolution techniques which are an alternative to the court system is not new, the more recent advent of the acronym is essentially taken to describe the use of a third party mediator who assists the parties to arrive at a voluntary, consensual, negotiated settlement.

Whilst the origins of mediation may be ancient and eastern the recent more formalised technique has principally developed in the USA (Pheng, L. S.: 1996). In the UK, mediation was initially taken seriously in the resolution of family disputes (Roberts: 1996). But, has mediation, or other alternative methods, attracted equal attention in construction? Not only is the construction industry important nationally and internationally, but it is also, arguably, the largest industry in the UK, attracting an equally large volume of diverse disputes, across a wide range of values.

The literature available indicates that ADR is a widely discussed discipline within the jurisprudence of construction disputes. Many writers provide an anecdotal review of the subject matter. Few writers venture beyond the normative to consider the reality of ADR, and many assume that this term relates only to mediation. In fact, many writers reveal their attitude towards the subject by suggesting that ADR may be taken to mean any of the following:

- alternative dispute resolution;
- appropriate dispute resolution;
- amicable dispute resolution;
- another dammed rip-off;
- another disappointing result;
- another drink required.

Nonetheless, some empirical research does exist. The Turner Kenneth Brown Report (1993) found that executives responsible for company legal services believed that ADR offered far more advantages than disadvantages, with 75% of the respondents considering ADR developments as a positive step and only 6% considering it negative. Watts and Scrivener (1994) provide a comparative analysis of construction arbitration in Australia and the UK. In the US, research by Stipanowich (1996) has documented the rise of mediation, which was first taken seriously by the US construction industry. Apparently the US Army Corp of Engineers pioneered the process in order to reduce the high costs of litigation. Stipanowich's recent survey indicates that 76% of the respondents had been involved in mediation during the 12 months preceding the completion of the questionnaire.

In the UK, Fenn and Gould (1994) completed a project based on Stipanowich's US survey. Surprisingly few mediations appear to have taken place in comparison to the size of the industry. Whilst 70% of the respondents could recount the benefits of ADR less than 30% had actually been involved in an ADR process. In fact none of the respondents had been involved in more than five mediations in the preceding 12-month period. More recently Brooker and

Lavers (1997) report on their work in the specific area of ADR in construction disputes, and accuse contractors of avoiding mediation.

## Benefits of ADR

*Maintains a business relationship*

The proponents of ADR argue that processes such as mediation can maintain existing business relationships as the parties are aided towards a settlement.

*Speed*

The average mediation lasts 1–2 days. The proponents of ADR frequently compare this to a trial lasting years. It is, however, important to remember that the parties may not be in a position to forge a settlement early on in the dispute process and it may in fact take many months or even years before they are in a position to mediate effectively.

*Lower cost*

Clearly a short mediation is a cheaper event than a trial or arbitration. Some argue that lawyers are unnecessary in the process (and therefore a further cost saving is made) while others consider lawyers a valuable addition.

*Confidentiality*

The proceedings of a mediation are confidential. Contrastingly, litigation is in the public domain and arbitration may become public if there is an appeal. Confidentiality is an advantage as some clients wish to keep their disputes from the public domain.

*Flexibility*

Arbitration and litigation is based upon the rights and obligations of the parties to the dispute. On the other hand a mediated settlement focuses on the parties' interests and needs. The mediator encourages the parties to search for a commercial solution that meets with both parties' needs.

*Greater satisfaction*

Many proponents of ADR argue that the ADR process and the outcomes are more satisfying for the parties than a trial or arbitration. Apparently the reaching of a settlement by consensus is viewed as producing high levels of satisfaction for the parties. Research has suggested that high levels of satisfaction are not attained. However, a mediated outcome is still more satisfactory than other forms of imposed decisions such as litigation, arbitration or adjudication.

## Perceived disadvantages of ADR

*I will disclose my hand*

Parties are frequently concerned that they may disclose some important aspect of their argument that will then aid the other side in the event that the mediation is not successful and the matter proceeds to trial. Mackie *et al.* (1995) suggests that this belief is more perceived than real and notes three points. First, if a party has a strong case then disclosure of the strengths is likely to assist in settlement. Second, if the party has a weak case then there is perhaps little advantage in "prolonging the agony". Third, if as in the majority of instances the case is not particularly strong or weak then surely it is best to consider ADR.

*There is pressure to settle*

Some of those individuals who have experienced mediation suggest that as the process goes on the pressure to settle builds. This is no doubt borne out by the fact that many mediations are over during the course of one day and that frequently the parties and the mediator will work late into the evening in order to forge a settlement.

*I will give the impression of weakness or liability*

Some have argued that to suggest ADR or mediation demonstrates a weakness in the case. While this may have been true at the start of the 1990s it is arguably less of a disadvantage today.

## Court annexed ADR

The concept of court annexed ADR and the ability for litigating parties to attempt mediation at court was initially developed in the USA. In May 1996 the Central London County Court launched a pilot court annexed ADR scheme on the initiative of Judge Butter QC. The scheme applied to dispute in the £3,000 to £10,000 range. The court wrote to both parties early on in the proceedings and offered them the option to mediate at the Central London County Court in an attempt to resolve their dispute amicably economically. The mediations took place between 4.30pm and 7.30pm and was therefore outside of the usual court hours. Parties were, therefore, given three hours in order to attempt to reach a mediated settlement. But is three hours adequate? One lawyer mediator who has participated in the pilot scheme commented:

"Well, the answer is that I've never failed to come to a conclusion within three hours. At $2\frac{1}{2}$ hours you've got nowhere but somehow the guillotine hanging is a great aid in resolving the thing if people want to. The thing is, most of this is based upon peoples misconceptions anyway. The vast majority, I would say close on 90%, of all mediations last for half a day or less. Now three hours or half a day, there's not very much in it. One thing I have mixed feelings about is that when you go in you know you have got three hours full stop. That's it. That's what I have reservations about, but the amount of time is adequate. I never actually had it go beyond. In all bar one of my mediations, the court has succeeded and that was nothing to do with time, it was due to dishonesty on the part of the parties. I've been at almost half-past-six without having a settlement. Its very useful to remind them that in ten minute's time they book their place to go upstairs [to the court] to have the matter dealt with. That helps focus the mind."

Each side paid £25 towards the mediator's expenses. Professor Genn (1997) observed a large proportion of the mediations that were carried out and reported that there had only been a 4% to 5% take-up rate. She reported that of those few cases which did come to mediation the settlement rate was high. Nonetheless, she reported that most settlements were reached in the last 10 minutes of the three-hour session, and that in general both parties were confused as to the nature of the process, frequently believing that any final suggestion put forward by the mediator was in some way binding upon them. Interestingly, she pointed out that a good deal of these disputes were small building related disputes between owners and trades people and architects.

The Central London County Court scheme is not the first in its kind and was preceded by a pilot mediation scheme launched in June 1994 by the Bristol Law Society. Apparently, at the end of the first year of operation only 24 cases had been referred to the scheme with only two reaching the mediation scheme (Miles, D.: 1996). Further, a similar scheme commenced operation in 1996 in the Patents County Court in London.

More recently Verkaik (1998) has reported on research by Professor Hazel Genn of University College London in relation to the Central London County Court Mediation pilot scheme. The research concludes that legally represented litigants are less likely to accept the offer of court mediation or indeed to reach a mediated settlement. Out of the 4,500 litigants invited by the London County Court to mediate, only 160 (3.5%) took up the offer. In 84% of the rejected cases both parties were legally represented. This compares to 67% where neither party was legally represented. Further, the report suggests that lawyers have a negative influence on the success of mediation. Seventy-six per cent of those case mediated, where no lawyers are involved, settled. This compares to a settlement rate of 55% where both parties had solicitors advising them.

## NEGOTIATION

According to the *Concise Oxford Dictionary* (1995), "to negotiate" means to "confer with others in order to reach a compromise or agreement". Negotiation is merely the name given to that process. Goldberg *et al.* (1992) described negotiation as "communication for the purpose of persuasion; the pre-eminent mode of dispute resolution". Nonetheless, negotiation should not be considered as merely a dispute resolution process. Negotiation in its broadest form may be considered as the process by which individuals communicate in order to arrange their business affairs and private lives by establishing agreement and reconciling areas of disagreement.

Interest in negotiation as an art or science appears to have developed in the 1970s. Research in this area is still very much in its infancy. Most theoretical work in the area of negotiation appears to focus on negotiation strategy or tactics rather than the process itself. It is therefore possible to examine negotiation from two perspectives. First, the processual shape of negotiations and, second, the strategy of negotiation.

### *The process of negotiation*

Negotiation clearly involves some form of communication leading to joint decisions. Do these negotiations always maintain a processual shape with identifiable features regardless of the individuals involved or the conditions under which the negotiation takes place? Gulliver (1979) maintains that negotiation is essentially a developmental process with eight distinct but often overlapping phases.

Phase 1: The search for an arena;
Phase 2: Agenda and definition;
Phase 3: Exploring the field (emphasis on differences);
Phase 4: Narrowing the differences;
Phase 5: Preliminaries to final bargain;
Phase 6: Final bargain;
Phase 7: Ritualising the outcome;
Phase 8: Execution of outcome.

Gulliver goes on to argue that negotiation is developmental because the early stages involve a predominance of antagonism whilst the later stages involve a predominance of coordination. Roberts (1994) on the other hand argues that negotiation is about communication and information exchange which leads to joint-decision making. As the parties begin to explore their differences, the information exchange that occurs leads to a greater understanding of the situation. This may eventually lead to a convergence of goals and an agreement, or alternatively the abandonment of the negotiation process. In other words negotiation may lead to a valid outcome that does not in fact result in agreement. For example, the unilateral decision to end a negotiation in favour of a more formal dispute resolution technique.

There are two important aspects to Gulliver's processual model. First, bargaining becomes part of the process. Many writers on the subject consider that negotiation is simply a process of bargaining. Gulliver's model on the other hand considers that successful bargaining cannot take place until an agenda has been agreed and the differences explored. On the other hand, it could also be argued that bargaining must occur at each phase. For example, in order to reach agreement over the venue. The second aspect of Gulliver's model relates to the phases themselves. The model identifies the central or strategic actions within a negotiation. Negotiation may break down if the parties are unable to agree a venue or an agenda. The margin between each phase therefore represents the high pressure points during the negotiation.

To reduce negotiation merely to a process of bargaining limits our understanding of the negotiation process. The inability to agree upon the venue may lead the parties to abandon the process completely or to seek redress through some formal dispute resolution process. Alternatively, the process of information exchange may reveal that a dispute does not in fact exist. The parties begin at odds, perceiving themselves to be in a dispute.

## Negotiation strategies

The literature reveals two main approaches to negotiation. First is the "competitive", "distributional" or "positional" approach. Positional negotiators will make an initial offer that is considerably less than they are ultimately willing to pay. They will raise their offers gradually and seek whatever tactical advantages are available. A large body of literature exists on the subject which essentially explores how to win as much as possible during negotiations. Meltsner and Schrag (1973) consider a variety of techniques that a lawyer may employ during negotiation. These tactics may be considered under three headings.

*First, proprietary tactics.* These involve a range of simple positional tactics. For example, insisting that meetings be held in your own office or some other setting where you feel more comfortable than your adversary. Attempting to ascertain the number of persons the other side will bring to the meeting in order to ensure that you balance or slightly outnumber the other side. In the event that the other side requests a negotiation meeting, then demanding some sort of precondition which if the other side accepts may improve the chances of a favourable outcome. These simple tactics provide an opportunity to weigh up the negotiating clout of the adversary as well as an opportunity to put the other party at a psychological disadvantage.

*Second, initial tactics.* These tactics are used in order to attempt to extract the first offer from the other side. For example, the use of silence in the hope that the other side will tender an offer in order to keep negotiations under way. A first high demand provides the negotiator with the ability to manoeuvre and reduce subsequent demands. Furthermore, unreasonable and outrageous demands appear to become more justifiable after extended discussions. Another initial tactic involves placing your major demand first on the agenda. Many competitive negotiators believe that there is a "honeymoon" period at the outset of all negotiations during which negotiators make compromises more freely.

*Finally, a range of general tactics.* This may simply include raising some of your demands during the course of negotiation in the hope that this will put pressure on the other side to complete the negotiations quickly before the position stiffens yet further. Another approach involves the use of two negotiators who play differing or even opposing roles. One takes a very hard line offering almost no compromise whilst the other appears to desire compromise. Opposing parties who are unaware of such tactics frequently grasp at marginal concessions because they perceive them substantial in relation to the position of the hard liner.

An alternative approach to negotiation is that of, "principled", "interest-based", "cooperative", "problem solving" or "win/win" negotiation. According to Fisher and Ury (1991), there are five basic elements to this approach.

(1) *Separate the people from the problem.* In other words, the negotiators should focus and attack the problem rather than each other.
(2) *Focus on interests not positions.* The negotiators should focus on the reasons for their demand. Focusing on interest in this way may uncover the existence of mutual interests which may pave the way for an agreement. For example the ability to maintain a long-term relationship between the parties.
(3) *Invent options for mutual gain.* A competitive negotiator will seek to obtain as much as possible during the course of the negotiations. The principled approach recognises that there may be bargained outcomes that will advance the interest of both negotiators. The infamous example is that of two children arguing over an orange. After some competitive and frustrating negotiation where each seeks to demand the orange for his or her own use the mother intervenes and asks each child in turn why they want the orange. One wants the orange for its juice whilst the other wants to grate the rind in order to flavour a cake. This simple example is a stark reminder of how a clear exploration of the parties interests provides the opportunity to maximise the mutual gains.
(4) *Insist on using objective criterion.* To reduce the risk of inefficient bargaining or failure to reach agreement on price, Fisher and Ury suggest that the parties focus on some objective criterion to govern the outcome. For example looking up the book value of a second hand car.
(5) *Know your best alternative to a negotiated agreement (BATNA).* This final element involves a serious consideration of the alternatives to reaching a negotiated agreement with the other party. This may involve exploring the cost of an alternative supplier, or addressing the costs associated with court action against the probability of succeeding.

White (1984) suggests that Fisher and Ury's approach is frequently naive and occasionally self-righteous. His principal criticism is that the book overlooks the ultimate hard bargaining which he considers must occur in every negotiation. White does not accept that a negotiator can turn all negotiations in to some form of problem solving exercise. One might conclude that a competitive negotiator would win over a principled negotiator. Ury argues that this is not the case. He argues that it is possible to break through the other side's resistance and engage him or her in problem solving negotiation. This "breakthrough negotiation" involves five steps.

The first step requires one to avoid acting in the normal way. Rather than attacking the other side Ury invites us to suspend our reaction and assume the position of an objective onlooker. The second step involves listening and acknowledging the other side's point of view agreeing wherever possible. He refers to this other stage as stepping to their side. The third and trickiest stage involves directing the other's attention to the problem of meeting each side's interests. He suggests that we ask simple questions such as "why is that what you want" or "what would you do if you were in my shoes?". The fourth step involves building on their ideas in order to make it easy and convenient for them to agree. The final stage—"bringing them to their senses, not their knees"—involves making it hard for them to say no. This does not involve using threats or force, but rather focuses on educating the other side about the costs of not agreeing. You are effectively demonstrating your BATNA.

## MEDIATION AND CONCILIATION

The origins of mediation and conciliation can be traced to China some 3,000 years ago. More specifically, China has used these techniques as a primary dispute resolution process whilst other parts of the world have resorted to some form of adjudicative process. State courts have been used as a mechanism to support socialist ideals and, as such, have performed a controlling function with regard to activities considered as criminal (Palmer, M. J. E.: 1991). On the other hand, activities relating to commerce fall outside of socialist ideals, as do non-criminal matters relating to private individuals. The resolution of these disputes by informal processes were encouraged in order to maintain "harmony" in the community.

More recently, and probably during the past 10 to 15 years, there has been a growing international awareness of the benefits of mediation as a dispute resolution technique. In the US, research by Stipanowich (1994) has documented the rise of mediation, which was first taken seriously by the US construction industry. Apparently the Army Corps of Engineers pioneered the process in order to reduce the high costs of litigation.

In the UK, this recent move towards mediation under the banner of ADR first developed in the area of family disputes. The commercial sector began to take an interest in the late 1980s and CEDR was formed in 1990 in order to promote ADR in the general commercial setting, primarily through mediation. Specifically in relation to the construction industry, the ICE established a conciliation procedure in 1988. More recently, the courts have piloted a court based mediation scheme (Butler, N.: 1997).

### *What is mediation and conciliation?*

To mediate means to act as a peacemaker between disputants. It is essentially an informal process in which the parties are assisted by one or more neutral third parties in their efforts towards settlement. Mediators do not judge or arbitrate the dispute. They advise and consult impartially with the parties to assist in bringing about a mutually agreeable solution to the problem. Some definitions in circulation include:

"Mediation is negotiation carried out with the assistance of a third party. The mediator, in contrast to the arbitrator or judge, has no power to impose an outcome on disputing parties" (Goldberg, S. B., *et al.*: 1992, p. 103).

"Mediation is a facilitative process in which disputing parties engage the assistance of a neutral third party who acts as a mediator in their dispute" (Brown & Marriott: 1992, p. 108).

"Where two or more people or companies are unable to resolve a particular problem they invite a neutral person to help them arrive at a solution. The neutral person, or Mediator, will work hard with each side and help them to understand better their own and the other person's position, and explore alternative solutions" (British Academy of Experts: 1992).

"Mediation consists of the effort of an individual, or several individuals, to assist the parties in reaching the settlement of a controversy or claim by direct negotiations between or among themselves. The mediator participates impartially in the negotiations, advising and consulting the various parties involved" (American Arbitration Association: 1992).

There are two common threads. First, the form of the third party intervention. The primary role of the third party is to facilitate other people's decision making. The process builds on negotiation, and the mediator fundamentally sustains and reviews the situation with the parties. Second, the third party should be independent of the parties in dispute. The essence of mediation is that the mediator is impartial. The trust which develops during the process allows the mediator to perform "a bridging role" between the parties.

Confusingly, the term "conciliation" is often used interchangeably with mediation. In the UK conciliation is usually taken to mean a more interventionist or evaluative style of mediation. However, there is no internationally agreed norm. The conciliation of labour disputes by ACAS is generally considered to be more evaluative, as is ICE conciliation. If the parties fail to settle under the ICE procedure, the conciliator will make a recommendation. However, the terms mediation and conciliation are often used interchangeably:

"Now the norm for a mediator is purely facilitative. A conciliator can be suggestive or more proactive. The reality is that most of time the roles tend to be very interchangeable but you do have to remember your role."

In practice, a mediation or conciliation may tend to be more towards one end of the scale than the other. It is perhaps more useful to make a distinction between facilitative and evaluative techniques. The process can be facilitative in that a third party intermediary merely tries to aid communications between the parties. CEDR advocate a facilitative approach to mediation. At the other end of the scale is an evaluative approach where the third party comments on the subject matter and makes recommendations as to the outcome.

In summary, the main elements of mediation and conciliation are:

(1) that it is voluntary in the sense that the parties participate of their own free will;
(2) a neutral third party assists the parties towards a settlement;
(3) the process is non-binding unless an agreement is reached;
(4) the process is private, confidential and conducted without prejudice to any legal proceedings.

### *Benefits of mediation*

Many consider that mediation and conciliation offer a range of benefits when compared to the traditional formal adjudicative processes such as litigation and arbitration. These benefits include:

- reductions in the time taken to resolve disputes;
- reductions in the costs of resolving disputes;
- providing a more satisfactory outcome to the dispute;
- minimising further disputes;
- opening channels of communication;
- preserving or enhancing relationships;
- savings in time and money;
- empowering the parties.

### *The mediation process*

There are, in general terms, three main phases to mediation:

(1) Pre-mediation—agreeing to mediate and preparation.
(2) The mediation—direct and indirect mediation.
(3) Post-mediation—complying with the outcome.

This basic framework may be further developed. Goldberg, *et al.*, suggest a five-stage process, whilst Brown and Marriott divide mediation into 10 stages:

| **Basic framework** | **The practice of mediation (Goldberg, *et al.*, p. 106)** | **The stages of mediation (Brown and Marriott, p. 121)** |
|---|---|---|
| Pre-mediation | A: Pre-mediation—getting to the table | 1: The initial inquiry—engaging the parties |

| **Basic framework** | **The practice of mediation (Goldberg, *et al.*, p. 106)** | **The stages of mediation (Brown and Marriott, p. 121)** |
|---|---|---|
| The mediation | B: The opening of mediations<br>C: The parties' opening presentations<br>D: Mediated negotiations<br>E: Agreement | 2: The contract to mediate<br>3: Preliminary communications and preparations<br>4: Meeting the parties<br>5: The parties' presentations<br>6: Information gathering<br>7: Facilitating negotiations<br>8: Impasse strategies<br>9: Terminating mediation and recording agreements |
| Post-mediation | | 10: Post-termination phase |

### *Pre-mediation*

The preparation phase of mediation develops from the initial inquiry, which may involve an explanation of the process, and an attempt to persuade reluctant parties to participate. A contract to mediate is frequently used in order to agree the terms and the ground rules for the mediation. This will include items such as costs, confidentiality, the without prejudice nature of the mediation, authority to settle and timetable. In some instances, the parties may provide and exchange written summaries of the dispute, and occasionally furnish copies of supporting documents. During this process, the mediator will be identified, and will become a party to the mediation contract.

From the mediator's perspective, the pre-mediation objective is merely to get the parties to the mediation. The strategy of the parties is less clear. Are they preparing their best case, do they consider innovative ways to settle, do they really calculate their BATNAS?

### *The mediation*

Most commercial mediations are conducted over the course of one day, although some may extend over several days, weeks, or even months. Mediations are usually conducted on neutral territory, rather than the offices of one of the parties. This is an attempt to avoid the power imbalances which may occur as a result of one of the parties operating within familiar territory. The mediator's role involves managing the process, and so will receive and seat the parties, before carrying out the necessary introductions. During this first joint meeting, the mediator will establish the ground rules and invite the parties to make an opening statement.

The mediation process is flexible, and once the parties have made their opening statements, the mediator may decide to discuss some issues in the joint meeting or a "caucus". A caucus is a private meeting between the mediator and one of the parties. The mediator will caucus with the parties in turn, in order to explore in confidence the issues in the dispute and the options for settlement. In a caucus, the mediator is mediating "indirectly" with the parties, and this exploration phase of mediation serves to:

- build a relationship between the parties and the mediator;
- clarify the main issues;
- identify the parties' interests or needs;
- allow the parties to vent their emotions;
- attempt to uncover hidden agendas;
- identify potential settlement options.

While the mediator is caucusing with one party, it may be possible for the other party to work on a specific task set by the mediator. The mediator may also utilise further joint meetings in order to narrow the issues, allow experts to meet, or broker the final settlement. The aim of mediation is to develop a commercially acceptable, workable agreement which can be written into a binding settlement contract.

### Post-mediation

Post mediation will either involve execution of the settlement agreement, or a continuation towards the trial or arbitration hearing. The mediator may still be involved as a settlement supervisor, or perhaps further mediations. It has been suggested that just because the parties do not settle, does not mean that the mediation was not successful. The parties may have a greater understanding of their dispute, which may lead to future efficiencies in the resolution of the dispute, or the parties may settle soon after the mediation.

### The mediator's role

The mediator is the manager of the process. S/he should take control of the process, and aid the parties to settlement. CEDR (1997) state that the mediator fulfils several important roles during the mediation and should:

- manage the process firmly but sensitively;
- facilitate the parties towards settlement by overcoming deadlock;
- gather information in order to identify common goals;
- be a reality tester, helping the parties to take a realistic view of the dispute;
- act as a problem solver, thinking creatively in order to help the parties construct an outcome that best meets their needs;

- soak up the parties feelings and frustrations, re-channelling the parties' energy into positive approaches to the issues;
- act as a scribe who assists in the writing of the agreement;
- be a settlement supervisor, checking that the settlement agreement has worked and being available to help with further problems that may occur;
- prompt the parties towards settlement and keep the momentum towards settlement.

It is vital that the mediator gains the trust and confidence of the parties so that a full and frank discussion can be encouraged. A full exploration of the problems will help to generate settlement options.

Mediators may employ a variety of strategies to achieve a settlement. The literature suggests that there are five main activities which mediators should employ:

- investigation—questioning to (1) obtain information and (2) to point out the holes in a particular party's point of view;
- empathy;
- persuasion;
- invention—creating solutions;
- distraction—to avoid parties from assuming a set position.

The mediator should question and investigate not just the issues in dispute, but the underlying conflict. Apparently mediators have little chance of "steering" the parties to a settlement without understanding the hidden objectives of the parties. Mediators should avoid sympathy with either party. Nonetheless, a degree of empathy is required in order to build trust with the parties. Persuasion is required in order to drive the mediation forward, as is a degree of inventiveness and the ability to provide distraction. In this context, distractions refers to the ability to take the parties onto another related subject in order to explore settlement possibilities from another angle. This technique may be used to avoid the polarisation of positions which is frequently adopted by many during conflict.

### *Liability of mediators*

Clause 12 of CEDR's standard form of Mediation Agreement states the following:

> "Neither CEDR nor any Mediator appointed by CEDR shall be liable to the Parties or either of them for any act or omission whatsoever in connection with the services to be provided by them."

It is arguable that the mediator, if acting purely in a facilitative capacity, should never find him or herself in circumstances which may give rise to any liability. Nonetheless it is clearly sensible to include an immunity clause. The clause is an attempt at a complete exclusion of liability and may be contrast to

s. 29 of the Arbitration Act 1996 which relates to the immunity of arbitrators. In that clause arbitrators are immune unless the act or omission is shown to have been in "bad faith".

Many mediation agreements around the world include similar immunity clauses. Apparently a similar clause has been tested in Australia where the mediators inadvertently gave incorrect legal advice. There is another incidence where the mediator may lay him or herself open to a claim. This would be where s/he obtains some confidential information during a caucus which s/he then negligently reveals to the other party.

### *The qualities of a mediator*

A good deal of the literature focuses on the function, role and skills of mediators. A mediator is qualified not by the virtue of his or her expertise in a particular area, but rather by the individual's ability to aid the parties to a settlement. In this respect the mediator must manage the mediation process, gather information from the parties before evaluating and testing that information in order to facilitate the exchange of information which should hopefully then lead to a settlement. These processes can be described as the role or function of the mediator.

However, the skills or attributes required of a mediator in order to carry through a successful mediation are somewhat more subjective. Many of the skills are interpersonal skills of the individual, in particular his or her ability to communicate effectively. An effective mediator needs to be seen to maintain a carefully balanced neutral role. In some respects a mediator who has no specialist knowledge about the technical issues of a dispute will have the benefit of coming to the mediation without preconceived ideas arising from his or her own background. This contrasts to the skills expected of an arbitrator who is usually chosen for his or her particular area of expertise.

The skills of a mediator are based upon the ability to communicate rather than a firm grounding in a technical area. For example, the ability to carefully encourage a party to see the weaknesses of its own case without providing one's own evaluation of the situation requires care and skill. An engineering consultant who had trained as an arbitrator expressed these sentiments in relation to his mediation training:

> "Despite the fact that I have completed the [CEDR] course, I am still a bit wary of actually undertaking a mediation because it is not everyone who has that particular talent. I wonder whether I personally have that talent. The person you select as a mediator is extremely important because s/he has to be able to persuade, to twist the parties arms, to come to an agreement and it needs a lot of lateral thinking. Whilst I think I might be able to do it if push came to shove, I am not confident. What you have to do is persuade each party as to the weak parts of their argument. You have to be able to identify those and in fact undermine their own confidence in their position without jeopardising your role as a mediator" (Gould, N., *et al.*: 1999).

A manager for a large public body lamented on his experience in one mediation:

"Well there are good mediators and bad. We have a real mixture of those. Some extremely good and some not so good. One particular guy had already made his mind up before talking to us. I tried to get across to him that I thought that was not his role. He seemed to get mixed up between mediation and arbitration. He is well known in the industry, very high up. People see mediation as just a different type of arbitration rather than adopting a totally different approach" (Gould, N., *et al.*: 1999).

### *Informal mediation processes*

Many of the survey respondents who reported mediation experiences were more specifically referring to a process of "informal" mediation. The technique essentially refers to a wide-ranging and flexible process which develops over time, and focuses on a key third party neutral. This neutral is approached because of his or her position by one of the disputants. The individual representing one of the parties approaches the particular neutral because a situation of mutual trust and respect already exists as a result of a prior course of dealing.

Often, the previous course of dealing will be over an extended period of many years, possibly with the neutral in a senior commercial position. He or she is usually approached at a certain stage in the dispute. First, the parties are entrenched and unable to find common ground. Second, at least one of the parties recognises the importance of reaching a commercially sensible solution to the dispute. Finally, the approaching agent recognises that the neutral is in a position such that s/he has the ability to "talk" to the other side with a degree of trust and respect. A director of one major contractor described such an experience.

## ADJUDICATION

The term adjudication can be misleading. In its general sense it refers to the process by which the judge decides the case before him/her or the manner in which a referee should decide issues before him or her. More specifically, adjudication may be defined as a process where a neutral third party gives a decision, which is binding on the parties in dispute unless or until revised in arbitration or litigation. This narrow interpretation may refer to the commercial use of an adjudicator to decide issues between parties to a contract. The use of an adjudicator is found in a variety of standard forms of contract used in the construction industry (McGaw, M.: 1992).

Until recently, adjudication in the construction industry has displayed certain characteristics. First, the adjudicator is a neutral individual who is not involved in the day to day running of the contract. He or she is neither an arbitrator, nor a state appointed judge. Second, the adjudicator enjoys his or her powers by virtue of the agreement between the parties. In other words the parties have agreed by contract that the decision of the adjudicator shall decide the matter for them. Third, the adjudicator's decision is binding on the parties, and therefore, unlike mediation, the process does not require the cooperation of both parties. Fourth, adjudicators' decisions are usually expressed as being binding until the end of the contract when either party may seek a review of the decision, most commonly by arbitration. Finally, adjudication is not arbitration and is therefore not subject to the Arbitration Act 1996.

It follows therefore that an adjudicator's powers are limited to those which are contained in the contract. For example, the DOM/1 (a widely used standard form of subcontract) made use of an adjudication provision in relation to payment and set-off. However, the position has recently changed with the introduction of statutory adjudication under the Housing Grants, Construction and Regeneration Act 1996.

### *Statutory adjudication*

The introduction of statutory adjudication under s. 108 of the Housing Grants Construction and Regeneration Act 1996 was one of the key recommendations in the Latham Report (1994). Latham recommended that a system of adjudication should be introduced within all of the standard forms of contract, unless some comparable arrangement already existed for mediation or conciliation. He further recommended that the system of adjudication should be "underpinned by legislation", capable of considering a wide range of issues and that the decision of the adjudicator should be implemented immediately.

## Housing Grants Construction and Regeneration Act 1996

The Housing Grants Construction and Regeneration Act received Royal Assent on 24 July 1996. However, those parts relating to construction (Part II of the Act) were not brought into force until the Scheme for Construction Contracts had been affirmed by Parliament. The Scheme and that part of the Act relating to construction commenced on 1 May 1998. At the same time an exclusion order reduced the scope of adjudication in relation to certain statutory provisions, contracts relating to private finance initiative finance agreements, and development agreements.

The Act sets out a framework for a system of adjudication. All construction contracts must meet this minimum criterion. Should a contract fail to meet these minimum requirements then the Scheme for Construction Contracts will apply. A consultation document was issued by the then Department of the Environment in November 1996. This document indicated the likely content of such a scheme. However, this document received widespread attention and criticism (Enderson, G.: 1996).

## Statutory adjudication—the process

Under Part II of the Housing Grants Construction and Regeneration Act 1996 a party to a construction contract is unilaterally given the right to refer a dispute arising under the contract to adjudication. The Act only applies to "construction contracts" which fall within the detailed definition of s. 104. For example, "architectural design, surveying work or to provide advice on building, engineering, interior or exterior decoration or the laying out of landscape in relation to construction operations" are included within the scope of the Act, whilst contracts of employment are expressly excluded. In addition, a construction contract is defined so as to include an agreement to carry out "construction operations".

Construction operations are further defined in s. 105 to include a wide variety of general construction related work together with a list of notable exceptions. A further notable exception is a construction contract with a residential occupier. The provisions only apply where the construction contract is in writing, however this is given a wide interpretation and it would seem very little is needed to fulfil this requirement.

Section 108 sets out the minimum requirements for an adjudication procedure. These may be summarised as follows:

(1) *Notices*: A party to a construction contract must have the right to give a notice at any time of his intention to refer a particular dispute to the adjudicator.
(2) *Appointment*: A method of securing the appointment of an adjudicator and furnishing him with details of the dispute within seven days of the notice is mandatory.
(3) *Time scales*: The adjudicator is then required to reach a decision within 28 days of this referral. It will not be possible to agree in advance of any dispute that additional time may be taken for the adjudication. There are only two exceptions to this rule. First, the adjudicator may extend the period of 28 days by a further 14 days if the party refereeing the dispute consents. Second, a longer period can be agreed by consent of all the parties. Such agreement can only be reached after the dispute has been referred.
(4) *Act impartially*: The adjudicator is required to act impartially.
(5) *Act inquisitorially*: The Act requires that the adjudicator "takes the initiative in ascertaining facts and the law". This gives the adjudicator power to investigate the issue in whatever manner he or she deems appropriate given the short time scale available.
(6) *Binding nature*: The decision of the adjudicator is binding until the dispute is finally determined by legal proceedings, by arbitration or by agreement. Phillip Capper (1997) suggests that "the 'until' formulation gives an unfortunate interim air to the decision almost inviting the view that it ought to be reopened at a later stage". The

Act does, however, go on to say that the parties may agree to accept the decision of the adjudicator as finally determining the dispute.

(7) *Immunity*: The adjudicator cannot be held liable for anything done or omitted in the discharge of his function as an adjudicator unless acting in bad faith. This protection is extended to any employee or agent of the adjudicator.

In addition to this basic procedural framework the Act further requires that any construction contract complies with the provisions of the scheme for construction contracts.

## The Scheme for Construction Contracts

If the construction contract does not comply with the above eight requirements then the Scheme will be implied into the contract. Alternatively, if the construction contract does comply with the above provisions then the parties may include further more detailed provisions and perhaps a procedure for enforcement. Essentially then the parties can achieve compliance with the Act in one of four ways:

(i) the parties could adopt the Scheme;

(ii) adopt a standard forms contract which sets out a series of adjudication rules;

(iii) adopt one of the alternative sets of rules, for example, the Institution of Civil Engineers Adjudication Procedure, the Construction Industry Council Model Adjudication Procedure or the Centre for Dispute Resolution Rules for Adjudication, the Institution of Chemical Engineers Adjudication Rules, the Technology Court Solicitor's Association Rules;

(iv) draw up their own set of bespoke rules.

Section 114(1) provides that the Secretary of State for England and Wales and the Lord Advocate for Scotland "shall by regulation make a Scheme ('the Scheme for Construction Contracts') containing provisions about the matters referred to" in the Act. The Scheme for England and Wales was introduced by a statutory instrument which commenced on 1 May 1998 (SI 1998 No 649). In its consultation paper, the Department of the Environment (as it was) stated that:

> "The Scheme may be used to remedy deficiencies in contractual adjudication agreements . . . and also to provide payment terms."

The Scheme detailed in the statutory instrument is divided into two parts; the first dealing with adjudication, and the second with payment. If a construction contract does not contain adjudication provisions which satisfy the eight key requirements of the Act then the Scheme applies in its entirety. The aim of the Scheme is to provide a series of workable arrangements which detail the mechanics of adjudication in the event that either no provision is made in the contract or an inadequate provision is included in the contract.

The Scheme is therefore an attempt to provide a workable adjudication procedure which supplements the skeletal regime in the Act. For example the Scheme states that the written notice must briefly set out the nature and description of the dispute, the parties involved, details of where and when the dispute arose, the remedy sought and the names and addresses of the parties to the contract. Further, the Scheme contemplates that there may be more than two parties to the contract and requires the notice of referral to be given to "every other party". In addition, an attempt is made at joinder of related disputes and different contracts and the adjudication at the same time of more than one dispute, but only with the consent of all parties.

## Alternative standard form rules

A range of alternative standard form adjudication procedures have developed from different corners of the industry. The Construction Industry Council ("CIC") launched the first edition of the Model Adjudication Procedure. The CIC is an umbrella body which seeks to represent both the supply and demand side of the construction industry. At the same time the Official Referee's Solicitors Association produced an adjudication procedure. More interestingly, the Centre for Dispute Resolution (CEDR) was quick to establish an adjudication procedure. At the time 99% of CEDR's work was in the field of mediation, and one might speculate that the development of CEDR's rules related to market sector protection rather than market opportunities, as their rules remind parties that mediation can be used at any time.

From a legal perspective it is helpful to consider the construction industry as comprising the building sector and the civil engineering sector. Standard forms for building work have traditionally been dominated by the Joint Contracts Tribunal ("JCT"), while the Institution of Civil Engineers' standard forms have dominated the civil engineering side of the industry. These two bodies have adopted slightly different approaches to the Act. The most recent JCT Amendment 18 is clearly a large scale amendment to the JCT form, and one which includes its own adjudication procedures. On the other hand, the ICE have chosen to produce a stand alone adjudication procedure which is then referred to in the standard forms. In addition, the ICE have attempted to maintain conciliation within the framework of their multi-tiered dispute resolution clause, whilst leaving the engineer's decision as the primary tier.

## Preliminary points

A party contemplating reference of a dispute to adjudication must consider a number of preliminary points before proceeding. These include:

(1) Is there a dispute?

(2) Does the dispute arise under a construction contract within the meaning of s. 104?
(3) Is the contract in writing within the meaning of s. 107?
(4) What are the identities of the correct parties to the contract?

A party finding itself in the position of responding in a reference to adjudication where there is no legal right so to refer must also pay attention to these issues in order to give itself the best possible chance of stopping the process from taking its full course.

### *1. Is there a dispute?*

Under the HGCRA, there is no entitlement to adjudicate unless a "dispute" has arisen under the contract. A party may therefore challenge a purported reference to adjudication on the ground that there is no dispute. Similarly, enforcement of a purported decision may be defended on the grounds that, without a dispute, the adjudicator had no jurisdiction to make a decision that is binding on the parties.

The question of when a dispute crystallises has been examined in a large number of cases but there has unfortunately been some inconsistency in judicial analysis as to when the point of crystallisation occurs.

Judgements on the question of what constitutes a dispute for the purposes of statutory adjudication can mostly be assigned into one or other of two categories. The first category, the "narrow definition", is based on the proposition that for a dispute to arise, not only must a claim be made but also the recipient of the claim should have been given reasonable opportunity to consider, and respond to, it. The second category, the "wide definition", consists of the cases in which the court in question has applied the proposition that there is a dispute once a claim is made, unless and until the defendant admits that the claimant is entitled to what has been claimed.

More recently, there has been "the flexible approach",[1] when Mr Justice Jackson stated:

"1. The word 'dispute' which occurs in many arbitration clauses and also in s. 108 of the Housing Grants Act should be given its normal meaning. It does not have some special or unusual meaning conferred upon it by lawyers.

. . .

3. The mere fact that one party (whom I shall call 'the Claimant') notifies the other party (whom I shall call 'the Respondent') of a claim does not automatically and immediately give rise to a dispute. It is clear, both as a matter of language and from judicial decisions, that a dispute does not arise unless and until it emerges that the claim is not admitted.

4. The circumstances from which it may emerge that a claim is not admitted are Protean. For example, there may be an express rejection of the claim. There may be discussions between the parties from which objectively it is to be inferred that the claim

1. *AMEC Civil Engineering Ltd* v. *The Secretary of State for Transport* [2004] EWHC 2339.

is not admitted. The Respondent may prevaricate, thus giving rise to the inference that he does not admit the claim. The Respondent may simply remain silent for a period of time, thus giving rise to the same inference.

5. The period of time for which a Respondent may remain silent before a dispute is to be inferred depends heavily upon the facts of the case and the contractual structure. Where the gist of the claim is well known and it is obviously controversial, a very short period of silence may suffice to give rise to this inference. Where the claim is notified to some agent of the Respondent who has a legal duty to consider the claim independently and then give a considered response, a longer period of time may be required before it can be inferred that mere silence gives rise to a dispute.

6. If the Claimant imposes upon the Respondent a deadline for responding to the claim, that deadline does not have the automatic effect of curtailing what would otherwise be a reasonable time for responding. On the other hand, a stated deadline and the reasons for its imposition may be relevant factors when the court comes to consider what is a reasonable time for responding.

7. If the claim as presented by the Claimant is so nebulous and ill defined that the Respondent cannot sensibly respond to it, neither silence by the Respondent nor even an express non-admission is likely to give rise to a dispute for the purposes of arbitration or adjudication."

The validity of contractual provisions imposing mandatory pre-adjudication procedures, for example stating that the parties are first to attempt to resolve any difference by mediation before being entitled to refer such difference to adjudication, has been considered in a number of cases.[2] Such contractual provisions have been held to be void, as they conflict with the unqualified right under s. 108(1) of the HGCRA to refer a difference or dispute to adjudication "at any time" and thereby attempt to fetter a party's right to do so.

*2. Does the dispute arise under a construction contract?*

The statutory right to refer a dispute to adjudication only arises "under a construction contract" falling within the definition of s. 104. Where the contract does not fall within this definition, there is therefore no right to statutory adjudication.

However, adjudication is also possible under a contract outside the statutory definition where the parties have as part of that contract agreed to refer disputes under it to adjudication. Sometimes the parties agree to adjudicate after the dispute has arisen in circumstances where otherwise there would be no right to refer to adjudication or obligation to participate in it. This is referred to as "contractual adjudication", to distinguish it from statutory adjudication under the HGCRA.

2. *RG Carter* v. *Edmund Nuttall Ltd* [2002] EWHC 400; 82 Con. L.R., [2002] All E.R. (D) 325, *John Mowlem & Co. Plc* v. *Hydra-Tight Ltd (T/A Hevilifts)* [2002] LTL 21/7/2000, British Waterways Board (Judicial Review) Scotland, Outer House, Court of Session, Lord McCluskey.

As it is "contractual adjudication", the Scheme cannot be implied to fill in any gaps in the adjudication procedures provided for in the contract.[3]

*3. Is the contract in writing?*

Section 107(1) of the HGCRA provides that the right to refer a dispute to adjudication applies only where the relevant construction contract is in writing. Subsections (2) to (6) contain the rules for determining whether the contract is in writing and were initially regarded as providing a fairly wide definition.

However, in the case of *RJT Consulting Engineers Ltd* v. *DM Engineering (Northern Ireland) Ltd*,[4] the Court of Appeal applied a much stricter interpretation.

At first instance, H.H.J. MacKay had taken what he described as a "purposive" approach and held that it was not necessary to identify all the terms of the contract and, since there was in this case a "comparatively great" amount of written material, that would be sufficient. The material included a fee account, identifying the parties and the place of work, and meeting minutes, which identified the type of work being carried out.

The Court of Appeal disagreed with this approach. They said that invoices, for example, are evidence of the existence of a contract and do not define the contract as such. They held that the whole of the agreement had to be evidenced in writing, saying:

> "Certainty is all the more important when adjudication is envisaged to have to take place under a demanding timetable. The adjudicator has to start with some certainty as to what the terms of the contract are. The written record of the agreement is the foundation from which a dispute may spring but the least the adjudicator has to be certain about is the terms of the agreement which is giving rise to the dispute."

A record of an agreement must thus be a record of a complete agreement.

It should be noted that one of the judges, Auld L.J., differed slightly in his view, considering that it was the terms of the agreement which are material to the issue(s) giving rise to the dispute which were important to be recorded in writing, not that every single term, however trivial, should itself be expressly recorded.

*4. Identity of the parties*

Care must be exercised to state the correct party names not only in the contract documentation but also in all exchanges during the adjudication process, as otherwise there may well be jurisdictional difficulties.

3. For other distinctions between these two types of adjudication, see the decisions of the Court of Appeal in *Parsons Plastics (Research & Development) Ltd* v. *Purac Ltd* [2002] B.L.R. 334 and *Ferson Contractors Ltd* v. *Levolux AT Ltd* [2003] EWCA Civ 11.

4. [2002] EWCA Civ 270, [2002] 1 W.L.R. 2344, 83 Con. L.R. 99, [2002] All E.R. (d) 108.

### *The adjudication process*

The first step is to serve notice of adjudication, to inform the other party that a dispute has arisen and that it is intended to refer this dispute to adjudication.

The notice should set out in reasonable detail what the dispute is about, and the redress being sought; it establishes the jurisdiction of the adjudicator, who will not be entitled to decide any issue not specifically stated in the notice. If a new issue emerges during the adjudication, this may well amount to a new dispute and could therefore be outside the adjudicator's jurisdiction.

The next step is to appoint the adjudicator.

An adjudicator may have been named in the contract; if not, then the referring party has to apply to the adjudicator nominating body (ANB) named in the contract or, if none is named, an appropriate ANB for a nomination to be made.

The adjudicator must be appointed, and the dispute formally referred to him/her, within seven days of the notice of adjudication.

Referral to the adjudicator is achieved through service of the referral notice, which states the referring party's case. It should be supported by copies of, or relevant extracts from, the construction contract and all other documents, for example drawings, programmes, correspondence, meeting minutes, notices and calculations, upon which the referring party intends to rely by way of evidence to prove the events or support the assertions which it is claiming.

If the referral notice includes any documentation which the responding party has not seen before (other than witness statements) then the adjudicator will not have jurisdiction to consider it, as it will not have formed part of the "dispute" being referred to adjudication.

The responding party is entitled to serve a response to the referral notice, setting out its reply to the issues, arguments and facts relied upon by the referring party.

The adjudicator may entitle the referring party to serve a reply to the response; in some larger and more complex adjudications, exchanges of submissions continue even beyond this point, with the service of rejoinders.

The adjudicator may ask the parties questions, and may decide to hold a meeting at which the issues in dispute may be explored in full. He may decide to visit the site, or carry out tests, or obtain his own legal and/or technical expert evidence. In the exercise of all these powers, he must be careful to comply with the rules of natural justice, giving the parties the opportunity to comment on any information from whatever source that he wishes to rely upon in reaching his decision. He must not conduct the proceedings in such a way that will lead an outsider to conclude that that might be a risk of bias.

The adjudicator must make his decision on the matters referred to him. If he cannot do this, then he should resign, thus allowing the parties to refer the dispute to someone else.

There is no format prescribed by the HGCRA, the Scheme or any of the published adjudication procedures with which an adjudicator's decision must comply. He should, however, make his decision responsive to the remedies sought, stating clearly what the parties are to do, and when it is to be done.

The HGCRA does not require the adjudicator to give reasons for his decision; whether he does so therefore depends on the contract, which may provide that he is to give reasons only if a party requests them. Many adjudicators, however, now take the view that they should give reasons in any event, even if only briefly, in order to inform the parties of their thinking and engender greater acceptability of their decision and, perhaps, promote the final resolution of the dispute in a more efficient manner.

Generally, after making and publishing his decision, the adjudicator has no power to review it to reflect any changes in his views on the merits of the dispute. He may, however, revise his decision in order to correct clerical or other accidental errors.[5] The contract itself may also provide for this to be done.

Unless otherwise agreed by the parties, the adjudicator has no power to award the payment of costs, other than to determine payment of his own fees and expenses, for which the parties are in any event jointly and severally liable.

If the adjudicator's decision is not complied with, then it will be necessary to enforce it. The main methods of enforcing adjudicators' decisions are:

(1) Summary judgment/interim payment application in court.
(2) Mandatory injunction.
(3) Statutory demand.
(4) Part 8 proceedings, where the declaration of the court is sought on a question that is unlikely to involve a substantial dispute over fact.

The principal grounds for challenging the decision of an adjudicator include:

(1) The adjudicator did not have jurisdiction to make the decision.
(2) The adjudicator acted in breach of the requirements of natural justice/impartiality/ fairness.
(3) The adjudicator acted in breach of the applicable procedural rules, thereby going outside his jurisdiction.
(4) The decision is wrong on its merits.
(5) The paying party is entitled to set-off/abatement against the amount ordered to be paid.
(6) The payee, by reason of insolvency, will be unable to repay the payment ordered when final determination of the dispute requires such payment.
(7) The enforcement proceedings should be stayed to arbitration.

5. *Bloor Construction (UK) Ltd* v. *Bowmer & Kirkland (London) Ltd* [2000] B.L.R. 314.

# ARBITRATION

Arbitration is a process, subject to statutory controls, whereby formal disputes are determined by a private tribunal of the parties' choosing. According to Stephenson, Lord Justice Sir Robert Raymond provided a definition some 250 years ago which is still considered valid today (Stephenson, D. A.: 1998):

"An arbitrator is a private extraordinary judge between party and party, chosen by their mutual consent to determine controversies between them, and arbitrators are so called because they have an arbitrary power; for if they observe the submission and keep within due bounds, their sentences are definite from which there lies no appeal."

Providing arbitrators stay within the law, there is generally no appeal from the arbitrator's award, and the award may be enforced by the courts if necessary.

Arbitration is essentially a process which is available as an alternative to litigation. The parties must agree to submit their dispute to arbitration and a distinction is often drawn between existing and future disputes. The distinction is of historical importance because some jurisdictions, notably France, would not until comparatively recently recognise agreements to refer future disputes to arbitration.

The advantages of arbitration are well rehearsed and include; flexibility, economy, expedition, privacy, freedom of choice of arbitrator, and finality. On the other hand, the disadvantages of arbitration appear to have been on the increase. In comparison to litigation, where the judge and court facilities are provided at public expense the parties to an arbitration will ultimately have to bear the costs of the arbitrator and the facilities. Where, as is often the case in construction, more than two parties are involved in a dispute there is relatively little statutory power to consolidate the actions in one arbitration. Some forms of contract such as the JCT and the FCEC form of subcontract provide for consolidation in limited circumstances.

## *The Arbitration Act 1996*

The Mustill Committee in its 1989 report recommended the development of a new arbitration act. The committee recommended against the adoption of the UNCITRAL Model Law on international and commercial arbitration ("The Model Law") despite the fact that this has been adopted in a great many countries around the world. The Mustill Committee considered that the existing English arbitration law was sufficiently well developed that the practical disadvantages of enacting a model law would outweigh any advantages. However, the committee considered that the existing law was unsatisfactory for a variety of reasons. Firstly, most of the law on arbitration is to be found in case law and is often only accessible to specialist lawyers. Secondly, the existing statute law was dispersed in a variety of acts. Finally the disjointed and illogical arrangement of the existing statutes, together with the complex terminology, is incomprehensible to the layman.

The initiative for a new act moved gradually forward, first, in a drafting bid under the Marriot Working Group, and then under the umbrella of the Department of Trade and Industry. A draft bill was published in February 1994. According to Ambrose and Maxwell (1997), the bill was subject to much criticism and around 2,500 comments were received during the five month consultation period. In November 1994, Lord Justice Saville became the Chairman of the Departmental Advisory Committee (DAC). The new draft was published in a consultative paper in 1995. (A final report and supplemental report was published in 1997.) The bill was debated in the House of Lords and then passed on to the House of Commons before being committed to the Special Public Bill Committee procedure. The Act received Royal Assent on 17 June 1996.

### The aim of the Arbitration Act

Five main objectives underlie the Act:

(1) To ensure that arbitration is fair, cost-effective and rapid.
(2) To promote party autonomy, in other words to respect the parties choice.
(3) To ensure that the courts' supportive powers are available at the appropriate times.
(4) To ensure that the language used is user friendly and clearly accessible.
(5) To follow the model law wherever possible.

The first of these objectives is included in s. 1 of the Act:

"The provisions of this part are founded on the following principles, and shall be construed accordingly—

(a) The objective of arbitration is to obtain the fair resolution of disputes by an impartial tribunal without unnecessary delay or expense;
(b) The Parties should be free to agree how their disputes are resolved, subject only to such safeguards as are necessary in the public interest;
(c) In matters governed by this part of the Act the court should not intervene except as provided by this part."

Although it was anticipated that the Act would have heralded a new era in arbitration practice, many of the provisions of the Act remain under-used. In contrast to the CPR, the Act's provisions are not all obligatory; arbitration remains a matter of private contract and therefore susceptible to party, lawyer and arbitrator conservatism. In addition, there is a sharp decline in the number of cases being referred to arbitration, partly due to previous dissatisfaction with pre-1996 arbitration, which has led to arbitration clauses in contracts still being struck through as a matter of course, but principally due to the impact of adjudication.

At a practical level, the increasing complexity and range of disputes referred to adjudication has led to some problems, particularly where adjudicators have lacked the skill or experience to deal with complex claims, for example extension of time claims which require planning and programming expertise, or money claims which require forensic accounting skills. Unless extended, the statutory 28-day period may simply be too short properly and fairly to deal with the points in issue. Further, the parties' costs in adjudication are almost always irrecoverable, and significant.

Arbitration is therefore now beginning to enjoy something of a comeback, particularly if based on the 100-day scheme, championed by the Society of Construction Arbitrators and launched by them on 1 July 2004. This process is designed to act as a halfway point between adjudication and arbitration and is likely to gain significant momentum in the coming years. Where the parties agree to adopt this procedure, the arbitrator will have an overriding duty to make his award within 100 days of the date on which the statement of case is delivered to him or to the other party (whichever is the later).

## The process of arbitration

The process of arbitration can be considered under four main headings:

- the agreement to arbitrate;
- the arbitrator;
- the procedure;
- the award and enforcement.

## The agreement to arbitrate

Parties can agree to arbitrate once a dispute has arisen, or more commonly they may agree to refer future disputes to arbitration should the need arise. Section 6(1) of the Arbitration Act recognises this distinction and defines an "arbitration agreement" as "an agreement to submit to arbitration present or future disputes". The definition does not restrict arbitration to merely contractual disputes, and could include a range of matters such as tortuous claims. There are limits to the kinds of dispute which may be "arbitrable" for example criminal matters cannot be settled privately by arbitration.

Section 6(2) of the Act states that a reference to an agreement that does contain an arbitration clause constitutes a valid agreement to arbitrate. This resolves a frequently encountered problem in the construction industry. The case of *Aughton Limited* v. *M F Kent Services Limited* [1991] 57 B.L.R. 1 found that merely referring to a standard form contract which contained an arbitration clause did not amount to an agreement to arbitrate. The parties needed to include a written agreement to arbitrate in their primary agreement. Section 6(2) apparently solves this problem.

An arbitration agreement must be in writing, but this is interpreted widely and includes any method of recording the agreement such as electronically or on tape. The agreement to arbitrate need not be complicated. In fact, the words "English Law—arbitration, if any, London according ICC rules", has been held to constitute a valid arbitration agreement which provided for arbitration in London under the ICC rules in accordance with English Law (*Arab African Energy Corporation Limited* v. *Olieprodukten Nederland BV* [1983] 2 Lloyd's Rep. 419). In practice a detailed arbitration agreement is recommended in order to avoid arguments over the validity of the agreement, provide a method of appointing an arbitrator and establish the arbitrator's powers.

The JCT 80 form of contract provides an arbitration agreement which the parties may choose to adopt. Article 5 of the contract contains the agreement to arbitrate, whilst clause 41 deals with issues such as the appointment of the arbitrator, the joinder of additional parties, the reviewing of certificates and instructions, the nature of the award, ability to appeal and also confirms that English Law is applicable. It states what to do if the arbitrator dies or ceases to act and provides that the arbitration is to be conducted in accordance with the JCT arbitration rules. These rules provide a detailed structure for the arbitration process.

## The arbitrator

A variety of methods exist for the appointment of arbitrators. An arbitrator or arbitrators may be appointed by agreement of the parties. Alternatively, the parties may have agreed that an institution will appoint an arbitrator on their behalf. Alternatively, the Court may appoint an arbitrator. The most frequently used method in construction contracts is to provide a timescale within which the parties can agree the name of the sole arbitrator, failing which either party may request that the president of a professional institution select and appoint an arbitrator.

Section 33 of the Arbitration Act requires that the tribunal should:

> "(a) Act fairly and impartially as between the parties, giving each party a reasonable opportunity of putting his case and dealing with that of his opponent, and
>
> "(b) adopt procedures suitable to the circumstances of the particular case, avoiding unnecessary delay or expense, so as to provide a fair means for the resolution of the matters falling to be determined."

The arbitrator's dilemma is to progress the arbitration and issue an award which deals with the matters in dispute whilst acting fairly and impartially between the parties. At the same time the arbitrator must not exceed his or her powers but must observe the agreed procedures whilst dealing with all of the issues raised (s. 68).

Section 29 states that an arbitrator is not liable for anything done or omitted in the discharge of his function as an arbitrator unless the act or omission is in bad faith. This immunity does not apply if the arbitrator resigns. However, the court has a power to grant the arbitrator relief from liability if the court considers that it was reasonable for the arbitrator to resign (s. 25).

The arbitrator obtains his or her powers from the agreement between the parties, the applicable rules and the Arbitration Act 1996. The Act provides the arbitrator with wide ranging powers, all of which are subject to the agreement of the parties.

Section 38 sets out the general powers of the arbitrator. Section 38(1) states that:

"The parties are free to agree on the powers exercisable by the arbitral tribunal for the purposes of and in relation to the proceedings."

The balance of the section goes on to give examples of the powers that might be exercised, unless otherwise agreed by the parties, including:

(1) The power to order a claimant to provide security for costs.
(2) The power to inspect, photograph, preserve or take samples of any property being the subject of the proceedings.
(3) The power to direct that witnesses be examined on oath.
(4) The power to order the preservation of any evidence.

Other sections of the Act contain specific powers, as follows:

Section 37: Unless otherwise agreed, the tribunal has the power to appoint experts, legal advisers or technical assessors.

Section 39: The parties are free to agree that the tribunal shall have power to make a provisional award.

Section 41: The parties are free to agree that the tribunal shall, in the event of one party's failure to do something or delay, have the power to make peremptory orders and dismiss claims if that default continues.

### The procedure

Arbitration commences when one party sends the other a notice stating that a dispute has arisen between them and refers it to arbitration. If an arbitrator has not been named in the contract, then party will also send a "notice to concur" in the appointment of an arbitrator. If the parties are unable to agree on an arbitrator then it is common for the professional institutions to appoint one, although this can only be done if the parties have agreed that this mechanism is appropriate. Most commonly, a procedure for default appointment is included within their contract.

Arbitration rules may adopt one or more of the following three possibilities:

- procedure without a hearing (documents only);
- full procedure with a hearing; and
- short procedure with a hearing.

The procedure without a hearing anticipates that the arbitrator will make an award based on documentary evidence only. The parties support their statements with a list of relevant documents together with a copy of any documents upon which they rely. The short procedure may be appropriate for disputes which are simple in nature. The time scales are short, allowing only 28 days for the entire process. This procedure is not frequently used. However, when it is used it is not uncommon for the parties to agreed to extend the time scale. Finally, the full procedure with a hearing provides that the parties will serve their statements of case and that the arbitrator will conduct a full oral hearing. Often the parties will be legally represented, expert witnesses are appointed and evidence is given under oath.

Section 34(1) provides that the arbitral tribunal shall decide on procedural and evidential matters, subject to the parties' agreement.

Section 34(2) sets out a non-exhaustive list of procedural and evidential matters including the exchange of pleadings, disclosure of documents, the application of the strict rules of evidence and whether or not the tribunal should take the initiative in ascertaining the facts and the law.

As usual, the parties have the choice but the list of procedural and evidential matters included within Section 34(2) gives some idea of the possibilities offered by these provisions. For example, subsection 2(d) begins with the words "whether any . . . documents . . . should be disclosed". In many disputes where the parties have gone through the exchange of, for example, final account documentation in voluminous form, they will already have seen most if not all of the relevant material so can in this procedure make their own decisions as to whether or not to spend extra costs on lawyers, photocopying, etc, in making these documents available again.

## The award and enforcement

The arbitrator's award is final and binding on the parties unless they agreed to the contrary (s. 58). Section 66 of the Act provides that the award may, with leave of the court, be enforced as if it were a judgement of the court. The ability for a party to challenge the award is extremely limited. On issuing the award the arbitrator becomes "*functus officio*". This means that the arbitrator's duty and powers are at an end and save for minor corrections the arbitrator is relieved of his task.

Frequently, the arbitrator may make more than one award, each award dealing with different issues. These "partial awards" or "interim awards" could relate to a part of the claim or an issue which affects the whole of the claim (s. 47). An interim award is not provisional in nature but is final and binding with respect to the issues with which it deals. The benefit of interim awards is that a major issue can be dealt with by the arbitrator as a preliminary point which dispenses with the need to spend time and money on related issues. The resolution of an important issue early in the proceedings may lead the parties to settle the whole of the dispute.

Should the parties settle the dispute, then the arbitrator may issue a consent award which records the parties agreement. Such an award is capable of enforcement in the Courts. Unless the parties have agreed otherwise then the arbitrator has the power to award a wide range of remedies:

- order payment of money;
- make a declaration of the rights between the parties;
- order a party to do or refrain from doing something;
- order specific performance; and/or
- order the rectification, setting aside or cancellation of a deed or document.

In addition, s. 49 of the Act provides that the arbitrator can unless otherwise agreed by the parties award simple or compound interests. This is an interesting provision as in most instances the court can only award simple interests. Rarely does the court have the power to award compound interest.

### *Variations on arbitration*

Arbitration is a judicial process, which often proceeds in a similar manner to court based litigation. However, variants on the traditional process of arbitration exist:

*Documents only.* The hearings are dispensed with and the arbitrator makes an award based upon the written submissions of the parties. This is sometimes referred to as "desk-top" arbitration.

*Amiable Compositeur or Ex aequo et bono.* If an arbitrator is to act as an amiable compositeur then the arbitrator may within certain limits disregard the strict legal or contractual requirements in order to arrive at an equitable solution to the dispute. "Equitable" in this sense means "fair".

*Final offer or last offer arbitration.* Each disputant submits to the arbitral tribunal its final offer in monetary terms. The tribunal must then select one or the other and make an award on that basis. The tribunal may not modify either parties' offer. A dilemma is faced by each party. An over exaggerated demand may well lead the tribunal to award in favour of the other party.

## LITIGATION AND THE COURT SYSTEM

The courts provide the setting for the traditional mode of dispute resolution; namely, litigation. The Law Courts themselves are often considered the most visible feature of the English legal system, and their main function is the adjudication of disputes. Nonetheless, the number of disputes determined by the Court is negligible, compared to the number of disputes settled by other means. Furthermore, very few proceedings which are commenced result in a trial and subsequent judgment. In fact, in excess of 90% of the actions commenced in the High Court are disposed of before reaching trial, and only a few percent result in a judgment (Judicial Statistics).

The entire civil procedure was replaced on 26 April 1999 by the civil procedure rules. Originally the White Book governed the procedure in the

High Court and the Green Book governed the procedure in the County Court. A review of the existing rules and procedures of the civil courts in England and Wales by Lord Woolf led first to the *Access to Justice report*, which in turn led to the establishment of the Civil Procedure Rules which govern both the county court and the High Court.

### *The new Civil Procedure Rule "CPR"*

Lord Woolf published his *Access to Justice* report in 1999. He considered that the existing system was too expensive, too slow, too fragmented, too adversarial, too uncertain, and incomprehensible to most litigants. The aim of the review was to:

- improve access to justice and reduce the cost of litigation;
- reduce the complexity of the rules and modernised terminology; and
- remove unnecessary distinctions, practice and procedures.

The CPRs were implemented on 26 April 1996 and apply to all new actions commenced from that date. Further, actions commenced under the old system will be transferred onto the Woolf regime after the first interlocutory application made after the 26 April.

The rules are printed in one volume which comprises a series of parts. Practice directions will support each rule, intending to clarify and describe the particular rule and how it should be used. In addition, practice forms are included in the rules for use at various stages of the litigation process.

### The overriding objective

Part 1 of the CPR establishes the overriding objective upon which all rules must be interpreted. Essentially, the overriding objective is that cases should be dealt with justly and in accordance with five basic principles that the court will adopt:

- to ensure that the parties are on an equal footing;
- save expense;
- deal with the case in ways which are proportionate to;
  - the amount of money involved;
  - the importance of the case;
  
    the complexity of the issue; and
  - the parties financial position.
- deal with case expeditiously and fairly; and
- allocate an appropriate share of the court's resources to the case whilst taking into account the needs of other cases.

In addition, the courts are undertaking a new proactive role in managing the cases in order to ensure that the overriding objective is complied with. The management process of the courts will include encouraging the parties to use ADR, identify the main issues at an early stage, make appropriate use of IT, attempt to deal with the case without requiring the parties to attend court if possible and ensure the matter proceeds as fast as is sensibly possible. More importantly, a party who engages in gamesmanship which the court considers is other than in accordance with the overriding objective risks incurring severe cost penalties.

The court's general management powers are set out in Part 3 and are wide ranging. Unlike the old rules the court is now expected to be proactive and may therefore exercise any of its powers on his own initiative. In addition, time limits are to be strictly adhered to. Under the old system parties were not penalised for missing dates established by the courts. However, under the new rules sanctions apply should a party fail to meet a court designated time limit. If a party is unable to comply then it must apply to the court for relief from the sanction before the time limit expires.

### *The litigation track*

Cases are categorised under three main tracks:

- small claims track;
- fast track;
- multi-track.

The court considers the statement of case of the parties and allocates the cases to a particular track. To a large extent this is based on the value of the case.

#### 1. Small claims track

Referral to the small claims track will be automatic. The small claims track deals with cases with a financial value not exceeding £5,000. Personal injury claims of less than £5,000 will also be assigned to the small track providing that the element of the claim which represents pain and suffering and loss of amenity does not exceed a £1,000. In addition, claims for residential housing disrepair where a cost of the repairs is less than £1,000 will again be assigned to the small claims track.

#### 2. The fast track

The fast track deals with claims which exceed £5,000 but are less than £15,000. Generally the hearing will last for less than one day, involve only one expert with standard directions and fixed costs. Once the case has been assigned to the fast track the court will set a timetable taking the case to trial, which will not normally be more than 30 weeks from the date on which the court sets the directions.

### 3. The multi-track

Cases exceeding £15,000 in value would generally be assigned to the multi-track. Clearly, most construction cases will be assigned to the multi-track and will be transferred to the TCC. The court will use it's proactive management power together with directions which establish clear deadlines act by designated sanctions in order to manage and progress the case.

The Official Referees who sit in the TCC already use a wide variety of mechanisms to proactively manage their cases. For example, the ORs regularly hold pre-trial reviews in order to establish directions specific to the case in hand. Further examples include time saving written procedures, meetings with the parties in order to discuss the manner in which the trial will take place and a high level of computerisation.

## Track allocation

The financial value of the case is the main factor in allocating a case to a particular track. However, other factors are considered:

- the nature of the remedy;
- the complexity of the case;
- the value of any counterclaim;
- the requirement of oral evidence;
- the importance of the claim to the parties;
- the importance of the claim to non-party and public interest;
- the views of the parties; and
- the parties' circumstances.

Cases which do not have a financial value such as injunctions will be allocated to a track according to their complexity. A judge may also award more than £15,000 if s/he considers that the claim is worth more than £15,000.

The parties are required to complete an allocation questionnaire. The questionnaire provides the parties with an opportunity to request a particular track, state how many experts and witnesses of fact they intend to call. The questionnaire also establishes whether the parties have complied with a pre-actioned protocol and provides the parties with an opportunity to state the case in order to pursue the ADR.

## *Commencing proceedings*

The distinction of commencing proceedings in the High Court and the county court under the old system no longer applies. A single system based on the old High Court procedure has been adopted by the CPR. The plaintiff commences proceedings by issuing and serving a claim form which need not contain details of the claim. The plaintiff then files a separate particulate of claim detailing the claim. The person bringing the action is called the "claimant" and the responding party the "defendant".

This system means that a claimant can issue a claim form in order to stop any relevant limitation period expiring. Once the claim form is issued then the claimant has four months (six months for service out of jurisdiction) within which to serve the claim form from the defendant. The particulars of claim together with a blank form for the defence must be served within a maximum of 14 days after the service of the claim form.

The defence form provides the defendant with opportunity to:

- admit the claim;
- defend; or
- merely acknowledge service of the claim form.

The defendant has 14 days in which to file the defence. If the defendant merely acknowledges service then he has 28 days from the service of the particulars of claim in order to file a defence.

It is often suggested that the threat of litigation is enough to broker a settlement.

### *The statement of truth*

Either the claim form or the particulars of claim form must state that the claimant believes the facts are true. The claimant or the legal representative signing on the claimant's behalf must certify that the contents of the claim are true. If the facts are untrue then the claimant or the legal representative will be in contempt. Statements of truth are used widely throughout the new CPR, for example, in witness statements, expert reports, and further and better particulars, etc.

If a defendant wishes to deny allegations in the claim then he must give reasons for that denial. In addition, if a defendant does not agree with the claimant's version of events then the defendant must state his version stating why it is different.

The claimant need not reply to the defence and the lack of a reply is not taken as an admission. However, the claimant must respond to any issues raised in the defence which were not contained in the particulars of claim.

The defendant may choose to make a counterclaim when serving the defence. The claimant is not required to acknowledge service of a counterclaim but merely to serve a defence. In addition, third party claims for contributions or indemnities may also be issued.

### *Default judgments*

Default judgment means that a party can obtain judgment without trial. A claimant can obtain judgment when the defendant has either failed to acknowledge a service or failed to file the defence. If the claim was for a specific sum then judgment in default can be obtained by filing a request for judgment form. If the sum is unliquidated then the court will assess the damages.

The court may set aside judgment and default if the defendant can show that he has a defence with a real prospect of success or that there is some other good reason why the defendant should be allowed to defend.

### Interlocutory applications

A party may make an interlocutory application to the court by serving an application notice. Lord Woolf's intention to discourage parties from making these applications, and proactive case management of the court should reduce the need for parties to make interlocutory applications. Unlike the old system, interlocutory hearings will be held in public. In addition, witness statements will be used to support interlocutory applications other than the old style affidavits.

### Summary judgment

Summary judgment provides a method for the claimant to obtain judgment if the defendant is unable to show that he has a meritorious defence with a real prospect of success. Under the old system the defendant merely needed to show that there was a triable issue. It was therefore difficult for claimants to obtain summary judgment.

The new system makes it a lot more difficult for defendants to defeat an application for summary judgment. On the other hand, a defendant may use summary judgment against a claimant where the defendant considers that the claimant has no real prospect of succeeding with the claim.

### Disclosure

The discovery of documents relating to the litigation has now been replaced by a system of disclosure. Standard disclosure requires a party to disclose:

- documents upon which it intends to rely;
- documents which adversely affect its case;
- documents which adversely affect the case of another party; and
- documents which support the party's case.

The new rules are attempting to dispense with extensive discovery and the high costs associated with considering all documents relevant to the case

Parties are expected to make a reasonable search for documents using resources which are proportional to the case.

### Experts

Experts have been criticised for readily supporting their client's case rather than providing an unbiased opinion upon which the court can rely. Part 35 of the CPR clearly states that an expert's primary and overriding duty is to the court rather than the person from whom he receives instructions. In addition, Woolf is encouraging the use of court appointed experts in order to further reduce this problem, reduce time taken at trial and reduce costs.

### The Technology and Construction Court

The Technology and Construction Court (TCC), like the Official Referees' courts before it, is the specialist court of the construction industry, because civil engineering and building disputes form a significant part of its work.

The types of claim which it may be appropriate to bring in the TCC include:

(1) building and other construction disputes, including claims for the enforcement of adjudicators' decisions under the HGCRA;
(2) engineering disputes;
(3) claims by and against engineers, architects, surveyors, accountants and other specialised advisers relating to the services they provide;
(4) claims by and against local authorities relating to their statutory duties concerning the development of land or the construction of buildings;
(5) claims relating to the environment, for example, pollution cases; and
(6) challenges to decisions of arbitrators in construction and engineering disputes, including applications for permission to appeal, and appeals.

All claims allocated to the TCC are assigned to the multi-track: see CPR Rule 60.6(1). The case will be assigned to a named TCC judge, who will have primary responsibility for the case management of that case, and who, subject to the exigencies of the list, will be the trial judge.

There are full time TCC judges at Birmingham, Liverpool, London and Salford, and part-time TCC judges (in the sense that they take TCC work as and when required) in a number of courts in other parts of the country.

Proceedings cannot usually be instituted in the TCC without first complying with the requirements of the pre-action protocol for construction and engineering disputes (see below).

Where a claim has been allocated to the TCC either on issue or by transfer from another court, the TCC will fix the first case management conference within 14 days of the earliest of the filing by the defendant of an acknowledgment of service, or the filing of a defence, or the date of an order transferring the claim to the TCC.

The TCC will send the parties' representatives a case management directions form; the parties are encouraged to try to agree the directions, which will then be approved by the court, if suitable. The directions will usually include the fixing of the date for the trial of the case or of any other preliminary issue that it orders to be tried. The trial of a preliminary issue or of some other severable part of the case often leads to the disposal of the whole case; efficient case management can favour the making of such orders, particularly in complex litigation of the kind that is tried in the TCC. The court will also investigate the possibility of splitting the trial into separate parts; preparation of quantum issues for trial is often wasteful and inefficient unless and until there has been a decision on liability.

The court will want to know whether the parties wish there to be a stay of proceedings to enable them to try to settle the case by negotiations or by some other form of alternative dispute resolution procedure (ADR). The court is obliged by CPR Part 1.4(1) to further the overriding objective by "active case management". CPR Part 1.4(2)(e) defines this as including "encouraging the parties to use an alternative dispute resolution procedure if the court considers that appropriate and facilitating the use of such procedure". The court may therefore include in the programme of preparation for trial a short period of stay of the proceedings for ADR to take place.

The facility for a without prejudice, non-binding, early neutral evaluation (ENE) by a TCC judge of a dispute, or of particular issues in it, may be available in appropriate cases. The approval of the judge in charge of the list must be obtained before any ENE is undertaken. If the parties suggest it, and the judge considers that an ENE is likely to assist the parties in the resolution of the dispute, or particular issues in it, he may offer to provide that evaluation himself or to arrange for another judge to do so. If the parties accept, then directions will be given for the ENE. Where an ENE is provided by a judge, that judge will, unless the parties otherwise agree, take no further part in the case.

Another question that will be addressed by the court at the first case management conference is expert evidence. The parties will be expected to apply the provisions of CPR Part 35. Expert evidence must be restricted to that which is reasonably required to resolve the proceedings. The overriding duty of the expert is to help the court on matters within his expertise. The following points should be noted:

(1) In deciding whether to give permission for an expert to give evidence, the court will require to be satisfied that:

   (a) the issues to which that evidence will go are a proper subject for expert evidence; and
   (b) expert evidence from the proposed witness is justified, having regard to the overriding objective.

   Parties sometimes need permission to adduce expert evidence on issues which are either not the proper subject for expert evidence at all, or where the issues are peripheral to the central questions in the case.

(2) The court will exercise rigorous control over the number of experts on whose evidence the parties may rely.
(3) Where the court gives permission to the parties to adduce expert evidence, it will usually specify the issues to which their evidence may relate. If an expert's report goes beyond that permission, the offending parts of the report are not likely to be admitted in evidence and costs sanctions are likely to follow.
(4) The court will also want to explore with the parties at the first case management conference the possibility of making a direction for the use of single joint experts under CPR Part 35.7. The CPR do not specify the criteria for making such a direction; the court will, however, tend to favour the giving of such a direction in relation to issues which do not rely at the heart of the case and/or which are relatively uncontroversial and/or where the cost of expert evidence is disproportionate to the sum at stake in the case. Where the use of a single joint expert is contemplated, the court will expect the parties to cooperate in developing and agreeing, so far as possible, the terms of reference for the expert. In default of agreement, the court will define the terms of reference. In most cases, the terms of reference will detail what the expert is asked to do, identify any documentary material he is asked to consider and specify any assumptions he is asked to make.

At the first case management conference, the court will also usually deal with the question of witness statements, disclosure of documents, whether to make any order for the carrying out of inspections, a site view and the use of IT—the parties should carefully consider how the burden of preparing documents can be reduced by cooperation and the use of IT and in the TCC the IT protocol produced by the Technology and Construction Solicitors Association is often useful.

Usually, it will not be necessary to hold a further case management conference.

At the pre-trial review, the court will look at whether the previous directions have all been complied with and, if not, why not and, where necessary, will give any further directions that are required to ensure that the case will be ready to start on the day fixed for trial. The court will also give directions for the conduct of the hearing itself, including the preparation of the trial bundles, the service and lodging of opening statements, chronologies, copies of authorities and pre-trial reading lists for the judge, the use of technology, the timetable, etc.

It should be noted that TCC judges are also entitled to act as arbitrators, under s. 93(1) of the Arbitration Act 1996, which provides that he may "if in all the circumstances he thinks fit, accept appointment as a sole arbitrator or as an umpire by or by virtue of an arbitration agreement". A TCC judge cannot accept such an appointment unless the Lord Chief Justice "has informed him that, having regard to the state of (TCC) business, he can be made available": see s. 93(3).

Application should be made in the first instance to the judge who is wanted as arbitrator; if he is willing to accept the appointment, he will make the necessary application to the Lord Chief Justice for his approval. The rules governing the arbitration will be decided at the preliminary hearing, when appropriate directions will be given.

## *The pre-action protocol for construction and engineering disputes*

The protocol applies to all construction and engineering disputes, including professional negligence claims against architects, engineers and quantity surveyors.

A claimant will be required to comply with the protocol unless the proposed proceedings (i) are for the enforcement of an adjudicator's decision under the HGCRA, (ii) include a claim for interim injunctive relief, (iii) will be the subject of a claim for summary judgment, or (iv) relate to the same, or substantially the same, issues as have been the subject of recent adjudication under the HGCRA or some other formal ADR procedure.

The objectives of the protocol are:

(1) to encourage the exchange of early and full information about the prospective legal claims;
(2) to enable parties to avoid litigation by agreeing a settlement of the claim before commencement of proceedings; and
(3) to support the efficient management of proceedings where litigation cannot be avoided.

The general aim of the protocol is to ensure that before court proceedings commence:

(1) the claimant and the defendant have provided sufficient information for each party to know the nature of the other's case;
(2) each party has had an opportunity to consider the other's case and to accept or reject all or any part of the case made against him at the earliest possible stage;
(3) there is more pre-action contact between the parties;
(4) better and earlier exchange of information occurs;
(5) there is better pre-action investigation by the parties;
(6) the parties have met formally on at least one occasion with a view to defining and agreeing the issues between them, and exploring possible ways by which the claim may be resolved;

(7) the parties are in a position where they may be able to settle cases early and fairly without recourse to litigation; and
(8) proceedings will be conducted efficiently if litigation does become necessary.

The first step in the protocol is for the claimant, prior to commencing proceedings, to send to each proposed defendant a copy of a letter of claim which sets out:

(1) a clear summary of the facts on which each claim is based;
(2) the basis on which each claim is made, identifying the principal contractual terms and statutory provisions relied upon;
(3) the nature of the relief claimed: if damages are claimed, a breakdown showing how the damages have been quantified; if a sum is claimed pursuant to a contract, how it has been calculated; if an extension of time is claimed, the period claimed;
(4) where a claim has been made previously and rejected by the defendant, and the claimant is able to identify the reason(s) for such rejection, the claimant's grounds of belief as to why the claim was wrongly rejected; and
(5) the names of any experts already instructed by the claimant on whose evidence he intends to rely, identifying the issues to which that evidence will be directed.

Within 14 calendar days of receipt of the letter of claim, the defendant should acknowledge its receipt in writing. If there has been no acknowledgment by or on behalf of the defendant within 14 days, the claimant will be entitled to commence proceedings without further compliance with the protocol.

If the defendant intends to object to all or any part of the claimant's claim on the grounds that:

(1) the court lacks jurisdiction,
(2) the matter should be referred to arbitration, or
(3) the defendant named in the letter is the wrong defendant,

then that objection should be raised within 28 days after receipt of the letter of claim.

Otherwise, the defendant shall within 28 days from the date of receipt of the letter of claim, or such other period as the parties may reasonably agree (up to a maximum of four months), send a letter of response to the claimant, identifying:

(1) the facts set out in the letter of claim which are agreed or not agreed, and if not agreed, the basis of the disagreement;
(2) which claims are accepted and which are rejected, and if rejected, the basis of the rejection;

(3) whether the defendant intends to make a counterclaim, and if so, giving the information which is required to be given in a letter of claim;
(4) the names of any experts already instructed on whose evidence it is intended to rely, identifying the issues to which that evidence will be directed.

If no response is received by the claimant within the 28-day period, or such other period as has been agreed, the claimant shall be entitled to institute proceedings without further compliance with the protocol.

The claimant shall provide a response to any counterclaim within the equivalent period allowed to the defendant to respond to the letter of claim. As soon as possible after exchange of these various letters of claim/response/reply to counterclaim, the parties should normally meet.

This meeting is referred to as the pre-action meeting; its aim is for the parties to agree what are the main issues in the case, to identify the root cause of disagreement in respect of each issue, and to consider (i) whether, and if so how, the issues might be resolved without recourse to litigation, and (ii) if litigation is unavoidable, what steps should be taken to ensure that it is conducted in accordance with the overriding objective of CPR Part 1.1.

The court will normally expect that those attending the pre-action meeting will include a representative of each party who has authority to settle or recommend settlement of the dispute, a legal representative of each party, if one has been instructed, and a representative of a party's insurer, where the involvement of insurers has been disclosed.

If the parties are unable to agree on a means of resolving the dispute other than by litigation, they should try to agree:

(a) whether, if there is any area where expert evidence is likely to be required, a joint expert may be appointed, and if so, who that should be, and (so far as is practicable)
(b) the extent of disclosure of documents with a view to saving costs; and
(c) the conduct of the litigation with the aim of minimising costs and delay.

Any party who attended a pre-action meeting is permitted to disclose to the court:

(1) that the meeting took place, when and who attended;
(2) the identity of any party who refused to attend, and the grounds for such refusal;
(3) if the meeting did not take place, why not; and
(4) any agreements concluded between the parties.

Except as set out immediately above, everything said at the pre-action meeting is otherwise to be treated as "without prejudice"

## HYBRID AND PROJECT-BASED DISPUTE RESOLUTION

### *Hybrid and multi-stage techniques*

This section considers "hybrid" variations to the core processes, together with a range of "multi-stage" procedures. A variety of dispute resolution and conflict avoidance mechanisms are explored. Approaches such as the DRA and DRB seek to deal with conflict early on and avoid the formation of full-blown disputes. Mini-trial is a hybrid ADR technique. Multi-stage procedures are also considered.

### *Agreements to negotiate and the approach of the courts*

The starting point is the use of an "amicable" dispute resolution clause. In the international construction arena, the FIDIC form of contract for civil engineering and construction works introduced the concept of amicable settlement as a prerequisite to arbitration. This clause was introduced in the 1987 Fourth Edition to the FIDIC "Red Book" (Clause 67.2) as follows:

> "Where Notice of Intention to Commence Arbitration as to a dispute has been given in accordance with sub-clause 67.1, arbitration of such dispute shall not be commenced unless an attempt has first been made by the parties to settle such dispute amicably. Provided that, unless the parties otherwise agree, arbitration may be commenced on or after the 56th day after the day on which Notice of Intention to Commence Arbitration of such dispute was given, whether or not any attempt at an amicable settlement thereof has been made."

Until recently the enforceability of such agreements to negotiate was in some doubt. However, since the 1992 House of Lords' decision in *Walford* v. *Miles* [1992] 1 All E.R. 453 it is clear that an agreement to negotiate is not enforceable in law. The case related to the sale of a photographic processing business and the central issue related to the enforceability of a contract to negotiate based on a "lock out" agreement. A lock out agreement is an agreement not to negotiate with any other parties whilst negotiations are continuing with one specific party. In *Walford* v. *Miles* the vendors decided to sell the business and received an offer from a third party. At the same time they entered into negotiations with an alternative purchaser and agreed in principle to sell the business and premises for £2m.

It was further agreed that if the purchaser provided a comfort letter from their bank the vendors would terminate negotiations with any third party. In disregard of this agreement the vendors withdrew from negotiations and in fact sold to a third party. The proposed purchasers brought an action for breach of the lock out agreement on the basis that they had been given an exclusive opportunity to agree terms with the vendors and that this was collateral to the subject to contract negotiations.

The House of Lords held that a lock out agreement could constitute an enforceable agreement. However, an agreement merely to negotiate in good faith for an unspecified period of time was not enforceable. On this basis their agreement was unenforceable. The court concluded that if such an agreement were enforceable the purchaser would not know when he was entitled to withdraw from the negotiations and it was not possible for the court to decide whether an "excuse" for terminating negotiations by one party was reasonable.

The approach of the English Courts could be contrasted with the approach of Giles J. in the Australian case of *Hooper Bailie Associated Limited* v. *Natcom Group Pty Limited* (unreported, 12 April 1992). In that case Giles J. made a clear distinction between the enforceability of the agreement to reach some sort of result and the agreement to participate in the process:

> "Conciliation or mediation is essentially consensual, and the opponents of enforceability contend that it is futile to seek to enforce something which requires the consent of a party when cooperation and consent cannot be enforced; equally they say that there can be no loss to the other party if for want of cooperation and consent the consensual process would have led to no result . . . What is enforced is not cooperation or consent, but participation in a process from which cooperation and consent might come."

During the course of the judgment Giles J. considered several important issues concerning the enforceability of ADR clauses. First Giles J. considered the case of *Allco Steel (Queensland) Pty Limited* v. *Torres Strait Gold Pty Limited* (unreported, 12 March 1990). In that case the court found that a conciliation clause could not operate as a precondition to litigation. Some emphasis was placed on the proposition that an ADR clause is unenforceable because it seeks to oust the jurisdiction of the court. Second, the judge accepted that conciliation was futile due to the apparently entrenched and opposing positions of the parties.

Third, the judge considered that an ADR clause was an agreement to negotiate and such an agreement is unenforceable as it lacks the certainty required to create legally binding relations. This reasoning is not only based on the House of Lords' decision in the *Walford* case but also on the New South Wales Court of Appeal decision in *Coal Cliff Collieries Pty Limited* v. *Sijehame Pty Limited* (1992) 24 N.S.W. L.R. 1.

Nonetheless Giles J. in *Hooper Bailie* made a clear distinction between a contract to negotiate and a contract to conciliate or mediate. He held that provided the mediation or conciliation process had sufficient procedural certainty then it would be enforced. It is important to note that the judge did not impose an obligation to compromise any of the issues but merely that the parties would conduct the conciliation in good faith. In many respects the House of Lords' decision in *Channel Tunnel Group Limited* v. *Balfour Beatty Limited* and the Commercial Court Practice Directions suggest that the court may well support a conciliation or mediation prerequisite provided that the process is carried out during a defined time scale and the rules of the process are sufficiently clear.

## *Hybrid techniques*

### Facilitated negotiation

According to Berman (1996) facilitated negotiation "is the introduction of an independent and objective person into your negotiation obsessions to assist and expedite the parties in reaching agreement. The purpose of this neutral is to advance the discussions by ensuring mutual understanding of the parties' positions and to extract settlement strategies, not unlike a mediator. However, 'mediation' is an altogether different process". Berman maintains that the focus of facilitated negotiation is somewhat different to mediation.

Apparently the goal of the facilitator is centred on aiding communication between the parties whilst the focus of a mediator is to reach settlement. Further, the facilitator does not caucus with the parties separately and "never renders an opinion or judgement". One might conclude that facilitated negotiation is a form of supported negotiation developed under the ADR umbrella, and it is something less than mediation.

### Med-Arb

Med-Arb is essentially a hybrid ADR two-stage process. In the first stage the parties attempt to settle their dispute amicably in the forum of mediation. If settlement cannot be found then the parties move to the second stage; arbitration. The essential characteristic of this technique is that the mediator in the first stage becomes the arbitrator for the final and binding stage. The commitment by the parties to use this process may arise either through the contract in the form of a multi-stage dispute resolution clause or alternatively the parties may agree to bind themselves to Med-Arb once a dispute has arisen.

The apparent advantages of Med-Arb are that it combines the benefits and possibility of a mediated settlement with the finality of arbitration. As Newman, *et al* (1999) points out:

> "Med-Arb recognises that arbitration may not resolve all the issues between the parties but limits the arbitration solely to the intractable disputes, thereby bringing a cost and time saving to the parties."

Some commentators have expressed their concerns over such a procedure. Is it not the case that Med-Arb compromises the intermediary's capacity to act, initially as a facilitative mediator and then in an adjudicative capacity, without restricting the flow of information? The fundamental objection to such an approach is that the parties will not wish to reveal confidential information during private sessions with the mediator which may then taint the mediator/arbitrators' view of their during the arbitration. One barrister commented:

> "I do not see Med-Arb working in the way you describe it, if the parties do not reveal their true position to the mediator then there is little chance of reaching a settlement and more chance that the mediator will have to assume the role of an arbitrator."

## Mini trial or executive tribunal

According to Siedel (1992), the use of mini trials to resolve construction disputes is currently a new and developing phenomenon. Apparently the mini trial originated in 1994 when Telly Credit took action against TRW, claiming an infringement on its patent rights. The action proceeded over a period of approximately two and a half years and during this time the parties exchanged around 100,000 documents as part of the discovery process. In a bid to conclude the dispute, the parties agreed to an alternative process in order to resolve their dispute.

The lawyers for each party were given a limited time (four hours each) in which to present their case to the senior executives of each company. The executives had authority to settle the dispute. Following the presentations, a further two-hour time period was provided in order for the other side to reply and for a counter to the reply. The entire process lasted for two days. This meeting was moderated, or facilitated, by a neutral third party who in this case was a retired judge with patent law expertise. In the event that the parties could not settle he had agreed to provide a non-binding opinion. Apparently the executives were able to resolve the dispute in around half an hour of private meetings upon the conclusion of the presentations.

The process which later became known as the mini trial can lead to savings in time and money. In addition, Siedel points out that there are two major benefits to this approach. First, high ranking officials from each company are given an opportunity to hear both sides' arguments. Second, the executives are then able to meet and discuss settlement without being constrained by legal remedies which assume that there will be a winner and a loser.

Very few real experiences of executive tribunal have occurred. Those that have relate to major projects. Many in the industry are confused about the process, believing that it relates to site negotiations which had reached the point where company executives become involved. Executive tribunals are managed mediation based processes.

## Expert determination

Expert determination is a process by which the parties to a dispute instruct a third party to decide a particular issue. The third party is selected because of his or her particular expertise in relation to the issues between the parties. According to Kendal (1996):

> "There is nothing very new about expert determination. It has been a feature of English commercial and legal practice for at least 250 years. What is new about it is that it is being called in to help with the current crisis in commercial dispute resolution. Expert determination is a simple procedure by which valuation and technical issues are referred to a suitably qualified professional to determine 'acting as an expert and not as an arbitrator' . . . Unlike alternative dispute resolution (ADR), expert determination guarantees a result which is final and binding."

Expert determination is essentially a creature of contract. The parties to a contract agree that some third party will decide a technical or valuation issue between the parties. Expert determination has traditionally been used in rent reviews. According to Kendal approximately half of all commercial leases contain a provision for rent review by a surveyor acting as an expert whilst the other half state that the surveyor is to act as an arbitrator. Nonetheless expert determination is not restricted to mere land valuations.

The technique lends itself to valuation and complex technical issues. In this respect expert determination may be found in a wide variety of circumstances: valuing shares in private companies, certifying profits or losses of a company during sale and purchase, valuing pension rights on transfer, determining market values in long term agreements. Further, the use of expert determination may be used as part of a multi stage dispute resolution procedure. In this instance some technical matter may be referred to an expert leaving the other issues in dispute to arbitration or litigation.

*A creature of contract*

A typical expert determination clause should ensure that specific items are clearly dealt with. First, the issue or issues to be determined should be clearly and precisely expressed. Lack of clarity in relation to the issue to be determined may provide an opportunity to argue subsequently about the jurisdiction of the expert. Second, it is important to state that the expert is to act as an expert and not as an arbitrator. Much of the case law in the area of expert determination focuses on this point. If the third party is acting as an expert, then his or her opinion as to the value or opinion of the correct decision in relation to the issue in dispute is not capable of being challenged. On the other hand, if the third party is acting as an arbitrator, then the formalities of an adjudicative procedure must be adhered to.

Third, a further essential feature of expert determination is that the decision should be final and binding. On the other hand adjudication and decisions of dispute review boards are often expressed as final unless challenged by a subsequent arbitration.

*Finality*

Finality is a common feature of expert determination. The contractual machinery should provide some mechanism for appointment of an appropriate expert. This would usually provide for appointment by agreement between the parties or in default by some appointing authority stated in the contract. The default procedure will ensure that an expert is appointed regardless of the strategies associated with the other party. In addition, it is beneficial to include express provisions in relation to the expert's qualifications and state how the expert is to be paid. These are usually split equally between the parties with a further provision allowing the expert to decide otherwise.

The leading case in this area is *Jones* v. *Sherwood Computer Services Plc* [1992] 1 W.L.R. 277. This case involved a sale and purchase agreement where part of the consideration was to be deferred. The valuation of this deferred consideration depended upon the acquired company's sales figures exceeding a certain level. If the vendor and purchaser's accountants were unable to agree this figure then a third accountant was to determine the figure as expert. The vendor's and purchaser's accountants could not agree on the categories of transactions which should be included as sales.

Coopers & Lybrand were appointed as the expert firm who determined that the sales amounted to £2,527,135. The vendor was not satisfied and wished to challenge the reasoning behind the determination. The Court of Appeal stated that the expert had been asked to determine the level of sales and that is exactly what they had done. On the other hand, if the expert departed from their instructions—for example, by valuing shares in the wrong company —then that would be sufficient to upset an expert's decision. *Jones* v. *Sherwood* suggests then that an expert would need to make some manifest mistake in relation to its jurisdiction before the court would intervene.

*Nikko Hotels (UK) Limited* v. *NEPC Plc* [1991] 2 E.G. 86 considers the expert's jurisdiction in relation to points of law. If the expert had answered the wrong question, then his decision would be a nullity. On the other hand, if the expert had answered the right question but in the wrong way the decision would still be binding.

More recently the House of Lords considered expert determination in the case of *Mercury Communications Limited* v. *Director General of Telecommunications and Another* [1996] 1 All E.R. 575. In that case two companies, BT and Mercury, were granted licences to run telecommunication systems under s. 7 of the Telecommunications Act 1984. Clause 29 of the Agreement provided for a review of the Terms of the Agreement after five years. If either party was unable to agree to any fundamental changes of the Terms then a reference was to be made to the Director General of Telecommunications for the determination of any particular issue. An issue in relation to pricing was referred to the Director General. Mercury challenged the Director General's decision on the basis that he had misinterpreted the costs to be taken into account when setting the price.

Initially, the Director General applied to strike the action out on the basis that the action was an abuse of process. The Director General argued that as the Agreement was formed under the Telecommunications Act 1984 any determinations of the Director General were in the domain of public law and should therefore be subject to judicial review and not a private action. The House of Lords held that as the dispute related to a contractual matter (albeit by way of a statutory power) then an action in private law was appropriate. In relation to the exercise of that decision making function the House of Lords decided that they ultimately had jurisdiction to interpret the construction of the clause. They went on to say that provided the expert does not depart from his/her instructions then the decision cannot be challenged unless there is some allegation of fraud.

> **Case study (expert determination)—containing the cost**
>
> A branch director for a services sub-contractor reported on a positive experience with expert determination, which arose from a bespoke management contract. The work related to a private new commercial development with a value of around £200,000. The amount in dispute was £60,000. The technique was used because it had been included in the contract. The dispute centred on project delays and payment issues. The respondent considered that the attitude of the parties was key to the positive experience and considered that expert determination proved successful because it kept the costs to a minimum and also helped to preserve communication between the parties. In relation to cost, the interviewee considered that the legal costs were in proportion to the claim and went on to state that by comparison, litigation or arbitration for "a relatively small sum would outweigh the base claim".

## ICE conciliation

The Institution of Civil Engineers introduced the process of conciliation in 1988 in the form of a code of procedure and a provision in the ICE Minor Works contract. Clause 11 of the Minor Works contract provided that either party could serve a "notice of dispute" on the other, and either party then has 28 days in which to refer the dispute to conciliation. If a reference is not made, then the opportunity is lost, and the dispute may only be referred to arbitration. Clause 66 of the ICE Condition of Contract 6th edition, which is for use on larger projects, provides a more sophisticated provision.

The process is essentially consensual, non-binding, confidential, without prejudice and, according to the most recent code of procedure, aimed at reaching a "settlement". This is in contrast to the earlier code which seemed to place an emphasis on the ability of the conciliator to make a recommendation in the absence of party agreement. The ability for the conciliator to make a recommendation—should the parties fail to agree—is an important and fundamental distinction which clearly places conciliation at the evaluative end of the mediation spectrum.

The more recent Design and Build version includes conciliation as a mandatory step in the resolution of disputes arising under that form of contract. The contract operates without an independent engineer and so in many respects the conciliation procedure provides an opportunity for early resolution of the dispute. It could be argued, therefore, that conciliation in this context is clearly replacing the decision making process of the engineer in respect of dispute resolution.

The conciliation process is commenced when one party serves written notice on the other. This trigger event, which is referred to as the "notice of conciliation", should be accompanied with a brief statement of the matters in dispute. If the parties have not agreed upon a conciliator then a default process is provided in the ICE procedure. Should the parties fail to agree within 14 days of the notice, either party may request the president of the ICE to appoint a conciliator. The president should appoint within 14 days of the request. If the conciliator is unable to act then a further mechanism for appointment is provided.

Once the conciliator has been appointed, the party requesting the conciliation must send copies of all relevant documents to the conciliator. Any party may furnish the conciliator with written submissions outlining their version of events and any remedies claimed. The conciliator is then given a range of powers in order to aid the parties to settlement, such as the ability to arrange joint meetings, meet and question the parties (jointly or separately), carry out site visits, etc.

One important feature is the ability to suggest solutions which are not restricted to the legal problem at hand; a commercial settlement can be reached. Once settlement is reached the conciliator may assist the parties to draft the settlement agreement, which is then binding.

Should the parties be unable to reach agreement, then the conciliator proceeds to make a recommendation on how to resolve the dispute. There are three important factors to consider when drawing up the recommendation. First, the conciliator must not disclose any information given to him in confidence during private meetings with a particular party. Second, his recommendation need not be based upon legal consideration. Third, he/she need not give reasons. Parties are usually required to pay an equal share of these costs. Once payment has been received, the conciliator delivers his recommendations.

## Dispute Resolution Adviser

The basic concept of a Dispute Resolution Adviser "DRA" involves the use of a neutral third person who advises the parties to a disagreement or dispute and suggests possible settlement options. This concept is clearly similar to that of the Early Settlement Adviser. According to Wall (1992) the idea stemmed from Clifford Evans who, in 1986, suggested the use of an "independent intervener". The independent intervener would be paid for equally by the employer and contractor to settle disputes as they emerged, rather than wait until the end of the contract. The decision would be binding until the end of the project when either party could commence arbitration proceedings. Unlike the independent intervener the DRA does not make interim binding decisions, but advises on the means by which settlement could be achieved. The power to settle ultimately rests with the parties.

There are a variety of benefits with such an approach. First, disagreements at site level can be addressed before a full-blown dispute develops. Not only does this avoid the breakdown in working relationships which could then affect the rest of the project's duration, but it also allows the issues to be dealt with whilst they are fresh in the parties' minds. Further, neither the parties nor the adviser are limited to a "legal" outcome in the sense that the settlement could encompass wider solutions mutually beneficial to the parties and the project. The disadvantage is that the parties may be unable to agree or may reject the DRA's advice. Because they are not bound by the adviser's suggestions the dispute may continue to develop.

The logical conclusion was developed by a working party of the Chartered Institute of Arbitrators, and labelled the Dispute Adviser. Severn (1989) presents the working party's two stage solution, which classifies disputes as being either "minor disputes" or "major disputes", and makes use of a dispute adviser. Minor disputes are those initial disagreements which may be dealt with by the dispute adviser, or some other expert who the parties and the adviser call in.

If a settlement is not reached or the problem continues then the minor dispute becomes a major dispute. Major disputes may be conciliated, mediated or the dispute adviser may make a recommendation. In this context conciliation refers to a purely facilitative process whilst mediation may lead to a written reasoned opinion, binding until overturned by arbitration. The dispute adviser may make a recommendation about a likely settlement which the parties could accept or reject, or alternatively help the parties to select either conciliation or mediation in order to progress the resolution of the dispute. In any event major disputes lead to a binding recommendation, rather than allowing a reticent party the opportunity of delaying payment until post completion arbitration.

Wall presents the most widely recognised use of a Dispute Resolution Adviser in practice in the form of a complete process—the DRA System. His model was first developed for use by the Hong Kong Government's Architectural Services Department in the refurbishment of the Queen Mary Hospital in Hong Kong. It is a hybrid system which builds on existing concepts. He states that the:

> "DRA system draws upon the independent intervener concept as modified by the Dispute Adviser but provides a far more flexible approach. It embodies the dispute prevention attributes of the Dispute Review Board and Project Arbitration, it uses partnering techniques to re-orient the parties' thinking and encourages negotiation by using a tiered dispute resolution process. It is based on giving the parties maximum control through the use of mediation techniques but also includes prompt short-form arbitration which encourages voluntary settlement and, if necessary, provides a final and binding resolution to the dispute."

The complete process has several distinct stages. First, at the commencement of the project the DRA undertakes partnering styled activities in order to build a rapport with the parties whilst at the same time encouraging the parties to work as a team. Second, the DRA will then visit the site on a regular basis in order to maintain a level of familiarity with the project and its participants.

This also provides the opportunity for the DRA to assist in the settlement of any disagreements which may have arisen since the last visit.

Disagreement

↓

Partnering and informal dispute resolution activities

↓

Formal dispute

↓

Good faith negotiations with site personnel without the DRA

↓

"Notice of Dispute"

↓

DRA and site personnel attempt to resolve dispute

↓

"DRA's report"

↓

Senior management meeting

↓

Short form arbitration

↓

Arbitration

*Figure 2: Outline of the DRA system, adapted from Wall, C.*

The third distinct stage of the DRA's work relates to formal disputes. The contract provides a time limit of 28 days within which any decisions or certificates issued under the contract may be challenged. If a decision or certificate is not challenged then it becomes final and binding. In the event of a challenge, the parties have 28 days within which to try and resolve the matter by direct negotiations. If unsuccessful the aggrieved party is required to issue a formal notice of dispute within the 28-day period, otherwise the right to challenge is lost. It is most likely that the DRA will have tried to facilitate the early settlement of such disputes, but in the event that a notice of dispute is issued then the DRA and the site representatives have 14 days to attempt to resolve the dispute.

During this period the DRA may try almost anything to resolve the dispute, from mediation to calling in an expert in the particular area if the problem proves to be beyond his/her expertise. The important point is that any evaluation is carried out by another neutral third party and not the DRA. By maintaining a purely facilitative role the DRA does not jeopardise the impartial and neutral position which he/she has developed with the parties. Time limits may be extended under certain circumstances and the process comes to an end in the event of a successful settlement or resolution. The parties could agree on a settlement or they may agree to be bound by an expert's opinion.

The fourth stage relates to disputes which have not been settled at site level. The DRA produces a report which outlines the nature of the disputes and each party's viewpoint; this may contain a non-binding recommendation or evaluation of the dispute. The site representatives are given an opportunity to check the accuracy of the report and comment. This provides an important chance for the individual disputants to review their position before the report is passed to senior management. Senior management should be able to obtain a clear picture of the nature of the dispute and bring a non-emotional perspective to the problem. The DRA may continue to facilitate the resolution of the dispute at senior management level.

At the fifth stage, if the matter remains unresolved 14 days after the DRA's report, then a short-form arbitration may be employed. This should take place within 28 days from termination of the senior management's efforts. An arbitrator is selected by the parties or if they cannot agree, then the DRA will select an arbitrator. The contract provides the rules for the short-form arbitration which include the following key elements:

- one issue or a limited number of issues, conducted in one day per issue;
- each party is given the opportunity to present;
- each party to have an equal amount of time;
- the arbitrator has seven days to make a written award which is final and binding; and
- disputes over time or money are resolved using final offer arbitration where the arbitrator must select one or the other figure.

According to Wall (1994), the Queen Mary Hospital project has raised "numerous problems yet there have been no disputes". The Architectural Services Department has used the DRA on other large projects and apparently now ensures that the system is used on all building projects with a value in excess of HK$200 million.

### *Project mediation*

The construction industry benefits from a wide range of dispute resolution techniques. The traditional processes of arbitration and litigation have in part made way for mediation and more recently adjudication under the Housing Grants, Construction and Regeneration Act 1996. Mediation has developed slowly since around the start of the 1990s. Hybrid and multi-stage processes such as dispute review boards or dispute escalation clauses have become more widely used on some projects. At the other end of the scale management techniques such as partnering are attempts to avoid disputes arising.

"Contracted mediation" or "project mediation" attempts to fuse team building, dispute avoidance and dispute resolution in one procedure. A project mediation panel is appointed at the outset of the project. The impartial project mediation panel consists of one lawyer and one commercial expert who are both trained mediators. The panel assists in organising and attends an initial meeting at the start of the project and may conduct one or more workshops at the outset of the project or during the course of the project as necessary.

The panel may also visit the project periodically during the life of the project. In this respect the panel therefore has a working knowledge of the project and more importantly the individuals working on that project. That knowledge allows the panel to resolve differences before they escalate, because the panel provides an immediate forum for the confidential discussion and potential mediation of differences or disputes. Experiences with project mediation in practice are limited. However, project mediation was apparently used on Jersey Airport.

The only publicly reported project where project mediation has been used was Jersey Airport taxiway. The contract sum was approximately £15m, and the project mediation panel cost approximately £15,000. According to the article in *Construction Manager* a variety of disputes were resolved and the project finished one day ahead of schedule and approximately £800,000 below budget. Much of the project's success has been attributed to the use of the contracted mediation process.

The parties to the construction contract have recognised that there is a risk that they might have disputes during the course of the building work but they have also recognised that a standing mediation panel can help to avoid those disputes during the course of the work. This is because the parties to the construction contract will get to know the individual mediators, and those mediators will not only have an understanding of the project, but will get to know the individuals working on the project. There is, therefore, the potential for the project mediation panel to become involved not just in disputes, but also in the avoidance of disputes before the parties become entrenched and turn to adjudication, arbitration or litigation.

The experience at Jersey raises an important observation and that is the amount of the contract sum by comparison to the cost of the contracted mediation process. Most of the structured ADR procedures such as dispute review boards are only economically viable because they are used on substantial projects. This is because of the costs associated with establishing and running a three-man dispute review board. A dispute review board is established at the start of the project, and then follows the project by making site visits. Disputes are then referred to that board, which will make recommendations only or binding decisions depending upon the drafting of the contract between the contractor and the employer.

However, a project mediation panel is viable for projects with a much lower contract sum. Statistics indicate that around 80% of construction work carried out in this country has a contract sum in £10s of millions rather than £100s of millions. Therefore, project mediation has the potential for use on around 80% of the construction projects carried out in this country.

One of the authors of this chapter (N. Gould) has worked as a project mediator. The project concerned a large hospital development in the south east of the UK. Work commenced in the summer of 2002. It is, of course, too early to say whether the process should be adopted for many more projects. However, the feedback from the author's involvement was positive, and a variety of issues were explored and resolved through the panel.

## *Dispute Review Boards ("DRBs")*

The concept of the Dispute Review Board "DRB" appears to have developed in the USA. It is essentially a process where an independent board of three people evaluates disputes as they arise during the project and make settlement recommendations to the parties. The board is constituted at the commencement of the project, much like a panel of three arbitrators. Each party selects one board member. The parties may then agree on the third or, if they fail to do so, the two board members will select the third. The board periodically visits the site and receives project information to ensure familiarity with the project and the parties. The board meets regularly to discuss problems or disputes, hears presentations from the parties and suggests solutions.

It seems that the main benefit of the DRB is that its mere existence helps to prevent disputes. The parties themselves become familiar with the board's view on particular issues which then aids the negotiation and settlement process which the parties undertake before presenting their dispute to the board. The main disadvantage is the cost of such a system. The non-binding nature also implies a risk that disputes may not settle, and may therefore fester and disrupt the project. The board evaluates the disputes, and there is a danger that one party may perceive that the board is biased if a series of evaluations run contrary to that party's expectations.

### Dispute boards

The use of the term "Dispute Boards" or occasionally "Disputes Boards" (collectively "DBs") is a relatively new term. It is used to describe a dispute resolution procedure which is normally established at the outset of a project and remains in place throughout the project's duration. It may comprise one or three members who become acquainted with the contract, the project and the individuals involved with the project in order to provide informal assistance, provide recommendations about how disputes should be resolved and provide binding decisions. The one person or three person DBs are remunerated throughout the project, most usually by way of a monthly retainer, which is then supplemented with a daily fee for travelling to the site, attending site visits and dealing with issues that arise between the parties by way of reading documents and attending hearings and producing written recommendations or decisions if and as appropriate.

The term has more recently come into use because of the increased globalisation of adjudication during the course of projects, coupled with the increased use of Dispute Review Boards ("DRBs"), which originally developed in the domestic USA major projects market. DRBs were apparently first used in the USA in 1975 on the Eisenhower Tunnel. The use of DRBs has steadily grown in the USA, but they have also been used internationally. However, DRBs predominantly remain the providence of domestic USA construction projects. As adjudication developed, the World Bank and FIDIC opted for a binding dispute resolution process during the course of projects, and so the Dispute Adjudication Board ("DAB") was borne from the DRB system; the DRB provides a recommendation that is not binding on the parties.

The important distinction then between DRBs and DABs is that the function of a DRB is to make a recommendation which the parties voluntarily accept (or reject), while the function of a DAB is to issue written decisions that bind the parties and must be implemented immediately during the course of the project. The DRB process is said to assist in developing amicable settlement procedures between the parties, such that the parties can accept or reject the DRB's recommendation. Genton, adopting the terminology of the International Chamber of Commerce ("ICC") describes the DAB approach "as a kind of pre-arbitration requiring the immediate implementation of a decision".[6] He goes on to state that:

> ". . . the DRB is a consensual, amicable procedure with non-binding recommendations and the DAB is a kind of pre-arbitration step with binding decisions."[7]

Building upon this distinction, the ICC has developed three new alternative approaches:

- Dispute Review Board—the DRB issues recommendations in line with the traditional approach of DRBs. An apparently consensual approach is adopted. However, if neither party expresses dissatisfaction with the written recommendation within the stipulated period then the parties agree to comply with the recommendation. The recommendation therefore becomes binding if the parties do not reject it.
- Dispute Adjudication Board—DRB's decision is to be implemented immediately.
- Combined Dispute Board ("CDB")—this attempts to mix both processes. The ICC CDB rules require the CDB to issue a recommendation in respect of any dispute, but it may instead issue a binding decision if either the employer or contractor requests and the other

6. Pierre N. Genton, *Dispute Boards* (2003).
7. Para. 7–029.

party does not object. If there is an objection, the CDB will decide whether to issue a recommendation or a decision.

Genton suggests that the third stage of a CDB would be the referral of a dispute leading to a binding decision, which would need to be implemented immediately. The ICC's approach is that the DB decides (if either party requests a decision) whether to issue a recommendation or immediately binding decision at the second stage of the process.

According to the ICC the essential difference is that the parties are required to comply with a decision immediately, whereas the parties must comply with a recommendation but only if the employer and contractor express no dissatisfaction within the time limit. The combined procedure seems at first glance to be a somewhat cumbersome approach attempting to build upon the benefits of the DRB and DAB, without following a clear pathway. Nonetheless, it may prove useful for those parties that cannot decide whether they need a DRB or a DAB.

At the other end of the spectrum a DB could be considered as a flexible and informal advisory panel. In other words, before issuing a recommendation, the DB might be asked for general advice on any particular matter. The DB will then look at documents and/or visit the site as appropriate and, most usually, provide an informal oral recommendation which the parties may choose then to adopt. If the parties were not satisfied, the DB would proceed to the issue of a formal, albeit non-binding, written recommendation after following the formal procedure of exchange of documents and a hearing.

As the DB and CDB is a relatively new concept, it is more informative to consider development of DRBs before then considering the development and practice of DABs.

## Dispute review board

A DRB usually comprises a panel of three impartial professionals who are employed by the employer and contractor to assist in avoiding disputes and resolving disputes that may arise in respect of a project. The panel should ideally have some specialist knowledge in respect of the type of project. In order to be effective, therefore, the panel needs to be implemented on or around the outset of the project in order that the panel can follow the progress of the project and deal with issues as they arise.

Most frequently, DRB provisions are included within the contract, or may be incorporated later by variation or change order. There will also need to be a tripartite agreement between the DRB members and the employer and contractor dealing with the remuneration of the panel as well as establishing the procedural rules and applicable terms such as confidentiality and the rights and obligation of the DRB members and the employer and contractor.

The key factor that distinguishes DRBs from other dispute resolution processes is that a DRB follows the progress of the project and makes recommendations about disagreements or disputes. While the DRB procedure is formal and will involve exchange of written positions, evidence and a hearing the written recommendation of the DRB is non-binding. The parties are, therefore, not obliged to comply with the recommendation. A fundamental point then about DRBs is that the panel must have the respect of the employer and the contractor and must reach reasoned recommendations that the parties can understand and respect in order that the parties will comply with the recommendation.

DRBs initially developed in the USA. According to the Dispute Review Board Foundation ("DRBF") the first documented use of an informal DRB process was on the Boundary Dam and Underground Powerhouse project north of Spokane, Washington during the 1960s. Problems occurred during the course of the project, and the contractor and employer agreed to appoint two professionals each to a four member "Joint Consulting Board", in order that that board could provide non-binding suggestions.

The DRBF reported that as a result the recommendations of the Joint Consulting Board were followed, and these included several administrative procedural changes and the settlement of a variety of claims and also an improvement in relationships between the parties. The project was also completed without litigation.

Subsequently the US National Committee and Tunnelling Technology, Standing Sub-committee No 4 conducted a study and made recommendations for improving contractual methods in the United States.[8] Further studies were carried out, and the first official use of a DRB was made by the Colorado Department of Highways on the second bore tunnel of the Eisenhower Tunnel Project. This was as a result of the financial disaster encountered in respect of the first tunnel between 1968 and 1974.

The DRB was required to make non-binding recommendations about disputes that arose during the project. The Board was constituted at the commencement of the project and followed the duration of the project. The project was extremely successful. As a result the use of DRBs began to spread for large civil engineering projects in the USA.

The DRBF has catalogued 1062 projects representing more than US$77.7 billion worth of project work. The December 2003 schedule shows that there were 340 contracts comprising DRBs in 2003. Of those projects 1,261 recommendations were given by the DRBs and only 28 matters went beyond the DRB process. In other words, only 2.2% of those disputes referred to the DRB progressed to arbitration or litigation. A more positive way of looking at this is that DRBs have a success rate of more than 97.8%. The DRBF has reported a considerable rise in the number of projects using DRBs (see Figure 3).

8. 1972.

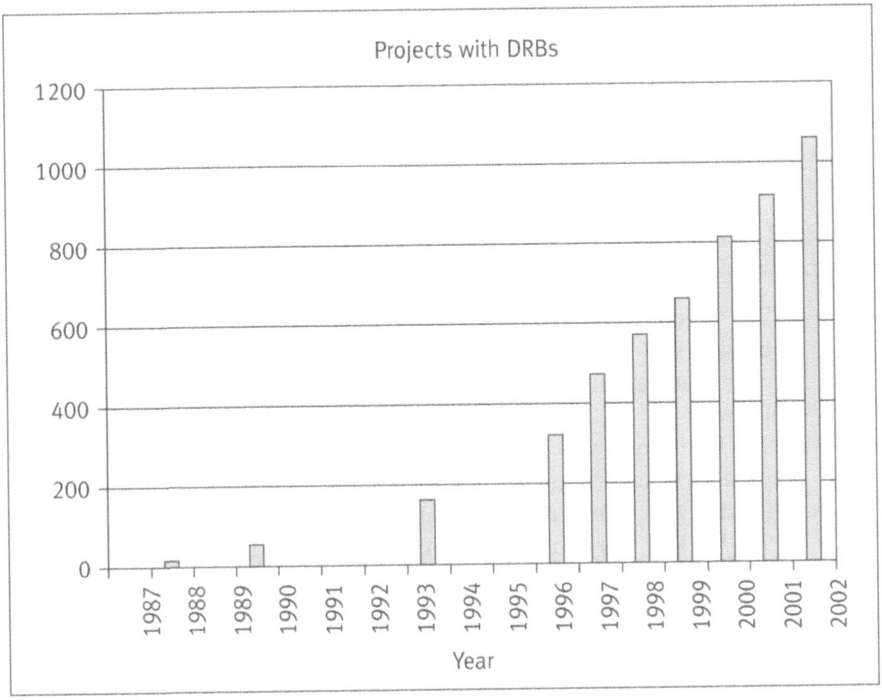


*Figure 3: Dispute Resolution Board Foundation, December 2003*

The DRBF has produced the following statistics, updated to December 2003:

***Table 3: Contracts complete and under construction (DRBF Schedule, December 2003)***

| | Projects with DRBs | Contract value | Disputes settled |
|---|---|---|---|
| **Year** | **Each** | **US$billion** | **Each** |
| 1988 | 19 | 1.4 | 16 |
| 1989 | | | |
| 1991 | 63 | 3.2 | 78 |
| 1992 | | | |
| 1994 | 166 | 9.7 | 211 |
| 1995 | | | |
| 1996 | | | |
| 1997 | 326 | 22.1 | 424 |
| 1998 | 477 | 28.8 | 596 |
| 1999 | 576 | 32.6 | 758 |
| 2000 | 666 | 35.4 | 869 |
| 2001 | 818 | 41.0 | 1021 |
| 2002 | 922 | 46.2 | 1108 |
| 2003 | 1062 | 50.3 | 1261 |

DRBs are now widely used on a range of civil engineering projects in the USA. Their use is no longer limited to the mega projects, and three man, or indeed one man DRBs are being used on smaller projects.

## Dispute Adjudication Board

The DAB has developed in parallel with DRBs. The key developments might be considered as follows:

- 1970: A contractual adjudication process was introduced into the domestic sub-contractor standard forms in the UK in order to primarily resolve set-off issues between the contractor and main contractor.
- 1994: Latham issues his final report reviewing procurement and contractual arrangements in the construction industry.
- 1995: FIDIC introduced a DAB in its Orange Book.
- 1996: FIDIC introduced as an option the DAB in the Red Book.
- 1996: Part II of the Housing Grants, Construction and Regeneration 1996 included adjudication provisions in Section 108.
- 1998: Part II of the Housing Grants, Construction and Regeneration 1996 is introduced on 1 May, together with the exclusion order (SI 1998 No 648) and the Scheme for Construction Contracts, England and Wales (SI 1998 No 649).
- 1999: FIDIC adopted a DAB/Dispute Review Expert ("DRE") procedure in favour of the additional approach of relying upon the engineer acting as the quasi arbitrator as well as an agent of the employer or owner. The DAB procedure became mandatory rather than an option. The three major model forms including DABs/DREs were:

  - Red Book: Conditions for Construction (a standing DAB comprising three members or one member).
  - Yellow Book: Plant & Design Build (ad hoc DAB).
  - Silver Book: Engineer Procure and Construct (Turnkey) again incorporating an ad hoc DAB.

- 2000: The World Bank introduced a new edition of Procurement of Works which made the "Recommendations" of the DRB or a DRE mandatory unless or until superseded by an arbitrator's award.
- 2002: ICC Task Force prepared draft rules for Dispute Boards ("DBs").
- 2004: The World Bank, together with other development banks, and FIDIC started from May working towards a harmonised set of conditions for DAB.
- 2004: (July): ICE published a DB procedure. Designed to be compliant with the HGCRA.

The introduction in the 1970s of the limited contractual adjudication procedure is perhaps now of limited historical interest. In the UK, the HGCRA was clearly a major turning point. However, it can certainly no longer be considered merely a domestic UK turning point; it also represents a major international turning point in the area of construction dispute resolution. On the international arena, FIDIC led the way by the introduction of DABs in its 1999 suite of contracts. The FIDIC Conditions of Contract typically comprise:

- Clauses 20.2–20.8 the Dispute Adjudication Board;
- Appendix—General Conditions of Dispute Adjudication Agreement;
- Annex 1—Procedural Rules; and
- Dispute Adjudication Agreement (three person DAB or one person DAB).

*FIDIC DAB (Clause 20)*

Clause 20 of the FIDIC form deals with claims, disputes and arbitration. Emphasis is placed upon the contractor to make its claims during the course of the works and for disputes to be resolved during the course of the works. Clause 20.1 requires a contractor seeking an extension of time or any additional payment to give notice to the engineer "as soon as practicable, and not later than 28 days after the event or circumstance giving rise to the claim".

Some have suggested that the contractor will lose its right to bring a claim for time and/or money if the claim is not brought within the timescale.[9] Under UK law this seems unlikely given that timescales in construction contracts are generally directory rather than mandatory,[10] and also because clause 20.1 does not go on to clearly state that the contractor will lose its right in the event of a failure to notify within a strict timescale.[11] Nonetheless, a contractor would be well advised to notify in writing any requests for extensions of time or money claims during the course of the works and within a period of 28 days from the event or circumstances giving rise to the claim.

The benefit then of the DAB is that it should be constituted at the commencement of the contract, so that the members of it will visit the site regularly and be familiar not just with the project but with the individual personalities involved in the project. They should, therefore, be in the position to issue binding decisions within the period of 84 days from the written notification of a dispute pursuant to clause 20.4.

The DAB is appointed in accordance with clause 20.2. It could comprise individuals that have been named in the contract. However, if the members of the DAB have not been identified in the contract then the parties are to jointly

9. Seppala, Christopher (2003) "Claims of the Contractor", a paper given at The Resolution of Disputes under International Construction Contracts, ICC, Paris, 6–7 February.

10. *Temloc* v. *Errill Properties* (1987) 22 B.L.R. 30 (CA).

11. *Bremer Handelsgesellschaft mbH* v. *Vanden Avenue-Izegem PVBA* (1978) 2 Lloyd's Rep. 109 (H.L.).

appoint a DAB "by the date 28 days after the Commencement Date". The DAB may comprise either one or three suitably qualified individuals. The appendix to the FIDIC contract should identify whether the DAB is to comprise one or three people. The appendix does not provide a default number, but clause 20.2 states that the parties are to agree if the appendix does not deal with the matter. If the parties cannot agree, then the appointing body named in the appendix will decide if the panel is to comprise one or three members.[12] The default appointing authority is the President of FIDIC or a person appointed by the President of FIDIC. The appointing authority is obliged to consult with both parties before making its final and conclusive determination.

On most major projects a DAB will comprise three persons. If that is the case, then each party is to nominate one member for approval by the other. The parties are then to mutually agree upon a third member who is to become the chairman. In practice, parties may propose a member for approval, or more commonly propose three potential members allowing the other party to select one. Once two members have been selected, it is then more common for those members to identify and agree upon (with the agreement of the parties) a third member. That third person might become the chairman, although, once again with the agreement of all concerned, one of the initially proposed members could be the chairman.

The terms of remuneration for each of the individual members of the DAB must be agreed between the parties. This is because each party will be responsible for paying 50% of the remuneration in respect of each member of the DAB.

Clause 20.2 states that a member can only be terminated by mutual agreement of both parties. The employer or contractor acting alone cannot terminate the DAB or a single member of the DAB once the DAB has been constituted. Once constituted the principle obligation of the DAB is to make binding decisions. However, the parties may jointly agree to refer a matter to the DAB simply for an advisory opinion.

If the parties do agree to terminate the appointment of an individual member of the DAB, then they should replace that person by agreement or if the parties cannot agree by nomination of the appointing entity. The parties might also need to replace a member if the member declines to act, resigns, becomes disabled or dies.

By virtue of clause 20.3 the parties have agreed that the appointing entity named in the appendix (the FIDIC President or his nominee by default) may appoint members to the DAB if the parties fail to agree within 28 days after the commencement date, or fail to agree the identity of a third member, or fail to agree on a replacement member within 42 days after the date on which the sole member declined or became unable to act.

12. Clause 20.3.

Clause 20.4 deals with referring a dispute to the DAB. The first paragraph of clause 20.4 states:

"If a dispute (of any kind whatsoever) arises between the Parties in connection with, or arising out of, the Contract or the execution of the Works, including any dispute as to any certificate, determination, instruction, opinion or valuation of the Engineer, the dispute shall be referred in writing to the DAB for its decision, with copies to the other Party and the Engineer. Such reference shall state that it is given under this sub-clause."

The parties are therefore obliged contractually to refer any dispute whatsoever that arises in connection with or out of the contract including the opening up and reviewing of notices and certificates. If the DAB comprises three members then the DAB is deemed to have received the notice of dispute when it is received by the Chairman alone. This means that the parties can simply direct all of their correspondence to the Chairman, but with copies to the other members, as well as providing a copy to the other party and engineer.[13]

Both the employer and the contractor are obliged to provide additional information and further access to the site and its facilities as the DAB may require in order for the DAB to make its decision.

The contractor, notwithstanding that a dispute has been referred to the DAB, is to continue to proceed with the works in accordance with the contract (unless abandoned, repudiated or terminated). Both parties are contractually obliged to properly comply with every decision of the DAB. DAB decisions are therefore immediately mandatory, unless or until revised by an arbitral award, litigation or settlement.

The DAB is obliged to provide its written decision within 84 days after receipt of the reference. The DAB must provide a reasoned award which must be issued pursuant to clause 20.4 of the contract.

The FIDIC contract, at clause 20.4, expressly states that the DAB is not acting in an arbitral capacity. The purpose of this express reference is to make it clear that the written decision of the DAB is not to be treated as an arbitrator's award, and so cannot be said to be immediately finally conclusive. Neither will the DAB's decision enjoy the status of an arbitrator's award in respect of enforcement. It will, however, be enforceable under the contract and depending upon the local law it may be possible to enforce payment required by a DAB's decision in the local court without recourse to the merits of the decision or a stay of litigation because of the existence of the arbitration clause.

If either party is dissatisfied with the decision of the DAB then either party may give notice of its dissatisfaction to the other party. However, this must be done within 28 days after receipt of the DAB's decision. If the DAB does not render its decision within 84 days of receipt of the reference then either party may simply serve a notice of dissatisfaction. A notice of dissatisfaction must set

13. Clause 20.4 and Procedural Rule 4.

out the dispute and reasons for the dissatisfaction. Matters that are the subject of a notice of dissatisfaction which are not resolved amicably in accordance with clause 20.5 may then be referred to international arbitration pursuant to clause 20.6.

The crucial point about the notice of dissatisfaction is that the decision of the DAB becomes final and binding upon both parties unless a written notice of dissatisfaction is served within 28 days of receipt of the DAB's decision. If either party is not satisfied with the DAB's decision then it is crucial for that party to serve a written notice of dissatisfaction. In the absence of such a notice the parties have clearly agreed by contract that they will accept the DAB's decision as being final and binding upon them.

In light of the House of Lords decision in *Beaufort Developments* v. *Gilbert Ash (NI) Limited* it is highly likely that a court will find that the parties are bound by such a clause and that a failure to serve a notice of dissatisfaction would result in either party's inability to raise a dispute in connection with the same subject matter of any DAB decision that has become final and conclusive.[14]

Clause 20.5 requires the parties to attempt to settle their dispute amicably before commencing arbitration. There is a 56-day cooling off period after the issue of the notice of dissatisfaction. Either party may not commence arbitration (unless the other party agrees) until after the 56th day after the date on which the notice of dissatisfaction was "given".

The final method of dispute resolution is international arbitration pursuant to clause 20.6. The applicable rules are the ICC rules, and disputes are referred to a panel of three arbitrators.

### *FIDIC General Conditions of Dispute Adjudication Agreement*

The appendix to the FIDIC form provides a tripartite General Conditions of Dispute Adjudication Agreement. It is tripartite in the sense that it is entered into between the Employer, Contractor and the sole member or three members of the DAB. The Agreement takes effect on the latest of:

- the commencement date defined in the contract;
- when all parties have signed the tripartite Dispute Adjudication Agreement; or
- when all parties have entered into a Dispute Adjudication Agreement.

The distinction between the last two points refers to the Dispute Adjudication Agreement appended to the FIDIC form, or alternatively provides for the parties to enter into an effective dispute adjudication agreement even if it is not in the form attached to the FIDIC contract.

14. [1999] 1 A.C. 266 (H.L.); [1998] 2 W.L.R. 860; [1998] 2 All E.R. 778; (1998) 83 B.L.R. 1; (1998) CILL 1386.

The engagement of a member from the DAB is a personal appointment. If a member wishes to resign then a member must give at least 70 days' notice. Members warrant that he or she is and shall remain impartial and independent of the Employer, Contractor and Engineer. A member is required to promptly disclose anything which might impact upon their impartiality or independence.[15]

The general obligations of a member of the DAB are quite extensive. Clause 4 requires that a member shall:

- have no financial interest or otherwise in the employer, the contractor or the engineer;
- not previously have been employed as a consultant by the employer, contractor or engineer (unless disclosed);
- have disclosed in writing any professional or personal relationships;
- not during the duration of the DAB be employed by the employer, contractor or engineer;
- comply with the Procedural Rules (see below);
- not give advice to either party;
- not whilst acting as a DAB member entertain any discussions with either party about potential employment with them;
- ensure availability for a site visit and hearings;
- become conversant with the contract and the progress of the works;
- keep all details of the Contract and the DAB's activities and hearings private and confidential; and
- be available to give advice and opinions if and when required by the employer and contractor.

By contrast, and pursuant to clause 5, the employer and contractor are obliged not to request a member to breach any of the obligations set out above. Neither is the employer or the contractor able to appoint a member as arbitrator under the contract or call a member as a witness to give evidence concerning any dispute arising under the contract. Further, the employer and contractor grant immunity upon the member of the DAB for any claims for anything done or omitted to be done in the purported discharge of the members functions unless those acts or omissions have been carried out by the member in bad faith. An indemnity is provided, joint and severally, by the employer and contractor in that regard.

Clause 6 deals with payment. There are two main elements to payment. The first is the retainer fee, which is paid on a monthly basis in consideration for the member being available for site visits and hearings, becoming conversant with the project and providing general services.

The second aspect of the fee comprises a daily fee for payment travelling to and from the site (a maximum of two days travelling in each direction) as well as for each day spent working on site, the hearings, preparing decisions and

15. Clause 3, Warranty.

reading submissions. Reasonable expenses together with taxes properly levied are then to be paid in addition. The retainer fee is paid from the last day of the month in which the DAB becomes effective until the last day of the month in which the taking over certificate is issued for the whole of the works. After that date, the retainer fee is reduced by 50% until the DAB is terminated or a member resigns.

It is therefore highly likely that each of the three members of the DAB will receive a different retainer fee and claim a different hourly rate. Each member submits their invoices for the monthly retainer and airfares quarterly in advance. Invoices for daily fees and other expenses are then submitted at the conclusion of a site visit or hearing. The contractor is to pay each of the members' invoices in full within 56 calendar days from receipt.

From a practicable perspective it is often sensible for the two "wing" members of the DAB to submit their invoices to the chairman who then submits those invoices together with his or her invoice in one go to the contractor. This means that the chairman can remain the single point of contact for any issues arising in respect of the DAB's charges and that the final date for payment for all of the members will be on the same date, thus allowing the chairman to take up the issue of late payment for the DAB if necessary.

If the contractor does not pay then the employer is obliged to pay the amount due. If a member has not received payment within 70 days from receipt of invoice by the contractor then that member may:

- suspend his or her services until the payment is received; and/or
- resign.

The employer or contractor may acting jointly terminate the DAB by giving 42 days' notice.[16] If the member fails to comply with the Dispute Adjudication Agreement, or the Employer or Contractor fail to comply with it then those affected may terminate the tripartite Agreement. If a member breaches the Agreement then he or she will not be entitled to any further fees. Any disputes arising under the tripartite Agreement are to be dealt with by ICC arbitration comprising a single arbitrator.[17]

### *FIDIC Procedural Rules*

The Annex to the General Conditions of the Dispute Adjudication Agreement sets out procedural rules for the DAB. The DAB is to visit the site "at intervals of not more than 140 days" and should visit the site during critical construction events. Consecutive visits should not be less than 70 days.[18] The timing and the agenda for each site visit should be agreed between the DAB and the parties.[19]

16. Clause 7, Termination.
17. Clause 9, Disputes.
18. Annex, Procedural Rule 1.
19. Annex, Procedural Rule 2.

In practice the DAB sets out the agenda, and the Chairman puts it to the parties and unless an objection is received from either of the parties the Board then proceeds upon that basis. At the conclusion of the site visit, the DAB is to prepare a report setting out its activities during the site visit and identifying those individuals who attended the site visit.[20]

Annex clause 4 requires the parties to furnish the DAB with a complete copy of the contract, progress reports, variation certificates and other documents which are "pertinent to the performance of the Contract" or communications between the DAB Employer and/or Contractor shall be copied to the other party, and all the members of the DAB.

Annex clause 7 states that the DAB has the power to act inquisitorially. Further, the DAB is to establish the procedure before deciding a dispute and may refuse admission to the hearings and proceed in the absence of any party who has received notice of the hearing.

The DAB may also decide upon its own jurisdiction, conduct any hearings as it thinks fit, take the initiative and ascertain the facts, make use of its own specialist knowledge, decide upon the payment of interest if any, provide provisional or interim relief, open up, review and revise any certificate, decision, determination, instruction, opinion or valuation of the engineer.[21]

Once a hearing has been concluded the DAB shall meet in private in order to discuss and prepare its decision.[22] Decisions should be reached unanimously, but if this "proves impossible", then a decision may be made by the majority. In practice, a single decision is usually issued by the DAB: a majority decision and a further section where the minority member sets out his or her written report. If a member fails to attend the hearing then the other two members may proceed to a unanimous decision unless the employer and contractor agree otherwise or the absent member is the Chairman and he instructs the other members not to proceed. The contractor and employer could of course ask the other two members to proceed and make a unanimous decision.[23]

### *FIDIC Dispute Adjudication Agreement*

The appendices to the FIDIC Form of contract contain two Dispute Adjudication Agreements. The first is for use on a one-person DAB, and the second for use on three-person DAB. The Dispute Adjudication Agreements are, for all intents and purposes, the same for a one- or three-person DAB, except that where a three-person DAB applies then those three persons are to act jointly as the DAB.

20. Annex, Procedural Rule 3.
21. Annex, Procedural Rule 8.
22. Annex, Procedural Rule 9(a).
23. Clause 9(c).

The terms of the General Conditions of Dispute Adjudication Agreement are incorporated by reference on clause 4 of the Dispute Adjudication Agreements. The retainer fee and daily fee of each member is set out in both Dispute Adjudication Agreements. The employer and contractor bind themselves jointly and severally to pay the DAB member in accordance with the General Conditions of the Dispute Adjudication Agreement. Details of the specific FIDIC contract between the employer and contractor also need to be recorded, as it is from this document that the Employer and Contractor agree to be bound by the DAB and it is also from that document that the DAB obtains its jurisdiction in respect of the project.

## *The move towards legislation for international adjudication*

The legislation that has been introduced in the UK, and other jurisdictions introducing adjudication has merely dealt with the domestic position. However, it has been radically suggested that adjudication legislation could be provided by a two part statute.[24] The first part of the Bill would deal with the domestic territorial position, whilst the second part could provide for adjudication in respect of a construction contract anywhere in the world. This follows the concept of international arbitration. Most arbitration acts provide for domestic arbitration in the country of origin, whilst also supporting, recognising and enforcing international arbitration. In other words, the international adjudication section of the Bill would provide an adjudication procedure together with the ability of a local court to support the process in terms of nominating adjudicators by default, or identifying or nominating a body by default and enforcing decisions. Parties anywhere in the world could choose the adjudication procedure of another jurisdiction.

An International Adjudication Bill might include the following aspects:

(1) be drafted on a "minimum interference, maximum enforceability" basis;
(2) adopt the New York Convention for the purposes of enforcement;
(3) provide for the local courts to identify an adjudicator or nominate an adjudicator nominating body in the appropriate part of the world. This could be done by a judge on a documents only (email) basis;
(4) provide a limited ability for challenges. There would always be the ability to challenges on the basis of no jurisdiction, but how restricted should challenges be based upon grounds of natural justice?;
(5) a decision would be binding, unless or until subsequent arbitration, litigation or settlement; and
(6) detailed procedural rules would need to be included.

24. Robert Fenwick Elliott.

The advantages of such an approach would mean that international projects could make use of adjudication procedures in a country supported by a competent court system, which is not always the case in some developing countries where considerable construction projects are being carried out. Further, the parties could choose an adjudication system that appears to be more effective than others, or adopt a system whose procedurals appear to suit their project or their needs to a greater extent than their domestic adjudication process, if any.

## *Summary*

### Spectrum of dispute resolution

- There are three core dispute resolution techniques: negotiation, mediation or conciliation and umpiring.
- Negotiation is the process of working out an agreement by direct communication, it is voluntary and non-binding.
- Mediation is a private informal process in which the parties are assisted by one or more neutral third parties in their efforts towards settlement.
- Umpiring refers to dispute resolution processes where the third party imposes a binding decision on the parties in dispute.
- Mediation can be facilitative or evaluative. The mediator may merely facilitate communication towards settlement, or may evaluate the issues in dispute.
- The terms mediation and conciliation are often used interchangeably. In the UK, mediation usually refers to a facilitative process whilst conciliation is evaluative.
- Hybrid processes have developed which are a combination of the core processes. For example, Med-Arb where the mediator becomes the arbitrator if the dispute cannot be settled during the mediation phase.

### Negotiation

- Negotiation involves conferring with others in order to reach a compromise or agreement.
- It is the most frequently employed dispute resolution technique.
- Negotiation is basically a developmental process with eight distinct, but often overlapping phases.
- There are two recognised approaches to negotiation. First, "positional" or "competitive" or "distributional" negotiation. Second, "principled" or "interest-based" or "cooperative" or "problem solving" or "win/win" negotiation.
- Positional negotiators barter over the outcome, whilst principled negotiators try to solve the problem in a mutually convenient way.

- Innovative structured approaches to negotiation can be and employed to deal with multi-issue disputes.
- Legal principles can provide the framework for negotiations.
- Litigation or arbitration can provide the pressure to negotiate a settlement.
- Negotiators should ensure that they: (1) are expert in their field; (2) research the technical issues of the dispute; and (3) explore every avenue with proberty.

## Mediation

- Mediation is an informal process in which the parties in dispute are assisted by one or more neutral third parties in their efforts towards settlement.
- Mediation is not a new process, but has been widely used throughout the world. It can be traced back to ancient China.
- The key elements of mediation are:

  It is *voluntary*. The parties choose to use the process.
  A *third party neutral*, who is independent of the parties, aids the parties towards settlement.
  It is *non-binding*. The mediator cannot impose a decision on the parties.
  It is *private*. The dispute is kept from the public domain.

- The terms "*mediation*" and "*conciliation*" are used interchangeably.
- *Facilitative* mediators merely try to aid communication between the parties in order to develop a settlement.
- *Evaluative* mediators will openly express opinions on the issues and make recommendations as to settlement.
- There are three main stages to mediation.

  (1) Pre-mediation—agreeing to mediate and preparing for the mediation.
  (2) The mediation—*direct mediation* with all the parties present, and *indirect mediation* during caucus.
  (3) Post-mediation—settlement supervision.

- It is a flexible process and a variety of approaches are adopted by different sectors. A typical commercial mediation will last for one day and pass through the following phases:

  (1) introductions;
  (2) mediation opening, and establishing the ground rules;
  (3) parties opening statement;

(4) private meetings or caucusing.
(5) joint meetings for particular issues, the experts or to record the outcome of the mediation.

- The aim of mediation is to reach a negotiated settlement. The mediator is there to facilitate that settlement.
- Mediators may employ five main activities to steer the parties towards settlement:

(1) investigation;
(2) empathy;
(3) persuasion;
(4) invention;
(5) destruction.

- There are three main approaches to mediation and conciliation in the construction industry:

(1) facilitative CEDR styled mediation;
(2) evaluative ICE styled conciliation;
(3) informal mediation.

- Informal mediations are not institutionally based. The mediator is appointed because of his or her experience, and the mutual respect of that individual by the parties. Informal mediations in the construction industry are more common than institutionally based CEDR styled mediations or ICE conciliation.

## Expert determination

- Expert determination is a process by which the parties instruct a third party to decide a particular issue.
- The third party is selected because of his or her particular expertise.
- Expert determination is a creature of contract. An expert determination clause should exhibit the following minimum requirements:

  – A clear and precise definition of the issue or issues to be determined.
  – The expert is to act as an expert and not as an arbitrator.
  – The decision should be final and binding.
  – A mechanism for the appointment of an appropriate expert.

- The court is extremely reluctant to intervene in an expert decision, and will only do so if the expert has made some manifest mistake in relation to his or her jurisdiction (*Jones* v. *Sherwood*).

- Only if the expert has answered the wrong question will the court declare a decision a nullity (*Nikko Hotels* v. *MEPC*).

## Adjudication

- The term adjudication is not a term of art. In the general sense it means a process by which a judge or referee decides the case before him or her. More specifically adjudication refers to a process where a neutral third party makes a decision which is binding on the parties in dispute unless or until revised in arbitration or litigation.
- A variety of construction contracts makes use of an adjudicator, who can make a "temporal" binding decision. Originally, the adjudicator obtained his or her powers from the contract between the parties in dispute. However, a right for one party in a construction contract to call on an adjudicator was introduced by the Housing Grants, Construction and Regeneration Act 1996.
- Under this Act the adjudicator receives wide statutory powers in order to decide the issues in dispute. A party may call on an adjudicator providing that the construction contract comes within the definition included in the Act, and a dispute has come into existence.
- The Act sets out a basic procedure which all construction contracts must incorporate. For example, strict time limits for the appointment (seven days) and the making of a decision (28 days) are a mandatory requirement of the Act.
- Providing that the construction contract meets with these minimum requirements then the contract may go to set out a more detailed procedure. If the contract does not include a right to adjudication, then the Act will imply a right into the contract and the Scheme will apply. The Scheme lays out a detailed procedure for the carrying out of the adjudication.
- The parties may choose to adopt a standard set of adjudication rules, or rely on those set out in one of the standard forms of construction contract, or could draft their own set of bespoke rules.

## Arbitration

- Arbitration is a private formal dispute resolution process, which subject to statutory controls, allows disputes to be determined by a tribunal of the parties choosing.
- An Arbitrator's award is final and binding upon the parties and may be enforced in the court if necessary.
- The advantages of arbitration over litigation include flexibility, economy, speed, privacy, freedom of choice of arbitrator, and finality.
- The disadvantages of arbitration are that the parties are, in effect, paying for the judge and the courtroom, and that often the apparent

economy and time saving advantages of arbitration do not materialise.

- Parties may agree to refer existing disputes to arbitration, or more commonly, they have chosen to refer future disputes to arbitration. The agreement is usually contained within some wider commercial contract.
- The Arbitration Act 1996 provides a statutory framework which supports the arbitration procedure.
- The Act allows the parties to agree on the procedure which the arbitrator will use to determine the dispute.
- The Act also contains mandatory provisions which the parties cannot vary. The mandatory provisions underpin the arbitration process and include the ability to stay legal proceedings in favour of arbitration and provide the arbitrator with immunity.
- The arbitration procedure may include a full hearing, a short hearing or even dispense with the hearing such that the arbitrator decides the dispute and document only.
- Once the arbitrator has issued his final award he is "*functus officio*" which means that the arbitrator's duties and powers are at an end.

## Litigation

- Litigation in the courts is the most visible feature of the English legal system, and the traditional mode of dispute resolution.
- Very few disputes which are commenced in the Courts result in a trial and subsequent judgment. Only a few percent of the actions commenced result in a judgment.
- The Civil Procedure Rules govern the litigation procedures in the County Courts, High Courts and Courts of Appeal. The Civil Procedure Rules were implemented on 26 April 1999 and are printed as a series of parts. Each part relates to one aspect of litigation. Practice directions support each part intending to clarify and describe the particular rule and its application.
- The Civil Procedure Rules are based on the overriding objective that cases should be dealt with justly and in accordance with five basic principles. The principles are equality, saving expense, proportionality, expedition and fairness, and allocated an appropriate share of the Court's resources to the case.
- Litigation is conducted under three main tracks. The small claims track, the fast track, and the multi-track. The small claims are those with a financial claim not exceeding £5,000. The fast track deals with claims between £5,000 and £50,000. Cases exceeding £50,000 are generally dealt with on the multi-track. However, financial value is not the only factor in allocating a case to a particular track.

- Judges are now expected to be more proactive in the management of disputes. In addition, more opportunities are provided to prompt the parties towards settlement and consider the use of ADR techniques.

## READING LIST AND USEFUL REFERENCES

### *Reading list*

De Bono, E. (1985) *Conflicts*, Penguin.

Fisher, R., Ury, W., and Patton, B. (1991) *Getting to Yes: Negotiating an Agreement without Giving In* (2nd edn) (London: Century Business).

Goldberg, S. B., Sander, F. E. A., and Rogers, N. H. (1992) *Dispute Resolution: Negotiation, Mediation and Other Processes* (2nd edn) (Boston: Little, Brown & Company), p. 17.

Mackie, K., Miles, D., and Marsh, W. (1995) *Commercial Dispute Resolution* (London: Butterworths).

Riches, J. L., & Dancaster, C. (2004) *Construction Adjudication* (2nd edn) (London: Blackwell Publishing).

Simmonds, D. (2003) *Statutory Adjudication: A Practical Guide* (London: Blackwell Publishing).

### *Useful references*

#### Cases and statutes

*Arab African Energy Corporation Limited* v. *Olieprodukten Nederland BV* [1983] 2 Lloyd's Rep. 419.

*Aughton Limited* v. *MF Kent Services Limited* [1991] 57 B.L.R. 1.

*Jones* v. *Sherwood Computer Services Plc* [1992] 1 W.L.R. 277.

*Mercury Communications Limited* v. *Director General of Telecommunications and Another* [1996] 1 All E.R. 575.

*Nikko Hotels (UK) Limited* v. *NEPC Plc* [1991] 2 E.G. 86.

Arbitration Act 1996.

Housing Grants, Construction and Regeneration Act 1996.

#### Book, journals and other material

Ambrose, C., and Maxwell, K. (1997) *London Maritime Arbitration* (London: LLP), p. 9.

American Arbitration Association, Construction Industry Mediation Rules (1 January 1992).

British Academy of Experts, *What is Mediation?* (January 1992).

Brown and Marriott (1999) *ADR Principles and Practice* (2nd edn) (Sweet & Maxwell).

Butter, N. (1997) "Mediation and the Courts: first official pilot mediation", *The Expert*, September 1997, p. 17.

Capper, P. (1997) Adjudicator, Dispute Resolution 97, CIC Conference on Arbitration, Adjudication and Expert Determination in Construction (London Hilton, 15 January 1997).

CEDR, *Mediator Training Handbook* (1997).

CEDR Mediation Agreement.

DAC Report on the Arbitration Bill (1997) Chaired by the Rt Hon. Lord Justice Mustill (now Lord Mustill). Also known as the Departmental Advisory Committee on arbitration law.

Enderson, G. (1996) *Disputes, Draft Provokes Fury in Construction*, 28 March, p. 2.

McGaw, M. (1992) "Adjudicators, Experts and Keeping out of Court" in *Legal Obligations in Construction* (Constructional Press), pp. 605–664.

Gould, N., Capper, P., Dixon, G., and Colen, M. (1999) *Dispute Resolution in the UK Construction Industry* (London: Thomas Telford).

Gulliver, P. H. (1979) *Dispute and Negotiations: A Cross Cultural Perspective* (London: Academic Press), pp. 121–177.

Judicial Statistics, HMSO.

Kendall, J. (1996) *Expert Determination* (2nd edn) (Harlow: Longman).

Latham, M. (1994) *Constructing the Team* (London: HMSO).

Mackie, K., Miles, D., and Marsh, W. (1995) *Commercial Dispute Resolution* (London: Butterworths).

Meltsner & Schrag (1973) "Negotiating Tactics for Legal Services Lawyers", 7 *Clearing House Review*, p. 259.

Palmer, M. J. E. (1991) "Mediation in the People's Republic of China: some general observations" in Macke, K. J. (ed.) *A Handbook of Dispute Resolution* (London: Routledge), pp. 221–230.

Roberts, S. (1994) "Re-Exploring the Pathways to Decision-Making", 12 *Law in Context* 9.

Schapiro, M. (1981) *Courts: A Comparative and Political Analysis* (Chicago and London: The University of Chicago Press).

Stephenson, D. A. (1998) *Arbitration Practice in Construction Disputes* (4th edn) (London: Spons).

Stipanowich, T. (1994) "What's Hot and What's Not", DART Conference Proceedings (Lexington, Kentucky, USA), 16–19 October 1994.

Thompson, D. (ed) (1995) *The Concise Oxford Dictionary of Current English* (Oxford: Clarendon Press), p. 912.

Ury, W. (1991) *Getting Past No: Negotiating with Difficult People* (New York: Bantam Books).

White, J. (1984) "The Pros and Cons of Getting to 'Yes'" 34 *Journal of Legal Education*, pp. 115–117.

Woolf (1996) *Access to Justice: Final Report* (London: HMSO).

## TEST YOUR UNDERSTANDING

1. Explain the spectrum of dispute resolution techniques.
2. Identify the key differences between the three pillars of dispute resolution.
3. Identify and distinguish the key elements in the escalation of a dispute.
4. Discuss the process of negotiation and contrast negotiation strategies.
5. Justify the approach of the courts to agreements to negotiate.
6. What is mediation?
7. Distinguish the various approaches to mediation.
8. Consider how a mediator affects the mediation or conciliation process.
9. Explain what is meant by ADR.
10. Discuss the development of ADR from the growth of informal justice.
11. Contrast the advantages and disadvantages of ADR by comparison to the traditional methods of dispute resolution.
12. Assess the advantages and disadvantages of expert determination over other forms of dispute resolution.
13. Contrast three hybrid or multi-stage approaches to dispute resolution.
14. From your own experience consider how an alternative approach to the resolution of dispute might improve the efficiency of your organisation.
15. Explain the adjudication process.
16. Contrast the key distinctions between arbitration and litigation.
17. Justify the CPR approach to track allocation.
18. Contrast three of the hybrid approaches to dispute resolution.
19. Compare and distinguish between the project based dispute resolution techniques.

# CONSTRUCTION LAW AND MANAGEMENT—ANSWERS TO SELF TEST QUESTIONS

## Chapter 1—Introduction to the English and EU Legal Framework

1. (d) adjudication provisions
2. (c) a Regulation
3. (b) contract for insurance
4. (d) must relate to a contract dealing with land
5. (a) a sum of money stated in the contract to be damages payable in the event of a specified breach of contract
6. (b) the terms of the Scheme will override the terms in your contract
7. (d) any period greater than all those listed as possible answers to this question as agreed between the parties
8. (d) the decision of the adjudicator is always binding
9. (d) the concrete supplier
10. (c) site survey work lasting 1000 person days

## Chapter 2—Materials and Communications

1. (e) all of the above
2. (c) a bill of quantities
3. (a) install 5000 $m^2$ of plasterboard and paint 5 coats
4. (a) whether the BOQ rates are commercially reasonable
5. (b) to minimise the risk of variation claims from the contractor
6. (d) a performance specification
7. (b) 21
8. (c) shifting the dates for the delivery of free-issue materials to later in the programme
9. (a) the employer should grant the contractor a 14-day extension of time, but should not have to compensate the contractor for its site and head office overheads
10. (c) he wishes to encourage the lowest possible bids from tenderers

## Chapter 3—Procurement

1. (b) traditional
2. (a) prime cost plus management fee

3. (b) traditional
4. (c) traditional
5. (c) early commitment from the contractor as to the project cost
6. (c) output
7. (c) the certainty of project costs prior to commencing on-site
8. (b) the length of time taken to design the project before it can be put out to tender
9. (c) design and build
10. (d) buildings requiring a highly regarded aesthetic appearance

## Chapter 4—Standard Forms of Contract I

### *1. Explain the term "compensation event" in an ECC Contract.*

A compensation event is an event which if it occurs potentially entitles the contractor under the form of contract to either an extension of time for completion of the works or additional monies, or both. It is subject to various procedures within the contract for approval but provided those procedures are complied with and the event falls within the various definitions of compensation events the contractor is entitled to receive the additional time and/or money. It is similar to relevant events under JCT forms of contract.

### *2. Outline the key advantages and disadvantages of the adoption of standard form contracts in the construction industry.*

Three key advantages accrue to those who use standard forms, and they are as follows:—

1. Huge economic advantage in not negotiating each individual contract;
2. Widespread knowledge among parties of the terms and conditions which are agreed;

and

3. Standardisation of bargaining power and position.

The most often raised criticism of using standard forms is that it produces a "one size fits all" mentality where a particular standard form is adopted simply because it was the form that was used previously. The risk with this approach is that it leads to insufficient thought being given as to how the terms and conditions set out in the standard form will operate for the particular project in question. This is not really a criticism of the standard form itself or its use, rather a criticism of the lack of intellectual rigour in the decision making process leading to the adoption of a particular standard form.

### *3. How does ICE 7th Edition measurement version deal with ground risk?*

Under Clause 11(2) the contractor shall be deemed to have inspected and examined the site. Under Clause 12 the contractor may claim additional time and/or money if during the carrying out of the works he encounters physical conditions (excluding weather) or artificial obstructions which could not in his opinion reasonably have been foreseen by an experienced contractor. It can thus be seen that the risk of ground conditions is not totally allocated either to the employer or the contractor but is rather shared between them in a way which, given the existence of the ICE contract, has created many disputes. It should be noted that this arrangement in respect of ground risk is broadly followed by the ECC contracts as well.

### *4. How is design liability dealt with in the JCT Management Contract suite of contracts?*

On the issue of design liability the JCT Management Contract is basically a traditional approach in that the employer is usually required to appoint a professional team and consequently design liability usually remains with the employer's professional design team. The exception will be certain specified elements of work which are in fact designed by specialist sub-contractors, in which case the design liability properly rests with the specialist sub-contractors.

### *5. What type of client/contractor is it envisaged that the JCT Major Projects form will be used by?*

The JCT Major Projects form is the nearest contract to be published by the JCT and was formally released in 2003. It represents a radical departure from previous JCT contracts. The guidance notes indicate that the MFP is intended to respond to the specific needs of employers who have in-house contractual procedures and who regularly undertake major projects under the contractors for whom they work. As a consequence of such parties familiarity with construction contracts it has been possible to reduce the overall level of detail in the contract from 80,000 words to 12,000.

### *6. Where would you normally find the FIDIC set of standard forms being used?*

FIDIC is the International Federation of Consulting Engineers (the acronym represents the French version of the name) which represents the international business of firms belonging to national member associations of engineering based consulting companies. FIDIC is based in Geneva, Switzerland and was founded in 1913, and to date its membership includes 64 member associations. FIDIC contracts are used predominately on international projects and are very much considered the standard form of contract for use in such projects, a fact that is recognised by international institutions such as the World Bank and the International Monetary Fund.

### *7. Outline how PPC 2000 attempts to encourage partnering and team work.*

PPC 2000 remains the only published standard form of tendering of team partnering contract. PPC 2000 envisages that the main parties ("partnering team members") involved in a project (including the employer, the contractor, the employer's representative/project manager and other professional team members) will enter into the contract together. This includes design sub-consultants and sub-contractors as well. The concept is that a client should also appoint a partnering facilitator to advise all the parties on relevant matters relating to the contract. The contract is entered into from project inception thus setting out a timetable governing all the activities of the parties including those prior to the start on site. Parties are contractually required to carry out their agreed activities regularly and diligently in accordance with the partnering timetable. It is by encouraging all the parties to work collaboratively and to be place in one contractual "melting pot" that the contract attempts to encourage partnering and team work.

### *8. How do the extension of time events in the JCT Major Projects form differ from those found in the JCT 98 Private with Quantities form?*

The key difference between the JCT Major Projects form and other JCT forms is that the contract envisages a greater degree of risk transfer to the contractor and consequently the number of relevant events is significantly less in the MPF than it is in other JCT standard forms. In many respects the scope of the relevant events within the MPF equates to what is often achieved by bespoke amendments by developers and their legal advisers to the JCT design and build form.

### *9. Explain the term "remeasurement" in context of a construction contract.*

The term "remeasurement" in context of a construction contract usually refers to the mechanism for ascertaining the amount to be paid by the contractor where it is not a lump sum contract. An example of a remeasurement contract is the ICE Conditions of Contractor where the quantities are taken to be approximate and the actual amount to be paid to the contractor is recalculated once the works have been carried out and the actual quantity has been ascertained. This actual quantity is then multiplied by the rate applicable in the relevant schedule of rates to arrive at the actual amount of payment to the contractor. Thus the process of remeasurement refers to the exercise of measuring the actual quantities as opposed to the approximate quantities included within the original tender.

### 10. For projects below £100,000 in value with no design responsibility being placed on the contract what contract form would you recommend?

The contract to recommend for such a project would be the JCT Minor Works Agreement. The JCT indicate that this form of contract is suitable for contracts up to a value of £100,000 (2001 prices) but that it is not suitable for use where bills of quantity would be normally required. It should only be used for work of a simple nature. Since the module was prepared the JCT have reissued a number of their standard forms and the JCT Minor Works Agreement 05 version now comes with a design portion supplement. Consequently the form could therefore now be used where some contractor design requirement was needed.

### 11. Provide an outline of the payment provisions within a JCT 98 Private with Quantities form.

The JCT Private with Quantities form is a lump sum contract. The contractor's obligations are to carry out and complete the works described by the contract documents for the contract sum. The payment provisions in the contract are set out in Clause 30. The contract provides two alternative mechanisms for payment to the contractor based either upon monthly valuations with payment being made monthly to the contractor or (if the appropriate appendix is completed) by way of stage payments at specified stages of the work as set out in the appendix. In both payment arrangements payment is certified by the architectural contract administrator and the final date for payment is fourteen days from the date of issue of each interim certificate. Provisions are included within Clause 30 to deal with advance payment for equipment that needs to be ordered early, retention and payment for off site materials. Detailed provisions with regard to the preparation of a final account are included within Clause 30.6, such account to be submitted by the contractor to the architect no later than six months following practical completion. Clause 30.8 envisages the final task of the architect under the contract to be the preparation and issue of the final certificate at the end of the defects liability period or the date the issue of certificate of completion of making good defects, whichever is the later. Although the JCT98 Private with Quantities contract is a lump sum contract there are numerous contractual mechanisms by which the contract sum can be increased or decreased.

### 12. JCT 98 Private with Quantities places no responsibility for design on the Contractor. Identify the two mechanisms which enable design responsibility to be placed on a contractor in the context of a Private with Quantities contract.

The core provisions of the JCT 98 Standard Form of Building Contract do not envisage the contractor having design responsibility (this remains with the designers appointed by the project client). The JCT do publish a supplemental option which allows the introduction of contractor design by way of the Contractor's Design Portion supplement (CDP), which provides for specific areas of design responsibility to be passed to the contractor. Most commonly this operates where the contractor is sub-contracting specific areas of design to sub-contractors. An example of this would be the mechanical and electrical engineering works. The Contractor's Design Portion supplement is published as a separate standalone supplement but it introduces a set of provisions which broadly match those contained within the JCT Standard Form of Building Contract with Contractors Design. The design obligations only apply to the pre-specified portion of the design for which the employer and the contractor have agreed the contractor will be responsible. An alternative provision contained with the standard form of building contract for part of the design responsibility to be cast to the contractor is to use the performance specified work mechanism. This is set out in Part 5 of the JCT at Clause 42. This provision allows for work to be specified by way of a performance specification of the contractor to then produce a finished product which meets the performance specification. It should be noted that the latter approach has been dropped from the new JCT05 suite of contracts.

### *13. How does the ECC suite of contracts deal with the amount of design liability placed on the Contractor and the level of responsibility to be expected with regard to that design liability?*

The ECC contract is unusual in its approach to design in that it is envisaged that this suite of contracts can be used in situations where the amount of contractor design is zero or 100%, or any point in between. As indicated above, the ECC contract has been drafted to provide maximum flexibility. The ECC contract itself is silent with regard to the level of design liability which results in the applicable standard being a fitness for purpose obligation. Secondary option M contains a mechanism to allow for the contractor's liability for its designs to be reduced to that of reasonable skill and care.

### *14. When would you use a target cost contract?*

Target cost arrangements are of most use where it is not possible in advance of the contract to be completely certain about the extent of the work that is to be done. The primary purpose of such arrangement is to provide an economic incentive to the contractor to come in on target and also to provide an economic disincentive for the stated target to be exceeded. This is usually achieved by way of a pain/gain arrangement with the contractor receiving a benefit if he comes in below the target cost or a penalty if he exceeds the target cost.

### *15. What were the main reasons behind the production of the ECC Form of Contract and what were the goals the drafters sought to achieve?*

The ECC have three clear aims.
First: flexibility. The idea behind the ECC contract is that it can be used for building and/or civil engineering works and where the contractor has some or no design responsibility. It can also be used for a variety of pricing mechanisms ranging from target costs through lump sum procurement to management contracting and can be used both in the UK and abroad. Second: clarity and simplicity. The drafters of the ECC contract wanted a distinct departure from the approach adopted particularly in JCT and ICE forms. Third: effective project management. The drafters of the ECC identified what they considered to be a weakness in many standard form contracts, mainly, they did not encourage and promote effective project management and this was in part a reason why so many disputes and problems were encountered on major building and civil engineering contracts. The ECC deliberately avoided the traditional style of drafting and technology. The ECC introduces unique terminology such as compensation events, contract data and site information.

## Chapter 5—Standard Forms of Contract II

1. Design and Build Forms; FIDIC Plant Design and Build (yellow book); FIDIC Turnkey (silver book); JCT Design and Build Contract; JCT Major Projects Form; ICE Design and Build Form; GC/Works/1 Design and Construct Form.
2. Reasonable skill and care.
3. FIDIC Plant Design and Build (yellow book); FIDIC Turnkey (silver book).
4. JCT, ACA, PPC 2000, ECC and ECC short form, FIDIC short form and the Change Management Supplements
5. PPC 2000; ICE.
6. JCT Standard Building Contract; GC/Works/1; PPC 2000.
7. JCT forms other than MPF, IFC, Management Contract and With Contractor's Design.
8. The effect of nomination or re-nomination of a sub-contractor or supplier is excused under Clauses 35, 36 and 25.4.5 of the 1998 version of the Standard Form of Building Contract. The effects of the nomination or re-nomination of a supplier, but not of a sub-contractor are excused under Clause 2.13.2 of the JCT Management Contract and clause 2.10.5 of the JCT Works Contract, and the renaming and replacing of a named sub-contractor are excused under clauses 3.7 and 2.20.2.2 of the JCT Intermediate Building Contract.
9. FIDIC.

10. A warranty by the employer that the specified information will be provided by the date stipulated.
11. IFC98.
12. All.
13. ECC and ECC short form.
14. GC/Works/1, GC/Works/1DC and ECC
15. IChemE.
16. FIDIC Plant Design and Build (yellow book); FIDIC Turnkey (silver book).

## Chapter 6—Powers and Duties of the Employer and Contractor Part I

1. (d) the contractor and those persons authorised by him to come onto the site are the only persons permitted onto the site
2. (b) information which describes the works and the way in which they are to be carried out
3. (c) the works will achieve the purpose for which they are said to be constructed
4. (c) collateral warranties simply confirm the obligations which the parties already owe

## Chapter 7—Powers and Duties of the Employer and Contractor II

1. FALSE
2. (c) half on practical completion, half on making good of defects
3. (b) under JCT 98, notice of delay is a condition precedent
4. (a) the works are completed but for minor items
5. (b) defects are not considered serious

## Chapter 9—Provisions for Managing Change

1. Under which type of contract does the contractor usually take the risk of variations required by the employer?
    (a) all the standard forms
2. In connection with change management, the word "change" means:
    (d) any departure from the contract documents
3. A CPM programme is important to change management because:
    (a) it is the baseline from which to measure the effect of change
4. The activities on a CPM programme should always be specified to be
    (e) able to react dynamically to change
5. The Change Management Supplements are
    (a) conditions of contract
6. The failure to produce a programme can be compensated by means of

(d) liquidated damages

7. The role of the risk manager during construction is to

(b) manage the employer's risks for him

8. The contractor should amend the programme from time to time because

(c) it is impossible to get it right first time

9. The employer can always mitigate the effects of employer-caused delays by

(b) agreeing with the contractor appropriate measures

10. Acceleration is usually most cost effectively achieved by:

(c) resequencing the work to change the critical path.

## Chapter 10—Remedies for Breach

1. (a) Liquidated damages obviate the employer's necessity to prove the actual losses he has suffered in the event of delay—which can be a difficult and onerous task.
1. (b) Liquidated damages clauses can be held to be invalid if they are not a genuine pre-estimate of loss.
1. (c) The right to liquidated damages can be lost where time becomes at large, i.e. where there ceases to be a defined contract completion date.
2. (a) The common law right to damages is founded upon the principle that the governing purpose of damages is to put the party whose rights have been violated in the same position, so far as money can do, as if his rights were observed.
2. (b) There has to be a limit on the extent of damages that can be recovered. Thus, in contract, damages must either arise naturally from the breach or, alternatively, be of a kind that the parties might have expected to be incurred as a consequence of breach, having regard to their knowledge at the time of contract.
2. (c) The full extent of damages may not be recovered:
   (i) where a party has failed to mitigate his loss;
   (ii) where putting the injured party precisely in the position he would have been in if the breach had not occurred would be disproportionate to the cost of doing so; or,
   (iii) where there is an element of betterment.
2. (d) The parties can agree to exclude or limit their liability but subject to certain exceptions: in particular, where one party deals as a consumer or on the other's written standard terms of business, that other party cannot exclude or restrict liability beyond what is reasonable.
3. (a) In contract, time for commencing proceedings for breach runs from the date of the breach, whereas in tort it runs from the date when the damage was suffered.

3. (b) It is more difficult to recover pure economic loss in tort (save where there is negligent misstatement).
4. (a) Important statutes having an impact on construction include:
   - the Defective Premises Act 1972 which fixes contractors and developers with liability to any person who acquires an interest in a dwelling where the construction work is not done in a workmanlike or professional manner, or carried out with proper materials, as a consequence of which the dwelling is unfit for habitation;
   - the Housing Grants Construction and Regeneration Act 1996 which provides that a contractor is entitled to periodic payments and the receipt of certain contractual notices respecting payment, and gives the right to suspend for non-payment. It also gives each party the right to adjudicate disputes;
   - the Building Act 1984 includes a right to compensation for a contractor's breach of the Building Regulations;
5. (a) A contract may be terminated lawfully where the contract specifically gives that right.
5. (b) termination of a party's employment under the contract depends upon the contract terms, whereas repudiation brings a party's obligation to perform further to an end where a repudiatory breach is accepted. Rescission, however, is an entitlement to treat a contract not merely as terminated, but extinguished, and is regulated largely by the Misrepresentation Act 1967.

## Chapter 11—Claims and Dispute Resolution

<u>Outline solutions</u>

The purpose of these outline solutions is quite simply to identify the main points that a student should consider in any answer to the self-test questions. These solutions are not suggested answers, but instead quite simply identify key points arising from the question. For a student to pass such a question at diploma level, the student would be required to write a carefully constructed essay dealing with these key characteristics, identifying authorities supporting the student's propositions and then identifying further issues arising from the referenced reading material identified in the Chapter.

<u>Dispute resolution generally</u>

**1 Explain the spectrum of dispute resolution techniques.**

The student should identify that there is a wide range of dispute resolution techniques. In particular, the student should identify that there are three "pillars" of dispute resolution. These are negotiation, mediation (or conciliation) and then adjudication. The term adjudication here is used to identify some form of umpiring process, such as litigation, or arbitration. The key characteristic of this third process is that some third party decides the outcome. In negotiation, the parties decide their own fate. The same is true of mediation; however they use an entirely neutral third party who aids their discussions towards settlement.

The key characteristics of the dispute resolution procedures available should be identified and the processes compared and contrasted.

**2 Identify the key differences between the three pillars of dispute resolution.**

The key characteristics of the dispute resolution procedures available should be identified and the processes compared and contrasted.

The important point here is for the student to identify a wide range of dispute resolution techniques that are available. The student could draw upon any of the material within the Chapter. The important point is to identify the ideal "model court", and then identify the three pillars of dispute resolution. The student should then compare and contrast the different techniques such as "facilitative" or "evaluative" mediation, and the distinction between mediation and conciliation in different parts of the world. Mediation is usually a conciliatory process in many parts of the world, but can be coercive in other parts of the world. The dispute resolution landscape diagram could be used to identify, describe and explain the wide variety of techniques that are available.

**3 Identify and distinguish the key elements in the escalation of a dispute.**

The student is encouraged to draw upon reading material referred to in Chapter 10 such as Mackie (1995) and the chapters specifically devoted to dispute escalation in N. Gould (1999). There are a variety of ways to consider the escalation of a dispute. At its simplest, a dispute cannot arise until one party has made a claim that the other party has rejected, either expressly or implicitly.

Some commentators in the area focus on wider aspects such as human conflict and the distinction between "functional" and "dysfunctional" conflict. Dysfunctional conflict is unhelpful, while functional conflict is good, in that disagreement between individuals can lead to progress. For example, disagreement between designers might in fact lead to a better design. It is dysfunctional conflict that leads to disputes. Most dysfunctional conflict starts from clashes of personality between individuals which then lead to formal, recognisable disputes.

Negotiation

**4. Discuss the process of negotiation and contrast negotiation strategies.**

Many of us negotiate all of the time, and not just in disputes, but in our everyday lives and also quite clearly during construction projects. The process could be considered a relatively simplistic one, but this is often misplaced. Gulliver (1979) provides the most useful explanation of the developmental process of negotiation. He identifies eight distinct overlapping phases. Each of these should be explored and considered by the student.

Negotiating strategies on the other hand can be divided into those that are "competitive", and compared to those that might be said to be "principled" or "interest based". A competitive negotiator adopts certain tactics that a principled negotiator would not adopt.

Commentators argue that a principled approach is best, although many negotiators are often in fact inexperienced and not sufficiently strategic to maximise their positions.

**5. Justify the approach of the courts to agreements to negotiate.**

An agreement to agree, or an agreement to negotiate, is unenforceable (*Walford* v. *Miles*). A student should also consider the House of Lords case of *Channel Tunnel Rail Link* v. *Balfour Beatty & Others* and also more recently, *IBM* v. *Cable and Wireless*. The key point is that the courts cannot force people to negotiate to an agreement. However, the court can force parties to negotiate within a limited timescale, although the court cannot compel the parties to agree any particular outcome. Therefore, those dispute resolution clauses that require the parties to engage in some form of ADR or negotiation will be upheld, but only so far as the court can force people to follow the procedure and stick to the timescales.

Mediation

**6. What is Mediation?**

In its basic terms, mediation is a process whereby the parties in dispute engage an entirely neutral third party to assist the disputing parties to settle their dispute. A variety of definitions have been circulated and these are set out in Chapter 10. The student should also consider the benefits and disadvantages of mediation and contrast mediation with other dispute resolution processes.

**7. Distinguish the various approaches to mediation.**

The fundamental distinction is between "evaluative" and "facilitative" mediation. A facilitative mediator will simply try to aid the parties towards settlement without making any recommendation. An evaluative mediator will state his or her opinion during the course of the mediation, or more likely at the end of the mediation in the form of a recommendation. In practice, mediators tend to be somewhere between the two. A very effective facilitative mediator can maintain his or her neutrality whilst putting questions to the parties in a forceful and direct way but without giving away his or her view.

**8. Consider how a mediator affects the mediation or conciliation process.**

This is a variation on the last question. However, here the student should focus upon the qualities of a mediator and possibly the informal mediation processes that sometimes arise. The qualities of a mediator can affect both the mediation and the mediation process. The ability of the mediator to communicate with the parties and gain their trust early on in the mediation is vital to progressing the mediation to the point where a resolution of the dispute can be identified.

ADR

**9. Explain what is meant by ADR?**

One could simply say that ADR means Alternative Dispute Resolution. However, on a more detailed analysis, one could trace the development of alternative dispute resolution procedures from the complaints based systems in the 60s towards a process of "appropriate dispute resolution" that is now adopted more widely in the commercial world. It is interesting to compare the approach of trying to identify the most appropriate dispute resolution process for the project against the background of statutory imposed adjudication in the construction industry.

**10. Discuss the development of ADR from the growth of informal justice.**

This is essentially a review of the historic development of ADR and is more focused than the preceding question. The interesting aspect of this is that each development could be seen to be an opportunity for new professionals to try to sell their dispute resolution skills to an audience that has traditionally relied upon litigation lawyers. In other words, the movement towards informal justice in the 60s in the United States was an attempt to get away from expensive litigation.

At the same time however, "unqualified" dispute resolvers were "getting in on the act" in order to develop their own industry and profit from it. There has clearly been a vying for business between litigation lawyers and the new breed of commercial mediators. Lawyers have in some instances re-branded themselves in order to ensure that they maintain a grip on this new developing market. In addition, the government has encouraged this approach perhaps cynically in order to reduce the cost of the provision of judges and courts rather than to promote conciliatory dispute resolution.

If parties pay for their private dispute resolution processes (such as in adjudication) then fewer courts and fewer judges are necessary.

An interesting debate could develop about how far the government should go in encouraging these moves. Whilst adjudication in the construction industry might be one thing, should private adjudication in respect of asylum seekers be kept from the public (because, of course, these processes are not heard in open court where the public and press have access unless and until they proceed to judicial review)?

**11. Contrast the advantages and disadvantages of ADR by comparison to the traditional methods of dispute resolution.**

The benefits and disadvantages of ADR are set out in the Chapter. This is a relatively straightforward exercise.

Hybrid processes

**12. Assess the advantages and disadvantages of expert determination over other forms of dispute resolution.**

The key point about expert determination is that it is the most binding of all dispute resolution processes. It is possible to appeal from an arbitrator's award in respect of a point of law. It is possible to appeal from a first instance judge to the High Court, Court of Appeal and (sometimes) the House of Lords. Many dispute resolution procedures, such as tribunals, provide for an appeal to a judge. However, expert determination is a contractual process, and providing that the contract states that the decision of the expert shall be final, binding and conclusive, then no court can or will interfere with the decision provided that the expert has determined the question put to him or her (*Nikko Hotels*).

The advantage is finality. If the parties refer a matter to an expert then they know that the matter will come to an end. The disadvantage is that if the expert issues a somewhat surprising result (but still one that the expert was empowered to make) then the parties will be bound by it. A surprising decision will almost always be in one party's favour and so they will not wish to overturn the decision. In the absence of both parties agreeing to ignore the decision, it will be final and binding.

Other advantages include cost, speed and expertise.

**13. Contrast three hybrid or multi-stage approaches to dispute resolution.**

Many are set out within Chapter 10. The reader could consider Colin Wall's dispute review adviser, "DRA", based in Hong Kong, or dispute review boards, "DRBs", or indeed the more modern dispute adjudication boards, "DABs", used in the FIDIC contracts or those proposed in the World Bank's procurement documentation.

Med-Arb is another multi-stage process. In addition, contracts now frequently include dispute escalation provisions. For example, a dispute is referred to the senior executive of a company, then mediation, before either arbitration or litigation. If adjudication is applicable, then that will simply form another process that is available to the parties at any time.

**14. From your own experience consider how an alternative approach to the resolution of a dispute might improve the efficiency of your organisation.**

This provides the student with the opportunity to apply the material set out in Chapter 10, together with their wider reading, to their own workplace. It may involve identifying a dispute with which the student has been involved, then considering how alternative methods for resolving it could have been used. The student does not, however, need to have been involved in any particularly lengthy or detailed dispute resolution procedures. The student could quite simply consider an ongoing conflict on a project that might benefit from some third party input in order to resolve the issues and allow the parties to be more efficient in moving the project onto completion.

Adjudication

**15. Explain the adjudication process.**

Adjudication was introduced into the UK in May 1998 as a result of Part II of the Housing Grants, Construction and Regeneration Act 1996. Section 108 of that Act implies into all construction contracts (as defined within the Act) a right for any party to a construction contract to refer a dispute to an adjudicator. That right is a unilateral one. This means that consent of the other side is not required. An adjudicator must be appointed within 7 days. The dispute is referred to the adjudicator who then has 28 days to decide the matter. That period can be extended by a further 14 days by the referring party, or longer, with the consent of both parties. The adjudicator is under an obligation to ensure that a decision is reached within the applicable time period.

Adjudication was introduced in order to try to improve cash-flow within the construction industry. However, it is now being used for substantial final account disputes and there is some debate as to whether it is really suitable for such large and complex disputes. Can a large dispute really be dealt with within a limited 28-day process?

Adjudication is spreading internationally. New Zealand has introduced adjudication, as has the whole of Australia and most recently, Singapore. Hong Kong is considering a draft bill, as is Texas. It seems that this process will be spreading over much of the world, and may expand into other areas beyond construction.

Arbitration and litigation

**16. Contrast the key distinctions between arbitration and litigation.**

Arbitration has been referred to as "litigation in suits". There are, however, many serious distinctions between arbitration and litigation. For example, the freedom in choice of the arbitrator. There is flexibility in the process. A documents only procedure could, for example, be adopted. As could a 100 day time limited arbitration. There is a distinction in cost. Arbitration should really be more economic than litigation, although often it is not. Arbitration should also be a faster process than litigation, although once again in recent times, it has not been. Arbitration is a private process, unlike the courts which are open to the press or the public.

The disadvantages of arbitration are that the parties have to pay for the arbitrator and the hearing facilities, whereas in litigation these are provided by the State. Having said that, Legal Aid is not available in arbitration. There is also the difficulty of joinder. For the parties to arbitrate, they must have agreed in their contract that they would refer disputes to arbitration; multi-party arbitrations are therefore rare. However, a court can join in parties where the subject matter is related.

**17. Justify the CPR approach to track allocations.**

The justification of the new Civil Procedure Rules, and indeed the distinction between track allocation, is one of cost saving and expedition. An attempt is being made to allocate smaller or more simple claims to the fast track, thus allowing them to be dealt with quickly. Limited rules apply and the aim is to deal with litigation in respect of those matters more economically. On the other hand, more complicated matters are then referred to an appropriate judge with the appropriate experience and all the Civil Procedure Rules apply. Most of the Technology and Construction Court's work is multi-track work comprising relatively complex construction issues and large sums of money.

Hybrid techniques

**18. Contrast three of the hybrid approaches to dispute resolution.**

This question has been dealt with above under the heading "Hybrid Processes".

**19. Compare and distinguish between the project based dispute resolution techniques.**

The reader should consider the various approaches that could be used during the course of a project. In simplistic terms, one could of course refer to adjudication as being a process that can be used during the course of a project. A greater degree of sophistication is introduced by way of dispute boards, comprising dispute review boards and dispute adjudication boards. These processes anticipate that the parties will agree to appoint a board at the start of a project. The board could comprise one or three persons that will follow the project and deal with any disputes that arise. The ICC's dispute board procedure anticipates that the dispute board may make recommendations, or, indeed, binding decisions, and so is a variation on the strict distinction between DRBs and DABs. DRBs make only recommendations while DABs only issue decisions.

Another alternative is project mediation. Two mediators are appointed at the start of the project in order to help the parties resolve their differences. The mediators do not make any recommendations or issue any decisions. Nonetheless, they are able to facilitate problem solving between the parties and help the parties settle a dispute that may arise.

There is also the dispute review advisor who will follow the project and help the parties to try to resolve their differences. The DRA might act as a mediator or might assist the parties to find an external mediator. He or she will help the parties crystallise their dispute and present it to senior executives who will then try to settle it. Any disputes that are not resolved are sent to a rapid arbitration process. The DRA does not sit as arbitrator, and so the DRA's neutral function is maintained.

For Product Safety Concerns and Information please contact our EU representative GPSR@taylorandfrancis.com Taylor & Francis Verlag GmbH, Kaufingerstraße 24, 80331 München, Germany